The
Antimonopoly
Laws and
Policies of Japan

H. Iyori and A. Uesugi

Federal Legal Publications, Inc. / New York

Library of Congress Catalog Card Number: 94-70047

ISBN #0-87945-076-2 (Cloth)
ISBN #0-87945-077-0 (Paper)

Manufactured in the United States of America

CONTENTS

i

Part II: Conduct Prohibited Under
the Antimonopoly Laws

vii

Part III: Enforcement and Procedures

Part IV: Selected Policy Issues

Appendices: Antimonopoly Laws, Regulations and Various FTC Guidelines

TABLES AND FIGURES

TABLES

FIGURES

PREFACE

The first edition of this book, written by H. Iyori, appeared in 1969; the second edition, which was revised by A. Uesugi, working closely with Mr. Iyori was issued in 1983. Mr. Uesugi was then working as a First Secretary at the Embassy of Japan in Washington, D.C. (1981-1984).

Almost 10 years have elapsed since our last publication, and there have been so many developments in the antimonopoly field during this decade that the second edition has become almost obsolete. In addition, interest by the world community in antimonopoly law enforcement in Japan recently has grown due in part to the trade negotiations between the United States and Japan. Because of this, our commentary on the antimonopoly law and policy of Japan should be more than of academic interest. The new edition is meant for the world community in order to enhance its understanding of Japanese antimonopoly law enforcement, its history, and its enforcement philosophy.

In the preface to the second edition, we wrote "Various reasons for such a remarkable achievement have been pointed out, but doubtless, the vigorous and incessant competition among Japanese firms themselves was one of the major factors for such performance." This was a rather bald statement 10 years ago but almost common sense in present-day Japan, reflecting the profound change that Japan observed in the early 1990s in the antimonopoly policy field.

Japanese antimonopoly law has inherited basic ideas from the U.S.A., however, it also shares many characteristics of European competition laws. Therefore, if it is restored to its original effectiveness there should be no problems in harmonizing the competition laws of Japan, the U.S.A. and Europe, which occupy a significant role in international trade. As internationalization of economic activities becomes prevalent, the business community needs more and more common rules of competition in order to engage in free and fair competition. This has been the authors' biggest concern.

The former two versions of this book were organized so as to describe substantive provisions and the exceptions to the rule of competition and did not cover an analysis of Japanese antimonopoly thinking itself. It did not fully cover procedural aspects such as criminal penalties and civil damage suits. When we were planning our new book, it was clear that it should have a completely new structure. The current edition concentrates on a balanced description of the substantive rules and procedural character of the antimonopoly laws, and offers a comparative analysis with U.S. counterpart laws as much as possible. We also eliminated the descriptions of the two supplemental laws, namely the Act Against Unjustifiable Premiums and Misleading Representation and the Act Against Delay in Payment Proceeds, etc. to Subcontractors. On the other hand, we added various policy issues on the antimonopoly laws of Japan that have been the subject of debates in recent years in the world community.

English-language analysis of Japanese antimonopoly laws is still rare, in particular compared with English materials describing industrial policy of Japan. We believe that Japanese antimonopoly policy should be evaluated in the world community in the context of Japanese economic development as favorably as industrial policy by MITI. It would be most unfortunate for Japan if industrial policy was widely believed to be a cause of Japanese economic success without knowing fully about antimonopoly law enforcement in Japan. The industrial policy was a product of Japanese origin and could only have such influence on the business community within the context of economic development that Japan experienced during the 1950s and 1960s. We believe that the information necessary for such analysis has been provided in this book.

The manuscript was prepared as of December 1992 and contains as much as was feasible up to that date. However, antimonopoly law enforcement is moving so quickly that for the convenience of our readers we want to supplement our text with the following new developments that have taken place thereafter.

a. On April 20, 1993, after many comments were filed on the draft, the Guideline for Joint R & D was finalized.

b. In April 1993, a guideline for the financial sector was announced for the first time. Its aim is to prevent unfair trade practices in view of financial reform that lowers walls between banking and security houses and could have a significant impact on the financial markets of Japan.

c. The Tokyo High Court reached a decision on May 21, 1993 as to the food wrapping material price-fixing cases. (The FTC had filed a criminal accusation to the prosecuting authority in December 1992.) The Tokyo High Court found that those indicted persons had violated the Antimonopoly Act and sentenced 15 officers and employees to prison terms ranging from 6 months to 1 year with 2 years suspension for each. The High Court also imposed 6-8 million yen fines on eight corporations.

The FTC had filed another accusation on February 24, 1993 against four printing companies that conspired to bid rigging for the procurement of special seals used for mailing notices for pension recipients by the Social Securities Agencies.

d. In the field of deregulation, 89 out of 90 exemption cartels were permitted under the Small and Medium-Sized Enterprise Organization Act covering various textile industries production facilities restricting cartels at the end of October 1993. By this measure, the number of exemption cartels would be less than 100 for the first time. Various deregulation measures are contemplated under the new leadership of the Hosokawa Cabinet. The importance of the FTC activities is increasing more and more and widespread expectancy to the FTC is mounting not only in Japan but also in foreign countries.

e. As to bid rigging, on October 21, 1993, the FTC announced its intention to issue a new guideline on public bidding that covers activities by entrepreneurs as well as trade associations, and that fully describes illegal activities and permissible conduct so far as

remedy to the ongoing bid-rigging scandals in the construction industry.

f. The Cabinet Ordinance was enacted under Sections 18-2 and 2(7) in order to change the market size requirements for monopolistic situations and parallel price increase regulation (the amount was doubled from 30 billion yen to 60 billion yen for parallel price increase and from 50 billion yen to 100 billion yen for a monopolistic situation).

This book is the result of our analytical work for many years, and needless to say, the opinions expressed in this book are strictly our own and not that of the FTC. We have expressed our observations concerning Japanese antimonopoly policy as candidly as possible within the constraints imposed upon us as a government official and a former government official, believing that more information and analysis would be necessary to make it possible to engage in an objective evaluation of Japanese antimonopoly laws for the world community.

We want to thank Mr. Christopher Hearth who prepared the bibliography of English and German for this book, and provided many suggestions from a non-Japanese perspective on what should be covered in this third edition. We also wish to thank Mr. Martin Greenberg of Federal Legal Publications, Inc. for making it possible to publish the third edition.

October, 1993
Tokyo, Japan

Hiroshi Iyori
Professor of law,
Chuo University
and former commissioner
of the FTC

Akinori Uesugi
Director, Trade Practices
Division
Fair Trade Commission
and Lecturer of law,
Chuo University

INTRODUCTION

The purpose of this book is to explore how Japanese antimonopoly laws evolved; the philosophy of their enforcement agency; how those provisions of the Antimonopoly Act[1] that were adopted from American antitrust laws—the Sherman, Clayton and Federal Trade Commission Acts[2]—were accepted as rules of competition in Japan; and lastly, how they differ from American antitrust laws. (Throughout the book, "antimonopoly laws" refer not only to the Antimonopoly Act, but also to related orders and regulations. In order to make comparisons with other countries, we sometimes use "competition laws" or "antitrust laws" when referring to laws on competition in general.)

Japanese antimonopoly laws and their enforcement policies can never be truly understood without knowing their history; this is why we have given so many pages over to describing their development. By knowing their history, one can get a clear idea of the destiny of laws and legal concepts imported into Japan, as well as how economic development later necessitated effective competition laws for Japan.

By understanding how antimonopoly laws could take root in Japan, one can understand Japan's transformation into a truly market economy country and the difficulties associated with such a process.[3]

Studying Japanese antimonopoly laws may be meaningful to non-Japanese readers for two reasons: for the purpose of doing business in Japan; or as one aspect of studies of the Japanese economy, in particular to explore the reason behind its rapid economic expansion. We mean this book to serve both these purposes.

In part I, the historical development of Japanese antimonopoly policy is described. ("Antimonopoly policy" also refers to the enforcement policy aspect of antimonopoly laws.) We begin with a look at antimonopoly policy in the pre-World War II period. Procartel policy can be traced back to the cartel legislation of the prewar period. By doing this analysis, we tried to show that Japanese antimonopoly policy established its current status gradually through difficult policy conflicts with procartel policy.

In part II, various substantive provisions of the Antimonopoly Act are explained. This part is intended to show how these provisions are interpreted by the Fair Trade Commission (FTC) and the courts, and especially to show the FTC's enforcement priorities.

In part III, procedural aspects of antimonopoly law enforcement are explained by using various statistical data. In this part the character of Japanese antimonopoly law enforcement is also explained. We hope this will enhance the reader's understanding of Japanese antimonopoly laws and policies.

In part IV, we selected several issues related to antimonopoly policy that might be of interest to foreign observers. There is some duplication to be found with material appearing in earlier chapters, but we felt it would be helpful to keep all the material on policy issues in one place.

NOTES

[1] Its full name is the Act Concerning Prohibition of Private Monopoly and Maintenance of Fair Trade. See appendix A for full text of translation.

[2] Sherman Act, 15 U.S.C.A. §§ 1–7, Clayton Act 15 U.S.C.A. §§ 12–27, Federal Trade Commission Act, 15 U.S.C.A. §§ 42–51.

[3] For further analysis of Japan as a developmental state, see C. JOHNSON, MITI AND THE JAPANESE MIRACLE (1982). He said, "Japan is a good example of a State in which the developmental orientation predominates. A regulatory, or market-rational state concerns itself with the forms and procedures—the rules . . . of economic competition, but it does not concern itself with substantive matters. . . . The developmental, or plan-rational state, by contrast, has as its dominant feature precisely the setting such substantive social and economic goals." at 19.

PART I

Historical Development of the Antimonopoly Laws and Policies

1

THE SITUATION BEFORE
AND AFTER WORLD WAR II

(A) THE SITUATION BEFORE WORLD WAR I

(1) UNTIL WORLD WAR I

(i) The Meiji restoration

To prepare for the development of modern capitalism in Japan, institutional reforms had been achieved under the Meiji government, which took over power from the Tokugawa government in 1868. The Meiji government understood the inferiority of the traditional economic systems in Japan as compared with the West, and actively tried to introduce Western technologies and various Western systems, including the legal system.[1]

At the time, there was not sufficient funds to finance a huge introduction of foreign goods and services, so that for the most part, industrial development was achieved through the initiative of the private sector. For example, starting from small factories located in the country, silk spinning was one of the first industries of the early Meiji period. Lacking money to buy Western spinning machines, traditional spinning machines were improved by Japanese craftsmen who were acting as true entrepreneurs.[2]

As was the case with silk spinning, other entrepreneurs of the Meiji period could not rely on foreign technologies and therefore developed technologies of their own. Sugar refining and beer breweries were established and, amazingly, within a decade they were able to supply goods of quality comparable to imports.[3]

Looking back, Japanese capitalism seemed to develop fairly successfully. Recent studies emphasize the importance of infrastructure during the Tokugawa period, which provided the highly skilled craftsmanship and technical capabilities needed to adapt to Western technologies.[4]

The Meiji government was forced to accept certain unequal provisions in the treaties on commerce and navigation, among which the power to set tariff rates was the most important.[5] This meant that after the abolition of the closed door policy in the Tokugawa period, the Japanese economy was faced with direct competition with Western goods that could be imported under low tariff rates. Because under the treaties the Meiji government could not set tariff rates to protect the domestic sector, it was forced to begin economic expansion under free trade conditions. Of course, the lack of foreign currency prevented imports; and transportation, which was not well developed at the time, also hampered the bringing of imports to Japan. However, at the very least there were no tariff barriers at the time.[6]

The difficulties of the domestic industries, which were completely isolated from international trade under the Tokugawa regime, were quite significant, but they were overcome by those entrepreneurs who were glad to meet the challenge for the first time in nearly 300 years.

Looking back, it is clear that the Japanese economy started its capitalistic development under very competitive circumstances. Many businesses that could not overcome such difficulties disappeared, but it was the difficulties that later made it possible for entrepreneurs to become true competitors in the world market.

What the Meiji government could do was to offer various assistance and protection such as soft financing, privatization measures (selling factories in which the government had invested or government-owned property to the private sector at low prices) and to introduce technology within its limited budget.[7] (The Meiji government had hired many foreign engineers and scholars at very high salaries and also sent many young Japanese to study in the West.)

Beginning in 1885 when the privatization program was started, the Meiji government sold a cement factory to Asano, a copper mine to Hurukawa, and a shipbuilding factory to Kawasaki and Iwasaki (founder of Mitsubishi). It is interesting to see that these firms, which later became *zaibatsu* (family controlled combines), started their businesses as individual entrepreneurs, whereas textile spinning was started by companies and did not later grow into *zaibatsu* concerns.[8]

(ii) The start of cartels and trusts

The first traces of cartel activity in Japan were the formation of the Paper Manufacturing Federation in 1880 and the Spinning Federation in 1882. True cartels started to develop as early as 1890 in the cotton spinning industry, which was the most developed industry at that time, in order to curtail production.[9]

However, the turning point was the recession that followed the Russo-Japanese War (1904-1905). Japanese industries that had flourished during the war suffered severely in the recession that followed. Those industries that expanded during the war-created demand did not have sufficient capacity to tolerate the recession. As a response to recession, cartels were formed in such industries as chemical fertilizer, paper, sugar, petroleum, and flour.[10]

Around this time, the Meiji government recovered tariff power through treaty negotiations and, in 1910, established protective tariff rates. Protective tariffs would greatly enhance the effectiveness of cartel activities.[11]

(iii) The start of zaibatsu concerns

The origin of the *zaibatsu* dates back to the 16th century for Sumitomo, the 17th century for Mitsui, the 18th century for Yasuda, and the 19th century for Mitsubishi.[12] All of them had started as merchants or moneylenders. These *zaibatsu* concerns had solid bases in the mining industry and in the financial sector. They were, therefore, suited to move into heavy industry and the chemical industry, both of which were promoted by the government. Zaibatsu concerns such as Mitsui, Mitsubishi, Sumitomo, Yasuda, etc. had emerged mainly during the depression. They had increased their influence in many markets, and tried to acquire those companies that had suffered business difficulty. Their closeness to the government had also helped their expansion. The Meiji government had sold the Nagasaki Dockyard, the biggest dockyard of the time, to Mitsubishi in 1884 and the Miike Coal Mine, the biggest coal mine at that time, to Mitsui in 1893.[13]

(iv) Attitudes toward cartels and trusts

During this period, no laws concerning cartels and trusts existed. The government had maintained a favorable attitude toward cartels and trusts, because they could serve as useful policy tools to combat the recession, which was the most important economic problem the government faced at that time.

Academically, Japanese scholars were influenced by German thought on cartels and trusts, as was the case in other legal fields.[14] Specifically, they thought that cartels and trusts were useful in eliminating the harmful side effects of free competition, and only misuse or abuse of their monopolistic position should be regulated, if necessary. High prices were feared as a result of cartels and trusts, but it was thought that price regulation could solve such problems and no influential scholars seemed to favor the idea of the promotion of competition or the idea of regulating cartels and trusts.[15]

The courts also maintained a favorable attitude toward cartels and trusts. In 1907 the Osaka High Court, in the case of the Retailers Association of White Sand, stated that the restriction on business territories by the Association had the "merit of preventing unfair competition among retailers in the same fields of business" and the restriction on retail prices had "merits to prevent unreasonable below cost sales, to promote business ethics in commerce, and further to strengthen credibility of the fellow businessmen." Based on this recognition, the court decided that "the agreement in question did not damage in any way the economic or social order" and therefore, held that it should be honored as a lawful agreement. (Contracts or agreements that were held to be against the economic or social order were invalid under the Civil Code of Japan.[16])

Later, the Supreme Court (*Daishin-In*) repeatedly decided that price agreements among competitors were valid under the Civil Code.[17]

(2) AFTER WORLD WAR I

(i) Enactment of cartel laws

The challenge to the newly created industries of Japan came after World War I (1914-1919). The war had provided Japanese industries with huge windfall profits. Many companies tried to expand into heavy industry and the chemical industry in order to share those profits. However, the recession after World War I was so severe and prolonged that many companies could not remain in the market. Many companies went bankrupt.[18]

To cope with the recession by gaining economies of scale, mergers also took place in paper, iron and steel, and in textiles. As of 1896, in terms of total assets, 57 of the top 100 companies were textile companies; by 1911, the number had declined to 31. After World War I, seven big textile companies had established their dominant position through mergers.[19]

To combat periodic recessions, cartels were formed in many industries. The great depression of the 1930s caused additional cartels to emerge in such fields as wool, copper, pulp, coal, cement and various steel products.[20] However, they could not exert dominant power in their respective markets because there still existed competitive outsiders, or because members of cartels did not necessarily observe agreements when market conditions started to improve. Government intervention was needed in order to make the cartels effective.

The government was in favor of strengthening cartels and trusts because they were deemed effective to restrict excessive competition and to stabilize, organize and rationalize industry. The government started to protect cartels and trusts through "administrative guidance."[21]

During this period, the Diet also started to react through cartel legislation. In order to promote export trade by small and medium sized manufacturers, the Diet, in 1925, enacted two specific laws to promote and strengthen association activities and cartel formation, namely, the Export Association Act and the Important Export Commodities Industrial Association Act.[22]

Under the Export Association Act, exporters of important export commodities, designated by ministerial order, were allowed to set up an export association (sec. 1). The association could inspect the members' commodities and was authorized to impose certain restrictions on the members' activities (sec. 3). The competent minister could order outsiders (non-members) to observe the same restrictions set by the association, when, under certain circumstances, it deemed it necessary (sec. 9).[23]

Similar provisions were authorized with respect to manufacturers of important commodities designated by ministerial order under the Important Export Commodities Industrial Association Act of 1925.[24]

This was the first attempt to compel outsiders to observe rules set by members of the association, and thereafter set a precedent for compulsory cartels—even following World War II.[25]

(ii) Enactment of industry control laws

As seen above, during the recession which began in 1929, cartels were formed in many important industries. The government, believing that the rationalization of industries could be achieved by regulating excessive competition, and thinking that this was its most important task, set up the Industry Rationalization Committee in the Council of Commerce and Industry, and started evaluating measures to cope with the problems of recession.[26]

The Council submitted a report in December 1929, saying

> that [the] coexistence of too many competing enterprises in the same industry brings about overinvestment of capital and it is not a suitable situation for reducing production cost and stabilizing the foundation of business activities.
>
> Therefore, considering good balance among production, distribution and consumption for each industry, promotion of corporate mergers, and solicitation to form cartels and similar agreements are especially needed, and by these means, it is essential to prevent unnecessary competition.[27]

After the report was submitted, with very little discussion in the Diet, the Important Industries Control Act was enacted in 1931. This Act provided that:

(A)   When market control agreements were set up among enterprises within important industries designated by ministerial order, the same agreement should be notified to the competent minister (sec. 1);

(B)   The minister could order, under certain circumstances, members of the agreement, as well as non-members, to observe the restrictions incorporated in the notified agreement (sec. 2);

(C)   Under certain circumstances, the minister could modify or revoke the notified agreement (sec. 3); and

(D)   As an organ to give advice to the minister for the application of the Act, a control committee was established (sec. 5).

The Act was enacted as a temporary law for 5 years, but in 1936 it was extended, with some amendments, for another 5 years in order to provide policy tools for the economic control of war mobilization.[28]

Eighteen industries were designated under this act. They included cotton spinning, silk spinning, paper, carbide, cement, sulfuric acid, flour, pig iron, ferro-alloy, various steel products, sugar refining, beer and coal. In most of these industries, common joint sales companies were established that eliminated competition in distribution. Cartels were also formed in non-designated fields such as wool, linen, fertilizer, copper, petroleum and canned foods.[29]

A ministerial control order to non-members under section 2 was actually issued on only one occasion. However, a formal order was unnecessary because the market-dominating powers of cartels were significantly strengthened by the existence of these provisions themselves, and the competent minister had used administrative guidance based upon these provisions. Under unusual political circumstances—the movement toward war—voluntary compliance was virtually secured.[30]

This act covered industries where large enterprises prevailed and under their leadership, control of markets was facilitated. As to smaller enterprises, two separate measures were taken. The Important Export Commodities Industrial Association Act of 1925 was transformed into the Industrial Association Act of 1931. In addition, the Mercantile Association Act was enacted in 1932 which provided similar measures for smaller merchants (distributors). Through these revisions of law, the legal status of cartels was significantly strengthened.[31]

In those days, the government also promoted mergers under an industrial rationalization policy. For example, as a consequence of these mergers, the Oji Paper Co. was created which controlled 96 percent of pulp production and 85 percent of paper production. The Japan Beer Co. controlled 64 percent of the beer brewing industry.[32]

(iii) War-time legislation

In 1936, the Important Industrial Control Act was extended for another 5 years, with revision of the following:

(A) The introduction of an authorization system to new entry under certain circumstances (sec. 2-2).
(B) New regulations on trusts (secs. 2-4 & 3).
(C) The strengthening of regulatory power concerning the misuse of cartels and trusts (sec. 3).

These revisions were added under the influence of related German legislation such as the Act Concerning the Establishment of Compulsory Cartels (1933) and the Ordinance Against Misuse of Economic Power.[33]

In order to include import trade restrictions, in 1937 the Export Association Act of 1925 was changed to the Foreign Trade Association Act.[34]

The Important Industrial Association Ordinance of 1941 was issued, based on section 18 of the National General Mobilization Act of 1938, and transformed the industrial associations into war time control associations established in each industry to effect necessary government control.[35]

The Commerce and Industry Association Act of 1942, which was formed by merging the Industry Association Act of 1931 and the Mercantile Association Act of 1932, provided for the compulsory establishment of control associations (sec. 12) and had a provision for the compulsory participation of related entrepreneurs (sec. 15). These provisions were thought to be influenced by the German Act Concerning Establishment of Compulsory Cartels of 1933 (sec. 1).[36]

The number of associations carrying out cartel resolutions increased rapidly under these acts. The number of industrial associations was 20 in 1925, 51 in 1927, 82 in 1929, 152 in 1931, 344 in 1933, 662 in 1935, and 850 in 1936.[37]

The major industries in which industrial associations had been formed included cotton spinning, silk spinning, various metal products, electric bulbs, china, matches, pencils, toys, and weighing and measuring tools.[38]

(iv) Other laws

During the recession of the 1920s, the Trust Banking Business Act of 1922 and the Banking Business Act of 1927, which provided for a minimum capital requirement for incorporating banks and trust banks, were enacted. Through these acts, as well as by administrative guidance under them, the concentration in financial fields increased remarkably. The number of trust banks, 488 in 1921, was reduced to 28 in 1924. The number of banks, 1,417 in 1926, was reduced to 779 in 1930.[39]

During this process of financial concentration, the *zaibatsu* concerns also strengthened their relative positions in each industry. Due to their stronghold in financial fields, these *zaibatsu* could buy out many companies that were weakened during the periodic depressions. However, such a dominant position had invited criticism from the military, and anti-*zaibatsu* feeling ran high among the public in general.[40]

Beginning about 1930, new middle-sized *zaibatsu* concerns such as Nissan, Nakajima, Nicchitsu, Mori, Nisso and Riken had started to emerge. They were mainly in heavy industry and the chemical industry sectors, and lead the economic expansion of Japan into heavy industry.[41]

In the 1930s, many monopolistic companies were established by law. For example, three giant companies were established under the Japan Iron and Steel Company Act of 1933, the Japan Power Generation Company Act of 1938, and the Greater Japan Aviation Company Act of 1939, respectively. In 1934, the Japan Iron & Steel Co. was established by merging the government-owned Yawata Iron & Steel Foundry and seven other privately owned iron and steel companies. This company thereafter produced 95.2 percent of the total pig iron production and 50.7 percent of the total steel production in Japan.[42]

Also, in the 1930s, many business control laws were enacted in important industries in which the government had exercised control on business activities, on one hand, through it's authorization power, and on the other, through protection of business by restricting new entry or imports, or by giving tax reductions, etc.

During World War II, financial institutions and small enterprises were further compelled to disappear through mergers and government reorganization plans. As a result, the number of banks, 426 in 1938, was reduced to 61 by 1945.[43]

(v) Positions of zaibatsu *concerns*

The *zaibatsu* concerns' market control power was enhanced through war time control of the economy. The position of the four major *zaibatsu* concerns at the end of the war was as follows:

The ratio of the aggregate paid-in capital of 544 companies directly and indirectly controlled by Mitsui, Mitsubishi, Sumitomo and Yasuda was 24.5 percent of that of the total industrial sectors, 49.7 percent of that of financial businesses, and 32.4 percent of that of heavy industry. In light industry, it was 10.7 percent, but in marine transportation, it was 60.8 percent. Low figures for light industry were one of the characteristics of the Japanese *zaibatsu*.

The top 10 *zaibatsu* groups comprised 35.2 percent of the aggregate paid-in capital. Furthermore, the four major *zaibatsu* concerns controlled 131 subsidiary companies abroad, which comprised 80 percent of the total Japanese private foreign investment.[44]

Following the Meiji period, the *zaibatsu* families established holding companies to control various subsidiary companies. In the *zaibatsu* structure, a holding company such as Mitsui Honsha, generally controlled its subsidiary companies through stockholdings, the right to appoint and recall board members of subsidiaries, interlocking directorates and other contractual terms or financial ties.

All business activities were coordinated uniformly by the single decision making of a holding company. However, this does not necessarily mean that family members dominated group activities. They were assisted by many of the best and brightest graduates of the

Imperial Universities. *Zaibatsu* headquarters recruited many of these graduates and dispatched them to its subsidiaries.

(vi) Court decisions

As was previously the case, the courts' attitude was very favorable to anticompetitive conduct. But, the decision of the Supreme Court of August 30, 1940 on a boycott by the Taiwan Banana Middlemen's Association was a very important exception. Rejecting the lower court decision, the Court found that such refusal to deal by the Middlemen's Association with a certain dealer who enjoyed a monopolistic position in the selling market of Taiwan Banana, without a justifiable reason, constituted "a misuse of a monopolistic position by middlemen, and therefore is illegal conduct which is against public order, because this conduct goes beyond a proper scope of conduct which can be accepted within a society."

This decision referred to a series of German Supreme Court decisions in which refusal to deal by a person with a monopolistic position or an association with the same position was declared illegal.[45]

This incident suggests that, if Japan took this course of action, it would have become a country with European-type competition laws concerning abuse regulation. It is also noteworthy that in Japan only the 20 years between 1925 and 1945 can be characterized by compulsory cartels. Even before World War II, cartels could dominate the relevant market of Japan only through government intervention and the regulation of outsiders.

(B) ECONOMIC DEMOCRATIZATION MEASURES AFTER WORLD WAR II

(1) ECONOMIC DEMOCRATIZATION MEASURES

Japan's fundamental economic policy assignment after World War II was stated in the U.S. President's directive of September 6, 1945 as follows:[46]

Encouragement shall be given and favor shown to the development of organization in labor, industry and agriculture, organized on a democratic basis. Policies shall be favored which permit a wide distribution of income and of ownership of the means of production and trade.

Those forms of economic activity, organization and leadership shall be favored that are deemed likely to strengthen the peaceful disposition of the Japanese people, and to make it difficult to command or direct economic activity in support of military ends.

To this end it shall be the policy of the Supreme Commander:

(A) to prohibit the retention in or selection for places of importance in the economic field of individuals who do not direct future Japanese economic effort solely toward peaceful ends; and

(B) to favor a program for the dissolution of the large industrial and banking combinations which have exercised control of a great part of Japan's trade and industry.

The economic democratization measures effected in the following three areas were called "the three basic policies for economic democratization:"[47]

(A) farmland reform,
(B) labor legislation reform,
(C) democratization of industry.

With regard to the democratization of industry, Directive No. 244 of the Supreme Commander for the Allied Powers (SCAP), entitled, "Dissolution of Holding Companies," dated November 6, 1945 was issued.[48] This directive made it clear that its ends would be attained by:

(A) Dissolution of the *zaibatsu* and other enterprise combinations;
(B) Abolition of various measures to promote private monopolization;
(C) Establishment of a free competitive system.

In January 1946, prior to the execution of *zaibatsu* dissolution, a special mission headed by Dr. Corwin D. Edwards was sent to Japan to survey the *zaibatsu* combines.[49] The essential findings and recommendations of this mission were published in October 1946. The summary said that:

(A) The domination exercised by the *Zaibatsu* over the Japanese economy was so powerful as to be unprecedented in any other capitalistic industrial country.

(B) The responsibility of the *Zaibatsu* for Japan's aggressive program existed chiefly in its organization. Whether or not leaders of the *Zaibatsu* were individually promoters of war was not important. The important point was that the *Zaibatsu* organization offered a convenient support for military aggression.

(C) A few great *Zaibatsu* controlled Japanese industry and foreign trade, were made powerful by the Companies Act of Japan and were backed by the Japanese government. The concentration of dominating economic power made it possible to preserve semi-feudal relations between employers and employees, to control wages, and to prevent the development of independent political thought, thereby delaying the rise of a middle class such as had opposed militarism in democratic countries.

Based on such findings of fact, it recommended the following:

The chief aim of American policy is to destroy the organization which may bring about the above result and to foster diffusion of economic control adequate to prevent militarists from dominating government policy.

(2) ZAIBATSU *DISSOLUTION*

As the first step in eliminating the *zaibatsu* combines, SCAP Directives Nos. 215, 403 and 408 of 1945 had ordered a freeze on the assets of 18 *zaibatsu* combines, including Mitsui, Mitsubishi, Sumitomo, and Yasuda.[50]

Then, under the Holding Company Liquidation Commission Ordinance enacted in April 1946, companies designated as holding companies were ordered to transfer securities in their possession to the Holding Company Liquidation Commission (HCLC) and to dispose of them under the supervision of HCLC.[51]

Eighty-three companies were designated by HCLC by September 1947; among them 42 were dissolved, including Mitsui Honsha and Mitsubishi Honsha.[52]

In order to eliminate combinations through stockholdings or personal or contractual relationships with the *zaibatsu*-affiliated companies, Imperial Ordinance No. 567 of 1946—Restriction of Securities Holding, Etc., by Companies[53]—was issued. Initially, 1,204 companies were designated by this ordinance, but after review, the number was reduced to 616.[54]

HCLC was further assigned by SCAP to enforce restrictions on the *zaibatsu* families, and by Imperial Ordinance No. 592 of 1946, 56 persons from 14 *zaibatsu* families were designated and ordered to transfer the securities in their possession to HCLC. They were also restricted from holding executive positions in companies, in accordance with the provisions of the Act for Termination of *Zaibatsu* Family Control of 1948 (Act No. 2 of 1948).[55]

SCAP Directive No. 550 of 1946 also ordered about 2,200 executives of 245 *zaibatsu*-affiliated companies to retire.[56]

In 1948, by amendment of Imperial Ordinance No. 567 of 1946, HCLC was authorized to prohibit the use of names and trademarks of the former *zaibatsu*. The names and trademarks of Mitsui, Mitsubishi and Sumitomo, among others, were scheduled to be prohibited after June 1950, but this deadline was postponed to 1952, and finally, the ordinance itself was repealed in 1952 without any prejudice to the companies designated.[57]

(3) ECONOMIC DECONCENTRATION

In December 1947, the Act Concerning the Elimination of Excessive Concentration of Economic Power (Act No. 207 of 1947) was passed. It empowered HCLC to designate and eliminate "excessive concentration of economic power."[58]

Initially, there were 325 companies designated by the Act, but application of this Act was later relaxed due to changes in the Occupation policy by the U.S. As a consequence, the number of companies that were ordered to restructure their organizations was reduced to 18.[59] In addition, under the special measures applicable to electric power companies, the Japan Electric Generation and Transmission Co. was divided into nine local power companies.

Out of these 18 companies, 4 companies were ordered to dispose of their stock in other companies, 3 companies were ordered to dispose of a part of their factories, and 11 companies were actually dissolved into several companies to change their corporate structures. For example, the Japan Iron & Steel Co. was divided into two companies, the Fuji Iron & Steel Co. and the Yawata Iron & Steel Co.; and the Japan Beer Co. was divided into the Asahi Beer Co. and the Supporo Beer Co.[60]

The Mitsui Mining Co. and the Mitsubishi Mining Co. each transferred its metal business to separately created companies. The Mitsubishi Heavy Industry Co. and Oji Paper Co. were divided into three separate companies respectively.[61]

The Mitsui Bussan (Mitsui & Co.) and the Mitsubishi Shoji (Mitsubishi Trading Co.), which were the most important enterprises of the *zaibatsu* combines, were dissolved by SCAP Directive No. 1741 (dated July 3, 1947). The Mitsui Bussan was divided into 200 companies and the Mitsubishi Shoji into 139 companies. However, *zaibatsu*-affiliated banks were not subjected to dissolution measures, but when the Antimonopoly Act was enacted, their stockholding in other companies in Japan was restricted.[62]

(4) THE BREAK-UP OF PRIVATE CONTROL ORGANIZATIONS

Prewar cartel organizations were closely regulated and protected by the government and the government made use of these cartel organizations for the purpose of economic control during the war. As a result, after the war, these organizations were dissolved or reformed by the Closed Institutions Ordinance of 1947, Cabinet Order No. 238 of 1947, issued in accordance with section 104 of the Antimonopoly Act, and SCAP Directive No. 1860 of 1948.

Laws that supported the development of such organizations were also abolished. The control of the distribution of scarce goods, which was necessitated by their short supply after the war, was carried out directly by government organizations.

(C) ORIGINAL ANTIMONOPOLY LAWS

(1) BACKGROUND OF THE ENACTMENT OF THE ANTIMONOPOLY LAWS

SCAP Directive No. 244 of November 6, 1945 had required the enactment "of such laws as will eliminate and prevent monopoly and restraint of trade, unreasonable interlocking directorates, undesirable intercorporate security ownership and assure the segregation of banking from commerce, industry and agriculture, and as will provide equal opportunity to firms and individuals to compete in industry, commerce, finance and agriculture on a democratic basis."

The Japanese government ordered the ministries concerned to draft a bill to implement the contents of this directive.

In early 1946, a Bill for Industrial Order (*Sangyo Chitsujo Hoan*) was drafted by the Ministry of Commerce and Industry. (Later, this ministry became the Ministry of International Trade and Industry. Hereinafter referred to as MITI). As the name implies, the bill was based on the abuse regulation principle on cartels and trusts of pre-war times. However, contrary to the expectation of the Japanese government, the draft was rejected by the SCAP as inadequate. SCAP prepared its own draft and presented it to the Japanese government. Its ideas were based on American antitrust law, and it also incorporated some provisions recommended in the U.S. in October 1943 by the Temporary National Economic Committee, chaired by Senator O'Mahoney.[63]

Therefore, in December 1946, a committee was established composed of various ministry representatives. It drafted a new bill, keeping close liaison with SCAP.

A Bill Concerning the Prohibition of Private Monopoly and Maintenance of Fair Trade was thus prepared and approved by SCAP, then presented to the Imperial Parliament on March 25, 1947. Parliamentary discussion was held on March 28 and without much argument, the bill passed on March 31, the final day of the Imperial Parliament.

The government promulgated the new act on April 12 and it became effective on July 20, 1947 (Act No. 547 of 1947). This day is celebrated as "Foundation Day" of the Fair Trade Commission (FTC).

(2) OUTLINE OF THE ORIGINAL ANTIMONOPOLY ACT

The Antimonopoly Act originally consisted of 10 chapters, 100 sections and 14 supplementary provisions. It contained both substantive provisions and procedural provisions, as well as organizational provisions for the enforcement agency, the FTC.

As was clear from the background of its enactment, the Act was patterned after the American antitrust laws and had combined the three basic antitrust laws, namely, the Sherman Act, Clayton Act and Federal Trade Commission Act into a single law.[64] It also contained a number of provisions not existing even in the American antitrust laws.

There are three basic prohibitions under the Act, namely private monopolization, unreasonable restraint of trade, and unfair methods of competition. The first two concepts were adopted from sections 1 and 2 of the Sherman Act and the third concept was adopted from section 5 of the Federal Trade Commission Act. The latter was intended to supplement the former two prohibitions by regulating the incipient level of impacts on competition.

In addition, those practices regulated under the Clayton Act were also included supplementally, namely regulations on mergers, transfers of business, acquisition of stocks and interlocking directorates.

Among others, the following provisions were important:

(i) Prohibition of concerted activities per se unless their impact on competition is minor. (sec. 4)
(ii) Prohibition of establishing private control organizations. (sec. 5)
(iii) Prior approval system and restriction on international agreements. (sec. 6)
(iv) Restriction on undue and substantial disparity in economic power that cannot be justified by technological reasons. (sec. 8)
(v) Prohibition against establishing a holding company. (sec. 9)
(vi) General prohibition of intercorporate stockholdings by non-financial companies unless authorized by the FTC. (sec. 10)
(vii) General prohibition of stockholdings by a financial company in excess of 5 percent of another company. (sec. 11)
(viii) Restriction on debenture holdings by companies in excess of 25 percent of another company's capital in Japan. (sec. 12)
(ix) Prohibition on interlocking directorates among companies in a competitive relationship, or on holding a position as a director in four or more companies in Japan. (sec. 13)

(x) Prior approval system by the FTC for all mergers or transfers of business. (secs. 15 & 16)

As seen above, one of the characteristics of the Original Anti-monopoly Act was the existence of many preventive or supplemental provisions. It was feared that, for the Japanese who were not familiar with antitrust concepts, vague prohibitive provisions like those of the American antitrust laws would not offer an effective guide to serious enforcement. These detailed regulations were intended to make sure that any types of anti-competitive conduct would be covered by the Act.

However, to those who did not appreciate the antitrust laws, these supplemental regulations were thought intolerably severe and unrealistic. The provisions were deemed nothing but a disturbance of the legitimate activities of Japanese business. Major prohibition provisions were thought problematic by those lawyers who were familiar with continental legal thinking, and it was thought that these concepts lacked the preciseness needed for a law, thus leaving too much room for the discretion of its enforcers. (See chapter 22 (A) Policy Evaluations.)

The FTC was created as an enforcement agency, modeled after the U.S. Federal Trade Commission. The idea of an independent regulatory commission was new to the Japanese government's organization system and most of what had been created during the Occupation period was abolished when the Occupation ended. The FTC was an exception; a quasi-judicial administrative agency that could continue to exist.[65]

The organization and procedures were quite similar to the Federal Trade Commission, and the FTC was attached to the Prime Minister's office to enable independent exercise of its power (see Chapter 14 FTC Organization.)

The Original Antimonopoly Act also had strict provisions on exemptions. Unlike American antitrust law, the Antimonopoly Act had provisions on exemptions in the Act (secs. 20-24). In addition, the Act Concerning Exemption, etc., of the Application of the Act Concerning Prohibition of Private Monopoly and Maintenance of Fair Trade was enacted in 1947 (Act No. 138 of 1947). It was meant to be the exclusive source of exemptions provided under section 22 of the Antimonopoly Act. However, this principle was easily broken by enacting separate exemption laws later (see chapter 2 (B) Enactment of Various Exemption Laws).

(3) OUTLINE OF THE TRADE ASSOCIATION ACT

As explained, in the prewar period, private control organizations or compulsory cartels were utilized as War-time control machines. SCAP suggested the necessity of having separate laws of trade associations, in view of their strong influence on business behavior in Japan. The Trade Association Act (Act No. 191 of 1947) was enacted on July 29, 1947. The essential purpose of this act was to define the legitimate scope of trade association activities, and to make it clear that anything other than legitimate kinds of conduct would be prohibited. It also adopted a notification system to place trade associations under effective regulation by the FTC (sec. 3).

Permitted conduct specified in the Act were: compiling statistics, public relations activities, labor relations activities, chambers of commerce and industry activities, arbitration of disputes among entrepreneurs, and cooperation with the FTC. In addition, the FTC was empowered to approve other types of legitimate conduct (sec. 4).

Prohibited conducts were: control of production and distribution, concerted activities, unreasonable restraint of trade, price control, limiting the number of entrepreneurs, limiting the functions of constituent members, owning business facilities, owning natural science research facilities, owning patents, financing, engaging in business enterprises, acting as an agent for transactions, collecting accounts for entrepreneurs, arbitration of commercial matters, unduly influencing legislation and rigging bids (sec. 5).

Some activities of cooperatives, etc. were exempted from the application of the Trade Association Act.

(4) ECONOMIC CONTROL

Direct economic regulation to control scarce goods was carried out by government agencies, according to a SCAP directive, because giving such power to private organizations might revive prewar control organizations. Control organizations could handle the necessary control of scarce goods effectively, but their elimination was favored by SCAP. For example, when the Temporary Adjustment of Demand and Supply of Commodities Act was passed it also established various public corporations exclusively to distribute the designated commodities.[66] This temporary economic control was abolished around 1950 as the economy recovered.

NOTES

[1] The Japanese legal system was adopted first from the French and then, as the Meiji government became hostile toward the republican ideal of French style, more and more influence was exerted by the German legal system or jurisprudence.

[2] The economic liberalization policy of the Meiji government was necessary for these potential entrepreneurs to start on the road to growth. The Meiji government had a very significant role in the economic development of Japan, but these private initiatives were the most important factors for Japanese economic development. For example, one of the first silk spinning industries was developed in farmland near Lake Suwa in the Nagano Prefecture, a rural district.

[3] Apparently, these were not the kinds of industries that the Meiji government had tried to encourage. The beer brewing business was started in 1869 by a foreigner, and after his business failed, a Japanese beer brewing company was established in 1886. Sugar was one of the important imports of the 1870s.

[4] In the late Tokugawa period, many *daimyo* (feudal lords), in order to increase their revenues, tried to encourage businesses such as textile spinning, mining and agricultural products in their own fiefdoms. Many of these businesses had failed after the Japanese market was opened to foreign products, but some of them would later grow as private businesses. The *daimyos* were financed by moneylenders in Osaka and Edo (Tokyo), which were becoming Japan's financial centers.

[5] Under these treaties concluded in 1854, Japan was bound to a maximum tariff of 5 percent ad valorem on a wide range of items. This was regarded as shamelessly unequal and became a target of government criticism from opposition groups. Full independence in tariff matters was achieved in 1911.

[6] Competitiveness in the Japanese textile industry was achieved during this period mainly through private investment. It should be remembered that free trade conditions in this period made it possible to purchase cheap raw materials such as cotton from India. From 1868 to 1876, cotton thread occupied about one-third of all imports and provided cheap raw materials for the cotton spinning industry. H. Ohuchi, *Keizaishi* (Economic History), in T. Yanaihara ed., GENDAI NIHON SHOSHI (The Short History of the Modern Japan), Vol. 1 (1961), at 79.

[7] The Meiji government started a tax reform program in 1872, changing from a rice-based feudal system to a modern tax system. The Meiji government used the new revenues from tax reform as capital investments for modern factories, for inviting foreign engineers and technicians and for the purchase of new machinery. Also, the government used these revenues as funds for financing these industries.

[8] Here we meant to emphasize that *zaibatsu* concerns did not grow out of the textile spinning industry, Japan's first modern industry. Of course, there existed many influential textile companies which were even designated by the GHQ as holding companies. Among 83 holding companies designated were the Katakura Partnership, the Kurashiki Spinning, the Fuji Cotton Spinning, the Great Japan Spinning, the Nisshin Spinning, the Shikishima Spinning, the Imperial Rayon, and the Oriental Spinning. See note 52 below.

[9] In 1888, the Spinners Federation (*Boseki Rengo Kai*), to overcome the depression following the Japan-China War, had engaged for 3 months (8 days per month) in the first production curtailment. The second production curtailment was effected in 1890, and the third was effected in 1892. This was the first cartel activity in Japan. As to the second curtailment, a penalty for a violation was even provided. See R. Minobe, *Karuteru, Torasuto, Kontzerun* (Cartel, Trust and Konzern), KEIZAIGAKU ZENSHU, Vol. 47-2 (1931), at 21–23.

In 1902, by expanding their membership, the Federation was reorganized into the Greater Japan Spinners Federation (*Dai Nihon Boseki Rengokai*). It had also functioned as an important export promoter into the Chinese market by assessing necessary funds from its members and distributing them to exporting members. It also engaged in import restriction activities. See R. Minobe, at 23–24.

[10] In 1904, a joint sales organization was formed in flax spinning. In 1907, the Chemical Fertilizer Federation was established, and three fertilizer companies had formed a price-fixing agreement on superphosphate. In 1908, these three companies had formed a joint sales organization; in 1908, three coal companies in the Joban coal field formed a joint sales organization. In 1908, three sugar refining companies formed a production restriction agreement and a joint sales organization, and in 1910, the Taiwan Sugar Refining Federation was established. In 1909, three railroad car manufacturers concluded an order allocation agreement for railway goods. In 1909, three flour mill companies formed a production restriction agreement, and in 1914, the Flour Mill Federation was established. In 1910, four petroleum companies including the Standard Oil Co. and the Rising Sun Co. formed a price-fixing, customer and supply allocation agreement (this was an international cartel). In 1911, a joint sales organization was formed by the Paper Boards Manufacturers. As to the spinning industry, the Greater Japan Spinners Federation engaged in production curtailment 11 times from 1890 to 1930. See R. Minobe, *supra* note 9, at 30–31, 367 371.

Among the above-mentioned cartels, the price-fixing agreements on superphosphate, the fertilizer companies' joint sales organizations, the railroad car manufacturers' order allocation agreements, the petroleum companies' price fixing customer and supply allocation agreements, and the sugar refining companies' joint sales organizations were broken within a year due to internal conflicts.

[11] Unequal provisions of the Treaty were amended first in 1894 with the United Kingdom, then with 14 other countries thereafter. This was a significant diplomatic achievement for the Meiji government, and opened the door for Japan to join in the world as a superpower. See E. HADLEY, ANTITRUST IN JAPAN (1970), fn. 18, at 38 and references therein.

[12] For discussion on the definition of *zaibatsu* see E. HADLEY, *supra* note 11, at 21–23. The Sumitomo had its origin dating back to the latter 16th century when it started copper smelting works. The Mitsui had its basis in a draper store opened in Edo in 1673.

[13] For the Miike coal mine transfer to Mitsui, see E. HADLEY, *supra* note 11, at 35.

[14] H. Iyori, *A Comparative Analysis on Japanese Competition Law: An Attempt to Identify German and American Influences*, in H. Coing et al. eds., DIE JANANISIERUNG DES WESTLICHEN RECHTS (1988), at 228. For example, I. GOTO, KIGYOKAN NO RENGO TO GODO (Combination and Trust Among Enterprises) (1901); U. TODA, GODO-KARUTERU OYOBI TORASUTO (Combination, Cartels and Trusts) (1910); H. SEKI, KOGYO SEISAKU JOU (Industrial Policy 1st Vol.) (1911).

[15] H. Iyori, *supra* note 14, at 233. As an example of exceptional views, see S. Tanaka, *Karuteru Horitsuron* (Legal Theory on Cartels), HOGAKU KYOKAI ZASSHI, Vol. 40, No. 12 (1922), where he insisted upon the necessity of control against cartels. T. Umeda also supported the free trade theory and criticized the enactment of the Important Industries Control Act. He stated that, "Foreign governments have been considering how to control abuses of cartels, but the Japanese government is trying to promote cartels. There is certainly a fear that the Control Act prepared by the Industrial Rationalization Bureau would ironically result in delaying progress of rationalization." T. Ueda, *Gorika wo Samatageru Sangyo Toseiho* (The Industrial Control Law Hindering Rationalization), JIYU TSUSHO, Vol. 4, No. 4 (1931), recompiled in Ueda, Teijiro Zenshu Vol. 7 (1956), p. 684.

[16] I. Nakaguchi et al. v. T. Hata, Osaka High Court, Feb. 15, 1907, Horitsu Shinbun No. 426, at 9.

[17] For example, B. Yokoi v. Osaka Liquor Retailers Associations, Supreme Court, July 19, 1920, Minroku No. 26, p. 992; N. Nagai v. Tokyo Pharmaceutical Associations, Supreme Court, Nov. 26, 1935, Hanketsu Zenshu No. 1, p. 1,246. The Supreme Court also had confirmed the legality of group boycotts in Z. Kawaura v. J. Fukuda et al., March 4, 1910, Minroku No. 16, P. 185.

[18] The Mogi Gomei Co., The Seventy-four Bank was the biggest of those that went into bankruptcy during this recession.

[19] During the depression starting in 1920, the Big Six merged many other spinning companies. As of 1930, members of the Greater Japan Spinners Federation numbered 62 and occupied 91 percent in terms of spindlage capacity. Among 62 companies, the Big Six occupied 80 percent in terms of spindlage capacity. See R. Minobe, *supra* note 12, at 350–351 & 356.

According to E. HADLEY, the Big Ten in spinning accounted for 60 percent of spindlage capacity in 1937, and 98 percent in 1945, *supra* note 11, at 369.

[20] *Id.* at table 15-1, p. 359. Between 1920 and 1924, six cartel organizations (bleaching powder, wool, canned crab sales, copper, coal mining, and cement) were established, whereas between 1926 and 1931, 21 cartel organizations (pig iron, bar steel, western paper, steel sales in the Kanto district, spun silk, sugar, rayon, gasoline, bars and flat steel, lime nitrate sales, sheet iron and medium thick steel sales, wire sales, flour milling sales, petroleum, ammonium sulphate, hemp, medium-sized chevron bars sales, small sized chevron bars sales, thick sheet iron and steel sales, black sheet sales, canned salmon) were established. After 1930, most cartels were in the form of joint sales organizations.

[21] H. Iyori, *supra* note 14, at 230. E. Hadley wrote; "Earlier in Japan's modernization, 'guidance' was handled through conversations between the pertinent ministers and the favored business houses. By the 1930s, however, with the expansion of the economy and an increase in the number of majors, more formal machinery was required. The recently developed cartels were the economic instruments relied on." *supra* note 11, at 363.

[22] According to Y. Kanazawa, E. Eggman pointed out that these two laws were the first compulsory cartel laws in the world in his DAS STAAT UND DIE KARTELLE (1945), at 32; Y. KANAZAWA, KEIZAI HO (Economic Law) (1961), at 51; KEIZAI HO NO SHITEKI KOSATSU (Private Observation on Economic Law), at 79 and note 15 therein. E. Hadley wrote; "While at no point during Japan's modern period had cartels [been] viewed unfavorably, the government in 1925 gave positive encouragement to their formation through passage of two laws. . ." *supra* note 11, at 365.

[23] H. Iyori, *supra* note 14, at 229. Y. Kanazawa, *Regulation of Corporate Enterprise*, in A. Mehren ed., LAW IN JAPAN (1963), at 482.

[24] H. Iyori, *supra* note 14. It should be noted that export promotion or antirecession measures had provided good excuses for legalizing cartel activities in general, even in a country where no strong antitrust philosophy existed.

[25] See reemergence of such laws after the war at chapter 2 (B) Enactment of Various Exemption Laws. We found much similarity in their philosophy and approach.

[26] MITI, SHOKO GYOSEI SHI (History of Commercial and Industrial Policies), Vol. 9, at 12–14.

[27] Just after this report, the Temporary Industrial Rationalization Bureau, which afterwards had tried to promote cartels and trusts, was set up within the Ministry of

Commerce and Industry. See MITI, *supra* note 26. According to E. Hadley, the Hamaguchi cabinet appointed the Temporary Inquiry Commission in Jan. 1930, which recommended encouragement of the amalgamation of enterprises on a large scale and encouragement of combinations and agreement such as agreements on production amounts, division of markets, sales prices, and other measures for the prevention of unnecessary competition, *supra* note 11, at 366–367.

[28] H. Iyori, *supra* note 14, at 230. In 1933, a new clause to compel manufacturers to send reports on the quantity and value of monthly output and sales, and stocks at the end of each month was added. The most important amendments in 1936 were the provisions that the participants in the recognized cartel agreements must represent not merely more than half of the producers but also more than half of the aggregated output or sales of the industry, which strengthened the position of cartels very much. See E. Hadley, *supra* note 11, at 366.

[29] E. Hadley, *supra* note 11, at table 9 in appendix VII, pp. 485–487, which lists the names of 32 cartels formed under the law. As to other cartels, see note 20 above.

[30] A control order was issued as to the cement industry. Under tightened economic control, cartels were entrusted with the right to determine the quantity of production, allotment of production quantity for each company and control prices, and could threaten to suspend allotments of raw materials to those who did not cooperate. E. HADLEY, *supra* note 11, at 369.

[31] Although Japanese cartel policy was greatly influenced by German law, Japan went further. For the comparison of Japanese and German policy on cartels, see H. Iyori, *supra* note 17, at 230–231. The Ordinance Against Misuse of Economic Power enacted in 1923 in Germany was the most important. As analyzed in the above article, Japanese economic law contained stronger characteristics of collectivism compared with German law.

[32] As to the process of concentration in the hands of the Oji Paper Co., see R. Minobe, *supra* note 9, at 233–236. The competitors of Oji, the Fuji Paper Co. and the Karahuto Kogyo Co. had the same process of concentration. *Id.* at 237–242.

[33] H. Iyori, *supra* note 14, at 232. Even in the U.S., the National Industrial Recovery Act was enacted in 1933 which contained a provision to allow a cartel agreement under a specified condition.

[34] It was a natural course for cartel legislation to have import restriction clauses in order to be effective. This was the course that the Export-Import Trading Act also took after the war. H. Iyori, *supra* note 14, at 232.

[35] This ordinance seems to be influenced by the German Act Concerning Preparation of Organic Construction of German Economy of 1934. *Id.* at 232.

[36] However, the German court declared certain conduct as misuses of economic power and, therefore, null and void, whereas, we can find no instances of such regulation by the Industrial Authority. The Japanese court had some power to declare the

illegality of such agreements, but the court can use such power only when asked by the plaintiffs in a law suit, which was very rare in Japan. See note 45 below.

[37] T. Tsuchiya and Y. Yoshi, *Chusho Kigyo Soshikika no Hensen* (Change of the Policies Concerning Small Enterprise Organizations) TSUSHO SANGYO KENKYU, Vol. 60 (1959), at 37. E. Hadley wrote that "it is reported that at the national level there were 1,538 control organizations 'coming to the attention of SCAP', and at the local level, 6,588." *supra* note 11, at 368.

[38] MITSUBISHI ECONOMIC RESEARCH INSTITUTE, NIHON NO SANGYO TO BOEKI NO HATTEN (Development of Industry and Trade in Japan) (1935), at 121–129.

[39] S. Asajima, *Honpo Shintakugyo no Shuchu Katei* (Concentration Process of the Trust Banking Business in Japan), in KINYU KEIZAI (Finance and Economy), Vol. 57 (1959), at 59–67; M. Fukushima and S. Haishi, *Kinyu Ho* (Financial Laws), in NIHON KINDAI HO HATTEN SHI (History of the Development of Modern Laws in Japan), Vol. 8 (1958), at 82–86.

[40] This movement was backed by fascist groups. E. Hadley wrote "the two major parties were primarily only spokesmen for the two largest combines—the Seiyukai for the Mitsui and the Minseito for the Mitsubishi. A major element in the rise of the military in the thirties was the contempt the Japanese people felt toward the political parties, which they regarded as pawns of the *zaibatsu*. The army was thought of as a purifying element." *supra* note 11, at 441.

[41] These enterprise groups were called newly created *zaibatsu* or newly created *konzerns*. Major shareholders of these newly created *zaibatsu* were companies and founders, and were more widely distributed, whereas almost all the capital of the Zaibatsu Honsha were owned by family members. As of 1937, more than a majority of mainstream subsidiaries were owned by the Zaibatsu Honsha. For example, 88.24 percent was owned by Mitsui, 59.2 percent by Mitsubishi, 56.74 percent by Sumitomo, and 59.34 percent by Yasuda.

Newly created *zaibatsu* depended on capital investments by persons other than their founders for their expansion, whereas the old *zaibatsu* could expand by their own capital investments. The lower shareholding ratios of the founders of newly created *zaibatsu* were the results of the different processes in their development.

[42] Other examples of such laws are the Petroleum Industry Act of 1934, the Automobile Manufacturing Act of 1936, the Iron and Steel Manufacturing Industry Act of 1937, the Airplane Manufacturing Industry Act of 1938 and the Shipbuilding Industry Act of 1939. These laws were abolished after the War, but the idea of enacting industry-by-industry laws was revived soon after the conclusion of the Peace Treaty in September 1951.

[43] The reorganization was carried out under the Enterprise Licensing Ordinance of 1941, the Financial Institutions Reorganization Ordinance of 1942 and the Enterprise Reorganization Ordinance of 1942, all of which were issued in accordance with the National General Mobilization Act of 1938. For example, in April 1943, the Mitsui Bank and the Daiichi Bank merged into the Imperial Bank.

[44] These findings were made by HCLC, *Nihon no Zaibastu to Sono Kaitai* (Japan's Zaibatsu and Their Dissolution), cited in E. HADLEY, *supra* note 11, at 45–57. These figures were as of 1946. For comparison with the Big Four, the Other Six represented 10 percent in terms of aggregated paid-in capital, 3.3 percent in finance, 16.6 percent in heavy industry, 6.1 percent in light industry, and 2.6 percent in others. Strong positions in heavy industry and light industry was characteristic of the Other Six.

By comparing the figures of 1937 and 1946, E. Hadley argues "It will be observed that in contrast to the 24.5% position of paid-up capital which the Big Four represented at the end of the war their position at the start was 12%" "The really significant increase in position in the economy for the Big Four, however, came during the Pacific War. . . . The Pacific War period was a striking success for the largest businesses in Japan." *Id.* at 56–57.

[45] The 1940 Taiwan Banana Middlemen's Association case, Supreme Court, August 30, 1940, Minji Hanrei Shu Vol. 19, No. 18, p. 1,521. The pertinent cases of the German Supreme Court are: Decisions of April 11, 1901, of Nov. 19, 1926 and of June 1, 1937 which are related to misuse of monopolistic positions; Decisions of June 25, 1890, of April 6, 1922 and of Dec. 18, 1931 which are related to misuses of economic power by trade associations. In these decisions, the alleged conduct was declared illegal, therefore, null and void.

[46] The First Stage of U.S. Policy toward Japan after the surrender, Directive by the President of the United States to General MacArthur, Sep. 6, 1945. According to T. Bisson, "The occupation officials who worked on the dissolution program soon learned that Japan 'had no real tradition or experience in the basic aspects of democratic capitalism.'. . . A competitive economy, regulated by government to maintain competition, Japan did not know. No favoring climate of opinion existed; the occupation would have to create it." T. BISSON, ZAIBATSU DISSOLUTION IN JAPAN (1954), at 39–41.

[47] For a short description on these reforms, see E. REISCHAUER, THE JAPANESE (1977), at 107–108.

[48] This Directive was issued in response to an official Japanese proposal for holding company dissolution incorporating the Yasuda Plan, Nov. 4, 1945. The Yasuda plan was proposed by the Yasuda Hozensha, a top holding company for the Yasuda Zaibatsu, as a voluntary measure for dissolving their *zaibatsu* structure.

By this Directive, the Japanese government is asked to present SCAP promptly for its approval;

"a. Plans for the dissolution of industrial, commercial, financial, and agricultural combines. . .

"b. Its program to abrogate all legislative or administrative measures which create, foster or tend to strengthen private monopoly.

"c. Its program for the enactment of such laws as will eliminate and prevent private monopoly and restraint of trade, undesirable interlocking directorates, undesirable intercorporate security ownership, and [assure] the segregation of banking from commerce, industry and agriculture and as will provide equal opportunity to firms and individuals to compete in industry, commerce, finance, and agriculture on a democratic basis."

For full text, see E. HADLEY, *supra* note 11, at 460–463.

[49] The State-War Mission on Japanese Combines. *Id.* at 125. THE FTC ANNUAL REPORT FOR FY 1947 (1948), at 2.

[50] The big four *zaibatsu* concerns were designated on Nov. 6, 1945, and the other 10 *zaibatsu* concerns, namely Ayukawa, Asano, Furukawa, Kawasaki, Matsushita, Nakajima, Nomura, Okochi, Okura and Shibusawa were designated on June 3, 1946. As a result, the property of the 56 persons belonging to the 14 *zaibatsu* families designated above were placed under the control of the Ministry of Finance, then under HCLC. These 56 persons were the heads of 11 houses and their family members belonging to 10 *zaibatsu* concerns.

Matsushita, Okochi and Shibusawa were eliminated from the designation thereafter in view of their scale.

[51] Imperial Ordinance No. 233, 1946. This ordinance was abolished on July 12, 1951.

[52] These were the number of holding companies, and about 1,200 companies could be counted as companies coming under their respective control, meaning companies owning 10 percent. According to E. Hadley, "That 83 holding companies were named does not indicate that there were 83 combines. As has been seen, combines numbered about 15 or 20. Rather, the designation of 83 holding companies came about out of the inclusion of major second-level holding companies within the combines." E. HADLEY, *supra* note 11, at 70.

Among these 83 holding companies, which included many operating companies, 16 companies were pure holding companies (first category) and eventually were dissolved, and 26 companies were operating companies (second category), as a result, these companies were dissolved but successor companies were created to continue their business activities. Among the remaining 41 companies, 30 were not ordered to make changes in their corporate structure, and 11 companies could survive after separate companies were created to make necessary changes in their corporate structure. *Id.* at 196.

The Mitsui Honsha was a first category company, but the Mitsubishi Honsha, the Sumitoino Housha and the Yasuda Hozensha were second category companies.

[53] Imperial Ordinance Concerning Restriction of Securities Holding, etc. by Companies, Nov. 25, 1946. Firms were continually added and subtracted. At its peak, it numbered about 1,200. See E. HADLEY, *supra* note 11, at 74 and fn 18.

[54] According to E. Hadley, "Although at peak the number of restricted firms was some 1,200, only 468 concerns participated. Furthermore, of the shares transferred, only approximately 60 percent were disposed of." *Id.* at 185.

DOKUSEN KINSHI SEISAKU 30 NEN SHI (The 30 Years History of the Antimonopoly Policies) [hereinafter 30 YEARS] published by the FTC said that the total number of companies that were subjected to the restriction were 682 designated companies, 1,383 affiliated companies and 769 related companies. As a whole, 40 million shares the equivalent to 1.67 billion yen were placed under such restrictions. 30 YEARS, at 21.

The voting rights on these shares were transferred to HCLC until they were disposed of.

[55] The list is given in E. HADLEY, *supra* note 11, at 466–467.

[56] These persons were persons holding key positions in 160 companies in Japan and 85 companies outside Japan between the outbreak of the War in China and the end of the war. *Id.* at 88.

Six hundred and thirty-nine executives were removed from their positions directly, 896 executives had resigned in anticipation of their removal or had retired earlier.

In addition, 405 officers were removed from 240 other companies. See *id.* at 91–92.

30 YEARS, *supra* note 54, at 21, said 2,192 persons were removed from executive positions. This number included 758 persons who were expelled from any official positions for other reasons.

[57] Imperial Ordinance Concerning Trade Name, Company Name and Trademark Which Were Used in Common by a Designated Holding Company and Companies Under the Same Ownership with Excessively Concentrated Companies, July 29, 1948; according to this ordinance, the HCLC Ordinance was amended on Aug. 19, 1948 by Cabinet Ordinance No. 240 of 1948.

[58] Act No. 207 of 1947. This Act was abolished in 1955.

[59] Overall, HCLC designated 257 companies from the industrial sector and 68 companies from the distributive and service sector, making a total of 325 companies. However, after the change in the U.S. Occupation policy, 225 companies were eliminated from the list of 325 companies on May 1 and July 1, 1948. After careful review, only 11 companies were subjected to the structural reorganization order, and eight companies were ordered to make adjustments in their assets, subsidiaries, etc. See table 9-1, in E. HADLEY, *supra* note 11, at 178–180; 30 YEARS, *supra* note 54, at 652–655.

In addition to the 19 companies above, 60 companies modified their corporate structures voluntarily to cope with economic difficulties.

[60] Initially, the Japan Iron and Steel Co. was dissolved and four new companies were created, namely, the Yawata Iron and Steel Co., the Fuji Iron and Steel Co., the Nittetsu Steamship Co. and the Harima Fire Brick Co.

The Japan Beer Co. was dissolved and the Asahi Beer Co. and the Japan Beer Co. were created. The latter changed its name to the Sapporo Beer Co.

[61] The Mitsubishi Heavy Industries were dissolved and the East Japan Heavy Industries, the Central Japan Heavy Industries and the West Japan Heavy Industries were created. In the case of the Oji Paper Co., the original proposal was to create six

companies, but finally three companies were created, namely, the Tomakomai Paper Mfg., the Jujo Paper Mfg. and the Honshu Paper Mfg.

In the case of the Mitsui Mining Co., the company continued to engage in coal mining and the Kamioka Mining Co. was created to engage in metal mining. In case of the Mitsubishi Mining Co., the Taihei Mining Co. was created to engage in the metal business. See note 59 above.

[62] In order to separate finance from commercial activities, sec. 11(1) puts a 5 percent ceiling on stockholdings in any other company. See chapter 11 (B) Restrictions on Stockholdings by a Financial Company.

[63] For example, it called for compulsory registration by companies residing or doing business in the U. S. of any international contract they may enter into that provided for restriction of output or sales, fixing of prices, dividing of markets and limiting or cross-licensing of patents. This idea was incorporated in section 6 of the Act. See Y. Ohara, *International Application of the Japanese Antimonopoly Act*, SWISS REVIEW OF INT'L COMP. L. Vol. 28, No. 5 (1986), at 7–9.

[64] Sherman Act, 15 U.S.C.A. §§ 1–7, Clayton Act, 15 U.S.C.A. §§ 12–17; Federal Trade Commission Act, 15 U.S.C.A. §§ 42–51.

[65] The Boards of Audit and the National Personnel Board are such exceptions. Most of the administrative commissions were attached to a ministry or an agency and do not have independent status like the FTC. However, when the Securities Inspection etc. Commission was established in 1992 within the Ministry of Finance, there existed strong opinions in favor of establishing an independent administrative commission. This episode seems to suggest that an administrative commission-type agency would have more public confidence in its neutral decision making nowadays.

[66] SCAP Directive Concerning Method of Control Under the Temporary Demand and Supply Adjustment Act (SCAP Directive No. 643, Dec. 11, 1946); E. Hadley wrote, "Because it was thoroughly unpalatable to continue the wartime control associations with their domination by the combines, and yet control organs were necessary, MacArthur resorted to the creation, in a limited number of cases, of agencies completely under government control, of 'kodan.' " *supra* note 11, at 371.

2

THE RETREAT OF THE ANTIMONOPOLY POLICY

(A) AMENDMENTS TO WEAKEN THE ANTIMONOPOLY ACT

Shortly after the enactment of the Antimonopoly Act, businesses started lobbying for its relaxation, but during the Occupation, any relaxation attempt could hardly succeed. The 1949 Amendment was an important revision of the Original Act, but cannot be viewed as a serious relaxation of it. Most of the modifications of the original provisions were thought unrealistic for Japan, at least at that time.

Soon after the conclusion of the Peace Treaty in September 1951, requests to relax the Antimonopoly Act by business circles and competent ministries became very demanding and this resulted in the 1953 Amendment. Various exemption laws were also enacted to bypass the Antimonopoly Act.

Furthermore and most importantly, production curtailments by way of administrative guidance by competent ministries, without any specific authority under law, began around 1951. These movements greatly influenced the FTC, compelling a very low level of enforcement activities (see chapter 15(B)(1) Trends of FTC Decisions).

However, through this process of relaxation, it became clear which groups in Japan actually supported the idea of the Antimonopoly Act. Business circles, in general, were hostile to the Antimonopoly Act but they also rejected the idea of giving stronger regulatory power to MITI even for the promotion of industrial policy. This decade, namely, the 10 years following the Peace Treaty, was a very interesting time in the history of Japan's economic policy. It was a time to determine whether Japan would accept a foreign-style antimonopoly act or move into a developmental state based on industrial policy different from other developed market economy countries.[1]

Let us examine the major incidents from this point of view.

(1) THE 1949 AMENDMENT

Beginning in early 1948, the implementation of the U.S. Occupation policy started to change, and the original Occupation policy was subject to review by the Japanese government. The Original Act had many unrealistic provisions and, in particular, some that could become obstacles to allowing the smoother and easier introduction of foreign technology and procurement of foreign capital in Japan, both of which were vitally needed at the time.

On July 31, 1949, the amendment to the law passed the Diet (Act No. 214 of 1947). The major points of the amendment were as follows:

(i)   A company may hold stock of other companies which do not compete with it, so long as such stockholding does not substantially restrain competition (new sec. 10).

(ii)   A company may hold the debentures of another company so long as such debenture holding does not substantially restrain competition (deletion of sec. 12 and amendment of sec. 10).

(iii)   Interlocking directorates among companies not in a competitive relationship are permitted (new sec. 13).

(iv)   The approval system of international contracts was changed to a post-notification system (new sec. 6).

(v)   The approval system of mergers or transfers of business was changed to a prior notification system (new secs. 15 & 16).

(vi)   Inclusion of a definition of competition (sec. 2(2)).

These changes were deemed as an amendment of the unrealistic provisions of the original Act, and did not constitute any retreat from antimonopoly policy.

(2) THE 1953 AMENDMENT

Soon after the conclusion of the Peace Treaty, in May 1951, the Ordinance Review Committee was established to review the various regulations issued during the Occupation period.[2] It submitted a report to the government in June, and pointed out, among other things, the necessity of relaxing the Antimonopoly Act and the Trade Association Act. Due to the depression following the end of the Korean war, requests from business circles became very intense.

Preparation of the amendment was started around the end of 1952.

In July 1952, as a first step in this movement, the Trade Association Act was relaxed substantially because it was the target of disgust by business circles and the industrial ministry. Then, in August 1952, the Specific Small and Medium Enterprise Stabilization Temporary Measures Act (Act No. 294 of 1952) and the Export Trading Act (Act No. 299 of 1952) were enacted. These laws were the first cartel exemption laws; later, others emerged frequently. These laws had provisions allowing the formation of cartels, and furthermore, allowed the issuance of ministerial orders to nonmembers of the cartel agreement to make them observe the restrictions of the cartel agreement.[3]

It should be remembered that these provisions were modelled after prewar cartel promotion laws. These laws were expanded through several revisions, for example, the Specific Small and Medium Enterprise Stabilization Temporary Measures Act was expanded into the Small and Medium Enterprise Organization Act (Act No. 185 of 1957); and the Export-Import Trading Act was expanded into the Export-Import Trading Act. This was the same course that cartel laws had followed in prewar days.[4]

Interestingly, the West German government's original bill against restraint of competition was made public about this time and those provisions in the bill to allow depression cartels, rationalization cartels and exports cartels had a great impact on the Japanese discussion of what kinds of antimonopoly laws were suitable for Japan. To those who favored cartel policy as an industrial policy tool and insisted on the introduction of these significant exemptions from the Antimonopoly Act, the German bill offered an encouraging sign.[5]

The bill prepared by the government received Cabinet approval in February 1953. At first, significant objections were raised to this amendment. In general, consumer organizations, small and medium enterprises, and agricultural associations took a critical stance against the bill. Scholars and opposition parties, in particular the Socialist Party raised strong objections. Newspapers and magazines carried critical comments and articles on the issue.

Although the objections were not strong enough to kill the bill, they showed that, at last in Japan, there existed groups outside of the FTC and academics, to support the Antimonopoly Act.

The amendment bill passed the Diet with a minor modification and was promulgated on September 1, 1953 (Act No. 259 of 1953).

The major amendments were as follows:

(i)   Deletion of section 4, the per se prohibition of certain concerted activities.

(ii)   Deletion of section 5, the prohibition of the establishment of private control organizations.

(iii)   Deletion of section 8, the remedial measures against undue and substantial disparity of economic power.

(iv)   Deletion of the provision on the restriction of debenture holdings (sec. 10 (1)).

(v)   Stockholdings, interlocking directorates, mergers, and transfers of business could be regulated only when they may substantially restrain competition, or when unfair trade practices are employed.

(vi)   "Unfair method of competition" was changed to "unfair trade practices" and abusive practices by entrepreneur with dominant bargaining positions were added so that they could be regulated as unfair trade practices (sec. 2(7)).

(vii)   Resale price maintenance contracts may be approved by the FTC under specified conditions (sec. 24-2).

(viii)   Depression cartels may be approved by the FTC under specified conditions (sec. 24-3).

(ix)   Rationalization cartels may be approved by the FTC under specified conditions (sec. 24-4).

(x)   Due to the abolition of the Trade Association, (ACT?) some of the provisions in the Act were adopted as a new section 8 of the Antimonopoly Act.

As a result of this amendment, most of the so-called preventive or supplementary provisions for the prohibition of cartels and trusts were deleted. Interestingly, holding company provisions (sec. 9) and 5-percent rules on financial company's stockholdings (sec. 11) were untouched.

The evaluation of the 1953 Amendment was mixed. To those who support strong antimonopoly policy, the 1953 Amendment represents a major retreat. In their view, this amendment caused the Antimonopoly Act to lose most of its effective provisions. To those who do not appreciate antimonopoly policy, the Act after the 1953 Amendment was still so strict that the cooperation necessary to promote the rationalization of industry could not be effected due to the Antimonopoly Act.

From that time on these two opinions clashed many times, and it was through these policy struggles that the Japanese antimonopoly policy was established.

Here again, we would like to draw your attention to the influence of Germany. We already indicated that provisions for depression cartels and rationalization cartels were adopted from sections 2 and 3 of the German bill proposed in 1952. The new exemption for resale price maintenance was also influenced by the German bill, although as to resale price maintenance, we can also see the influence of the Miller-Tydings Act of the U.S.[6]

New power to regulate abusive practices by entrepreneurs with dominant bargaining positions was also adopted from the German bill. This new power given to the FTC was favorably accepted even by those groups opposed to the Antimonopoly Act. This was accepted as small and medium firm policy because the abuse of buying power by larger retailers and the abuse of buying power by parent companies vis-a-vis their subcontractors, were thought of as a sort of social problem. With this new provision, it was expected that it would be possible for the FTC to regulate these abusive practices (see chapter 8 (H) Abuse of a Dominant Bargaining Position).

Abuse of buying power by parent companies vis-a-vis their subcontractors was thought so important that a separate law, the Act Against Delay in Payment Etc., to Subcontractors of 1956 (Act No. 120 of 1956) was enacted for the effective control of such abusive practices.

(3) THE PROPOSED 1958 AMENDMENT

In spite of the introduction of the approval of depression and rationalization cartels, business circles and industrial ministries further requested the relaxation of the conditions for FTC approvals.

Also, expanded coverage by these cartels was requested. In October 1957, the Kishi government established the Antimonopoly Act Review Committee for the purpose of "conducting a general review of the Antimonopoly Act." Members of this committee consisted primarily of representatives from the industrial sector. Because of this, the committee was referred to by its critics as the "Committee of Friends of Cartels."

The committee reviewed the materials presented by the FTC and MITI, as well as the opinions of various private organizations. In all, 64 organizations presented their views to the committee. The industrial sector requested urgent and wide-ranging relaxation of the Antimonopoly Act, saying that the existence of the Antimonopoly Act itself had caused unfavorable influences by stimulating excessive competition among businesses. They insisted that excessive competition should be blamed as a major cause of business instability at that time.

Consumer organizations, small business organizations, agriculture and fishery organizations expressed strong opposition to the further relaxation of the Antimonopoly Act. These groups took the view that the Antimonopoly Act was necessary for the protection of the weaker segments of society. It is noteworthy that these groups supported the Antimonopoly Act not because they believed that competition should be promoted, but because they believed that the Antimonopoly Act might be useful in eliminating the abusive conduct of big business in Japan.

After 4 months' deliberation, the committee came up with a recommendation to the effect that some provisions of the Antimonopoly Act were not suitable to the current situation in Japan, which was suffering from excessive competition. They suggested the Act be amended in the following ways.

(i) To relax the criteria for forming depression cartels and simplify the procedure for their approval, so that depression cartels could be approved when there exists a reasonable fear of depression and in a more expeditious way.

(ii) any kind of rationalization cartels shall be approved under a simplified procedure. Investment adjustment cartels shall be legalized, which means that new investment will be adjusted among competitors so as not to produce overcapacity or oversupply. Export promotion cartels, in addition to simple export cartels should be permitted by law.

(iii)   A merger or transfer of a business which may substantially restrict competition shall be approved if it is particularly necessary for the attainment of rationalization and the enhancement of international competitiveness.

(iv)   Unfair methods of competition provisions should be strengthened so that abusive conduct can be more effectively regulated.

In accordance with the report of this committee, a bill was drafted for an Antimonopoly Act amendment. The idea of export promotion cartels was incorporated into the amendment bill of the Export-Import Trading Act.

There was strong opposition to the bill. The Japan Socialist Party opposed the bill, and some Liberal Democratic Party members who represented agricultural and fishery interests and small business interests, raised objections.

In support of the FTC's opposition, scholars and journalists raised strong opposition to passage of the bill.

These movements to oppose the bill effectively prevented its reaching the discussion stage in the Diet, and at the end of the session, the bill was nullified. Although the Cabinet decided to submit the same bill again, because of the fierce opposition this was never done.[7]

After excluding the provisions regarding export promotion cartels, in 1961, the amendment to the Export-Import Trading Act finally passed the Diet.

This movement was the most significant event in antimonopoly policy development, because it meant that the Antimonopoly Act as amended in 1953 was accepted de facto for the first time by the Diet, and the public had been made to realize that it could not be relaxed easily.

However, this did not mean that the Antimonopoly Act was solidly accepted. It only meant that attempts to amend the Antimonopoly Act had failed. Besides, there were two other ways to effectively contain the importance of the Act.

Firstly, although the amendment movement had failed, it had greatly influenced the FTC, so that the enforcement activities of the Act became extremely passive around 1958. Only one case was reported in 1958, and only a few cases were taken up by the FTC (see table 15-1). In this period, many big mergers took place that had little trouble clearing the Antimonopoly Act. For example, in 1958 a merger was effected between the the Snow Brand Dairy Co. (Yuki-jirushi Nyugyo) and the Clover Dairy Co. (the combined market share of butter was 57.7 percent and that of cheese 75 percent) and between the Chuo Textile Co. and the Teikoku Linen Co. in 1959 (the market share of linen thread was 56.8 percent.) A decade before, these companies were divided by the Elimination of Excessive Concentration of Economic Power Act (see chapter 10 (A) (3) Other Cases).

In addition, by this time the Mitsubishi Shoji and the Mitsui Bussan, which had been split into more than a hundred small companies, were reunited to their predissolution level through a series of mergers and transfers of business.

(B) ENACTMENT OF VARIOUS EXEMPTION LAWS

From 1953 to 1957, more than 10 special laws that contained exemption provisions were enacted. These special laws provided for depression cartels and rationalization cartels in specific industries under conditions that were more relaxed than those in the Antimonopoly Act. The Coal Mining Industry Rationalization Temporary Measures Act of 1955 (Act No. 156 of 1955), had a provision that allowed depression cartels if done in accordance with a directive from MITI. The Textile Industry Facilities Temporary Measures Act of 1956 was another example of such a depression cartel (see chapter 25 (A) In General).

The idea of utilizing such cartels for the purposes of industry-wide rationalization or recovery from a depression was quite similar to prewar industrial policy. However, the big difference was that consultation with or consent of the FTC was needed. At first, for MITI, this provision did not constitute much of an obstacle to utilizing such cartels, but later, as the FTC regained its influence, it became difficult to do so.

These special exemption laws were enacted for declining industries and were justifiable because of the industries' declining status. They were enacted as temporary laws, ordinarily with a 5-year sunset clause. However, they were extended several times and some of them lasted for more than 20 years.

MITI was not satisfied to keep these exemption laws for declining industries only, and intended to extend the same idea to future industries, the so-called picking-the-winner policy. The Machinery Industry Promotion Temporary Measures Act (Act No. 156 of 1956) was enacted in 1956 and provided for an exemption of rationalization cartels if done in accordance with a directive to effect rationalization or an industry promotion plan prepared by MITI. The Electronics Industry Promotion Temporary Measures Act of 1957 (Act No. 171 of 1957) was the other example of such a rationalization cartel.

In 1956, MITI prepared similar bills which were applicable to the chemical and iron and steel industries, among others. But this idea never came to fruition because of opposition by business circles that feared that such laws would increase government control over their industries. This incident could be interpreted as a sign of recovery of the confidence of Japanese businessmen.

(C) PRODUCTION CURTAILMENT BY ADMINISTRATIVE GUIDANCE

Even before the 1953 Amendment to the Antimonopoly Act, MITI effected production curtailment based on administrative guidance, namely, a method to informally recommend that the industry concerned restrict production to a suitable level in order to recover from a depression. The 1953 Amendment, so far as depression cartels were concerned, had offered and excuse for MITI to utilize administrative guidance. MITI could insist that if production curtailment could be permitted under the Antimonopoly Act, MITI should be able to effect them through its administrative guidance in order to achieve industrial policy purposes.

It is widely accepted in Japan that a competent ministry can issue an administrative guidance even without a specific legal basis because administrative guidance is a mere moral suasion and simply calls for a voluntary act of cooperation with government offices. Therefore, the remaining legal question is whether business activities based on such an administrative guidance could be subject to the FTC's remedial power when such conduct falls under any one of the conducts prohibited under the Antimonopoly Act. (For further analysis, see chapter 5 (D) "Contrary to the Public Interest.")

In the Toyo Tayon case, the FTC took legal action against production curtailment that was found to constitute an antimonopoly law violation, and in other cases the FTC found it difficult to prove antimonopoly law violations due to the lack of communication of wills among companies. Thereafter, the FTC formally requested MITI to discontinue the use of administrative guidance.

If such production curtailment was carried out independently along the lines of a recommendation issued by government authorities to individual companies, it did not violate the Antimonopoly Act. This was because there is no concerted action among companies to constitute a mutual understanding (see chapter 6 (A) Definition of Cartels).

The FTC's request or criticism was disregarded by MITI, and recommended production curtailments were carried out frequently thereafter. This was true especially during the 1958 depression, when about 30 recommendations were issued concerning such industries as petroleum, electrolytic copper, lead, crude steel, various steel products, phosphoric acid, fertilizer, carbide, methanol, paper, textiles and sugar refining.

These production curtailments could be pursued as long as the FTC criticism could be disregarded. Beginning around the fall of 1963, criticism of production curtailment became so strong, not only from the antimonopoly policy side but from the price stability policy side, that it became an important national concern of that time. Production curtailment was finally abandoned in the spring of 1964 (see chapter 3 (A) (1) Policies Against Raising Prices).

NOTES

[1] C. Johnson looks at current Japan as a developmental state, however, we differ in this aspect from him. For his argument, see C. JOHNSON, MITI AND THE JAPANESE MIRACLE (1982), at 1-34.

[2] KEIZAI HOREI NO KAIHAI NI KANSURU IKEN (Views on Amendments or Elimination of Economic Laws and Orders), which was reported to Prime Minister Yoshida on June 21, 1931.

[3] This is called an outsider restriction order and is the most problematic aspect of the Japanese cartel exemption system. An outsider restriction order is based on the idea that cartels can serve the public interest by eliminating excessive competition. See chapter 25 (B) Cartel Exemption Laws.

[4] Y. Kanazawa wrote "MITI can order both members and nonmembers of the society to observe restrictions on competition imposed by MITI to accomplish the purposes of the society and order medium and small enterprises which are non-members to enter it. The parallel with the prewar statutory supported cartels is obvious." Y. Kanazawa, *Regulation of Corporate Enterprise*, in A. Mehren ed., LAW IN JAPAN (1963), at 498-499.

[5] See H. lyori, *A Comparative Analysis on Japanese Competition Law: An Attempt to Identify German and American Influences*, in H. Coing et al. eds., DIE JANANISIERUNG DES WESTLICHEN RECHTS (1988), at 238; F. Furuuchi, *Nishi Doitsu Renpo no Kyososeigen Boshi Ho* (Law Against Restraints of Competition of West Germany), KOSEI TORIHIKI (Sep., Oct. and Nov. 1952); F. Furuuchi, *Nishi Doitsu Tsusin* (Letters from West Germany), KOSEI TORIHIKI (April 1953).

[6] Miller-Tydings Act, 50 Stat. 693 (1937), 15 U.S.C. 1 (1970); McGuire Act, 66 Stat. 632 (1952), 15 U.S.C. 45 (1970).

[7] Small business feared that the bill would facilitate market control by big business. Agricultural organizations feared that production or sales restriction cartels such as in fertilizers or agricultural machinery would be formed, or buying cartels such as in dairy products would be formed.

3

THE CONFLICT BETWEEN ANTIMONOPOLY POLICY AND INDUSTRIAL POLICY

Just when antimonopoly policy took root in Japan is a difficult question and the answer depends on one's view of antimonopoly policy. One might say that the further relaxation attempt that failed in 1958 could be interpreted as a sign of the establishment of antimonopoly policy in Japan. However, the best way to evaluate antimonopoly policy is to examine its actual impact on business behavior.

In this chapter we will consider policy conflicts between antimonopoly policy and industrial policy, or conflicts between those who supported procompetition policy and those who insisted that a procartel policy was necessary to alleviate the negative impact of excessive competition in Japan.

(A) SIGNS OF INCREASING POLICY SUPPORT FOR THE ANTIMONOPOLY ACT

(1) POLICIES AGAINST RISING PRICES

During 1960, rising consumer prices became a phenomenal problem in Japan, and policies against rising prices started to arouse public interest. The general public became keenly aware of rising price levels and thought that inflation was depriving them of what they should be entitled to as a result of rapid economic expansion. It was the general feeling that rapid economic expansion benefitted big corporations only, and economic disparity between big business and small business was growing.

In view of the increasing importance of inflation, in September 1960, the government had announced countermeasures to curb inflation, and in the Cabinet's policy statement, the FTC was, for the first time at the Cabinet level, requested to strictly enforce the Antimonopoly Act as an effective means for curbing inflation.

The Price Problems Conference established by the Economic Planning Agency, one of the government offices, had published a *Report on the Recent Price Problems* in December 1963. This report pointed out that elimination of the causes that impeded free determination of prices was one of the fundamentals for achieving price stability. From this standpoint, the report concluded that: "Elimination of causes which impede free determination of prices is important from the viewpoint of bringing about changes of relative prices based on economic rationality (keizai gorisei), ensuring well-balanced development of the economy through optimum resource allocation, and effecting stabilization of prices as a whole. Recently, price increases by cartel agreements among small and medium enterprises and downward inflexibility of prices by the large enterprise sector have become conspicuous, and therefore, it is considered necessary to strengthen the enforcement of the Antimonopoly Act on price fixing agreements and to review government guidance policies such as the recommended production curtailment or restriction of production facilities through administrative guidance."[1]

This conclusion seems a very orthodox statement in 1980, but this was quite an important document that specifically requested stronger enforcement of the Antimonopoly Act, and this report set a course for government price policy thereafter. The 1964 Cabinet decision concerning the urgent countermeasures against rising prices had again called for stricter enforcement of the Antimonopoly Act and, more importantly, abolition of recommended production curtailment.

In 1966, the Price Problems Conference and its successor conference submitted various specific recommendations to the government. Measures to promote competition were stressed, and in particular, measures to strengthen the prohibition of resale price maintenance. The practice of resale price maintenance was looked upon as a mechanism used by large enterprises to maintain high prices in the domestic market for goods they produced, in spite of the cost savings of increased productivity.

The FTC, learning from U.S. arguments, started to engage in an industry-by-industry analysis of competitive conditions of oligopolistic industries. The above-mentioned conference recommendations had also called for the FTC to conduct research on so-called administered prices—the downward inflexible prices seen in highly concentrated industries.[2]

Under these circumstances, the FTC enforcement activities obtained policy support at the Cabinet level, and the FTC issued many decisions against price-fixing cartels and resale price maintenance practices. Examples include among others, the cement cartel case of 1966 (April 22, 1966, 14 KTIS 1), the color TV cartel case of 1966 (July 27, 1978, 25 KTIS 37) and the Matsushita Electric Co. resale price maintenance case in 1967 (March 12, 1971, 17 KTIS 187). It seems that the FTC tried to use its formal remedial power to focus on consumer-related goods.[3]

(2) GENERAL CONSUMER PROTECTION POLICY

Once price policy was emphasized, consumer protection policy also started to gain the general public's support. The consumer protection policy established by the Kennedy administration influenced such policy formulation in Japan.[4] The Committee for Raising the National Living Standard established at the Economic Planning Agency in June 1963 examined the matter and submitted a report concerning consumer protection. It emphasized that cartel activities were against consumer interests because consumers should be entitled to receive goods or services with prices established under free and fair competition. This philosophy began to be reflected in the government's policy toward consumer protection.

In May 1968, the Consumer Protection Basic Act (Act No. 78 of 1968) was enacted. The elimination of misleading representation for the purpose of protecting consumer interests, and maintenance of free competition were among the basic policy objectives of this act. However, in general, consumer protection policy was relatively weak and mainly promoted by the FTC and Economic Planning Agency.

(B) CHANGE OF INDUSTRIAL POLICY

(1) NEW INDUSTRIAL STRUCTURE POLICY

Emphasis on price policy and consumer protection policy did not mean that the era of industrial policy was over. In this period, industrial policy was going to be transformed into a policy to enhance the competitiveness of Japanese firms in order to cope with the liberalization of international trade. The policy tried to justify itself by emphasizing that the enhancement of competitiveness was necessary in order to compete in the world.

It was called the New Industrial Structure Policy because it emphasized structural reform of the Japanese economy. Traditional industrial policy was anti-antimonopoly policy, and regarded the Antimonopoly Act as a burden or obstacle to business activities.

The new industrial structure policy took a bit more favorable attitude toward procompetition policy. Namely, in November 1964, the Research Committee on Industrial Structure (*Sangyo Kozo Singikai*), established in MITI, presented a report concerning the new industrial structure policy. This report had one dissimilarity to the previous report by MITI, that was, evaluation of the role of free competition and the importance of the antimonopoly policy.

It stated that:

> It goes without saying that national economy admits freedom of activity for enterprises and finds its driving power in the originality and invention of enterprises. In order to advance the efficiency of industrial activities, full utilization of the function of competition should be made, and without it the above purpose cannot be attained. It is also considered important to promote the sense of responsibility on the part of enterprises through the function of competition, in view of the fact that the enterprises of this nation used to show a lack of such sense of responsibility in the past.
>
> Furthermore, the benefits earned through the improvement in efficiency of industrial activities could faithfully be returned to general consumers by way of competitive order in a best way. . . The role of the Antimonopoly Act to maintain competition is very important. In this sense, it is necessary to develop wider recognition concerning the role and the effect of the Antimonopoly Act.[5]

The report also emphasized the necessity of rationalization cartels and mergers in order to make an enterprise's activities more efficient. It envisioned that promotion of standardization of products, specialization of production, expansion of the scale of production, and expansion of corporate scale were necessary to structure Japan to compete in the world market.

In other words, new industrial structure policy favored market concentration through expansion of corporate scale. In particular, it favored the establishment of a leading company in each important industrial sector. To those who favored industrial policy, an oligopolistic market was desirable or at least unavoidable in order to enjoy economies of scale and thus to assure international competitiveness.[6]

The report suggested the establishment of a coordination conference between the government and business organizations where they could prepare a plan for the creation of a desirable industrial structure. The government would be able to guide business toward a desirable industrial structure by means of tax incentives or other financial measures.[7]

(2) RECOMMENDED PRODUCTION CURTAILMENT V. DEPRESSION CARTELS

The Japanese economy entered into a recession in mid-1964, and large-scale bankruptcies were reported. Under these circumstances, government agencies took measures for production curtailment as well as financial and fiscal measures to cope with the recession. In view of the difficult economic conditions, the FTC insisted, when necessary, upon using depression cartels under the Antimonopoly Act instead of the production curtailment method recommended by MITI.

Thereafter, many industries chose to file applications for depression cartels with the FTC. By the end of 1965, depression cartels were permitted in the following fields: pentachlorophenol weed killers, structural steel alloy, automobile tires and tubes, cameras, sugar refining, steel plate, vinyl chloride tube, paper board, cotton yarn, spun rayon, and vinylchloride plates and drills. For technical reasons, recommended production curtailment was undertaken as to crude steel (see chapter 6 (E)(1) Depression Cartel System).

The experts' evaluation of this incident is mixed. The major differences were in its approval procedure and rigid requirements for forming and terminating depression cartels. Remember that there was an attempt in 1958 to relax these requirements.

The FTC was criticized for being too lenient toward depression cartels, and criticism even came from the leading participants in depression cartels. The FTC terminated these depression cartels by the end of 1966.[8]

(3) INVESTMENT ADJUSTMENT

It was said that one of the factors that had caused the recession of 1964 was excessive investment in equipment by the private sector which had placed too much confidence in the continuation of Japan's rapid economic growth. In this connection, the problem of investment adjustment had been debated in early 1965. MITI called for informal cooperative conferences with leaders of such industries as petroleum, petrochemicals, synthetic fibers, and paper and pulp, to adjust the amount or timing of their investments in large-scale equipment.

Although only a few industries could reach an agreement at this conference, MITI's guidance had a big influence on the investment attitudes of these industries. The idea to adjust investment was justified because, it was believed, disorderly investment competition would result in overcapacity and thus excessive competition later.

With hindsight, the need to adjust investment was doubtful and the actual impact of these efforts by MITI can hardly be described as successful. However, it should be noted that this kind of interventionist idea was widely supported at that time and the FTC had great difficulty in resisting these efforts.

Investment adjustment was undertaken as a government action, and because investment adjustment did not bring about immediate anticompetitive behavior in a market, it was difficult for the FTC to find antimonopoly violations (investment adjustments took effect a few years later, and no immediate effect can be seen on competition in a market).

(C) BIG MERGER MOVEMENT

(1) LIBERALIZATION OF TRADE AND CAPITAL

As liberalization of the Japanese economy became inevitable after Japan had joined GATT, IMF and OECD, MITI undertook various measures to improve the international competitiveness of key industries, and the need to expand corporate scale through mergers and consolidation was emphasized.

Japanese firms were compared with U.S. companies in terms of paid-in capital, sales figures, and total assets, and most people concluded that Japanese firms were too small to compete in the world market with the huge American companies. It was feared that the liberalization of capital would bring about the drastic intensification of competition in the Japanese market.

As an incentive to promote mergers, MITI set up a preferential credit system, through the Japan Development Bank, offering preferential tax incentives. The Ministry of Transport arranged for 12 shipping companies to merge into 6 companies by April 1964, and the remaining shipping companies were to be affiliated with one of these six shipping companies. For this purpose, the Shipping Industry Reconstruction and Reorganization Temporary Measures Act (Act No. 118 of 1963) was enacted in 1963.[9]

Another idea advocated by MITI and business circles for facilitating mergers was to again legalize holding companies. In 1966, MITI and business circles announced their proposal to relax section 9 of the Antimonopoly Act. This idea did not have support outside of the business community and so did not come to fruition. However, because no country other than Japan prohibits holding companies and the idea of prohibition originated with the *zaibatsu* dissolution, section 9 has a symbolic meaning among the many provisions of the Antimonopoly Act.

This issue was raised several times thereafter.

(2) BIG MERGER MOVEMENT

In this period, liberalization measures sent a strong signal to Japanese business concerning merger and consolidation. The number of mergers involving big companies had increased. Natural partners in these mergers were companies that were separated after the war, or were members of the same business group.

Three Mitsubishi heavy-industry companies merged in 1964. The Nissan Motor Co. had merged with the Prince Motor Co. in 1966.

In the spring of 1968, the three largest paper manufacturing companies—the Oji Paper Mfg. Co., the Honshu Paper Mfg. C. and the Jujo Paper Mfg. Co.—that together accounted for 60 percent of newsprint, made public their merger plans. Soon after, the two largest Japanese steel manufacturers—the Yawata Iron & Steel Co. and the Fuji Iron & Steel Co.—that together held a 35.6 percent share of crude steel production, announced their merger plans. These two merger plans caused a public sensation because of their size and their market position (see chapter 10 (A)(2) Yawata-Fuji Merger Case).

These merger plans received the immediate support of MITI and business circles. However, about 90 economists made a joint announcement opposing such mergers and indicating their concerns about the mergers' impact on competition. Because events were reported in detail, the case became a litmus test for the Antimonopoly Act. In the case of the paper companies, the three companies voluntarily gave up their plans to merge after they got a negative informal reaction from the FTC.

The Fuji-Yawata merger case was settled in favor of a merger, but the case sent a strong message to business that the Antimonopoly Act could prevent big mergers even if they were supported by the competent ministries. Thereafter no mergers were attempted that could have an impact comparable to the Fuji-Yawata merger. It can be said that the merger movement prompted by fear of foreign competition, ended after this incident. More importantly, after this case, relevant companies tended to seek advance merger clearance from the FTC.[10]

Viewed with hindsight, this fear was totally unjustified. The trade and capital liberalization measures did not bring about any appreciable intensification of competition in the Japanese market. Besides, newspaper reports and analytical works carried in magazines concerning the Fuji-Yawata merger case provided the FTC with good public relations. It became, for the first time, a well known name throughout the nation. Therefore, in spite of its outcome, the case made a great contribution to enhancing the understanding of antimonopoly policy by those outside the FTC and academia. It had set a new starting point for the FTC's next decade.

(D) DEVELOPMENT UP TO THE 1977 AMENDMENT

(1) INCREASE IN ANTIMONOPOLY LAW ENFORCEMENT

(i) Establishment of the antimonopoly conference

The Fuji-Yawata merger case had indicated the importance of enhancing the public's understanding of the FTC's policy. In 1969 the FTC set up an advisory body called the Antimonopoly Conference. This was one of the council-type forums that were used by other ministries for policy making. The Conference was made up of law and economics professors, representatives of industry, commerce and finance, consumer and labor organizations, and journalists.

The Conference viewed FTC materials in advance of their publication. It enabled the FTC to learn the public's response to its activities beforehand, in particular when new policy was formulated. By going through this conference, the FTC could expand the understanding of antimonopoly policy, and also could get various suggestions from members of the Conference concerning its policies.

In the 1970s, the Conference became a forum to study administered prices in oligopolistic industries. This study revealed the weakness of the Antimonopoly Act as to oligopolistic industries. Through examination of possible measures that could be taken against administered prices, the idea for the Antimonopoly Act amendment was born.

As to resale price maintenance, the FTC had conducted a major review of designated commodities, and in 1973, abolished its designations on some commodities in order to eliminate their exempted status. The Antimonopoly Conference had provided the necessary policy support for this movement.

Various documents and materials submitted to the Conference were published as a series of books, providing researchers and scholars with information on antimonopoly law enforcement in Japan.

(ii) Economic research

The FTC had conducted economic research on various aspects of business activities in Japan. The Research Division and Trade Practice Division have been responsible for this research (see figure 14-1).

Beginning in 1949, the FTC tried to compile statistics on concentration ratios of major commodities. The first research covered only 63 items but the 16th, conducted in 1990, covered 581 items. Since 1967, the FTC has included the Herfindahl index, as well.[11]

Using the information contained in stockholding reports, the FTC also surveyed the stockholdings of six major business groups, of general trading companies, or sometimes, the stockholdings of the top 100 companies in the non-financial sector (see chapter 24 (B) FTC Study on Keiretsu).

The FTC had conducted various research on particular industries in order to examine their competitive conditions. These activities were quite useful in themselves, and also had great impact on the public, providing a basis for understanding antimonopoly policy.

(iii) International development

Since Japan had joined the Organization for Economic Cooperation and Development (OECD), the FTC had a chance to participate in the Committee of Experts on Restrictive Business Practices and the Committee on Consumer Policy. Through the exchange of information at these meetings, the FTC could learn what was happening in other developed countries and could share enforcement experiences for the same kinds of antimonopoly problems in these countries.

By participating in these OECD meetings, the FTC could get to know other OECD countries' enforcement agencies and using this network, the FTC sent its staff to the U.S. and European countries to study their experiences with particular policy issues that it faced.

In the 1970s, the United Nations Conference on Trade and Development (UNCTAD) examined the impact of restrictive business practices on trade and development and tried to establish a code of conduct on restrictive business practices, transfer of technology and multinational corporations. These developments made it necessary for the Ministry of Foreign Affairs, and other related ministries, to study the Antimonopoly Act and broadened antimonopoly issues from those for experts to issues for the Japanese government.

Since 1972, the FTC has dispatched staff to the Japanese Delegation to OECD in Paris, France; and since 1978, to the General

Consul Office in Berlin, Germany. Since 1981, the FTC has a secretary position at the Japanese Embassy in Washington, D.C. And since 1991 to the Japanese Delegation to the EC in Brussels, Belgium. These diplomatic positions contributed to the exchange of information on antimonopoly issues with the OECD, Germany, the U.S. and the EC.

(2) OIL SHOCKS AND CARTEL ACTIVITIES

We have already touched on the FTC's enforcement emphasis on regulating cartel activities in support of price policy in the 1960s. However, they were mostly section 8 cases. Section 8 cases met with less resistance from business, partly because only the identity of the trade association concerned was revealed in the decision. At that time, bad publicity was the most effective sanction against cartel activities.

Around 1972, section 3 cases started to increase, which meant that the FTC took a tougher stance toward cartel activities by revealing the identities of the cartel participants. Then the first oil shock shook Japan by quadrupling the import price of crude oil. Domestic prices rose drastically, and the nation as a whole was panicked.

Generally, businesses large and small tried to absorb this cost increase by forming cartels. In 1973 the FTC issued 67 decisions against cartel activities, 35 section 3 violations and 32 section 8(1)(i) violations. In 1974, 31 section 3 violations and 10 section 8(1)(i) violation cases were handed down. This was a record number for cartel regulation by the FTC (see chapter 15 (B)(1) Trends of FTC Decisions).

In February 1974, the FTC passed along to the Public Prosecutor's Office the names of 12 oil wholesalers and five of their directors accused of price fixing, and the Japan Petroleum Federation and its four representatives for production quantity restriction cartels. This was, in effect, the first criminal accusation for violation of the Antimonopoly Act. Again, this incident showed the public the tougher stance of the FTC against cartel activities (see chapter 18 (B)(2) Oil Cartel Cases).

These incidents convinced the public of the evils of cartel activities and, thereafter, no outright attempts to justify cartel activities were heard from business circles. However, these incidents also revealed the weaknesses of cartel regulation because they had shown a lack of effective deterrence to prevent their repetition.

(3) THE 1977 AMENDMENT

As the result of studies of administered prices, proposals for divestiture orders against monopolistic entrepreneurs and certain disclosure requirements for parallel price increases came about. As the result of studies of the stockholdings of major business groups and general trading companies, proposals for setting ceilings on stockholdings by giant companies and the tightening of stockholding restrictions by financial institutions came about.

Disclosure of widespread cartel activities during the oil shock also revealed to the public the insufficiency of sanctions against cartels. From this incident, proposals for the introduction of a surcharge system and an increase in criminal penalties arose.

In December 1973, a study group consisting of law and economics professors was established in order to make recommendations for antimonopoly amendments. Based on these recommendations, which were submitted in July 1974, the FTC announced its ideas for the amendment of the Antimonopoly Act.

Reaction to the FTC's ideas for an amendment were as expected. Business circles and MITI raised strong objections. Scholars and consumer organizations were in favor of the amendment. This announcement coincided with Prime Minister Tanaka's resignation due to scandals and criticisms of his economic policy. Miki, the new Prime Minister, when he formed his Cabinet in December 1974, expressed his support for the antimonopoly law amendment. The move toward amendment was therefore given policy impetus.

In April 1975, the Antimonopoly Act Amendment bill was submitted to the Diet. In June, the House of Representatives had, after partial revision, passed the bill unanimously. However, the bill could not pass the House of Councilors due to the short time set aside for deliberations.

In May 1976, the government submitted the second version of the bill, eliminating some controversial provisions, but the bill could not get any support from the Diet.

Prime Minister Miki was replaced by Mr. Fukuda, and when he formed his Cabinet in December 1976, he made the Antimonopoly Act Amendment one of his Cabinet's priorities. Due to this new political support, the third version of the bill, which was close to the first version, was submitted in April 1977. By this time, opposition to the amendment had weakened, and with minor modifications, the bill passed the Diet on May 27, 1977. It became law on June 3, 1977 (Act No. 63 of 1977), and became effective on December 2, 1977. More than 3 years had passed since the first ideas for the antimonopoly law amendment had surfaced.

The 1977 amendment empowered the FTC

(A) to order payment of surcharges against cartel participants (sec. 7-2);

(B) to order divestiture of a part of a business when a monopolistic situation was found to exist (sec. 8-4);

(C) to order the filing of reports by concerned entrepreneurs when parallel price increases took place in highly oligopolistic industries (sec. 18-2);

(D) to impose restrictions on aggregated total stockholdings by giant companies (sec. 9-2);

(E) to tighten restrictions on stockholdings by financial companies to 5 percent (sec. 11);

(F) to take remedial measures against past violations (sec. 7(2));

(G) to take broader remedial measures against unfair trade practices violations (sec. 20);

(H) to enforce new procedural requirements to insure the rights of respondents and fairness in hearing proceedings;

(I) to notify the person who provided information to the FTC of the disposition of the matter (sec. 45(3)).

The maximum fine for a violation was also raised, and the punlshment of representatives of juridical persons was incorporated (sec. 95-2).

NOTES

[1] The first Cabinet decision on price policy was made in September 1960, but the price rise at this stage was regarded as of a cyclical nature. This Conference was established in August 1963 when the price rise was regarded as persistent in nature, thus necessitating certain countermeasures against the rising trend of prices.

[2] Through these detailed studies, the problem of an oligopolistic market was clearly presented. However, the problem lay in the measures to be taken. This examination brought about the basic ideas reflected in the 1977 Amendment.

[3] See chapter 15 (B)(1) Trends of FTC Decisions. It seems that, around this time, the FTC had obtained some government-level support to enforce the Act. The Price Problems Conference had made 11 proposals and two proposals were related to the FTC. One was the necessity to enforce the Act in such fields as household items such as drugs, cosmetics, soaps, and detergents. The other was competition restricting factors in the big business sector.

[4] In particular, emphasis on competition policy from the viewpoint of consumer interest was influenced by U.S. consumer policy under the Kennedy administration.

[5] MITI, NIHON NO SANGYO KOZO (Industrial Structure in Japan) (1964).

[6] This meant that industrial policy is shifting from outright encouragement of conduct in violation of the Act to certain policy measures that are in conflict with antimonopoly policy.

[7] MITI could rely on the Japan Development Bank created in 1951 for financing important industries. C. Johnson wrote; "Within a year of its creation the JDB became one of MITI's most important instruments of industrial policy." "A JDB loan, regardless of its size, became MITI's seal of approval on an enterprise, and the company that had received a JDB loan could easily raise whatever else it needed from private resources." C. JOHNSON, MITI AND THE JAPANESE MIRACLE (1982), at 219-220.

[8] See H. IYORI & A. UESUGI, ANTIMONOPOLY LAWS OF JAPAN (1983), at table XI List of Depression Cartels Approved Under Section 24-3 of the Antimonopoly Act. Altogether 18 depression cartels were approved during this depression and most of them were terminated by September 30, 1966. Sugar, liner board and cotton yarn and spun rayon yarn lasted up to February 28, March 30 and June 30, 1967, respectively.

[9] Under this reorganization, the Mitsui O.S.K. Lines group had 19.8 percent, the Nippon Yusen group had 19.5 percent, the Kawasaki Kisen group had 13.2 percent, the Yamashita Shin Nihon group had 9.5 percent, the Japan Lines group had 9.1 percent and the Showa Line group had 8.7 percent in their markets.

[10] The FTC had announced the Merger Guideline in 1980 (see chapter 10 (C) Merger Guidelines), but even before the issuance of this guideline, since the Fuji-Yawata merger case, big mergers were notified informally in advance of the filing of a notification to clarify the possible antimonopoly problems.

[11] Since 1982 the U.S. Merger Guidelines has used the Herfindahl Hirschman Index (HHI) for case selection. See the Department of Justice and Federal Trade Commission Horizontal Merger Guidelines, April 2, 1992. HHI is calculated by summing the squares of the individual market shares of all the participants.

4

THE DECADE UNDER THE 1977 AMENDMENT AND THEREAFTER

(A) THE DECADE UNDER THE 1977 AMENDMENT

(1) PREVENTIVE LAW APPROACH

With hindsight it seems that, following its newly created power under the 1977 Amendment, the FTC took a cautious approach to enforcement. Even though the 1977 Amendment had passed the Diet by an overwhelming majority, this did not mean that it was fully appreciated in business circles and by industrial policy authorities. In order to have the 1977 Amendment get off to a smooth start in a harmonious society, the FTC had to try to broaden the understanding of the Antimonopoly Act as amended. This was achieved by emphasizing a preventive law approach.

Under this approach, the FTC announced various guidelines and took measures to secure compliance with them, instead of stressing remedial measures against those who had violated the law.

When various guidelines were prepared, they tended to cover formerly unstipulated areas or to reflect a rather rigid interpretation of the law. Thus, the FTC interpretation expressed in these guidelines appeared tougher than before. It is noteworthy that these guidelines were the result of analytical work and not necessarily reflections of case law. In other words, guidelines could cover areas where there was no previous case law or could cover practices that were widely regulated in other developed countries. Under this approach, the tightening of enforcement took place gradually without causing much friction in business circles.

In 1979 guidelines for trade associations were announced (see chapter III-5-(e) of the Guidelines for Trade Association Activities). This was followed by the enactment of merger guidelines, in 1980, and guidelines on stockholdings in 1981 (see chapter III-6-(c) of the Merger Guidelines). The 1986 guidelines on administrative guidance were an important step toward eliminating competent ministries' anticompetitive intervention into business activities and enlarging the coverage of the Act (see chapter 6 (B) Administrative Guidance and Cartel Regulation).

In 1982, after nearly 30 years, the FTC Notification on Unfair Trade Practices was revised. This was also an important step toward enhanced enforcement efforts because it clarified the rules applicable to daily business practices (see chapter 8 (A)(5) Old General Designations and New General Designations).

Around this period, the FTC had started to initiate legal action against professional associations such as those of construction engineers, dentists and doctors, thus the meaning of "entrepreneurs" in the Act was given a broad interpretation (see chapter 5 (A)(1) Entrepreneurs).

These FTC measures were adopted after careful analysis of the U.S. antitrust law enforcement experience as well as that of the European countries, Germany in particular. Therefore, although the above-mentioned measures were adopted as a rule of competition for Japan, because of the internationalization of business activities, the content of the competition laws tended to be compatible among developed market economy countries.

(2) ENFORCEMENT OF AMENDED PROVISIONS

The surcharge system adopted in 1977, seemed to be the most effective provision among the amended provisions of the Act. The amount collected from cartel participants within the first 10 years had amounted to roughly 10 billion yen (9.8 billion yen or roughly $750 million at current value). Most importantly, the surcharge system was quite well accepted in Japan even though such a system did not originate in our legal system (see chapter 19 (C) Enforcement).

When the 10-year grace period was over concerning the newly created restriction for stockholdings under sections 9-2 and 11, no serious problems of compliance were observed. During this grace period, those companies that would have to dispose of excess stockholdings had 10 years to meet the target. As to section 11 restrictions, many companies expanded their paid-in capital in this decade, therefore when the stock issuing company issued new stocks, financial companies could clear the 5 percent rule without disposing of the stock in their possession.

As to the section 9-2 restriction, giant companies could clear the restriction by expanding their net assets so that the net assets exceeded the amount of total stock held at the start of the grace period. However, the speed of expansion of stockholdings by the eight largest trading companies was slowed down significantly compared with a decade before (see table 24-13). For this reason, contrary to the fears raised at the time of amendment, there was no appreciable impact on the stock market.

As a whole, within 10 years, enforcement of the Act was significantly tightened under the 1977 Amendment. Interestingly, what was tightened was the enforcement of provisions that existed before the 1977 Amendment. The 1977 Amendment greatly improved circumstances for antimonopoly enforcement, and the FTC seemed to get more policy support than ever for its enforcement.

On the other hand, the evaluation of the enforcement record of the amended provisions was mixed. In particular, one criticism held that the smoothness of the decade under the 1977 Amendment was the result of insufficient use of the power authorized by the 1977 Amendment.[1]

Generally speaking, antimonopoly law enforcement was tightened not through vigorous enforcement of the new provisions incorporated into the 1977 Amendment, but through that of existing provisions of the Act (surcharge power was an exception because this was not a substantive regulation, created newly). No big changes in business behavior could be identified under the 1977 Amendment.

For example, in spite of the tougher limitations on stockholdings set by sections 9-2 and 11, there seemed no apparent reduction of cross-shareholding relationships among *keiretsu* (groups of firms). These regulations had resulted in the elimination of relatively unnecessary stocks of a giant company or financial company, but shares held for the purpose of cross shareholding remained in their possession. Sometimes those shares were transferred to other friendly firms in the same *keiretsu*, ones that did not face a ceiling.

Of course, there is no doubt that the 1977 Amendment had a positive impact on *keiretsu* relationships by putting restrictions on their expansionist trends. Recent arguments concerning *keiretsu* would necessitate the reevaluation of the 1977 amendment from the *keiretsu* viewpoint (see chapter 24 *Keiretsu* Relationships).

(3) SIGNS OF CHANGE

(i) Support for cartel exemptions

There are many positive signs to make one believe that the change that took place in the latter half of 1980s was a real one, and that business behavior started to change. On the other hand, there are some signs that the change was not yet a real one. One interesting example can be seen in the cartel exemption laws.

Only in 1985 did MITI abandon the idea of extending the Specific Machine and Information Industries Promotion Temporary Act of 1978 (Act No. 84 of 1978). The basic idea for this law started in 1956. The law had exemption provisions to authorize rationalization cartels in order to enhance their international competitiveness (see chapter 25 (B) Cartel Exemption Laws).

In 1978, the Specific Depressed Industries Stabilization Temporary Measures Act (Act No. 44 of 1978) was enacted to ease the difficulties of structurally depressed industries and eliminate excessive capacity. The Act had a provision for the exemption of production facility restriction cartels. In 1982 the Act was succeeded by a similar law. In 1987, MITI gave up an attempt to extend the latter law. Instead, the Industrial Structure Improvement Smoothing Temporary Measures Act (Act No. 24 of 1987), was enacted which did not contain any provision to exempt the application of the Antimonopoly Act.

This shows that the idea that some laws were necessary to promote rationalization had continued, but the idea that cartels were necessary for effecting rationalization measures was finally abandoned. Nowadays, MITI takes a more positive view concerning antimonopoly policy, and the other ministries, to a lesser extent, have started to show more understanding of competition policy.

This development also shows that domestic considerations were overwhelmed by international considerations, namely, the fact that the above-mentioned policy cannot be tolerated by the other developed market economy countries anymore.

Of course, this does not mean that every cartel exemption law that was enacted for the purpose of improving international competitiveness was eliminated. But, this was an important further step for the development of Japanese antimonopoly policy.

(ii) Reasons for change

The major reasons for the enhanced evaluation of antimonopoly policy in Japan by business circles and industrial policy authorities seemed to come from confidence in its success in overcoming two oil shocks, in particular the second oil shock in late 1970s. As to the first oil shock caused by the third Arab-Israeli war, there were still pessimistic views concerning Japanese businesses ability to overcome such a huge crisis. Japan had experienced a minus growth rate for the first time after World War II.

However, nowadays, it is apparent that Japanese business overcame the crisis by huge equipment investment, less energy consumption and more efficient use of resources. The second oil shock showed the world that Japan's economy's ability to adapt to changing economic conditions was the most effective among the developed countries.

This achievement was the result of private initiatives, not government leadership. Many businessmen had realized that this achievement became possible because they faced domestic and international competition. In other words, if they did not face serious competition to absorb the huge upward cost pressure, and relied on government protection, they could not adapt to changing economic conditions. Once these confidences were shared among business circles, support for competition became very solid for the first time in our history.

(iii) Internationalization

When the first decade under the 1977 Amendment was over, a new challenge for Antimonopoly policy began. Trade friction problems had compelled the antimonopoly policy to play a new role. In the past, antimonopoly policy in Japan had been susceptible to the strong influence of the antitrust law enforcement experiences of the U.S. and European countries, as seen above.

Rules of competition that were sustainable only in Japan could not survive, and would not benefit Japanese business interests. In short, Japanese antimonopoly policy would face increasing pressure for harmonization with other developed market economy countries. Trade friction would continue to apply pressure for the reevaluation of the antimonopoly policy of Japan. This process was drastically heightened by the Structural Impediments Initiative begun in 1989.

(B) STRUCTURAL IMPEDIMENTS INITIATIVE

(1) TRADE FRICTION AND THE ANTIMONOPOLY ACT

Although there was constant friction concerning trade between the U.S. and Japan, the Antimonopoly Act or its enforcement did not become a target before 1980. Before 1980, the weakness of Antimonopoly Act enforcement was discussed by some scholars in the U.S., but mostly it was confined to academic debates.[2]

Around the mid-1980s, allegations of possible anticompetitive practices by Japanese firms and trade associations were raised by U.S. Trade Representatives. The 1983 soda ash case was highly publicized as an example of an import restricting conspiracy by Japanese firms.[3] The existence of this outright restriction on imports was questioned by the American side. Upon investigation, the FTC found that import restricting cartels existed. After the FTC's remedial measures, the import of soda ash actually increased.

In 1985, MOSS (Market-Oriented Sector Selective) talks were started in which a few sectors were chosen and intensively evaluated in order to eliminate all barriers to imports. The sectors chosen were telecommunications, electronics, forest products, medical equipment, and pharmaceuticals.[4] Anti-competitive conduct by Japanese firms was one of the targets for scrutiny in these talks.

The FTC had surveyed the distribution practices of the paper industry as part of the examination of competitive conditions of forest products, and the result was published in 1985.[5] In 1986 the FTC examined the problems of continuous transactions among Japanese firms and the results were published in 1987.[6]

(2) STRUCTURAL IMPEDIMENTS INITIATIVE

In July 1989, both governments agreed to start Structural Impediments Initiative (SII) talks. Six topics were decided upon as targets of the talks; they being possible problem areas for the Japanese side. Among them, exclusionary trade practices, distribution systems, *keiretsu* relationships, and pricing mechanisms were related to antimonopoly problems.

Concerning exclusionary trade practices, the improvement of Antimonopoly Act enforcement was questioned, and many measures for improving enforcement activities were agreed upon (see appendix I). They included:

(A) An increase in the number of FTC investigators.

(B) The use of formal remedial power, particularly in such fields as price-fixing cartels, production restriction cartels, market allocation, bid rigging and group boycotts.

(C) An increase in the publicizing of enforcement by the disclosure of the identities of persons committing violations, the facts of the violations and the relevant information concerning formal decisions and surcharge orders. Similar information was also to be disclosed concerning "warning" cases (see chapter 15(B)(2) Informal Enforcement).

(D) An increase in the surcharge rate fixed by the law in order to increase the deterrent effects of cartel regulations.

(E) The establishment of a liaison organ between the FTC and the Ministry of the Judiciary and the Public Prosecutor's Office, and the announcement of FTC policy statements on criminal accusations.

(F) Measures to improve the effectiveness of damage suits under section 25.

(G) Enhanced enforcement of the Act against bid rigging.

The details of each of the above measures are described in the relevant chapters in part II.

Under the distribution system, the so-called distribution *keiretsu*'s impact was at issue, and antimonopoly law enforcement was thought important in order to open distribution channels to foreign goods. For this purpose, the announcement of the Guidelines for Distribution System and Business Practices was promised.

Concerning *keiretsu* relationships, some measures to make public the keiretsu relationships were promised, and the FTC promised to conduct a survey of the major business groups every 2 years. There is a big difference in the evaluation of *keiretsu* relationships between the two countries, and a detailed analysis is given in Chapter 24 *Keiretsu* Relationships.

(3) IMPACT OF STRUCTURAL IMPEDIMENTS INITIATIVE

As is analyzed separately in chapter 22, the basic system to enforce the Japanese Antimonopoly Act was established when the FTC was weak and lacked sufficient political support. Therefore, many of the measures promised at SII had been insisted upon for a long time by the FTC and scholars, but remained unchanged due to lack of sufficient political support to effect such changes.

As seen above, the 1977 Amendments were an important step toward strengthening the Act, but the enforcement mechanism remained unchanged. The most effective way to strengthen enforcement is to improve the enforcement mechanism by way of increased appropriations and improved public support.

Most of the measures promised by the Japanese government at SII were, essentially, what were advocated by the FTC up to then, or at least matters that were felt to be of importance by the FTC. The measures could be achieved because in view of the development of SII, their importance was finally shared by the government.

The most important effect of SII is seen in the business community's reaction toward the antimonopoly compliance program. The economic success of Japan gave Japanese businessmen confidence, and no business organizations nowadays oppose the necessity for competition policy. However, this does not necessarily mean that businessmen regard antimonopoly violations as seriously as they did tax evasion or embezzling in the past.

Now, we can observe sweeping changes in business behavior, or at least some signs of it. We believe three factors are important.

(A) Firstly, SII itself is sufficient to convince businessmen that this is the time to undertake compliance programs with the Antimonopoly Act as a company policy.

(B) Secondly, after the SII interim report in 1990, the FTC started to enforced the Act as promised, and that had sent a clear signal to business that antimonopoly risks would be enhanced significantly.

(C) Thirdly, SII had provided a good excuse to change some Japanese business practices. These problems were already understood by relevant entrepreneurs, but could not be alleviated due to the strong opposition of the affected parties.

Whether these movements give only the appearance of or do represent true change is a question to be answered in the future.

(4) ENHANCEMENT OF FTC ENFORCEMENT

As of March 1993, the FTC enforcement record is significantly improved. In FY 1990, the FTC issued 22 recommendations. In FY 1992, the FTC issued 37 recommendations and 1 formal decision. Beginning in October 1990, almost all warning cases were released to the press. Surcharge orders were frequent and their amounts were significantly increased setting records for a single year in FY 1990. The effects of quadrupled surcharge rates would soon be seen as an actual increase in the amount. (The new rate would apply to cartel activities ended after July 1991. See chapter 15(B)(2) Informal Enforcement.)

Most significantly, the FTC started to use its criminal accusation power in appropriate cases (see Chapter 18 Criminal Cases and Penalties). The FTC took formal action against companies in situations where, formerly, informal warnings might have been utilized (see chapter 8 (L) Other Unfair Trade Practices).

The FTC, through consultation with the competent ministries, is trying to eliminate unnecessary exemption laws and abolish some exempted cartels (see Chapter 25 Deregulation and Antimonopoly Exemption Laws).

At present, the FTC seems to be running at full strength.

(C) A PROSPECT
(1) THE FUTURE OF COMPETITION POLICY IN JAPAN

As seen above, the second decade after the 1977 Amendment may be characterized by SII. The decade would be characterized by how to respond to the challenge of SII and how to improve market access to Japan. In other words, we believe that Antimonopoly Act enforcement becomes more important for the next decade because eventually a significant foreign presence will be achieved in the Japanese market.

When foreign firms are exporting into the Japanese market, keen competition through antimonopoly law enforcement may not favor foreign exporters' interests. After entry obstacles into the Japanese market are overcome, Antimonopoly Act enforcement may gain more importance for foreign firms competing in Japan. This is because only rules for competition based on competition law can provide a fair chance of competition to foreign firms.

In this sense, the most important task for Japan's antimonopoly policy is to make it easily accessible to foreign firms. To achieve this, the following would be necessary:

First, antimonopoly law violations should be spelled out as clearly as possible, and antimonopoly laws should be in harmony with the U.S. and EC antitrust laws as much as possible. When foreign firms enter the Japanese market, they should be able to rely on a meaningful competition policy. If they are forced to compete using different rules of competition, foreign firms would never have a fair chance of competing in Japan.

Second, foreign firms should either be able to file a petition to the FTC for alleged violations or be able to file private suits to protect themselves from antimonopoly law violations.

As a matter of general practice, not many complaints are filed by foreign firms in Japan, and so far there have been no attempts to file private antitrust suits by foreign firms. After the measures were put into effect as mentioned in the final report of SII, would there be any change in the attitude of foreign business in Japan? Does the recovery of damages by the U.S. government in bid-rigging cases as to the Yokosuka Naval Base and Yokota Air Base trigger a more active use of private damage suits by foreign firms in Japan? (See chapter 6 (D) Bid Rigging.) These answers could predict the policy direction of antimonopoly enforcement for the next decade.

(2) JAPANESE LESSONS

Japanese experience could provide at least two lessons. One lesson is in the process of foreign-made legal philosophy taking root in the Japanese soil. The other is in the transformation of procartel policy into procompetition policy. By looking at the transformation of Japanese procartel policy to procompetition, we can count Japan as a case for competition policy, in other words, a convincing case to prove the universal applicability of competition policy in a developed market economy country. A free and democratic society needs a meaningful procompetition policy, but this simple fact was not well accepted until recently in Japan.

For an overall evaluation from these lessons, see the analysis in Chapter 22 How Antimonopoly Policy Relates to Rapid Economic Growth in Japan.

NOTES

[1] K. Imamura, *Dokkinho Kaisei Go 10 Nen* (A Decade after the Antimonopoly Act Amendment), Keizai Ho Gakkai Nenpo No. 8 (1987).

[2] *Notes, Trustbusting in Japan: Cartels and Government Business Cooperation,* Harvard. L. Review, Vol. 94 (1981), at 1064.

[3] H. First, *Japan's Antitrust Policy: Impact on Import Competition,* in T. Pugel and R. Hawkins eds., Fragile Interdependence: Economic Issues in U.S.-Japanese Trade and Investment (1986), at 63.

[4] For example, the U.S. Government and the Japanese Government (issued jointly), Final Report on the MOSS Talks on Transportation Machinery, Aug. 18, 1987. The MOSS talks had provided the basic idea leading to the SII talks.

[5] FTC, Kami no Ryutsu to no Jittai ni kansuru Chosa (Economic Research on Distribution of Paper Products), May 1986.

[6] FTC, Wagakuni Kigyo no Keizokuteki Torihiki ni kansuru Chosa (Economic Research on Continuous Transaction Relationship Among Firms in Japan), April 1987.

PART II

Conduct Prohibited Under the Antimonopoly Laws

5

GENERAL
DEFINITIONS

In the chapters that make up part II, various conducts that are prohibited under the Antimonopoly Act are explained. However, we tried to avoid making part II merely a section by section commentary, therefore, the full text of the Act and guidelines that appear in the appendices should be referred to along with each explanation below.

In Japan, court decisions on antimonopoly cases are not abundant. Of course, as long as case law exists, it sets clear precedents and strongly influences the FTC's interpretations. However, in most areas, scholars' opinions also have great influence on the FTC's interpretations. Because private antimonopoly suits are still small in number,[1] the FTC's interpretations as shown in decisions and guidelines are very important to the understanding of how the Act will be enforced. Therefore, the following explanations focus mainly on how the FTC interprets and enforces the Act.

(A) GENERAL TERMS

(1) ENTREPRENEURS

Section 2(1) of the Act defines an entrepreneur. If a person is not regarded as an entrepreneur the Act cannot be applied to his conduct, however objectionable it is. This provision is interpreted to cover economic activities such as mining, agriculture, forestry, transportation, warehousing and services, as well as those sectors mentioned specifically in section 2(1).

It could cover non-profit organizations, such as trade associations, or a public entity.[2] On the other hand, labor is not considered an economic activity.

Initially, the FTC was cautious in expanding the coverage of the Act to professional services. In 1979, the FTC had ordered remedial measures against a civil engineers association for fixing the fee schedule of its member engineers (Japan Civil Engineers Association, FTC, Sep. 16, 1979, 26 KTIS 25). In 1980, the FTC applied the Act against a doctors association (Chiba Prefecture Doctors Association, FTC, June 19, 1980, 27 KTIS 39). The 1981 Guideline on Doctors Associations made clear that restrictions on new entry, establishment of uniform fee schedules, and restrictions on advertisements could violate the Act (sec.5-(e) Guideline for Trade Association Activities). Thereafter, professional services were treated in the same manner as other economic activities.

Fee schedules for attorneys or fees for the insured medical care services of a doctor are established by law,[3] and for this reason, the Act is not applicable. However, when a doctors association decides the fee for non-insured medical care services, it could be a violation of section 8(1). Therefore, it makes a difference whether professional services are covered under the definition of "entrepreneur."

In the 1989 Michiko Murakami case (March 7, 1989, 35 KTIS 129), the Fukuoka District Court ruled that the defendant, a veterinarian association, was a trade association within the meaning of section 2(3) of the Act, even though it engaged in such public service work as anti-hydrophobia inoculation. This ruling was sustained by the Fukuoka High Court (Aug. 29, 1990, 37 KTIS 222).

A municipal government can also be an entrepreneur when it engages in economic activities. If, for example, a division of a municipal government provides a scheduled bus service, this "division of municipal government" could be an entrepreneur.

In the 1989 Nippon Shokuhin Co. case (Dec. 14, 1989, 36 KTIS 570), the Supreme Court ruled that a municipal government can be an entrepreneur as long as it engages in economic activities. This was the case of a slaughter house business that was competing with a privately operated slaughter house.

Section 2(1) also says that "an officer, employee, agent or any other person who acts for the benefit of any entrepreneur shall be deemed an entrepreneur" with respect to section 8 violations. This provision is included to cover situations where a person participates in a trade association in his personal capacity. However, usually any act of an officer or employee carried out in his business capacity would be deemed an act of the entrepreneur he works for, and section 8 is applicable without using this provision. When an officer or employee participates in a trade association and he personally pays the membership fee etc., then it might be necessary to apply section 8 to the entrepreneur for whom he works.

(2) OFFICERS

The term "officers" is used to describe a board member, a partner, an auditor or any other employees in similar positions, or employees in charge of the business of a main or branch office (sec. 2(3)).

This concept is used in section 13 (interlocking directorates). Moreover, whenever necessary, the FTC can take some remedial measures against officers in addition to the related entrepreneurs (secs. 8-2 & 17-2).

(B) SUBSTANTIAL RESTRAINT OF COMPETITION

(1) COMPETITION

The definition of the term "competition" was added by the 1949 Amendment. Under the definition of section 2(4), "competition" means:

(A) a situation in which two or more entrepreneurs do or may, within the normal scope of their business activities and without undertaking any significant change in their business facilities or types of activities

(B) engage in supplying the same or similar goods or services to the same consumers or customers, or engage in receiving supplies of the same or similar goods or services from the same suppliers.

This definition makes clear that competition covers actual competition and potential competition, and it also covers supply competition and buying competition. This definition also made clear that competitive relationships shall be examined as to the same goods or services and to goods or services similar thereto. In this way, potential competition is examined as to kinds of goods or services, and as to business facilities or types of activities. And when potential competition is at issue, whether other entrepreneurs can start to compete within the normal scope of their business activities will be examined, then if necessary, whether other entrepreneurs can start competing without undertaking any significant change in their business facilities or types of activities will be examined.

This definition is useful in evaluating whether competitive relationships exist among entrepreneurs, and ultimately when potential competition needs to be evaluated. However, which competitive relationships need to be examined varies depending on the nature of the violation. There is no doubt that unreasonable restraint of trade needs to be regulated without considering potential competition. Easy new entry into a market does not cause much pressure on or does not nullify the effects of cartel activities. The regulation of unfair trade practices does not require a detailed market definition. In most cases, the existence of potential competitors does not give any justifiable reason to engage in unfair trade practices (see chapter 8 (B)(1) Tendency to Impede Fair Competition).

On the other hand, regulation of mergers and acquisitions requires a more detailed analysis of how to define a market, including potential competition and the possibility of new entry (see Chapter 10 Mergers and Acquisitions). Private monopolization also requires a bit broader definition of a market, in this sense, potential competition needs to be evaluated. However, so far as acts of exclusion or control are concerned, ease of new entry cannot effectively prevent exclusionary conduct in order to achieve private monopolization. Therefore, the existence of potential competition does not seem to give a justifiable reason for private monopolization, too (see Chapter 7 Private Monopolization).

In the case of a monopolistic situation, the broadest definition of a market was given in the Act itself (sec. 2(7)).

Whether this definition allows a flexible understanding of competition is not made clear by court decisions. However, the FTC needs to define "a particular field of trade" as to section 3 cases and section 10, 13, 14, 15 and 16 cases (section 10-16 cases), and in these cases, a market is defined by the FTC without considering ease of new entry in particular. Instead, ease of new entry is considered as a factor to evaluate the anticompetitive effects of alleged conduct (see Chapter 10 Mergers and Acquisitions).

(2) SUBSTANTIAL RESTRAINT OF COMPETITION

The court ruling on "substantial restraint of competition" was given as to section 15 cases, instead of section 3 cases.[4] Therefore, it is a ruling on interpretation of the term "may substantially restrain competition." As to section 3 cases, alleged conducts are objectionable in themselves because cartel agreements or acts to exclude or control other entrepreneurs are involved. However, as to section 10-16 cases, alleged conducts are not objectionable in themselves. This is why the requirement of "substantial restraint of competition" is heavily argued in section 10-16 cases. The FTC and the court are confronted with this question because of their need to inform respondents as to why such ordinary business activities shall be restricted.

In the 1951 Toho-Subaru case (Sep. 19, 1951, 3 KTIS 166), the Tokyo High Court established a general interpretation of the term "substantial restraint of competition" and it controlled the courts and the FTC rulings thereafter.

According to the FTC decision in the Toho-Subaru case mentioned above (Sep. 29, 1950, 2 KTIS 146), "[s]ubstantial restraint of competition as referred to in this Act should be construed as effective restraint of competition, and it shall mean a situation where effective competition is made impossible."

The Tokyo High Court ruled at the appeal of the Toho-Subaru case (Sep. 19, 1951, 3 KTIS 166), that

> [s]ubstantial restraint of competition under Section 15(1) does not refer to individual market behavior in itself, but rather the question to be considered is whether a situation appears or at least is about to appear where competition itself has decreased and whereby a certain entrepreneur or a group of entrepreneurs can, according to its own will, manipulate price, quality, quantity, or other various conditions, thereby controlling the market to some extent.

Thus, the reduction of the number of competitors, the reduced means of competition. . . . necessarily lead to some restraint of competition, but the existence of these individual facts does not *per se* mean that there is substantial restraint. In determining whether or not the restraint is substantial, it must be decided whether the reduction of competition results from the above mentioned situation.

This ruling was sustained by the Supreme Court in 1954 (May 25, 1954, 8 KTIS 102).

In the subsequent 1953 case of Toho and Shin-Toho (Dec. 7, 1953, 5 KTIS 118), the Tokyo High Court said

"[s]ubstantial restrain of competition" may be defined as the establishment, maintenance or strengthening of market control. . . . The question of under what circumstances a market control is established is a relative one and cannot be determined uniformly, but depends on economic conditions of the case. It cannot be determined only by the share of the suppliers (or demands) of concerned entrepreneurs in a market.

The scale of business, capital procurement ability, marketing ability, the abilities of competitors, the possibility of new entry or the countervailing power of buyers or suppliers are some factors necessarily taken into consideration. Thus, market control is brought about not only by a mutual restraint of competition, but also by such activities as preventing or eliminating market participation by other competitors.

Sections 10-16 have a common effect requirement, namely, "may substantially restrain competition." This means that a particular merger or stockholding would result in control of the business activities of an acquired company or companies, and consequently would be likely to cause "substantial restraint of competition in a particular field of trade." It is not necessary that such a situation be present for competition to be substantially restrained. This is evaluated as a matter of probability of market control. It does not matter whether a company acts individually or in combination with any other entrepreneurs.

In the above-mentioned Toho and Shin-Toho case (Dec. 7, 1953, 5 KTIS 118), the Tokyo High Court ruled "It does not prove that competitors are mutually restricted their business activities merely by showing one-third of distribution business of Japanese movies are controlled by the respondents."

According to FTC decisions, an 80 percent or more market share gives a strong presumption that any agreement on price, etc. among the respondents would restrain competition substantially. When the market share is around 50 percent, some additional factors, such as the competitive situation vis-a-vis outsiders and the influence of the respondents in a market are analyzed before the FTC finds substantial restraint of competition. It is rare that the FTC finds in its decision substantial restraint of competition where the combined market share of the respondents is less than 50 percent.[5]

(C) "IN ANY PARTICULAR FIELD OF TRADE"

In the Act, various concepts are used to describe a market. One is "in any particular field of trade," under sections 2(5), 2(6), 8(l)(i), 10, 13, 14, 15 and 16. Sections 2(7) and 18-2(1) use "in any particular field of business," and section 8(l)(iii) uses "in any particular field of business," as well.

Sections 2(9) and 8(l)(iv) do not contain any requirement as to a market. However, a concept of fair competition can exist only in a market, and "unduly restricting the functions or activities" under section 8(l)(iv) is interpreted to supplement section 8(l)(i), therefore, it is clear that the latter shall be evaluated in any particular field of trade.

"Any particular field of business," under section 8(l)(iii) is interpreted to cover a narrower area than "a particular field of trade."[6] On the other hand, "any particular field of business" under sections 2(7) and 18 2(1) is a concept based on goods or services. By definition, "any particular field of business" under section 2(7) is broader than "any particular field of business" under section 18-2(1) (see chapter 12 (A) Market Structure Test).

As explained concerning the term "competition," although sections 2(5) and 2(6) use the same market concept of "any particular field of trade," they could cover different product lines or items.

It is possible to define "a particular field of trade" according to the different stages of a transaction, namely, at the manufacturing level, the wholesale level or the retail level. It is also possible to define various submarkets within a market according to goods or services, geographic area or types of specific customers.

The above analysis shows that, although the Act uses various concepts to describe a market, the same term could be interpreted to cover narrower or broader product or service lines or items depending on the type of violation. Therefore, it seems that the different wording in the Act is not so important, and competitive relationships shall be examined according to the nature or type of illegal conduct. The different wording used in various sections of the Act does not seem to preclude such interpretations of the law.

(D) "CONTRARY TO THE PUBLIC INTEREST"

"Contrary to the public interest" is used in the definition of unreasonable restraint of trade and private monopolization, but not in section 8(l)(i), which has the same effect requirements as the former two.

There are roughly two contrasting views concerning how to interpret this term.

The first view is that "contrary to the public interest" does not require any additional proof to find a violation of section 3. For this purpose, "public interest" is interpreted to mean nothing but maintenance of or promotion of economic order based on free competition. Therefore, when a substantial restraint of competition occurs, it automatically fulfills the requirement of "contrary to the public interest." This view concludes that eliminating such acts of substantial restraint of competition is in the public interest.

The second view is that there could be some situations where a substantial restraint of competition does not constitute a violation of section 3 because it is not "contrary to the public interest." There are many variations to this view depending upon how large in this sense the exception could be.

The FTC takes the first view, and in the 1949 Yuasa Lumber Co. case (Aug. 30, 1949, 1 KTIS 62), it made clear that

> The act of joint price fixing by entrepreneurs on occasion of open competitive bidding is against the spirit of the provision of section 1 of the Act, of which the primary purpose is to ensure free competition. . . . Such activity as price fixing should be recognized as being contrary to the public interest. Whether the agreed price is appropriate or not, or whether the national economy has suffered any loss or not, all

these considerations should not furnish any basis for deciding whether the activities in question are contrary to the public interest or not.

In the past, those who opposed antimonopoly policy tried to justify their position through the interpretation of the term "contrary to the public interest." According to this view, some activities of cartels are not illegal when they are not "contrary to the public interest." For example, it was widely believed in Japan that excessive competition was undesirable and could constitute an important obstacle for the promotion of the democratic and wholesome development of the national economy.[7] Under this view, cartels formed to eliminate excessive competition would be deemed not against the ultimate objectives described in section 1 of the Act, and therefore, not "contrary to the public interest."

In particular, there is an extreme view that holds that "public interest" equals consideration of the interests of the national economy as a whole, including the interests of producers. This view tries to reflect industrial policy considerations in the enforcement of the Act.[8]

The first view has been maintained by the FTC in order to reject any attempt to justify cartel activities that lack a specific basis in the exemption laws.

The Tokyo High Court, in the 1980 oil cartel price-fixing case (Sep. 26, 1980, 28-2 KTIS 299), ruled that

> "contrary to the public interest" means contrary to the goals of the Act, and generally speaking, it follows that the public interest is violated when economic order based on the principles of free competition is infringed. This economic order is what the Act intends to protect through its enforcement. The public interest clause is incorporated because some exceptional cases might be exempted from the application of the Act simply because they are not deemed contrary to the public interest.
>
> For example, some acts may fall under one of the prohibited conducts in form, but in reality, the purpose of the Act is not infringed by these acts. Careful examination of related interests associated with the conducts in question and the goals of the Act will be the key factor to look at.

The Tokyo High Court took a restrictive version of the second view, which is supported by the Supreme Court (Feb. 24, 1984, 30

KTIS 244), but these rulings try to keep the exception within very narrow limits. Anyhow, although an exception is declared possible by the Supreme Court, it is also clear that the courts have not so far accepted any exception to cartel prohibition through interpretation of the term "contrary to the public interest."

Sometimes, the FTC refrains from taking any formal action as to small-scale cartel activities by small businesses. However, this is the exercise of its discretionary power under section 48 of the Act, and does not mean that such small cartel activities are deemed not "contrary to the public interest" by the FTC.

NOTES

[1] See Chapter 17 Civil Damage Suits. There is no official compilation of antimonopoly suits. Section 709 suits and section 25 suits are clearly antimonopoly suits and could easily be identified as such, but other types of claims partially based on antimonopoly law violations are difficult to compile. The FTC is trying to compile related antimonopoly cases and report them in its official compilation, namely, *Kosei Torihiki Iinkai Shinketsushu* (in this book, this is refered to as KTIS). However, KTIS is not inclusive of all such cases.

The FTC decisions cited in this book are expressed by the English name of the companies or trade associations involved, and in abbreviated style, therefore, e.g., only one company involved in a cartel case is named.

[2] Public entities are often tightly regulated as to their business activities, therefore, insofar as doing business as it is regulated, the Act could not apply to their activities. This exemption can immunize only their legitimate activities (sec. 21). Due to the privatization program, the number of public entities are declining in Japan. See chapter 25 (C) Deregulation and Privatization.

[3] The Ministry of Health and Welfare establishes fee schedules for insured medical care service, and doctors or hospitals cannot charge more than the fee in the schedules because most of medical services are insured by the ministry's health care program. In the case of attorney's fee, it is a standard fee schedule, and actual attorney's fees leave and actually do have a much room for negotiation.

[4] Interpretation of "substantial restraint of competition" by a court is a good example of attitudes and how Anglo-American law concepts are interpreted by continental legal thinking. See chapter 22 (A)(1) Why the Japanese Antimonopoly Policy Looks Different.

[5] K. UEKI & K. KAWAGOE, HAN SHINKETSU DOKUSEN KINSI HO (Antimonopoly Act Cases and Decisions) (1986), which said, "Almost no decisions can be found where the market share of the cartel participants is below 50 percent. . . .", at 190.

[6] These are literal translations of the terms used in the Act, therefore, the term itself does not show whether the term could cover a larger market or a smaller market. This is the reason why the market can only be determined by examining alleged conduct, even if the Act used the same term to define the relevant market.

[7] See chapter 2 Retreat of the Antimonopoly Act. The opponents to the Antimonopoly policy relied on the term "public interest" to confine the effectiveness of the Antimonopoly Act in this period.

[8] M. IZUMOI, SHIN DOKUSEN KINSHI HO KAISETSU (New Commentary on the Antimonopoly Act) (1953), at 90-91.

6

CARTELS AND BOYCOTTS

(A) DEFINITION OF CARTELS

(1) DEFINITION OF CARTELS

For "unreasonable restraint of trade" to be found, the following conditions must exist (sec. 2(6)) when entrepreneurs

- (A) by contract, agreement, or any other concerted activities,
- (B) mutually restrict or conduct their business activities,
- (C) in such a manner as to fix, maintain, or enhance prices, or limit production, technology, products, facilities, or customers or suppliers,
- (D) thereby causing a substantial restraint of competition,
- (E) in any particular field of trade,
- (F) contrary to the public interest.

The requirements of (D), (E) and (F) are considered in the former chapter. (A), (B) and (C) are examined here.

(2) PROOF OF AGREEMENT OR MUTUAL UNDERSTANDING

"By contract, agreement, or any other concerted activities" is an essential requirement of a cartel. It is equivalent to mutual understanding among entrepreneurs. In an FTC decision, usually the terms "decided" or "agreed" are used to describe this requirement.

However, it is a mutual understanding as a result of a liaison of wills that may constitute a cartel agreement. Therefore, the FTC must show some kind of liaison of wills among competitors in order to prove the existence of an agreement or mutual understanding.

In the 1949 Yuasa Lumber Co. case (Aug. 30, 1949, 1 KTIS 62), the FTC stated that "In order to establish concerted activities, the existence of an external uniformity as a result of acts of entrepreneurs is not enough, and it is further required that a liaison of wills of some sort exists among the entrepreneurs concerned."

A liaison of wills of some sort needs to be established by evidence, and the investigatory activities of the FTC are meant to collect evidence to show a liaison of wills of some sort as much as possible. However, it is clear that a liaison of wills can be found by an overall evaluation of all the available evidence. It is possible to find a liaison of wills even though no direct evidence is available. Circumstantial evidence can be used to show the existence of a mutual understanding.

In the Yuasa Lumber Co. case mentioned above, the FTC found that "Under the condition of this case, some entrepreneurs take the same conduct with the other entrepreneurs anticipating the subsequent parallel behavior of those entrepreneurs, it can be found that liaison of wills is established."

Ordinary cartel cases (sec. 3 or sec. 8(1)(i) cases) contain the following fact finding by the FTC.

(A) Communication of wills by way of meetings or telephone conversation among competitors.

(B) The fact that some discussion took place on such matters as prices at such meetings, using memos at such meetings, facsimile messages, desk diaries, notebooks, reports, or any other such kinds of documents that can be used as evidence.

(C) Parallel activities among competitors thereafter indicating that such mutual understanding was actually reached.

When possible, the place and date of such meetings are described in the decision, but sometimes such places and/or dates are unspecified. The place and date of such a meeting is not a necessary requirement to prove mutual understanding among cartel participants. In the 1981 Honshu Paper Co. case (June 5, 1981, 28 KTIS 32), only the name of the committee under which the competitors met and the approximate meeting dates, by month, are indicated in the decision.

In the case of absentees, some facts concerning the communication of the outcome of the meetings to those who were absent are found in the decision. A gentlemen's agreement is sufficient so far as it is effectively binding on the participating companies. No penalty needs to be stipulated. So far as mutual understanding is interpreted, tacit understanding, or any acts to follow the competitor's behavior without explicitly agreeing on specifics are held sufficient.

It does not matter whether mutual understanding is reached at the managerial level or board level, as long as the mutual understanding is effected as a conduct of each participating company.

There may be an impression that the FTC is relying too much on direct evidence to prove mutual understanding among competitors. However, coordinating business activities of many entrepreneurs is not a simple task, and it is virtually impossible not to leave any documentary evidence of some sort. Even when only a few entrepreneurs are concerned, in order to coordinate business activities in such a big market as Japan, offices or branches may be involved, thus some documentary evidence could be seized through the investigatory activities of the FTC.

(3) HORIZONTAL AGREEMENTS V. VERTICAL AGREEMENTS

Whether unreasonable restraint of trade covers only horizontal agreements or could cover vertical restraints was debated early on. For the first 6 years, the FTC had been applying section 3 to vertical restraints, but after the Tokyo High Court decision mentioned below, the FTC abandoned this interpretation.

In the 1953 Asahi Newspaper Co. case (March 9, 1953, 4 KTIS 145), the Tokyo High Court decided that the latter part of section 3 does not cover vertical restraints and ruled that

> Unreasonable restraint of trade is formed where independent entrepreneurs in mutual competition jointly impose certain restrictions upon each other and, thereby restrain their free business activities. . . . If mutuality is lacking in the restriction, an unreasonable restraint of trade does not occur.

According to the Tokyo High Court, the requirement "to mutually restrict or conduct" could be found only among competitors, and if entrepreneurs in different fields, for example, distributors are included, no mutual restriction covering all of them can be found. This interpretation prompted the FTC to find separate cartels at each distribution stage when manufacturers and their distributors had participated in cartel operations. Or when manufacturers had agreed on resale prices of their products, and then forced their distributors to maintain the retail price set by each manufacturer, only manufacturers are made respondents of cartel cases.

When a single manufacturer and its distributors reach a cartel agreement to fix retail prices, it is treated as a unilateral act of the manufacturer and is regulated as an unfair trade practice (see chapter 8 (D) Resale Price Maintenance).

So far as cartel activities are concerned, no serious problem was felt by such constraints. It is possible to impose a surcharge order on those conspiring manufacturers (see Chapter 19 Surcharge Orders), and it seems acceptable, in view of its nature of restraint, not to impose a surcharge order against distributors who actively participate in a resale price maintenance scheme.

However, in so far as group boycotts are concerned, this limitation could cause serious problems in the application of section 3 (see (F) below). Only a few group boycotts are effected by only a group of competitors. When their suppliers or their distributors participate in group boycotts, more effective exclusion of new entry can be achieved.

In view of this constraint, and in order to expand the traditional interpretation of this subject, the Distribution System and Business Practices Guidelines (DSBP Guidelines; see appendix H) made clear that the FTC will adopt a slightly different interpretation of the law thereafter. It said "The content of restrictions of business activities in this context does not need to be identical with respect to all firms (for example, distributors and manufacturers), but is sufficient if the conduct restricts the business activities of each firm and is effected for the purpose of achieving a common purpose, such as the exclusion of any specific firm." (Note 3 of part 1 of the Guidelines.)

This interpretation made possible the application of section 3 to group boycotts. Whether this interpretation is applicable to ordinary cartel cases is not clear.

(B) ADMINISTRATIVE GUIDANCE AND CARTEL REGULATIONS

As is referred to in part I, administrative guidance cartels were used by MITI in the 1950s. Although such an outright attempt was eliminated in the 1960s, administrative guidance and cartel regulation has continued to be the target of hot academic debate.

Two problems need to be examined. One is the legality of government action to issue administrative guidance itself, the other is the applicability of the Antimonopoly Act to conduct that was effected based on administrative guidance.

It is almost undisputed in Japan that administrative guidance is the legal exercise of government power even if does not have a specific basis in law (oil cartel price-fixing case, Supreme Court, Feb. 24, 1984, 30 KTIS 244). Only in such extreme cases where administrative guidance is being used to solicit the committing of an illegal conduct, is such guidance thought illegal.

In 1984, the Supreme Court (oil cartel price-fixing case, Feb. 24, 1984, 30 KTIS 244) held that "the most important objective of the Antimonopoly Act is to guarantee that price is determined freely in a market, and it is clear from the aim or purpose of the Act that an administrative agency should not intervene in free price formation."

It also held that

> even an administrative guidance, which tries to affect price and does not have a clear basis in the Petroleum Act, should not be held illegal, if done from the standpoint of smooth administration to cope with changing circumstances, and as far as it is executed by such appropriate means as are socially acceptable, and as far as it is not substantially incompatible with the ultimate purpose of the Act, which is defined as promotion of the democratic and wholesome development of the national economy as well as assurance of the interest of consumers in general.
>
> Even when an understanding on price among entrepreneurs seemed to violate the letter of the act, the illegality of such understanding is removed if it is done in accordance with and in cooperation with lawful administrative guidance.

On the second issue, the general principle was now fairly clear. Since as early as 1953, the FTC had maintained the position that the formation of a cartel effected in response to administrative guidance could constitute a violation of the Act (Toyo Rayon Case, Aug. 6, 1953, 5 KTIS 17). An output restriction cartel was declared illegal in this FTC case, which was begun in response to the administrative guidance of MITI.

Administrative guidance is by definition not in itself compulsory. On the other hand, it is not simply an informal approval or an encouragement from some government office. It is an administrative agency's action to induce or encourage a person or persons to do some acts or not to do some acts in order to achieve the task or responsibility of the agency prescribed in the law that they administer. It is used to achieve certain policy purposes through the voluntary cooperation of a person or persons.[1]

Four patterns of administrative guidance need to be examined.

The first pattern occurs when administrative guidance results in the restriction of competition, but does not directly foster cartel activity. Illustrative of such a guidance is the favoring of large firms to establish price leadership, to encourage large-scale mergers and acquisitions, to encourage the taking of some rationalization measures in selected industries, to restrict entry or investment, or to promote joint technology development.

Guidance of this sort increases market concentration or changes market structure. However, it is clear that such a guidance does not limit the FTC's jurisdiction at all, and the FTC maintains a final voice in the outcome of the matter. This kind of administrative guidance could sometimes be in serious conflict with competition policy. It may not be desirable for one agency of the government to apply the Act that is encouraged by one branch of the government. Therefore, the FTC urges other government agencies to hold advance consultations with it before undertaking such guidance.

The second pattern consists of cases where administrative guidance is issued to a group of entrepreneurs or a trade association by indicating the total amount of output or investment, or range of prices acceptable to the competent agency. This kind of administrative guidance would inevitably be followed by some concerted action on the part of entrepreneurs or trade associations to comply with the guidance. For example, in order to implement output restraint there needs to be an allocation of production quotas among the related entrepreneurs, unless each entrepreneur were told the specific amount of its production.

The third pattern consists of cases where administrative guidance is issued to individual entrepreneurs to restrict their respective outputs to a certain level or to set certain prices on their products.

The fourth pattern consists of government action prior to or in lieu of the formal disposition pursuant to a law. Guidance of this type presents less of a problem than the three types mentioned above. However, even administrative guidance of this type could pose some problems because such acts may go beyond what is authorized by the law. When it goes beyond what is authorized by the law, such administrative guidance cannot immunize the conduct effected from the application of the Act.

As to the second and the third patterns, the FTC's statement on the Antimonopoly Act and Administrative Guidance (1981 Statement) on March 16, 1981 and the Tokyo High Court (Sep. 26, 1980, 28-2 KTIS 299) and the Supreme Court decisions (Feb. 24, 1984, 30 KTIS 244) relating to the oil cartel cases mentioned above, established the rule.

The 1981 Statement said that administrative guidance, which does not have a clear legal basis and so far as it affects such vital market conditions as price or production quantity, could pose serious antimonopoly problems. When guidance is directed at a trade association by indicating the total level of acceptable output, it is highly likely to induce cartel activities by a trade association or a group of entrepreneurs, and thus shall be restrained.

Even when a guidance is issued to each company, it could still induce cartel activity when it is made based on a uniform standard to restrict output of each company equally, or to show a master plan that indicates each company's quota. It would induce cartel activity because each company will decide to follow the guidance knowing that the other companies would also be following it.

On the other hand, the 1981 Statement said that an administrative guidance that is used when every requirement is fulfilled for taking formal action based on a law does not pose any antimonopoly problem, however, if it does not, the FTC would apply the above-mentioned general principle to such case.

The Tokyo High Court said in the 1980 oil production curtailment cartel case (Sep. 26, 1980, 28-2 KTIS 299) that some of the defendants were not conscious of the illegality of production adjustments because they were done according to the administrative guidance of MITI. The FTC had not taken any action for a long time concerning this guidance, therefore, the defendants could not be held criminally responsible for their conduct (see Chapter 18 Criminal Cases and Penalties).

(C) TYPES OF CONCERTED ACTIVITIES CONDEMNED AS CARTELS

Section 2(6) gives specific examples of cartel activities according to their type. Those that

(A) fix, maintain or enhance prices,
(B) limit production,
(C) limit technology,
(D) limit products,
(E) limit facilities,
(F) limit customers or suppliers.

(A) covers all sorts of price-fixing cartels, (B) covers production restriction cartels, (C) covers technology restricting cartels such as those restricting the use of a particular technology, (D) covers specialization cartels and standardization cartels, (E) covers one type of production restricting cartel, but could also cover investment adjusting cartels, and (F) covers customer allocation, bid-rigging or market allocation cartels. It also covers cartel agreements not to sell to competitors' customers, and joint sales agreements.

(A) could include indirect ways to fix prices. Therefore, if certain conduct influences price competition even though it directly restricts trade terms other than price, for example, the amount of a rebate, transportation charges, service fees, etc., such conduct could be that of a price-fixing cartel. Information exchange agreements concerning prices could indicate a price-fixing cartel when it is found that the participants have a mutual understanding to fix price.

In general, it still seems true that there is little hesitation to talk of prices among competitors in Japan, and as a result, it increases the difficulty for the FTC to prove mutual understanding as something different from an exchange of price information.

Production restriction cartels also could influence price, but they are separately proscribed. In Japan, it is rare for production restricting cartels not to involve any price-fixing activities. In the 1991 cement cartel case in the Chugoku District (Jan. 25, 1991, 37 KTIS 66), nine respondents had agreed, beginning in July 1985, to fix production share among themselves. They established a secretariat office where they compared sales figures on a monthly basis and adjusted sales figures so that quotas could be achieved. Sometimes, companies that exceeded their quotas would have to buy cement from other companies in order to adjust their sales figures. In September 1989, they had also formed price-fixing cartels to raise prices. The FTC ordered these nine companies to pay a 6.62 billion yen surcharge (see chapter 19 (C) Enforcement).

Among these cartels, technology restricting cartels may have a less direct effect on competition, e.g., the joint adoption of certain technology to prevent public hazards, and specialization cartels may sometimes have a cost-saving aspect and are not treated as per se illegal. Under certain conditions, they can be exempted from the Act (see (E)(2) Rationalization Cartels, below).

(E) and (F) are more naked restraints, whereas (C) and (D) may not necessarily have the same degree of anticompetitiveness. It seems necessary to evaluate the existence of actual and potential competition in the case of standardization cartels, investment restricting cartels or technology restricting cartels, but not other types of cartels. Although these types of cartels are not differentiated in the definition provision, it is necessary to evaluate them according to the nature of their individual conduct and effect on competition.

Import restricting cartels are also covered by the Act. In the 1983 Asahi Glass Co. case (March 31, 1983, 29 KTIS 104), respondents had engaged in restricting imports of soda ash produced in the U.S. by restricting import quantities, having quotas among the respondents, designating importers, and fixing import prices. So far, this is the only case where the import market was found to constitute a particular field of trade.

(D) BID RIGGING

(1) FTC ENFORCEMENT CONCERNING BID RIGGING

Bid rigging could be a violation under article 96-3 of the Criminal Code (Act No. 45 of 1907), as well as under the Antimonopoly Act. However, the Code was interpreted fairly narrowly so that only bid rigging that unreasonably profited from public

Table 6-1. Bid-Rigging Cases 1977-1991

FY	Number of Bid-Rigging Cases[1]	Total Price Related Cartel Cases	Share of Bid-Rigging Cases (%)	The Amount of Surcharges on Bid-Rigging Cases[2] (In Thousands of Yen)	Share of Bid-Rigging Cases (%)
1978	0	2	0	0	0
1979	7	12	58.3	122,595	78.0
1980	4	5	80.0	29,336	22.0
1981	2	8	25.0	30,916	8.3
1982	4	10	40.0	31,080	64.3
1983	1	6	16.7	1,259	0.9
1984	2	5	40.0	125	0.4
1985	0	3	0	0	0
1986	2	4	50.0	1,018	3.7
1987	0	4	0	0	0
1988	1	5	20.0	28,980	69.2
1989	1	7	14.3	12,596	15.7
1990	4	11	36.4	21,771	1.7
1991	1	10	10.0	25,341	12.9

NOTES:

[1] Bid-rigging cases include not only designated bidding by a procuring agency, but also private procuring bids.

[2] For the total amount of surcharges of all cases, see table 19-1.

funds could be condemned under the Criminal Code. Article 96-3 was added to the Criminal Code in 1941, during World War II, as an emergency package. It could be applied only to competitive bidding or designated bidding on publicly funded projects.

The Supreme Court ruled in 1944 (April 28, 1944, 23 Keishu 97) that "fair price" meant the price was to be achieved as a natural result of competitive bidding, in other words, the price was to be established as a result of free and fair competition. However, free and fair competition is thought to exclude competition disregarding ordinary profits. For example, in 1953 the Tokyo High Court ruled that fair price meant the price that enables one to earn actual costs plus appropriate profits (July 20, 1953, 39 Kousai Keihantokuhou 37).

In 1968 The Otsu District Court ruled that bid rigging for the purpose of securing normal profits, in other words, bid rigging to avoid loss-making bids could not be bid rigging within the meaning of the Criminal Code (Aug. 27, 1968 Keishu 10 ka 8 gou 866). Thus, the Criminal Code could only be applied to bid-rigging cases that were effected to gain unreasonable profits by such means as distributing profits among conspirators.

On the other hand, the Antimonopoly Act could have broader applicability than the Criminal Code and has much more flexibility due to its nature as administrative law, not criminal law. Nowadays, there are many FTC cases on bid rigging as well as criminal bid rigging cases prosecuted by the Public Prosecutor's Office.[2]

Before 1950, under the influence of the American Occupation Forces, five bid-rigging cases were brought (for example, the Yuasa Lumber Co. Case, Aug. 30, 1949, 1 KTIS 62). However, during the 1950s and 1960s, no bid rigging cases were taken up by the FTC. At that time, the construction industry was promoted under the primary jurisdiction of the Ministry of Construction, and the FTC did not seem to have sufficient political backing to challenge its jurisdiction.

Bid-rigging cases started to appear in the 1970s, and since 1977 when surcharge power was given to the FTC, the number of bid- rigging cases has increased dramatically. In terms of surcharge amounts, bid-rigging cases are the most noticeable group of violations among the various cartel cases (see table 6-1). Most of them were related to publicly funded projects, but some of them were related to procurement by private entities.[3]

(2) THE DESIGNATED BIDDING SYSTEM

As one form of competitive bidding, Japan had developed a very unique bidding system called a "designated bidding system." Here, only designated firms selected among registered entrepreneurs are invited to bid by a procuring agency.[4] Under ordinary procedures, firms such as construction firms are required to be registered in order to be eligible to bid on publicly funded projects. The procuring agency classifies these registered firms according to their capability and corporate size so that competitive bidding is done among equally qualified firms. In municipal government, the procuring agency often maintains a policy favoring local entrepreneurs.

In Japan, the idea of letting only qualified firms bid is justified from the point of view of fairness. It is said that the idea of separating large firms from small firms and letting them compete with other equally qualified firms has a strong foothold in Japan. This idea is explained from a public policy standpoint, as assuring that small firms have equal access with respect to publicly funded projects as do large firms.

Another consideration is to avoid so-called excessive competition. A procuring agency carefully selects a number of equally qualified bidders, normally around 10 firms, and sometimes a joint partnership is formed between large firms and local firms to increase their chances of business. It is argued that the designated bidding system is necessary to avoid destructive competition in the construction industry.

In Japan, the idea of a designated bidding system is widely supported, even though it limits bidding competition. By limiting the number of bidders, bid rigging becomes easy and bidders need not worry about the participation of third-party bidders. The designated bidding system is thought justifiable in the construction industry because the procuring agency is powerful enough so that unrestricted bidding would result in unprofitable work and might result in unreliable work.

On the issue of wasting public funds, it is argued that restraint of bidding competition is not a major problem. This is because the procuring agency prepares estimated prices in advance and, anyway, rigged prices cannot exceed the estimated prices, which means that no significant defrauding of public funds for profit could take place.

In Japan these two rationalizations of the designated bidding system are widely supported as to publicly funded projects, and the designated bidding system is routinely used by the procuring agencies. In view of the potential risk of bid rigging under the designated bidding system, the FTC's efforts to eliminate bid rigging will continue unless the current system itself is reformed and antimonopoly compliance programs are effected.

However, this view is not shared by the world community. Not only that, the designated bidding system is starting to be criticized as an entry inhibiting element to Japan's lucrative construction market. In view of the fact that large-scale publicly funded construction is projected in Japan in order to improve the social infrastructure (this was another important promise of SII), foreign firms' interest in the Japanese market is also increasing. From their perspective, the designated bidding system is subject to criticism as the main obstacle for foreign entry into the Japanese construction market.

For example, "From Washington's perspective, it stood as another serious impediment to foreign participation in Japan's construction market. For many in Washington, dango and the designated-bidding system became synonymous."[5]

(3) BID RIGGING AND TRADE FRICTION

In November 1988, the U.S. Trade Representative (USTR) started a section 301 investigation of Japan's construction industry as mandated under the Omnibus Trade and Competitiveness Act of 1988. Another important movement took place at the Structural Impediments Initiative talks (see chapter 4 (B) Structural Impediments Initiative). At first, the bid rigging issue was not a subject of SII, and was left solely as a subject of section 301 investigation. However, bid rigging has more general a nature and is thought to be a more appropriate subject for SII.

After several talks at SII, the Japanese and United States governments had agreed to take the following measures to prevent bid rigging.

> The Government of Japan will continue to make efforts to eliminate bid rigging on government-funded projects. The procuring agency will vigorously apply administrative measures, including suspension from designation, that are effective in deterring bid rigging activities. The procurement agency will on their own judgement report relevant information regarding such activities to the FTC.
>
> Through revision of the model guideline on designation suspension in certain cases, the minimum period of designation suspension has been doubled and it is to be applied on a nation wide level.
>
> The FTC will enforce the Antimonopoly Act strictly against bid rigging in all industries. (See appendix I.)

(4) CASES

(i) Shizuoka bid-rigging cases

Bid rigging cases have some more or less common features. In the 1982 Shizuoka Construction Contractors' Association case (Sep.

8, 1982, 29 KTIS 66), bid rigging was carried out in the following manner.

Under a bid rigging scheme, member firms were obliged to inform the secretariat of the association when they were designated to bid by either the procuring agency belonging to the Shizuoka Prefecture or to Shizuoka City.

Member firms that were designated by the procuring agency were obliged to meet in advance and select among themselves a champion who would get the project contract. When no agreement could be reached at the meeting, the matter would be referred to a coordinating board and the decision of the board would become final.

Each designated bidder's bid was coordinated in advance so that the champion's price would become the lowest.

If any member did not obey the rules, it would be subject to disciplinary action, such as expulsion from the ring.

The FTC, finding that such a bid rigging scheme had violated section 8(1)(i), issued a recommendation decision and imposed surcharges totaling 15.8 million yen against 44 construction firms (see chapter 19 (C) Enforcement).

(ii) Yokosuka Naval Base bid-rigging case

In the 1988 Yokosuka Naval Base case (FTC Surcharge Order, Dec. 9, 1988, 35 KTIS 57), the respondent, the Study Group on U.S. Military Constructors Safety Techniques (Star Flag Association) had engaged in a bid rigging scheme since 1984.

It was agreed that member firms were obliged to inform the secretariat of the Association about the names and project numbers of upcoming bidding at the Base. Where feasible, in order to decide a champion among those member firms who were going to bid, the secretariat would routinely gather information on possible bidders and notify dates and places for meetings. The Kajima Corp. (Kajima) was not a member of the Association but had actively participated in this bid rigging scheme.

The Study Group was abolished voluntarily in October 1987. But the existence of the bid rigging scheme was revealed in 1988. Because a 1-year statute of limitation prevented the FTC from taking remedial measures, it issued a surcharge order against 70 entrepreneurs finding a section 3 violation for Kajima and a section 8 violation for the Association. The total amount of the surcharge was about 290 million yen (see chapter 19 (C) Enforcement).

Thereafter, the U.S. Department of Justice demanded that Star Flag Association member firms pay damages. Most of the member firms settled by agreeing to pay about 4,700 million yen as a whole, about 20 times as much as the total amount of the surcharges. This incident had revealed the fact that only 70 entrepreneurs, who were actually awarded construction contracts through a bid rigging scheme, were ordered to pay surcharges, whereas 145 member firms were asked to pay damages by the U.S. government because of their participation in the bid rigging scheme.

This case had also revealed the fact that, under the current system, surcharges can recover only a small fraction of the profits gained from illegal conduct. No one would dare to be involved in a bid rigging scheme only to get a 1.5 percent overcharge. This incident prompted the U.S. Government, at the SII talks, to insist upon a substantial increase in surcharges. (For more detail, see Chapter 19 Surcharge Orders.)

(iii) Yokota Air Force Base bid-rigging case

In the 1991 NEC Information Technologies Co. case (FTC Surcharge Order, May 9, 1991, 38 KTIS 188), a group called *kabu-to-kai* was formed by those 10 firms who routinely participated in bidding for operation and maintenance work on telecommunications equipment at the various U.S. military bases located in Japan (two additional firms participated later). Member firms of *kabuto-kai* who participated in each bid at the base, met after orientation meetings or on the spot orientation, chose or confirmed a champion among themselves and thereafter exchanged bidding price information beforehand so that a champion could get the award at the price he wanted.

Thus, as to 27 biddings conducted by the 475 Air Base Wing Contracting Center at the Yokota Air Base between April 1981 and June 15, 1988, 26 bids were awarded to three member firms as a result of collusion.

In May 1991, the FTC issued surcharge orders totalling 275 million yen, against three member firms. On the same day, the NEC Information Technologies Co. and the Justice Department announced a settlement agreement totalling $34 million, about 4.7 billion yen.

One of the respondents, the Kyowa Densetsu Co. (Kyowa) had moved to deny the FTC allegation, and after the FTC had issued a complaint against Kyowa, a hearing proceeding was started. The Department of Justice had negotiated a settlement agreement as to the rest of the *kabuto-kai* members, with the exception of Kyowa, and the claim was settled in February 1992 by the payment of $2.7 million, about 350 million yen over all.

Because Kyowa is litigating all the FTC's fact-finding, until a final fact finding is made, the above description does not mean Kyowa was involved in illegal bid rigging.

(E) DEPRESSION CARTELS AND RATIONALIZATION CARTELS

(1) DEPRESSION CARTEL SYSTEM

Section 24-2 permits the formation of depression cartels. This system was adopted by the 1953 Amendment and modelled after the original bill of the German cartel law. Interestingly, this version did not pass the German Parliament (see chapter 2 (A) Amendments to Weaken the Antimonopoly Act).

The idea of allowing depression cartels is an adjustment policy that shifts adjustment costs downstream and ultimately to consumers.[6] Nowadays, the importance of free entry is well accepted in Japan, but there is much resistance to accepting the idea of free exit. The bankruptcy of inefficient entrepreneurs, in particular a possible chain reaction of bankruptcies, is thought an unacceptable solution to recovery from overproduction in a market.

Anyway, adjustment by way of free exit sometimes requires a heavy social cost. It still seems true that adjustment cost shifting via depression cartels is preferred in Japan, at least it is viewed as one of the useful adjustment mechanisms. By providing for temporary relief, some firms would stay in the market and would be given a chance to restore their ability to compete, whereas bankruptcy would immediately totally eliminate such a chance. Proponents of depression cartels also emphasize their positive impact on business, namely, uneasiness among business people might be ameliorated by renewed confidence in the future prospects of business.

Such relief could be provided by the government as a special assistance program to a particular firm, therefore, if carefully enforced, a depression cartel system could function as an effective adjustment mechanism.[7]

However, such cartels cannot remove the cause of the depression, prevent phasing out of inefficient entrepreneurs, and may create an unhealthy tendency to rely on cartels. These are domestic problems, but such cartels may also create international problems, namely, they may export adjustment costs to other countries, ones that do not accept the necessity for such an adjustment. Thus, the idea of depression cartels becomes a target of international dialogue (see chapter 25 (A) In General).

Section 24-2 gives two positive requirements (sec. 24-2(1)) and four negative requirements (sec. 24-2(2)) for depression cartels. A depression cartel is permissible only in the manufacturing sector, and with respect to "restrictions on production, sales or facilities." Restrictions on facilities is one form of cartel that restricts production, and it is so-called because the operating ratio of production facilities is agreed to by such means as limiting working hours or the non-use of some production facilities.

When restrictions on production, sales, or facilities are entirely inadequate to overcome the depressed situation or when such restrictions are difficult to achieve for technical reasons, then a price-fixing cartel is permissible (sec.24-(3)).

In the past, only 5 out of 96 depression cartels (73 if the same depression cartels that were extended more than twice are excluded) are price-related. More than half (54) are related to restrictions on the amount of production, and 25 are related to restrictions on facilities. Restrictions on sales volume were authorized in 12 cases.

In general, in Japan, cyclical depression is viewed as caused by the existence of excessive production; thus production adjustment through cartels was favored by related entrepreneurs. However, the relevance of excessive competition to depression is dubious from any standpoint, and support for depression cartels is diminishing.

Related entrepreneurs or a trade association must obtain authorization from the FTC in order to engage in a depression cartel (secs.

24-3(2) and 24-3(3)). The average duration of depression cartels was as follows.

Table 6-2. Length of Authorized Depression Cartels

Depression Period (Number of Depression Cartels Authorized)	Average Duration
1956-61 depression (6)	23.3 months
1962-64 depression (2)	8.5 months
1963-66 depression (18)	10.7 months
1971-73 depression (13)	9.2 months
1974-76 depression (5)	4.6 months
1976-79 depression (15)	10.5 months
1981-82 depression (8)	6.1 months
1982-83 depression (3)	6.3 months
Shipbuilding depression (3) cartels in 1979 and 1984	26.7 months
Total (73)	

After the depressed situation is examined upon a petition to extend, cartel duration may be extended several times. The longest depression cartels lasting more than 5 years (April 1956 to September 1961), were those for flax and ramie yarn. Most of the depression cartels were terminated within a year after fulfilling their objectives. In the case of worsted yarn, the cartel was extended six times and lasted for 21 months. The initial period of cartel authorization is ordinarily short, say about 3 months. However, as to the shipbuilding depression cartel, a 2-year period was authorized initially.

The FTC must consult with the competent minister before disposing of a cartel application (sec. 24-3(8)). If an objection is raised, the FTC must conduct a public hearing (sec. 24-3(7)). After a hearing, the FTC may revoke or modify an authorization for a depression cartel (sec. 66(1)).

(2) RATIONALIZATION CARTEL SYSTEM

Section 24-3 provides for rationalization cartels. This system was also modelled after the German cartel law and enacted by the 1953

Amendment (see chapter 2 (A) Amendments to Weaken the Antimonopoly Act). Rationalization cartels are used to effect the advancement of technology, improve the quality of goods, reduce costs, increase efficiency, and for any other rationalization measures in the manufacturing sector (sec. 24-4(1)). They can restrict technology or kinds of products, utilization of facilities for storage of raw materials or products, or transportation thereof, or utilization or purchase of by-products, waste, and scrap (sec. 24-4 (2)).

Technological collaboration seems useful to enhance the value of technology, however, no such rationalization cartels have been utilized so far. As is explained in (C) Types of Concerted Activities Condemned as Cartels, above, restrictions on technology, or on products are not necessarily per se illegal. Rationalization cartels, therefore, may not be necessary for this purpose as long as they are formed by minority groups in the industry. In addition, there are special laws for rationalization, and these laws offer very convenient mechanisms for joint action on technology (see chapter 25 (A)(1) Rationalization Cartels).

It is arguable whether there would be a situation where rationalization could not be achieved without cartel activities. Business would have plenty of reason to rationalize by its own efforts. However, this provision might be useful for prompting several entrepreneurs to take some joint action for rationalization which did not necessarily violate the Antimonopoly Act. Or sometimes, as with recycling, joint action might be necessary in order to accomplish acts that are socially desirable. From this aspect, this system can provide a safe harbor for such desirable joint action.

In the past, specialization cartels were formed in cotton and staple fiber, mixed yarn, rayon fiber yarn, margarine, flax and ramie yarn, and automobile tires and tubes. Standardization cartels were formed in ball bearings and synthetic dye stuffs. Joint purchase cartels in scrap iron were formed because scraps from each factory were relatively small in quantity and such factories tended to be scattered throughout Japan, therefore, a joint program would enhance the recycling of scrap iron.

No cartel to use warehouse or storage, or transportation facilities has been formed so far. In the case of specialization cartels, too much concentration in the hands of a particular entrepreneur is not permissible (sec. 24-4(3)(v)).

If the necessity for rationalization continues, these cartels could last forever, but in reality, cartel activities might have negative side effects. Therefore, these cartels were permitted for a limited time period, and extended if no problem could be seen.

(F) GROUP BOYCOTTS

As mentioned in (A)(3) Horizontal Agreements v. Vertical Agreements above, the most noticeable consequence of limiting unreasonable restraint of trade to a horizontal one only appears in the treatment of boycotts. Traditionally, boycotts are regulated as one type of unfair trade practice, thus no surcharge can be ordered (see chapter 19 (A)(1) Types of Cartels That Are Subject to a Surcharge) and no criminal penalty is possible against boycotts. So far as remedial measures are concerned, there isn't much difference.

Boycotts will be evaluated according to their effect on actual or potential attempts at new entry. They are very effective ways to exclude competitors from entering into a market or preventing them from expanding their market shares. Their anticompetitive effects are not limited to those who are excluded, but could be found broadly among those who intend to enter into the market. Thus, boycotts could have very anticompetitive effects on new entry. Particularly from the U.S. point of view, where cartels and boycotts are treated similarly, this approach had serious problems concerning the lack of deterring effects. This is why boycotts became one of the topics at the SII talks.

The final report of SII said "Moreover, group boycotts will also be regulated as cartels if they substantially restrain competition, and will be subject to surcharges if they influence prices. . . . The FTC will rigorously deal with such conduct as price cartels, supply restraints cartels, market allocations, bid-rigging, and boycotts." (See appendix I.)

The DSBP Guidelines which adopted a new interpretation (see (A)(3) Horizontal Agreements v. Vertical Agreements above) said that "A concerted refusal to deal, if it makes it very difficult for a firm to enter a market, or its effect is to exclude a firm from the market, . . . thereby resulting in substantial restraint of competition in the market, is illegal as unreasonable restraint of trade."

Then it gives concrete examples of where substantial restraint of competition can be found. (DSBP Guidelines Note 2, part I.)

(i)   It is made very difficult for any firm:

      (A)   manufacturing or selling products superior in price and quality

      (B)   adopting innovative selling methods

      (C)   having superior overall business capabilities to enter a market, or such firm is to be excluded from the market.

(ii)   A concerted refusal to deal is conducted toward any potential entrant, and if it is very difficult for the potential entrant to enter a market.

(iii)   It is made difficult for any firm having superior overall business capabilities to enter a market where no active competition is taking place.

In essence, when capable entrepreneurs are effectively excluded from entering a market by a group boycott, such a case would be deemed to cause a substantial restraint of competition.

When the effect is less than a substantial restraint of competition, such acts still could violate section 19 (see chapter 8 (C) Refusal to Deal).

NOTES

[1] K. Yamanouchi, *Administrative Guidance and Rule of Law*, LAW IN JAPAN: AN ANNUAL, Vol. 7 (1974), at 14; K. Sanekata, *Administrative Guidance and the Antimonopoly Law*, LAW IN JAPAN: AN ANNUAL, Vol. 10 (1977), at 65.

[2] The number of criminal bid-rigging cases are as follows: 1979, 9 cases; 1980, 10 cases; 1981, 4 cases; 1982, 22 cases; 1983, 9 cases; 1984, 6 cases; 1985, 4 cases; 1986, 7 cases; 1987, 7 cases; 1988, 9 cases. Cited in J. Abe, *Kensetsu Dango to Keiho* (Bid Rigging in the Construction Industry and the Criminal Code), KOSEI TORIHIKI No. 476 (June 1990).

[3] For example, the 1980 Chubu Toyota Forklift Co. case (April 4, 1980, 27 KTIS 1), the 1981 Nobi Bosai Industries Co. case (July 2, 1981, 28 KTIS 51).

[4] Under procurement law, there are two types of competitive bidding, namely, general competitive bidding and designated competitive bidding. In the former method, bids are solicited among any registered persons who are interested in the bid, and supposed to be a general rule. However, for the reasons stated in this chapter, in the actual practice of procuring agencies, only designated competitive bidding was employed.

[5] E. Krauss & I. Coles, *Built-in Impediments: The Political Economy of the U.S.-Japan Construction Dispute,* in K. Yamamura ed., ECONOMIC STRUCTURE: SHOULD IT CHANGE?, at 340.

In this article, the author said, "Japanese industry officials defend the practice as necessary to avoid 'confusion', a code word for excessive competition. Tokunosuke Hasegawa . . . argues that the aim of bid-rigging in Japan is not to defraud the government for profit, but to defuse destructive competition." at 340.

[6] For further analysis, see A. Uesugi, *Japan's Cartel System and Its Impact on International Trade,* HARVARD INTERNATIONAL L. J. (Special Issue), Vol. 27 (1986), at 389.

[7] *Id.* at 390-392. If depression cartels are not followed by import restrictive measures, it could serve as an effective adjustment mechanism. However, there are additional problems of international implications as examined in my article.

7

PRIVATE
MONOPOLIZATION

(A) DEFINITION OF PRIVATE MONOPOLIZATION

According to section 2(5), private monopolization refers to business activities by which any entrepreneurs, individually or by combination or conspiracy with other entrepreneurs or in any other manner, exclude or control the business activities of other entrepreneurs, thereby causing, contrary to the public interest, a substantial restraint of competition in any particular field of trade.

Therefore, the effect requirement and the public interest requirement are the same with respect to unreasonable restraint of trade. The conduct requirement to exclude or to control other entrepreneurs is particular to private monopolization. This conduct requirement is what divides monopoly and private monopolization. It means that some condemnable activities of entrepreneurs must exist that could establish, maintain or strengthen their monopoly position in a market. Such activities would be distinguishable from those of the normal means of competition in a market.

As of March 1992, there have been six cases concerning private monopolization. Two of them relate to very exceptional practices over scarce goods by a private control association dating back to 1947 (Kimura Risaburo Case, March 27, 1948, 1 KTIS 13 etc.). This number is very small compared with unreasonable restraint of trade cases. One reason is the existence of unfair trade practices regulations. Most conduct to exclude or to control other entrepreneurs may fall under any one of the conducts designated as unfair trade practices. As far as a cease and desist order is concerned, applying sections 3 or 19 does not matter. The FTC will determine as to each case whether section 3 should be applied for meeting higher standards of proof.

Conduct to control other entrepreneurs may also constitute a violation under sections 10, 13, 14, 15 or 16 (see Chapter 10 Mergers and Acquisitions). This conduct is the most typical way for controlling other entrepreneurs, and when a substantial restraint of competition is brought about, such conduct would violate section 3 rather than the sections in part IV of the Act. But for the same reason, there is no strong need to rely on section 3 for meeting higher standards of proof.

(B) EXCLUSION OF BUSINESS ACTIVITIES OF OTHER ENTREPRENEURS

Exclusion of business activities does not necessarily mean the actual exclusion of other entrepreneurs from a market. It could cover activities that make it difficult for other entrepreneurs to engage or continue to engage in normal business activities.

Two cases relate to exclusion. In the 1950 Saitama Bank case (July 13, 1950, 2 KTIS 74), the Saitama Bank tried to effect control over the raw silk export business in the Saitama Prefecture, one of the most prominent raw silk producing districts. In making a loan agreement to silk mills to purchase cocoons, the Saitama Bank made the loan available to silk mills on condition that they sold all their raw silks to the Marusa Raw Silk Co. (Marusa), an affiliated company of the Saitama Bank.

Thus through its lending policy, the respondent bank attempted to exclude the competitors of Marusa and to establish substantial control over the raw silk market. The FTC found that this conduct violated section 3.

In the 1956 Snow Brand Dairy Co. (Snow Brand) case (July 28, 1956, 8 KTIS 12), Snow Brand and the Hokkaido Butter Co. (these two companies together controlled more than 80 percent of the purchase of raw milk in Hokkaido, the largest milk producing district) tied to exclude the purchase of raw milk from other dairy companies. They acted to maintain their monopolistic position regarding the purchase of raw milk in Hokkaido, in collusion with the Agriculture and Forestry Central Bank and the Federations of Hokkaido Agricultural Credit Cooperative Associations, by having

them limit loans for buying milk cows only to agricultural cooperative associations that agreed to sell all of their raw milk to Snow
Brand or the Hokkaido Butter Co.

These two cases are examples of private monopolization by combination or conspiracy with other entrepreneurs. In the Saitama Bank
case, those excluded from a market were not competitors of the
Saitama Bank, but competitors of its related company. Such exclusion of a third party can also come under "to exclude business activities of other entrepreneurs" within the meaning of section 2(5).

(C) CONTROL OF BUSINESS ACTIVITIES OF OTHER ENTREPRENEURS

There are two cases in which the FTC found acts of "control" of
other entrepreneurs. In the 1955 Noda Soy-Sauce Co. case (FTC,
Dec. 27, 1955, 7 KTIS 108), the Noda Soy-Sauce Co. (Noda) was a
national brand soy-sauce manufacturer and the famous Kikko-man
brand. Noda with a 30.5 percent market share in the Tokyo area,
established a policy to refuse to sell to dealers who did not observe
its newly established retail price.

This was not a resale price maintenance case because, due to a
market structure particular to soy sauce, the other two national brand
manufacturers were forced to follow Noda's pricing policy, and had
to set their retail prices at the same level as Noda. Thus, by establishing a new price and carrying out a resale price maintenance
scheme, Noda effectively controlled the soy-sauce market in the
Tokyo area, because two national brand competitors were forced to
follow their pricing policy.

After the FTC had issued a decision against Noda in 1955, the
matter was litigated by the Tokyo High Court (Dec. 25, 1957, 9
KTIS 57). The Tokyo High Court acknowledged the nature of the
market structure, and found that owing to a very strong brand image
among consumers, the other two national brand manufacturers were
compelled to follow the pricing policy of Noda, and did not have the
power to challenge it. As a result, Noda could effectively control the
retail market of soy sauce by establishing a resale price maintenance
scheme for its own goods. Such an indirect way of maintaining control was found to come under "control of business activities" within
the meaning of section 2(5).

In the 1972 Toyo Can Co. case (Sep. 18, 1972, 19 KTIS 87), a direct way of controlling competitors was questioned. The Toyo Can Co. (Toyo) had controlled 56 percent of the can manufacturing industry, and had a policy of refusing to supply specialty cans to those manufacturers of canned products who had produced or tried to produce ordinary type cans for their internal use. Specialty cans required high technology to produce, and were beyond the capability of those who produced ordinary cans for their internal use. These two cases are examples of "to exclude business activities of other entrepreneurs" within the meaning of section 2(5).

Toyo also held stock in three can manufacturing companies, dispatched directors to these three companies and tried to influence the management of these companies. In particular, the Hokkai Can Co.'s business expansion activities were prevented. This conduct was found to come under "control" within the meaning of section 2(5) and the FTC ordered Toyo to dispose of the stock of these competitors, among others.

According to the 1957 Tokyo High Court decision on Noda Soy-Sauce (Dec. 25, 1957, 9 KTIS 57), "control" is an act "taking away from other entrepreneurs their free decision in business activities," and such an act must be distinguishable from those normal means of competition in a market. These two cases are examples of private monopolization effected by an individual.

8

UNFAIR TRADE PRACTICES

(A) IN GENERAL

(1) DEFINITION

For an activity to qualify as an unfair trade practice, it must fall within the scope of activities set forth in subparagraphs (i) to (vi) of section 2(9) of the Act, such activity must tend to impede fair competition, and the FTC must have designated the activity as an unfair trade practice.

When the FTC designates an unfair trade practice, it takes the former two requirements fully into account, therefore, once such activities are designated as unfair trade practices they can be regarded as prohibited conduct under section 19 of the Act.

(2) FTC DESIGNATIONS

(i) Procedure

Section 71 provides that, before designating a specific business practice in a particular field of business, the FTC shall obtain the views of entrepreneurs engaged in the same line of business as the entrepreneurs who employ the business practice under consideration, and hold a public hearing to obtain the views of the public. Section 72 provides that the FTC shall make its designation by means of a Notification.

(ii) General designations and specific designations

As a matter of practice, the FTC has two sets of designations of unfair trade practices. One is a General Designation, and the other is a Specific Designation. The General Designation specifies a broad category of practices coming under the purview of section 2(9), and could apply to all fields of business.

The Specific Designations are limited by their terms to particular industries and employed by the FTC where very specific rules are warranted resulting from particular situations or other special factors in an industry.

Once designated, there are no substantive differences between the General Designations and the Specific Designations, but the Specific Designations have by their nature, primary applicability. The practices not covered by the Specific Designations would still be susceptible to application of the General Designations.

The FTC has designated practices that are inherently unfair or unreasonable employed in a particular industry by Specific Designations. Thus, a case-by-case appraisal is not required for these practices. The Specific Designations impose explicit and often absolute prohibition of practices that might be regulated under the broad standard of reasonableness of the General Designations.

Explicit and absolute prohibition under the Specific Designations may, although it has the merit of clear-cut rule making, sometimes cause a problem of overregulation. Recently, the FTC favored relying on General Designations even if this approach required a greater expenditure of resources than the Specific Designation approach.

It also seems true that Specific Designations would invite much criticism due to their specific applicability, whereas the General Designations face less objection from related entrepreneurs and the public in general. In August 1973, the FTC attempted to make a Specific Designation with respect to loss leader selling. This attempt met with much criticism from consumer organizations, and could not proceed further.

(3) UNFAIR TRADE PRACTICES V. SECTION 3 PROHIBITIONS

Although three major substantive prongs—unreasonable restraint of trade, private monopolization, and unfair trade practices—each have their own applicability, they sometimes overlap. In particular, because unfair trade practices could be employed as a means to achieve a monopoly position, unfair trade practices by a dominant entrepreneur could constitute a private monopolization or some conduct that is regulated as an unfair trade practice could be regulated as an unreasonable restraint of trade when horizontal agreements or contracts are involved. Therefore, it should be noted that there are some activities that would be equally vulnerable to attack under one or the other of the two major substantive prongs of the Act.

One benefit of applying the unfair trade practice provision consists of less stringent standards for establishing violations of the Act. When a cease and desist order is what is aimed for, proceeding under an unfair trade practices provision has a great advantage.

However, as far as criminal penalties are concerned, there exists a huge difference. (There are no criminal penalties placed upon unfair trade practices.) In order to increase the deterring effects of Antimonopoly Act violations, it is expected that the FTC will rely on section 3 as much as is feasible.

(4) SCOPE OF FTC AUTHORITY

The FTC authority to designate unfair trade practices, or whether designated practices are within the scope of subparagraphs (i) to (iv) of section 2(9) of the Act is questioned in some litigated cases. In these cases, the court supported the FTC's authority to designate unfair trade practices, and confirmed the legality of the General Designations. For example, in the 1971 Meiji Trading Co. case (July 17, 1971, 18 KTIS 167), the Tokyo High Court ruled that

> Now, we consider the problem of whether the General Designations fit with the power delegated under Section 2(7). The FTC categorized 12 items of business conduct throughout various fields of business and designated them as unfair trade practices. . . . If we compare the designated conducts with each subparagraph of Section 2(7), it is evident that the General Designations have further clarified and specified such subparagraphs within the context of law. Therefore, it cannot be said that the General Designations do not fit with the delegated power under Section 2(7) or are illegal.

In the 1975 Wakodo Co. case (July 10, 1975, 212 KTIS 173), the Supreme Court said "the present General Designations have specified each subparagraph of Section 2(7), and we do not think that it goes beyond the delegated power under the law, if we consider the fact that they are intended to have general applicability to all industries in a changing economic world."

As to the extent of the FTC's statutory authority, it is the FTC's policy to include in unfair trade practices a wide range of practices based on a standard of unfairness or unreasonableness where the effect on competition is less direct. There is a debate as to whether the FTC's authority in this area should be restricted primarily to practices that have direct anticompetitive effects, or should be extended to practices that are unreasonable or unfair in nature.[1]

(5) OLD GENERAL DESIGNATIONS AND NEW GENERAL DESIGNATIONS

The first set of General Designations was issued in 1953 (FTC Notification No. 11 of 1953) when such power was first authorized under the Act, and consisted of 12 items (Old General Designations). These were in effect for about 20 years without any amendment or addition.

In 1982, after a careful review conducted by a special study group established for the purpose, the FTC adopted a new set of General Designations (General Designations, FTC Notification No. 15 of 1982). The amendments concerned mainly clarification of some phrases or reclassification of items of the Old General Designations in order to increase the predictability of prohibited conduct under the Act.

From September 1953 through August 1982, the FTC rendered 91 cases under the Old General Designations. Among them, 37 cases are related to resale price maintenance falling under item 8, and 16 cases are related to exclusive dealing falling under item 7 (see table 8-1).

(6) INCREASED IMPORTANCE OF UNFAIR TRADE PRACTICES REGULATIONS

Distribution *keiretsu* (see Chapter 24 *Keiretsu* Relationships) may work to foreclose the access of foreign products into the Japanese market. A manufacturer's dominant position might work as a disincentive for distributors to lower their prices. A distributor's dependence on a particular manufacturer would make distribution channels exclusive and raise entry barriers significantly.

The final report of the Structural Impediments Initiative said, "The FTC will formulate and publish guidelines . . . which will clarify, as concretely and clearly as possible, the criteria regarding the enforcement of the Antimonopoly Act so that fair competition with regard to trade practices in the distribution sector will not be hindered."

The FTC had announced the Guidelines on Distribution System and Business Practices on July 11, 1991 (DSBP Guidelines). Part II of the DSBP Guidelines is the one thus formulated.

In view of the flexibility of unfair trade practices regulation, it seems useful in securing market access to foreign goods to rigorously enforce the Antimonopoly Act. Unfair trade practice regulation could make a great contribution toward making business practices in Japan more open to foreign products and more compatible with market mechanism principles. The FTC's enforcement of the rules as prescribed in the DSBP Guidelines, would make a very important contribution to the improvement of market access.

(B) GENERAL DESIGNATIONS—16 DESIGNATED CONDUCTS

(1) TENDENCY TO IMPEDE FAIR COMPETITION

The General Designations contain general language such as "without proper justification," "unjustly," and "unjustly in the light of normal business practices." This language was added to show that, in individual cases, these designated conducts are prohibited when a tendency to impede fair competition is found. "Without proper justification" is used to show that the designated practices are illegal in principle, but if any justifiable reason is available, they could be excluded. Item 1 (group boycotts) and item 12 (resale price maintenance) fall into this category. "Unjustly" is used to show that the practices designated are evaluated under a broad rule of reason. "Unjustly in the light of normal business practices" has the same meaning, except that the unjustness of the practices shall be evaluated in the light of normal business practices.

(2) THREE TYPES OF TENDENCIES TO IMPEDE FAIR COMPETITION

According to the study group that prepared a report on unfair trade practices,[2] fair competition is interpreted to mean that any one of the following situations exists in a market. This view was shared by the FTC and, reflected in the General Designations.

First, free competition among entrepreneurs is not restricted and an entrepreneur is not prevented from entering into free competition (maintenance of free competition).

Second, competition is centered on price, quality, and service, thus the free competitive order is maintained (maintenance of fairness in competitive method).

Third, trading partners can engage in transactions based on free and voluntary decision making, thus the basis for free competition is maintained (maintenance of the basis for free competition).

The tendency to impede fair competition, therefore, shall be found where any harm could be caused under any one of the above situations.

Items 8, 9, and 10 are provisions to maintain fairness in competitive method, thus, they do not necessarily require the same level of impact on a market as do the other items. Items 14, 15, and 16 are provisions to maintain the basis for free competition, in other words, to try to remove market factors that disturb the operation of free competition. From this aspect, their impact on a market shall be evaluated a bit differently than the rest of the unfair trade practices.

To understand unfair trade practice regulations, it is necessary to keep in mind these three types of conduct and the difference in the analytical methods employed in evaluating the tendency to impede fair competition.

(3) "ILLEGAL" IN PRINCIPLE CASES V. RULE OF REASON CASES

As to unfair trade practices, the term "illegal in principle" instead of "illegal per se" is used to show that there could be a situation where those practices are still justifiable in individual cases.

In the DSBP Guidelines, the FTC classified conduct into illegal in principle cases, and rule of reason cases. As to the rule of reason cases, in a further clarification, the DSBP Guidelines found that rule of reason cases would constitute an unfair trade practice if such practice was employed by an influential entrepreneur and if it produced specified effects on a market or on price competition.

(4) "INFLUENTIAL ENTREPRENEUR"

In view of the importance of the term "influential entrepreneur," the DSBP Guidelines give the following criteria for the term (DSBP Guidelines note 4 of part II), namely, whether an entrepreneur has a market share of 10 percent or more, or he is among the top three in a market. On the other hand, if the entrepreneur has less than a 10 percent market share, or he is in the fourth position or less in a market, he is presumed not to be an influential entrepreneur. A new entrant into a market is also deemed not to be an influential entrepreneur.

However, market position is a criteria in the first instance, and each case shall be evaluated as to

(A) whether the conduct in question has a tendency to result in reducing competitors' business opportunities and making it difficult for them to easily find alternative trading partners, or

(B) the conduct has a tendency to result in making it difficult for new entrants or competitors to easily secure alternative distribution channels. (See DSBP Guidelines note 4, part II.)

Therefore, market position criteria are important in offering easy-to-understand guidance to related entrepreneurs, and to offer a safe harbor for those who are not influential entrepreneurs in a market to utilize non-price vertical restraints.

(C) REFUSAL TO DEAL

(1) CONCERTED REFUSALS TO DEAL (GROUP BOYCOTTS) (ITEM 1)

When formulated, item 1 of the General Designations was meant as the sole source for regulating group boycotts. However, due to an important policy change adopted in the DSBP Guidelines, the FTC will look at group boycotts primarily as an unreasonable restraint of trade, and when the conduct falls short of this, then item 1 applicability shall be examined.

The DSBP Guidelines say that group boycotts will fall under either unreasonable restraint of trade or item 1 of the General Designations (DSBP Guidelines chapter 2-1, part I). The Guidelines give examples of where competition is substantially restrained, which means that a group boycott has the effect of making it very difficult for any firm refused to deal with to enter into a market, or has the effect of excluding any firm refused to deal with from the market (DSBP Guidelines chapter 2-2-(1), part I).

Subparagraphs (i), (iii), (iv) and (v) of section 8(1) could be applied to group boycotts by a trade association, depending on the effects on a market (DSBP Guidelines chapter 2-4, part I; also see Chapter 9 Trade Association Activities, *infra*).

The number of cases in which items 1 or 2 were applied (item 1 in the Old General Designations) was relatively small (see table 8-1). In contrast, group boycott cases by a trade association amounted to 27 (see table 8-3). Among section 8(1)(v) cases, there were six cases in which item 2 of the General Designations was applied.

Most item 1 cases were related to private monopolization cases, not collective refusal to deal cases. The relatively small number of group boycott cases under item 1 can be explained by the fact that section 8(1)(v) cases could, for the most part, cover group boycotts. This also means that a trade association would offer a convenient forum to carry out group boycotts, and thus, strict regulation of trade association activities is warranted in Japan. (See chapter 9 (A) Trade Associations and Section 8 Regulation.)

(2) OTHER REFUSALS TO DEAL (ITEM 2)

(i) Individual refusals to deal

In Japan, in applying the Act, freedom of choice of trading partners is respected. A firm is thought free to select its trading partners and to have or not to have a business relationship (see DSBP Guidelines chapter 3-1, part I). An individual refusal to deal would be illegal only when it is used as a means to secure the effectiveness of illegal conduct under the Antimonopoly Act, or when it is used as a means to achieve such unjust purposes, under the Antimonopoly Act, as excluding competitors from a market.

The DSBP Guidelines describe concrete examples of the following two types of conduct (DSBP Guidelines chapter 3-2, part I).

(A) Refusal to deal as a means to secure the effectiveness of illegal practices under the Act.

In this case, refusal to deal is used as a means of other illegal conduct. In the past years, the FTC rarely applied item 2 to cases where refusal to deal was used to secure the effectiveness of such unfair trade practices as resale price maintenance; only item 12 was applied. The DSBP Guidelines declare that the FTC would apply various items relevant to a particular case as much as is feasible.

In the 1955 Taisho Pharmaceutical Co. (Taisho) case (Dec. 10, 1955, 7 KTIS 99), where the respondent ceased to deal with some of its retail outlets because they also handled competitors' pharmaceutical products, the FTC applied item 1 of the Old General Designations. These actual refusals to deal were employed in order to convince other Taisho chain stores to refuse to serve as retail outlets for competitors, and cause those member stores that had already started to deal with competitors to return those competitors' products.

(B) Refusal to deal as a means to achieve such unjust purposes as excluding competitors from a market.

To fall under this conduct, the effect of a refusal to deal must be such that makes it difficult for the refused firm to carry on normal business activities.

In the past, sections 3 and 19 were applied when refusal to deal by a market-dominating firm took place in order to maintain or strengthen its market dominating position, or could be deemed as abusive conduct of its market-dominating position.

For example, in early cases such as the 1950 Saitama Bank case (July 13, 1950, 2 KTIS 74) or the 1956 Snow Brand Dairy Co. case (July 28, 1956, 8 KTIS 12) (see chapter 7 (B) Exclusion of Business Activities of Other Entrepreneurs), in violation of the former part of section 3, refusal to deal was utilized as a means to effect the exclusion of competitors. However, because unfair trade practices are effected as a means of private monopolization, it is a recent FTC practice to apply only section 3. Therefore, item 2 would be applied to cases that fall short of private monopolization.

The DSBP Guidelines give as an example of item 2 violations (DSBP Guidelines chapter 3-2, part I), that "an influential manufacturer in a market, by causing its distributors not to deal with its competitors, reduces business opportunities of the competitors, and prevents them from easily finding alternative trading partners, and refuses to deal with its distributors not yielding to such requests."

As shown by this example, the FTC would apply item 2 to refusals to deal by influential firms in a market, not be limited to that of market-dominating firms.

Group boycotts need some horizontal aspect, and collective refusals to deal by a manufacturer and a distributor cannot qualify as group boycotts (see chapter 6 (F) Group Boycotts). Therefore, when such conduct still has the effect of excluding competitors from a market, it could nonetheless be condemned under item 2.

(D) RESALE PRICE MAINTENANCE (ITEM 12)

Item 12 deals with resale price restrictions on goods. Its predecessor, item 8, was the most heavily utilized among the various items of the Old General Designations. As a whole, 37 cases were handed down under item 8 (see table 8-1). Most of them are related to resale price maintenance. Because resale price maintenance is a conduct illegal in principle, and other dealings on restrictive terms are deemed to be rule of reason cases, the General Designations divided conduct falling under item 8 into item 12 (Resale Price Maintenance) and item 13 (Other Dealings on Restrictive Terms).

(1) RESALE PRICE MAINTENANCE

Resale price maintenance is thought illegal in principle. The question is whether there could be any proper justification as provided for in item 12. The standard of illegality of resale price maintenance was litigated in the 1975 Wakodo Co. (Wakodo) case (Supreme Court, July 10, 1975, 22 KTIS 173). The respondent raised the following basic issues:

(A)   Can small entrepreneurs employ resale price maintenance to strengthen their market positions, or is it always a violation of item 8 (currently item 12)?

(B)   What is the meaning as to resale price maintenance of "without proper justification" under item 8?

(C)   What is the relationship between section 24-2, which exempts certain resale price maintenance contracts from the Act, and "proper justification" under item 8?

The Supreme Court stated that since it was thought that resale price maintenance was illegal in principle, section 24-2 was enacted as a specific provision to legalize resale price maintenance as to designated goods and copyrighted works. The Supreme Court further stated that "proper justification" would not be found as to resale price maintenance if that was employed without obtaining the FTC's designation and was not applied to all of its distributors generally and systematically.

Wakodo was a small entrepreneur of baby formula with a less than 5 percent market share, and it insisted that it had a justifiable reason to employ resale price maintenance in order to enhance its market position, thus Wakodo's conduct could encourage competition in a market where a small number of firms dominate.

> The Supreme Court rejected Wakodo's argument, stating that: Item No. 8 mainly aims at preventing restriction on competition as to the business activities of one's customers. And even though resale price maintenance may strengthen one's competition vis-a-vis one's competitors, it does not necessarily produce the same economic effects as free price competition among the distributors of the goods concerned: therefore, the injurious effects on competition cannot be denied.

According to the Supreme Court, a weak position in a market does not justify the use of a resale price maintenance scheme. It is established that resale price maintenance is illegal in principle, and the FTC and the courts have so far not accepted any proper justification as to resale price maintenance.

It is also made clear that secondary level resale price maintenance, namely, instructing another distributor to employ resale price maintenance to its customer/retailer, also falls under item 12.

(2) DEFINITION OF RESTRICTIONS

The DSBP Guidelines say that when some artificial means is employed to assure the effectiveness of sales at the price indicated by a manufacturer, it would be regarded as a resale price restriction (DSBP Guidelines chapter 1-2, part II). For example, when disadvantageous treatment such as curtailment of shipments is notified or suggested to distributors in cases where sales at an indicated price were not observed, or a manufacturer patrols retail stores, or a manufacturer tries to identify suppliers who sold the products to discounting retailers, this conduct would constitute such artificial means that make maintenance of resale prices illegal.

(E) EXEMPTION OF RESALE PRICE MAINTENANCE

(1) REQUIREMENTS FOR DESIGNATION

Under section 24-2(1), the FTC may designate commodities by a Notification as to which resale price maintenance can be permitted. Copyrighted works are designated in the Act (sec. 24-2 (4)).

In order to be designated by the FTC, commodities should be for daily use by consumers in general and of uniform quality that can be easily identifiable. Free competition should exist with regard to the commodity (sec. 24-2 (2)).

As a justifiable reason for resale price maintenance, the possibility of loss leader selling is often cited. As a result, only consumer goods that are sold with the brand name of a manufacturer on them, and as a result may be suitable targets for loss leader selling tactics, can be designated.

The following conduct by manufacturers and distributors could be exempted.

(A)   Making it a contractual obligation to observe a resale price, and imposing penalties for non-compliance.

(B)   Making it a condition for its dealers to conclude resale price maintenance contracts with their retailers/customers.

(C)   Refusing to deal with those who do not have resale price maintenance contracts, or those who do not observe resale prices.

However, collective resale price maintenance or horizontal agreements to maintain the retail price of particular products are not allowed, and could violate either sections 3, 8(1)(iv) or 8(1)(v). (See chapter 9 (D) Restrictions on Functions or Activities of Constituent Entrepreneurs.)

Section 24-2 allows only resale price maintenance that is uniformly enforced and non-discriminatorily applied by a manufacturer or by distributors.

When an entrepreneur has entered into a resale price maintenance contract, he must file a report with the FTC within 30 days (sec. 24-2(6)).

Organizations formed in accordance with the specified laws in section 24-2 shall not be compelled to have resale price maintenance contracts with respect to the designated commodities or copyrighted works (see. 24-2(5)). These organizations are to supply inexpensive goods to members, and thus shall have the freedom to negotiate lower prices for the members. In the 1965 Kao Soap Co. case (May 20, 1965, 13 KTIS 14), the Kao Soap Co. had concluded resale price maintenance contracts with dealers in which dealers were compelled to have resale price maintenance contracts with consumer cooperatives with respect to soaps and detergents, which were designated as commodities at that time. The FTC held that such contracts were unlawful.

(2) ENFORCEMENT

In the 1950s, the FTC designated several commodities such as hair coloring, toothpaste, soap, whisky and brandy, caramel candy, cameras, and ready-made shirts with collars. The designated commodities were first reviewed in February 1966, then again in April 1971, and the major review was held in September 1974 when most of designated commodities were eliminated. Thus, only drugs for daily use, and cosmetics for which the retail price is 1,000 yen or less (1,030 yen after the introduction of the consumption tax of 3 percent in April 1989) remained as designated commodities.

In July 1991, a study group commissioned by the FTC proposed a further review of the designated commodities and the total elimination of designated commodities was proposed.[3] The study group indicated two basic problems with designated commodities.

First, once retail price maintenance is legalized as to particular commodities, most of the manufacturers of such commodities tended to utilize the exemption system and, therefore, the impact on a market in Japan became fairly significant. Besides, pricing policy tends to be similar among these manufacturers in Japan, which causes a concern as to the impact of retail price maintenance on the national economy.

In particular, it is said that the exemption system had great impact on non-exempted items within the same product category, namely, cosmetics whose retail price exceeded 1,030 yen or some drugs or drug-related products marketed by the same manufacturers.

Another problem is the ill-balance with non-designated commodities. Resale price maintenance worked to eliminate interbrand price competition in Japan, and the probability of loss leader selling tactics for the designated commodities is not persuasive enough under Japan's current economic conditions.

After the submission of this report, the FTC had conducted its own hearings with related entrepreneurs and the general public, and decided that immediate elimination of all the designated commodities would be inappropriate in spite of the study group's recommendation. And, in the meantime, about half of the subproducts of drugs and cosmetics were eliminated from the designation by April 1993 (two subproducts of drugs would be eliminated by the end of FY 1994). The FTC had announced its policy to make a thorough review in 1998.

(3) COPYRIGHTED WORKS

Section 24-2 provides for the exemption of copyrighted works. Originally, the FTC had interpreted that books, magazines, newspapers and records are the copyrighted works under section 24-2. Since this provision was enacted in 1953 copyright protection was significantly expanded, and new technology has produced new types of copyrighted works.[4] For example, music tapes, compact discs (CDs), and digital audio tapes did not exist at all at that time, and such audio-visual equipment as video and laser discs have since been invented and protected as copyrighted works. The question is whether these new types of copyrighted works shall be entitled to receive exemption status automatically or if a different interpretation is warranted.

In view of this development, the study group mentioned above had reviewed in late 1991, whether these new types of copyrighted works should also be entitled to maintain resale price. As long as records are permitted resale price maintenance, there seems less justification to deny the same status to CDs. On the other hand, there are no other countries that permit resale price maintenance of CDs, and, as a result, the price of CDs tended to be high in Japan.

The study group was skeptical of the exempted status afforded to CDs. The FTC decided, in April 1992, that records, music tapes and CDs should be afforded the same treatment under the current law and the related provisions be amended, if necessary, to eliminate their exemption status for the sake of legal stability. The FTC started its review on copyrighted works from this perspective.

(F) CUSTOMER AND TERRITORIAL RESTRICTIONS (ITEM 13)

(1) DEALING ON UNDULY RESTRICTIVE TERMS

Item 13 could be applied to non-price vertical restraints such as customer restrictions and territorial restrictions as a dealing on unduly restrictive terms. Item 13 covers rule of reason cases, but dealings on unduly restrictive terms that cause the same effects as resale price maintenance are considered illegal in principle cases.

(2) CUSTOMER RESTRICTIONS

(i) Cases

The FTC's decisions had constantly made it illegal for a manufacturer to demand that its customers/wholesalers suspend shipments to or refuse to deal with particular retailers who sell below the suggested retail price. Although this conduct restricts customers of a manufacturer's customers, it is treated as secondary level resale price maintenance, and it falls under item 12.

However, a manufacturer may restrict its wholesalers' customers with an aim to stabilizing retail price. When wholesalers are prohibited to deal with certain retailers, but not specifically for the purpose of restricting resale prices, the applicability of item 13 comes into question.

In three related 1977 cases concerning baby formula manufacturers (the Meiji Trading Co., the Morinaga Trading Co., and the Wakodo Co.) the FTC issued complaints to remedy the "one wholesaler/one retailer system" where the respondents independently had requested their respective wholesalers not to deal with any retailers who maintained business relations with other wholesalers with respect to the manufacturers' products.

In 1968, after a hearing, the FTC issued a formal decision finding that these three companies had engaged in resale price maintenance, and ordered remedial measures against them (Oct. 11, 1968, 15 KTIS 67, 15 KTIS 84, 15 KTIS 98). These cases were appealed to the Tokyo High Court (July 17, 1971, 18 KTIS 167, 18 KTIS 198), and finally resolved by the Supreme Court in 1975 in favor of the FTC (Supreme Court, July 11, 1975, 22 KTIS 173; July 10, 1975, 22 KTIS 198; the Morinaga Trading Co. dropped the appeal at the Tokyo High Court). After the FTC decision became final, with an aim to stabilizing retail prices without directly engaging in resale price maintenance, a new distribution system was introduced simultaneously by these companies.

The issue of concern in these cases was whether such a distribution system still could violate item 8 (currently item 13) of the General Designations when there was no specific evidence to show the respondents' intention to effect resale price maintenance, although an aim of such a scheme is to stabilize retail prices. The FTC pointed out that the respondents had suggested or implicated that there would be possible sanctions against those who did not comply with these requests, and under this system, both wholesalers and retailers had their rights to freely select customers restricted. The FTC found that the system's effect was to lessen competition both at the manufacturers' level and at their wholesalers' level.

Although the FTC ruling seems to say that restrictions on customers are themselves illegal, this was a case of a dealing on unduly restrictive terms that had the same effect as resale price maintenance. In this particular case, one wholesale/one retailer restrictions seem to have no other objective than resale price maintenance, and the impact on retail prices could be presumed because the system was introduced as a substitute for resale price maintenance.

(ii) Distribution system and business practices guidelines

The DSBP Guidelines made clear that "in cases where a manufacturer imposes a requirement of designated accounts on wholesalers, and if price level of the products covered by the restriction is likely to be maintained, such restriction is illegal." (DSBP Guidelines chapter 2-4, part II.)

Under the DSBP Guidelines, three types of customer restrictions are declared illegal if as a result of such conducts the price level of the products is likely to be maintained. These types of conduct are:

(A) Requiring dealing with designated wholesalers, or to have only one account with wholesalers;
(B) Prohibiting sales among distributors; and
(C) Prohibiting sales to price cutters.

As to (C), the effects on price are obvious and particular examination of the impact on the price level of the products would be unnecessary.

(3) TERRITORIAL RESTRICTIONS

Territorial restriction is not illegal per se. There are two aspects to examine. One is the restrictiveness of the conduct in question. For example, assignment of an area of primary responsibility or a so-called location clause in which store location is subject to control by a manufacturer is regarded as legal from this perspective (DSBP Guidelines chapter 2-3-(2), part II).

The other is the market position of a manufacturer. When utilized by an influential person in a market, territorial restriction could have the tendency to impede fair competition (DSBP Guidelines chapter 2-3-(3), part II).

There have been only two FTC decisions relating to territorial restrictions. In the 1981 Fuji X-Ray Co. (Fuji X-Ray) case (May 11, 1981, 28 KTIS 10), the respondent who controlled more than 50 percent of the X-ray film market had distributed products made by the Fuji Film Co. parent company of Fuji X-Ray. Fuji X-Ray had distribution contracts with many distributors that contained provisions restricting the handling of competitive products, sales territory and sales price. The FTC found that, as a whole, these provisions fell under the prohibition of item 8 of the Old General Designations, and ordered Fuji X-Ray not to restrict sales territories of its distributors among others.

In the 1965 Yaculto Honsha Co. case (Sep. 13, 1965, 13 KTIS 72), the FTC ordered the deletion of a territorial restriction clause from process patent and trademark licensing agreements, as well as a clause to restrict the sales price of retailers/licensees.

The DSBP Guidelines made clear that exclusive territorial assignment, and restriction of sales to outside customers are illegal when the following two conditions are met (DSBP Guidelines chapters 2-3-(3) & (4), part II):

(A)   it is employed by an influential person in a market, and
(B)   if the price level of the product covered by the restriction is likely to be maintained.

"Exclusive territorial assignment" refers to the assigning of a specific area to each distributor and restricting the distributor from selling outside that area. "Restriction of sales to outside customers" means assigning a specific area to each distributor and restricting the distributor from selling to customers outside each sales area even if requested from such outside customers.

(4) EFFECTS ON PRICE LEVELS

The DSBP Guidelines give more concrete standards, which are used as a common requirement for the illegality of non-price vertical restraints, for evaluating the impact on price levels (DSBP Guidelines note 7 of part II). For this requirement, the FTC would take into account whether interbrand competition was effective or the degree of product differentiation. Therefore, when interbrand competition is not working well due to such market factors as oligopolistic market structure, or because product differentiation is advanced, then, price competition for the product may be impeded by non-price vertical restraints. In such a situation, the FTC would think that price level is likely to be maintained.

(5) PROHIBITION ON ADVERTISING DISCOUNT SALES

A case where a manufacturer prohibits its retailers from attaching a price tag showing a discount price at their sales outlets, or to advertise a discount price, or where a manufacturer causes magazines, newspapers or other advertising media that carry his own advertisement, to reject advertisements by retailers that announce discount prices would fall under an item 13 prohibition (DSBP Guidelines chapter 2-5-(2), part II).

(G) EXCLUSIVE DEALING (ITEM 11)

Item 11 covers three kinds of exclusive dealing: (1) exclusive supply arrangements, (2) exclusive buying arrangements, and (3) reciprocally exclusive arrangements. Exclusive buying arrangements would pose anticompetitive problems only when such arrangements were forced to some extent, therefore, item 10's applicability needs to be examined, as well. In other words, exclusive buying arrangements need to be examined to see whether full-line-forcing or similar practices are employed.

(1) GENERAL PRINCIPLE

In the 1954 Hokkaido Newspaper Co. case (Dec. 23, 1954, 6 KTIS 89), the Tokyo High Court stated the following general prin-

Table 8-1. Unfair Trade Practices Cases Under the Old General Designations

Year	§1	§6	§7	§8	§9	§10	§11	Other Items[2]	S.D.[3]	Sum Total	Net Total
1953	0	0	0	0	1	1	0	0	—	2	1
1954	0	0	1	1	0	0	0	0	—	2	2
1955	2	1	1	0	0	1	0	1	—	6	3
1956	1	0	0	1	0	0	0	1	0	3	2
1957	0	0	0	0	1	1	0	0	0	2	1
1958	0	0	0	0	0	0	0	0	0	0	0
1959	0	1	1	0	0	0	1	0	0	3	1
1960-61	0	0	0	0	0	0	0	0	0	0	0
1962	0	0	0	0	0	0	1	0	1	2	2
1963	0	1	1	0	0	0	2	0	5	9	9
1964	0	0	0	1	0	0	0	0	0	1	1
1965	0	0	0	3	0	0	0	0	0	2	3
1966	0	0	0	2	0	0	0	0	0	2	2
1967	1	3	0	1	0	0	0	0	0	5	5
1968	0	0	0	3	0	0	0	0	0	3	3
1969	0	0	0	1	0	0	0	0	0	1	1
1970	0	0	0	1	0	0	0	0	0	1	1
1971	0	0	0	0	0	0	0	0	0	0	0
1972	0	0	0	1	0	0	0	0	1	2	2
1973	0	0	0	0	0	0	0	0	0	0	0
1974	0	0	1	1	0	0	0	0	0	2	1
1975	0	1	3	2	0	0	1	0	0	7	5
1976	0	0	2	2	0	0	0	0	0	4	4
1977	0	0	0	5	0	2	0	1	0	8	6
1978	0	0	0	4	0	0	0	0	0	4	4
1979	0	0	2	1	0	0	0	1	0	4	4
1980	1	0	2	1	0	0	0	0	0	4	3
1981	0	0	2	3	0	0	0	0	0	5	3
1982[1]	0	0	0	3	0	1	0	2	0	6	6
Total	5	7	16	37	2	6	5	6	7	91	75

NOTES:
[1] FY 1982 covers from April 1982 to August 1982.
[2] "Other Items" covers sections 2, 3, 4 and 5.
[3] "S.D." refers to the Specific Designations.

ciple regarding exclusive dealing, and this ruling has been supported ever since.

Generally speaking, dealing with another party on the condition that the said party not receive any supplies from one's competitor is not in itself illegal. Even if entrepreneur A adopts such a policy, entrepreneur B—A's competitor—is not prevented from entering into the market through price, quality, quantity, or service competition, so long as he can easily find distributors other than those who are dealing with entrepreneur A. In such a case, A's practice cannot be said to have a tendency to impede fair competition.

Thus, exclusive dealing is a rule of reason case, and when an entrepreneur makes an exclusive dealing or sole agency arrangement, its impact on his competitor would be a determining factor.

Table 8-2. Unfair Trade Practices Cases Under the General Designations

Year	§1	§2	§3	§9	§10	§11	§12	§13	§14	§15	§16	S.D.[2]	Sum Total	Net Total
1982[1]	0	0	0	0	0	0	1	0	0	0	0	0	1	1
1983	0	0	0	0	0	0	3	1	0	0	0	0	4	4
1984	0	0	0	0	0	0	0	0	0	0	0	0	0	0
1985	0	0	0	0	0	0	7	0	0	0	0	0	7	7
1986	0	0	0	0	0	0	0	0	0	0	0	0	0	0
1987	0	0	0	0	0	0	1	1	0	0	0	0	2	1
1988	0	0	0	0	0	1	0	1	0	0	0	0	2	2
1989	0	1	0	0	0	2	0	1	1	2	0	0	7	3
1990	0	0	0	0	5	0	0	0	0	1	0	0	6	6
1991	0	0	0	4	1	0	2	2	0	1	0	0	10	9
1992	0	0	0	0	0	0	0	4	0	0	0	0	4	4
Total	0	1	0	4	6	3	14	10	1	4	0	0	43	37

NOTES:
[1] FY 1982 covers September 1982 to March 1983.
[2] "S.D." refers to the Specific Designations.

(2) CASES

In the 1953 Chukyo Lion Dentifrice Co. case (March 7, 1953, 4 KTIS 104), the respondent was the sole agent of the Lion Dentifrice Co. (Lion) in the Chubu District. In order to prevent the entry of Lion's competitors into the Chubu District, the respondent told its distributors that if they wished to continue their business relationships with the respondent, they could not deal the products of other dentifrice companies. The FTC found that use of exclusive dealing in order to prevent the entry of one's competitors into the market where one is in a dominant position falls under item 7 (currently item 11).

In the 1955 Taisho Pharmaceutical Co. case (Dec. 10, 1955, 7 KTIS 99), the respondent's refusal to deal with its retail outlets because they started to handle competitors' products is held an exclusive dealing falling under item 7 (currently item 11), in addition to items 1 and 2.

In the 1976 Pigeon Co. case (Jan. 7, 1976, 22 KTIS 115), the respondent had about 80 percent of the market share of baby nursing bottles, 35 percent of paper diapers, and 10 percent of baby formula. The Pigeon Co. (Pigeon) concluded agency agreements with its distributors that contained a provision that no agency was to handle competitors' products that are the same or similar to Pigeon's baby products without first obtaining Pigeon's approval. Thereafter, on many occasions, the respondent suggested that its distributors refrain from handling its competitors' products and declared that it would refuse to deal at all or reduce its rebate payments to those who did not follow its suggestions. The FTC ordered the respondent to cease its exclusive dealing arrangements as to all of its baby products, including baby formula, where the respondent was not in a market-dominating position.

In the 1974 Muto Kogyo Co. case (Nov. 22, 1974, 21 KTIS 148), the respondent had a two-thirds market share of the drawing board and instrument field. In the 1976 France Bed Co. case (Feb. 20, 1976, 22 KTIS 127), the respondent had a 40 percent market share in the bed manufacturing field. In both cases the FTC held that exclusive dealing arrangements with their distributors fell under item 7 (currently item 11) of the General Designations.

(3) THE DISTRIBUTION SYSTEM AND BUSINESS PRACTICES GUIDELINES

The DSBP Guidelines made it clear that a restriction on the handling of competing products by an influential manufacturer in a market, that may result in making it difficult for new entrants or competitors to easily secure alternative distribution channels, was illegal (DSBP Guidelines chapter 22, part II).

The difficulty in securing alternative distribution channels may depend on other manufacturers' behavior in a market, therefore, other manufacturers' behavior in a market needs to be considered. For example, if other manufacturers independently and simultaneously restrict the handling of competing products, it is more likely to produce the anticompetitive effects stated above (see DSBP Guidelines note 5 of part II).

In the past, the FTC seemed to evaluate only the impact of restrictions on a relevant market imposed by the respondent. However, when the impact on a market is to be evaluated, the other major competitors' conduct in the same market seems very important. Such analysis seems more important in Japan because parallel behavior is prevalent among Japanese firms.[5]

(H) ABUSE OF A DOMINANT BARGAINING POSITION (ITEM 14)

(1) IN GENERAL

The regulation of abuse of a dominant bargaining position was introduced as one unfair trade practice by the 1953 Amendment (see chapter 2 (A) Amendments to Weaken the Antimonopoly Act). The idea comes from European competition policy, and aims at eliminating those types of conduct that impede fair competition. In other words, fair competition can be expected among equally capable entrepreneurs, but in the actual market there could be a large disparity of competitive capability. There are many provisions in the Antimonopoly Act that aim at preventing excessive concentration of economic power, but in reality, large disparities in economic power among entrepreneurs are inevitable.

Through the regulation of the abusive conduct of entrepreneurs in a market-dominating position, the Act aims at making it possible for customers that are in a weaker position vis-a-vis their trading partners to obtain fair terms of trade and thus to strengthen their relative competitive positions.

This regulation may sound as if the FTC will intervene at its will in matters to be freely decided by contractual parties. However, this is not the idea of the regulation, and the FTC will intervene in order to maintain fair competition among various parties in a market. For this purpose, "unduly unfavorable" shall be evaluated in the light of normal business practices. Based on this standard, only those practices that impede fair competition, namely, are contrary to the concepts of equal footing shall be regulated.

As seen above, abuse of a dominant bargaining position had developed in a different way from the concept of abuse of market-dominating positions in Europe. The former is a relative concept, and relationships such as banks vis-a-vis non-financial companies, parent company vis-a-vis subcontractors, department stores vis-a-vis their suppliers are covered. Therefore, it is not necessarily a market-based concept. Sometimes fairness in transaction terms is questioned.

As to franchising agreements where a franchisor may be in superior bargaining position vis-a-vis franchisees, the FTC issued a Guideline on Franchising Systems on September 20, 1983. This guideline indicates the factors to be evaluated when franchising systems as a whole fall under item 14. In addition, it also indicates cases for tie-in sales, price restriction, and non-competition clauses after the termination of franchising contracts.

Item 14 consolidates items 9 and 10 of the Old General Designations. There were two FTC decisions relying on item 9, but in both cases item 10 also was applied (see table 8-1). This fact also shows that these two items are similar in nature. Item 14 is interpreted to cover mainly the terms of transactions exclusive of price.

(2) FTC DECISIONS

So far there have been seven cases concerning items 9 and 10 (currently item 14) of the General Designations (see tables 8-1 and 8-2). The FTC relied exclusively on item 10 in two of these cases and applied item 10 supplementarily in the others. The cases where the FTC relied on item 10 exclusively were the 1985 Nihon Musical Instrument Co. case (June 18, 1985, 32 KTIS 107) and the 1982 Mitsukoshi Co. case (June 17, 1982, 29 KTIS 31).

In the 1957 Mitsubishi Bank case (June 3, 1957, 9 KTIS 1), the Mitsubishi Bank (Mitsubishi Bank) made a loan agreement with the Omi Silk Yarn Spinning Co. (Omi) to finance its new factory. In addition, it forced Omi to appoint Mitsubishi Bank's officers to various important positions at Omi, including those of president and vice president. Mitsubishi Bank claimed that these acts were necessary to avoid Omi's default and secure its financial interests.

The FTC held that Mitsubishi Bank's conduct was beyond that necessary to protect its financial interest and therefore, fell under item 9 (currently item 14(v)) and item 10 (currently item 14(i)). The FTC ordered the resignations of the president, vice president and other officers dispatched by Mitsubishi Bank.

In the 1985 Nihon Musical Instrument Co. case (June 18, 1985, 32 KTIS 107), the respondent, a manufacturer of musical instruments, had more than a 50 percent market share in the field of pianos, organs, and wind instruments. It sold its products only to those dealers who concluded a contract with it. Under the dealership contract, when a dealer sold the products to a non-contracting distributor, the dealer who sold such products, upon a complaint from other dealers, had to pay a penalty to the complaining dealers. In addition, by threatening to cancel the dealership contract, the respondent forced the dealer who sold such products to buy back the products and to stop such sales thereafter.

The respondent also prohibited its dealers from selling their products to certain local government offices and stopped delivery to dealers who did not comply with this restriction. The respondent also established an installment payment plan, and when a dealer sold a keyboard instrument to a customer without arranging for the use of the installment payment plan, the respondent required the dealer to pay a penalty to the complaining dealer. Finally, the respondent compelled its dealers to establish music classes and the respondent restricted delivery of the products or canceled the dealership contract if the dealer did not cooperate with this policy.

The FTC found that these acts as a whole fell under item 10. After the respondent refused to accept the recommendation, the matter went to hearing proceedings which lasted for 8 years; the hearing proceedings were terminated in June 18, 1985. The respondent's voluntary remedial measures were cited as one of the reasons for terminating the hearing proceedings (see chapter 16 (B) Hearing Proceedings).

In the 1982 Mitsukoshi Co. (Mitsukoshi) case (June 17, 1982, 29 KTIS 31), the respondent was the most prestigious department store in Japan and ranked second in terms of total sales in the retail industry. Mitsukoshi was in a dominant bargaining position vis-a-vis suppliers, and those suppliers desired to have or maintain business relations with Mitsukoshi. Mitsukoshi started a sales campaign in which each employee was assigned a sales target as well as a time limit in which to achieve that target, and suppliers to Mitsukoshi became the victims of the campaign.

During this campaign, most suppliers were forced to buy various goods, e.g., jewelry, air conditioners, movie tickets that were promoted by Mitsukoshi, tickets for fire works festivals, and overseas tours. Suppliers were forced to buy these goods in proportion to their sales figures to Mitsukoshi. Mitsukoshi also forced them to share a part of the expenses for the sales campaign, e.g., advertisement costs and costs of remodelling the sales floor, and these suppliers were obliged to accept these requests in order to maintain business relations with Mitsukoshi.

The FTC held that the respondent's conduct came under item 10 (currently item 14(i)), but because Mitsukoshi rejected the recommendation, the matter went to hearing proceedings and was finally settled, after many years, by a consent decision.

In the 1990 National Agricultural Cooperatives Federation (Zen-no) case (Feb. 20, 1990, 36 KTIS 53), the market-dominating position of Zen-no, a powerful nationwide agricultural cooperative association that consisted of regional agricultural cooperatives, and a prefecture level association of agricultural cooperatives etc., was abused. Under section 24, acts of cooperatives are exempted, but when unfair trade practices are employed, their exemption status cannot immunize their conduct from violation of the Act.

Zen-no had controlled nearly 60 percent of the distribution of corrugated cardboard boxes for fruits in the eastern half of Japan. Zen-no concluded basic agreements with manufacturers of such boxes in which Zen-no and these manufacturers agreed that Zen-no would provide the major raw materials, namely, corrugated cardboard, after which the boxes produced by the contracting manufacturers were to be shipped to regional agricultural cooperatives. Sales of boxes manufactured outside the assigned territories were prohibited. The price of boxes sold in this way tended to be higher than the price of ordinary corrugated cardboard boxes sold by contracting manufacturers through their own distribution channels.

When member agricultural cooperatives complained of the higher prices of boxes, Zen-no paid back the amount equal to the spread to the complaining cooperatives, then forced contracting manufacturers to pay an equal amount by using its dominant position vis-a-vis these box manufacturers.

Zen-no also engaged in activities to stop sales by contracting manufacturers to agricultural cooperatives outside the assigned territory.

The FTC found that these conducts fell under item 14 as well as items 2 and 13 of the General Designations.

As shown by these cases, item 14 could be applied when other items could be applied due to the existence of a dominant bargaining position.

(3) PRIVATE SUITS

In the 1977 Gifu Credit Union case (Supreme Court, June 20, 1977, 24 KTIS 291), which has been litigated for more than 10 years as a whole, the practice of compensatory balance was questioned. The Gifu Credit Union (Gifu) loaned 11.5 million yen instead of the 7 million yen that was the amount actually requested from the plaintiff, then forced the plaintiff to deposit 6 million yen as a fixed term deposit, and also deducted interest and other expenses in advance, resulting in the plaintiff getting only 4.4 million yen. Each court held that this practice fell under item 10 (currently item 14) and constituted a violation of the Antimonopoly Act. The main question was what portion of the loan agreement should be held invalid due to a violation of the Antimonopoly Act.

By these practices, the net interest rate exceeded the legal maximum allowed (i.e., an annual rate of 15 percent), and the ratio of compensatory balance exceeded 50 percent. The Supreme Court held that the defendant had violated section 19 of the Act. However, it should not be considered that the contract that violated section 19 of the Act was void and unenforceable, unless the contract itself was contrary to the public interest. The Supreme Court said only that the portion of the interest payment that exceeded the legal limit set by the Interest Rate Restriction Act (Act No. 195 of 1954) due to compensatory balance should be void and unenforceable.

(4) BUYING POWER PROBLEMS

Large-scale retailers may sometimes be in a dominant bargaining position vis-a-vis their suppliers. Suppliers are obliged to accept the large-scale retailers' requests even if they are excessively disadvantageous to the suppliers, since discontinuance of transactions with the such retailers would significantly damage the suppliers' businesses. This is called a buying power problem. There are four patterns of conduct that constitute an abuse of the dominant bargaining positions of large-scale retailers.

(A)   return of unsold goods,
(B)   request for dispatch of sales persons to shops,
(C)   coercion to purchase, and
(D)   coercive collection of contributions.

The DSBP Guidelines clarify requirements for illegality in the above four patterns of conduct. Degree of dependence on the retailer, and the position of the retailer in a market will be examined to find a dominant bargaining position of the large-scale retailer (DSBP Guidelines chapter 5, part II).

Reasons to regulate these conducts are mixed. These practices reflect a lack of bargaining power in certain distribution sectors of Japan. These practices had lasted for a long time and, therefore, could be regarded as merely domestic problems. However, they have a market access aspect as well, and these practices could constitute barriers to enter into the Japanese market.

When these practices were widely applied in some distribution sectors, which are unknown to foreign entrants, regulation of these practices might work procompetitively by encouraging new entry into the Japanese market.

This conduct could only be regulated under item 14. Because of the wide applicability of item 14 to these business practices, it could offer a legal basis for the FTC to regulate Japanese business practices from the viewpoint of making fair and transparent trade practices. This is why this conduct is specifically described in the DSBP Guidelines. In this regard, reference shall be made to the Specific Designations applicable to large-scale retailers, too (see (M)(3) Large-Scale Retailing Industry, below).

(I) TIE-IN SALES AND RECIPROCAL DEALINGS (ITEM 10 ETC.)

(1) TIE-IN SALES AND COERCIVE DEALINGS

Tie-ins and other coercive dealings can be regulated under item 10 of the General Designations. Tie-in sales cause trading partners to purchase other goods or services as well if they want to purchase goods or services from oneself. In many cases, these coercive dealings are effected by a market-dominating entrepreneur, or by an entrepreneur in a dominant bargaining position. Therefore, when employed by an entrepreneur in a dominant bargaining position, the same kind of conduct can fall under item 14(i).

However, tie-in sales by non-market-dominating entrepreneurs can also fall under item 10 when the conduct, unless regulated, has a tendency to spread or be repeated by other entrepreneurs. The 1990 TV game tie-in cases mentioned below are examples.

Tie-in sales and coercive dealings are regarded as unjust methods of transaction, and, therefore, separately proscribed as unfair trade practices.

There were 13 cases concerning this item, and six of them relate to the TV game tie-in sales.

In the 1955 Chubu Nippon Newspaper Co. case (Feb. 15, 1955, 6 KTIS 16), the Chubu Nippon Newspaper Co. was alleged to have forced its dealers not to deliver morning newspapers unless customers also subscribed to its evening newspapers, which were newly started. In its decision the FTC found that no violation was established because acts of coercion by the respondent were not established by evidence.

In the 1964 Nagano School Textbook Wholesaler case (Feb. 11, 1964, 12 KTIS 100), the respondent, who was the only authorized wholesaler of school textbooks in the Nagano Prefecture, established a policy whereby any textbook dealers wanting to purchase textbooks had also to purchase other kinds of books to be used in school equalling more than one-third of the total purchase price of the textbooks. In addition, the respondent required those dealers to place orders exceeding 3 million yen per year and said it would discontinue dealing with anyone who failed to meet this requirement. The FTC found that the respondent's conduct should be deemed a coercion under item 6 (currently item 10).

In all six 1990 TV game tie-in sales cases, the FTC ordered one TV game primary wholesaler and five secondary wholesalers not to force tie-in sales to secondary wholesalers and retailers respectively. In this case, TV game software called "Dragon Quest IV," which was very popular among kids and temporarily in short supply at the time of the sales campaign, was sold by the respondents on condition that other unpopular TV game software that was in stock at the respondents were tied-in.

In view of repetitive nature and tendency to spread to other wholesalers, the FTC rendered a recommendation against six wholesalers. The other five wholesalers accepted the recommendation, and a non-repetition order was imposed on them (Nov. 30, 1990, 37 KTIS 32, 37 KTIS 35, 37 KTIS 39, 37 KTIS 43, 37 KTIS 47). One of the respondents, the Hujitaya Co., rejected the recommendation and hearing proceedings were started. After relatively short hearing proceedings, the FTC rendered a formal decision finding illegal tie-in sales practices by the Hujitaya Co. (Feb. 28, 1992, 38 KTIS 41).

(2) UNJUST RECIPROCAL DEALINGS

Reciprocal dealing refers to transactions in which the purchases or sales of one party are linked to the purchases from or sales to the other party reciprocally. When one party has buying power and can compel reciprocal dealing by the other party, it may create the effect of reducing business opportunities of the party's competitors by foreclosing a significant portion of a market.

According to the DSBP Guidelines, there could be three types of unjust reciprocal dealings,

(A)   those that are used by an influential person in a purchase market (item 13),

(B)   those that are compelled by making use of its buying power (item 10),

(C)   those that are induced by making use of a dominant bargaining position (item 14) (DSBP Guidelines chapter 5, part I).

As to (A), reciprocal dealings are effected by making them a condition of purchasing agreements, and the same effect requirement must be fulfilled with respect to an item 13 violation. In other words, to reduce business opportunities of firms not buying under such conditions or of competitors of the influential firm and making it difficult for those firms to easily find alternative trading partners.

When reciprocal dealings are carried out based on voluntary consent between those firms, it could still fall under item 13, as long as the above effect requirements are met (DSBP Guidelines chapter 5-3, part I).

As to (B), the above-mentioned coercion or compulsion is a requirement for unjust reciprocal dealing. So far as coercion or compulsion was effected, no more effect requirement needs to be found.

As to (C), there must be a dominant bargaining position for one party over the other.

Reciprocal dealing among firms belonging to the same business group can be regulated when the above requirements are met (DSBP Guidelines chapter 5-3-(2), part I).

(J) DISCRIMINATORY PRACTICES (ITEMS 3, 4 AND 5)

Three items of the General Designations relate to discrimination—discriminatory pricing (item 3), discriminatory treatment of transaction terms (item 4), and discriminatory treatment in a trade association (item 5).

(1) DISCRIMINATORY PRICING (ITEM 3)

(i) In general

Four kinds of conduct could be prohibited under item 3 of the General Designations.

- (A) Supplying at prices that discriminate against customers in different places,
- (B) Receiving at discriminatory prices from customers in different places,
- (C) Supplying at prices that discriminate against particular customers,
- (D) Receiving at discriminatory prices from different customers.

In general, discriminatory pricing could have a procompetitive effect by encouraging price reduction in a market where an entrepreneur faces competition. Or, by lowering prices, it would be possible for an entrepreneur to enter into a different geographical market. When price discrimination is prohibited per se, an entrepreneur may hesitate to lower his price as a whole to enter into a different market or to meet price competition by new entrants.

On the other hand, when an entrepreneur who lowers his price has very deep pockets, this practice could be objectionable. For smaller firms, price discrimination is an objectionable practice. This is why regulation of discriminatory pricing is controversial.

(ii) Cases

There is only one case where item 4 of the Old General Designations was applied. And in one injunction case, geographical price discrimination was at issue. In the 1957 Hokkoku Newspaper

Co. case (Tokyo High Court, March 18, 1957, 8 KTIS 82), the respondent published a newspaper called "Hokkoku" in the Ishikawa Prefecture and "Toyama" in the Toyama Prefecture. Although these two newspapers were identical, in order to undercut his competitor, the Kita-Nihon Newspaper Co., the respondent charged a lower subscription fee (280 yen per month) for Toyama (Kita-Nihon charged 330 yen per month). Because of this systematic price discrimination, Kita-Nihon suffered severely.

The FTC filed a motion for an injunction to the Tokyo High Court to stop discriminatory pricing, and this motion was granted. Because this injunction was sufficient to stop the practice, no further decision was issued by the FTC.

In the other Hokkoku Newspaper Co. case (Dec. 17, 1954, 6 KTIS 13), the respondent offered a fee lower than that for general advertising to those movie theaters who promised not to use competitors' newspapers for their advertisements. In this case, the FTC tried to apply item 8 rather than item 4 of the Old General Designations, but this could be a price discrimination case.

In the 1980 Toyo Linoleum Co. case (Feb. 7, 1980, 26 KTIS 85), the respondent companies had formed a trade association and set different prices for member and non-member firms. In order to encourage participation in the trade association activities, rebates were offered only to member firms. The FTC found that this practice fell under item 4 of the General Designations.

(iii) Guideline

The guideline on Unjust Low Price Sales explained at (K) Sales Below Cost, *infra*, says that the following cases might fall under item 3.

(A) When an influential entrepreneur, in order to exclude his competitors, lowers his price only at places where he is competing with the competitors (geographical price discrimination).

(B) When an entrepreneur lowers prices only to customers of his competitors, thus interfering with his competitors' transactions (systematic price discrimination against a particular group of customers).

Similar justifiable reasons might be available for price discrimination as described in the above mentioned guideline. Cost justification is accepted as a justifiable reason, e.g., delivery costs, purchase volume or method of payment. A meeting-competition defense is also accepted as a justifiable reason for such price discrimination.

(2) DISCRIMINATORY TREATMENT OF TRANSACTION TERMS (ITEM 4)

This item covers transaction terms other than price. It could cover discrimination in quality, terms of delivery and payment, amount of rebate, etc.

In the 1955 Taisho Pharmaceutical Co. case (Dec. 10, 1955, 7 KTIS 99), item 3 (currently item 4) of the Old General Designations was applied. This is the only occasion where item 3 (currently item 4) was applied.

(3) DISCRIMINATORY TREATMENT BY A TRADE ASSOCIATION (ITEM 5)

This item deals with discriminatory treatment of members joined in concerted activities or within a trade association. Because these concerted activities allow some kind of regulation of members' activities, only conduct that gravely affects the competitive ability of members who are discriminated against is covered by this item.

When a law allows concerted activities for a group of firms, it also requires free entry and free exit, therefore, cases falling under this item are rare.

In the 1957 Hamanakayama Livestock Agricultural Association case (March 7, 1957, 8 KTIS 54), the only case reported on this item (item 3 of the Old General Designations), the respondent imposed discriminatory treatment such as refusal to make a loan agreement to those who sold raw milk to dairy companies other than the Hokkaido Butter Co. and the Meiji Dairy Co., on some member firms in violation of a resolution of the association, The respondent also urged those members dealing with other dairy companies to leave the association. In view of the particular importance for farmers of membership in an agricultural cooperative association the exclusionary effects of such discrimination are clear.

(K) SALES BELOW COST (ITEM 6)

(1) GENERAL PRINCIPLE

Selling at unjustly low prices means to sell goods or to supply services at prices so low that other efficient entrepreneurs cannot cope with them. It is generally thought that selling at unjustly low prices equals sales below cost, but, these two are not the same concept. Whether sales below cost are a necessary requirement for sales at unjustly low prices is a fundamental question. Too much regulation on this item merely protects less efficient entrepreneurs from normal price competition.

The general principle for regulating selling at unjustly low prices was established by the 1975 Tokyo High Court decision in the Chubu Yomiuri Newspaper Co. case (April 30, 1975, 22 KTIS 301).

On March 25, 1975, the Chubu Yomiuri Newspaper Co. (Chubu Yomiuri) began to sell daily newspapers at 500 yen per month in the Chubu District. At that time, the competitor's price range was 1,000 to 1,300 yen per month. Because of its low subscription price, the company estimated that within 6 months its sales could amount to 500,000 copies per month.

The FTC filed a motion for an injunction asking the Tokyo High Court to order the company temporarily not to sell the newspaper below 812 yen per month. Chubu Yomiuri had no stockholding relationship with the Yomiuri Newspaper Co., but did have a cooperative agreement with it to publish "Chubu Yomiuri," in the Chubu District, as a sister newspaper to "The Yomiuri," the largest selling national newspaper in Japan.

Eight hundred and twelve yen was calculated to reflect the possible cost of manufacturing, but it could be lower because of some factors that were made possible because of its cooperative agreement with or financial assistance from the Yomiuri Newspaper Co. In other words, according to the FTC finding, without such special assistance, a 500 yen subscription fee per month was impossible.

The Tokyo High Court granted the FTC's motion and ruled that

> a so-called unjust low price which may constitute an unfair trade practice means a low price not only below prevailing market prices, but also below the manufacturing costs of the product. . . . Unjust low price sales shall be evaluated using the cost as a standard, and the cost data as a standard of unjust low price sales shall be calculated based

on normal necessary expenses for average and independent entrepreneurs in pursuance of their business activities without special assistance from other entrepreneurs. These costs will include general and administrative expenses and other necessary sales expenses.

As a result, the Court accepted 812 yen as the cost, and ordered the company to temporarily set its subscription price above 812 yen.

On September 9, 1975, without first issuing a recommendation, the FTC served a complaint and started hearing proceedings. The matter was settled by a consent decision where the respondent agreed not to sell its newspaper below 1,000 yen per month (Nov. 24, 1977, 24 KTIS 50).

In the 1989 Nippon Shokuhin Co. case (Dec. 14, 1989, 36 KTIS 570), the Supreme Court ruled that

[s]upplying a commodity or service continuously at a low price which is excessively below cost incurred in the said supply is prohibited in principle under Item 6 of the General Designations, because such conduct does not reflect business efforts or normal competitive process and tends to cause harmful effects on fair competitive order by making it difficult for competitors to engage in business activities. Then, the General Designations put the requirement "without justifiable reasons" in order to exclude such cases which cannot be deemed undue as to concrete cases.

(2) LOSS LEADER SELLING

Item 6 could also be used to regulate loss leader selling which is used by large-scale retailers with a great many sales items and where selective price-cutting could hurt small retailers who have a limited number of sales items. This practice is often cited as a justification for resale price maintenance.

In 1982, the FTC took for the first time, a formal action against loss leader selling by supermarkets. In the Maruetsu Co. (Maruetsu) (May 28, 1982, 29 KTIS 13) and the Haro Mato Co. (Haro) (May 28, 1982, 29 KTIS 13) cases of 1982, the respondents, chain stores competing with each other in the suburbs of Tokyo, had engaged in a price war against each other using milk among other things, as a loss leader. The FTC found that Maruetsu's actual invoiced cost for milk was 155-158 yen per 1-liter carton, and the ordinary sales price was

178 yen or more. Beginning in July 1981, Maruetsu started selling milk at 158 yen, then lowered the price to 155 yen, and finally in mid-September, to 100 yen for the first carton, and 150 yen for an additional carton. This price war was stopped in early November when the FTC started its investigation.

Haro, with its invoice price of 157-160 yen, sold at the same price to counter Maruetsu's action. The price war had an impact on milk retailers whose incomes relied on home delivery of milk or sales at their retail outlets. Their invoice price was about 185 yen and their sales price was about 190-230 yen at their sales outlets, and 225-230 for home delivery.

The FTC decided that this conduct fell under item 5 of the Old General Designations.

(3) GUIDELINE ON UNJUST LOW PRICE SALES

On November 20, 1984, in response to mounting criticism against loss leader selling by large-scale retailers, the FTC announced the Guideline on Unjust Low Price Sales. In particular, milk, soy sauce, and soy bean curd were the targets of loss leader selling, and many requests asking that necessary measures be taken by the FTC were filed under section 45(1).

The Guideline limits its applicability to the retail industry and describes three requirements for unjust low prices.

(A) degree of low price sales,
(B) degree of impact on competition,
(C) availability of justifiable reason.

As to (A), the guideline says that as to the retail industry, unjust low price means that the price is less than the invoice price that is posted on a continuous basis in actual transactions. Rebates or discounts shall be deducted from the invoice price so that real cost rather than posted cost can be used.

Unjust low price sales shall be the one to be repeated to some extent, or at least to be effected as a business policy when not repeated.

As to (B), it must cause difficulty to the business activities of other entrepreneurs, however, it is not necessary to cause actual difficulty to their businesses. The likelihood of causing difficulties is sufficient for this requirement. Difficulty at the retailer level and at the manufacturer's level shall be examined.

As to (C), close-out sales or low price sales of perishable goods or seasonal goods can be justified. Low quality goods, which are clearly marked as such, can also be sold below the invoice price.

(4) 1-YEN BID ISSUE

In the fall 1989, a 1-yen bid for a computer system programming contract by municipal governments was investigated by the FTC. At least three system programming contracts were awarded by a 1-yen bid to the Fujitsu Corp. In one case, a computer system programming contract was awarded to the Fujitsu Corp. for a 10,000 yen bid.

The FTC found that this conduct was carried out by a very influential entrepreneur in the computer system programming industry as well as in the computer hardware manufacturing industry. When such a low price bid was repeated by computer hardware manufacturers it could cause difficulty to their competitors, in particular to those who specialized in system programming. Computer hardware manufacturers could easily recover any loss incurred in software programming if they could also sell computer hardware.

It may also be used to induce municipal governments to award computer hardware to the same computer manufacturer. Therefore, the FTC warned Fujitsu and the NEC Corp., in November 1989, finding that these conducts may fall under unjust low price selling or customer inducement by unjust benefits (item 9).

The FTC explained its reason for not taking formal action against these companies by saying that very few contracts for system programming were as yet awarded by competitive bidding and so competitive bidding cannot be said to be a general method of awarding system programming by the municipal government (FTC press release, Nov. 24, 1989).

(L) OTHER UNFAIR TRADE PRACTICES

There exist some particular practices that could be regulated by the General Designations. Some of them are practices that could be regulated as unfair competition in other countries, however, in Japan, these practices are regulated as unfair trade practices.

(1) DECEPTIVE CUSTOMER INDUCEMENTS (ITEM 8)

The FTC first designated deceptive practices in the canned and bottled foods industry, and after the enactment of the Act Against Unjustifiable Premiums and Misleading Representations (Act No. 134 of 1962), most deceptive practices were regulated in a summary procedure under this Act. In so far as deceptive practices are concerned, so far there are no cases under item 6 of the Old General Designations.

Because the Act Against Unjustifiable Premiums and Misleading Representations is a special law regulating unfair trade practices, there must be some provisions applicable to deceptive practices in the General Designations. This is the reason for item 8.

On September 20, 1983, the FTC issued a guideline on franchising systems. In this guideline, non-disclosure or insufficient disclosure of material information on business chances to potential franchisees, or provision of deceptive or misleading information on a franchising business are said to fall under item 8. There are some difficulties in applying the Act Against Unjustifiable Premiums and Misleading Representations to acts of franchisors against franchisees, therefore, item 8 could be a useful source of regulation of deceptive practices directed at franchisees.[6]

(2) UNDUE CUSTOMER INDUCEMENT BY UNJUST BENEFITS (ITEM 9)

(i) Excessive premium offerings

Before the enactment of the Act Against Unjustifiable Premiums and Misleading Representations, the FTC applied item 6 (currently item 9) to regulate excessive premium offerings.

In the 1955 Osaka Yomiuri Newspaper Co. (Osaka Yomiuri) case (Tokyo High Court, Nov. 5, 1955, 7 KTIS 169), the respondent had announced in its newspaper ("Osaka Yomiuri") in September 1955 that 200 million yen's worth of prizes would be offered in order to celebrate its third anniversary. The prizes would be offered by way of a lottery among those who subscribed to "Osaka Yomiuri" after October 1955. More than 50,000 prizes were planned to be offered.

The FTC filed a motion to the Tokyo High Court for a temporary injunction to stop the premium campaign, and after the motion was granted, it pursued its investigation and ordered Osaka Yomiuri to cancel the drawings, finding that Osaka Yomuiri's act fell under item 6 (currently item 9) (Dec. 8, 1955, 7 KTIS 96).

Another case in 1968 involved a premium offering, here the Tsunashima Trading Co. (Tsunashima) (Feb. 6, 1968, 14 KTIS 99) was an exclusive agent for the General Electric Co. (G.E.) on air conditioners in the eastern half of Japan. As a sales promotion, Tsunashima offered to give a color TV (of an approximate retail value of 165,000 yen) when a person bought a G.E. air conditioner for a retail price ranging from 335,000 to 465,000 yen, and to give a coupon for a trip worth 25,000 yen to those who purchased models ranging from 159,000 to 280,000 yen.

The FTC, finding that ordinary premiums offered in the air conditioner industry had never exceeded 5,000 yen in retail value, held that Tsunashima's premium offering fell under item 6 (currently item 9). (Similar remedial measures were ordered against the Nihon Air Conditioning Co., which was an exclusive agent for Admiral air conditioners and the Nikko Aircon Co., which was an exclusive agent for G.E. in the western half of Japan.)

(ii) Pyramid selling (multilevel marketing systems)

(A) FTC CASES   In the 1975 Holiday Magic Co. case (June 13, 1975, 22 KTIS 11), the Holiday Magic Co. had established a four-tier system of distribution to sell its cosmetics. Distributors at the top two levels could earn not only from their sales activities but also by recruiting new distributors into the system and/or by inducing distributors to advance to higher levels in the system. Distributors were compelled to purchase fixed amounts of cosmetics and/or to pay a certain amount of money to the company in order to become distributors or to be promoted to higher levels of distribution (a portion of the payment would be paid back to those who had recruited others or induced them to seek promotions).

The FTC decided that such an offering of benefits to those who recruited new participants into the system should be deemed as an undue advantage in the light of normal business practices, and thus fell under item 6 (currently item 9).

(B) THE DOOR-TO-DOOR SALES ACT   After pyramid selling had caused a wide range of consumer injuries, the Door-to-Door Sales Act (Act No. 57 of 1976) was enacted. It had provisions concerning pyramid selling or multilevel marketing systems.

Pyramid sales organizers or other participants were prohibited from intentionally failing to tell the truth or telling lies with respect to material items of pyramid sales at the time they recruit participants. In addition, if MITI finds that an organizer's method of recruiting is improper (the standards are determined by a Cabinet Order), and that there is a risk that such sales method may be repeated, the organizers may be ordered to stop recruiting activities for a period not exceeding 1 year.

Those who violate a MITI order can be punished by penal servitude for not more than 1 year and/or by a fine of not more than 500,000 yen.

When an organizer advertises a pyramid selling plan, he must disclose material facts in the advertisement. Moreover, he must issue a notice to participants giving a general outline of the pyramid selling system before concluding contracts with distributors. At the time of contract, the organizer must issue a written notice revealing the kinds of goods to be handled, participants' obligations as distributors, conditions for cancellation of the contract, etc.

A 14-day cooling off period should be offered to participants starting from the date when they received the notice, and no penalty or damages may be assessed on account of such cancellation. When a fixed amount of goods are required to be purchased in order to become a distributor, a 14-day cooling off period shall start from the date when those goods are delivered.

(iii) Commercial bribery

Item 9 could be a source of regulation of commercial bribery. By specific designation, the FTC regulates commercial bribery in the textbook industry (see (M)(5) Textbook Industry, below).

(iv) Investment loss compensation

In December 1991, the FTC issued decisions against four securities companies finding that investment loss compensation practices fell under item 9 as constituting unjust profits in the light of normal business practices. (These included the Nomura Securities Co. case of 1991, Dec. 2, 1991, 38 KTIS 134 and similar decisions against the Daiwa Securities Co., the Nikko Securities Co. and the Yamaichi Securities Co.)

Starting around 1985, many securities companies had promoted securities investment accounts called "particular money trusts." However, around 1987 when stock prices started to fall significantly, these securities companies offered loss compensation to important investors in order to maintain their position as main underwriters or security brokers for these important customers.

In December 1989, the Ministry of Finance issued an administrative guidance against investment loss compensation, and for a moment the practice was discontinued, but as stock prices continued to be depressed these companies started to practice loss compensation with their most important investors.

The FTC found that investment loss compensation was against normal business practices and, therefore, was an undue method to induce transactions with oneself.

(3) INTERFERENCE WITH A COMPETITOR'S TRANSACTION (ITEM 15)

There have been five cases under item 11 (currently item 15) (see tables 8-1 and 8-2). This item is directed at unethical methods of exclusion of competitors.

In the 1963 Tokyo Juki Kogyo Co. case (Jan. 9, 1963, 11 KTIS 41), the respondent, a manufacturer and distributor of sewing machines, induced competitors' customers to cancel installment payment contracts they had concluded. It did this by providing special discounts equivalent to money already paid for competitors' sewing machines under their installment payment plan (the maximum amount was 1,000 yen).

The FTC found that this conduct was an unjust interference with competitors' transactions in a way to induce a cancellation of competitors' contracts.

In the 1963 Kashiwazaki Fish Market case (Dec. 11, 1963, 12 KTIS 48), the respondent, a privately operated fish market, prohibited its buyers from dealing with the respondent's competitor and compelled them to sign a statement promising not to deal with other fish markets. The FTC found this act was an unjust interference with competitors' transactions.

(4) INTERFERENCE WITH THE INTERNAL OPERATION OF A COMPETING COMPANY (ITEM 6)

This is a sister regulation to item 15, but is directed at rather rare acts of interference with the internal operations of competitors. Therefore, there have been no cases based on this item.

(5) UNJUST HIGH PRICE PURCHASING (ITEM 9)

Unjust high price purchasing is directed at the very particular situation where an influential person in a market tries to monopolize a market through buying goods at a high price. No case is reported under this item nor its predecessor (item 5 of the Old General Designations).

(M) SPECIFIC DESIGNATIONS

The FTC is empowered to designate specific unfair trade practices applicable to a specific industry. The FTC has utilized this power in a limited manner and relied on the General Designations, which have more general applicability.

In the 1950s and 1960s, many specific designations were issued. In most cases, the standards of illegality are clearly stated. In some industries, a fair trade conference to monitor violations of the specific designation was established by the entrepreneurs concerned. Such conferences were sometimes empowered to impose sanctions on those who violated the designated practices.

(1) PREMIUM OFFERINGS

Before the enactment of the Act Against Unjustifiable Premiums and Misleading Representations (Act No. 134 of 1962), the FTC issued many specific designations regulating premium offerings. These specific designations were abolished and similar notifications were issued in accordance with the above-mentioned Act. The only exception is the prohibition against premium offerings in the large-scale retailing industry. This is because the Specific Designation in the department store industry (see (3) Large Scale Retailing Industry, below) regulates premium offerings as well as other abusive practices of a dominant bargaining position of large-scale retailers.

(2) CANNED AND BOTTLED FOOD INDUSTRY (NOTIFICATION NO. 12 OF 1961)

In the canned and bottled food industry, the Specific Designation prohibits misleading representation, advertising, etc. as to contents, date of manufacturing, raw materials, cooking method, kinds of food additives and other contents with respect to product quality.

(3) LARGE-SCALE RETAILING INDUSTRY (NOTIFICATION NO. 7 OF 1954)

This designation covers various abusive conducts by large-scale retailers such as department stores or supermarkets vis-a-vis their suppliers. Large-scale retailers that are subject to this designation are those that sell various kinds of common consumer goods, and whose floor dimensions exceed 3,000 square meters in Japan's largest 13 cities as a whole, and 1,500 square meters or more in other cities and towns.

On April 21, 1987, the FTC issued a guideline concerning the Unjust Return of Unsold Goods (see appendix G). This covers the unjust return of unsold goods, which is regulated by the Specific Designation, but also explains situations where the unjust return of unsold goods falls under item 14 of the General Designations. As this shows, most of the conduct designated by this Specific Designation, in particular, the unjust return of unsold goods, and requests for dispatch of sales persons to shops may also fall under item 14.

However, these practices also reflect some conduct that is particular to transactions among department stores and their suppliers. For example, department stores often use a consignment basis contract but the term of such a consignment basis contract tend to be too disadvantageous to their suppliers. Therefore, consignment basis contracts are prohibited when the term is too disadvantageous compared with normal consignment basis contracts. Most of these practices reflect the fact that, in Japan, the terms of transactions are not spelled out in advance in a written contract, and as a result, department stores may demand *ex post* discounts on supplied goods that are sold through bargain sales, and may refuse to receive goods that are ordered with specifications particular to the department store.

In these cases it is thought that the suppliers are obliged to accept the retailer's requests even if they are excessively disadvantageous to the suppliers, since discontinuance of transactions with the retailer would significantly damage the suppliers' business. Therefore, a continuous transaction relationship among Japanese businesses is one of the reasons necessitating a particular regulation against large-scale retailers (for this aspect, see (H)(4) Buying Power Problems, above).

Practices that are prohibited under this designation are:

(A)   Undue return of unsold goods,
(B)   Undue *ex post* demand of discounts,
(C)   Disadvantageous terms of a consignment basis contract,
(D)   Compulsion of low price supply on account of bargain sales,
(E)   Undue refusal to receive those goods produced with a particular specification,
(F)   Request for dispatch of sales persons to shops,
(G)   Retaliation due to non-compliance to the above-mentioned request,
(H)   Premium offerings.

(4) NEWSPAPER PUBLISHING INDUSTRY (NOTIFICATION NO. 14 OF 1959)

The FTC issued a Specific Designation that set very strict regulations on geographical price discrimination and forcing of sales.

(i) Publishers or dealers of daily newspapers shall not, directly or indirectly, charge different subscription prices, or allow any discounts thereon, according to geographical area or customers.

(ii) Publishers of daily newspapers shall not supply their dealers with more than the number of copies actually ordered.

With exemption status given to resale price maintenance as to copyrighted works, national newspapers in Japan can charge the same subscription price throughout the country.

Coercive sales practices (forcing-in-sales) are prohibited because advertising fees are normally set in proportion to the daily sales figures of national newspapers, thus there exists some incentive for newspaper publishers to try to increase sales figures by forcing their dealers to accept extra copies.

(5) SCHOOL TEXTBOOK INDUSTRY (NOTIFICATION NO. 5 OF 1956)

In the school textbook industry, acts of entertaining teachers who are in a position to choose which textbooks to use at a school are questioned. The FTC issued Notification No. 5 of 1956 to regulate commercial bribery as an undue inducement to transactions.

The Specific Designation prohibits the publishers or dealers of textbooks, directly or indirectly, from providing or offering to provide money, goods, entertainment or similar economic benefits to those who use textbooks as teaching materials, or to those who are in charge of textbook selection, as a means of inducing the use or selection of textbooks published by them or persons specified by them.

The same conduct is prohibited even when it is used as a means of inducing the use or selection of books, magazines, teaching materials, etc. other than textbooks that are published by them.

Providing such economic benefits to make someone induce those who use textbooks as teaching materials, or to those who are in charge of textbook selection, is also prohibited.

Lastly, slandering or defaming of other publishers or their textbooks to prevent the use or selection of textbooks published by them is prohibited.

In 1963, the FTC rendered six decisions finding a violation of this Specific Designation (the Tokyo Books Co. case of 1963, Feb. 13, 1963, 11 KTIS 63 et al.).

(6) MARINE TRANSPORTATION INDUSTRY (NOTIFICATION NO. 17 OF 1959)

Notification No. 17 of 1959 is a unique designation in the sense that it specifies a relationship between the Marine Transportation Act (Act No. 187 of 1949) and the Antimonopoly Act. Section 28 of the Marine Transportation Act exempts shipping conference agreements from cartel regulations, but when unfair trade practices are employed, or when competition is substantially restrained resulting in undue enhancement of freights rates, fares and charges, the exemption status would not be afforded.

The purpose of this regulation is to check abusive conduct of the market-dominating position afforded to shipping conferences, thus protecting the interests of shippers.[7]

The specific designation specifies the following practices of shipping conferences or ship operators:

(i) *Discriminatory treatment*: Imposing unjustly discriminatory terms for freight rates and charges or other terms of transportation among particular shippers or geographical areas, based on the volume of cargo, or on the cargo's loading or unloading place.

Injustice will be evaluated in view of its impact on competitive difficulty as a result of such discrimination.

(ii) *Admission to a shipping conference*: Causing a substantial disadvantage to the business activities of a ship operator applying for admission to a conference, etc., by making the terms of admission unjustly discriminatory as compared with those of other members, or by refusing the ship operator's admission thereto without justifiable reason.

This so-called closed conference system is accepted in Japan in contrast to an open conference system where free admission and free exit are required to obtain cartel exemption status.

Oversupply of bottoms is accepted as a justifiable reason, moreover, a reasonable difference in the treatment of newly admitted member liners is also allowed. This includes differences in voting rights, allocation of cargoes, etc.

(iii) *Exclusive patronage contracts (also called a double- decker system) that fulfill the following three conditions:*

(A)   Granting undue advantageous treatment as to transportation conditions to shippers who have concluded an exclusive patronage contract.

(B)   Stipulating undue conditions for termination of an exclusive patronage contract by shippers.

(C)   Demanding payment of unreasonably high penalties or damages when a shipper has violated an exclusive patronage contract.

In the 1959 Far East Freight Conference case (Dec. 23, 1959, 10 KTIS 51), the FTC stipulated the following three standards to further clarify the terms of this provision:

(A)   The spread of freight rates between contract shippers and non-contract shippers shall be less than 9.5 percent;

(B)   Either of the contracting parties may terminate the contract upon giving a written notice 3 months in advance;

(C)   The "liquidated damages" to be paid to the ship operators by contract shippers who make a shipment in violation of the terms of the contract shall be 50 percent of the freight rates applicable to the shipment of the cargo by conference vessels.

(iv) *Dispensation:* Demanding from shippers the payment of penalties or damages, or giving them disadvantageous treatment with respect to freight rates, etc., when such shippers have used non-conference vessels to carry their shipments for a justifiable reason (e.g. they were unable to secure sufficient space in conference vessels within a reasonable period of time).

In the above-mentioned Far East Freight Conference case, the FTC stipulated the following standards to further clarify the terms of this provision:

(A) Where a foreign buyer reserves the right to designate a vessel under an F.O.B. shipment contract, this shall be accepted as a justifiable reason.

(B) When a contract shipper asks the local shipping conference representative to find a space on a vessel, and if he does not confirm the requested space within 7 business days on a vessel scheduled to sail within 30 days, the shipper shall be able to find an appropriate non-conference vessel without any injury to his contract rights.

(v) *Unilateral modification of terms and conditions for deferred rebate detrimental to the interests of shippers:* Unduly prolonging the date of return, or unreasonably decreasing the amount of freight rates and charges to be returned when any portion of the freight rates and charges received within a given period of time are to be returned, or a shipper who has within such period of time exclusively utilized conference vessels for the transportation of a certain class of cargo (such deferred rebate is also called a fidelity rebate).

(vi) *Refusing to allow a choice between the deferred rebate system and an exclusive patronage contract:* Whenever the deferred rebate system is employed, ship operators shall allow a choice between the deferred rebate system and exclusive patronage contracts. And the terms of an exclusive patronage contract shall be no less favorable than those of the deferred rebate system.

(7) OPEN LOTTERY (NOTIFICATION NO. 34 OF 1971)

Offering excessive premiums by way of an open lottery is designated as an unfair trade practice. Premiums exceeding 1 million yen are considered excessive.

An open lottery means a lottery scheme where any person is eligible to participate and no purchase is required. To be an open lottery, winners can be selected by way of a lottery or any other method having an element of chance, e.g., game, performance, answering questions or sending in a card.

(N) OTHER UNFAIR TRADE PRACTICES

(1) UNFAIR TRADE PRACTICES BY A TRADE ASSOCIATION

Section 8(l)(v) prohibits a trade association from causing entrepreneurs to commit acts constituting unfair trade practices. Entrepreneurs may be non-member firms as well as member firms.

"To cause" is not limited to acts of compulsion, but could cover any resolution or decision of a trade association to do such acts as will constitute unfair trade practices. Agreement among member firms to do such acts as will constitute unfair trade practices is what is required by the term "to cause."

When a trade association decides to boycott particular non-members in the same industry by asking their suppliers not to supply to the particular non-members, it is construed as an act to cause the suppliers to commit an act that falls under item 2 of the General Designations, namely, not to deal with the particular non-members.

Section 8(1)(ii) could apply to a trade association that enters into international agreements or contracts that contain such matters as constitute unfair trade practices. However, it is very rare for a trade association in Japan to enter into international contracts, thus this provision has never been used.

As table 8-3 shows, item 1 of the Old General Designations or item 2 of the General Designations are involved in most section 8(1)(v) cases. In other words, these cases are dealing with secondary boycotts.

Table 8-3. Relevant Items of General Designations as to Section 8(1)(v) Cases

Year	Item 1	Item 2	Item 7	Item 8	Item 11	Item 2*	Sum Total	Net Total
1953	0	0	0	0	0	–	0	0
1954	0	1	0	0	0	–	1	1
1955	1	0	0	0	0	–	1	1
1956	0	0	0	0	0	–	0	0
1957	3	0	2	1	0	–	6	4
1958	1	0	0	0	0	–	1	1
1959	0	0	0	0	0	–	0	0
1960	1	0	0	0	0	–	1	1
1961	0	0	0	0	0	–	0	0
1962	2	0	0	0	0	–	2	2
1963	3	1	0	0	0	–	4	4
1964	2	0	0	0	0	–	2	2
1965	4	0	0	0	0	–	4	4
1966	1	0	0	0	0	–	1	1
1967	1	0	0	0	0	–	1	1
1968	3	0	0	2	0	–	5	4
1969	1	1	0	2	0	–	4	3
1970	0	0	0	0	0	–	0	0
1971	0	0	0	1	0	–	1	1
1972	1	0	0	1	0	–	2	2
1973-74	0	0	0	0	0	–	0	0
1975	1	0	0	1	0	–	2	2
1976	0	0	0	0	0	–	0	0
1977	1	0	0	0	0	–	1	1
1978	1	0	0	0	0	–	1	1
1979	0	0	0	0	0	–	0	0
1980	0	0	0	0	1	–	1	1
1981-82	0	0	0	0	0	–	0	0
1983	–	–	–	–	–	1	1	1
1984	–	–	–	–	–	1	1	1
1985	–	–	–	–	–	1	1	1
1986	–	–	–	–	–	0	0	0
1987	–	–	–	–	–	1	1	1
1988-90	–	–	–	–	–	0	0	0
1991	–	–	–	–	–	1	1	1
1992	–	–	–	–	–	0	0	0
Total	27	3	2	8	1	5	46	42

NOTE:
* Refers to item 2 of the General Designations. All other items refer to the Old General Designations.

(2) UNFAIR TRADE PRACTICES BY OTHER PROVISIONS

One thing unique to unfair trade practice regulation is its wide applicability. For example, section 24, which exempts acts of cooperatives that have been formed in accordance with the provisions of other laws, does not authorize such exemption status when unfair trade practices are employed. This means that when these cooperatives employ unfair trade practices, the FTC can even find a violation of unreasonable restraint of trade or private monopolization.

When separate laws authorize an exemption from the application of the Antimonopoly Act, they usually contain provisions excluding cases in which unfair trade practices are employed, thus unfair trade practice regulation could give the FTC the power to regulate certain activities even as to exempted industries.

The FTC sometimes utilized this power with agricultural cooperatives (see the 1990 Zen-no case at (H) Abuse of a Dominant Bargaining Position, above).

As to section 23, which exempts acts that are not recognized to be within the scope of rights under the Patent Act etc., when unfair trade practices are effected, these acts are not recognized to be within the scope of rights under the Patent Act etc.

As to section 21, which exempts acts of enterprises that are monopolies by the very nature of their business activities, unfair trade practices may be regarded as acts that go beyond the exempted acts.

In the 1965 Yakulto Honsha Co. case (Sep. 13, 1965, 13 KTIS 72), the respondent, a patent and trademark holder and a manufacturer of condensed lactic acid bacilli, sold its product called *Yakulto* to only those processors who concluded a licensing agreement in which the processors agreed not to sell to retailers who did not conclude a retail sales contract with the respondent. The retail sales contract contained provisions on resale price maintenance and territorial restrictions, and prohibitions on the handling of competing products.

The FTC ruled that these restrictions were not within the scope of the rights granted under the Patent Act or Trademark Act, and found that these restrictions constituted a violation of section 19 of the Antimonopoly Act.

NOTES

[1] Economists tended to be critical of the regulation on practices unfair in their nature. The most controversial one is the regulation on sales below cost or discriminatory pricing. See related sections (H), (I), (J), (K) and (L) in this chapter.

[2] ANTIMONOPOLY LAW STUDY GROUP, HUKOUSEI NA TORIHIKI HOHO NI KANSURU KIHONTEKI NA KANGAEKATA (Basic Thinking on Unfair Trade Practices), July 8, 1982.

[3] STUDY GROUP ON GOVERNMENT REGULATION ETC., AND COMPETITION POLICY, DOKUSEN KINSI HO TEKIYO JOGAI SEIDO NO MINAOSHI (Reviews on Antimonopoly Law Exemption Systems), July 29, 1991. For an English summary, see *Report of the Study Group on the Review of the Exemption Systems from the Antimonopoly Act, July 29, 1991*, FTC/JAPAN VIEWS, No. 12, (Sept. 1991), at 70-73.

[4] When section 24-2 was enacted, the meaning of copyrighted works was clear and it was not expected that copyrighted works would expand their coverage to such a magnitude. This was the reason why the term copyrighted works was used in the Act without much thought to its implication on resale price maintenance systems.

[5] The idea of a coverage ratio was used as one of the primary standards for market structure screening on vertical restraints by the Department of Justice. The U.S. DEPARTMENT OF JUSTICE, VERTICAL RESTRAINTS GUIDELINES, 4.1. The Guidelines think there are no antitrust problems if the coverage ratio is less than 60 percent in both relevant markets.

[6] The Act Against Unjustifiable Premiums and Misleading Representations could apply to misleading representation directed at consumers, but not those directed at entrepreneurs. Franchisees sometimes are persons inexperienced in business such as housewives, but legally speaking, they shall be looked at as entrepreneurs.

[7] When a law provides for cartel exemption but excludes cases from cartel exemption in which unfair trade practices are employed, it means that abusive conduct could still be regulated by the FTC. This is one of the characteristics of unfair trade practices regulation in Japan.

9

TRADE ASSOCIATION ACTIVITIES

(A) TRADE ASSOCIATIONS AND SECTION 8 REGULATION

(1) TRADE ASSOCIATION ACTIVITIES IN JAPAN

Trade associations are very active in Japan. Some of them had functioned as controlling organizations during World War II (see chapter 1 (A)(2) After World War II). Most of them not only consist of competitors but also have a high coverage ratio in a relevant market. Competitors would get together in the same trade association and engage in a wide range of activities that were very important in the pursuit of their business interests. For these reasons, the temptation to form a cartel agreement at a trade association is very high and a trade association can provide a convenient forum for this purpose (see table 9-1).

Another reason for being greatly concerned, from an antimonopoly point of view, is the existence of a close government-business relationship. This fact in itself is not only undesirable, but because much important government information flows through relevant trade associations, membership in a trade association has a very important meaning in the pursuit of business activities in Japan.

With this background, the Trade Association Act (Act No. 191 of 1947), a sister law to the Antimonopoly Act, contained very strict provisions. It specified permissible conduct for trade associations, and also specified a detailed list of prohibited conduct (see chapter 1 (C)(3) Outline of the Trade Association). This law was so hated by business circles that it was one of the first laws to be eliminated after the end of the Occupation period (see chapter 2 (A)(1) The 1949 Amendment).

Table 9-1. Types of Violations of Sections 8(1) and 8(2)

Year	Related Subparagraphs					Section 8(2)*	Sum Total	Net Total
	(i)	*(ii)*	*(iii)*	*(iv)*	*(v)*			
1953	1	0	0	4	0	0	5	4
1954	0	0	0	1	0	0	1	1
1955	1	0	0	0	1	0	2	2
1956	2	0	0	0	0	0	2	2
1957	0	0	1	3	4	0	8	4
1958	1	0	0	1	1	0	3	2
1959	1	0	0	0	0	0	1	1
1960	0	0	0	1	1	0	2	1
1961	1	0	0	1	0	0	2	2
1962	8	0	2	0	2	0	12	10
1963	20	0	0	1	4	0	25	25
1964	18	0	0	1	2	0	21	20
1965	13	0	1	9	4	0	27	22
1966	13	0	0	3	1	0	17	15
1967	5	0	0	1	1	0	7	6
1968	14	0	0	6	4	0	24	22
1969	18	0	0	5	3	0	26	24
1970	39	0	0	1	0	0	40	40
1971	32	0	0	1	1	0	34	34
1972	9	0	0	0	2	0	11	11
1973	32	0	0	2	0	0	34	33
1974	10	0	0	1	0	0	11	11
1975	8	0	0	2	2	0	12	10
1976	6	0	0	0	0	0	6	6
1977	7	0	0	1	1	0	9	9
1978	1	0	0	1	1	0	3	2
1979	8	0	0	2	0	1	11	10
1980	2	0	4	6	1	0	13	8
1981	3	0	0	1	0	0	4	4
1982	5	0	0	2	0	0	7	7
1983	0	0	1	1	1	0	3	2
1984	3	0	1	1	1	0	6	5
1985	2	0	0	0	1	0	3	3
1986	1	0	0	0	0	0	1	1
1987	4	0	0	1	1	0	6	5
1988	0	0	0	0	0	0	0	0
1989	3	0	0	1	0	0	4	3
1990	5	0	1	1	1	0	8	7
1991	3	0	0	3	0	0	6	6
1992	11	0	0	0	0	0	11	11
Total	310	0	11	65	42	1	428	391

NOTE:

* Section 8(2) provides for a filing obligation.

Section 8 was added to the Antimonopoly Act by the 1953 Amendment so that some of the conduct regulated by the Trade Association Act could be regulated under the Act.

(2) TRADE ASSOCIATIONS AND CARTELS

Trade association activities cover a very detailed area of business activities, and it is normal to have special committees with respect to each subproduct that is covered by the trade association. Such committees are also organized at multiple levels so that many problems can be examined at the staff level first, then go up to the management level or vice versa.

For example, in the 1974 Sumitomo Light Metals Industry Co. case (March 15, 1974, 20 KTIS 329), there existed within a trade association a principal committee consisting of company board members, a central committee consisting of managers, and a price committee consisting of staff-level employees. These committees were used to form a cartel agreement to raise the prices of various rolled aluminum.

(3) REASONS FOR SPECIAL REGULATION

As stated above, the reason for having stringent provisions covering trade associations can be explained by:

(A)   the history of trade association activities in prewar days,
(B)   the fact that there exist so many trade associations that are horizontal in nature and have a high coverage ratio in a relevant market, and
(C)   convenience to effect cartel activities through trade association activities.

It is also important that each entrepreneur be free of undue restrictions on its business activities, and organizational restrictions imposed by trade associations are sometimes in conflict with the freedom of business activities.

(B) SUBSTANTIAL RESTRAINT OF COMPETITION

(1) REQUIREMENTS FOR A SECTION 8(1)(i) VIOLATION

Section 8(1)(i) prohibits a substantial restraint of competition in any particular field of trade, and it does not add any further requirements. For example, it does not contain such requirements as "contrary to the public interest" or "mutually restrict their business activities." In other words, compared with section 3, the law does specify only the anti-competitive effects of conduct by a trade association.

As to the relationship between sections 3 and 8(1)(i), the Supreme Court (Oil Cartel Price-Fixing case of 1984, Feb. 24, 1984, 30 KTIS 244) ruled that

> section 8(1)(i) is a provision to supplement prohibition under section 3, and is intended to prohibit trade associations to engage in unreasonable restraint of trade by such means as forcing concerted activities on the member firms, or being involved in concerted activities in restraint of trade by combining with the member firms, or to put restrictions on business activities of member firms through the controlling power of the trade association.

This provision covers unreasonable restraint of trade and private monopolization by a trade association. There is no case where private monopolization is questioned. In the case of section 8(1)(i) violations, a surcharge order can be imposed even if the conduct of a trade association amounted to private monopolization (see Chapter 19 Surcharge Orders).

Whether section 3 and section 8(1)(i) could be applicable to the same conduct is questioned, and the FTC has been negative concerning such an application.[1]

(2) REMEDIAL MEASURES AGAINST MEMBER FIRMS

Sometimes, remedial measures only against the trade association are not sufficient to eliminate concerted activities by member firms. In such a case, section 8-2(3) allows the FTC to take remedial measures against individual member firms, too. However, in these situations, the FTC can apply section 3 against individual member firms, therefore, there are as yet no cases where the FTC has used section 8-2(3).

(3) DECISIONS BY A TRADE ASSOCIATION

A trade association makes its decisions by way of its resolution. Therefore, it is interpreted that a trade association's resolution, which is binding on its member firms, is an essential requirement for a section 8 violation.

Any activities that can objectively be recognized as those of the trade association can be regulated under section 8. A trade association's decision-making organ is the general meeting of its members, but on many occasions it selects representatives such as the president, vice president, secretary, etc. to form a board so that daily matters can be decided at the board meeting, or a special committee is delegated such de facto decision-making power. Therefore, any decision by a trade association shall be examined whether it has the power to bind its relevant member firms or it is an agreement only among participants to the decision. In the latter case, section 3 shall be applied.

It is less troublesome to prove the existence of such a resolution by a trade association compared with that of an agreement among many competitors. This explains the large number of trade association cases handled in the late 1960s and early 1970s. In some situations, a trade association resolution and any agreement among individual member firms are indistinguishable, and either section 3 or section 8 may be applied.

The Supreme Court ruled that the choice of applicable provisions can be made with reasonable discretion either by the FTC or the prosecuting authority (Oil Cartel Price-Fixing case of 1984, Feb. 24, 1984, 30 KTIS 244). The FTC will apply section 8(1)(i) when a trade association is made up of a great many member firms so that decision-making power tends to be delegated to a board meeting, special committee, or panel of representatives.

(4) COMMON INTEREST REQUIREMENT

A trade association is defined in the Act as any combination of two or more entrepreneurs having as its principal purpose the furtherance of their common interest as entrepreneurs (sec. 2(2)). At a minimum, it shall have some covenant or code, have representatives, collect membership fees, and have some common purpose to pursue. A mere temporary association of entrepreneurs may not constitute a trade association.

Sometimes, internal groups at a trade association such as regional branches, committees or subcommittees, are regarded as a trade association when they act independently from the mother organization. For example, in the 1980 Ohita Gasoline Station Commercial Association Beppu Branch price-fixing case (Feb. 7, 1980, 26 KTIS 96), the respondent was one branch of the prefecture-wide commercial association.

(C) LIMITING THE NUMBER OF ENTREPRENEURS

Section 8(1)(iii) prohibits a trade association from limiting the present or future number of entrepreneurs in any particular field of business.

"Any particular field of business" is used to imply a narrower market than "any particular field of trade" under section 8(1)(i) or section 3.

This provision can be interpreted as a prohibition of restraint of competition in any particular field of business by way of limiting the present or future number of entrepreneurs. This provision covers restraint of competition that is less than substantial.

A trade association can achieve this effect by restricting admission to it. When a trade association is in a dominant position in a market, membership becomes crucial in order to engage in business activities in that particular field. Membership in a local doctors association is an example of such a dominant position, and refusal to admit a member to a doctors association for such a reason as oversupply can cause a problem under section 8(1)(iii). In the 1980 Chiba Prefecture Doctors Association case (June 19, 1980, 27 KTIS 39), the doctors association restricted the new entry of hospitals or clinics by making them get the permission on their scale of entry (number of beds) from the doctors association.

In the 1963 National Federation of Phonograph Record Retailers Association case (Feb. 13, 1963, 11 KTIS 58), the Federation restricted admission of newcomers, who were mainly retailers of household electric appliances, and made an agreement with record manufacturers not to sell to non-members. This conduct was found to fall under section 8(1)(iii).

Limiting the number of entrepreneurs could fall under this provision when refused entrepreneurs are deprived of the chance to participate freely in a market. This could happen when some member firms were discriminated against by not being allowed to use particular facilities belonging to the association. However, the FTC has been applying section 8(1)(iv) in such cases as restriction of member firms' activities by a trade association.

(D) RESTRICTIONS ON FUNCTIONS OR ACTIVITIES OF CONSTITUENT ENTREPRENEURS

Section 8(1)(iv) prohibits undue restriction of the functions or activities of the constituent entrepreneurs of a trade association.

This provision was utilized to prohibit conduct having less direct anticompetitive effects compared with a substantial restraint of competition. The borderline between a section 8(1)(i) case and a section 8(1)(iv) case is unclear, and in the past there were some section 8(1)(iv) cases where section 8(1)(i) could have been applied.

The conduct of a trade association that is held to violate section 8(1)(iv) is as follows:

(A) Price fixing within a small geographical area.

(B) Price fixing where cartel participants do not include a majority of entrepreneurs in a particular field of trade.

(C) Restrictions on members' business activities other than price.

(D) Price-fixing agreements among an association of dealers or agents of a particular manufacturer (intrabrand restriction).

(E) Prevention of price reductions of member firms.

(F) Restrictions on rebate rates or advertising methods among member firms.

(G) Restrictions on customers.

(H) Restrictions on location of stores or sales outlets, or of change of location.

(I) Exclusive purchasing arrangements for raw materials among member firms.

The major difference between section 8(1)(i) and 8(1)(iv) is that no surcharge can be ordered for the latter (see Chapter 19 Surcharge Orders). To increase the deterring effects of cartel prohibitions, section 8(1)(i) needs to be used as much as is feasible.

(E) GUIDELINES FOR TRADE ASSOCIATION ACTIVITIES

(1) 1979 GUIDELINE

In August 27, 1979, the FTC announced a Guideline on Trade Association Activities. In view of the large area of activities engaged in by trade associations in Japan, this guideline covered 10 areas of activities that trade associations might engage in, and tried to classify these activities into:

(A) acts that violate the Act in principle,

(B) acts that may constitute a violation of the Act depending on circumstances,

(C) acts that are not considered a violation of the Act.

As to acts that violate the Act in principle, the Guidelines gives the following examples:

(A) To decide minimum sales prices, rates or amounts of price increases of member firms.

(B) To establish prices to be used as a standard, such as standard price, basic price, target price of member firms.

(C) To establish prices of member firms by preparing a common pricing formula giving concrete figures for calculation.

(D) To set limits on such factors of price as rebates, fees and commissions or discounts.

(E) To determine or revise prices, rebates, or commissions by way of collective bargaining with purchasers or suppliers on behalf of member firms.

(F)   To exert pressure on suppliers to stop or to restrict supplies of goods or raw materials to discounters in order to maintain price.

(G)   To cause member firms to maintain resale prices.

(H)   To control production or sales quantities of member firms.

(I)   To control production or sales quantities of member firms by restricting the purchase of raw materials or use of production facilities.

(J)   To adjust production or sales quantity by setting a concrete standard for limiting production or sales quantity of member firms.

(K)   To restrict customers of member firms.

(L)   To restrict sales territories of member firms.

(M)   To decide upon the allocation of bids, or determine winning bidders in advance, or to decide ways to select bidders to win among member firms.

(N)   To restrict participation of member firms to bidding.

(O)   To restrict new facilities, or increase of facilities, or use of facilities, or jointly decide to scrap production capacity.

(P)   To restrict technology development or use of technology of member firms.

(Q)   To restrict competition substantially by way of joint production, joint sales, or joint purchases by member firms, or to force the use of joint facilities, or to discriminate in their use among member firms.

(R)   To exert pressure on member firms by requesting them not to deal with, or to restrict transactions with non-member firms.

(S)   To exert pressure on trading partners by requesting them not to deal with, or to restrict transactions with non-member firms.

(T)   To exert pressure on trading partners by requesting them to engage in disadvantageous treatment of non-member firms without justifiable reasons.

(U)   To obstruct transactions of non-member firms by means of defaming or vilification of such firms.

(V)   To restrict any increase in the number of entrepreneurs by means of obstructing or discouraging new entry, or by excluding existing entrepreneurs.

These conducts can violate either sections 8(1)(i) or 8(1)(iv) depending on their impact on competition. Some of the above-mentioned conduct could violate section 8(1)(v).

It is one of the important characteristics of section 8(l)(iv) regulation to cover cases with lesser effects on competition than substantial restraints of competition.

(2) DOCTORS AND CONSTRUCTION COMPANIES GUIDELINES

On August 7, 1981, a supplementary guideline was issued dealing with doctors associations. In the past, applicability of the Antimonopoly Act to doctors' activities was not clear, and as a result, there was much confusion concerning restrictions on new entry and uniform fee schedules by doctors associations. The FTC, after four decisions against doctors associations in 1980 and 1981 (see the Chiba Prefecture Doctors Association case of 1980, June 19, 1980, 27 KTIS 39 et al.), thought that illegal conduct should be clarified by way of a guideline and then, if necessary, enforcement activities should follow in view of the special status afforded to doctors.

The guideline gives more concrete examples of conduct by doctors associations along the general principles explained in the Guidelines on Trade Association Activities. It covers such areas as:

(A) Restrictions on new entry by doctors.
(B) Undue interference in the use of medical facilities in nearby districts.
(C) Establishment of a fee schedule for non-insured medical care and medical certification.
(D) Restrictions on medical care hours and advertising by doctors.

In February 21, 1984, the FTC announced a Guideline for Construction Companies with respect to Public Works. The FTC was asked to issue a guideline regarding the limit of legitimate information exchange among construction companies with respect to public works.

It was customary among construction companies to try to obtain information on competitors' bidding intentions in order to make sure of who was interested in winning the bid. Of course, these activities have the potential high risk of leading to bid rigging. This guideline gives some examples of those exchanges of information that are permissible for a construction company trade association in so far as public works bidding is concerned (see chapter 6 (D) Bid Rigging).

(3) CLEARANCE SYSTEM

The Guideline on Trade Association Activities provides for a clearance system procedure whereby a trade association can ask for an FTC opinion on specific conduct by the trade association. The FTC will give its opinion in writing and make public an outline of its opinion. Most clearances were obtained through informal consultation with the FTC, and in the latter case, the FTC discloses an outline of the facts and its opinions for reference to other trade associations. By disclosing outlines of such opinions, further clarification of the guideline is expected.

(4) PUBLIC RELATIONS ACTIVITIES CONCERNING THE GUIDELINES

There are many small trade associations who need guidance and advice so they will not violate the rules established by the guidelines. The FTC has a senior officer for guidance who is responsible for answering questions from relevant trade associations (see Chapter 14 FTC Organization). Through this guidance program, the FTC is trying to educate trade associations to comply with the guidelines.

NOTE

[1] This is the same with violations of the first part of section 3 (private monopolization) and section 19 (unfair trade practices).

10

MERGERS AND ACQUISITIONS

(A) REGULATION OF MERGERS AND ACQUISITIONS

(1) MERGER REGULATION

Section 15(1) prohibits a company from entering into a merger if it may cause a substantial restraint of competition in any particular field of trade, or if unfair trade practices are employed in the course of the merger.

Under the Commercial Code (Act No. 48 of 1899), mergers are divided into two kinds. One is where one company acquires other companies as a whole and inherits all the assets and liabilities of the acquired companies. The other is when a new company is established that acquires existing companies including all their assets and liabilities. Because the first method has advantages in the tax treatment of assets to be acquired, more than 99 percent of Japanese mergers are made using the first method (in FY 1990, 3 out of 1,751 filings on mergers used this method).

Only the methods described above are considered mergers within the meaning of section 15. For example, acquiring 100 percent of a company's stock, or acquiring all the assets of a company is not a merger and is not subject to section 15.

In view of its impact on market concentration, premerger notification is required (see Chapter 20 Reporting Requirements). The parties may not effect a merger until the 30-day waiting period expires. The FTC must take action against the merger within the 30-day waiting period (sec. 15(3)).

(2) YAWATA-FUJI MERGER CASE

The only case in which the FTC decision applied section 15 was the 1969 Yawata-Fuji Merger case (Oct. 30, 1969, 16 KTIS 46). The Yawata Iron & Steel Co. (Yawata) and the Fuji Iron & Steel Co. (Fuji) were the top and second largest companies in the steel industry, and these companies were divided in 1946 by the Elimination of Excessive Concentration of Economic Power Act (see chapter 1 (B)(3) Economic Deconcentration).

In April 1968, these two companies announced their plan to merge and this caused very contrasting reactions in various sectors of Japan. The market shares of the merged company would be 44.5 percent in pig iron (the second largest market share would be 16.9 percent), 35.4 percent in crude steel (the second largest would be 12.4 percent), 34.2 percent in hot rolled bars (the second largest would be 11.5 percent), 93.3 percent in heavy rails (the second largest would be 2.7 percent), 55.1 percent in large shaped steel (the second largest would be 10.5 percent), 45.4 percent in steel wires (the second largest would be 16.9 percent), 34.9 percent in cold rolled sheet (the second largest would be 9.8 percent), 55.4 percent in tin plate (the second largest would be 23 percent), and 98.3 percent in steel pile (the second largest would be 1.1 percent).

Both business circles and MITI welcomed this plan as a good model to follow to prepare for international competition that was forthcoming after a series of liberalization measures on trade and capital. This merger also had the symbolic meaning of restoring the pre-*zaibatsu*-dissolution status. A group of economists had raised strong objections to the plan and demanded fair evaluation of the merger by the FTC (see chapter 3 (C) Big Merger Movement).

In view of this development, the companies had asked the FTC for its informal opinion of the proposed merger. After careful examination, the FTC stated that the merger would be illegal because of three product lines: rails for railways (combined share 100 percent), tin plates for food cans (combined share 61.2 percent), foundry pig iron (combined share 56.3 percent). The FTC also said that the legality of sheet pile would be doubtful (combined share 98.3 percent).

The companies then filed a premerger notification with some plans for proposed remedies to the problems indicated by the FTC. However, the FTC was not satisfied with the proposal, and issued a recommendation to them not to merge. The companies did not accept the recommendation and the matter went into hearing proceedings.

After 13 hearings, the companies filed a motion for a consent decision. The proposed remedial measures were:

> Concerning rail for railway, Fuji agreed to transfer its manufacturing facilities of railway rail, along with technology assistance, to its competitor and manage the manufacturing of railway rail for the competitor until it was able to start its own production.
>
> Concerning tin plates for food cans, Yawata would sell the stock of its affiliated company, of which it held 20 percent, to the other company. The company had a market share of 29.2 percent as to tin plate for food cans.
>
> Concerning foundry pig iron, Yawata agreed to transfer its manufacturing facilities along with technology assistance to its leading competitor, which had a 17 percent market share.
>
> Concerning sheet pile, the two companies agreed to give technology assistance to two of their competitors.

Altogether, the proposed remedial measures consisted of 24 items, two-thirds of which were related to technology assistance. The FTC accepted the proposal and issued a consent decision. The merger was effected on April 1970.

(3) OTHER CASES

(i) Snow Brand Dairy Co. merger case

In 1958, the FTC examined the proposed merger of the Snow Brand Dairy Co. and the Clover Dairy Co (reported in the FY 1958 Annual Report). As a result of this merger, the companies would have a 57.2 percent market share in butter production, 75 percent in cheese production, and 76.2 percent in milk collection from farmers in Hokkaido, a major milk producing area. The FTC decided that this merger would not violate the Act because,

(A)   influential competitors existed;

(B)   dairy companies could not refuse to buy milk from farmers or their cooperatives;

(C) milk was in excess in Hokkaido and couldn't be shipped outside by the regulation of the Ministry of Agriculture, Forestry and Fishery, therefore, dairy companies must make butter, cheese or the like from milk they collected in Hokkaido; and

(D) dairy companies' power to determine the purchase price of milk was limited by collective bargaining with farmers' cooperatives.

(ii) Chuo-Sen'i Co. case

In 1959, the FTC examined the proposed merger of two fiber manufacturers, the Chuo-Sen'i Co. and the Teikoku Seima Co. (reported in the FY 1959 Annual Report). The merger would give a market share of 56.8 percent in flax yarn, but the FTC decided that the merger did not violate the Act because some synthetic fibers would be considered as a close substitute, which brought the merged company's share down to about 10 percent.

(iii) Mitsunishi Heavy Industry Co. case

In 1963, the FTC examined the proposed merger of Shin-Mitsubishi Heavy Industries Co., the Mitsubishi Nippon Heavy Industries Co., and the Mitsubishi Shipbuilding and Engineering Co. (reported in the FY 1963 Annual Report). These three companies were a single company that had been dissolved after the war, and had been in competition in many fields. The company's market share would be 28 percent in shipbuilding, 27 percent in diesel engines, 35 percent in turbines and boilers for ships, 24 percent in turbines and boilers for thermal power generation, 35-42 percent in turbines and boilers for industrial use, 63 percent in paper manufacturing machines, 25 percent in truck production, and 26 percent in bus production.

The FTC found that the merger would not violate the Act, but some remedial measures were necessary. These products, except trucks and buses, are capital goods produced after orders were placed. In view of the users' strong bargaining position, strong business ties with customers, and the existence of competitors with technological capability, the FTC thought that the companies could not control these markets. In the field of trucks and buses, there existed strong competitors.

As to paper manufacturing machines, the FTC found that the increase in market share was small even though market share of the companies was high, and thus would not create a problem under the Act. But as a result of the merger, the companies would have two of the most widely known patents as their exclusive licensees in Japan. In view of the fact that new companies accounted for 63 percent of this submarket, the FTC advised them to cancel one of these licensing agreements. The companies accepted this advice, and the merger was effected as proposed.

(B) REGULATION OF TRANSFERS OF BUSINESS

(1) TRANSFERS OF BUSINESS REGULATIONS

Section 15 applies *mutatis mutandis* to the following five kinds of asset transfer:

(A) Acquiring the whole or a substantial part of the business in Japan of another company;

(B) Acquiring the whole or a substantial part of the fixed assets in Japan of another company;

(C) Taking on the lease of the whole or a substantial part of the business in Japan of another company;

(D) Undertaking a management agreement of the whole or a substantial part of the business in Japan of another company;

(E) Entering into a contract that provides for a joint profit and loss account for business in Japan of another company.

(C) to (E) are rarely used in business circles, and the most important kind of asset transfer is (A). Transfers of "business" are not merely transfers of assets. When business is transferred, it means business operations as a whole are transferred including assets and customer relations.

"Substantial part of the business" means a substantial part of the business to those who transfer the business, but where the transferred business constitutes a substantial part of the business of the acquiring company is also covered. Therefore, this provision can cover most forms of asset transfer.

"Fixed assets" means things such as factories, buildings, etc.

(2) TOHO-SUBARU CASE

The 1950 Toho-Subaru case (Sep. 29, 1950, 2 KTIS 146) is the only case where section 16 was applied. The Toho Co. (Toho), a motion picture producing, distributing and exhibiting company, had a contract with the Subaru Kogyo Co. (Subaru), a motion picture exhibiting and other recreational facilities operating company, for the lease of two theaters owned by Subaru. The contract had provided for joint operation of these theaters, and for sharing the profits from them.

These theaters are located in the center of Tokyo called Marunouchi and Yurakucho. There are 10 theaters in this district, and by this contract, Toho came to control eight of them, and 90 percent of the audience capacity. If the adjacent Ginza area is included, Toho would control 58 percent of the audience capacity of the area.

The FTC found that this contract violated section 16(1) and ordered Toho to stop leasing the theaters from Subaru. It also ordered them not to take part, directly or indirectly, in the operation of the theaters, nor to engage in any future acts causing the same effect.

The FTC decision was appealed to the Tokyo High Court, which sustained the FTC decision (Tokyo High Court, Sep. 19, 1951, 3 KTIS 166).

(C) MERGER GUIDELINES

(1) MERGER GUIDELINE

The FTC has been reviewing mergers and transfers of business for many years and has developed internal standards to be used for such review. On July 15, 1980, the FTC announced the Merger Guideline which also covered transfers of business (in this section mergers refer also to transfers of business). This guideline specifies cases that need closer examination and various considerations that must be taken into account in reviewing mergers.

In Japan, every merger and most transfers of business are subject to a prior notification obligation, therefore, the first thing the FTC must do is to select cases that require closer examination.

The standards for selecting cases that need closer examination are as follows:

(i) The market share of any party or the combined market share of the parties is:

(A) 25 percent or more;
(B) the largest in the market, and the market share is 15 percent or more;
(C) the largest in the market, and the difference between the market share of the second or the third largest is substantial.

(ii) The market share of the party or, in the case of a horizontal merger, the combined market share of the parties, is among the top three, and the aggregated market share of the largest three exceeds 50 percent;
(iii) The number of competitors is few;
(iv) The total assets of any party exceed 100 billion yen, and those of the other party exceed 10 billion.

By the subsequent Guidelines on Stockholdings, one-fourth is now considered as substantial as to (i)(C), and less than seven is considered few as to (iii). The factors to be considered as to a horizontal merger are, among others, market share after the merger, ranking in the market, difference of market share with competitors, and change in these factors by the merger.

The FTC reviews and examines more closely mergers that exceed the thresholds. Secondly, the FTC will examine market share after the merger—ranking in the market, difference of market share with competitors, change of these factors by the merger. As to those cases that still need further evaluation, the FTC will consider various market factors. This approach is very close to what is described in the U.S. Justice Department's 1992 Merger Guidelines.[1]

(2) RETAIL MERGER GUIDELINE

In addition to the Merger Guideline, in July 24, 1981, the FTC issued a separate guideline for the retail sector. This guideline gives the following criteria for selecting retail sector merger cases for closer examination.

(A) In more than three cities or towns, the combined market share exceeds 25 percent based on annual retail sales data, and the merger creates the largest firm in the market concerned;

(B) The combined annual sales amount to 500 billion yen or more;

(C) The merger involves more than two companies whose annual retail sales are 150 billion yen or more, respectively.

In the retail sector, three types of retailers can be identified—department stores, supermarkets, and retail stores in general. The guideline states that in big cities (13 in all) like Tokyo or Osaka, each of these different kinds of retailers shall be deemed to compete, thus each market can be distinguished. On the other hand, in local towns and cities, there could be only one retail market comprised by many kinds of retailers. This guideline was issued in view of large merger movements in the retail sector in the late 1970s.

(3) OTHER FACTORS

In determining the asset amount or the market share requirement in reviewing mergers, the FTC will take into account subsidiaries controlled by the merging company, or companies that control the merging company. In principle, the holding of 25 percent of a company's stock is used as a criterion of control, therefore, those companies where more than 25 percent of their stocks are held or which hold more than 25 percent of their stocks are included in these evaluations.

There is no mention of market definition in the guideline. Generally speaking, the filing form for merger asks the parties to describe their market positions as to each relevant product line, and the FTC will use these data as a starting point for its evaluation. In other words, the FTC examines data for narrow market definition and explores whether the market should be expanded.

(D) REGULATION OF STOCKHOLDINGS

(1) REGULATION OF STOCKHOLDINGS BY A COMPANY

A company is prohibited from acquiring or holding stock in companies in Japan where the effect of such acquisition or holding may be to substantially restrain competition in any particular field of trade (sec. 10(1)).

Stock acquisition or holding through unfair trade practices is also prohibited.

Examination of stock acquisition or holding requires a two-step evaluation. First, it is determined whether a company acquired or held stocks that are sufficient to control or at least to cause considerable influence over the business activities of other companies. This is called a joint relationship. Secondly, if a joint relationship is found after the first analysis, then the same analysis of the merger will be attempted.

(2) REGULATION OF STOCKHOLDINGS BY A PERSON

The same regulation as to a company is imposed on individuals other than a company (sec. 14(1)). Therefore, a natural person, cooperatives, association, public entity, public association, any juridical person other than companies come under this regulation.

(3) CASES

There were eight cases with respect to section 10, but those cases were rendered before the 1949 Amendment when acquisition of stocks were per se illegal and so do not now have the value of case law. In the 1957 Nippon Musical Instrument Co. (Nippon) case (Jan. 30, 1957, 8 KTIS 51), Nippon was charged with a violation of section 17 by virtue of stockholdings in the Kawai Musical Instrument Co. (Kawai). Nippon had a market share of 54 percent in pianos, 64 percent in organs, and 28 percent in harmonicas. Kawai was the second largest in the field and its market share was 16 percent in pianos, 13 percent in organs, and 7 percent in harmonicas.

Nippon acquired 24.5 percent of Kawai's stock as a whole, but the major part of its stock was held in the name of one of Nippon's suppliers, the Mitani Shindo Co. However, the funds necessary to purchase such stocks were provided by Nippon. In this case, in view of such intentional acts of evasion, the FTC relied on section 17 instead of section 10.

In the 1973 Hiroshima Railway Co. (Hiroshima Railway) case (July 17, 1973, 20 KTIS 282), a private railway company, Hiroshima Railway, held 110,000 shares out of 130,000 outstanding shares, (85 percent) of the Hiroshima Bus Co. The FTC found that such stockholdings would cause a substantial restraint of competition in the passenger transportation field in the Hiroshima City area and ordered Hiroshima Railway to dispose of 85,000 shares out of the 110,000 shares it held.

(4) GUIDELINE ON STOCKHOLDINGS

In September 11, 1981, the FTC announced a guideline on stockholdings, and specified a two-step guide to evaluating stockholding relationships among companies.

The first thing to determine was whether a "joint relationship" could be found. The guideline says that a "joint relationship" shall be found in the following cases.

(A) Where the stockholding ratio is 50 percent or more, or

(B) Where the acquired company satisfies the requirements of an "affiliated company" as defined in the Ministry of Finance Ordinance No. 59 of 1963.

An affiliated company is defined as a company for which 20 to 50 percent of its voting rights are controlled by, and its financial and management policy are importantly influenced by the acquiring company through such relations as personnel, financial or technological assistance or business relationships.

In the following cases, a joint relationship will be found after a case-by-case examination:

(i) Where the stockholding ratio is 25 percent or more,

(ii) Where the stockholding ratio is 10 percent or more and less than 25 percent, and,

    (A) where the acquiring company is the largest among shareholders,

    (B) where the acquiring company is among the top three shareholders, when it is in competition with the acquired company, or

(C) when the stockholding is related to a joint venture among
competitors.

In essence, where the stockholding ratio is less than 25 percent, a
case-by-case analysis is required to determine whether a joint relationships can be found, and personnel, financial, technological assistance or business relations are considered for this purpose. Once
"joint relationships" are found, these companies are examined as
though they were merged, and the same principle for closer examination is applied as with the Merger Guideline.

This guideline is more specific in certain aspects. For example, it
says that where the amount of difference between the second or the
third largest firm is a quarter of the largest or more, the difference is
substantial. It also says that the number of competitors are few when
it is less than seven.

(5) DISTRIBUTION SYSTEM AND BUSINESS PRACTICES GUIDELINES

In this guideline, the FTC indicated its intention to utilize remedial power to order the disposition of stocks under section 20, when
unfair trade practices are employed and, in view of stockholding
relationships, such illegal practices might be repeated (chapter 7-1-
(3), part I of the Guidelines).

These guidelines also show examples of where stock acquisition
is done through unfair trade practices that violate section 10(1) or
where it falls under unfair trade practices (chapter 7-2, part I of the
Guidelines).

The guidelines say:

(A) Where a finished product manufacturer is in a dominant bargaining
position vis-a-vis its suppliers of parts or raw materials, and by
requesting to let it acquire stocks of such suppliers, or suggesting
refusal to deal or unjustly disadvantageous terms with such suppliers unless such demand is accepted, such acquisition would violate
section 10(1) (item 14 of the General Designations)

(B) Where an influential finished product manufacturer acquires stocks
of parts manufacturers by inducing material suppliers to the parts
manufacturers to refuse further supply of such materials to them,

such acquisition would violate section 10(1) (item 2 of the General Designations).

(C) Where a firm is in a dominant bargaining position vis-a-vis its trading partners, and by suggesting to the trading partners suspension of transactions with the firm, then such firm's acquisition of stocks of the trading partners would fall under item 14 of the General Designations.

(D) Where a manufacturer supplies its products on condition that the distributors of its products who have stocks of the manufacturer do not dispose of stocks of the manufacturer, then such conduct would fall under item 14 of the General Designations.

In addition, exclusionary conduct by means of or by reason of the holding of stocks of trading partners are described in the guidelines (chapter 7-3, part I of the Guidelines).

(E) REGULATION OF INTERLOCKING DIRECTORATES

Interlocking directorates are prohibited when they may substantially restrain competition in any particular field of trade (sec. 13(1)). A company may not coerce another competing company into admitting interlocking directorates through unfair trade practices (sec. 13(2)).

The term "interlocking directorates" refers to an officer or an employee of a company who holds, at the same time, a position as an officer in another competing company or companies in Japan (sec. 13(1)).

In the 1973 Hiroshima Railway Co. case (July 17, 1973, 20 KTIS 282), officers and employees of the respondent, the Hiroshima Railway Co., held certain key positions in the Hiroshima Bus Co., which was in competition with the respondent in the field of passenger transportation within Hiroshima City. The FTC ordered these officers to resign from either one or the other of these companies.

NOTE

[1] The Department of Justice and Federal Trade Commission Horizontal Merger Guidelines, April 2, 1992.

11

SPECIAL REGULATION
ON STOCKHOLDING

(A) PROHIBITION OF HOLDING COMPANIES (SECTION 9)

A holding company was utilized as the core or the headquarters of such *zaibatsu* groups as Mitsui, Mitsubishi, Sumitomo and Yasuda (see chapter 1 (A)(2) After World War I). These holding companies not only controlled the stocks of affiliated companies, but also dispatched key personnel to exercise effective control of these affiliated companies. The first measure of *zaibatsu* dissolution was to abolish these holding companies and force them to dispose their stock (see chapter 1 (B)(1) *Zaibatsu* Dissolution). It still seems true that a holding company provides an effective and easy means of establishing a large concern such as a *zaibatsu* or a huge conglomerate company.

Section 9 was enacted to effect permanent prohibition of the establishment of a holding company (sec. 9(1)) and to prohibit a company from operating as a holding company (sec. 9(2)). A "holding company" is defined as a company whose principal business is to control the business activities of a Japanese company or companies by means of holding stock (sec. 9(3)).

The business activities of a company need to be evaluated as a whole to see what its "principal business" is. The most important factor to look at on its balance sheet is the percentage of the total value of stock owned by a company, namely, the percentage in total value of assets of the company.

For example, when it exceeds 50 percent, the company is highly likely to be a holding company. However, when all the stocks held by a company total less than the controlling stocks of each company held, it is not a holding company. The nature and scale of business other than stockholding is also a relevant factor to consider.[1]

The prohibition of section 9 is absolute. All holding companies are prohibited irrespective of their corporate scale or effect on a market.

Shares in a partnership are included in the term "stocks" so that shares in a partnership, limited or unlimited liability companies, can qualify a company controlling these entities as a holding company (sec. 9(3)).

In the event any holding company is formed within Japan, the FTC may bring a legal action to have such a company declared null and void by a court (sec. 18).

Because this is a unique regulation particular to Japan and foreign holding companies may own stock in a company in Japan as a means to enter into the Japanese market, only activities within Japan are taken into account so far as a foreign holding company is concerned. For this reason, it is not a holding company within the meaning of section 9 when a company in Japan controls business activities of other companies in foreign countries. It is also possible for a Japanese company to establish a holding company in a foreign country and to control business activities of other companies therein.

When a foreign holding company controls only a single company in Japan and this can be regarded as a means of entering into the Japanese market, then such stockholding may not be prohibited. However, if a foreign holding company functions as a controlling entity of various companies in Japan, it shall be regarded as a holding company.

(B) RESTRICTIONS ON STOCKHOLDING BY A FINANCIAL COMPANY

(1) REASONS FOR A SPECIAL REGULATION

In order to limit its influence over the business activities of nonfinancial companies, a financial company is restricted in its holding of stock in other companies in Japan. This idea of separating financial companies from non-financial companies is not a purely antitrust idea, and, for example, in the U.S. the same kind of regulation is effected by the Federal Reserve Board as a means of regulating banking.[2]

The original Antimonopoly Act had set a 5-percent limitation on a financial company, and this limitation was relaxed to 10 percent in 1953 (see chapter 2 (A)(2) The 1953 Amendment). During the rapid economic expansion of the Japanese economy, non-financial companies relied on banks for their financing and banks had a very strong influence over business activities of non- financial companies.

In the 1970s, FTC studies revealed that banks were among the top three shareholders of major Japanese corporations listed on the Tokyo Stock Exchange Market. If stockholding is not limited, it is feared that a financial company will increase its influence over non-financial big businesses in Japan.

In 1977, in view of the above-mentioned influential position of banks, the limitation was again lowered to 5 percent. However, as before, insurance companies can own up to 10 percent of a company's stock because stockholding is an important part of the assets on their balance sheets.

When the 10-year grace period was over in 1987, financial companies could clear the restriction.[3] They could clear the limitation without actually disposing of their shares on the stock market because most companies expanded their capital during the 10 years so that the percentage went down to 5 percent.[4]

Restrictions on stockholding by a financial company has regained its importance from the viewpoint of the *keiretsu* issue. Banks, trust banks, life insurance companies, and marine and fire insurance companies are important members of the major business groups, and they are important shareholders of member companies of the major business groups (see tables 24-1 & 24-2 in chapter 24 Keiretsu Relationships). As a whole, these financial companies in the major business groups had a large percentage of shares of member companies (see table 24-5).

Generally speaking, influence over non-financial companies has lessened due to the expansion of equity financing. Non-financial companies rely less and less on financial companies. However, as described above, the importance of the 5-percent rule remains high from the *keiretsu* point of view. The 5-percent rule imposed on financial companies in Japan works as an important antimonopoly policy tool by placing an effective limitation on business group expansion (see Chapter 24 *Keiretsu* Relationships).

(2) DEFINITION OF A FINANCIAL COMPANY

"Financial companies" are defined in the Act as "banking, trust banks, insurance, mutual financing or securities business" (sec. 11(1)). It applies to any financial company irrespective of its size or position in a market.

(3) EXEMPTIONS

The proviso of section 11(1) gives three exemptions, namely:

(A) Acquisition or holding of stocks as a result of the enforcement of a lien, pledge, mortgage, or of payment in kind,

(B) Acquisition or holding of stocks by a company engaging in securities trading in the course of its business,

(C) Acquisition or holding of stocks in the form of a trust of a pecuniary interest or securities trust, where the trustor or the beneficiary of such trust property can exercise his voting rights, or where such trustee or beneficiary can issue instructions regarding the exercise of such voting rights.

Besides, a financial company may acquire stock of another company in excess of 5 percent if prior approval of the FTC is obtained.

Three exemptions are provided so as not to disturb normal financial business activities. In the case of (A) and (B), these stocks can be held for less than 1 year, and when the financial company wishes to hold them for more than 1 year, it must obtain prior approval from the FTC (sec. 11(2)). The approval will be granted with the condition that stock in excess of 5 percent will be promptly disposed of (sec. 11(3)).

The prior approval power of the FTC is discretionary, and the Act does not specify any situation or conditions for approval. Because such absolute and uniform regulation under section 11(1) lacks flexibility, this power can be used by the FTC to provide necessary room for flexibility in the enforcement of section 11(1).

Section 11(1) covers stocks of any other company, including another financial company. In view of this severe restriction, the FTC grants approval where a financial company acquires stock in another company whose business is exclusively, or almost exclusively, for the benefit of the financial company.

.

For example, the FTC granted approval to acquire 100 percent of the stock of a research company, a computer operation company, a building maintenance company or any supporting business company whose business is done for the financial company. The FTC granted approval for foreign financial companies that established a subsidiary financial company in Japan or a joint venture company to engage in financial business in Japan.

Due to the financial reform adopted in 1992, the wall between banks, trust banks and securities companies was substantially lowered, and after April 1993, banks can establish security companies and securities companies can establish banks as their subsidiaries. The parent financial company must hold more than 50 percent of its stock.[5] Therefore, these financial companies must obtain FTC approval under section 11(1) in order to establish these subsidiary financial companies.

Because the FTC can place conditions for approval on these companies, the FTC is preparing a guideline on financial sectors.

(4) CASES

In 1961, in the Daiwa Bank case, acquisition of the newly issued stock of a failing company for the purpose of rehabilitating it, was charged as a violation of section 11(1) by the FTC (June 26, 1961, 10 KTIS 36). In this case, a chemical company borrowed 350 million yen from the Daiwa Bank and issued 690 million shares whose preemptive rights were assigned to the bank. The company's duty to repay the loan was set off against the bank's duty to pay for the new shares. As a result of this arrangement, the bank possessed most of the company's stock. The FTC held that the acquisition was not deemed to fall under the exemption provided in section 11(1)(i), since the stock was not acquired as the result of the enforcement of a lien, pledge, mortgage, or of payment in kind.

In the 1991 Nomura Securities Co. case (Nov. 11, 1991, 38 KTIS 115), the Nomura Securities Co. (Nomura) was charged with a violation of section 11 for effectively controlling the stock of the Nomura Real Estate Co. (Nomura Real Estate). Nomura Real Estate's stock was held by Nomura and its officers, but, since 1966, those shares held by individuals had been transferred to other companies.

In order to maintain effective control over Nomura Real Estate, Nomura exchanged a side letter with the new shareholders of Nomura Real Estate, namely the Obayashi Co., the Sanwa Bank, the Asahi Fire and Marine Insurance Co., among others, that promised that those stocks would not be transferred without prior consent of Nomura, and that Nomura could buy back those stocks at their acquisition costs.

In 1987, when the grace period above-mentioned had ended, stocks owned by Nomura that exceeded 5 percent were also transferred to other friendly companies under the same conditions. Nomura had exercised the right conferred by this side letter as to stocks held by the above new shareholders (10 as a whole) so that the stocks were transferred to other friendly companies at their acquisition costs.

The FTC found that Nomura acted to evade the 5-percent restriction imposed by section 11(1), and therefore violated section 17.

(C) RESTRICTIONS ON STOCKHOLDINGS BY A GIANT COMPANY

(1) REASONS FOR A SPECIAL REGULATION

Based on the FTC study, a general trading company's large amount of stockholdings was revealed (see table 24-3). General trading companies were increasing their importance among each business group and becoming a "core" company of *keiretsu*. The above-mentioned table shows that the speed of expansion of stockholdings in the mid-1970s was abnormal. This trend of rapid expansion of shareholding could not be stopped by the case-by-case approach provided under sections 9 through 17 of the Act. Aggregated power accumulated through shareholding was beyond the reach of the Act, but could still have a great impact on a market that couldn't be ignored from an antimonopoly view point (see Chapter 24 *Keiretsu* Relationships).

This could mean that these companies were becoming quasi-holding companies as a core of each business group. In order to lessen the chance of becoming a core company in a *keiretsu*, new regulations on stockholding by a big corporation were proposed by the FTC. And, because the case-by-case approach is already well prescribed in the Act, a total ceiling on shareholding for a giant company was proposed.

Restrictions on shareholding by a giant corporation were introduced in the 1977 Amendment.

(2) DEFINITION OF A GIANT COMPANY

Because the purpose of this regulation is to lessen the chance of a big corporation becoming a "core" company in a *keiretsu*, the restriction is imposed on those big corporations in Japan that rank among the top 200 in the non-financial sector. For this reason, "giant company" is defined as a company whose paid-in capital is 10 billion yen or more, or whose net assets are 30 billion yen or more. Financial companies are excluded because they are subject to the more stringent restrictions described above.

(3) CEILING ON STOCKHOLDINGS

Section 9-2(1) prohibits a giant company from acquiring or holding shares of companies in Japan when the value of these stocks exceed its paid-in capital or net assets, whichever is larger.

Only companies in Japan are covered. Acquisition costs of stocks are measured by book value on the latest balance sheet. Book value normally reflects the acquisition cost of stocks, but when the value of stocks are revalued, new values are reflected on the latest balance sheet. Because this restriction is directed at stocks of any company in Japan, in other words it covers non-listed companies or private companies, book value is the only feasible and objective way of measuring the value of stocks.

For the purpose of this regulation, net assets mean total assets minus total liabilities, as reflected in the latest balance sheet of a giant company. But newly issued stocks, those stocks that are converted from debentures, or assets acquired as a result of a merger etc. are taken into account for net assets calculation even if these events took place after the close of the latest business year (sec. 9-2(1)).

(4) EXEMPTIONS

Section 9-2(1) specifies various kinds of stocks that are excluded from this restriction. Stocks of companies that are partially owned by the government or a municipal government, or by those entities whose capital is wholly invested by the government (sec. 9-2(1)(i)); stocks of companies whose business is to further industrial development and the progress of the economy and society, and require large sums of funds (sec. 9-2(1)(ii)); stocks of companies whose business is undertaken outside Japan, or that engage in an investment business in foreign countries (secs. 9-2(1)(iii) and (iv)) are excluded.

These stocks have nothing to do with *keiretsu* and their exclusion does not raise any problem as to the effectiveness of this regulation.

There are more technical exemptions such as stocks of joint ventures with foreign companies (sec. 9-2(1)(vi)), or stocks of a company that is established to separate some business from a giant company (sec. 9-2(1)(v)), or company stocks that are newly issued (sec. 9-2(1)(vii)) etc. Besides, the FTC is authorized to grant prior approval when imperative reasons are available to acquire such stocks (sec. 9-2(1)(ix)).

Because of these exemption provisions, the system looks too complex, but in essence, it tries to set the ceiling for stockholdings of a giant company, and thus to put the breaks on *keiretsu* expansion through shareholding.

(D) EVALUATION

As mentioned in the antimonopoly laws, it is very rare to find restrictions on the stockholding of a financial company. But the idea for the regulation covered by section 11(1) is not peculiar to Japan. The other two regulations are specific to Japan, and should be evaluated from the *keiretsu* point of view, or in terms of their implications for the *keiretsu* issue (see Chapter 24 *Keiretsu* Relationships).

Generally speaking, a giant company holds stock in three different kinds of companies. One group of stocks are those for subsidiaries and affiliated companies over which it exercises control over their business activities. One group of stocks are held for the purpose of so-called mutual or cross stockholding. The last group of stocks are held as an investment.

Of course, motives for stockholdings are mixed, particularly in the second and the third kind of company may have mixed reasons for such stockholdings. However, the priority of holdings are certain. When a giant company faces the ceiling, it may dispose of stocks held as investments and as cross holdings, but not those stocks of subsidiaries or affiliated companies. Therefore, the impact of section 9-2 on a *keiretsu* is certain. A giant company could become a "core" company of a *keiretsu*, and by restricting its shareholding, section 9-2 could put some limitation on *keiretsu* expansion.

Prohibitions against holding companies will serve to eliminate a chance to restore a "core" company in a business group. Section 11(1) could also serve to restrain banks and other financial companies from reviving as a "core" company in business groups or to expand financial *keiretsu*. It can be said that as a whole these regulations are aimed at eliminating a chance for the restoration of "core" companies in business groups.

Whether or not *keiretsu* themselves are undesirable or not is argued. Whether these regulations are effective enough will depend heavily on how one looks at the *keiretsu* issue. In Japan, the existence of *keiretsu* is positively accepted by most commentators,[6] but this does not mean that these special regulations are meaningless. It seems too simplistic to say that these special regulations on stock-holdings cannot be justified because no other developed countries have comparable regulations. In view of the *keiretsu* problems, they have a good raison d'etre in Japan. Effectiveness of these regulations will be evaluated by looking at their actual impact on *keiretsu*, and it is certain that unrestricted expansion of *keiretsu* in Japan is not desirable (see Chapter 24 *Keiretsu* Relationships).

NOTES

[1] Section 9 is based on the hostility to such traditional methods of corporate control, due to historical reasons. On the other hand, it simply allows a company to hold controlling stock in other companies so long as the company has some business activities besides stockholding. There are some companies that engage in businesses such as the management of real estate, etc. in order to avoid becoming holding companies. It is not yet clear whether a company falls under a holding company if it establishes a subsidiary in order to engage in some of its business. It may become a holding company if it controls more than two companies that are established by the company itself to make them engage in some of its businesses.

[2] In the U.S., commercial banks cannot have stock of other companies in their own account, but the Federal Reserve Board can give necessary authorization for stockholdings with respect to companies that engage in other financial business or

other businesses affiliated with banking (Regulation Y, 12 CFR § 225.25). As a result, a very similar regulation was effected by the FRB in the U.S.

[3] *A Decade of the Antimonopoly Act as Amended,* FTC/VIEWS, No. 1 (Jan. 1988), which said, "It is reported that most would comply with this ceiling by December 1, 1987 by either stock disposal or a share increase in the company concerned." at 13-14.

[4] *Id.* As of December 2, 1977, there were 2,851 companies in which banks had holdings of over 5 percent, among them, 134 companies received authorization under the sec. 11(1) proviso in 1987. In the case of security companies, the number was 286 and 4, respectively. As a result, financial companies' stockholding in 2,999 companies could clear the ceiling imposed by the Act. See *id.,* at 13-14.

[5] The Financial Reform Act (Act No. 87 of 1992). The kinds of business allowed for such subsidiaries can be prescribed by a Cabinet Ordinance and the MOF Regulations, which are still under examination as of December 1992.

[6] X. Imai, *Japanese Business Groups and the Structural Impediments Initiative,* K. Yomamura ed., JAPAN'S ECONOMIC STRUCTURE: SHOULD IT CHANGE? at 167-202. He argues, "The business transactions of corporate groups are clearly carried out on the basis of economically rational calculations." at 171; "The long-term, continuous transactions in recent Japanese industrial networks have an economic rationale and are in no way a unique phenomenon. The key role of user-producer interactions in creating continuous innovation is well-established theory in recent economics of technological change." at 200.

12

MONOPOLISTIC SITUATIONS

Section 8-4 authorizes the FTC to order the entrepreneur concerned to transfer a part of the business or to take any other measure necessary to restore competition relating to goods or services where a monopolistic situation is found to exist.

This provision was incorporated in the 1977 Amendment. The original Antimonopoly Act had a provision that authorized the FTC to take measures against undue and substantial disparity in economic power that could not be justified for technological reasons (see chapter 1 (C)(2) Outline of the Original Antimonopoly Act).

The term "monopolistic situation" is defined by two requirements: (1) market structure and (2) market performance.

(A) MARKET STRUCTURE TEST

A particular field of business where a monopolistic situation can be found must fulfill the following conditions as to the market structure requirement:

(1) DOMESTIC SHIPMENT AND MARKET-SHARE REQUIREMENTS

The aggregated total value of goods or services that are supplied within Japan during the latest 1-year period, exceeds 50 billion yen (sec. 2(7)).

Goods are divided into three different but interrelated categories in order to evaluate the competitive effects on the entrepreneurs concerned.

(A) Goods of the same description (same goods).
(B) Goods capable of being supplied without making any significant change to business facilities or kind of business activities.
(C) Goods having a strikingly similar function (similar goods).

The market structure test is used in a market consisting of (A), (B) and (C), but market performance is examined as to (A) and (B). For this purpose, a particular field of business is defined as a market consisting of (A) and (B). This is why (A) and (B) combined are called "particular goods." "Similar goods" are counted only for the purpose of calculating market share and domestic shipment value.

As to services or non-goods, no reference to (B) and (C) is given in section 2(7). Therefore, a relevant market for services should be analyzed by examining the description of the services concerned.

The following two aspects shall be examined.

(A) The market share of a single entrepreneur, with respect to the particular goods plus similar goods, exceeds one half of the market, or the combined market share of the top two exceeds three-fourths of the market (sec. 2(7)(i))).
(B) There exist conditions in a market that make it extremely difficult for any other entrepreneur to be newly engaged in this particular field of business (sec. 2(7)(ii)).

The latter requirement is to consider barriers to entry, and by definition, low entry barriers to "similar goods" are not taken into account.

(2) FTC GUIDELINE

On November 29, 1977, the FTC announced, in the form of a guideline, its interpretation of the term "particular field of business" within the meaning of section 2(7). In order to clarify the way to define a particular field of business, this guideline also contains examples of industries (see table 12-1). However, by the guideline's listing concrete names of industries that satisfy or are about to satisfy market structure requirements, it also meant that the relevant entrepreneurs in the industries concerned should be cautious as to whether their market performance might not fall under the criteria given in the Act.

The following explanation is given in this guideline.

"Same goods" mean a group of goods that have the same function and utility. In this sense, the external limit of the same goods is determined by examining their function and utility. In the manufacturing sector, a six-digit classification under the "Census of Manufacturing" is deemed, in principle, to constitute "same goods." In other words, the examination of "same goods" will be started by looking at the six-digit manufacturing sector classification.

"Particular goods" are defined so as to take into account potential competition among various kinds of goods. When an entrepreneur can produce the same goods without a significant change to his business facilities or kind of business activities, in view of his potential ability to exert competitive pressure on a monopolist, he should be considered as a competitor so far as the monopolistic situation is concerned.

In view of the availability of drastic remedial measures to be taken against monopolistic situations, the time frame for considering potential competition is also extensive. Therefore, when competitive relationships can be expected, in view of business facilities or kind of business activities, the law assumes that a competitive relationship would eventually arise.

By taking into account a rather broad range of goods or services, thus broad market competition, section 8-4 is meant as the "last resort" for a monopolistic situation.

The term "similar goods" means close substitutes of any goods constituting particular goods. Because similar goods is included as a mitigating factor of the market-share requirement, direct competitive relationships rather than potential competitive relationships with the particular goods will be examined.

(3) LATEST 1-YEAR PERIOD

"The latest 1-year period" is defined by a Cabinet Ordinance (No. 317 of 1977, sec. 1). When the aggregated total amount of prices of "particular goods" and "similar goods," as well as the market share of the entrepreneurs concerned can be identified by the newest statistics prepared by the government or other equivalent data covering a 1-year period, this 1-year period shall be the latest 1-year period.

Table 12-1. *Examples of Industries Satisfying the Market Structure Requirement Under Section 2(7) of the Act[1]*

Part I (Manufacturing Sector)

Particular Goods		A Particular Field of Business	Similar Goods
Same Goods			
1. Sodium Glutamate	Other Chemical Seasonings	Chemical Seasoning Mfg.	—
2. Chewing Gum	—	Chewing Gum Mfg.	—
3. Beer	—	Beer Mfg.	—
4. Whisky	—	Whisky Mfg.	—
5. Instant Coffee	—	Instant Coffee Mfg.	Regular Coffee
6. Cigarettes	Pipe Tobacco, Cut Tobacco, Cigars	Tobacco Mfg.	—
7. Synthetic Detergent for Laundry	Synthetic Detergent for Kitchenware, Synthetic Detergent for Household	Household Synthetic Detergent Mfg.	Laundry Soap
8. Dentifrice	—	Dentifrice Mfg.	—
9. Photographic Color Film (excluding Instant Color Film)	Color Film for Movies	Color Film Mfg.	Instant Color Film
10. Tires & Tubes for Motor Vehicles	—	Tires & Tubes for Motor Vehicles Mfg.	—
11. Polished Sheet Glass	Common Sheet Glass, Figured Sheet Glass, Laminated Sheet Glass, Toughened Sheet Glass, Complex Sheet Glass,	Sheet Glass Mfg.	—
12. Glass Bulbs for Cathode-ray Tubes	Glass Bulbs for Other Electronic Tubes	Glass Bulbs for Electronic Tubes Mfg.	—
13. Tin Cans (including Aluminum Cans)	—	Tin Cans Mfg.	—
14. Ventilators	Electric Fans	Ventilator Mfg.	—
15. Pushbutton Telephones	—	Pushbutton Telephone Mfg.	—
16. X-ray Equipment for Medical Purposes	—	X-ray Equipment Mfg. for Medical Purposes	—

Table 12-1. Examples of Industries Satisfying the Market Structure Requirement Under Section 2(7) of the Act[1] (cont.)

Part I (Manufacturing Sector)

Particular Goods		A Particular Field	Similar
Same Goods		of Business	Goods
17. Passenger Cars (Regular and Compact Size)	Subcompact Cars[2]	Passenger Car Mfg.	—
18. Motorcycles	—	Motorcycle Mfg.	—
19. Pianos	—	Piano Mfg.	—

Part II (Service Sector)

The Same Kind of Service	Particular Field of Business
1. Scheduled Domestic Passenger Flights	Scheduled Domestic Passenger Flight Business
2. Scheduled Domestic Cargo Flights	Scheduled Domestic Cargo Flight Business
3. Domestic Basic Telecommunications	Domestic Basic Telecommunications Business
4. International Basic Telecommunications	International Basic Telecommunications Business
5. Elevator Maintenance	Elevator Maintenance Business

NOTES:

[1] These lists were compiled from the data as of FY 1988 and were published on Aug. 1991. They include those industries for which market share or aggregated domestic shipment may fulfill the market structure requirements prescribed in section 2(7) in the near future, in other words, some of these industries have not satisfied the market structure requirements as yet, but are very close to meeting it.

[2] Subcompact Cars means those with less than 550 c.c. engine.

A 1-year period can be a fiscal or calendar year, and when monthly data are available, the latest 1 year could be calculated on a monthly basis.

This requirement is meant to limit the kind of data used for this purpose to that of government offices or their equivalent.

(4) AGGREGATED TOTAL AMOUNT OF PRICES

The formula for calculation can be described as follows:

(A)   The aggregated total amount of shipments of the "particular goods" and the "similar goods," or services of the same description; minus

(B)   Those exported; plus

(C)   Those imported; minus

(D)   The total amount of taxes levied directly on those goods or services mentioned above.

When the figure calculated in this way exceeds 50 billion yen, the market is large enough from a national economy standpoint to have its market performance carefully watched.

Exports and imports are taken into account in order to evaluate a monopolistic situation in a global market for Japan. By doing this, foreign competition can be taken into consideration.

In order to see the market size as a net rather than a gross figure, taxes levied directly on goods or services are also deducted. In such industries as tobacco, beer or whisky, the amount of tax is a significant amount of the value of a shipment, and may be the cause of an unfair disadvantage compared with those goods or services not heavily taxed. Examples of these taxes are: liquor taxes, sugar consumption taxes, gasoline taxes, and customs and duties.

(5) MARKET-SHARE CALCULATION

Market share is calculated by dividing each entrepreneur's total volume of domestic shipment by the aggregate total volume of domestic shipments. Taxes levied on those goods or services need not be considered because market share is not affected by the amount of tax.

Quantity data are principally used to make this calculation. However, in a case where calculation by quantity is not appropriate, price data may be used. The FTC will calculate market share in the way it is done in the industry concerned. For example, price data will be used when price differences among goods belonging to the same category are so large that the quantity data cannot properly show the relative size of the entrepreneurs concerned. Computers and carrier supply equipment are examples of where price data are more appropriate.

(6) BARRIERS TO ENTRY

This requirement is normally counted as a market structure test but it also has some characteristics similar to the market performance test.

The following items will be examined to evaluate the difficulty of entry into a particular field of business:

(A) Economies of scale in both production and distribution;

(B) Aspects of past entry into, or exit from the market;

(C) Absolute cost advantages associated with superior technology or control of such technology;

(D) Control of raw materials or control of distribution channels;

(E) Need to commit larger amounts of capital to enter into the market;

(F) Strong consumer preference favoring differentiated products.

When excessive profits are obtained by monopolists for a long period of time, in other words, the profitability requirement in the performance test is fulfilled, it can be assumed that entry into a market may be difficult and at least some of the barriers described above may exist.

(B) MARKET PERFORMANCE TEST

Three kinds of requirements are described in the Act. Namely, fulfillment of the requirement of downward inflexibility of prices, and either one of the following requirements are necessary to qualify as a monopolistic situation; i.e. the existence of (a) excessive profits or (b) excessive selling costs and general and administrative expenses (sec. 2(7)(iii)).

(1) DOWNWARD INFLEXIBILITY OF PRICES

This phenomenon is generally thought to be a symptom of an oligopolistic or monopolistic market. However, in order to take into account whether this phenomenon prolongs, beyond a cyclical price movement in a market, a 3- to 5-year price movement is examined, and the price movement trend as a whole would be a key in evaluating this requirement. Whether price shows some inflexible movement during the examined period would not be sufficient.

(2) EXCESSIVE PROFITS

The kinds of profit rates that shall be used for evaluating excessiveness of profits and the industrial sectors with which it shall be compared are specified by a Cabinet Ordinance.

Cabinet Ordinance No. 317 of 1977 designated two sets of profit rates to see whether profits were excessive (sec. 3).

(A) $\dfrac{\text{Operating Profits*}}{\text{Total Assets}}$

(B) $\dfrac{\text{Recurring Profits**}}{\text{Net Worth ***}}$

    * = total operating income minus total operating cost and expenses.

  ** = total operating income minus general and administrative costs as well as total operating cost and expenses.

*** = total assets minus total liability.

In order to calculate these profit rates, the amount of assets, net worth, or profits shall be allocated to each particular field of business according to a fair standard of accounting.

The Cabinet Ordinance also designated 12 classes of business fields (sec. 2). The profit rates observed in these broad classes of business fields are used as the norms for evaluating whether there exists excessive profits in any particular field of business belonging to such a class of business field.

These designated classes of business field are equivalent to the large categories of industry classification established under the *Japan Standard Industry Classification*, which is prepared by the General Affairs Agency. Agriculture, mining, construction, manufacturing, wholesaling and retailing, real estate, transport and communication are examples of such designated categories.

The term "far exceeding" is interpreted to mean approximately 50 percent above the normal profit rates of the class of business field to which the entrepreneur belongs.

*(3) EXCESSIVE SELLING COSTS AND GENERAL AND
ADMINISTRATIVE EXPENSES*

This requirement is included in order to cover a situation where profit rates are normal due to wasteful spending of selling costs or general and administrative expenses. Therefore, change in the pattern of spending by the entrepreneur concerned with respect to selling costs or general and administrative expenses, for example, sudden expansion of these expenses in order to reduce the total profit rate level, would be an important factor to examine.

For evaluating the excessiveness of general and administrative expenses, when the entrepreneur engages in multiple fields of business, such expenses should be allocated to a particular field of business. The method of allocation is not prescribed in the guideline. It may be allocated in proportion to total sales of the goods or services concerned.

According to the guideline, "norm for the field of business" means a level that is deemed to be normal for the particular field of business, therefore, the norm would be evaluated based on a much narrower business field as compared with that used to examine excessiveness of profit rates.

(C) NEGATIVE REQUIREMENTS AND PROCEDURAL REQUIREMENTS

(1) NEGATIVE REQUIREMENTS

Although the FTC is authorized to take measures against monopolistic situations, the Act requires certain very strict pre-conditions before remedial measures may be ordered (sec. 8-4).

The FTC cannot order remedial measures when they may reduce the scale of business to such an extent that:

(A)   The costs of supplying the goods or services concerned would rise sharply;

(B)   The financial position of the entrepreneur concerned is undermined;

(C)   Maintenance of international competitiveness becomes difficult.

In addition, when other alternative measures are available, the FTC also cannot take remedial measures, so long as the alternative measures are sufficient to restore competition with respect to the goods or services concerned. It is up to the FTC to evaluate whether the alternative measures are sufficient for the purpose of restoring competition.

Section 8-4(2) specifies eight items that the FTC must consider for the purpose of insuring that the remedial measures would be consistent with the smooth running of business and the preservation of the livelihoods of its employees.

(2) PROCEDURAL REQUIREMENTS

(A) When the FTC starts a formal investigation with respect to a monopolistic situation, the competent minister shall be notified of such facts, and thereafter, he can state his opinion as to whether there exists a monopolistic situation and whether there are any appropriate remedial measures available under his control (sec. 45-2).

For example, the competent minister may have the power to lower or abolish tariffs to lower entry barriers for foreign goods, or may have licensing power so that more entrepreneurs can get licenses. Whether these measures are sufficient to restore competition depends on the FTC's evaluation. This requirement is meant to give appropriate balance between antimonopoly policy and industrial policy or any other policy considerations by competent ministers.

(B) A public hearing must be held before issuing a complaint, and the FTC is not authorized to issue a recommendation with respect to a case involving a monopolistic situation. This means that the case must go through hearing proceedings (sec. 72-2).

(C) The competent minister shall be consulted before a complaint is issued by the FTC, and he can express his opinion concerning whether a complaint should be issued (sec. 49(4)).

(D) More than three members of the FTC must give their consent in order to issue a final order to the entrepreneurs concerned (sec. 55(3)). Under an ordinary situation, only two members' consent may constitute a majority when three members are present (sec. 55(2)).

(E) The FTC order cannot be enforced until it becomes final, and no administrative fine can be imposed on account of non-compliance while the case is pending in court (sec. 58(2)). An appeal to the Tokyo High Court can be filed within 3 months (sec. 77(1)). All of these are exceptions to the general rules, and mean that the FTC order may take effect only after all the available procedures are exhausted.

(D) ENFORCEMENT AND EVALUATION

Since enactment in 1977, no action has been initiated by the FTC under this provision. The FTC has regularly made public a new list of industries that satisfy the market structure test. Since 1985, service sectors have been included in the list (see table 12-1). The list of industries might be interesting to foreign observers as it would help them to learn in what business fields in Japan there exist truly oligopolistic industries.

The FTC has regularly conducted research on the listed industries, and has carefully watched to see whether their market performance requirement has been met. These efforts to subject highly concentrated industries to constant scrutiny by the FTC had some positive impact on their behaviors. The accumulation of data on highly oligopolistic industries by the FTC also provides a useful source of information for future analyses.

During the 1980s, antitrust thinking was influenced to some extent by the economic theory espoused by the U.S. Chicago school, and Japan was no exception.[1] So-called structural measures against monopoly were less emphasized and thought fruitless in view of the high administrative cost of achieving such measures. It is also argued that associated efficiency loss would outweigh any gain expected from the structural measures.

However, this does not mean that monopoly causes no welfare loss problems, or that such problems are negligible. In the meantime, it seems important for the FTC to keep to its current "watch and study" approach toward monopolistic situations.

NOTE

[1] R. BORK, ANTITRUST PARADOX (1978); R. POSNER, ANTITRUST LAWS: AN ECONOMIC PERSPECTIVE (1976)

In our opinion, the most positive aspects of such influence can be seen in the emphasis on cartel regulations, rather than the regulation based on the abuse principle. In view of the Chicago school's thoughts on cartel regulation, there is much room to improve in Japan in the way of proving the existence of cartel agreements among competitors.

13

PARALLEL PRICE INCREASES

Section 18-2 of the Antimonopoly Act is a controversial provision. It is directed at the so-called conscious parallelism problem. It is said that in an oligopolistic market structure, entrepreneurs can coordinate their conduct without specific communications. For some, this is only a problem of finding proof of a cartel agreement, therefore, it may be solved by relying more on circumstantial evidence.[1]

For others, proof is not a simple problem and new regulation is warranted. The FTC's enforcement experience demonstrated difficulty in finding cartel agreements in an oligopolistic market. The original idea was to give the FTC the power to make public the cost structure of oligopolistic entrepreneurs. By doing so, sound business decision making may be expected, in particular when price is going to be raised. But whether sound business decisions can be expected from such regulation is not clear, and whether parallel price increases justifiable by cost data are desirable is also unclear. The negative impact of such cost data disclosure is also feared.

As a compromise, a reporting system was adopted. Under section 18-2, the FTC is empowered to order the filing of a report describing the reasons for a price increase by major entrepreneurs in an oligopolistic industry.

(A) STRUCTURAL REQUIREMENTS

"The particular field of business" is defined by the following structural requirements (sec. 18-2(1)):

(A)   The aggregated total amount of prices of goods or services of the same description supplied within Japan is in excess of 30 billion yen;

(B)   The aggregated market share of the top three entrepreneurs is in excess of 70 percent.

As is the case for monopolistic situations, those goods that are exported, and the amount of tax levied directly on such goods or services are excluded. Those goods that are imported are included in the aggregated total amount of prices. Market share is calculated in terms of supply volume and, in principle, the quantity data are used for the purpose of such calculations. But if such data are not appropriate, price data can be used to calculate the market share.

The 1-year period during which structural requirements are measured is different from that used for monopolistic situations. Cabinet Ordinance No. 317 of 1977 designated that the latest calendar year data should be used for which these structural requirements could be identified by government statistics or any other equivalent data (sec. 11). Therefore, the 1-year period is always expressed on a calendar year basis.

The "same goods" means a group of goods that have the same function and utility. In the manufacturing sector, a six-digit classification under the "Census of Manufacturing" is deemed, in principle, to constitute the same goods. In the case of services, a four-digit classification under the *Japan Standard Industrial Classification* is referred to in order to see the external limits of the same services.

(B) DEFINITION OF A PARALLEL PRICE INCREASE

A parallel price increase is defined as when two or more major entrepreneurs, including the largest, raise the prices they use as the base of their transactions by an identical or similar amount or percentage within a period of 3 months.

"Major entrepreneurs" mean any one of the top five entrepreneurs whose market share exceeds 5 percent. "The price they use as the base of their transactions" refers to the so-called quoted prices, suggested wholesale or retail prices, or list prices that are usually made known to customers or to the public.

The 3-month period starts from the date when a new price is applied in an actual transaction for the first time. This means that the time when the price increase is decided or announced, or when the new price is made public or is notified to their customers, does not start the 3-month period. Nor rebate provided to offset a price increase does start the 3-month period.

If the largest entrepreneur's price hike is not followed by other major entrepreneurs, it is not considered a parallel price increase. The law assumes that, if an actual price increase by the largest firm did take place, and the other major entrepreneurs raised their prices 3 months later (the vice versa case is also true), this would cause customers of the largest firm to change their suppliers, thus restoring price competition.

"Similar amount or percentage" means that the price difference with the largest firm is so small that the price increase can be regarded as a parallel one. The FTC will use the following formula for this purpose, and when it is 10 percent or less, the price increase will be considered similar.

$$\frac{(\text{Largest entrepreneur's price increase}) - (\text{other major entrepreneur's price increase})}{(\text{Largest entrepreneur's price increase})}$$

As to differentiated goods, a more than 10 percent, possibly a 30 percent or less difference could be regarded as a similar amount or percentage.

(C) EXEMPTIONS

There are two exemptions to the reporting obligation.

Those entrepreneurs whose price of goods or services are approved or authorized by, or registered with the competent ministers having jurisdiction over such businesses, are excluded from the reporting requirement. As to the registered price, exempted status is given only when the competent minister has the legal authority to order the entrepreneur concerned to change the registered price.

When the reason for the price increase is objectively clear to the public, the FTC will not ask that a report be filed. One example is when a tax is raised and the price of goods or services is raised by the amount exactly equivalent to the amount of the tax increase.

(D) ENFORCEMENT AND EVALUATION

In November 1977, the FTC issued a policy statement interpreting and making clear the important terms of section 18-2. Fifty-six items were revealed for which the FTC found that the structural requirements were satisfied. By announcing this list, the FTC made clear that it will regularly watch price increases of those listed and only those listed. In other words, new items would be subject to the reporting obligation only after their names appeared on the list. The FTC will revise the list every two years based on newly collected data.

When it has ordered relevant entrepreneurs to file a report, the FTC must outline the reported facts in its annual report (sec. 44(1)).

As of July 1991, the revised list was composed of 84 items (see table 13-1). The first year of enforcement, namely FY 1978, reports were filed with respect to motorcycles and prepared powdered milk. For FY 1979, reports were filed as to automobiles, sheet glass, tires and tubes for motor vehicles, synthetic detergent for kitchenware, and instant coffee.

Due to the strong upward pressures on price after the second oil shock, FY 1980 was a record year for number of reports filed. The FTC had asked for the filing of reports as to 20 items: photographic color film, photographic paper, beer, whisky, sheet piles, hot rolled wide steel sheet and plate, hot rolled hoop, cold rolled silicon steel sheet and plate, cold rolled wide steel sheet and plate, high tensile steel, tin plate, bearing steel, prepared powdered milk, tires and tubes for motor vehicles, synthetic detergent for kitchenware, electric welding rod, fish meat sausage, tractors used in construction, glass bulbs for cathode-ray tubes, tin cans, and cast iron pipe and tubes.

In contrast, in FY 1981, only automobiles and six steel related products and in FY 1982, butter, were asked to file reports. Thereafter, there was a period of price stability in Japan and very few parallel price increases were observed. Electric welding rod, beer and whisky in FY 1983, photographic color film, automobiles

Table 13-1. Items Satisfying Market Structure Requirements Under Section 18-2*

1	Prepared milk powder	43	Shutters
2	Fish meat sausage	44	Turbines
3	Sodium glutamate	45	Rice transplanters
4	Mayonnaise & dressing	46	Combines harvesters-threshers
5	Chewing gum	47	Cranes for construction
6	Beer	48	Excavators
7	Whisky	49	Tractors for agriculture
8	Instant coffee	50	Tractors for construction
9	Sanitary goods	51	Numerically controlled cutting
10	Baby diapers		machines using electric charging
11	Daily newspapers	52	Rolling machines
12	Metaclyric resins	53	Compressors
13	Synthetic detergent for laundry	54	Electronic calculating machines
14	Synthetic detergent for kitchenware		(table type)
15	Softeners	55	Coping machines
16	Dentifrices	56	Sewing machines (Heads)
17	Monochrome photographic film	57	Bearings
	(X-ray film)	58	High voltage crossing gates
18	Photographic color film	59	Charging generators
	(excluding instant color film)	60	Starting engines
19	Photographic paper	61	Ventilators
20	Tires & tubes for motor vehicles	62	Electric fluorescent lamps
21	Rubber transmission belts	63	Electric fluorescents
22	Polished sheet glass	64	Automatic telephone switchboards &
23	Laminated glass		exchanges
24	Toughened glass	65	Pushbutton telephones
25	Glass bulbs for cathode-ray tubes	66	Transmission equipment
26	Optical fiber	67	Headphone stereos
27	Lightweight aerated concrete	68	Magnetic tape for recording
28	Sanitary wares	69	Communication control systems
29	Plaster board	70	X-ray equipment for medical purposes
30	Steel sheet pile	71	Video disk players
31	Cold rolled silicon steel	72	Cathode-ray tubes for TVs
32	Piping steel pipe & tubes	73	Dry cells
33	Tool steel	74	Ordinary/Compact passengers cars
34	Spring steel	75	Sub-compact passenger cars
35	Bearing steel	76	Bus or truck chassis
36	High tensile steel	77	Motorcyles
37	Tin plate	78	Forklift trucks
38	Cast iron pipes & tubes	79	Table clocks
39	Tin cans (including aluminium cans)	80	Pianos
40	Kitchen gas ranges	81	Toothbrushes
41	Aluminum saches	82	Thermos-bottles
42	Electric welding rods	83	Elevator maintenance contracts

NOTE:
* These lists were compiled from the data as of FY 1988 and were published in Aug. 1991.

and coking coal in FY 1984, instant coffee, mayonnaise and dressing, and cast iron pipe and tube in FY 1985, and daily newspapers in FY 1986.

After 10 years' enforcement, merely asking the reason for a price increase seemed to have lost its original impact on the behavior of oligopolistic firms. Evaluation found that section 18-2 had some influence on making oligopolistic firms cautious about their pricing behavior, and price increases by those companies in the listed industries were less frequent. It is difficult to quantify the effect of section 18-2, but it may be evaluated by looking at the low level of price increases for the listed industries as compared with those of the general price level.

In 1989, parallel price increases by beer brewery companies and daily newspaper publishers were observed, and impressed the public with the fact that oligopolistic firms had the power to raise prices with great ease. The subscription prices for national newspapers were raised twice simultaneously in the same amount within 2 months. In the case of beer, the suggested retail price was observed by virtually every retailer, partially because they needed a license to sell liquor, including beer. A newspaper's retail price can be maintained due to its exempted status under section 24-2 of the Act.

In order to encourage price competition, the FTC had asked four beer brewery companies to inform or make it clear to retailers that their suggested retail price was not binding, and each retailer was free to set his own retail price. This is a new development and shows that this provision could provide the FTC with some power to increase competition in oligopolistic industries.

NOTE

[1] Recent cases suggest that cartels can exist among very few competitors in a market, or with a single company occupying more than half of the market share. The 1991 Duskin Co. case, Oct. 18, 1991, 38 KTIS 104; the 1991 Shizuoka Hino Motor Co. case, Oct. 18, 1991, 38 KTIS 110.

PART III

Enforcement and Procedures

14

FTC ORGANIZATION

(A) THE STRUCTURE OF THE FTC

The FTC was created as an independent administrative agency to implement the Antimonopoly Act (sec. 27(1)). Administratively, the FTC belongs under the jurisdiction of the Prime Minister (sec. 27(2)), and was established as an extra-ministerial agency attached to the Prime Minister's Office under article 3 of the National Administration Organization Act (Act No. 120 of 1948).

The Chairman and Commissioners perform their duties independently (sec. 29). In order to assure their independent decision making, section 31 of the Act guarantees the Chairman and Commissioners' independent status.

The Chairman and Commissioners are appointed by the Prime Minister with the consent of both Houses of the Diet and are chosen from among individuals who are considered experts in law and economics (sec. 29(2)). The appointment or dismissal of the Chairman is attested by the Emperor (sec. 29(3)). The terms of office for the Chairman and Commissioners are 5 years (sec. 30(1)), and they must be at least 35 years of age at the time of their appointments (sec. 29(2)). Retirement at the age of 65 is compulsory (sec. 30(3)).

The majority of the past Chairmen have been appointed from among ex-officials of the Ministry of Finance (MOF). The four immediate past Chairmen were ex-officials of MOF. Commissioners are appointed mostly from among ex-officials of MITI, the Ministry of Judiciary, and MOF. Most of them served as a director-general of some bureau of these ministries, or held equivalent positions. Sometimes they are appointed from among ex-officials of the Staff Office of the FTC, the Ministry of Foreign Affairs, or the Bank of Japan. These appointment decisions are made by the Cabinet Secretariat, and tend to reflect a careful balance among relevant ministries and agencies in Japan.[1]

(B) THE STAFF OFFICE

The Staff Office executes the FTC's day-to-day operation. Technically, the FTC refers to a meeting of the Chairman and Commissioners, but it usually means the FTC and its Staff Office combined. As of FY 1992, the number of personnel in the Staff Office was fixed at 484. The organization of the FTC is shown in figure 14-1.

In 1947 the Staff Office began with 323 people but soon after the end of the Occupation, the number was reduced to 237. The staff began to increase after 1963, and it has constantly increased to the present level.

The Staff Office took its present form in 1953 when the Secretariat and two bureaus were established. In 1953, the Staff Office began with 10 divisions, and it expanded to 17 divisions as of FY 1992. By looking at what organizations were added within the Staff Office, one may come to understand how the Staff Office expanded.

The newly created divisions were the Subcontract Division in 1957, the International Transaction Division in 1960 (this division was eliminated in 1992 in view of its reduced responsibility), and the Trade Practices Division in 1961. Then, in 1966, the 4th Investigation Division and the Premium and Representation Division (in 1972 this division was divided into the Guidance Division and the Inspection Division) were added. In 1968 the Planning Division was added, and the last addition was the 5th Investigation Division, which was added in 1990.

The FY 1990 budget expanded the investigation staff by 20 percent—from 129 to 154. These numbers include investigation staff at regional offices. The FY 1992 budget further increased the

Figure 14-1. — Organization of the Fair Trade Commission
(As of Dec. 31, 1992)

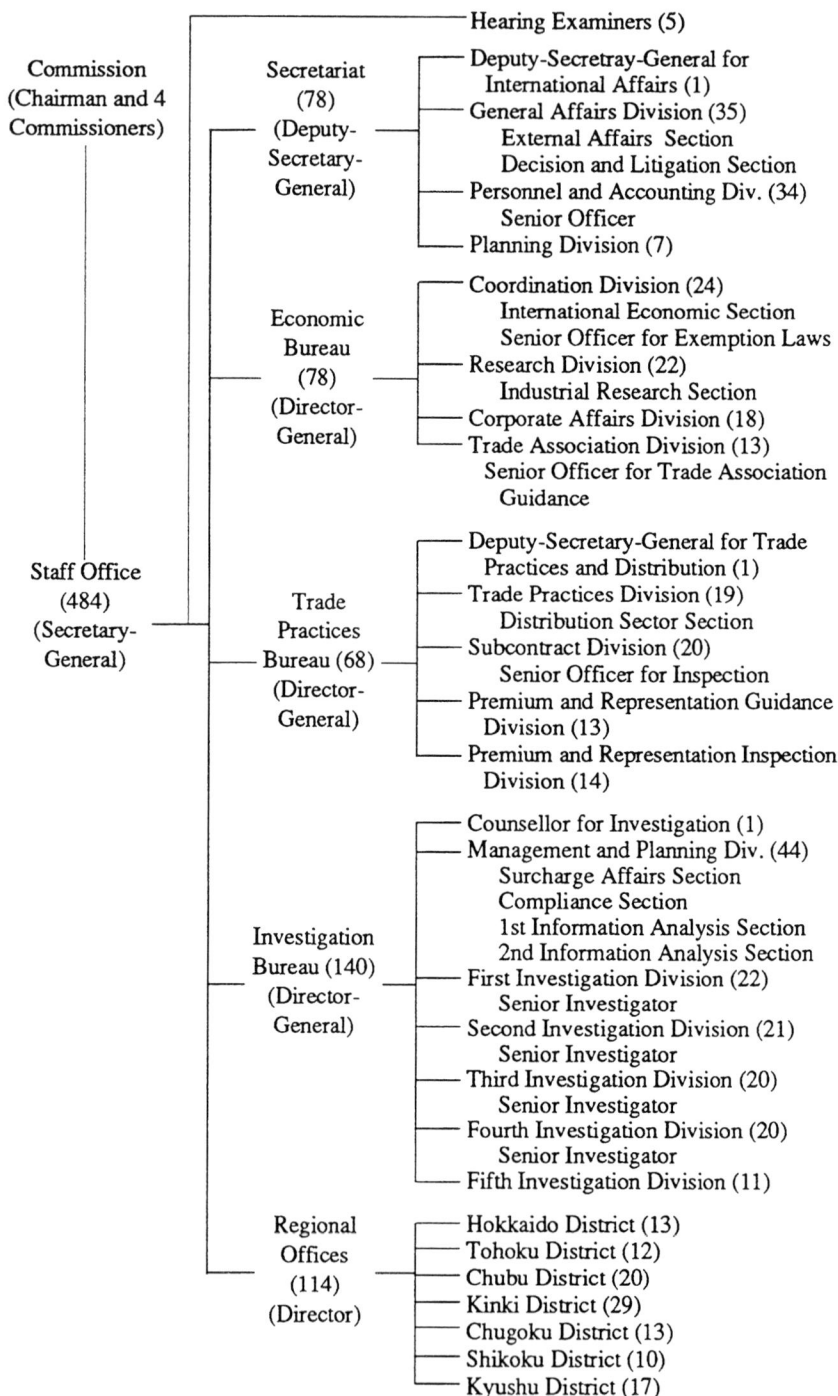

```
                                                    ┌─ Hearing Examiners (5)
                                                    │
Commission              Secretariat                 ├─ Deputy-Secretray-General for
(Chairman and 4          (78)                        │   International Affairs (1)
 Commissioners)                                      ├─ General Affairs Division (35)
                        (Deputy-                     │    External Affairs Section
                        Secretary-                   │    Decision and Litigation Section
                        General)                     ├─ Personnel and Accounting Div. (34)
                                                     │    Senior Officer
                                                     └─ Planning Division (7)

                                                    ┌─ Coordination Division (24)
                                                    │    International Economic Section
                        Economic                    │    Senior Officer for Exemption Laws
                        Bureau                       ├─ Research Division (22)
                        (78)                         │    Industrial Research Section
                        (Director-                   ├─ Corporate Affairs Division (18)
                        General)                     └─ Trade Association Division (13)
                                                         Senior Officer for Trade Association
                                                         Guidance

Staff Office                                        ┌─ Deputy-Secretary-General for Trade
(484)                                               │   Practices and Distribution (1)
(Secretary-             Trade                        ├─ Trade Practices Division (19)
General)                Practices                    │    Distribution Sector Section
                        Bureau (68)                  ├─ Subcontract Division (20)
                        (Director-                   │    Senior Officer for Inspection
                        General)                     ├─ Premium and Representation Guidance
                                                     │   Division (13)
                                                     └─ Premium and Representation Inspection
                                                         Division (14)

                                                    ┌─ Counsellor for Investigation (1)
                                                    ├─ Management and Planning Div. (44)
                                                    │    Surcharge Affairs Section
                                                    │    Compliance Section
                        Investigation               │    1st Information Analysis Section
                        Bureau (140)                │    2nd Information Analysis Section
                        (Director-                  ├─ First Investigation Division (22)
                        General)                    │    Senior Investigator
                                                    ├─ Second Investigation Division (21)
                                                    │    Senior Investigator
                                                    ├─ Third Investigation Division (20)
                                                    │    Senior Investigator
                                                    ├─ Fourth Investigation Division (20)
                                                    │    Senior Investigator
                                                    └─ Fifth Investigation Division (11)

                        Regional                    ┌─ Hokkaido District (13)
                        Offices                      ├─ Tohoku District (12)
                        (114)                        ├─ Chubu District (20)
                        (Director)                   ├─ Kinki District (29)
                                                     ├─ Chugoku District (13)
                                                     ├─ Shikoku District (10)
                                                     └─ Kyushu District (17)
```

NOTE: The number of fixed personnel allocated to each bureau, division, and regional office is shown in parentheses.

Investigation Bureau, and the Management and Planning Division was created in order to coordinate all the investigation activities. Now, under the Division's coordination, five Divisional Directors and four senior investigators are conducting investigations of cases by supervising investigators in charge of each case. As a whole, the number of investigators was expanded by 40 percent within 3 years (see Final Report of SII, appendix I).

These measures were prompted by the SII talks. The guidance or preventive approach had been working well in so far as educating Japanese business, but on the other hand, it also had the problem of lacking deterring effects. Through the SII talks, the FTC started to emphasize law enforcement activities by taking more remedial measures (chapter 4 (B) Structural Impediments Initiative).

The head of the Staff Office is a secretary-general, and he functions as a chief-of-staff. He clears every matter that goes up to the Commission, and coordinates matters between the Commission and the Staff Office.

Each bureau is headed by a director-general, and assisted by a division chief called a director. A Cabinet Ordinance (Cabinet Ordinance No. 373 of 1952) stipulates each division's function and responsibility, and a director is responsible for the function assigned by the Cabinet Ordinance.

The Investigation Bureau is exclusively delegated the power to utilize the compulsory investigatory power provided by section 46 of the Act (see chapter 2 (A)(2) Compulsory Power for Investigation).

When necessary, upon Commission authorization, the other two bureaus can use the general research power provided under section 40 of the Act. In order to initiate a case, other bureaus must transfer the matter to the Investigation Bureau.

As shown above, the Staff Office is expanding its staff each year. In Japan, the Act Concerning Total Number of Government Employees (Act No. 33 of 1969) set an absolute ceiling on the total number of government employees at 509,508. Within this limit, and in view of new societal needs, the Ministry of General Affairs tries each year to re-allocate the number of personnel among each government agency.[7] But because the total number is fixed, those agencies that need quick expansion are at a disadvantage. Therefore, it should be remembered that in Japan an increase in an agency's personnel takes quite some time.

In Japan, each agency recruits personnel who, in principle, stay in the same agency up to their retirement. And each agency maintains an exchange program called *shukko*, or dispatch of personnel in order to introduce flexibility into its recruiting method.[3] The FTC relies heavily on these dispatched personnel because it is difficult to recruit personnel in proportion to its expansion. Many personnel were transferred from such agencies as the Prime Minister's Office, MOF, MITI, the Public Prosecutor's Office, the Ministry of Agriculture, Forestry and Fishery, and the Economic Planning Agency.

(C) POWERS

As an independent administrative agency, the FTC has the power to exercise quasi-legislative and quasi-judicial powers, in addition to its administrative power to take remedial measures.

As an administrative agency, the FTC has the power to conduct investigations with respect to a case, to render a recommendation or to issue a complaint and start hearing proceedings, and has the power to render a formal decision. It has a duty to receive various reports required to be filed with it (see Chapter 20 Reporting Requirements), to authorize depression cartels or rationalization cartels upon a petition by related entrepreneurs (see chapter 2 (E) Depression Cartels and Rationalization Cartels), to authorize exceptional stockholdings in excess of 5 percent by a financial company or to authorize stockholdings by a giant company under section 9-2(6). When required under the Act, it will consult with other ministers (secs. 9-2(5), 11(3) etc.).

As a quasi-legislative power, the FTC has a rule-making power to designate commodities for which resale price maintenance is permissible (sec. 24-2) and to designate unfair trade practices (sec. 2(9)). It can also establish the procedures for handling cases and for hearing proceedings (sec. 76). It determines the form of reports to be filed with it and any necessary attachments thereto.

As a quasi-judicial power, the FTC will issue a decision after hearing proceedings. An appeal to an FTC decision goes directly and exclusively to the Tokyo High Court. This is very exceptional in Japanese jurisprudence and reflects the importance attached to the expertise of the FTC on antimonopoly matters.

The FTC also has the power to accuse individuals and corporations who are involved in antimonopoly violations and to pass the cases along to the Public Prosecutor's Office for indictment. Without the FTC accusation, no criminal proceeding against antimonopoly violations can be initiated.

The FTC is required to submit an annual report to the Diet (sec. 44).

NOTES

[1] This idea can be found in many fields. The most typical one is in the way of choosing the Justices of the Supreme Court.

[2] The Ministry of General Affairs establishes a 3-to-5-year plan for personnel cutbacks and imposes a mandatory quota on each agency each year. Each agency then places a request for a personnel increase to the Ministry by showing increasing demand for the work to be done by the agency. Under this scheme the Ministry can allocate personnel that were to be cut back to such an agency.

[3] This exchange program is commonly utilized among the central government offices. Sometimes, exchanges of personnel are negotiated among rival agencies such as MITI and the FTC. In addition, this exchange program is used as a training program to broaden staff experience.

15

FTC INVESTIGATORY AND REMEDIAL POWERS

(A) INVESTIGATORY POWERS

(1) INITIATION OF AN INVESTIGATION

Any person may request that the FTC institute an investigation as to any suspected acts in violation of the Antimonopoly Act and ask for necessary measures to be taken (sec. 45(1)). The FTC can initiate an investigation upon its own authority as a result of its research of available information or reports filed under the provisions of the Act (sec. 45(4)).

The Prosecutor General may notify the FTC of a suspected violation of the Act and may request an investigation and a report thereof (sec. 74). The Small and Medium Business Agency has a similar power to refer cases to the FTC and request appropriate measures when it finds that business activities of small and medium businesses are disrupted as a result of undue restraints of trade or unfair trade practices by other entrepreneurs. These powers have never been utilized and the FTC has reacted to its own information sources.

Upon receipt of information as to the existence of a violation of the Act, the Investigation Bureau (Information Analysis Section) conducts a preliminary investigation without relying on compulsory investigatory powers. When the existence of suspicious acts violative of any provisions of the Act are established, the matter is referred to the Commission, and the Commission decides whether the matter should be investigated formally. At this stage, the matter gets a formal docket number, and the Commission authorizes inves-

**Figure 15-1. Flow Chart of the FTC Procedures
(Section Numbers Appear in Brackets)**

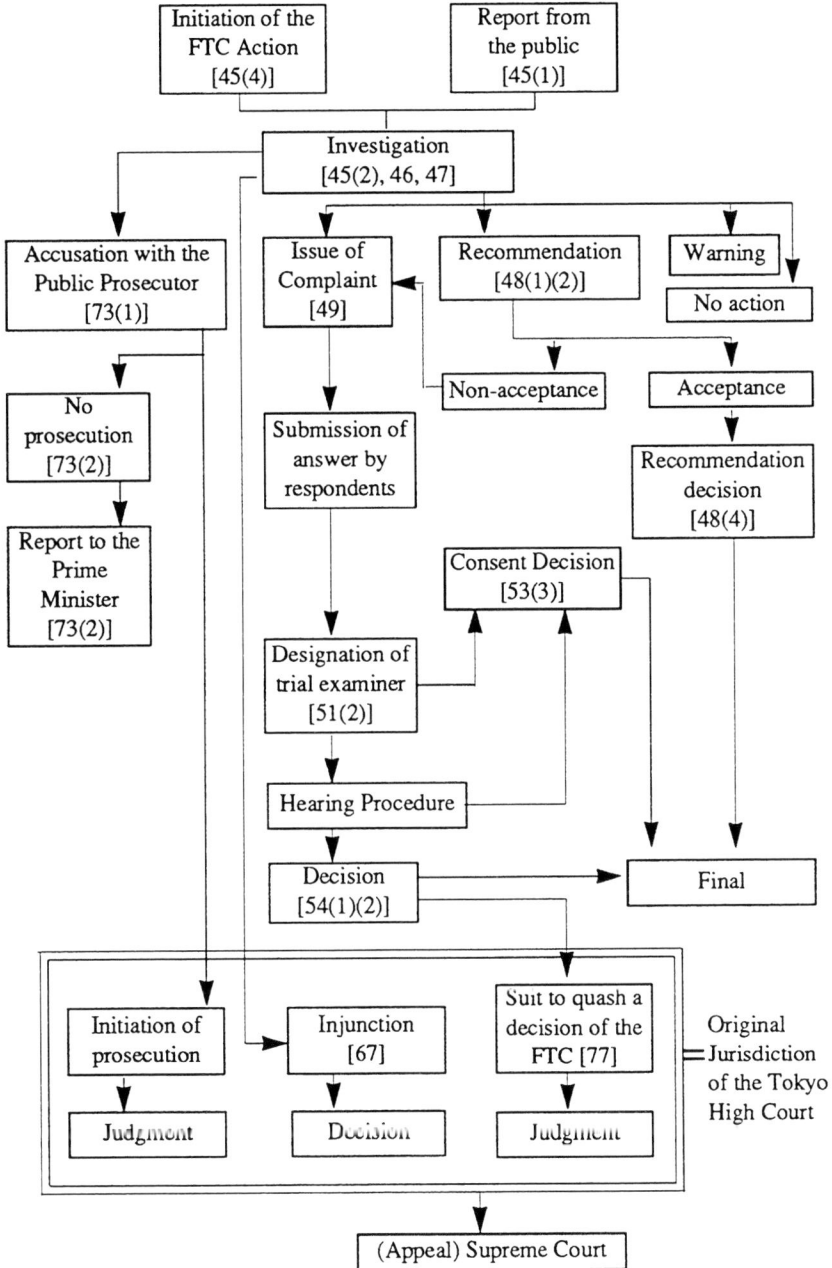

tigators designated with respect to a case among the Investigation Bureau's senior staff to exercise their power under section 46 of the Act (sec. 46(2)).

(2) COMPULSORY POWER FOR INVESTIGATION

The FTC is empowered to take the following measures to conduct the necessary investigation of a case (sec. 46[1]):

(A)   To order persons involved in a case or any other relevant persons to appear at a designated time and place to testify or to produce documentary evidence;

(B)   To order experts to appear and to give expert testimony;

(C)   To order persons holding account books, documents and other materials to submit them, and to retain such submitted materials;

(D)   To enter any place of business of persons involved in a case and other necessary places and to inspect the conditions of business operation and property, account books, documents and other materials.

This power is not self-enforcing and in the case of intentional non-compliance (sec. 94), any person who refuses, obstructs or evades the inspection described in (D) above can be punished by penal servitude and/or a fine. In the case of (A), (B), and (C), a fine could be imposed (sec. 94-2).

It is the investigators assigned to each case who exercise these investigatory powers (sec. 46(2)). The most important power of the investigators is to enter into places of business and to inspect documents and other materials (D). This is done without any advance notice to the person concerned, and has proven to be an effective way to collect evidence for a case. When investigators order persons to submit the documents and other materials that are found at the spot of investigation, they can retain the submitted materials (C).

Based on this submitted material, investigators order or ask persons involved in a case to testify (A). Normally, testimony is given on a voluntary basis, but when necessary, compulsory testimony may be ordered. In almost all cases, investigators will order the respondents and other related persons to file a report by answering and providing necessary information to the questionnaires prepared by the investigators (A).

The investigators, after they have conducted an appropriate investigation of a case, keep a record of the main points thereof (sec. 47).

This document is called an investigation record (*chosho*), and will be used as evidence at hearing proceedings or court proceedings.

A person involved in a case may file with the FTC an objection to an order issued by investigators within 1 week from the day of the receipt of such order (section 17-2 of FTC Regulation No. 5 of 1953).

When a report submitted by a person specifies in writing any fact, and when the FTC decides to take or not to take measures with respect to the matter referred to in the report, the FTC must promptly notify the person of the measures taken by it (sec. 45(3)).

(B) DISPOSITION OF CASES

(1) TRENDS OF FTC DECISIONS

Table 15-1 shows the number of cases disposed of by the FTC by applicable provision. The number of cases disposed of may roughly-

Table 15-1. Classification of FTC Decisions by Applicable Provisions

FY	Sections							No[6]	PRA[7]	Sum Total	Net Total[8]
	3F[4]	3L[5]	6	8[9]	10~17	19[9]	Others				
1947	2	4	0	—	0	0	4[1]	0	0	10	5
1948	0	2	0	—	0	0	1[1]	0	0	3	2
1949	0	5	1	—	1	2	13[1]	0	0	22	14
1950	1	25	21	—	20	20	29[1]	3	0	119	59
1951	0	4	0	—	5	1	17[1]	0	0	27	18
1952	0	5	0	—	0	4	13[1]	8	0	30	15
1953	0	1	1	4	0	3	5[1]	2	0	16	12
1954	0	0	0	1	0	2	0	3	0	6	5
1955	1	5	0	2	0	3	0	1	0	12	11
1956	1	1	0	2	1	2	0	0	0	7	6
1957	0	2	0	4	0	1	0	0	0	7	7
1958	0	0	0	2	0	0	0	0	0	2	2
1959	0	0	0	1	0	1	0	0	0	2	2
1960	0	0	0	1	0	0	0	0	0	1	1
1961	0	0	0	2	1	0	0	0	0	3	3
1962	0	0	0	10	0	2	0	1	0	13	13
1963	0	2	0	25	0	9	0	0	0	36	36
1964	0	9	0	20	0	1	0	0	0	30	30
1965	0	1	0	22	0	3	0	2	0	28	27
1966	0	0	0	15	0	2	0	0	0	17	17
1967	0	2	0	6	0	5	0	0	0	13	12
1968	0	6	0	22	0	3	0	0	0	31	31

Table 15-1. (cont.) — Sections

FY	3F[4]	3L[5]	6	8[9]	10~17	19[9]	Others	No[6]	PRA[7]	Sum Total	Net Total[8]
1969	0	3	1	24	1	1	0	0	2	32	32
1970	0	3	0	40	0	1	0	0	0	44	44
1971	0	3	0	34	0	0	0	0	0	37	37
1972	1	10	6	11	0	2	0	0	4	34	34
1973	0	35	0	33	2	0	0	0	0	70	69
1974	0	31	0	11	0	1	15[3]	0	2	60	60
1975	0	12	0	10	0	5	7[2]	0	1	35	34
1976	0	14	0	6	0	4	0	0	1	25	25
1977	0	2	0	9	0	6	0	0	1	18	18
1978	0	1	0	2	0	4	0	0	1	8	8
1979	0	3	0	10	0	4	0	0	0	17	15
1980	0	4	0	8	0	3	0	0	1	16	16
1981	0	6	0	4	0	3	0	0	0	13	13
1982	0	5	0	7	0	7	0	0	1	20	20
1983	0	5	0	2	0	4	1[3]	0	0	12	12
1984	0	4	0	5	0	0	0	0	0	9	9
1985	0	1	0	3	0	7	6[3]	0	0	17	17
1986	0	3	0	1	0	0	0	0	1	5	5
1987	0	0	0	5	0	1	0	0	0	6	6
1988	0	5	0	0	0	1	0	0	0	6	6
1989	0	4	0	3	0	3	0	0	0	10	10
1990	0	4	0	7	0	6	0	0	0	17	17
1991	0	12	0	6	1	9	0	0	1	29	29
1992	0	23	0	11	0	4	0	0	0	38	38
Total	6	267	30	391	32	140	111 (29)	21 (11)	16	1013	902

NOTES:

[1] Shows violations of the provisions that were repealed, namely, sections 4, 5 and The Trade Association Act. When these cases are excluded, "others" consists of 29 cases as is shown in parentheses.

[2] Shows 7 FTC decisions ordering surcharge payments after hearing proceedings under section 7-2.

[3] Shows 9 FTC decisions to terminate the authorized rationalization cartels under section 65 of the Act, and 13 decisions to exclude large-scale entrepreneurs from cooperatives under section 107 of the Small and Medium Enterprise Cooperative Act.

[4] 3F means a violation of the former part of section 3.

[5] 3L means a violation of the latter part of section 3.

[6] "No" shows FTC decisions where no violations were found and declared so in the decision. Some of them found no violation on two counts, therefore, net figures are 11 as a whole as shown in parentheses.

[7] "PRA" shows violations of the Act Against Unjustifiable Premiums and Misleading Representations (Act No. 134 of 1962).

[8] In the early period, the FTC applied various related provisions to a single case, therefore, the sum total and net total differ greatly in these years. But such duplicative application of various provisions became rare in recent years.

[9] For the breakdown of sections 8 and 19 cases, see tables 8-1, 8-2, 8-3 and 9-1.

correspond to the density of the FTC's enforcement activities. In the first 2 to 3 years we see few cases because the war-impoverished economy had been placed under direct government control. Then as decontrol of the economy progressed, the case numbers increased rapidly.

The latter half of the 1950s was the low point in FTC enforcement activities, as shown in part I (chapter 2 (A) Amendments to Weaken the Antimonopoly Act). In the 1960s the FTC relied on section 8(1)(i), which had some advantage in proving the facts of a violation.[2] Most cartel agreements were formed at trade association meetings, and used to be easier to prove at that time. Section 8(1)(i) cases do not disclose individual entrepreneurs' names, therefore, as compared to section 3 cases, it met with less resistance from business circles. Since around 1970, section 8(1)(i) cases and section 3 (the latter half of 1970) cases became more balanced. The FTC relied on section 3 cases increasingly by improving the methodology of proving cartels. During the 1960s and 1970s, most section 19 cases were related to resale price maintenance (see table 8-1).

Enforcement activities by the FTC reached their peak in 1973 and 1974 during the oil crisis when many trade associations and companies resorted to cartels in order to shift the increased cost of energy to downstream industries or consumers. Since 1977 when surcharge power was given to the FTC, the number of cases has dropped sharply. Business seemed to react to the enhancement of sanctions against cartels by being cautious about not leaving outright evidence.

For example, instructions not to produce any memos or to destroy related papers with respect to meetings among competitors were sometimes found in the course of an FTC investigation. In the Oil Cartel Price-Fixing case, a sign of a "bird" was stamped on important documents to warn each participant about the FTC investigation.[3] Increased sanctions also prompted related entrepreneurs not to accept easily the recommendations of the FTC. Thus, after the 1977 Amendment, contrary to its summary nature, the FTC must clear higher levels of proof before issuing a recommendation.[4]

After the 1977 Amendment, it became hard to make as many cases as were made in the pre-1977 period. Cases where hard evidence of cartels can be seized became rare, and less cooperation with the FTC investigation can be expected from the related entrepreneurs due to increased sanctions. This would increase the burden of proof for the FTC to make as many cases as possible. The FTC has been coping with this difficulty by increasing the number of investigators and by improving their investigation capabilities.

(2) INFORMAL ENFORCEMENT

Tables 15-2, 15-3, and 15-4 show how cases are disposed of by the FTC. They show that the workload has been very heavy as a whole but relatively few cases have been disposed of under formal procedures. A "warning" is a kind of administrative guidance that is used as a substitute to a formal order by the FTC. It is used when:

(A) The facts of a violation cannot be proved to warrant ordering formal remedial measures, but there remains suspicion of a violation in view of the collected evidence;

(B) The illegal conduct was voluntarily discontinued more than 1 year before, and no remedial measures can be ordered under sec. 7-2(2);

(C) The trade association concerned was dissolved voluntarily in case of section 8(1)(i) violations;

(D) The impact of illegal conduct are so limited that informal solutions might be sufficient.

Table 15-2. Disposition of Cases by the FTC 1970-1977

FY	1970	1971	1972	1973	1974	1975	1976	1977
Total cases disposed of	*143*	*116*	*87*	*119*	*128*	*94*	*103*	*101*
Recommendations	44	37	30	66	58	30	31	10
Complaints	(3)[1]	(2)	(1)	(2)	(4)	1(3)	(2)	(4)
Indictments	1	0	0	(2)	0	0	0	0
Voluntary acts of discontinuance[2]	75	57	48	47	55	52	63	78
No evidence	23	22	9	6	15	11	9	13

NOTES:

[1] ( ) shows number of complaints or indictments issued among those recommendation cases, therefore, it is excluded from the total number in order to avoid duplication.

[2] Voluntary acts of discontinuance cases also include those cases where no violation was found.

SOURCE: Compiled from the FTC Annual Reports.

Table 15-3. Disposition of Cases by the FTC 1978-1986

FY	1978	1979	1980	1981	1982	1983	1984	1985	1986
Total cases disposed of	37	41	67	146	297	233	204	168	148
Recommendations	6	16	14	11	19	10	7	10	4
						(11)[2]	(6)	(10)	(8)
Complaints	(1)[1]	1(2)	(2)	(2)	0	0	1	0	0
Indictments	0	0	0	0	0	0	0	0	0
Surcharge orders	(1)	2(3)	1(11)	(6)	(8)	(10)	(2)	(4)	(4)
Warning cases	26	22	39	91	151	118	94	80	88
Caution cases	N.A.	N.A.	N.A.	N.A.	49	60	66	62	37
No violation[3]	5	0	13	44	78	45	36	16	19

NOTES:

[1] ( ) shows number of complaints, indictments or surcharge orders issued among those recommendation cases, therefore, it is excluded from the total number in order to avoid duplication.

[2] Since FY 1983, recommendation means number of recommendation decisions, and number of recommendations issued during the fiscal year is shown in parentheses.

[3] Caution cases are included in this category before FY 1981.

SOURCE: Compiled from the FTC Annual Reports.

Table 15-4. Disposition of Cases by the FTC[1] 1987-1992

FY	1987	1988	1989	1990	1991	1992
Total cases disposed of	132	95	169	180	150	173
Recommendations	6	5	10	17	27	37
	(4)[2]	(6)	(7)	(22)	(30)	(34)
Complaints	0	0	(1)	2	2(1)	0
Indictments	0	0	0	0	(1)	(1)
Surcharge orders	(6)	(3)	(6)	(11)	(10)	(17)
Warning cases	84	65	115	60	24	21
Caution cases	28	17	28	85	88	73
No violation	14	8	16	16	9	42

NOTES:

[1] ( ) shows number of complaints, indictments or surcharge orders issued among those recommendation cases, therefore, it is excluded from the total number in order to avoid duplication.

[2] Recommendations mean number of recommendation decisions, and number of recommendations issued during the fiscal year is shown in parentheses.

SOURCE: Compiled from the FTC Annual Reports.

These informal methods of enforcement made it possible for the FTC to handle as many cases as possible with its limited personnel. Since FY 1978, the FTC Annual Report carries a number of warning cases; before FY 1978, it carried the number of cases where alleged conduct was voluntarily discontinued.

For various reasons, informal disposition has increased in Japan. Before 1977, it was interpreted that once the respondents discontinued the alleged conduct voluntarily, the FTC could not order any remedial measures.[5] Therefore, under such circumstances, informal dispositions tended to increase. It seems also true that when the FTC's policy objective for law enforcement was to stop the illegal conduct itself, not to punish the respondents, any formal order would not be necessary if the FTC could expect full compliance from the respondents. In the past, in order to secure less resistance to the antimonopoly policy from business circles, informal ways of enforcement were also preferable.

Because of the convenience attached to informal disposition, the practice had lasted until it met criticism from the U.S. government at the SII talks. Of course, this did not mean that in the past informal ways of enforcement were always emphasized or preferred by the FTC as a matter of policy. From time to time, there has been some difference in the emphasis placed on informal enforcement. There was also the problem of the lack of deterrent effect. By disposing of cases informally, many firms did not think seriously about the significance of Antimonopoly Act violations. Because informal disposition was not disclosed to the public, it also lacked the openness of the FTC enforcement activities.

The last report of SII said,

> The Fair Trade Commission (FTC) will strictly exclude, through resorting more to formal actions, activities violating the Antimonopoly Act . . . In order to ensure transparency, to enhance the deterrent effect and to prevent similar illegal activities from occurring, the contents, . . . , of all formal actions such as recommendations and surcharge payment orders will be made public. Warning will also be made public other than in exceptional cases. [See Appendix I.]

Informal ways of enforcement had the problem of lack of transparency. By making the FTC "warning" public, effectiveness of the warning as an informal way of enforcement would increase. It should be remembered that public announcement or disclosure has an aspect of effective remedy in such a country as Japan where bad publicity is of very serious concern to business.[6]

One of the related enforcement mechanisms is the use of a "caution" as an administrative tool. It is often used when facts of a violation cannot be proven after investigation, but when the parties engage in suspicious conduct that might lead to antimonopoly violations under certain circumstances. In these cases, the FTC will sometimes indicate to the parties that the alleged conduct would constitute a violation of the Act if such conduct were actually committed. The FTC would not engage in a detailed investigation of these cases and summarily dispose of them. This method has been used and could be used to enhance the understanding of the Act or to remind Japanese businessmen of the possibility of a violation of the Act.

(C) FTC DECISIONS

(1) FTC DECISION TO DROP A CASE

If, in the course of its investigation, the FTC finds that (A) there has been no violation of the Act, or (B) a violation cannot be proven to the extent warranting the issuing of a recommendation, the FTC will drop or close a case. The FTC's decision to drop a case is not appealable in court.

However, in the case of (B), the FTC may issue a "warning" or a "caution" as explained in the preceding section.

(2) RECOMMENDATIONS

When the FTC finds the existence of a violation of any substantive provisions of the Act, it may recommend that the respondents take appropriate remedial measures (secs. 48(1) or (2)). The respondents must notify the FTC within a designated period of time whether they accept the recommendation. The FTC usually allows 14 days for a trade association, and 10 days for an individual company. These answering periods can be extended upon a request from the respondents.

When the recommendation is accepted, the FTC issues a decision without resorting to an adjudicative procedure. This is called a recommendation decision.

In the 1975 Novo Industri Co. case (Nov. 28, 1975, 22 KTIS 260), the Supreme Court explained the nature of the FTC recommendation as follows:

> The recommendation system was established with the purpose of achieving the objectives of the Act summarily and promptly where the person alleged to violate the Act is freely willing to take recommended remedial measures. In such cases, there is no need to establish the existence of violations through adjudicative procedures and to order remedial measures. Therefore, on the one hand, a decision issued after an adjudicative procedure is based on the establishment of a violation through evidence; on the other hand, a recommendation decision is based on a person's willing acceptance of the recommendation.

The Supreme Court then ruled that the recommendation decision "did not establish the fact that the alleged conduct did violate the Act."

Recommendation decisions make up about 75 percent of all FTC decisions (see table 16-1). Most consent decisions were rendered during the 1949-1951 period and at that time consent decisions were issued without holding any hearing proceedings. Therefore, after the introduction of the recommendation system in 1953, the ratio between recommendation decisions and cases that went to adjudicative procedures is roughly 10 to 1.

The term "recommendation" may give the impression of informality, but this term is used to signify that a choice is given to the respondents to take remedial measures as recommended and thus to end the case summarily, or to resort to adjudicative procedures. Because rejection of the recommendation would start adjudicative proceedings, the FTC tends to make precise fact finding at the time of the recommendation.

(3) COMPLAINTS

When a person rejects a recommendation or fails to notify his response to the recommendation, the FTC may issue a complaint against the person and initiate an adjudicative procedure.

In cases where rejection of a recommendation is highly probable, the FTC may also issue a complaint without first issuing a recommendation. In the 1981 Komatsu-Bucyrus case (Nov. 26, 1981, 28 KTIS 79) and the 1975 Chubu Yomiuri Newspaper Co. case (April 30, 1975, 22 KTIS 301), the FTC issued complaints without first issuing a recommendation. However, it has become customary under normal conditions for the FTC to first issue a recommendation.

As indicated by the Supreme Court, the recommendation decision system was intended as a summary procedure (Novo Industri Co., Nov. 28, 1975, 22 KTIS 260). However, the FTC tries to fully establish the existence of a violation before issuing a recommendation. This may explain why so few cases go to adjudicative proceedings and a recommendation was accepted in most cases by the respondents.

(D) REMEDIAL POWERS AND INJUNCTIONS

(1) REMEDIAL POWERS

The Act authorizes the FTC to order the entrepreneur concerned to take remedial measures, such as "to file a report, or to cease and desist from such acts, to transfer a part of his business, or to take any other measures necessary to eliminate such acts in violation of the said provisions" (sec. 7(1)). As to trade association cases, "to dissolve the said association" is specifically mentioned in section 8-2(1), and as to part-IV violation cases, "to dispose of the whole or a part of his stocks," or "to resign from his position as an officer in a company," are illustrated specifically in section 17-2.

As to unfair trade practices cases, "to delete the clauses concerned from the contract" is illustrated specifically in section 20.

As to unreasonable restraint of trade, the FTC will order the respondents to eliminate the agreement or decision on price or on production etc., to notify each of their customers that the cartel agreement was terminated, and thereafter price or production would be decided individually by each entrepreneur; and to file a report with the FTC on actual remedial measures taken by the respondents. These notices would be delivered to each customer by mail, or when appropriate, newspaper advertisements are used to inform customers/consumers.

Sometimes, when it is deemed necessary, the FTC decision will order the respondents not to engage in similar conduct in future (non-repetition order). Such an order can be issued when future repetition might be plausible in view of the nature of the conduct or the respondents' behaviors.

When section 6 is violated, the FTC can take remedial measures against a Japanese party if no personal jurisdiction can be claimed on a foreign party. By such measures, a Japanese party cannot enforce any unlawful provisions, or unlawful activities cannot be effected within Japan, therefore, so far as the Japanese market is concerned, anticompetitive effects could effectively be eliminated (see Chapter 21 International Application of the Antimonopoly Act).

One of the characteristics of Japanese remedial measures is their uniformity, and similar remedial measures are ordered in almost every case. Flexible remedial measures like the U.S. courts' equity powers are not accepted in Japan.[7] So far as remedial measures on price raising cartels are concerned, they are not effective enough to restore price competition because the price usually remains at the same level even after these remedial measures are effected.

These remedial measures are ordered expecting long-term effect, so that competition would be restored in the industry concerned eventually. Those who favor a short-term effect insist that the FTC should take such remedial measures as to order the roll back of prices or at least renegotiation of prices that are raised through cartel agreements in order to restore price competition.

Whether remedial measures should aim at such a short-term effect on price, or at a long-term effect on price competition is debated among scholars.[8] Even if the FTC tried to take as wide a range of remedial measures as possible, remedial measures in themselves may not be sufficient to restore price competition. Therefore, such measures as surcharge orders or criminal penalties might be necessary to provide effective deterring effects on cartel prohibitions. So long as such effective sanctions are utilized, the necessity for flexible remedial powers does not seem strong.

As to unfair trade practices, cease and desist orders are common, and in most cases non-repetition orders are provided for in the decision.

(2) INJUNCTIONS

The FTC may apply to the Tokyo High Court asking that a person committing acts suspected of violating any one of the substantive provisions of the Act be temporarily ordered to stop the said acts (sec. 67). The FTC must make it clear to the Court that the act would gravely injure fair competition if left unchecked and that normal remedial measures after full investigation would come too late to effectively restore competition. However, the FTC does not need to prove the existence of a violation at this stage.

If the Court deems the matter to be one of urgent necessity, it may order the person suspected of committing an act in violation of the Act to temporarily cease and desist from the said act (sec. 67). For example, the Court may order someone not to exercise voting rights, not to execute his duties as an officer in a company, or not to proceed with a merger, etc.

The execution of the Court's order may be stayed by the respondent's depositing of such bond or security as the Court may fix (sec. 68), but the court has so far never permitted a stay of injunction petition.

The FTC has requested an injunction to the Tokyo High Court in six cases. The motion was granted in five cases, and in the 1969 Fuji-Yawata merger case (see chapter 10 (A)(2) Yawata-Fuji Merger case), the FTC withdrew its motion because the respondent voluntarily agreed not to proceed with the merger until the FTC made a decision on the merits of the case.

NOTES

[1] Traditionally, it is deemed that section 3 violations can be established when a liaison of wills can be found among all the cartel participants, whereas section 8(1)(i) violations could be established by merely showing a decision making by a trade association, therefore, by the force of the organization, the decision is binding on member firms.

[2] In chapter 4 (B)(3) Impact of Structural Impediments Initiative, we presented rather an optimistic view in this regard, namely, our observation that Japanese firms are changing. However, there is much evidences to make us pessimistic in this regard.

[3] Oil Cartel Price Fixing case of 1983, Tokyo High Court, Sep. 26, 1980, 28-2 KTIS 177. The abbreviated name for the FTC is *Kotori* which sounds like the name of bird in Japanese.

[4] The fact that surcharge orders must follow the acceptance of a recommendation makes it harder for the respondents to accept them easily. Therefore, the FTC must inevitably meet a higher level of proof in view of the higher possibility of formal hearing proceedings. Use of criminal penalties will also enhance this tendency.

[5] This finding depends on how to find facts of the discontinuance of cartel agreements. So far as the cartel agreement was revoked by participants a cease-and-desist order cannot be issued after its revocation.

[6] J. Haley, *Antitrust Sanctions and Remedies: A Comparative Study of German and Japanese Law,* WASHINGTON LAW REVIEW, Vol. 59 (1984), at 471. He argues, "In both the Federal Republic and Japan, publicity of violations appears to have been the most significant sanction imposed on the offender, and the most effective deterrent." at 505.

[7] Haley argues; "The concept of an equity power to fashion nonstatutory remedies in order to provide effective relief is alien to both German and Japanese notions of juridical and administrative power." *id.* at 474.

[8] Y. Tsuji, *Kakaku no Genjo Kaihuku Meirei no Touhi* (Pro-and-Con of Price Restoration Order to the Precartel Level), Vol. 10 Nos. 3 and 4, Kagawa Hogaku KAGAWA UNIV. LAW JOURNAL (1991), at 11.

16

FTC DECISIONS, HEARING PROCEEDINGS, AND APPEALS TO COURTS

(A) FTC DECISIONS

After hearing proceedings have started there are the following ways to terminate them:

(1) DECISION TO QUASH A COMPLAINT

In three cases the FTC has quashed the complaint for the following reasons:

(A) The violation had ceased to exist.
(B) Relevant provisions had been amended during the hearing proceedings.
(C) There had been illegal service of process.

As to (A), it was possible to render a formal decision, and the FTC did issue such a decision early on.

(2) DECISION TO DISCONTINUE HEARING PROCEEDINGS

The FTC has decided to discontinue hearing proceedings for the following reasons:

(A) Relevant provisions of the Act were eliminated during the hearing proceedings.

(B) The respondent had discontinued his business activities or the trade association was dissolved voluntarily.

(C) The FTC found a formal order unnecessary on the following grounds:

    (i) Violating acts in question were eliminated voluntarily by the respondents.

    (ii) Changes in the situations after the issuance of the complaint.

    (iii) Alleged conduct was no longer considered illegal (change in interpretation of law).

The FTC has decided to discontinue hearing proceedings in eight cases that came under (C). In most of these cases, the FTC decided to do so after the completion of hearing proceedings, or at the very last stage of the proceedings. The FTC could have issued a formal decision in these cases, and the appropriateness of such decisions were questioned because injured persons might be deprived of their rights for damage claims under section 25 of the Act (see chapter 17 (B) Damage Suits).

(3) CONSENT DECISIONS

After issuance of a complaint the respondent can submit a written statement in which he states that he admits the findings of fact and application of laws stated in the complaint and that he will accept a decision without resorting to further proceedings. He then files a plan describing the concrete measures he proposes to take for eliminating the violation. The FTC may render a consent decision if it considers that the respondent's proposal is acceptable (sec. 53-3). The respondent can do so during the pendency of the hearing proceedings, and he can even propose a consent decision in the answer he submits to the complaint served upon him (sec. 51 of the Act; FTC Regulation on Investigation, secs. 22 and 23).

In the 1969 Yawata Fuji Merger case (Oct. 30, 1969, 16 KTIS 46), the respondents submitted a motion for a consent decision after the final statement by investigators, but before the respondents' own final statement. In one case (Sanyo Electric Co., July 27, 1978, 25 KTIS 37), a motion for a consent decision was submitted after the respondent was served with a certified copy of an initial decision prepared by the hearing examiners. In both cases the FTC had accepted such motions and issued consent decisions.

(4) FORMAL DECISIONS

After the completion of the hearing proceedings, hearing examiners prepare an initial decision and serve a certified copy of it on the respondent (FTC Regulation on Investigation, sec. 66).

The FTC will render a decision in keeping with an initial decision when it finds, after reviewing all of the hearing records and respondent's additional opinion, if any, that the initial decision is acceptable (FTC Regulation on Investigation, sec. 69).

When it finds that a violation had existed prior to the issuance of a complaint, but had ceased to exist thereafter, the FTC must issue a decision to confirm the existence of a violation (sec. 54(3)). No remedial measures can be ordered in such cases.

The FTC must make clear that no violation existed at the time of the issuance of a complaint if, after hearing proceedings, it so finds (sec. 54(3)).

(5) LEGAL EFFECTS OF FTC DECISIONS

The FTC decision takes effect when a certified copy thereof is served on the respondent or his attorney (sec. 58). The respondent may apply to the court for a stay of execution of the FTC decision until it becomes final and binding by depositing such bond or security as may be fixed by the court (sec. 62). In this case, the respondent may apply to any district court that has jurisdiction over the subject matter.

Among 15 petitions for a stay of execution, 11 were accepted by the courts. Only three petitions were rejected, and one petition was withdrawn. Therefore, the courts have accepted most of such petitions applied for by respondents. The court may, upon a motion by the FTC, forfeit the whole or a part of such bond or security thus deposited (sec. 63), and in four cases, the FTC filed such a motion and the court accepted such a motion of forfeiture. In two of these cases, the court forfeited the whole amount (Meiji Trading Co., Tokyo High Court, Dec. 27, 1968, 15 KTIS 181) and in two cases, the court forfeited half of the deposited money (Snow Brand Dairy Co., Tokyo High Court, March 31, 1978, 24 KTIS 287). In four

Table 16-1. Classification of FTC Decisions and Appeals Cases[1]

Year	Formal Decision	Consent Decision	Recommen- dation	Tokyo High Court Decisions[2]	Supreme Court Decisions[2]
1947	0	5	0	0	0
1948	0	2	0	0	0
1949	1	11	2	0	0
1950	10	45	4	0	0
1951	8	6	4	2	0
1952	8	4	3	1	0
1953	2	5	5	2	0
1954	3	2	0	1	1
1955	5	1	5	0	0
1956	1	0	5	1	0
1957	0	0	7	1	0
1958	0	0	2	1	0
1959	0	0	2	0	0
1960	0	0	1	0	2
1961	0	0	3	0	0
1962	1	5	7	0	0
1963	1	11	24	1*	0
1964	0	0	30	0	0
1965	1	0	26	0	0
1966	0	0	17	0	0
1967	1	0	11	0	0
1968	3	0	28	0	0
1969	4	1	26	0	0
1970	0	1	43	1	0
1971	0	0	37	4(1#)	0
1972	5	1	27	0	1
1973	1	1	67	0	0
1974	4	0	47	1**	0
1975	1	2	31	6	3
1976	0	1	24	0	0
1977	4	1	13	1	1**
1978	0	1	7	1#	6
1979	2	1	12	1#	0
1980	2	1	12	1#	0
1981	1	0	12	1**	1
1982	0	1	18	1**	0
1983	0	1	10	2	0

Table 16-1. Classification of FTC Decisions and Appeals Cases[1] (cont.)

Year	Formal Decision	Consent Decision	Recommen- dation	Tokyo High Court Decisions[2]	Supreme Court Decisions[2]
1984	1	1	7	0	0
1985	1	0	10	0	0
1986	1	0	4	1	0
1987	0	0	6	0	1
1988	0	1	5	0	0
1989	0	0	10	0	0
1990	0	0	17	0	0
1991	2	0	27	0	0
1992	1	0	37	0	0
Total	75	112	695	31	16
	—	—	—	(23)	(15)

NOTES:

[1] This table covers only the FTC decisions under sections 48, 53-3, and 54. Therefore, such FTC decisions ordering surcharges after adjudicative proceedings, or those decisions based on the Act Concerning Excessive Premiums and Misleading Representations, or section 65 of the Act were excluded.

[2] The decisions by the Tokyo High Court and the Supreme Court cover only appeals cases against FTC decisions under section 77. However, by this definition, it also covers settled cases (*), withdrawn cases (#) and those cases based on the Act Concerning Excessive Premiums and Misleading Representations (##). Therefore, the net total excluding those cases is shown in parentheses.

* indicates that the case was settled out of the Court voluntarily, and the Court had accepted such settlement.

** indicates that the case was related to the Act Concerning Excessive Premiums and Misleading Representations.

# indicates that the case was withdrawn by the respondents, and no decision was rendered.

SOURCE: Compiled from the FTC Annual Reports.

cases, the FTC did not file a motion and the deposited money was returned to the respondents.

Unless the interests of the respondents may be injured thereby (sec. 66(2)), the FTC may amend or modify its decision by a subsequent decision when it deems that further maintenance of the original decision would be improper and contrary to the public interest because of changes in economic conditions or for other reasons.

A person who contravenes an FTC decision is liable to an administrative fine (*karyo*), and anyone who contravenes it after it becomes final and binding may be punishable by penal servitude and/or a fine (see Chapter 18 Criminal Cases and Penalties).

The factual finding by the FTC that a violation of the Act existed or not can be used in private suits under section 25 of the Act and in other private suits (see Chapter 17 Civil Damage Suits). In the 1971 Novo Industri Co. case (May 19, 1971, 17 KTIS 297), the Tokyo High Court held that the FTC's finding of facts merely had the effect of presumptions as to the existence of violative acts in private suits, and the court can make its own fact findings.

In the case of a formal decision rendered after adjudicative proceedings, the effect of presumption would be stronger than in the case of a recommendation decision or consent decision. The Supreme Court in the 1975 Novo Industri Co. case (Nov. 28, 1975, 22 KTIS 260), acknowledged that a decision issued after an adjudicative procedure was based on the establishment of a violation through evidence, and can have stronger presumptive effects than a recommendation decision.

(B) HEARING PROCEEDINGS

(1) PARTICIPANTS

The FTC itself may conduct a hearing proceeding, and this was done on four occasions. In such cases, the Chairman and at least two of the Commissioners are present (FTC Regulation on Investigation, sec. 25). Usually the FTC will designate hearing examiners from among five hearing examiners attached to the case (see figure 15-1). The FTC may not designate such persons who have been involved in the investigation of the case (sec. 51-2). The hearing is conducted by a three-member panel designated as to Antimonopoly Act violation cases; one hearing examiner will hear the case that is related to the Act Concerning Excessive Premiums and Misleading Representations.

The respondents can be represented by an attorney, but when necessary approval is given, persons other than attorneys can represent the respondents (sec. 52(2)). In the past, the managing director of a corporation and secretaries of trade associations have been approved by the FTC.

The FTC may, when it deems necessary, cause a third person interested in the result of the decision to be made a party to the hearing proceedings (sec. 59). There has been no such case up to now. An injured person may be a third person interested in the result of the decision. In addition, upon the approval of the FTC, any government agency or public organization concerned with a case may become a party to the hearing proceedings (sec. 60).

As to the 1971 Ishikawa Chuo Fishery Market case (Dec. 28, 1971, 18 KTIS 149), the City of Kanazawa, which had the power to regulate operation of the fishery market, had participated as a party to the hearing proceeding.

(2) PROCEDURES

A hearing proceeding is initiated upon service of a certified copy of a complaint (sec. 50(2)). After he receives a certified copy of a complaint, a respondent must file an answer with the FTC without delay. The date of the first hearing shall be at least 30 days after the service of the complaint (sec. 50(4)), and normally it will proceed at a once a month pace. All proceedings must be public except where in camera proceedings are deemed necessary in order to protect an entrepreneur's trade secrets or the public interest (sec. 53). All oral presentations given during hearing proceedings are recorded and constitute the hearing record (sec. 53(2)).

Investigators designated under section 46(2) can be present at hearing proceedings, and can submit evidence and engage in other necessary acts in support of the complaint. Generally speaking, submission of evidence in support of the complaint by investigators comes first, defense activities by the respondent would follow. The respondent would present his evidence and ask to take the testimony of necessary witnesses.

In the course of investigation, the results of the necessary examination of those persons related to a case are recorded as an investigation record and submitted as evidence. Sometimes, the respondent side may contest the value as evidence of such an investigation record by calling those persons to the hearing room in order to cross-examine them. Ordinarily, the examination of witnesses would constitute a major battle field at the FTC hearing proceedings.

If any evidence submitted during the course of the hearing proceedings is not accepted by the hearing examiners, or by the FTC ultimately, the hearing examiners or the FTC must specify their reasons for such non-acceptance (sec. 52-2). This rule is interpreted as submitted evidence shall be accepted in principle.

The respondent or investigators may file an objection with the FTC as to any dispositions made by the hearing examiners when they consider that such dispositions violate any rules or laws or are deemed unreasonable (FTC Regulation on Investigation, secs. 61-2 and 62). When the FTC sustains such an objection, it instructs the hearing examiners to cancel, revoke, or change the disposition in question.

(3) INITIAL DECISION

Upon the conclusion of the hearing proceedings, the hearing examiners must prepare an initial decision within 30 days and must hand over all records of the case to the FTC (FTC Regulation on Investigation, sec. 66). The FTC may issue a decision in keeping with the initial decision, issue a different decision, or order the re-opening of the hearing proceedings to clarify specified points of argument (FTC Regulation on Investigation, sec. 69).

In cases where the hearing examiners are entrusted to conduct hearing proceedings the respondent may ask to have an opportunity to state his case directly to the Commission (sec. 53 2-2). This motion can be made after the preparation of an initial decision (FTC Regulation on Investigation, sec. 68-2). Anyway, if he desires to do so, the respondent can file an opinion to the initial decision within 2 weeks after the service of a certified copy of it (FTC Regulation on Investigation, sec. 68).

(4) INSPECTION OF HEARING RECORDS BY A THIRD PERSON

Any interested person may inspect or copy the record of a case after issuance of a complaint (sec. 69). "The record of a case" refers to any documents prepared during the hearing proceedings, including all evidence submitted at the proceedings, but does not include documents in the possession of investigators, or any documents produced by investigators in the course of their investigation that were not submitted as evidence.

As to the scope of "interested person," the 1975 Wakodo Co. case (Supreme Court, July 10, 1975, 22 KTIS 173) set a precedent. In this case, the hearing examiners denied the respondent's motion to obtain a copy of the record of a sister case that was simultaneously pending at the FTC, and the Wakodo Co. filed an objection with the FTC. The FTC denied the motion saying that "interested person" within the meaning of section 69 is limited to the respondent, those who may participate in the hearing proceedings under sections 59 and 60, and any person injured by the violation in question (Jan. 26, 1967, 18 KTIS 289).

(C) APPEALS TO COURTS
(1) EXCLUSIVE JURISDICTION OF THE TOKYO HIGH COURT

As to an FTC decision rendered after hearing proceedings, the respondent may seek to quash the decision by bringing suit in the Tokyo High Court (sec. 77). The Tokyo High Court has exclusive jurisdiction in suits to quash an FTC decision (sec. 85).

No appeal from a consent decision will be made by the respondent. Standing to sue is limited as explained below. Therefore, the remaining question is whether an appeal to a recommendation decision is possible by the respondents. In the 1975 Shell Oil Co. case (Sep. 29, 1975, 22 KTIS 220), the Tokyo High Court rejected an appeal by the respondents of the recommendation decision saying that respondents/plaintiffs cannot revoke their acceptance of the FTC recommendation after the decision is rendered. Even if there were some mistakes in the motive to accept the recommendation, it did not affect the validity of their acceptance, therefore, the recommendation decision was valid and could not be revoked.

In this case, the FTC did bring a criminal accusation against respondents after they had accepted the FTC recommendation (see chapter 18 (B)(2) Oil Cartel Cases), therefore, the respondents argued that they would not have accepted the recommendation if they had known that the FTC would bring a criminal accusation against them.

(2) SUBSTANTIAL EVIDENCE

In a suit to quash an FTC decision, the Tokyo High Court is bound by the FTC's findings of fact as long as they are supported by substantial evidence (sec. 80). In other words, an FTC decision can be canceled if the facts on which the decision was based are not supported by substantial evidence or if the decision is contrary to the Constitution or other laws (sec. 82). Introduction of new evidence at the Tokyo High Court is limited to such cases where such evidence was not accepted by the FTC without good cause, or where it was impossible to adduce such evidence at the hearing proceedings and there was no negligence on the respondent's part in failing to adduce evidence at the hearing proceedings (sec. 81 (1)).

The Tokyo High Court may remand the case to the FTC when it judges that a further adjudicative procedure is necessary (sec. 83).

In the 1984 Toyo Rice Cleaning Machine Co. case (Feb. 17, 1984, 30 KTIS 136), the Tokyo High Court remanded the case to the FTC saying that the FTC decision was not supported by substantial evidence.

Specifically, the Court questioned the basis of the respondent's market share calculations because other kinds of rice cleaning machines were included in such calculations. Also, the Court questioned the FTC finding of tendency to impede fair competition, because such a finding should be done concretely in each case by examining the market foreclosure effects on competitors of such exclusive dealing, whereas the FTC merely found that the respondent was in an influential position in a market based on market share data only, then without examining further, the FTC had found that the exclusive dealing in question had a tendency to impede fair competition. According to the Court's reasoning, such fact finding lacks substantial evidence and the case should be remanded to the FTC for further hearing proceedings. After hearing proceedings were reopened, this case was settled by a consent decision (May 17, 1988, 35 KTIS 15)

(3) STANDING TO SUE

The Japanese rule on standing to sue on administrative cases is rather rigid. A person has standing to sue when his legal interests are adversely affected by the conduct of a government office. Only legal interests that are within the range of protection of the related law can be recognized.

The 1975 Novo Industri Co. (Novo) case (Supreme Court, Nov. 28, 1975, 22 KTIS 260) was the one where a foreign party to an international contract filed a suit under section 76 of the Act to quash a recommendation decision rendered against a Japanese contracting party of Novo. The FTC rendered a recommendation decision against the Amano Pharmaceutical Co. (Amano), a Japanese party, in which a non-competition clause after the termination of a contract and resale maintenance clause were declared illegal under the Antimonopoly Act. Amano accepted the recommendation, and a recommendation decision was rendered against Amano thereafter (Jan. 12, 1970, 16 KTIS 134). (See chapter 21 (a)(3) Cases.)

The Supreme Court's rejection of the suit to quash the recommendation decision was twofold. First the recommendation was not directed against Novo, therefore, it had no binding effects on Novo. According to the Supreme Court's reasoning, a recommendation decision has binding effects only on persons to whom the decision is directed.

Secondly, a foreign party is free to bring a private suit such as an enforcement of a contract or damage suit, in which he can insist upon the illegality of the FTC decision. The finding in the FTC decision does not bind the court. Therefore, the legal interest of Novo was not adversely affected by the recommendation decision, thus standing to sue was denied to Novo.

(D) ENFORCEABILITY OF AN ILLEGAL CONTRACT

Once a contract or a provision in a contract is declared illegal, the contract or the provision becomes unenforceable. The question is whether the contract or the provision is treated as null and void even after it has been performed.

The Court showed reluctance to restore the status quo of an illegal contract or a particular provision in order to safeguard legal stability. In the 1953 Shirokiya Co. case (Shirokiya) (Tokyo High Court, Dec. 1, 1953, 9 KTIS 193), the defendant, the Yokoi Sangyo Co., a wholesaler of imported products, acquired stock of a competitor illegally, but was duly registered as a stockholder on the shareholder's list. Shirokiya, a department store plaintiff, sought a temporary injunction against the exercise of the defendant's voting rights.

The Tokyo High Court held that a contract that violated the Antimonopoly Act (old secs. 10(2) and 14(3)) was unenforceable, but the contract for the stock transfer should be held valid after the sales contract was performed and the purchaser was duly registered as a shareholder. Therefore, the exercise of voting rights could not be stopped.

In the 1977 Gifu Credit Union case (June 20, 1977, 24 KTIS 291), the Supreme Court held that an excessive compensatory deposit at the bank could be a violation of section 19 of the Act (see chapter 8 (H)(3) Private Suits). But, it also held that only those portions of the loan contract that exceeded the legal limit set by the Interest Restriction Law (Act No. 195 of 1954) shall be unenforceable, and thus relieved the plaintiff from its payment obligation to that extent.

As a whole, an illegal contract under the Antimonopoly Act is not held unenforceable per se. The court seems to try to carefully balance legal stability and illegality of the contract under the Antimonopoly Act. In particular, those contracts that were already performed were ordinarily held enforceable by the court.

However, cartel agreements are considered null and void and cannot be enforced in court. Most cartel agreements are effected as gentlemen's agreements, thus are not enforceable in court anyway.

17

CIVIL DAMAGE SUITS

(A) IN GENERAL

(1) BASIS FOR CLAIM

The enforcement powers of the Antimonopoly Act were concentrated in the FTC, and very little enforcement has been done by private parties alone. By allowing injured persons to protect themselves, damage suits have an important function for antimonopoly law enforcement. Although it is an act to recover the injuries a plaintiff has suffered, it has a function to enhance the deterring effects of antimonopoly violations, and could make an important contribution to maintaining competitive order.

There are two bases for damage suits for private parties. One is section 25 suits that provide for absolute liabilities, and the other is ordinary damage suits under the Civil Code (Act No. 89 of 1896). No injunction suit is possible for a private party; therefore, a private party who thinks he is injured by some acts in violation of the Antimonopoly Act can file such information with the FTC under section 45(1), and ask for an FTC investigation on the matter to be started. Once a decision rendered by the FTC becomes final, he can then file a damage suit under section 25 of the Act (section 25 suits).

However, the FTC will not take up cases that arise basically from private disputes, and thus would be better solved through private initiatives. In such cases, or any other situation where the FTC is not involved, the private party can file a damage suit under section 709 of the Civil Code (section 709 suits). In the latter case, such suits can be initiated any time, that is before or after the FTC decision, or when there is no FTC decision. Sometimes, a section 709 suit is filed because of the inconvenience of filing a section 25 suit due to exclusive jurisdiction to the Tokyo High Court.[1]

(2) SINGLE DAMAGE AWARDS

In Japan, there is no concept of awarding double or treble damages, nor punitive damages. Plaintiffs who prevail in damage suits can recover only single damages. The court can decide in the judgment which side should bear the cost of the legal proceedings. In general, the losing side should bear the cost, but the court tends to allocate the burden carefully between plaintiff and defendant. Legal proceeding costs consist mostly of allowances paid to witnesses for transportation and lodging and such allowances for expert testimony.

The court can award standardized attorney's fees for the plaintiff when he prevails. Up to now, they have been awarded in such limited cases as traffic accident suits.[2]

(B) DAMAGE SUITS

(1) DAMAGE SUITS UNDER SECTION 25

(i) Absolute liability

Section 25 provides for absolute liability for specified types of antimonopoly violations. Absolute liability means that one cannot be exempted from liability by proving the nonexistence of willfulness or negligence on his part. Ordinary liability means that to prevail in a damage suit the plaintiff must prove the existence of willfulness or negligence.

Only section 3 violations and section 19 violations are subject to absolute liability (sec. 25(1)). Other violations such as those of sections 6 and 8, although the nature of violations are the same as those of sections 3 and 19 violations, are excluded.

Section 25 is available as to damage suits but it is possible to use such claims in counterclaim suits as well.

(ii) Indirect injuries

Any person who has suffered injury as a result of violations of sections 3 and 19 may use section 25. Plaintiff may be his competitors, direct customers, and indirect customers including consumers. It becomes relatively difficult for indirect customers to prove the causal relationship of their injuries with violations, but this fact does not deny their standing to file a damage suit.

In a country like Japan where business relations tend to be continuous, it is less probable that injured persons who are direct customers would file damage suits against those who had violated the Act. So far as cartels and resale price maintenance are concerned, only consumers who do not have such disincentives may resort to filing damage suits. In Japan, if those indirect customers are denied standing to sue, no private party may be interested in filing such damage suits. It is also for this reason that only consumer goods have been subjected to damage suits in the past.

(iii) Exclusive jurisdiction

Section 25 cases are filed with the Tokyo High Court (sec. 85(2)), which has a special panel of five judges. Even at the High Court level, three judges will sit to hear the case, and a five-judge panel is very exceptional. The merit of this system is that one can expect consistent judgments by the same panel, but on the other hand, for those persons located in districts other than Tokyo and its vicinity, it is so inconvenient to pursue legal proceedings in Tokyo that they sometimes prefer to file a section 709 case instead of a section 25 case in spite of the absolute liability provisions afforded to section 25 suits.

(iv) FTC opinions

According to section 84(1), the court must request an opinion of the FTC as to the amount of damages. Although the law only speaks about the amount of damages, the FTC is not precluded from expressing its opinion concerning causal relationships with injuries,

Table 17-1. Private Damage Suits for Alleged Violations of the Antimonopoly Law

Basis of Claim	Number of Cases	Plaintiff		Win	Lose	Settlement	Withdrawal	Wrongful Action[1]		Claims Raised				Duration[2]			
		Consumers	Competitors					Restraint of trade	Unfair practices	1955-1964	1965-1974	1975-1984	After 1985	Up to three years	Three to five years	Five to ten years	More than ten years
Antimonopoly law sec. 25	6[3]	2	4	0	4[4]	1	1	1	5	2	3	1	0	3	0	2	1
Civil Code sec. 709	9[3]	2	7	0	8	1	0	3[5]	7[5]	0	1	7	1	3	3	2	1
Total	15	4	11	0	12	2	1	4	12	2	4	8	1	6	3	4	2

NOTES:

[1] Including the cases of a trade association under secs. 8(1)(i) and (iv).

[2] About one claim under sec. 709 the courts had not decided by April 1990. The figure is the duration until that date.

[3] The original number was 9 resp. 11, though some have been combined by the courts.

[4] Disregarding those individual plaintiffs that settled during the process.

[5] One claim was raised under both restraint of trade and unfair trade practices.

SOURCE: Study Group Report on Damage Suits (1991), at 35.

existence of damages etc. as well as submission of any evidence in support of its opinion.

(2) DAMAGE SUITS UNDER THE CIVIL CODE

Under the Civil Code, general damage provisions (sec. 709) applicable to damage claims can be used by private parties. The merits of these damage suits are:

(A) Local district courts throughout Japan are available for plaintiffs.
(B) Such suits can be initiated within the general statute of limitations of 5 years. It is also possible to file section 709 suits where there exists a final FTC decision.

It is clear that absolute liability is not available as to section 709 suits. As to the opinion of the FTC, the court can use its general power to get the opinions of the related government offices.[3] When there exists a final FTC decision, plaintiffs in section 709 suits can submit a copy of the FTC decision as evidence to the court to prove facts of violation, amount of damages, etc.[4]

(3) DIFFERENCES BETWEEN SECTION 25 AND SECTION 709 SUITS

Because the problem of section 25 suits is not negligible, the court tended to interpret section 25 suits and section 709 suits in a way that treats these two damage suits as much the same as is feasibly possible.

The Act seems to assume that whenever section 25 is available, a private party would use it, and only when no action is taken by the FTC, would section 709 suits be filed as a last resort. However, there could be a situation where there exists a final FTC decision and still a section 709 suit is preferred.

It is clear that the FTC decisions never have binding effects on courts. It is up to individual judges who sit on a private case how much weight is given to the FTC decisions. When there exists a final FTC decision, it may not be significant for the court whether the case before it is a section 25 suit or a section 709 suit so long as the FTC decision is not sustained by the court in the subsequent cases.

On the other hand, when the FTC decision becomes final after review by the Tokyo High Court, it is certain that other courts would give much weight to the FTC finding on the violation of the Act even if it is filed as a section 709 suit.

The FTC decision alone may not be sufficient to prove violations, but if the plaintiffs can submit the evidence produced at the hearing proceedings it gets easier for the plaintiffs to prevail in proving facts of violations as to suits based on section 25 or section 709.

From this aspect, the court's power to get access to evidence produced by the FTC or examined in hearing proceedings under section 319 of the Civil Procedure Code becomes important. In the past, this power was not utilized by the court, partly because of the uncertainty of the FTC response to such requests.

(C) PROOF OF DAMAGES AND CAUSAL RELATIONSHIP

(1) SECTION 25 CASES

Up to now, only six section 25 cases have been filed, and these six cases related to three FTC decisions. The first two cases related to the Matsushita Electric Industries Co. (Matsushita) (March 12, 1971, 17 KTIS 187), where plaintiffs asked damages caused by Matsushita's resale price maintenance. The FTC rendered a decision against Matsushita, finding a violation of section 19, and after the decision became final two groups of consumers brought damage suits. The claimed amount of damages was 7,000~64,000 yen.

Upon a request from the Court, the FTC filed an opinion that said that because no finding on retail price was made in the decision, it was not possible for the FTC to determine the amount of damages. The Tokyo High Court denied the plaintiffs' claim saying that there was no evidence to show the purchase price was actually inflated by Matsushita's conduct, thus the amount of damages was not proved (Tokyo High Court, Sep. 19, 1977, 24 KTIS 313).

As to oil cartel cases, in 1974 three groups of consumers had filed section 25 suits separately and two groups had settled the claim in 1981 (Tokyo High Court settlement record, July 2, 1981, 28 KTIS 188). In the remaining case, the Tokyo High Court denied the claim saying that there were other factors contributing to the increase of prices at the time of the cartel agreements, therefore it was not possible to determine whether any damages were caused by the defendants' conduct; and even if some damages were so caused, the amount could not be determined by evidence (July 17, 1981, 28-2 KTIS 3).

The Supreme Court also denied the claim and made clear that the plaintiff had a burden of proof as to the causal relationship of his injuries with violations, and as to the amount of damages (June 2, 1987, 34 KTIS 119).

The sixth case was filed in 1983 by one milk producer, Saeki Milk Co., who was refused to deal by the Ooita Dairy Farmers' Cooperatives. In 1981, the FTC rendered a decision against the Cooperatives because their imposition of a non-competition obligation on their member farmers had violated section 19 of the Act (June 8, 1981, 28 KTIS 56). The suit was dropped on December 26, 1988 before the FTC was asked by the court to file its opinion.

(D) ENHANCEMENT OF FTC INVOLVEMENT

As seen above, the records of section 25 and section 709 cases are miserable by any standards. The reason is clear. Ordinary plaintiffs, in particular consumer plaintiffs, could not have sufficient access to evidence to meet the burden of proof set by the Supreme Court. One way to solve this problem is via legislative change, but it does not seem an easy solution.

The other way is by improving access to the FTC produced documents and evidence collected for investigation purposes. In this evidence there might be some documents, besides those that prove the fact of violations, that could show a causal relationship between injuries and acts of violation or any data to be used for calculating the amount of damages.

At SII, lack of effective private suits was discussed as one of the problems of the Japanese antimonopoly laws. The FTC established a Study Group on Damage Remedy Systems under the Antimonopoly Act, and its report was prepared in June 1990. The recommendations of the Study Group were as follows:

(A) In order to contribute to a court's finding of facts, the facts stated in the FTC decisions should be more clear and more concrete.

(B) The FTC opinion under section 84 should indicate its view on the relevance or causal relationship between the violations and the injury, the amount of damages and also the method of calculating damages, in order to alleviate the plaintiff's burden of proof.

(C) The FTC should attach the necessary materials as the basis of its opinion. If necessary, the FTC should conduct a new investigation to obtain materials that provide for the basis of its opinion.

(D) When a request for documents is made by a court under section 319 of the Civil Procedure Code, the FTC should provide materials to the extent necessary to prove a fact of violation and injury. The FTC should establish principles by specifying types and kinds of materials to be submitted to the court.

(E) The FTC should provide for sufficient public relations to promote public awareness of section 25 suits.

On May 15, 1991, the FTC announced the following policy statement concerning private damage suits. According to this new policy, the following measures would be taken when there existed a final FTC decision.

(A) Before the injured person files a damage suit

The FTC would provide, upon the request of the injured person, the following documents:

(i)   A certified copy of the FTC decision,

(ii)   A certified copy of the surcharge order,

(iii) In the case of a trade association case, the name and address of constituent members of the trade association.

(iv)   In the case of a consent decision and a formal decision, all hearing records (this includes every piece of evidence submitted, stenographic records of the hearing proceedings, papers submitted by investigators and respondents). Access to these records are provided under section 69 of the Act.

(B) After the injured person filed a damage suit

Upon the request by the court under section 319 of the Civil Procedure, the FTC would provide the following documents:

(i)   Any documents and evidence used as the basis of the FTC fact finding in a recommendation decision.

(ii)   Copies of all hearing records, in the case of a consent decision and formal decision.

(iii) Any documents relating to a causal relationship of injuries with violations and the amount of damages.

When the matter is still pending at the hearing proceedings or at the court upon appeal, the FTC would provide a certified copy of the complaint, a formal decision, and permit inspection and copying of hearing records if requested under section 69 of the Act by the injured person.

In order to be ready for such a request, the FTC would keep necessary documents and records for 3 years.

NOTES

[1] This was exactly the reason why injured persons located in the Yamagata Prefecture had to file section 709 suits to the Yamagata District Court, instead of section 25 suits in Tokyo.

[2] Nowadays, courts will award about 10 percent of the amount of damages in various kinds of accident related cases. For example, in the damage suits filed by a pupil as to accidental injuries caused by another pupil, the court awarded 5.53 million yen as damages and 500,000 yen as an attorney's fee (Osaka District Court, Sep. 29, 1980, 429 Hanrei Taimuzu 140). Because of this case law, plaintiffs also tend to ask for about 10 percent of the claimed damage amount as attorney's fee, too.

[3] Sec. 310 of the Civil Procedure Code.

[4] As to the value of the FTC decision in this aspect, see chapter 16 (A)(5) Legal Effects of FTC Decisions. However, sec. 78 of the Act does not apply to such cases, therefore, transmission of the FTC's entire record of cases cannot be requested by the court.

18

CRIMINAL CASES
AND PENALTIES

(A) CRIMINAL PENALTIES

(1) CRIMINAL PENALTIES FOR ANTIMONOPOLY VIOLATIONS

Since the Antimonopoly Act was modeled after the U.S. antitrust laws, it provides for heavy criminal penalties against violations of the Act. However, in Japan, criminal penalties have never been considered as necessary sanctions against antimonopoly violations. There are several factors to explain this situation.

It is arguable whether it was the FTC or the Prosecuting Authority that was pessimistic concerning the use of criminal sanctions. It seems that the FTC tended to be more positive on the use of criminal sanctions if feasible. The most important factor was the legal principle of the prosecutor's exercise of discretion, and in general, prosecutors tended to be very selective in exercising the discretionary power to prosecute. Therefore, non-exercise of the accusation power of the FTC or discretionary power to prosecute by the Prosecuting Authority depended on the general public's attitudes toward particular crimes.

Up to 1990 it seemed true that antimonopoly violations were not thought to be as serious as tax evasion or other business crimes such as embezzlement. Probably, antimonopoly violations would be ranked by the general public in Japan slightly above traffic violations. This factor seems important for the Prosecuting Authority in selecting cases suitable to prosecute.

Another reason is separation of powers between the FTC and the Prosecuting Authority. By completely separating the administrative power of the FTC and criminal power of the Prosecuting Authority it was fairly difficult to coordinate effective criminal enforcement. It was only after SII had started that true coordination of the two agencies began.[1]

(2) CRIMINAL SYSTEM IN JAPAN

There are several characteristics in the Japanese criminal system, and for better understanding of criminal enforcement of the Act, the following should be borne in mind.

The first and most important characteristic is selectiveness in the use of criminal sanctions. The fact that a criminal penalty is stipulated in the law does not mean that such a sanction can be utilized. In addition, the amount of a fine is mostly symbolic and does not necessarily have sufficient deterring effects in itself. Sometimes, a fine was a nominal or meaningless amount because the amount had not been amended for many years.

Of course, the fact that a fine could be imposed on the offenders was seriously considered by related persons. In spite of the nominal amount of a penalty, the huge disadvantage one suffers as a defendant in a criminal case may also increase the deterring effects.

The second important factor is the nature of the Japanese criminal system itself. Criminal penalties are imposed on individual offenders who actually commit conduct that constitutes a crime, and when they commit a crime with regard to the business or property of a corporation, then such corporation can be fined in addition to the offenders (sec. 95, this is called double punishment). Representatives of related corporations may be punished when they fail to take necessary measures to prevent violations or failed to take necessary measures for the rectification of such violations in cases where they knew of the existence of such crimes (sec. 95-2, this is called triple punishment).

As a result, the maximum amount of a fine for a corporation in the case of double punishment was set at the same level as that for individual offenders, and the maximum amount of a fine, for example 5,000,000 yen for unreasonable restraint of trade, is meaningless as a penalty for a corporation.[2] In view of the importance of corporations as major actors in economic activities at present, criminal penalties need to take this reality into consideration.

In particular, offenders of antimonopoly violations in Japan may sometimes be merely acting on behalf of corporations they work for, and any benefits from such illegal conduct belong to the corporations, but not to the offenders. It makes it difficult for the judge to impose a severe criminal penalty if the offender was not personally enriched by the criminal act.

In the U.S., it was only in 1974 when fines for a corporation and for an individual were separately proscribed in the Sherman Act,[3] and this was about the time when criminal enforcement started to be emphasized in the U.S.

Antimonopoly violations are regarded as corporate crimes and the necessity of heavy fines on offending corporations is increasing. However, because of the general nature of the problem, this problem was taken up at the Ministry of the Judiciary.

(3) CRIMINAL PENALTIES

The criminal penalties set by the Act are shown in table 18-1. The maximum length of sentence appears quite sufficient. It is also noticeable that these penalties are determined carefully to reflect the seriousness of the crime. And, except for unfair trade practices, every substantive violation can be fined without regard to whether a criminal penalty is warranted for such conduct.

It is also noticeable that interference with the inspection or non-compliance with an FTC order is taken lightly in terms of criminal penalties. The necessity of criminal punishment is much higher for non-compliance or interference with the investigation activities of the FTC. Section 46(1)(i), (ii) and (iii) violations can be fined only up to a maximum of 200,000 yen.

(B) ENFORCEMENT

(1) EARLY CASES

Before 1991, only on six occasions were the criminal provisions of the Act utilized. However, the first three cases occurred during the Occupation period and have little value as precedents now.

In the 1952 Okawa Co. case (Tokyo High Court, May 12, 1952), the Okawa Co. was alleged to violate sections 105, 107, 108 and

Table 18-1. Criminal Penalties Against Various Violations of the Act

Relevant Provisions	Maximum Amount of Fine (Yen)	Maximum Length of Servitude
3 former half	5,000,000	3 years
3 latter half	5,000,000	3 years
8(1)(i)	5,000,000	3 years
In case of a juridical person and non-juridical organization (double punishment)	100 million	None
6(1) and 8(1)(ii)	3,000,000	2 years
8(1)(iii) and 8(1)(iv)	3,000,000	2 years
Infringement of final FTC decisions	3,000,000	2 years
9(1) and 9(2)	2,000,000	1 year
9-2(1)	2,000,000	1 year
10(1) former half	2,000,000	1 year
11(1) and 11(2)	2,000,000	1 year
13(1)	2,000,000	1 year
14(1) former half	2,000,000	1 year
17	2,000,000	1 year
Those who fail to file a notification or those who filed a false notification	2,000,000	None
Those who effect registration of the merger etc. in violation of sections 15 and 16	2,000,000	None
40	200,000	None
46(1)(i)	200,000	None
46(1)(ii)	200,000	None
46(1)(iii)	200,000	None
53-2 (Refusal to give oaths)	200,000	None
53-2 (Perjury)	None	3 months~10 years
39 (Divulging secrets)	100,000	1 year
46(1)(iv) (Interference with inspection etc.)	200,000	6 months

109, and the penalty for such violations was specially provided in sections 111 and 112 of the Act. The FTC accusation was made against the failure to submit plans for the disposal of stock in violation of the SCAP policy of deconcentration.

In the 1951 Yamaichi Securities Co. case (decision not to prosecute, Dec. 28, 1951), a section 16 violation was asserted but the Prosecuting Authority decided not to prosecute the Yamaichi Securities Co. in spite of the FTC accusation.

In the 1951 Agricultural and Forestry Liaison Conference case (Tokyo High Court, Feb. 27, 1951), the Conference was alleged to have violated the Trade Association Act. The FTC accused the Conference and 21 officers, but the Prosecuting Authority prosecuted the Conference and two officers, and a fine of 10,000 yen was imposed on each of the defendants by the court.

The fourth case was the San-ai Land Co. case. This was a case concerning a violation of the final FTC decision issued under the Act Concerning Excessive Premiums and Misleading Representations. The company was fined 200,000 yen, and an officer/defendant was fined 100,000 yen and given a 1-year suspended sentence.

(2) OIL CARTEL CASES

The most serious and controversial criminal cases were started by FTC accusations against the Petroleum Federation and 12 wholesalers of oil. These were the first criminal accusations against substantive provisions of the Act. This case involved very complicated legal issues such as relationships between administrative guidance and the illegality of conduct based on such guidance.

In July 1971, the FTC had issued a complaint against the Petroleum Federation alleging price fixing of oil products. In 1974, after hearing proceedings, the FTC rendered a formal decision (March 28, 1974, 20 KTIS 355). The Federation appealed to the Tokyo High Court (Aug. 15, 1977, 24 KTIS 155), and ultimately to the Supreme Court (March 9, 1982, 28 KTIS 165).

In this case, price fixing by one committee of the Federation was found to constitute a section 8(1)(i) violation. Thereafter, 12 wholesalers had established meetings separate from the official committee of the Federation and met regularly to exchange information on matters of mutual interest. On the eve of the oil crisis, of the 14 wholesalers of oil these 12 companies had regularly attended meetings to determine what price should be charged to absorb the increased cost of oil.

Under the Petroleum Industry Law (Act No. 128 of 1962), MITI had the authority to set the standard price for oil products. But this authority was rarely utilized, instead MITI preferred to intervene informally in such a way as to examine the price to be charged by oil companies in advance and to make sure that the price level was acceptable to MITT. Due to this policy, these 12 companies had consulted with MITI to comply with such policy objectives.

In general, MITI maintained such a policy in order to secure the sound economic condition of oil companies so as to secure a sufficient energy supply for Japan. But, in view of the panicked reaction of people to the first oil shock, MITI also had to try to make policy efforts to secure the interest of consumers, and for this reason, MITI tried to allow only a strict pass-over of increased cost of oil to oil products.

However, the 12 wholesalers were not simply complying with the policy expressed by the administrative guidance of MITI. Conversely, they agreed on the level of price increases on various kinds of oil products, and thereafter MITI accepted such price increases as a whole. MITI did not intervene on individual prices of various kinds of oil products. It was left to each wholesaler of oil to allocate the increased cost among various oil products.

On the production allocation issue, since the enactment of the Petroleum Industry Law, the Federation has been allocating production amounts for each members' oil companies. This allocation was effected to make sure that each oil company's projected production amount met the total production estimates of MITI. The Federation collected each company's production estimates and if there was any discrepancy with the MITI estimates of total production, the necessary adjustment was effected by the Federation.

On February 5, 1974, the FTC issued a recommendation to the Federation as to production allocations, and to 12 wholesalers of oil as to price fixing, both recommendations were accepted on February 15.

Thereafter, there were two important developments in this case. First, the FTC filed accusations against the Federation and four officers as to a production restriction charge, and 12 companies and 15 officers as to price fixing under section 96(1). And subsequently, the Prosecuting Authority filed indictments against the Petroleum Federation and its officers for a production restriction charge in violation of section 8 (production curtailment case), and 12 wholesalers of oil and 15 of their officers for price fixing charges in violation of section 3 on May 28, 1974 (price-fixing case).

Secondly, 6 of 12 companies had filed a suit to quash the FTC decision alleging that the acceptance of the FTC recommendation was based on a mistake. They claimed that, if they had known that the FTC was going to accuse them, they would never have accepted the recommendation.

As to the production curtailment case, the Tokyo High Court found the three indicted persons and the Federation not guilty (Sep. 26, 1980, 28-2 KTIS 177). The Court found the conduct of these defendants fulfilled the necessary requirements for illegality, and there were no factors to justify or immunize the illegal conduct. However, the Court found that the crucial factor to punish these offenders was missing in this particular case, namely, the defendants were not conscious of the illegality of their conduct and there were justifiable reasons for their not knowing that the conduct was illegal, therefore, their conduct could not be condemned as criminal.

One of the reasons the Court indicated was that the FTC had not taken any action since 1962, even though production curtailment was effected continuously (except in FY 1967 and 1968). In particular, the FTC had issued a complaint against the Federation for price fixing in July 1971, and the FTC did not take any action against production curtailment even though this was done quite openly and the FTC could have known about it. The Court found that the defendants believed that the production allocation that was effected by the Federation in order to comply with the MITI administrative guidance was legal, and there were justifiable reasons for these offenders to believe so.

As to the price-fixing case, the 12 defendant companies and 14 individual defendants were found guilty (Sep. 26, 1980, 28-2 KTIS 299). Two companies were fined 2,500,000 yen, one company 1,500,000 yen, and nine companies 2,000,000 yen; two individuals were sentenced to 10 months' imprisonment, seven individuals to 4 months' and five individuals to 6 months' imprisonment (all of them got 2-year suspended sentences). The Court found five separate violations of law, therefore, the 2,500,000 yen fine was five times the maximum amount of fines for section 3 violations at that time. It should be remembered that the FTC found one violation of law as to the same facts.[4]

As a reason for the suspended sentence, the Court indicated some mitigating factors such as: the defendants had tried in essence to shift cost up due to a series of imported oil price increases, and did not unreasonably profit from this price fixing; besides MITI approved the price increase thereafter.

On appeal, the Supreme Court acquitted two companies and one individual among the defendants (Feb. 24. 1984, 30 KTIS 244).

As to the suit to revoke the FTC decision, the Tokyo High Court said that once a recommendation decision was issued, it becomes a legitimate decision binding respondents and the decision cannot be revoked for such reason as was cited by the plaintiffs (Aug. 15, 1977, 24 KTIS 155).

(C) ENHANCEMENT OF CRIMINAL ENFORCEMENT

(1) CRIMINAL ENFORCEMENT AND THE STRUCTURAL IMPEDIMENTS INITIATIVE

The final report of SII in 1990 emphasized the importance of criminal enforcement of the Antimonopoly Act and said, "More criminal penalties will be utilized in the future by the FTC's accusation of illegal activities violating the Antimonopoly Act to seek criminal penalties for them." (Appendix I.)

On June 20, 1990, the FTC announced a new policy statement expressing its intention to seek criminal penalties for vicious and serious cases that are considered to have a widespread influence on people's lives, these violations included price fixing cartels, supply restraint cartels, market allocation cartels, bid rigging, and group boycotts.

Criminal penalties would also be sought as to violation cases involving those businessmen or industries who are repeat offenders or those who do not abide by FTC decisions, in other words, when administrative measures by the FTC are not considered sufficient to fulfill the purpose of the law.

In January 1991, a liaison-coordination organ was set up between the Prosecuting Authority and the FTC, where information and opinions on concrete problems of each case for which an accusation was being considered would be exchanged.

In November and December 1991, under the above-mentioned new policy on criminal accusation, the FTC filed an accusation against eight companies' managers and seven directors who were involved in price-fixing cartels in plastic wrapping materials. The

Prosecuting Authority prosecuted these defendants and this criminal case is pending at the Tokyo High Court.

(2) INCREASE IN CRIMINAL PENALTIES

The advisory group of the Ministry of the Judiciary had studied the possibility of increasing criminal penalties for a juridical person, and on December 2, 1991, the advisory group made a recommendation to the Ministry to authorize the increase of criminal penalties for a juridical person in the case of double punishment. Double punishment is provided where any person in the service of a juridical person commits a violation specified in the Act (sec. 95).

By this authorization it became possible for each agency to propose the increase of criminal penalties for a juridical person in the case of double punishment. The study group organized by the FTC has been examining this issue concurrently since 1990, and in December 1991, the group submitted a report in favor of increasing the criminal penalty for a juridical person from 5 million yen as to violations provided for in section 89.

Based on this recommendation, a bill to increase the maximum fine up to 100 million yen for a juridical person or non-juridical organization in case of double punishment, which is applicable only to violations provided for in section 89, was submitted to the Diet, but could not go through during 1991 ordinary session. The bill was passed on December 10, 1992 during the extraordinary session (Act No. 107 of 1992).

This amendment raised the fine for a juridical person or non-juridical organization by 20 times. The amendment is applicable only to double punishment situations, therefore, it is still necessary in Japan for an act of violation by the offender to be established before a juridical person or non-juridical organization can be punished when such act was committed with respect to the business or property of the juridical person. The majority view in Japan denies a juridical person's capacity to commit a crime.

This increase applies only to section 3 and 8(1)(1) violations. This is because these violations represent the most serious violations of the Act, and according to the 1990 policy statement on criminal accusation, these violations cover almost all types of vicious and serious violations to which criminal penalties shall be sought.

(3) RELATIONS WITH OTHER SANCTIONS

With this amendment, sanctions against cartel activities are significantly tightened, and four kinds of de facto sanctions could be applicable against cartel activities—cease and desist orders and surcharge orders by the FTC, criminal prosecution by the Prosecuting Authority, and single damage suits by any injured person. Whether the latter two sanctions would become a feasible means of sanctions in Japan needs more time for evaluation by looking at actual enforcement. However, developments described in this chapter and chapter 17 (D) Enhancement of FTC Involvement would certainly increase the possibility of the effective use of these two systems, which have not worked effectively in the last 45 years.

It should be noted that Japan is the only country in which these four kinds of sanctions could be imposed on the same case. In view of the significant deterrent effects of these four sanctions as a whole, and the increased feasibility of using such sanctions in recent years, Japan can be described as one of the countries with the most severe sanctions against cartel activities.

Because the latter two sanctions inevitably involve court participation in antimonopoly matters, much desired case law would increase in Japan, which could increase the transparency of Antimonopoly Act enforcement.

NOTES

[1] Kokuhatu Mondai Kyogikai (Liaison Conference on Accusation Matters) was established in January 1991 between the FTC and the Prosecuting Authority.

[2] J. Haley argues, "The criminal justice system in Japan does not operate as a penalty-imposing process but a corrective one in which defendants are given the opportunity and incentive to repent, compensate the victims, and be absolved." J. Haley, *Antitrust Sanctions and Remedies: A Comparative Study of German and Japanese Law*, WASHINGTON LAW REVIEW, Vol. 59 (1984), at 487.

[3] Before 1974, fines were set at $50,000 for all persons. In 1974, fines for an individual were raised to $100,000, and fines for a corporation were raised to $1 million. Currently, the fine is set at $350,000 for an individual and $10 million for a corporation.

[4] So far as remedial measures are concerned, the FTC does not need to find several violations in a single decision. The FTC decision is directed to respondents, therefore, plural violations can be found in a single case.

19

SURCHARGE ORDER

The 1977 Amendment introduced a surcharge system aimed at increasing the effectiveness of preventing cartel activities. Before this amendment, partly due to lack of effective sanctions, there were an increasing number of cases where cartel activities were repeated. The FTC power to take remedial measures was limited, and once the illegal conduct was stopped voluntarily after the initiation of an investigation by the FTC, the FTC had difficulty in even using its remedial power.[1]

Before the 1977 Amendment, in order for the FTC to issue a decision, acts in violation of the Antimonopoly Act had to exist at the time of the FTC recommendation. Private suits to recover damages were almost nonexistent, and criminal penalties were not feasible under the circumstances.

In the pre-1977 Amendment period, economic benefits gained through cartel activities were left untouched, which made cartel activities profitable and with small risk of public disclosure of a cartel's activities. This prompted repeated cartel activities, even by prominent Japanese firms.

In order to break this vicious cycle by increasing economic sanctions against cartel participants, the surcharge system was introduced in 1977.

(A) OUTLINE OF THE SURCHARGE SYSTEM

(1) TYPES OF CARTELS THAT ARE SUBJECT TO A SURCHARGE ORDER

Surcharge orders can be imposed on those unreasonable restraints of trade that are related to price or that would result in affecting the price of goods or services by curtailing the volume of their shipment (sec. 7-2(1)).

Price raising cartels, price maintaining cartels, rebate cartels and bid rigging are typical examples of restraints of trade that are related to price. Production curtailment cartels, shipment restricting cartels, agreements to set quotas for production or shipments are examples that will result in affecting the price of goods or services.

A case-by-case analysis is necessary to see whether non-price related cartels such as investment adjustment cartels, cartels to restrict the use of facilities, or cartels to restrict the use of technology or customers would result in affecting the prices of goods or services by curtailing the volume of their shipment. Surcharges can also be imposed on cartels that violate sections 6(1) or 8(1)(i) or (ii).

(2) HOW TO CALCULATE THE AMOUNTS OF SURCHARGES

Surcharges are calculated by multiplying a fixed percentage by the amount of "turnover" of the goods or services during the cartel period. Cabinet Ordinance No. 317 of 1977 states that surcharges shall be equivalent to the total amount of prices of goods delivered or of services supplied for the period of the cartel (Cabinet Ordinance No. 317, sec. 5).

It is not necessary that all of the prices of goods or service delivered be cartelized or affected specifically by the cartel. For example, the goods for which price was negotiated before the start of cartel activities still would be counted as "turnover" so far as the goods are delivered during the cartel period.

The amount equivalent to any discount or rebate or the price reduction for goods returned will be deducted from the "turnover" (Cabinet Ordinance No. 317, sec. 5).

The cartel period starts from the date when goods that are cartelized are delivered to the customer for the first time, therefore, the cartel period is determined as to individual cartel participants. This means that the date set as an effective date by cartel agreements is not necessarily the starting date of the cartel period.

The cartel period ends when the cartel activities cease to exist. Ordinarily, this is the date when the FTC remedial measures are effected by the respondents. But, the respondents may take some voluntary measures to stop the alleged conduct before the FTC formally orders them to do so, and the FTC may sometimes acknowledge that such a date would be the date when the cartel period had ended.

The 1991 Amendment introduced a new system to limit the maximum length of the cartel period to 3 years. It means that whatever the cartel period, surcharges can be imposed as to the last 3 years of the cartel's activities. This amendment reasoned that account books showing the detailed sales records would not be available as to old sales figures, and so the 3-year period might ease the FTC's burden to calculate surcharges in cartel cases that had started years before. A significant increase in the fixed rate for surcharges may also justify such a summary way of enforcement.

(3) PERCENTAGE OF SURCHARGES

When the surcharge system was introduced, the percentage of surcharges was generally set at 3 percent. But a special rate of 4 percent was applied to manufacturing, 1 percent to wholesale, and 2 percent to retailing. Besides, the amount of surcharges was halved, because under the Act, for simplicity's sake, only one half of the total profits are assumed to be derived from illegal cartel activities.

These figures were determined based on the long-term profit rates for each industrial sector, and were meant to reflect the difference in the average profit rates among various industrial sectors.

On April 26, 1991, the Diet amended the Antimonopoly Act to increase the fixed percentage of surcharges in order to increase the deterring effects of the surcharge system. The assumption that one half of the total profits are derived from illegal cartel activities was eliminated.

The long-term profit rates for each industrial group that were used as the basis to determine the fixed percentage for surcharges was reviewed so as to reflect the difference in average profit rates according to the scale of firms. The special rates for the manufacturing sector were eliminated.

As a result of these amendments, the fixed percentage was raised to 6 percent in general, but the percentage for the retail and wholesale sectors remained at the same level.

On the other hand, the law provided specially reduced rates for smaller firms and individuals. For the purpose of the surcharge system, smaller firms are defined in the law as firms with less than 100 million yen paid-up capital or firms or individuals with fewer than 300 employees in other than wholesale, retail and service industries.

As to the retail or service industries, firms with less than 10 million yen of paid-up capital or firms or individuals with fewer than 50 employees are designated as smaller firms. In the wholesale industry, firms with less than 30 million yen of paid-up capital or firms or individuals with fewer than 100 employees are designated as smaller firms.

Accordingly, after the amendment, the fixed percentage for surcharges was changed as follows:

Industry	In general	Smaller firms or individuals
Manufacturing	2.0%—6.0%	2.0%—3.0%
Others	1.5%—6.0%	1.5%—3.0%
Wholesale	0.5%—1.0%	0.5%—1.0%
Retail	1.0%—2.0%	1.0%—1.0%

This amendment takes effect as to cartel activities that were effected after July 1, 1991 and the old surcharge rate would be applicable to those cartel activities effected before that date.

(4) UNIQUE NATURE OF THE SURCHARGE SYSTEM

The Japanese surcharge system has the following two characteristics, as compared with its European model.[2] Firstly, any discretion on the part of the FTC is denied. When the FTC finds cartel activities in its decision, it must order payment of surcharges as calculated according to the law. Secondly, there is no discretion concerning the percentage of a surcharge, as a result, the amount of a surcharge does not correspond to the amount of overcharge. Even when the price is raised 20 percent, the surcharge percentage is at a maximum of 6 percent. There is also a problem with its deterrent effect, because if cartel participants were to know beforehand the ultimate burden when cartel activities are found by the FTC, those persons would try to include the necessary amount in their overcharge.

The first characteristic is justified by reason of avoiding double punishment. If the FTC is authorized discretionary power as mentioned above, a surcharge assumes the nature of a penalty, and co-existence with a criminal penalty is not justifiable under the Constitution. Therefore, a surcharge can be imposed as an administrative measure to deter any recurrence of cartel activities.

The second characteristic is justified by reason of administrative convenience. Under the current system, the FTC is not required to calculate the amount of overcharge in individual cases. Even the current system places a huge administrative burden on the FTC, therefore, the current method could have a huge advantage for enforcing the system.

The 1991 Amendment raised the percentage of surcharge to the level sufficient to have deterring effects. It is clear that a fixed percentage of surcharge may not have a sufficient deterring effect in individual cases. However, when the amount of surcharge is considered insufficient as to an individual case, that is the case where a criminal penalty should be considered.

(B) PROCEDURES TO IMPOSE SURCHARGES

When the FTC finds the existence of cartel activities that are subject to surcharge it must order the entrepreneurs concerned to pay a fixed amount to the Treasury within a specified period of time (sec. 48-2(1)). In case of a section 8(1)(i) violation, the FTC will order each member of the trade association concerned to pay a surcharge (sec. 8-3).

The FTC may not order the payment of surcharges when more than 3 years have elapsed from the date the cartel activities ended; in other words, there shall be not more than 3 years since the date on which the entrepreneurs had discontinued their business activities based on a cartel agreement (sec. 7-2(5)). In case the amount thus calculated is below 500,000 yen, the entrepreneurs concerned are exempted from the payment of surcharges (sec. 7-2(1)). Before the 1991 Amendment, the amount was set at 200,000 yen.

The order shall state the amount of the surcharge to be paid, the basis for such calculation, the provisions of the Act that were violated causing them to be paid, and the deadline for such payment (sec. 48-2(2)).

The FTC must provide the entrepreneurs an opportunity in advance to present their opinions and to submit evidence in support thereof (sec. 48-2(4)). This opportunity is offered by serving a certified copy of the draft order of the surcharge payment to the entrepreneurs concerned.

Ordinarily, the FTC would start the surcharge collecting procedure after the fact of violation was established, in other words, after the FTC decision was rendered finding a violation of the Act. However, when 1 year has elapsed from the date on which the cartel activities ended, or in case of a section 8(1)(i) violation, when the trade association was dissolved before any FTC decision, the FTC will issue a surcharge order only.

The deadline for the payment of a surcharge shall fall on a date 2 months after the service of the order. If any person is dissatisfied with the order, he may demand, within 30 days from the date on which he was served a certified copy of the order, the initiation of a hearing proceeding on his case (sec. 48-2(5)).

(C) ENFORCEMENT

During FY 1978, the first year of enforcement, there was one surcharge case and the amount of the surcharge assessed was 5.07 million yen. However, during FY 1979, there were five surcharge cases, and a total payment of 1,571.74 million yen was ordered against 134 entrepreneurs. In the 1979 Ishikawajima-Harima Heavy Industries Co. case (Surcharge order, March 31, 1980, 26 KTIS 169), the respondents were ordered to pay a total of 897.32 million yen.

Table 19-1. The Amount of Surcharge Ordered Per Year

FY	Number of Cases	Number of Entrepreneurs Who Were Ordered to Pay Surcharge	Amount of Surcharges Ordered Per Year (In Thousands of Yen)
1978	1	4	507
1979	5	134	157,174
1980	12	203	133,111
1981	6	148	373,020
1982	8	166	48,354
1983	10	93	149,257
1984	2	5	35,310
1985	4	38	40,747
1986	4	32	27,554
1987	6	54	14,758
1988	3	84	41,899
1989	6	54	80,349
1990	11	175	1,256,214
1991	10	101	197,169
1992	17	135	268,157
Total	105	1,426	2,823,580

During FY 1981, a total of 3,730.2 million yen in surcharges was ordered; a record as to surcharge amount per year up to FY 1991. The largest amount for a single cartel case involved the 1981 Dai-o Paper Co. case (Surcharge order, Feb. 24, 1981, 28 KTIS 110), and the respondents were ordered to pay a total of 1.17 billion yen. This was also a record as to an individual case up to FY 1991.

From FY 1982 to FY 1989, the annual amount of surcharges collected remained at a low level. By far the largest surcharge case was observed in FY 1991 when cement manufacturing companies were ordered to pay to the Treasury a total of over 11.2 billion yen. This cement cartel consisted of two regional cases. The single company's surcharge record was also broken by this case. The Nippon Cement Co. was ordered to pay 2.4 billion yen (Surcharge order, March 18, 1991, 37 KTIS 174).

As to a single case, the cement cartel case in the Chugoku District was the largest, a total of 6.62 billion yen in surcharges was ordered against nine companies. The cement cartel case in Hokkaido was the second largest single case; a total of 4.61 billion yen in surcharges was ordered against eight companies.

These were the cases before the 1991 Amendment took effect. For FY 1991, the total amount was the fourth largest per year, but there were no cases where an increased percentage was applied. FY 1992 was the third largest per year, but most of the cartel activities had covered conducts before June 1991. The effect of the amendment will be seen after FY 1993.

NOTES

[1] This finding depends on how to find the fact of discontinuance of cartel agreements. So far as the cartel agreement was revoked by participants, a cease-and-desist order cannot be issued after its revocation.

[2] As to the German system of surcharges, see J. Haley, *Antitrust Sanctions and Remedies: A Comparative Study of German and Japanese Law,* WASHINGTON LAW REVIEW, Vol. 59 (1984), at 490-492. In Germany, a surcharge equal to three times any excess proceeds realized as a result of violations can be imposed. See sec. 38(4) of the German antitrust law. However, J. Haley sees that "The problem lies in the proof of the amount of illegal proceeds in Germany or damages in the United States. To meet the legal requirements of proof in either case is a difficult and extremely costly task." "As a consequence of the problems associated with the illegal proceeds surcharge, the Federal Cartel Office has made use of the excess proceeds surcharge provision of GWB section 38(4) in relatively few instances." *id.* at 491-492.

20

REPORTING REQUIREMENTS

(A) IN GENERAL

One of the major characteristics of Japanese antimonopoly enforcement is its reliance on the reporting or filing obligation. The Antimonopoly Act liberally provided a power to obligate related entrepreneurs to file a report with the FTC. This is a method that requires relatively little manpower to enforce the Antimonopoly Act. This power made it possible for the FTC to engage in a wide range of activities in spite of a limited number of personnel. Also, it helped the FTC to engage in various economic research on the competitive conditions of industry. This accumulation of economic study helped very much to enhance the understanding of the Act by providing a sound basis for the antimonopoly policy.

Reliance on the filing obligation is one of the common methods for the government offices in Japan to obtain the necessary information for law enforcement with a minimum burden on business. For example, under section 29 of the Foreign Exchange and Foreign Trade Control Act (Act No. 228 of 1949), foreign technology assistance agreements are required to file, within 30 days of their conclusion, with the Bank of Japan.

Reliance on reporting had some impact on the FTC's informal way of enforcement. When the FTC takes remedial measures triggered by a filed report, it does not necessarily utilize the formal power authorized under the Act.

By emphasizing the informal way of enforcement, understanding of the Antimonopoly Act on the part of business was greatly enhanced. This had proved to be a very effective enforcement method as to regulation of mergers and acquisitions, and regulation of unfair trade practices. Reliance on such a soft or informal enforcement mechanism has helped to broaden the acceptance of the basic notion of antitrust among business, and could be called a compliance-oriented approach.

Business could start to accept the basic notion of antitrust by facing the high risk of severe punishment. Apparently, this was the path the U.S. took, and could be called the punishment-oriented approach.[1] But this was not a feasible approach for such a country as Japan because, here, antitrust was an alien concept for ordinary businessmen.

Too much reliance on informal enforcement could produce a lack-of-transparency problem. Sometimes, non-disclosure becomes an important component of informal enforcement, that is, non-disclosure makes it easy to get the compliance of the related entrepreneurs. On the other hand, non-disclosure has a problem of it own, namely, it does not educate other businessmen who engage in the same conduct, and the general public will not have sufficient information concerning enforcement of the Act.[2]

Japan was the first country in the world to introduce a premerger notification system, and has been enforcing the system for more than 40 years. Premerger notification has proven to be an effective policy tool and in the 1970s and 1980s was adopted by the United States, West Germany, France, and the European Community.[3]

Other filing obligations seem to be unique to Japan, and would constitute one of the important characteristics of the Japanese antimonopoly laws. Reliance on a filing obligation will continue in view of the limited resources available to the FTC, but cases to be disclosed arc going to increase in order to enhance transparency and the deterrent effects of the FTC's enforcement activities.

(B) FILING OBLIGATIONS

(1) INTERNATIONAL CONTRACTS

(i) Nature of the obligation

An entrepreneur who has entered into a specified international agreement or contract must file a report with the FTC within 30 days of the execution of such an act (sec. 6(2)). An oral contract or agreement also is subject to the filing obligation. This is an *ex post* notification requirement and has nothing to do with its effectiveness.

This obligation was criticized as discriminating against international contracts vis-a-vis domestic contracts. The filing obligation of international contracts was criticized not because it is burdensome to a foreign party, but because only international contracts were required to file, therefore, domestic contracts may remain unchecked whereas international contracts may be regularly checked by the FTC.

When antitrust risk is high, business benefits by filing a report and enjoying a negative clearance thereafter. Legal stability, in particular, is important for international business activities, which face a higher risk of troubles than do domestic business activities. The solutions to international troubles are more difficult than for domestic disputes. In this sense, the filing requirement on international contracts could serve to lessen business risk, and even could serve the interests of foreign business.

In order to learn the usefulness of the filing obligation, it is wise to look at its history. In 1943, S.1476 was introduced in the U.S. by Senator O'Mahoney. It called for compulsory registration with the Attorney General of companies residing or doing business in the U.S. of any international contracts that contain such matters as restriction of output or sales, fixing of prices, dividing of markets and limiting or cross-licensing of patents. This bill was prompted as the result of an investigation conducted by the Temporary National Economic Committee.[4]

The compulsory registration system relating to the above-mentioned international contracts was effectuated in Japan first by Imperial Ordinance No. 33 on the Prohibition of Any Agreement or Contract of International Character on January 23, 1946. This ordinance was issued in accordance with the memorandum from the Supreme Commander for the Allied Powers (SCAP). Section 6(2) of the Antimonopoly Act succeeded this compulsory registration system.

(ii) The 1982 Amendment

As shown above, the filing obligation on international contracts in itself could serve a useful purpose. However, it is also clear that only those international contracts that face higher antitrust risk should be required to be filed.

In 1982, section 6 was amended, and by this amendment only those international contracts that are designated by the FTC regulation need to be filed. The FTC must designate only those types of international contracts wherein it finds a tendency to contain such matters constituting unreasonable restraint of trade or unfair trade practices.[5]

According to the FTC regulation, the following six kinds of international contracts were designated:

(A) Technology licensing agreements (software licensing agreements are included),
(B) Import or export distributorship agreements,
(C) Joint venture agreements,
(D) Trademark and copyright licensing agreements,
(E) Joint export or import agreements among domestic competitors,
(F) International agreements that contain restrictions on price, volume, or area etc. of exports or imports.

(iii) The 1992 Amendment

In view of the continued criticism concerning discrimination, the FTC reviewed the extent of the filing requirement with a view to confine such a requirement to the minimum necessary.

As a result, on March 30, 1992, the filing obligation was significantly reduced by introducing additional standards for selection.

As to technology licensing agreements and import or export distributorship agreements, the following changes were adopted.

(A) Non-exclusive agreements were excluded completely from the filing obligation.

(B) When a party to the contract does not have a market position exceeding 10 percent or is not within the top three in the relevant market of Japan, then his international contract is excluded from the filing obligation.

(C) When the contract contains a price restriction clause, such a contract needs to be filed without regard to the market position of the contracting parties.

(D) As to trademark and copyright licensing agreements, the filing obligation was completely eliminated.

(E) As to joint venture agreements, those agreements by medium and small businesses were excluded from the filing obligation. (For a definition of medium and small business, see chapter 19 (A)(3) Percentage of Surcharges.)

In view of their horizontal nature, joint export or import agreements among domestic competitors and international agreements that contain restrictions on export or import prices, volumes, or area etc. remain unchanged.

Because of this amendment, it is estimated that about two-thirds or four-fifths of all international contracts would be excluded from filing obligations.

(2) TRADE ASSOCIATIONS

Every trade association shall file a report with the FTC within 30 days of its formation (sec. 8(2)). When there have been any changes in the matters reported or when the association is dissolved, a report thereof is also required to be filed (secs. 8 (3) and 8(4)). The form to be filed is given in FTC Regulation No. 2 of 1953. Certain trade associations that are established according to specific laws are exempted from the application of section 8, including the filing obligation.

This filing obligation may be meaningful in making known the existence of a trade association, but most problems of trade associations lie in their day-to-day activities, not articles of incorporation or memberships. In view of the need to keep a close watch on trade association activities, the FTC regulation was amended in December

1991 so that more market related information could be gathered by the FTC.

For example, market share occupied by the trade association in the relevant market, the internal organization of the trade association (many cartel activities are effected by these internal organizations), and the names of member firms now need to be filed so that the FTC can keep a closer watch on the activities of trade associations.

(3) MERGERS AND TRANSFERS OF BUSINESS

(i) Mergers

Every company in Japan that intends to become a party to a merger, regardless of its corporate size, is required to file a report with the FTC (sec. 15(2)). This is a prior notification obligation, and the parties cannot effect a merger until the expiration of 30 days from the date of filing. The FTC will issue an "acknowledgement of filing" after it confirms fulfillment of the filing obligation, including necessary information and attachments. Under its rules, the Commercial Registration Office will not register a merger without the "acknowledgement of filing" issued by the FTC.

The FTC, when it intends to take an action against the merger, is required to do so before the expiration of the 30-day waiting period. With the consent of the parties, this waiting period can be extended for up to an additional 60 days (sec. 15(3)).

(ii) Transfers of business

The same prior notification obligation is applicable to transfers of business. Prior notification is mandated when the whole or "a substantial part of the business," "the fixed assets" etc. is transferred. Therefore, in contrast to the case of mergers, some uncertainty remains concerning the notification obligation. It is not necessary that the transferred business be a substantial business for the transferor. For example, the business of a branch office, factory, or a division of the transferor's business activities could be a substantial part of the business within the meaning of section 16(2).

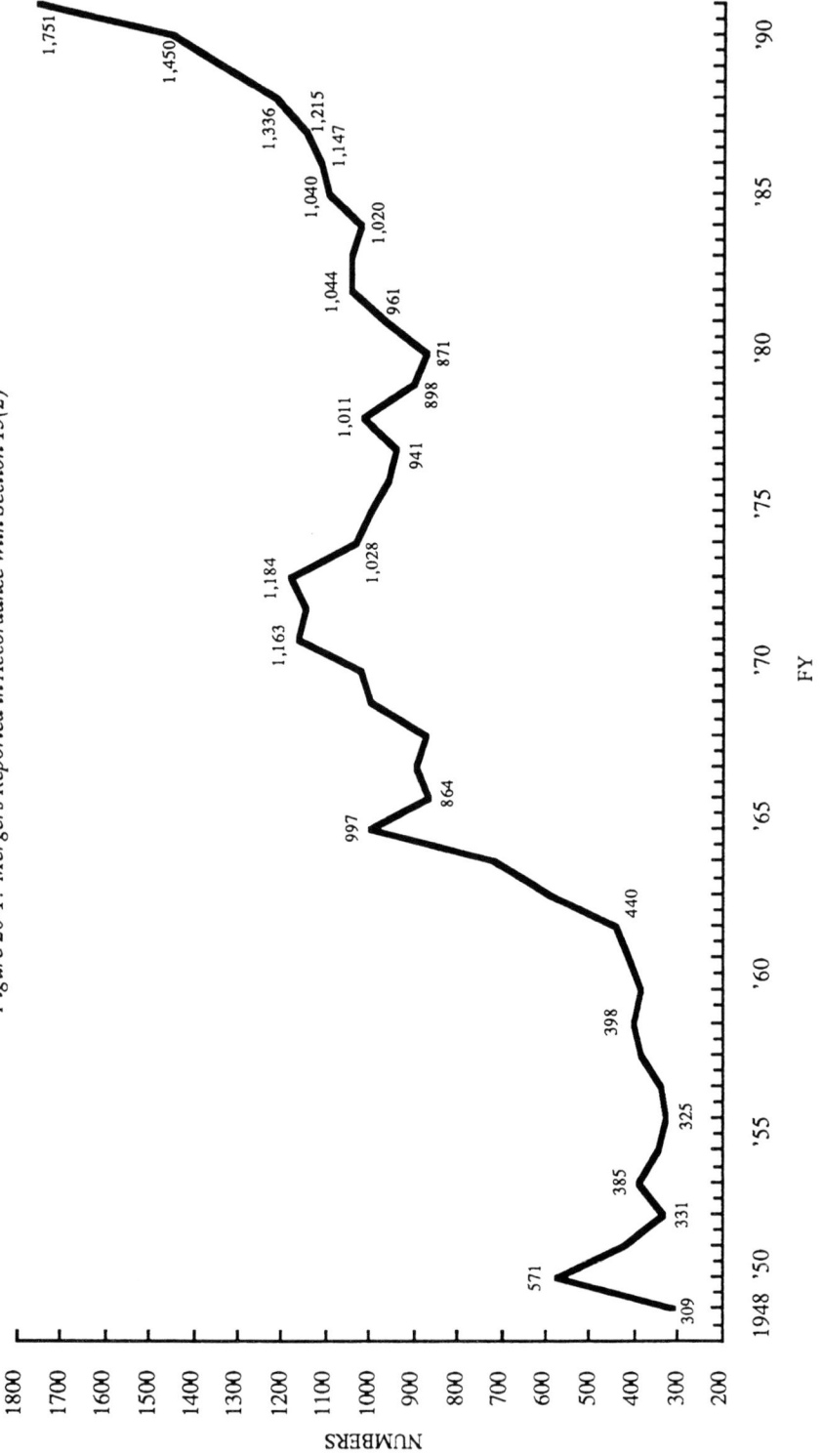

Figure 20-1. Mergers Reported in Accordance with Section 15(2)

Figure 20-2. Transfers of Business Reported in Accordance with Section 16

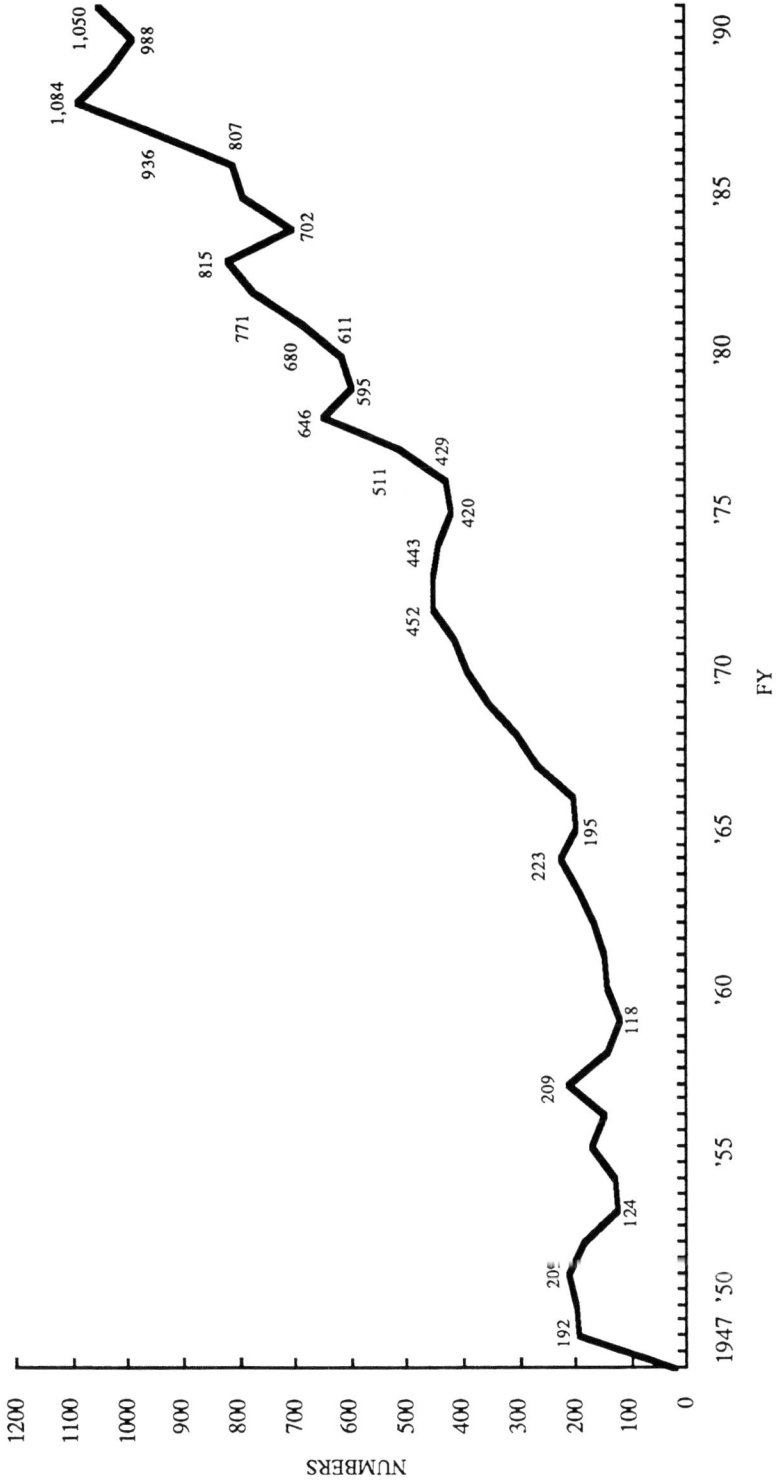

Table 20-1. Classification of Mergers by Scale of Company*

(FY)	Less than 100	100– 500	500– 1,000	1,000– 5,000	5,000– 10,000	More than 10,000	Total
1947	–	–	–	–	–	–	23
1948	–	–	–	–	–	–	309
1949	–	–	–	–	–	–	571
1950	413	7	0	0	0	0	420
1951	317	12	2	0	0	0	331
1952	359	19	4	3	0	0	385
1953	315	19	5	5	0	0	344
1954	293	23	5	4	0	0	325
1955	311	15	4	7	1	0	338
1956	359	13	2	6	1	0	381
1957	367	18	4	9	0	0	398
1958	348	23	2	7	1	0	381
1959	368	30	7	8	0	0	413
1960	381	41	8	9	0	1	440
1961	519	45	9	13	3	2	591
1962	585	91	10	23	3	3	715
1963	821	116	15	28	5	12	997
1964	730	90	14	17	4	9	864
1965	771	93	16	8	3	3	894
1966	763	67	11	23	2	5	871
1967	852	94	9	29	4	7	995
1968	876	100	16	19	2	7	1,020
1969	965	142	20	29	5	2	1,163
1970	925	142	37	34	3	6	1,147
1971	981	131	27	23	9	7	1,178
1972	939	171	29	37	1	7	1,184
1973	803	163	25	26	3	8	1,028
1974	773	157	30	19	0	16	995
1975	776	128	17	24	6	6	957
1976	763	119	27	27	1	4	941
1977	781	164	29	29	5	3	1,011
1978	657	158	51	26	4	2	898
1979	647	153	33	28	3	7	871
1980	733	158	37	22	6	5	961
1981	759	198	43	36	4	4	1,044
1982	813	140	40	35	4	8	1,040
1983	764	184	24	30	10	8	1,020
1984	856	174	19	34	6	7	1,096
1985	874	162	29	33	7	8	1,113
1986	891	167	37	31	12	9	1,147
1987	868	226	42	51	12	16	1,215
1988	941	286	33	48	18	10	1,336
1989	959	347	53	51	14	26	1,450
1990	1,137	409	74	88	15	28	1,751
1991	1,442	422	79	101	21	26	2,091

NOTE:
* The scale of company is classified by the amount of paid-in capital after the merger was completed in million yen.
SOURCE: Compiled from the FTC Annual Reports.

Table 20-2. Classification of Transfers of Business by Scale of Company*

(FY)	Less than 100	100– 500	500– 1,000	1,000– 5,000	5,000– 10,000	More than 10,000	Total
1947	–	–	–	–	–	–	22
1948	–	–	–	–	–	–	192
1949	–	–	–	–	–	–	196
1950	184	15	8	2	0	0	209
1951	164	9	1	5	3	0	182
1952	106	12	6	0	0	0	124
1953	103	15	3	5	0	0	126
1954	131	21	3	11	1	0	167
1955	104	17	7	13	2	0	143
1956	164	26	8	11	0	0	209
1957	98	26	5	11	0	0	140
1958	93	15	5	5	0	0	118
1959	89	24	11	15	0	0	139
1960	100	21	7	16	0	0	144
1961	122	29	2	8	1	0	162
1962	146	29	5	11	1	1	193
1963	169	32	5	14	1	2	223
1964	147	25	9	14	0	0	195
1965	148	30	8	10	2	4	202
1966	203	34	9	11	4	6	267
1967	216	51	14	12	4	4	301
1968	298	36	8	8	0	4	354
1969	296	62	12	18	2	1	391
1970	317	49	16	20	3	8	413
1971	352	54	10	22	7	4	449
1972	335	65	13	29	5	5	452
1973	244	95	26	38	16	24	443
1974	329	46	11	18	4	12	420
1975	324	53	9	30	0	13	429
1976	398	61	13	24	4	11	511
1977	455	104	17	50	6	14	646
1978	442	91	16	24	5	17	595
1979	454	83	26	30	5	13	611
1980	522	93	12	25	13	15	680
1981	599	96	23	36	7	10	771
1982	589	132	24	38	5	27	815
1983	514	115	16	31	10	16	702
1984	567	158	6	22	10	27	790
1985	544	155	24	51	7	26	807
1986	652	158	24	48	10	44	936
1987	752	205	17	45	11	54	1,804
1988	709	197	11	52	9	50	1,028
1989	651	191	36	51	19	40	988
1990	692	196	40	46	21	55	1,050
1991	835	224	29	74	18	86	1,266

NOTE:

* The scale of company is classified by the amount of paid-in capital after the merger was completed in million yen.

SOURCE: Compiled from the FTC Annual Reports.

Table 20-3. Number of Mergers by Type

FY	Horizontal	Vertical	Market Extension[1]	Product Extension[2]	Conglo- merate	Others[3]	Total[4]
1970	472(36.1)	107 (8.2)	205(15.7)	109 (8.4)	260(20.0)	150(14.5)	1,303
1971	389(28.5)	176(12.9)	238(17.5)	132 (9.7)	315(23.1)	113 (8.3)	1,363
1972	319(24.4)	183(14.0)	199(15.2)	129 (9.9)	369(28.2)	108 (8.3)	1,307
1973	264(23.2)	159(14.0)	135(11.9)	144(12.7)	330(29.0)	104 (9.2)	1,136
1974	242(20.6)	153(13.0)	130(11.5)	143(12.2)	392(33.3)	115 (9.8)	1,175
1975	261(23.4)	159(14.2)	129(11.5)	128(11.5)	357(31.9)	84 (7.5)	1,118
1976	239(22.5)	128(12.0)	126(11.8)	143(13.4)	338(31.8)	90 (8.5)	1,064
1977	267(23.3)	173(15.1)	141(12.3)	146(12.7)	337(29.4)	83 (7.2)	1,147
1978	257(25.2)	164(16.1)	158(15.5)	122(12.0)	231(22.7)	86 (8.5)	1,018
1979	213(20.5)	216(20.7)	160(15.4)	118(11.3)	236(22.7)	98 (9.4)	1,041
1980	204(16.7)	119 (9.7)	372(30.3)	119 (9.7)	342(27.9)	70 (5.7)	1,226
1981	278(23.2)	123 (9.8)	279(22.3)	104 (8.3)	412(33.3)	54 (4.3)	1,250
1982	255(20.7)	185(15.1)	213(17.3)	116 (9.4)	406(33.0)	54 (4.4)	1,229
1983	277(22.6)	161(13.1)	249(20.3)	98 (8.0)	402(32.8)	38 (3.1)	1,225
1984	340(27.2)	189(15.1)	138(11.0)	132(10.6)	412(33.0)	38 (3.0)	1,249
1985	360(28.2)	204(16.0)	221(17.3)	99 (7.8)	349(27.4)	43 (3.4)	1,276
1986	312(22.6)	240(17.4)	240(17.4)	161(11.7)	391(28.3)	36 (2.6)	1,380
1987	399(25.8)	232(15.0)	236(15.3)	215(13.9)	414(26.8)	50 (3.2)	1,546
1988	514(30.1)	285(16.7)	274(16.1)	177(10.4)	401(23.5)	56 (3.3)	1,707
1989	517(28.9)	249(13.9)	278(15.6)	218(12.2)	466(26.1)	59 (3.3)	1,787
1990	771(33.9)	310(13.6)	352(15.5)	238(10.5)	512(22.5)	92 (4.0)	2,275
1991	803(30.7)	466(17.8)	329(12.6)	193 (7.4)	720(27.5)	107 (4.1)	2,618

NOTES:

[1] Market extension refers to one type of conglomerate merger where the acquiring company merges with a potential competitor to expand into a different geographical market.

[2] "Product extension" refers to one type of conglomerate merger where the acquiring company merges with a company whose product is not directly in competition with the acquiring company but is closely related to it.

[3] "Others" refers to mergers effected to change the face amount of stocks, or to change the corporate form from an unlimited liability company to a stock company etc.

[4] Because one merger can involve several companies engaging in different markets, the total in this table is not equal to the total number of filed reports.

(4) STOCKHOLDING AND INTERLOCKING DIRECTORATES

(i) Report on stockholding by a company

Every company in Japan whose business is other than financial and whose total assets—the total amount of the assets according to the latest balance sheet—exceed 2 billion yen, or every foreign company whose business is other than financial, shall, in the event that it holds stocks of another company or companies in Japan, submit a report on stockholdings that are held in its name or in the name of a trustee, to the FTC within 3 months from the end of every business year (sec. 10(2)).

FTC Regulation No. 2 of 1953 describes the form to use. On the form, such matters as the total amount of the stocks according to the latest balance sheet, names of major shareholders of companies, names and details of companies of which it holds more than 10 percent of stocks, among others, shall be disclosed.

(ii) Report on stockholding by a person other than a company

Every person other than a company, in the event he holds stocks of two or more companies that are mutually competing in Japan, and he holds stocks in excess of 10 percent of the total outstanding stocks of each, must submit a report of such stockholdings to the FTC within 30 days therefrom (sec. 14(2)).

(iii) Report on interlocking directorates

Every officer or employee of a company who holds concurrently the position of an officer in another company or companies in Japan (interlocking directorates) that are in competition with it in Japan, shall, in case the total assets of either company exceed 2 billion yen, file a report thereof with the FTC within 30 days from the date of assuming the position of an officer (sec. 13(3)).

(5) RESALE PRICE MAINTENANCE

When entrepreneurs intend to conclude resale price maintenance contracts with their distributors, they must file a report with the FTC within 30 days from the date of such conclusion. This applies to designated commodities only, therefore, copyrighted works are excluded from this filing obligation (sec. 24-2(6)). Based on this report, the FTC will make sure that resale price maintenance was conducted complying with all the requirements given in section 24-2.

NOTES

[1] J. Haley, *Sheathing the Sword of Justice in Japan: An Assay on Law without Sanctions*, JOURNAL JAPANESE STUDIES, Vol. 8 (1982), at 265. J. Haley, *Antitrust Sanctions and Remedies: A Comparative Study of German and Japanese Law*, WASHINGTON LAW REVIEW, Vol. 54 (1984), at 471, argues, "If criminal prosecution in any society, as we have noted in Germany, is an unwieldy tool for antitrust enforcement, in Japan it is even less useful. Japan is consequently left with an extraordinary weak system of law enforcement." at 482.

[2] This view is contradictory to the use of publicity as a sanction. J. Haley, *Antitrust Sanctions . . . , supra* note 1 argues, "If it is true that adverse publicity is as meaningful a penalty as a fine, must its use be subject also to the procedural restrictions applied to the imposition of other penalties to protect the citizens from arbitrary government action?" at 507.

Publicity shall not be regarded as a means of sanction, rather it shall be treated as a measure to improve the transparency of governmental action, even if in Japan it has de facto deterrent effects.

[3] Germany adopted the premerger notification system in 1957, the United States adopted it in 1976. France adopted a voluntary merger notification system in 1977. Canada adopted a merger notification system in 1986, which became effective on July 15, 1987. The EC adopted Council Regulation (EEC) No. 4064/89 on the control of concentrations between undertakings on Dec. 21, 1989, which became effective on Sep. 21, 1990.

[4] TNEC, FINAL REPORT AND RECOMMENDATIONS (Senate Doc. 35, 77 Cong., 1 Sess., 1941); Y. Ohara, *International Application of the Japanese Antimonopoly Act*, SWISS REVIEW OF INTERNATIONAL COMPARATIVE LAW, Vol. 28 (1986), at 6-9; E. HAWLEY, THE NEW DEAL AND THE PROBLEM OF MONOPOLY (1966), in which he wrote "About all that a majority of the Committee could agree upon were some minor changes in the antitrust laws and minor reforms in patent procedures, and few of these were ever implemented." at 465.

[5] This amendment was effected as one of the packages to simplify government administration and procedures. Act No. 75 of 1982, effective Oct. 1, 1982.

INTERNATIONAL APPLICATION OF THE ANTIMONOPOLY ACT

(A) INDIRECT APPLICATION OF THE ANTIMONOPOLY ACT

(1) REGULATION UNDER SECTION 6(1)

The Antimonopoly Act is applicable to conduct undertaken within Japan by foreign entrepreneurs. Whether the foreign entrepreneurs reside in Japan is irrelevant. Whether Japan adopts an "effect doctrine" is not yet settled.[1] But because section 6(1) could reach foreign entrepreneurs who had an agreement or a contract with Japanese entrepreneurs, it could be extended indirectly to foreign entrepreneurs. This is called an indirect application of the Antimonopoly Act.

Section 6(1) deals specifically with international agreements or contracts that may have a harmful influence upon the Japanese market by prohibiting entrepreneurs from entering into an international agreement or contract that contains matters constituting "unreasonable restraint of trade" or "unfair trade practices." Section 8(1)(ii) prohibits a trade association from entering into an international agreement or contract that contains matters constituting "unreasonable restraint of trade" or "unfair trade practices."

(2) SECTION 6 V. SECTIONS 3 AND 19

Section 6 is a special provision directed at an international agreement or contract. However, section 3 could be applicable to international "unreasonable restraint of trade" because entrepreneurs who are subject to section 3 regulation are not limited to Japanese entrepreneurs. Section 6 prohibits the conclusion of an international agreement or contract as long as it contains matters constituting "unreasonable restraint of trade" or "unfair trade practices." Therefore, section 6(1) does cover the act of concluding such an agreement or contract, and does not require that the restraints contained in the agreement or contract were actually effected.

As to section 3 violations, it is argued[2] that a cartel agreement, before it becomes effective could be prohibited, but in the case of section 6(1), it is very clear that such an agreement or contract is itself prohibited at the time of conclusion, not at the time it becomes effective. In particular, section 6 as compared with section 19, enlarges the applicability of the law as to unfair trade practices because it could cover entrepreneurs other than those who carry out unfair trade practices, and also could cover those agreements or contracts where the restrictive provisions are not yet in effect.

(3) CASES

The FTC applied section 6(1) in 30 cases, 22 of them were cases rendered in 1949 and 1950. As to 21 of these cases, foreign entrepreneurs had imposed restrictions on the activities of Japanese entrepreneurs, and except for one exclusive distributorship contract case all were related to technological assistance agreements.

Most of them involved restrictions on sales territories, handling of competitive products, or on the purchase of raw materials. In the 1953 Mitsubishi Shipbuilding Co. case (April 23, 1953, 5 KTIS 1), the FTC found that royalty payments even where licensed patents were not used were illegal as was stipulated in the international contract with the Sulzer Freres S.A. of Switzerland.

In the 1950 Marukin Soy Sauce Co. case (March 20, 1950, 1 KTIS 129), the respondent imposed a non-competition clause on its exclusive exporters of soy sauce, and the FTC found that this provision did violate section 6(1).

However, in the 1952 Nihon Kogaku Kogyo Co. case (Sep. 3, 1952, 4 KTIS 30 and 4 KTIS 46), the FTC had revoked two complaints against the Nihon Kogaku Kogyo Co. because no violation shall be found when exclusive export sales rights were granted and in this connection a non-competition obligation was imposed on such exporters.

Six cases in 1972 were directed against Japanese exporters of various synthetic fiber products who had participated in international agreements that restricted exports from Japan to Europe and other world markets with the exception of the U.S. (Asahi Kasei Kogyo Co., Dec. 27, 1972, 19 KTIS 124 et al.).

In two cases, foreign entrepreneurs were made respondents. In the above-mentioned 1953 Mitsubishi Shipbuilding Co. case, a Swiss corporation was ordered to cancel patent licensing agreements concluded with the Mitsubishi Shipbuilding Co. In the other case, the 1950 Takeda Pharmaceutical Co. case (June 15, 1950, 2 KTIS 46), the Chiba Co. of Switzerland was made the respondent.

Foreign companies were also made the respondents in the 1972 Far East Freight Conference case (Aug. 18, 1972, 19 KTIS (197), mentioned at (C)(1) below.

In one instance, the FTC had issued a complaint to an American company, the Bucyrus-Erie Co., which had a joint venture agreement with a Japanese party, the Komatsu Co. The FTC alleged that some of the restrictive provisions in the joint venture agreement constituted unfair trade practices. The complaint was dismissed after the joint venture agreement was voluntarily canceled by the parties (Oct. 26, 1981, 28 KTIS 79).

In 1966, the Amano Pharmaceutical Co. (Amano) had concluded an international distributorship contract with the Novo Industri Co. (Novo), a Danish company, granting an exclusive sales right throughout Japan for alkaline bacterial proteinase. The contract provided that Amano would maintain the retail price established by Novo, and refrain from selling competing products for 3 years after the expiration of the contract, and finally not manufacture and sell any competing products for an indefinite period after the expiration of the contract. The FTC, finding that these restrictive provisions constituted unfair trade practices, issued a recommendation. Because Amano accepted the recommendation, the FTC rendered a recommendation decision ordering Amano to eliminate these provisions (Jan. 12, 1970, 16 KTIS 134).

(B) PROCEDURAL PROBLEMS OF REGULATION UNDER SECTION 6(1)

Because section 6(1) of the Antimonopoly Act could be used as an indirect way of applying the Act, there are several problems from the view point of due process. Four kinds of procedural problems are indicated.

First is the unilateral nature of regulation under section 6(1) of the Act. It is suspected that the FTC will make decisions based only on the facts offered by one party to an international agreement, namely, the Japanese party.

Second, the FTC intervenes after international agreements are concluded, therefore, a foreign party faces difficulty in coping with the FTC intervention because at that time it is difficult to renegotiate the contractual terms of the agreements *de novo*. Foreign parties may sometimes be forced to accept, reluctantly, revisions of the provisions in question.

Third, FTC regulation is based on a wrong assumption that a foreign party is always in a dominant bargaining position vis-a-vis a Japanese party, thus a nationalistic bias exists.

Fourth, only international agreements are subject to filing obligations, and similar domestic agreements are not regulated with the same intensity.

(1) UNILATERAL NATURE OF REGULATION

The first question stems from the jurisdictional limitation of the FTC's investigatory powers. Under the Antimonopoly Act, the FTC has no power to compel a foreign party to appear and present its views. However, when they voluntarily appear before the FTC, their views can be listened to. For example, in the case of patent or know-how licensing agreements, any views presented by foreign licensors would be evaluated by the FTC.

Ordinarily, a foreign party rarely tries to present its views to the FTC. The FTC is not in a position to compel a foreign party to appear, therefore, under ordinary circumstances, the FTC will have contact with a foreign party only through a Japanese party and on a voluntary basis.

The Guidelines on Patent and Know-How Licensing Agreements had introduced a procedure to permit contracting parties to present justification for the alleged restrictive provisions in the contract (see Chapter 23 Technology Licensing and Joint R & D). Under this procedure, a foreign party can present justification when the FTC indicates to the party its views on a particular restrictive provision. The FTC's action at this stage is an important one, and by its nature is not a final disposition of a case. Therefore, in fact it could mean the start of a series of procedures to solve antimonopoly problems informally.

(2) INTRODUCTION OF A CLEARANCE SYSTEM

In order to solve the second problem, that is to say, the FTC's *ex post* intervention problem, a clearance system was started so as to give a foreign party the chance to know beforehand what the FTC will say on particular restrictive provisions in a contract.

An *ex post* notification system is a weaker form of government intervention compared with an *ex ante* or prior notification system. The problem with an *ex post* notification system can be avoided by giving those who prefer legal stability a chance for advance clearance. Introduction of a clearance system could eliminate possible problems associated with an *ex post* notification system.

In addition, guidelines would give sufficient information to foreign parties, in advance, on what kinds of antitrust risks are involved in various international agreements.

When a foreign party is not sure what the FTC's reaction would be, this is the time for him to utilize a clearance system. A foreign party alone can file a petition for clearance to the FTC.

(3) CLEARANCE EFFECT

A clearance system has another merit for international agreements. Section 6(1) violations could happen at any time during the life of an international agreement. The filing of international agreements and lack of FTC reaction thereafter does not mean that the agreements become immune from attack under the Antimonopoly

Act. By obtaining the FTC's clearance, it becomes possible to secure immunity in so far as the clearance is effective.

Before the start of a clearance system, there is no such procedure for the party to learn, in writing, the result of the FTC's scrutiny. The FTC indicates its view only through informal guidance. This is the so-called administrative guidance and is done orally. With the introduction of a clearance system, a foreign party can rely on a more transparent administrative procedure.

(4) NATIONALISTIC BIAS

The third and fourth arguments relate to the problem of nationalistic bias (see Chapter 20 Reporting Requirements). These filing obligations have the common purpose of providing the necessary information for law enforcement. Therefore, the issue is whether the filing obligation imposed on international agreements will result in discriminatory enforcement of the law against foreign parties.

On the wrong assumption problem, see Chapter 23 Technology Licensing and Joint R & D. Although the potential for such bias cannot be denied, the FTC's actions have been taken regardless of the short-term interests of Japanese business. What is aimed at is fair terms in international agreements, and the anticompetitive effects they would produce within the Japanese market place. If these conditions are met, nationality is not a consideration at all. The regulation of outbound licensing agreements is one example of the disregard for the nationality of contracting parties.

(C) DIRECT APPLICABILITY OF THE ANTIMONOPOLY ACT

Regulation under section 6(1) is an indirect way to extend the FTC's jurisdiction to foreign firms. However, it is also possible to extend the FTC's jurisdiction over foreign firms directly.

(1) PERSONAL JURISDICTION

Section 69-2 provides for *mutatis mutandis* application of articles 175 and 178 of the Civil Procedure Code (Act No. 29 of 1890). This provision is interpreted to allow only service of process mentioned in section 69-2 of the Act. Because of this provision, service of process can be accomplished only within Japan.

The FTC interpretation further limited the way to serve a certified copy of a recommendation or a complaint on foreign firms. In the 1972 Far East Freight Conference case (Aug. 18, 1972, 19 KTIS 57), the FTC had issued complaints against 17 liner companies composing the Far East Freight Conference (Homeward) that carried cargo from Japan to Europe. The Conference's headquarters were in London and it had a branch office in Tokyo. As to 11 foreign companies, the FTC had served certified copies of complaints on their respective agents because no other appropriate persons were located within Japan.

The FTC, after hearing proceedings started, had quashed complaints against these 11 foreign companies (Aug. 18, 1972, 17 KTIS 117), whereas it rendered decisions against four foreign firms that had maintained representative offices in Japan (Nihon Yusen Co., Aug. 18, 1972, 19 KTIS 57), therefore, the service of process to these four companies was held valid.

The reason given by the FTC was that these agents were not duly authorized to receive such copies of complaints, and although the agents had in fact received the copies, such receipt was held invalid unless confirmed by the respondents thereafter, and there was no evidence produced to show such confirmation by these companies.

The presence of foreign firms is increasing and the extent of their presence is also expanding. As a result, the chances that the FTC could find foreign firms within Japan and serve its legal documents on foreign firms will increase.

In the 1981 Komatsu-Bucyrus case (Oct. 26, 1981, 28 KTIS 79), the FTC issued complaints against the Komatsu Co., the Bucyrus-Erie Co. and Mitsui & Co. The Bucyrus-Erie Co. was an American company, but the FTC said that it transacted a part of its business in Japan, held registered patents and had established a wholly owned subsidiary for the importing of construction machinery, therefore, the FTC found that the company can be found in Japan, and served a complaint to its legal representative located in Japan.[3] The hearing proceedings were terminated in their early stages because the international joint venture agreement in question was voluntarily canceled.

(2) STUDY GROUP REPORT

In view of the above problems on the international application of the Antimonopoly Act, a study group was organized to examine the issue. In February 1989, the Study Group on International Antimonopoly Problems prepared a report. This report did not make any specific recommendations to the FTC, but the Study Group's opinions on specific issues were indicated as possible future policy for the FTC.

Most importantly, the Study Group took a positive view that it is not necessary for a foreign company to maintain offices within Japan, i.e., a branch office, in order to be directly subject to the Antimonopoly Act. Therefore, it should be interpreted that section 69-2 does not preclude the FTC from directly serving processes to a firm that is located outside of Japan. The Group could find no justification to maintain a restrictive interpretation of law with respect to section 69-2. However, if this is held inappropriate, then the report said, necessary amendment of the law should be undertaken.

NOTES

[1] "Effect doctrine" was first articulated by Judge L. Hand in U.S. v. Aluminum Co. of America, 148 F.2d 416 (2d Cir. 1945).

[2] On this issue, the Supreme Court, in the 1984 oil cartel (price fixing) case (Feb. 24, 1984, 24 KTIS 155), declared that "it is not the necessary requirement for the violation of the Act that contents of a cartel agreement be implemented by each participating entrepreneur or the date as agreed to implement the cartel has arrived."

[3] See M. Suzuki, *Komatsu-Bucyrus Kokusai Keiyaku Jiken*, KOSEI TORIHIKI, No. 378 (April 1982). The author says that the investigators in this case had indicated the following three reasons for assuming jurisdiction over the Bucyrus-Erie Co. in the hearing proceeding.

a   A part of its business activities had been carried out in Japan through the joint venture, Komatsu-Bucyrus Co.

b   It registered patent rights in Japan under its name.

c   It had a wholly owned subsidiary, the Japan Bucyrus Co., to engage in the business of importing construction machinery.

PART IV

Selected Policy Issues

22

HOW ANTIMONOPOLY POLICY RELATES TO RAPID ECONOMIC GROWTH IN JAPAN

(A) POLICY EVALUATION

(1) WHY JAPANESE ANTIMONOPOLY POLICY LOOKS DIFFERENT

After World War II, under the overwhelming influence of the U.S. laws the Antimonopoly Act was enacted (see chapter 1 (C) Original Antimonopoly Laws). However, even though the Act had its basis in the concepts of American law, the legal thinking and enforcement mechanism to apply these new concepts had remained unchanged even after the reform of the court system in the post-war period (Japan adopted the so-called Continental legal system in the Meiji period[1]).

This is the most important factor to explain why the Antimonopoly Act had followed a different road than the original drafters had thought. The performance of the Antimonopoly Act was so different from what the English translation of the Act implies, that Americans who examine Japanese antimonopoly law enforcement can only think that there was a kind of negligence by the government of Japan, or a lack of effective enforcement efforts by the FTC.

The antitrust concepts need soil in which to take root, namely, a well developed market economy, and unfortunately Japan did not have that due to the war-devastated economic conditions at the time of its introduction. Business attitudes toward the Antimonopoly Act were mentioned in detail in part I. Lawyers, other than the FTC staff, and scholars tended to interpret these American concepts literally, based on traditional Continental legal thinking. From the point of view of traditional legal thinking, the terms used in the Antimonopoly Act were so vague and left so much room for discretion that the court tried to interpret these terms based on traditional legal thinking, that is, narrowly.[2]

The court's interpretation of "vertical agreement," "substantial restraint of competition" or "competition" are typical examples of such a traditional interpretation.

A second element existed that forced antimonopoly enforcement away from the influence of U.S. laws. When political pressure to weaken the Antimonopoly Act became evident, it took the form of a "look at the European countries instead of the U.S." movement, in particular the German competition laws were frequently referred to. For example, depression cartel and rationalization cartel systems were adopted from German competition law, and this exception prompted the introduction of many exemption laws as mentioned in Chapter 25 Deregulation and Antimonopoly Exemption Laws. In the 1950s, a French style government-business cooperation style was strongly promoted by MITI as a rationale for advocating the 1958 bill[3] (see chapter 2 (A) Amendments to Weaken the Antimonopoly Act).

Thirdly, there was no appreciation of the antimonopoly policy on the part of business circles, and the concept of freedom of business activities was not an essential component of business ethics in Japan. (Some signs of change are mentioned in chapter 4 (A)(3) Signs of Change.) Small business was not a strong supporter of the antimonopoly policy, and favored the protection of their interests vis-a-vis big business through more government regulation, rather than the chance of free and fair competition. In particular, they seemed to favor prevention of entry by large business into small business fields. There are specific laws established for this purpose.[4]

This could explain why so many business practices that could have been in conflict with the spirit of the Antimonopoly Act developed in Japan and were untouched for more than 40 years after the war.[5] Lack of effective private enforcement of the Antimonopoly Act may be one factor for this phenomenon.[6] However, this problem was not unique to antimonopoly laws.

It seems generally true in Japan that only strong enforcement activities by public authorities can influence these business practices. As a result, when injured persons demanded strong enforcement of some laws, the business practices in question changed. However, apparent victims of these practices did not move toward stronger antimonopoly law enforcement.[7]

In addition, liberal cartel exemption laws and the existence of administrative guidance cartels had promoted a so-called cartel mind set among Japanese business circles. Victims of these practices moved to ask for government protection of small business. As a result, Japan established a fairly strong small business protection system. The more these practices remained unchecked under the Antimonopoly Act, the more protection of small business was demanded.[8]

Therefore, in spite of the FTC's efforts, unique practices have been maintained and were not challenged under the Antimonopoly Act, and as a result, reflecting different business ethics, Japanese rules of competition departed significantly from those of the U.S.

All of the above had contributed to keep the Japanese market for Japanese firms. Most foreign interests were eliminated during the War, and few foreign firms showed interest in entering into the Japanese market during the Occupation. Thereafter, Japan had established strong foreign exchange and foreign capital regulations, and these regulations were lifted only at the time when no serious damage to domestic industries could be expected.[9]

(2) STRONG COMPETITION IN THE JAPANESE MARKET

All of these phenomena did not mean that competition was effectively restricted in Japan. On the contrary, in most of the manufacturing sectors there was effective competition. Rapid economic expansion was supported by new entry and the strong competitive spirit of Japanese firms.

This meant that effective competition in the Japanese market was maintained under conditions where market access by foreign firms was effectively restricted. The market was large enough to allow many participants to prosper. The Japanese firms had competed with other Japanese firms, and there had been effective competition anyway.[10] Therefore, when the systems that Japan had developed over the years were under review from the viewpoint of market access improvement, the reevaluation of antimonopoly policy was also requested.

We believe that, generally speaking, the Antimonopoly Act would function better if it could recover something that it had lost during 1950s and 1960s. During these periods, the Antimonopoly Act was under various restraints. The restraints that were intentionally or unintentionally imposed on the Antimonopoly Act in the early period need to be removed in order for the Antimonopoly Act to recover its full effectiveness. It also means that antimonopoly policy needs to be reevaluated so as to see whether a more expansive interpretation is possible under the circumstances.

The Antimonopoly Act itself is very much in harmony with its counterpart laws in the U.S. and Europe, the only problem is in its enforcement.[11] By recovering the essential function of the Antimonopoly Act in Japan, this trilateral trading area could enjoy very common conditions for competition.

Several movements toward an expansive interpretation have been attempted by the FTC. New interpretations of group boycotts to include some vertical agreements into the coverage of section 3, possible expansion of personal jurisdiction over foreign firms, a more liberal interpretation of various requirements for a cartel are some examples. Whether all of these expansive interpretations of law would be accepted by the court is an important question for the future.[12]

(B) ECONOMIC GROWTH AND COMPETITION POLICY

(1) JAPANESE ECONOMIC GROWTH

Japanese economic growth took place when antimonopoly enforcement was relatively weak. Many influential business leaders and politicians had believed that, at least up to the early 1960s, the economic democratization measures explained in chapter 1 and the enactment of antimonopoly laws thereafter were nothing but sanctions against Japan to assure that Japan never returned as an economic power.[13]

Proponents of this theory feel that antimonopoly law enforcement should be kept at a minimum level, in particular when it is at odds with industrial policy. For them, effective industrial policy should be credited for Japanese economic expansion. According to this view, the Japanese economy could grow faster because important sectors were promoted by industrial laws and policy while they were protected from foreign competition.[14]

Therefore, evaluation of Japanese antimonopoly policy cannot be complete unless one prepares an answer to such questions as why the Japanese economy could grow fast in spite of generous protection of key industries, lax enforcement of the Antimonopoly Act, or the almost negligible role that the Antimonopoly Act played during the 1950s and 1960s.

(2) JAPANIZATION PROCESS

Although the Antimonopoly Act was modeled after American antitrust laws as shown in chapter 1, hostile attitudes by business circles and industrial policy makers had compelled the Antimonopoly Act to follow a different course than originally anticipated by its drafters. We will refer to this course as the Japanization process. (In general, *Die Japanisierung des Westlichen Rechts*, in German.)

Roughly speaking, the Antimonopoly Act could maintain its fundamental structure during hard times by accepting many exemptions, administrative guidance cartels and a rather narrow interpretation of the law. Enforcement activities virtually stopped in the late 1950s. As a result, the Antimonopoly Act had a relatively weaker impact on the actual business behavior of Japanese firms in this period, and it took many years for the FTC to regain its influence over the actual behavior of Japanese firms.

In the case of American antitrust laws, it also took many years to establish their current position. It seems to us that for the first 50 years American antitrust laws had been relatively inactive, and corporate behavior had changed significantly only in the 1950s when merger regulation had been significantly tightened and criminal enforcement had started as to price-fixing cases.[15]

This will imply that it is normal to have some time pass before the Antimonopoly Act has a visible influence on the actual behavior of firms. It seems fair to say that business costs were significantly reduced because of the inactive enforcement of the Antimonopoly

Act in Japan. How these phenomena can be consistent with the economic achievement of Japanese business will be touched upon below.

(C) MARKET ACCESS AND ANTIMONOPOLY LAW ENFORCEMENT

(1) MARKET ACCESS

Competitive conditions and enforcement activities of competition laws are not necessarily the same. A market could be very competitive even though competition laws are not enforced as rigorously as they should be. Competitive conditions depend on market behavior or the function of market forces, and entrepreneurs will compete if there is enough incentive to do so.

Generally speaking, as we refer to below, industrial policy did try to offer incentive to promote rationalization or increase competitiveness. The problem seems to exist in the policy tools used to promote rationalization. Industrial policy tried to use measures in conflict with competition policy. In other words, industrial policy did not provide outright protection of industry, it only provided protective measures as a means of rationalization.

Fortunately, so far as the Japanese market was concerned, sufficient competition had been secured in spite of the fact that competent ministries tried to offer such protective measures. These protective measures may seem at odds with competition policy, but they were confined to the minimum necessary.

Competition laws had the important function of checking the mounting pressure for more regulation or more protection. In this sense, we believe that the FTC made much more of a contribution than normally thought. Rapid economic expansion meant expanding business chances for innovative entrepreneurs and there were many incidents to show that incumbent entrepreneurs tried to disturb the active investment of latecomers through the intervention of competent ministries or by their own activities.[16] The existence of the Antimonopoly Act and the FTC's efforts had successfully deterred these attempts and without these innovative entrepreneurs, economic expansion of Japan hardly could be expected.

However, the above explanation offers only one side of the story. One of the very frequent allegations concerning market access to Japan is that Japanese firms had gained their competitive strength in terms of advanced technology, economies of scale in production capacity at the time when they were effectively protected from foreign competitors, and that the Japanese market was opened only after it gained sufficient competitive strength.

The government of Japan carefully checked competitiveness before a relevant market was opened. Foreign firms were compelled to be latecomers and to face Japanese competitors who were well prepared to compete when they entered into the Japanese market. There remained few places in the market where foreign firms could claim competitive strength when they were afforded chances to compete. They claim they were not offered fair chances of competition based on equal footings.

On the other hand, a very popular opinion in Japan insists that if foreign firms did try hard they could have entered the Japanese market, and only lack of effort could explain the lack of successful entry cases. The former is criticizing the past policy of the government of Japan, and the latter is justifying the situation based on current market conditions. However, it is clear that foreign firms could not enter the Japanese market before liberalization measures were adopted in the 1960s. Therefore, even if the above allegation could be sustained by facts, it does not mean that no market access problem had existed.

By any means, the Japanese market has been a tough market in which to compete, and foreign firms without competitive strength cannot expect any significant shares in Japan. Besides, Japanese manufacturers could produce many goods that substituted for imports, thus imported products did not have as much time to enjoy their dominance. This applies to "capital goods" to a greater extent.

If the difficulty to enter the Japanese market could be fully explained by the very competitive conduct of Japanese firms, in other words, low prices and better quality of goods and services, then antimonopoly law enforcement could not have much impact on the market access issue. Under this theory, it might be true that less rigorous antimonopoly law enforcement would be better for foreign firms because it will reduce the competitiveness of Japanese firms and make the Japanese market less competitive.

On the other hand, if market access into Japan is difficult due to exclusionary practices by Japanese firms, or unfair protection of the Japanese market from foreign competitors, then active enforcement of the Antimonopoly Act could greatly improve the market access of foreign firms by removing these obstacles to entry.

We believe the possibility of the market access restraints of exclusionary practices cannot be denied. Various practices to disturb new entry or to make the expansion of new entrants harder had existed and could have been condemned under the Antimonopoly Act. Therefore, the Antimonopoly Act, if enforced properly, can provide a better chance of fair competition for foreign firms.

The Antimonopoly Act also has provisions against abusive conduct of a market dominating position. If there exists any problems associated with competitive advantage gained in the past, such problems might appear as some kinds of market position, and abusive conduct of such positions can be regulated under the Antimonopoly Act. This is one of the reasons why we believe regulation of abusive conduct can have market access implications in Japan.[17]

(2) PRICE DISPARITY

The big disparity in price for many imported products shows that price competition in the domestic market is not necessarily very strong. There are many studies that implicate the inefficiency of the Japanese distribution sector, and many practices of Japanese firms in distribution are said to raise the entry cost of foreign firms into Japan.[18]

Although further elaboration is necessary, the review of antimonopoly policy development in Japan shown in part I would be sufficient to conclude that Japanese firms' performances could not be explained solely by their competitive behaviors.

However, there is a further complication to this issue, because if the latter is the case, how can we explain the international competitiveness of Japanese firms in the world market? Lack of competition would only lead to a less efficient economy, and cannot be consistent with international competitiveness.

(3) COMPETITIVENESS IN THE MANUFACTURING SECTOR V. THE DISTRIBUTION SECTOR

It seems to be true that the manufacturing sector in Japan could establish its basis for expansion in the 1950s and 1960s due to investment in heavy equipment that provided technologically advanced production capability and large economies of scale. Domestic manufacturers were faced with international competition, indirectly, even if they did not export and not actually compete in foreign markets. Many Japanese firms expanded through import substitution.

On the other hand, the distribution sector had remained less efficient partly due to lack of competitive pressure from the outside world. Lack of investment and overstaffing in the distribution sector is common, and pursuit of economies of scale was disturbed by such laws as the Large Scale Retailers Law (Act No. 109 of 1973).[19]

Competition was relatively sparse in distribution, which in turn had prevented price competition among Japanese manufacturers in the domestic market. This had benefitted manufactures by stabilizing domestic prices, thus providing them with relatively stable profits in the domestic market.

In the manufacturing sector, there is no law like the Large Scale Retailers Law. On the contrary, there existed laws directed toward achieving economies of scale and increasing industry productivity, all of which were seriously enforced by MITI.

Price stability or lack of price competition in the domestic market due to distribution channelling by consumer goods manufacturers and relatively weak competition in the distribution sector had provided a comfortable profit source for Japanese exporting firms. This also explains why many consumer goods manufacturers had tried to establish their own distribution channels in order to stabilize their domestic prices. Fortunately, these profits did flow into R & D expenses and other equipment investments and were not distributed as generous dividends to shareholders or as very generous salaries for management.[20]

However, efficiency in the manufacturing sector was a sufficient driving force to penetrate into foreign markets, where they could rely on open and efficient distribution systems developed in such countries as the U.S.[21] General trading companies' information network could also be used for this purpose.

(4) INDUSTRIAL POLICY AND COMPETITIVENESS

How can we explain the coexistence of an anticompetitive policy toward industry or a protective policy stance toward industry with international competitiveness in many export industries of Japan? Did that give unfair advantage to Japanese firms or did that help them to penetrate into foreign markets?

If the answer is affirmative, how we can explain the long lasting international competitiveness of Japanese firms? Wouldn't protection of the home market necessarily lessen the incentive to compete?

It seems that industrial policy did offer significant protection, at least by reducing business risks, in such a way as to reduce the risk of price competition, or by enabling joint research activities and/or sharing of business information among Japanese firms. However, industrial policy did not offer a kind of protection functioning as a discouragement to innovate in these sectors.

In spite of MITI's intention, industrial policy could not have had more than a supplemental role. The fundamental promoter of economic growth in Japan was undoubtedly the market mechanism. The FTC's role to resist industrial policy and to block the movement toward a managed economy during the 1950s deserves a more positive evaluation. With hindsight, the FTC seems to have achieved more than it should have in view of the difficulty it faced in those days. The bad performance record in terms of enforcement activities of the FTC in the 1950s could be mitigated by these contributions.

Economic performance in simply protected sectors such as agriculture or transportation was much worse than in those industries that were subjected to industrial policy. The existence of strong competitors in the U.S. and Europe was always recognized, and seemed to offer sufficient incentive to innovate even though they were not in actual competition within the same market. In other sectors such as agriculture and transportation, simple protection was offered but no incentive to innovate. Sparseness in these sectors at present owes very much to the different policy stance of the competent ministry, and more fundamentally, different attitudes of firms in these sectors.

(D) POLICY IMPLICATIONS

It is too simplistic to assume that the Japanese market was a truly competitive market and/or anticompetitive conduct had been effectively regulated by the FTC. Firms who are bound by fair rules of competition would face difficulty in competing with those who were not. In this sense, foreign firms may not be completely free in their competitive conduct in Japanese markets. There seems to be much room to improve access into Japanese markets by effectively enforcing the Antimonopoly Act.[22]

If Japan had grown fast due partly to the advantage given by the government's protective policy, which reduced the business risks of Japanese firms, how should this advantage be evaluated? It is unrealistic to think that such an advantage rose to a significant level. Even if it could be significant in some sectors, the fact that management was encouraged toward more technological innovation seems a more important factor for explaining the economic success of Japan.

On the other hand, if above-market-price profits in the domestic market are the reason for the active technological equipment investment by Japanese firms, how should this be evaluated? Is this objectionable? If government subsidies should be opposed in a free trade regime, by the same reasoning we should oppose above-market-price profits through cartel activities. Those unfair sources of profits should be condemned in order to maintain a free trade regime.

Reaching agreement among governments on unfair sources of profits would be difficult because national interests, even among developed economy countries, would be in conflict in this regard. Therefore, the important task for experts is to try to identify the existence of and magnitude of such unfair advantages, if any. Such unfair advantages should not be confused with Japanese firms' legitimate advantages that could be emulated by foreign firms.

This should be an acceptable policy choice for Japan because it could enhance its competitive position in the world market by encouraging competition among Japanese firms and/or with foreign firms, thereby contributing to sustain international competitiveness.

Effective antimonopoly enforcement could benefit foreign firms, too, firstly by removing the unfair advantage of Japanese firms in terms of cost saving, and secondly by reducing the extra cost of distributing their goods in the Japanese market. Under this policy, those products that are competitive could find more opportunity in the Japanese market.[23]

However, it is also true that as the Japanese market becomes more competitive, entry into the Japanese market would become more difficult for those who cannot satisfy the needs of choosey Japanese consumers.

NOTES

[1] See chapter 1 (A)(1) Until World War I. J. Haley, *Antitrust Sanctions and Remedies: A Comparative Study of German and Japanese Law*, WASHINGTON LAW REVIEW, Vol. 59 (1984), at 471. He argues that "The basic institutions and concepts of German civil, criminal and administrative law provided the principal models for Japan's legal reforms during the late nineteen and early twentieth centuries." at 472.

[2] The 1977 Amendment was the result of traditional thinking from this aspect. It tried to avoid vague terminology as much as was feasible. This mixture can be seen in areas where the original law was drafted based on the thinking of American law such as the Antimonopoly Act. When the law is amended, the amended portion tends to be based on the traditional way of drafting.

J. Haley, *supra* note 1, wrote, "Despite the American origins of Japanese antitrust legislation, . . . the influence of German law and practice on Japanese antitrust law, at least since 1953, has been profound. . . . As a result, today Japanese antitrust law can be understood accurately only when read in terms of German rather than American practice." at 472.

[3] C. JOHNSON, MITI AND THE JAPANESE MIRACLE (1982), where he wrote; "Morozumi represented a new breed of officer in the ministry, men who combined overseas service, primarily in continental Europe rather than in the Anglo-American countries, with industrial policy expertise. . . . They were the authorities within the ministry on the Common Market, on the so-called invasion of Europe by American capital, and on such ideas for industrial development as the French concept of economie concertee, or what the Japanese call the 'mixed economy'." at 257.

[4] Two laws are important from this aspect. One is the Large-Scale Retail Stores Law of 1973 (Large Retailers Law). For a detailed analysis, see F. UPHAM, LEGAL REGULATION OF THE JAPANESE RETAIL INDUSTRY: THE LARGE SCALE RETAIL STORES LAW AND PROSPECTS FOR REFORM, ANNUAL REPORT 1989-90 THE PROGRAM ON U.S.-JAPAN RELATIONS, at 2.

The other is the Act Concerning Business Activity Adjustment of Large-Sized Enterprises to Preserve Business Chances of Small and Medium-Sized Enterprises (Small- and Medium-Sized Business Field Adjustment Law) of 1977 (Act No. 74 of 1977). This law tries to avoid friction arising from big businesses' new entry into the business fields that were traditionally and predominantly engaged in by small businesses.

[5] We cannot believe that all of these practices could have been condemned by the FTC while they were developing. Without private initiatives such as the filing of complaints with the FTC or the filing of private law suits, not much change in business practices could be expected. Simply, they could have demanded of the Diet significant increases in the FTC's personnel so that more complaints could be smoothly handled. We want to say that these practices might be significantly different form what we see now if Japanese businesses had been more serious about the strategic value of the Antimonopoly Act.

[6] Without private initiatives, the enforcement activities of the FTC could not cover these practices effectively. J. Haley observed that "Additional institutional barriers to litigation, such as delay and costs, the lack of the treble damage incentive, and a possible reluctance on the part of business firms to sue as a result of complex and close interrelationships even with their competitors also work to preclude effective use of the damage action as either remedy or penalty in antitrust enforcement." *supra* note 1, at 503.

J. Ramseyer, *The Costs of the Consensual Myth: Antitrust Enforcement and Institutional Barriers to Litigation in Japan,* YALE LAW JOURNAL, Vol. 94 (1985), at 604. He argues that "If public antitrust enforcement has been sparse, private antitrust enforcement has been almost nonexistent. Although the Antimonopoly Act grants the victims of a cartel a strict liability cause of action for actual damages, the private damage actions brought to date demonstrate the extent to which private Japanese antitrust litigation is a fiction." at 617.

[7] For example, small business could have demanded fairer terms of transactions by using more a expansive reading of unfair trade practice regulation. The Act Against Delay in Payment etc., to Subcontractors (Act No. 120 of 1956) was one of a few examples that could get political support toward fairer terms of transactions.

[8] See the two laws indicated in note 4 *supra*. Instead of enacting these laws, it might have been possible to move toward tighter regulation on price discrimination or sales below cost in favor of small-scale retail stores, which seems to be the course the U.S. took as evidenced by the enactment of the Robinson-Patman Act (49 Stat. 1526, 15 U.S.C. §§ 3, 13a-c, 21a (1970)). This is more acceptable from an antitrust viewpoint, as compared with straight protection of small business fields.

Whether the regulations on price discrimination or sales below cost should actively be pursued are difficult questions, and need to be evaluated from this policy choice perspective. We believe that, depending on the situation of economic development of each country, there is legitimate room for active regulations on these practices. See also chapter 8 (A)(4) Scope of FTC Authority.

[9] The MITI had classified all industries into three categories for the purpose of selecting suitable sectors for capital liberalization. As to category 1, foreign capital can be unconditionally authorized; as to category II, it can be authorized when less than 50 percent of the stock is held by foreign capital; and as to category III, as before, it shall be subject to a case-by-case scrutiny. The number of industry lines belonging to each category was increased year by year as follows;

FY	Category I	Category II
1967	13	33
1969	44	160
1970	77	447
1971	151 (27 %)	(66%)

(The total industry lines were about 850.)

Category III contained seven industry lines such as retail stores with more than 11 outlets, or real estate.

[10] For a more detailed analysis, see section (C)(3) *supra*. In the manufacturing sector, there seemed very keen competition among Japanese firms, even when the Japanese market was separated from international competition.

[11] There seems much consensus as to this aspect. See J. Haley, *Weak Law, Strong Competition, and Trade Barriers: Competitiveness as a Disincentive to Foreign Entry into Japanese Markets*, in K. Yamamura ed., JAPAN'S ECONOMIC STRUCTURE: SHOULD IT CHANGE? (1990), where he wrote, "Prior to the late 1970s, there was reasonably broad agreement that the continuation of Japanese industrial policies favoring special legislation to exempt various cartel agreements from antitrust control combined with the weakness of both the Japanese FTC's investigatory power and ultimate sanctions for antitrust violations to produce an environment conducive to significant levels of private anticompetitive output and price stabilization measures."

J. Ramseyer, *supra* note 6, said, "Drafted under the supervision of American authorities in 1947, the Act reflects American economic theory of the time and prohibits most acts illegal under American antitrust law." at 613.

[12] One of the difficulties in understanding the Japanese Antimonopoly Act is in the small number of cases tested in court. Because of this even the very key concepts are not well tested by the courts. This is the reason why we think that an expansive reading of the Act's terms faces practical difficulties.

[13] A 1958 report by the Japan Productivity Center stated, "There are many who profess, and in all appearance honestly believe, that the Antimonopoly Law, along with the Standards of Labor law, was forced by the victors upon the defeated nation for the covert purpose of keeping down her economy in a weak condition." cited in E. HADLEY, ANTITRUST IN JAPAN (1970), at 11.

[14] See note 9 *supra*. The categorization of all industrial sectors into three groups was made based on careful review of their current international competitiveness.

[15] For the history of criminal antitrust enforcement, see H. First, *Criminal Antitrust Enforcement* (Occasional Papers from the Center for Research in Crime and Justice, New York Univ. School of Law 1991), at 1-3. In 1960, 29 electrical equipment manufacturers, including the General Electric Co. and 31 executives of these companies were prosecuted for a long standing conspiracy to bid rig and fix prices on the sale of heavy electrical generating equipment. Seven executives were sentenced to 30 days' imprisonment, which gravely shook the U.S. business community, and prompted them to become very serious about antitrust compliance

programs. However, generally speaking, criminal antitrust enforcement was the phenomenon after 1974.

Merger regulation was tightened following the enactment of the Celler-Kefauver Act (64 Stat. 1125, 15 U.S.C. 18 (1950)).

[16] See, for example, the Sumitomo Metals incident, F. UPHAM, LAW AND SOCIAL CHANGE IN POSTWAR JAPAN (1987), at 176-184. This was an incidence in September 1965, in which the Sumitomo Metal Co., a steelmaker, declared that it could not abide by MITI's administrative guidance cartel to curtail steel production.

[17] See chapter 8 (A)(6) Increased Importance of Unfair Trade Practices Regulations. Regulation of abusive conduct occupies an important part in the Distribution System and Business Practices Guidelines (see appendix H).

[18] *Research on the Distribution of Nine Consumer Goods with Respect to Price Differentials Between Domestic and Overseas Markets, June 11, 1990,* FTC/JAPAN VIEWS, No. 10 (Nov. 1990), at 13-22. Prices of surveyed items in Tokyo were, as to almost all items, significantly higher than those in New York, London, Paris and Frankfurt.

See also *Japanese Market as Viewed by Foreign-Affiliated Companies (Outline),* FTC/JAPAN VIEWS, No. 10 (Nov. 1990), at 23-35, where it is said that "not a few of the respondents feel that Japanese companies maintain such strong ties with specified business partners because of human relations, keiretsu-relationships, groupings, etc., that the market tends to exclude others and is thus closed. They further feel that taking countermeasures is difficult because Japan's distribution channels and business practices are more complex and unique than those of other countries." at 34.

[19] See note 4 *supra*.

[20] In the United States, such profits might be spent as higher dividends and higher management bonuses. As for the Japanese firms' tendency to spend less as dividends or management bonuses and more for R & D expenditure, see R. Dore, *An Outsider's View,* in Y. Yamamura ed., *supra* note 11, where he argues; "the distribution of these unfair rents, *within* the companies that gain them, tends in Japan to be a good deal less unequal than it would be in the United States with the shareholders seeing less of the profits to begin with. . . and the dispersal of wages and salaries being much more compressed. A CEO's salary is usually not more than a single-figure multiple of his firm's average salary rather than the three-figure multiple not unusual in America. . . . some of these monopoly rents are channeled into R & D which does eventually benefit the consumer." at 365.

[21] A. Wolff, *U.S.-Japan Relations and Rule of Law: The Nature of the Trade Conflict and the American Response,* in Y. Yamamura ed., *supra* note 11, where he claims, "I said in Tokyo, . . . that the United States is, by any reasonable measure, the world's most open market. . . . Of the developing countries' exports of manufactured goods to the industrialized world, in recent years the United States has taken roughly two thirds. Japan lags behind Europe by far in sharing the remaining third." at 138-139. We believe this comes from a difference in distribution systems among these countries.

[22] A contrary view is presented by J. Haley, *supra* note 11, where he claims, "in increasingly larger segments of Japan's overall domestic market, competition has become a significant disincentive for new entry. Even for foreign incumbents with equal if not greater access to new technology and capital, the competitiveness of incumbent independents as well as firms with *keiretsu* affiliations as both established rivals and potential new product entrants poses a significant disincentive to entry." at 235.

[23] The performance of firms in Japan, foreign or domestic, depends upon their ability to adapt to changing market conditions and customer demands. In this sense, incumbents have huge advantages in maintaining their market positions. The problem is how large are such unfair advantages as measured quantitatively for incumbent firms, foreign or domestic.

CHAPTER

23

TECHNOLOGY LICENSING AND JOINT R & D

(A) ACTS CONCERNING INDUSTRIAL PROPERTY RIGHTS

Section 23 exempts acts recognizable as the exercise of rights under the Patent Act, Utility Model Act, Design Act, Trademark Act and Copyright Act (in this chapter, rights under these acts are called IPR). In other words, improper acts or misused acts are, even if they are based on IPR, not recognizable as the exercise of IPR, therefore, the Antimonopoly Act can be applied to such acts.

So long as holders of IPR utilize such rights by themselves, no misuse or improper use could happen. However, when they license IPR to third parties, the terms stipulated in such licensing agreements are not recognizable as the exercise of rights under IPR. Therefore, terms in such licensing agreements are subject to the Antimonopoly Act, and many contractual terms in licensing agreements may fall under unfair trade practices, when they are regarded as improper or misused exercise of IPR.

It is also possible to say that any acts to utilize IPR to effect unreasonable restraint of trade or private monopolization cannot be recognizable as the exercise of rights under IPR.

(B) NEW GUIDELINE AND BASIC OBJECTIVES OF REVISION

On February 15, 1989, the FTC had announced a new Guideline on Patent and Know-How Licensing Agreements (New Guideline) replacing its old Guideline on International Licensing Agreements (Old Guideline), which was promulgated on May 24, 1968.[1]

When the Old Guideline was adopted in 1968, significant technology licensing was limited to an international one in which Japanese firms introduced foreign technology as licensees. However, many Japanese firms have now become significant exporters of technology, and technology licensing among Japanese firms has increased significantly.

Therefore, firstly, the New Guideline ought to be made applicable to every kind of patent or know-how licensing agreement without regard to the nationality of the contracting parties.

Secondly, in order to increase clarity concerning possible anti-monopoly problems, as a guideline, restrictive clauses in patent and know-how licensing agreements are classified into the following three kinds:

(A) Restrictions that are considered, in principle, not to fall under unfair trade practices (white clauses).

(B) Restrictions that may fall under unfair trade practices depending on their impact on competition in a market (grey clauses).

(C) Restrictions that are highly likely to fall under unfair trade practices (black clauses).

Grey clauses refer to those that might be condemned depending upon the market position of a licensor or a licensee or other market factors. Grey clauses are not necessarily the ones to be avoided in licensing agreements. On the contrary, these clauses can be used freely unless the licensor's or licensee's market position is significant, or there exists some market factors that raise anticompetitive problems.

Black clauses are those that could be incorporated into the licensing agreement only when specific justifiable reasons are available. Room for justifiable reasons is provided because there may be a case where a black clause might be justifiable as to a particular industry or as to a particular technology. If a licensor or licensee is not sure what kind of justifiable reasons would be acceptable to the

FTC, a clearance system may be utilized for this purpose (see section (D)(3) below).

The FTC had included white clauses in the New Guideline believing that there should be a safe harbor for a licensor to enhance the incentive to license. A white list would be useful for clarifying various restrictive clauses about which licensors need not worry concerning antimonopoly problems.

The third objective for revision is the treatment of know-how licensing agreements. There are particular characteristics of know-how compared with patents, therefore, a different treatment of know-how licensing agreements is warranted, and such differences should be clarified as much as possible.[2]

The fourth is related to criticisms against the Old Guideline's two basic assumptions. Namely, it is said that the Old Guideline assumes that:

(A) A licensor of a patent or know-how is in a superior bargaining position vis-a-vis its licensee.

(B) In international patent or know-how licensing agreements, foreign entrepreneurs are assumed to be in a superior technological position vis-à-vis Japanese entrepreneurs.

These assumptions were not doubted in the late 1960s when the Old Guideline was formulated; these assumptions were explicit in the Old Guideline.

These two assumptions have lead to a situation where nine items of restrictive provisions stipulated in the Old Guideline were treated as the quasi Nine No-Nos.[3] The U.S. Department of Justice pronouncement of the Nine No-Nos in January 1975 had some influence on the enforcement policy of the FTC.[4] Around 1975, the number of disposed cases were at a high level (see table 23-1), and the FTC's quasi per se illegal approach was encouraged by American policy as expressed in the Nine No-Nos.

The fifth objective for revision is related to the so-called balancing approach upon which the Old Guideline was based. For example, reciprocal and well balanced grant backs and assign back clauses of improvements originating from the licensed technology, and non-competition clauses for exclusive licensing agreements are thought acceptable under the Old Guideline, but such a balanced approach is not always consistent with the concept of competition policy.

Under the New Guideline, the fact that the obligation of a licensor and its licensee is balanced will be treated as one of many factors to be evaluated in a case-by-case analysis, but not a factor to determine the legality or illegality of the restrictive clauses.

(C) FTC POLICY ON TECHNOLOGY TRANSFER

(1) EVALUATION OF ENFORCEMENT OF THE OLD GUIDELINE

A comparison of tables 23-1 and 23-2 will show that the FTC's enforcement policy was modified around 1980. The years 1975-1980 can be described as a period when the Old Guideline was most heavily enforced, whereas the years 1981-1988 can be described as a period when the Old Guideline was somehow less actively enforced.

At its peak, about 19 percent of the total international licensing agreements were deemed to contain restrictive provisions falling under the Old Guideline, and, on average, nearly 16 percent of the total international licensing agreements in the 1975-1980 period contained problematic provisions from the viewpoint of the Old Guideline (see table 23-1).

The number of disposed cases was also significant. Annually, in this period, 200 to 240 international licensing agreements were deemed to have restrictive provisions falling under the Old Guideline (see table 23-1).

Since 1981, the average ratio of these disposed cases dropped to about 7 percent, and the number of disposed cases dropped to around 140. As to the 1985-1990 period, the ratio was about 5 percent and the number of disposed cases was around 100 (see table 23-2). These tables imply that the quasi per se illegal approach was abandoned around 1980.

In the United States, the Nine No-Nos were abandoned specifically in November 1981.[5] It was said that the appropriateness of the Nine No-Nos approach was denied by the Department of Justice around 1979.[6]

The types of restrictions for which the FTC took remedial measures consistently have been few in kind. Restrictions on applied inventions of licensed technology ("grant back clauses") and restrictions on handling of competitive products or competitive technology ("non-competition clauses") in the 1975-1980 period always occupy

Table 23-1. FTC Enforcement of International Licensing Agreements 1975-1980

FY	'75	'76	'77	'78	'79	'80	Average
Unfair Trade Practices	*186*	*289*	*254*	*295*	*320*	*263*	*267.8*
(1) Grant back	94	199	174	173	149	140	154.8
(2) Non-competition	39	49	39	47	44	32	41.7
(3) Distributors	5	5	8	13	39	33	17.2
(4) Tie-in sales	16	6	12	22	6	4	11.0
(5) Resale price	3	2	0	0	20	15	6.7
(6) Advertisement	4	2	2	9	10	6	5.5
(7) Quality	0	0	0	6	15	10	5.2
(8) Royalty	6	5	1	2	3	8	4.2
(9) Business activities	0	13	8	1	1	1	4.0
(10) Parallel import	12	2	1	0	0	0	2.5
(11) Termination	–	–	–	–	–	2	0.3
(12) Sales method	–	0	0	0	0	2	0.3
(13) Trademark	–	–	–	–	–	1	0.2
(14) Others	7	6	9	22	33	9	14.3
Unreasonable restraint of trade	0	0	0	0	0	0	0.0
Sum total	186	289	254	295	320	263	267.8
Net total (A)	156	241	212	228	224	200	210.2
Total international licensing agreement (B)	1,198	1,260	1,211	1,356	1,499	1,522	1,341
(A) / (B)	13.0	19.1	17.5	16.8	14.9	13.1	15.7

NOTES:
* The restrictive provisions that are deemed to fall under unfair trade practices are defined as follows. For more detail, see relevant provisions of the Guideline given in parenthesis. (*See* also appendix F).

Type of restrictive clauses:
(1) Grant back (grant back and exclusive or non-exclusive grant back obligation (I-3-(6) and I-2-(3)).
(2) Non-competition (restrictions on handling of competing technology or competing products) (I-3-(3) and I-2-(1)).
(3) Restrictions on distributors (I-2-(2)).
(4) Tie-in sales (restrictions on purchasers of raw materials or parts) (I-2-(6)).
(5) Resale price (restrictions on resale price of patented products (I-3-(1)).
(6) Obligation on advertisement (none).
(7) Quality (restrictions on quality of patented products) (I-2-(5)).
(8) Royalty (royalty payment obligation after the termination of the licensed technology or on unpatented products) (I-3-(4) and I-2-(9)).
(9) Restrictions on business activities (none).
(10) Parallel import (undue hindrance of parallel import) (none).
(11) Termination (unilateral conditions for contract termination) (I-2-(11)).
(12) Obligation on the sales method (none).
(13) Obligation on the use of a trademark (I-2-(4)).
SOURCE: Compiled from the FTC Annual Reports.

Table 23-2. FTC Enforcement of International Licensing Agreements 1981-1900

FY	'81	'82	'83	'84	'85	'86	'87	'88	'89	'90	Average
Unfair Trade Practices	*122*	*170*	*131*	*143*	*110*	*76*	*85*	*113*	*169*	*137*	*125.6*
(1) Grant back	51	55	66	63	52	34	26	58	44	26	47.5
(2) Non-competition	36	56	29	43	36	34	38	35	32	32	37.1
(3) Resale price	3	5	1	1	3	1	3	5	21	24	6.7
(4) Distributors	6	9	5	0	1	0	0	3	9	17	5.0
(5) Advertisement	0	10	12	7	4	0	2	0	0	0	3.5
(6) Parallel import	0	3	3	4	1	0	2	2	11	6	3.2
(7) R & D	–	–	–	–	1	1	1	3	15	14	3.5
(8) Tie-in sales	2	3	2	4	5	1	1	1	9	1	2.9
(9) Sales price	–	–	–	–	–	–	–	–	17	15	3.2
(10) Termination	2	5	0	2	0	0	2	1	0	0	1.2
(11) Royalty	0	0	0	1	0	1	1	0	5	1	0.9
(12) Export	0	0	0	0	0	0	0	0	6	1	0.7
(13) Quality	4	1	0	0	0	0	0	0	0	0	0.5
(14) Business activities	3	0	0	0	0	0	0	0	0	0	0.3
(15) Trademark	2	0	0	0	0	0	0	0	0	0	0.2
(16) Sales method	0	1	0	0	0	0	0	0	0	0	0.1
(17) Others	13	22	13	18	7	4	9	5	0	0	9.1
Unreasonable restraint of trade	0	0	0	0	0	0	0	0	0	0	0.0
Sum total	122	170	131	143	110	76	85	113	169	137	125.6
Net total (A)	101	141	116	117	89	68	74	97	144	102	104.9
Total international licensing agreement (B)	1,468	1,717	1,557	1,675	1,607	1,543	1,710	1,892	1,916	1,996	1,708
(A) / (B)	6.9	8.2	7.5	7.0	5.5	4.4	4.3	5.1	7.5	5.1	6.9

NOTES:

  * See note table 23-1 for restrictive provisions other than those defined below. For more detail, see relevant provisions in the Guidelines (Appendix F) given in parentheses.

  (7) Restrictions on R & D (I-3-(5)).

  (9) Restrictions on sales price of patented products (I-3-(2)).

  (12) Restrictions on export area of patented products (I-2-(7)).

SOURCE: Compiled from the FTC Annual Reports.

almost 70 percent of all disposed cases by the FTC (the average was 73.3 percent).

Under the Old Guideline, up to 1980, only reciprocal grant back and non-competition clauses for exclusive licensing agreements were thought acceptable. The number of disposed cases on grant back clauses before 1980 suggests that quasi-per-se rules were applied. For example, during 1976-1980, 140 to 199 grant back clauses were deemed to fall under the Old Guideline. Since 1981, the number dropped to the one-third level (from 155 to 48, see tables 23-1 and 23-2). The drastic change in the number of cases concerning grant back clause seems to be the result of the case-by-case approach started around 1980.

The non-competition clause for non-exclusive licenses continued to receive negative evaluations by the FTC, in particular non-competition clauses after expiration of the licensing agreements are always thought unacceptable and could not be unjustified (see part I-3-(3) of the Guideline).

The number of disposed cases concerning non-competition clauses seems constant throughout the 1975-1990 period (the 1975-1980 average was 42, and the 1981-1990 average was 46). Therefore, the FTC's regulatory policy seemed unchanged insofar as non-competition clauses were concerned.

One of the changes adopted in the New Guideline is the treatment of non-competition clauses for non-exclusive licenses. Insofar as substitutable goods or technology are abundant, these clauses are thought acceptable (see part I-2-(1) of the Guideline).

(2) ENFORCEMENT METHODS

Table 23-3 shows the type of cases disposed of by the FTC. There are two kinds of disposed cases. One is the guidance case where the restrictive provisions are deemed anticompetitive enough so that the immediate start of renegotiation with the licensor to revise or to drop the provisions in question is requested (guidance cases).

In the other case, because the provisions may not pose a serious threat to competition, at least immediately, remedial measures need not be taken at this stage, and the FTC indicates to the party that, because such provisions are grey clauses or black clauses, they might, depending on the circumstances, raise antimonopoly problems (caution cases). The caution case means that when there is a chance to renegotiate the terms of the licensing agreement, it is better to clear up these problems as much as is feasible among the contracting parties.

Table 23-3. FTC Enforcement of International Licensing Agreements: Guidance and Caution Cases

FY	'85		'86		'87		'88		'89		'90		Average	
Unfair Trade Practices[3]	G[1]	C	G[2]	C	G	C	G	C	G	C	G	C	G	C
(1) Non-competition	29	7	27	7	20	18	11	24	16	16	18	14	20.2	14.3
(2) Grant back	30	22	18	16	10	16	20	38	15	29	17	9	18.3	21.7
(3) Resale price	3	0	1	0	1	2	2	3	9	12	15	9	5.2	4.3
(4) R & D	1	0	0	1	0	1	2	1	8	7	6	8	2.8	3.0
(5) Sales price	–	–	–	–	–	–	–	–	6	11	10	5	2.7	2.7
(6) Distributor	1	1	0	0	0	0	0	3	4	5	8	9	2.2	3.0
(7) Parallel import	1	0	0	0	0	2	0	2	5	6	1	5	1.2	2.5
(8) Royalty	0	0	0	0	0	0	0	0	1	4	0	1	0.2	0.8
(9) Export	0	0	0	0	0	0	0	0	2	4	0	1	0.3	0.8
(10) Tie-in sales	0	5	0	1	0	1	0	1	0	9	0	1	0	3.0
(11) Advertisement	0	0	0	0	0	0	0	0	0	0	0	0	0	0.0
(12) Termination	0	0	0	0	0	2	0	1	0	0	0	0	0	0.5
(13) Others	3	8	1	4	1	11	0	5	0	0	0	0	0.8	4.7
Sum total (A)	68	43	47	29	32	53	35	78	66	103	75	62	53.8	61.3
Total international licensing agreement (B)	1,607		1,543		1,710		1,892		1,916		1,996		1,777	
(A) / (B) G	4.2		3.0		1.9		1.8		3.4		3.8		3.0	
C	2.7		1.9		3.1		4.1		5.4		3.1		3.4	

NOTES:

[1] "G" refers to guidance cases to which the FTC issues guidances to the contracting party to modify the questioned provisions.

[2] "C" refers to caution cases to which the FTC indicated the contracting party had possible antimonopoly problems.

[3] See note table 23-1 for the definition of restrictive provisons.

SOURCE: Compiled from the FTC Annual Reports.

Therefore, as to a caution case, a licensor and its licensee have a chance to solve the possible antimonopoly problems in a way that would be acceptable to both of them. For example, when an exclusive grant back clause is to be changed to a non-exclusive one, a licensor may demand an increase in royalty payments in return.

Table 23-3 shows that guidance cases amounted annually to between 35 and 75; on average there were around 50 per year (these figures became available only after 1985). On the other hand, caution cases amounted annually to between 30 and 100, and this number tended to fluctuate. On average, about 60 caution cases were reported. The guidance cases are the ones to which the FTC gave administrative guidance to the Japanese party to start re-negotiation with its foreign party, and these represent the real number of cases that are disposed of by the FTC.

The increase in the number of disposed cases as to FY 1989 and 1990 seems to be caused by the FTC's efforts to insure the enforcement of the New Guideline by issuing many cautions to unfamiliar contracting parties.

The FTC guidance cases are limited, in principle, to such clauses that are classified as black in the New Guideline. As to FY 1989 and 1990 when the New Guideline was enforced, grant back clauses, non-competition clauses, resale price maintenance clauses, sales price restriction clauses, restrictions on R & D, restrictions on distributors, tie-in clauses and hindrance of parallel imports were the types of restrictions subjected to guidance by the FTC more than 10 times.

For FY 1989, the first year when the New Guideline was enforced, a noticeable change can be observed in the table, namely the types of restrictive clauses had increased. For the first time, grant back and non-competition clauses occupied less than half of the total disposed cases (in 1981-1990 the average was 67 percent).

There are other aspects to the increase of disposed cases. For example, there was a drastic increase in the number of disposed cases on resale price maintenance (in FY 1989 there were 21 and in FY 1990 there were 24), hindrance of parallel import cases (in FY 1989 were 11 and in FY 1990 there were 6), and restriction on distributors (in FY 1989 there were 9 and in FY 1990 there were 17). However, these are not the types of restrictive clauses contained in pure technology licensing agreements.

Licensing agreements to produce foreign branded goods in Japan are filed as know-how licensing agreements, therefore, the table contains guidance and caution cases as to these know-how licensing agreements. However, these are in fact functioning as alternatives to imports of branded goods, therefore, the increased number of guidance and caution cases reflects the tightened regulation of sole import agency agreements, motivated by significant price disparity on those branded goods sold in Japan.

The increase of disposed cases on restrictions on R & D and sales price on licensed products are the result of changes adopted by the New Guideline. As for FY 1989 and 1990, around 15 guidance cases are recorded, respectively, in the FTC Annual Reports.

It is also noticeable that in this area the FTC continues to rely on soft or informal methods of enforcement, such as guidance or cautions. This reliance on informal enforcement methods has the merit of making the guideline more widely understood among the businesses concerned. This does not mean that the FTC has been trying to intervene in matters that have minor effects on competition. The FTC disposed cases are focused on black clauses for which there is clear concern about their anticompetitive effects within a market of Japan.

(D) POLICY OBJECTIVES OF THE NEW GUIDELINE

(1) GRANT BACK CLAUSES

As tables 23-1 and 23-2 show, the FTC has been placing policy emphasis on grant back clauses. This reflects the FTC policy consideration that technology can be improved not only by the original innovator, but also through licensees of that technology.

The Japanese experience is a good example of how important it is to encourage innovative activities not only of original innovators but also of licensees of the technology. Japanese technological development could not have happened solely by relying on the introduction of foreign technology. One of the FTC policy goals is to secure higher levels of innovative activities within Japanese markets or to maintain maximum incentive to innovate through improvement of the licensed technology. Improvement is one of the important contributions to innovation, and with improvement the licensed technology can enhance its value or its marketability significantly.

By grant back clauses, a licensor can secure access to its licensee's improvements. Therefore, such grant back clauses could be procompetitive by enhancing the value of the original innovation. However, exclusive grant back is not necessary to serve this purpose. A licensee's access should not be restricted to his own improvement. This is why the FTC had designated exclusive grant back and assign back as black clauses.

Improvement is a very important form of innovation, in particular, for successful marketing of licensed products. On this issue, the OECD report described that

Some countries view prohibiting certain kinds of agreements as a way to protect licensees' freedom of action or to serve certain goals of fairness to licensees. Finally, some countries believe that certain license restrictions, such as exclusive grant-backs, reduce the incentive of licensees to innovate. Thus, they believe legal limitations on those restrictions are necessary to ensure a better balance between the licensee's and the licensor's incentives to innovate, which these countries believe is fundamental to higher levels of innovative activity in their economies.[7]

(2) OTHER SPECIFIC PROVISIONS

Here we will try to explain the basic policy objectives of specific provisions of the New Guideline. When the New Guideline was prepared, in view of its impact on foreign concerns, the chance to file comments to the draft guideline was offered, and many comments were filed by foreign parties, mostly Americans. Some of them indicated concerns on specific provisions in the New Guideline.

In view of these comments, the following implicit ideas reflected in the New Guideline are important.

(i) Export restrictions

The provision to grant exclusive licenses to particular licensees in specified territories is not an export restriction as defined in the New Guideline. Also, the export restriction on COCOM items, or export restrictions to comply with U.S. export regulations does not raise any question under the New Guideline.

The New Guideline designated three kinds of areas as white clauses. In addition, such provisions to reserve some area for the licensor or for the third party with which he has a plan to or is negotiating distributorship agreements or licensing agreements with would raise no problem under the New Guideline. Such provision to obligate licensees to obtain their licensor's approval in case of export might be justifiable to make sure that licensees would not export licensed products to the area reserved for licensors or for the third party.

On the other hand, if there is a provision to prohibit export of licensed products after the expiration of a patent or licensing agreement, it will be deemed to raise serious anticompetitive effects on the Japanese market.

(ii) Price restrictions

Because of the so-called General Electric Doctrine in the U.S.,[8] there is some concern on the enforcement policy for price restriction clauses that were newly designated as black clauses in the New Guideline. Price restriction in the case of non-exclusive licenses, in particular, where a licensor himself uses the patent in the licensed territory, could be justifiable after a case-by-case analysis.[9]

In the case of export of patented products as to the area reserved for the licensor or for the third party, export price restrictions on patented products are designated as white clauses under the Guideline.

(iii) Non-competition clauses following the expiration of licensing agreement

A non-competition clause may be necessary to secure the best efforts of the licensees as to the licensed technology, but this justification is lost after the expiration of a licensing agreement. This is why the FTC designated non-competition clauses following the expiration of licensing agreements as black clauses.

There seems to be no other country that divides non-competition clauses during and after the licensing agreements. Therefore, a foreign licensor might feel that the Japanese rule is too rigid. It should be remembered that a non-competition clause after the expiration of a know-how licensing agreement is acceptable as long as the restriction is less than 2 years and is necessary for preventing unauthorized use or disclosure of the licensed know-how.[10] By this exception, most of the licensor's need for a non-competition clause may be satisfied.

(iv) Assign back and exclusive grant back clauses

Finally, the definition of assign back and exclusive grant back in the New Guideline needs special attention.

(A) Assign back means an obligation to transfer any rights etc. on improvements made by a licensee to its licensor without any royalty payment. When royalty is paid to a licensor, this is not an assign back.

(B) Exclusive grant back is defined as a case where a licensee himself cannot use the improvement in his business territory. Therefore, when a licensee as well as its licensor can use the improvement, such obligation is regarded as non-exclusive under the New Guideline. This is an important difference because, "exclusive license" in American usage means "non-exclusive license" in the definitions of the New Guideline. In American usage, granting exclusive rights on an improvement does not prevent the innovator from using the improvement himself.

(C) Option back clauses and the right to first refusal clauses are not included in the term "grant back clause," and a licensor can use such clauses freely.[11]

(3) CLEARANCE SYSTEM

For international business in particular, legal stability is very much preferred. Business activities are disturbed merely by the *possibility* that there is a risk that the agreement might cause antimonopoly problems after its conclusion. It is highly desired to remove any antimonopoly problems as much as possible in advance. This is the reason why the FTC established a clearance system at the time of its announcement of the New Guideline.

A Japanese party or a foreign party can ask for clearance of any licensing agreement that they are going to conclude that is covered by the New Guideline. The FTC will answer in writing, and it guarantees clearance effect until it is canceled due to such reason as a changed situation. In other words, the FTC will not take any legal action against a licensing agreement once cleared by it unless and until the clearance itself is vacated.

This clearance system is established in view of the criticism of the FTC enforcement of the Old Guideline, namely, the undesirableness of *ex post* intervention, therefore, active use by foreign firms is expected.

(4) SUMMARY

A guideline shall be such that can give clear guidance to businessmen at the time of contract negotiations, and restrictive provisions in the contract shall be remedied without damaging the whole licensing agreement. Under the approach adopted by the New Guideline, the procompetitive effect through technology transfer can be secured, whereas, anticompetitive provisions can be removed.

Technology may flow only when exclusive rights to the technology are fully guaranteed in the licensed territory and contract terms are satisfactory to the licensor. This is a minimum condition for significant transfer of technology to happen. On the other hand, some restrictive clauses may raise anticompetitive effects that nullify the procompetitive effects expected from a transfer of technology. There are certain restrictive clauses that from a fairness viewpoint, should be avoided as much as possible. Certain restrictive clauses are unfair in nature, and cannot be justified even from a licensor's viewpoint. However, for the sake of legal stability, such clauses should be spelled out as clearly as possible. This is why a clear statement of policy such as this guideline is desirable in this field.[12]

A balanced approach to secure the maximum incentive for innovation both by the original innovator and his licensees is what the FTC aimed at with the New Guideline. From this point of view, the New Guideline tried to provide a wider chance to justify restrictive provisions from a licensor's perspective, compared with the old one.

(E) FTC POLICY ON JOINT R & D

(1) USE OF JOINT R & D

Joint R & D is a very common phenomenon in Japan. Among 790 big businesses surveyed in 1988, 65 percent answered that they had engaged in some kind of joint R & D activities, and about 10 percent of R & D expenditures were used for this purpose. On average, 30 joint R & D projects per firm were in progress. The majority of joint R & D was to effect the commercialization of technology (about 60 percent), and about 20 patent applications per firm were filed, which made up 7.4 percent of all patent applications per year. The most common form of joint R & D was concluded among firms in vertical relationships such as finished products manufacturers and their parts suppliers with the purpose of commercialization of new products. Joint R & D was actively engaged in in chemicals, electronics and precisions industries.[13]

In view of the increasing importance of joint R & D, the FTC set up a study group which submitted a report on *Joint R & D and Competition Policy* in June 1990.[14] Based on recommendations presented by this study group, the FTC prepared a draft guideline on joint R & D that it made public in September 1992, and encouraged relevant organizations, foreign or domestic, to submit their comments.

The major points of the draft guideline are as follows:

(A) Because of the plurality of relevant entrepreneurs, applicability of sections 3, 8(1)(i) and 10 needs to be evaluated. In addition, the applicability of section 19 needs to be evaluated. Possible antimonopoly problems concerning these aspects are examined separately.[15]

(B) There will be no problem as to joint R & D when it is engaged in by firms with no competitive relationships. However, potential competition needs to be evaluated.

(C) When participants' market share is less than 20 percent, joint R & D for product improvement purposes or for development of substitutable goods may not pose antimonopoly problems. The more market share of participants increases and the more influential entrepreneurs are involved, the more possible antimonopoly problems joint R & D will face.[16]

(D) Joint R & D relating to basic technology research poses an indirect impact on markets, whereas joint R & D relating to commercialization purposes poses a more direct impact on markets, therefore, the latter may face a greater chance of antimonopoly problems.[17]

(E) Joint R & D to cope with environmental or safety needs may face a lesser chance of antimonopoly problems.

(F) When risk and cost involved in the research are beyond an individual firm's capability, or the research capability of an individual firm is limited, joint R & D to cope with such difficulty will face a lesser chance of antimonopoly problems.

(G) When results of joint R & D are jointly utilized and price or quantity of products incorporating the technology is restricted, section 3's applicability shall be examined. Joint production or sales shall also be examined from this aspect.[18]

As to section 19 applicability, the draft guideline shows three categories of clauses as did the Patent and Know-How Licensing Guideline. Most of the black clauses proscribe those clauses that go beyond necessary restriction in order to pursue joint R & D projects. Other problematic clauses are almost the same as those condemned by the Patent and Know-How Licensing Guideline.[19]

NOTES

[1] As to the Old Guideline, see A. Uesugi, *Transfer of Technology and Joint Ventures in Japan*, ANNUAL PROCEEDINGS OF FORDHAM CORPORATE LAW INSTITUTE (1983), at 347.

[2] Protection of know-how depends heavily on contractual terms, whereas, patents can be protected under the Patent Law, therefore, licensors have relatively stronger reasons to put more restrictive terms in their licensing agreements to protect their know-how.

[3] See A. Uesugi, *supra* note 1.

[4] Remarks by B. Wilson, Deputy Assistant Attorney General, Antitrust Division, Before the American Patent Law Association (Jan. 21, 1975). This idea had prompted the Recommendation of the OECD Council Concerning Action Against Restrictive Business Practices Relating to the Use of Patents and Licenses (1974).

[5] Remarks by B. Lipsky, Deputy Assistant Attorney General, Antitrust Division, Current Antitrust Division Views on Patent Licensing Practices, before ABA Antitrust Section (Nov. 5, 1981).

[6] J. Davidow, *The New Japanese Guidelines on Unfair Practices in Patent and Know-How Licenses: An American View*, WORLD COMPETITION, Vol. 12 No. 4 (June 1989), at 6.

[7] OECD, COMPETITION POLICY AND INTELLECTUAL PROPERTY RIGHTS (1989), at 102. This portion reflects the views of Japan.

[8] U.S. v. General Electric Co., 272 U.S. 476 (1926); Newburgh Moire Co. v. Superior Moire Co., 237 F.2d 283 (3rd Cir. 1956).

[9] M. Matsushita, *Protection of Technology and the Liberal Trade Order: A Japanese View*, in Y. Yamamura ed., JAPAN'S ECONOMIC STRUCTURE: SHOULD IT CHANGE? (1990), where he presents a contrary view saying that "a licensor is prohibited from determining the price of the licensed product. Such a restriction by the licensor may not always be anticompetitive if the licensor is not producing." at 299.

[10] See part 2-3-(3) and 2-1-(4) in appendix F.

[11] An option back clause means giving the licensor an option right to negotiate licensing agreements on the improvements. A first refusal right clause means giving the licensor a first refusal right to conclude a licensing agreement on the improvements. Grant-back clauses condemned by the Guideline refers to the automatic grant back obligation on the part of licensees so that they might be discouraged from improving.

[12] This thinking is clearly expressed in Introduction 3 of the Patent and Know-How Licensing Guidelines. See appendix F.

[13] GIJUTSU TORIHIKI TO KENKYUKAI (Study Group on Technology Transaction etc.), KYODO KENKYU KAIHATSU TO GOKUSEN KINSHI HO (Joint R & D and the Antimonopoly Act) (June 1990), at 22-29.

[14] *Id.*

[15] This distinction corresponds to horizontal agreements v. vertical agreements. See chapter 6 (A)(3) Horizontal Agreements v. Vertical Agreements.

As seen above, in view of their procompetition aspects, the FTC will carefully try to balance them with the horizontal aspects of licensing agreements on patent or know-how.

[16] This draft guideline indicates possible problems in the technology transaction market, too. However, as to such markets, technology could easily flow beyond national borders, thus when evaluated, if foreign entrepreneurs are taken into consideration, there will be less chance of antimonopoly problems.

[17] Technological research can be classified into three categories: basic research, research for application, and research for commercialization.

[18] This does not mean that joint production or joint sales schemes are deemed illegal in principle. If undertaken by participants with less than a 20 percent market share, they will face less chance of antimonopoly problems.

Restrictions on production or sales quantity are declared grey clauses in this draft, and thus may pose problem under section 19. Price restriction is declared a black clause, thus highly likely be condemned under section 19.

[19] See appendix F.

KEIRETSU RELATIONSHIPS

(A) *KEIRETSU* CLASSIFICATIONS

Keiretsu relationships may be examined in three categories.

The first category refers to a business group or *kigyo shudan* and in view of the relationships among its member firms, this could be called a horizontal *keiretsu*. However, in the area of antitrust law, the term "horizontal" refers to relations among competitors and may not be suitable in view of the conglomerate nature of member firms within the same business group.

The second category refers to a group of firms weakly consolidated along a customer-supplier relationship, and this could be called a vertical *keiretsu*. Vertical *keiretsu* include a chain of distributors controlled or related to a particular manufacturer (this is most often called a distribution *keiretsu*) or a chain of subcontractors related to a particular manufacturer or a group of firms consisting of a manufacturer of finished products and its parts manufacturers (this is most often called a production *keiretsu*).

The third category is that of financial *keiretsu*, which refers to a group of firms coming under a single "main bank."

In a sense, a business group is a kind of financial *keiretsu*, but has a broader aspect than a financial *keiretsu*. A financial *keiretsu* usually is understood to cover a broader relationship of non-financial firms with their main bank. It could cover broadly smaller firms than members of a particular business group, and sometimes includes the relationship of non-financial firms with their main underwriters.

Contrary to the general impression, these various *keiretsu* relationships are the products of World War II. Business groups formed by three former *zaibatsu*-related companies are the products of the *zaibatsu* dissolution that occurred after the war. After holding companies were eliminated, and member firms were forced to become separate independent companies, as they expanded their capital they then started to have cross-shareholding relationships. As a natural course of action, they each formed president clubs.

In order to counter the formation of a business group by these three former *zaibatsu*-related companies, three other bank-related business groups were formed. In the case of Daiichi Kangyo, former Kawasaki *zaibatsu*-related firms and Hurukawa *zaibatsu*-related firms were combined due to the merger between the Daiichi Bank and the Nihon Kangyo Bank. The Fuyo Group consisted mostly of the former Yasuda *zaibatsu*-related firms.

The production *keiretsu* had expanded in the 1950s, and the distribution *keiretsu* was a product of 1960s and thereafter.[1] They became noticeable in steel and textile transactions where *keiretsu* relationships were established among finished product manufacturers and raw material suppliers.[2] Parent-subcontractor relationships, which have an aspect of *keiretsu*, also became evident in the 1950s.[3]

Therefore, it is clearly wrong to regard the *keiretsu* relationship as something particular to the Japanese industrial organization. The *keiretsu* relationships in these meanings were the products of the rapid economic expansion in the 1950s and 1960s.

(B) FTC STUDY OF *KEIRETSU*

(1) FTC STUDY OF BUSINESS GROUPS

(i) Definition of a business group

How to define a particular business group is in itself a big question. The FTC understood it as a group of big firms belonging to each of the six president clubs. The merit of this approach is its easiness in identifying member firms. In other words, these firms are by any means member firms of these business groups.

However, the problem is that the definition may be too narrow and too limited so that only firms that are definitely related are counted as member firms of the same business group. For this reason, the FTC includes affiliated companies of member firms when it evaluates the impact of the six major business groups on the national economy. In various research papers by private research institutions, a broader definition of a business group may be seen.[4] In the business world, many companies think that they are associated with a particular business group even though they are not members of the president clubs. For example, the Asahi Breweries Co. or the Toyo Kogyo Co., a car manufacturer of Mazdas, are sometimes regarded as one of the Sumitomo Group companies, but not members of the Hakusui-kai, a president club of the Sumitomo Group. Or many firms of production *keiretsu* identify themselves as members of these business groups.

For example, the Mitsui Group organizes different meetings at lower levels. Besides president clubs, there are meetings of the vice presidents and board members of 72 companies. The trademark and trade name of the Mitsui are controlled by 52 related companies. In the case of Mitsubishi, 41 companies are members that control trademarks and trade names and also hold public relations divisions meetings.[5]

These multilevel meetings show that a particular business group has "majors" and "minors" as its members.

At this writing, the FTC has conducted research on the six major business groups four times. The 1992 research was conducted after this matter was discussed at SII. Many interesting results were disclosed as a result of this research, most of them never before made public. For example, the FTC for the first time, made public data for each business group. The past three research projects disclosed only data showing the average for the former *zaibatsu* Groups and the non-former *zaibatsu* groups. There are small differences in the analytic methodology of each Research Paper on Business Groups and comparisons of these research papers is not easy.

Table 24-1 shows the number of big firms that make up the six major business groups, and how they have increased. Table 24-2 shows the names of the big and influential Japanese companies that are members of each president club, showing the industry classification to which they belong as well. There are cases where competing firms belong to the same business group.[6]

Table 24-1. Number of Companies in Each Business Group

	Mitsui	Mitsubishi	Sumitomo	Fuyo	Sanwa	Daiichi Kangyo[1]	Sum Total	Net Total[2]
1955	—	21	14	—	—	—	35	35
1960	—	22	15	—	—	—	37	37
1965	18	22	16	25	—	(47)	128	128
1970	19	26	16	29	22	(48)	160	158
1975	23	28	16	29	36	(58)	190	188
1979	24	28	21	29	39	45	186	181
1981	24	28	21	29	40	45	187	182
1985	24	28	21	29	42	46	190	187
1987	24	29	20	29	44	47	193	188
1989	24	29	20	29	44	47	193	188
1992	26	29	20	29	44	47	195	190

NOTES:

[1] Before 1979, member firms of the Daiichi Kangyo Group include the total of former Hurukawa, Kawasaki and Kangyo Groups' member firms.

[2] Those firms that participate in several president clubs are adjusted for in the net total.

(ii) Relationships of firms within each business group

The FTC has been studying the six major business groups regularly and some findings are made public through its research papers.

The critical point of the surveys is how these firms are related to each other, and tables 24-3 to 24-8 show, on average, how these firms are related by stockholding relationships and interlocking directorates. Individually, less than 2 percent of the stocks are held by each member firm on average (see table 24-3), but when accumulated, member firms hold 15 to 35 percent of stocks, on average, of a particular member firm (see table 24-4).

When the top 50 shareholders are examined, 35 percent of them are member firms of the same business group. However, at the same time, 24 percent of the top shareholders are member firms belonging to the other six major business groups. Most of them are financial companies (see table 24-5).

Sixty-five percent of the top shareholders are member firms of the same business group. Sixty-one percent of the top three share-

Table 24-2. Companies that are Members of the Six Major Business Groups

Industry	MITSUI Group (26 Companies)	MITSUBISHI Group (29 Companies)	SUMITOMO Group (20 Companies)	FUYO Group (29 Companies)	SANWA Group (44 Companies)	DAIICHI-KANGYO Group (47 Companies)
Financial Securities	Mitsui Bank Mitsui Trust & Banking Mitsui Life Insurance Mitsui Marine & Fire Insurance	Mitsubishi Bank Mitsubishi Trust Banking Meiji Life Insurance Tokyo Marine & Fire Insurance	Sumitomo Bank Sumitomo Trust & Banking Sumitomo Life Insurance Sumitomo Marine & Fire Insurance	Fuji Bank Yasuda Trust & Banking Yasuda Life Insurance Yasuda Fire & Marine Insurance	Sanwa Bank Toyo Trust & Banking Nihon Life Insurance	Dai-Ichi Kangyo Bank Asahi Life Insurance Hukoku Life Insurance Nissan Fire & Marine Insurance Taisei Fire & Marine Insurance Kankaku Securities
Commerce	Mitsui & Co. Mitsukoshi	Mitsubishi	Sumitomo	Marubeni	Nichimen Nissho Iwai Iwatani International Takashimaya	C. Itoh & Co. Nissho Iwai Kanematsu-Gosho Kawasho Seibu Department Stores
Forestry	—	—	Sumitomo Forestry	—	—	—
Mining	Mitsui Mining Hokkaido Tonko Kinsen	—	Sumitomo Coal Mining	—	—	—
Construction	Mitsui Construction Sanki Engineering	Mitsubishi Construction	Sumitomo Construction	Taisei	Obayashi Toyo Construction Zenitaka Sekisui House	Shimizu Construction

Table 24-2. Companies that are Members of the Six Major Business Groups (cont.)

Industry	MITSUI Group (26 Companies)	MITSUBISHI Group (29 Companies)	SUMITOMO Group (20 Companies)	FUYO Group (29 Companies)	SANWA Group (44 Companies)	DAIICHI-KANGYO Group (47 Companies)
Foods	Nippn Flour Mills	Kirin Breweries	—	Nisshin Flour Milling Sapporo Breweries Nichirei	Ito Ham Foods Suntory	—
Textiles	—	—	—	Nissinbo Industries Toho Rayon	Unitika	—
Pulp & Paper	Oji Paper	Mitsubishi Paper Mills	—	Snayo Koku-saku Pulp	—	Honshu Paper
Chemical	Mitsui Toatsu Chemicals Mitsui Petro-chemical Industries Toray Industries Denki Kagaku Kogyo	Mitsubishi Chemical Industries Mitsubishi Gas Chemical Mitsubishi Petro-chemical Mitsubishi Plastic Mitsubishi Rayon	Sumitomo Chemical Sumitomo Bakelite	Showa Denko Kureha Chemical Industry Nippon Oil & Fats	Teijin Tokuyama Soda Sekisui Chemical Ube Industries Hitachi Chemical Tanabe Seiyaku Fujisawa Phar-maceutical Kansai Paint	Denki Kagaku Kogyo Kyowa Hakko Kogyo Nippon Zeon Asahi Denka Kogyo Sankyo Shiseido Lion Asahi Chemical Industries

Table 24-2. Companies that are Members of the Six Major Business Groups *(cont.)*

Industry	MITSUI Group (26 Companies)	MITSUBISHI Group (29 Companies)	SUMITOMO Group (20 Companies)	FUYO Group (29 Companies)	SANWA Group (44 Companies)	DAIICHI-KANGYO Group (47 Companies)
Oil & Coal	—	Mitsubishi Oil	—	Tonen	Cosmo Oil	Showa Shell Sekiyu
Rubber	—	—	—	—	Toyo Tire & Rubber	Yokohama Rubber
Ceramics	Onoda Cement	Asahi Glass	Nippon Sheet Glass Sumitomo Cement	Nihon Cement	Osaka Cement Kyocera	Chichibu Cement
Iron & Steel	Japan Steel Works	Mitsubishi Steel Mfg.	Sumitomo Metal Industries	NKK	Kobe Steel Nisshin Steel Nakayama Steel Works Hitachi Metals	Kobe Steel Kawasaki Steel Japan Metals
Non-ferrous	Mitsui Mining & Smelting	Mitsubishi Materials Mitsubishi Shindo Mitsubishi Aluminum Mitsubishi Cable Industries	Sumitomo Metal & Mining Sumitomo Light Metal Industries Sumitomo Electric Industries	—	Hitachi Cables	Nippon Light Metal Hurukawa Hurukawa Electric
Machinery	—	Mitsubishi Kakoki	Sumitomo Heavy Industries	Kubota Nippon Seiko	N.T.N.	Niigata Engineering Iseki & Co. Ebara

Table 24-2. Companies that are Members of the Six Major Business Groups (cont.)

Industry	MITSUI Group (26 Companies)	MITSUBISHI Group (29 Companies)	SUMITOMO Group (20 Companies)	FUYO Group (29 Companies)	SANWA Group (44 Companies)	DAIICHI-KANGYO Group (47 Companies)
Electric	Toshiba	Mitsubishi Electric	NEC	Hitachi Oki Electric Industries Yokogawa Electric	Hitachi Iwasaki Electric Sharp Nitto Denko	Hitachi Fuji Electric Yasukawa Electric Mfg. Fujitsu Nippon Columbia
Transportation	Toyota Motor Mitsui Shipbuilding Ishikawajima Harima Heavy Industries	Mitsubishi Heavy Industries Mitsubishi Motors	—	Nissan Motor	Hitachi Zosen Shinmeiwa Industry Daihatsu Motor	Kawasaki Heavy Industries Ishikawajima-Harima Heavy Industries Isuzu Motors
Precision	—	Nippon Kogaku	—	Canon	Hoya	Asahi Optical
Real Estate	Mitsui Real Estate Development	Mitsubishi Estate	Sumitomo Realty & Development	Tokyo Tatemono	—	—
Land Transport	—	—	—	Tobu Railway Keihin Electric Express Railway	Hankyu Railway Nippon Express	Nippon Express

Table 24-2. Companies that are Members of the Six Major Business Groups (cont.)

Industry	MITSUI Group (26 Companies)	MITSUBISHI Group (29 Companies)	SUMITOMO Group (20 Companies)	FUYO Group (29 Companies)	SANWA Group (44 Companies)	DAIICHI-KANGYO Group (47 Companies)
Sea Transport	Mitsui O.S.K. Lines	Nippon Yusen	—	Showa Line	Navicks Line	Kawasaki Kisen
Warehouse	Mitsui Warehouse	Mitsubishi Warehouse & Transportation	Sumitomo Warehouse	—	—	Shibusawa Warehouse
Service	—	Mitsubishi Research Institute	—	—	Orix	Orient Corp. Korakuen Stadium

Table 24-3. Average Stockholding Ratios of the Group[1]

FY	1977	1981	1987	% 1989
Mitsui	2.08	1.77	1.58	1.42
Mitsubishi	2.10	2.20	1.85	1.75
Sumitomo	2.30	2.17	1.68	1.54
Average[2] for the Three	2.16	2.05	1.70	1.57
Fuyo	1.96	1.47	1.28	1.30
Sanwa	2.51	1.68	1.55	1.43
Daiichi Kangyo	2.18	1.39	1.16	1.08
Average[2] for the Three	2.22	1.51	1.33	1.27
Average[2] for the Six	2.19	1.78	1.52	1.42

NOTES:
[1] Average stockholding ratio = K/n

  K = Σ Stocks of company i held by other member companies in the Group/
    Total stocks issued of company i

  n = Σ Number of company i's shareholders who are members of the Group.

[2] Averages are simple averages of stockholding ratio of each Group.

SOURCE: This table is compiled from the 1992 FTC Research Paper on Business Groups.

Table 24-4. Cross-Stockholding Ratios of Each Group[1]

FY	1970	1975	1977[3]	1979	1981	1985	1987	% 1989
Mitsui	21.32	21.17	22.22	22.08	23.13	21.16	21.35	19.46
Mitsubishi	26.78	30.26	30.35	36.29	36.93	36.94	36.04	35.45
Sumitomo	28.94	29.58	34.00	36.77	36.57	29.68	29.40	27.46
Average[2] for the Three	25.68	27.00	28.86	31.71	32.21	29.41	28.93	27.46
Fuyo	16.04	18.28	19.11	19.29	18.80	17.36	17.11	16.39
Sanwa	12.50	20.30	20.98	20.26	19.95	18.03	17.05	16.46
Daiichi Kangyo	24.51	23.77	16.47	17.88	17.50	16.78	14.92	14.60
Average[2] for the Three	17.68	20.78	18.85	19.14	18.75	17.39	16.36	15.82
Average[2] for the Six	21.68	23.89	23.86	25.43	25.48	23.40	22.65	21.64

NOTES:
[1] Average cross-stockholding ratio = K/n

  K = Σ Stocks of company i held by other member companies in the Group/
    Total stocks issued of company i

  n = Number of member firms in the Groups.

[2] Averages are simple averages of cross-stockholding ratios of each Group.

[3] The figures before 1977 are based on those for listed companies and life insurance companies.
    They exclude unlisted companies and other financial companies.

SOURCE: This table is compiled from the 1992 FTC Research Paper on Business Groups.

Table 24-5. Top 50 Shareholders of Member Firms of Each Business Group[1]
(As of FY 1989)

	Top 50 Share- holders	Member Firms	Members of Other Groups	Non- Member Banks	Non-Member Financial Companies	% Foreign Firms
Mitsui	61.05	34.37	27.50	26.10	7.22	1.71
Mitsubishi	68.79	52.88	17.39	19.28	4.12	4.75
Sumitomo	60.61	48.63	21.09	19.41	7.34	1.73
Average[2] for the Three	63.48	45.29	21.99	21.60	6.23	2.73
Fuyo	64.67	27.65	33.14	26.25	6.40	4.37
Sanwa	66.38	26.25	27.64	26.26	11.86	2.04
Daiichi Kangyo	68.54	20.28	31.68	26.90	11.99	6.15
Average[2] for the Three	66.53	24.73	30.82	26.47	10.08	4.19
Average[2] for the Six	65.01	35.01	26.41	24.04	8.16	3.46

NOTES:
[1] Averages above are simple averages of stockholding ratios of each Group.
The figures are based on those excluding life insurance companies.
[2] The figures above show average stockholding ratios held by top 50 shareholders of each category of companies (= K/n)
K = Σ Stocks of company i held by other member companies in the same Group who are among top 50 shareholders/Total stocks issued of company i
n = Number of member firms of the Group.
SOURCE: Compiled from the 1992 FTC Research Paper on Business Groups.

holders are member firms of the same business group (see table 24-6). When other closely related companies are taken into account, more than a majority of shareholders can be counted as "stable shareholders."

However, as a matter of law, it is difficult to regard these firms as firms under the same control as were the former *zaibatsu* firms.

Business Week once carried an article about the Mitsubishi Group and said that a "huge network of companies is challenging antitrust laws—and the American culture." "Its structure doesn't conflict with U.S. statutes because Mitsubishi companies are legally independent and compete mainly in different industry segments." "Congressional critics argue that Mitsubishi-like keiretsu already are violating the intent of antitrust laws, but they have so far turned up no proof." "Mitsubishi's push into the U.S. is likely to force a reexamination of U.S. economic values, systems, and policies."[7]

Although it is difficult to regard member firms as a unified group of firms, it is possible to take into account the close relationships of

Table 24-6. *Top 10 Shareholders of Each Business Group[1]*

%

FY	Top Shareholder				Top Three Shareholders			
	1977	1981	1987	1989	1977	1981	1987	1989
Mitsui	68.18	63.64	N.A.	56.52	56.06	60.61	N.A.	65.28
Mitsubishi	86.95	89.96	N.A.	85.71	84.05	81.16	N.A.	79.31
Sumitomo	84.21	84.21	N.A.	100.00	80.70	78.95	N.A.	83.33
Average[2] for the Three	79.78	78.27	77.10	80.75	73.60	73.57	74.27	75.97
Fuyo	50.00	46.43	N.A.	46.43	48.81	50.00	N.A.	44.83
Sanwa	65.72	69.23	N.A.	55.81	53.33	51.28	N.A.	50.76
Daiichi Kangyo	53.66	69.23	N.A.	48.28	43.09	47.97	N.A.	40.43
Average[2] for the Three	56.46	60.51	48.52	50.17	48.41	49.75	50.38	45.34
Average[2] for the Six	68.12	69.39	62.81	65.46	61.01	61.66	62.33	60.66

FY	Top Five Shareholders				Top Ten Shareholders			
	1977	1981	1987	1989	1977	1981	1987	1989
Mitsui	53.64	56.36	N.A.	54.17	47.28	46.36	N.A.	41.25
Mitsubishi	72.17	73.91	N.A.	71.03	59.99	58.26	N.A.	51.03
Sumitomo	78.95	78.95	N.A.	66.00	63.16	64.21	N.A.	51.00
Average[2] for the Three	68.25	69.74	67.21	63.73	56.81	56.28	51.10	47.76
Fuyo	41.42	41.43	N.A.	42.76	35.36	36.79	N.A.	31.27
Sanwa	40.58	37.95	N.A.	40.91	29.43	30.26	N.A.	29.09
Daiichi Kangyo	35.12	35.61	N.A.	31.06	26.34	28.05	N.A.	22.55
Average[2] for the Three	39.04	38.33	40.08	38.24	30.38	31.70	29.70	27.64
Average[2] for the Six	53.65	54.04	53.65	50.99	43.59	43.99	40.40	37.70

NOTES:
[1] Ratio of member shareholders among top shareholders = K/n
  K = Σ Number of top shareholders of company i who are members of the same Business Group.
  n = Total number of top shareholders of member firms in the Group.
  The figures are based on those of listed companies only.
[2] Averages are simple averages of stockholding ratio of each Group.
SOURCE: Compiled from the 1992 FTC Research Paper on Business Groups.

these firms when the impact on competition is to be evaluated. The Distribution System and Business Practices Guidelines (DSBP Guidelines) said that "Whether or not a firm has close relations with another firm is to be judged on a case-by-case basis, taking comprehensively into account such factors as . . . common membership of so-called business groups."[8] (Note 6, Part 1 of the Guidelines.)

Table 24-7. Ratio of Interlocking Directorates[1]

	FY	Ratio Dispatched by Member Firms	Ratio Dispatched by Member Banks	% Ratio Dispatched by Member Trading Companies
Mitsui	1977[2]	47.83	47.83	17.39
	1981	47.83	39.13	4.35
	1987	45.83	41.66	4.17
	1989	41.66	37.50	4.17
Mitsubishi	1977	92.86	71.43	28.57
	1981	96.55	85.71	35.71
	1987	96.55	86.21	41.38
	1989	96.55	75.86	37.93
Sumitomo	1977	66.67	52.38	23.81
	1981	71.43	52.38	23.81
	1987	50.00	40.00	10.00
	1989	50.00	35.00	15.00
Average[3] for	1977	69.12	57.12	23.26
the Three	1981	71.94	59.07	21.29
	1987	64.13	55.96	18.52
	1989	62.74	49.45	19.03
Fuyo	1977[2]	58.62	51.72	0.00
	1981	62.07	55.17	0.00
	1987	68.97	58.62	0.00
	1989	44.83	37.93	0.00
Sanwa	1977[2]	61.11	41.67	8.33
	1981	67.50	50.00	2.50
	1987	68.18	50.00	2.27
	1989	68.18	54.54	2.27
Daiichi	1977[2]	57.78	51.11	2.22
Kangyo	1981	73.33	68.89	2.22
	1987	76.60	70.21	2.12
	1989	72.34	63.83	2.12
Average[3] for	1977[2]	59.17	48.17	3.52
the Three	1981	67.63	58.02	1.57
	1987	71.25	59.61	1.46
	1989	61.78	52.10	1.46
Average[3] for	1977[2]	64.15	52.69	13.39
the Six	1981	69.79	58.55	11.43
	1987	67.69	57.79	9.99
	1989	62.26	50.78	10.25

NOTES:
[1] Ratio of interlocking directorates = K/n
  K = Number of companies accepting directors from other member firms of the same Business Group.
  n = Total number of companies in the same Group.
[2] The figures for 1977 are based on those of listed companies and life insurance. They exclude unlisted companies and other financial companies.
[3] Averages above are simple averages of interlocking directorates ratio of each Group.
SOURCE: Compiled from the 1992 FTC Research Paper on Business Groups.

Table 24-8. Ratio of Interlocking Directorates Among Board Members[1]

	F Y	Ratio Dispatched by Member Firms	Ratio Dispatched by Member Banks	% Ratio Dispatched by Member Trading Companies
Mitsui	1977[2]	4.64	2.41	0.93
	1981	3.58	1.88	0.19
	1987	2.86	1.89	0.16
	1989	2.20	1.62	0.15
Mitsubishi	1977[22]	12.64	4.98	1.66
	1981	18.24	5.00	1.62
	1987	14.25	4.55	1.92
	1989	12.85	3.42	1.42
Sumitomo	1977[2]	13.60	4.47	1.57
	1981	11.61	3.87	1.02
	1987	8.87	6.10	0.37
	1989	8.68	3.99	0.52
Average[3] for	1977[2]	10.29	3.95	1.39
the Three	1981	11.14	3.58	0.94
	1987	8.65	4.18	0.82
	1989	7.91	3.01	0.70
Fuyo	1977[2]	4.60	3.16	0.00
	1981	4.21	3.26	0.00
	1987	3.94	3.18	0.00
	1989	2.37	1.66	0.00
Sanwa	1977[2]	6.25	3.00	0.72
	1981	5.47	2.84	0.21
	1987	5.49	3.34	0.09
	1989	5.03	3.00	0.08
Daiichi	1977[2]	7.00	3.35	0.19
Kangyo	1981	8.27	4.40	0.18
	1987	7.40	4.43	0.08
	1989	6.92	4.05	0.08
Average[3] for	1977[2]	5.95	3.17	0.30
the Three	1981	5.98	3.50	0.13
	1987	5.61	3.65	0.06
	1989	4.78	2.90	0.05
Average[3] for	1977[2]	8.12	3.56	0.85
the Six	1981	8.56	3.54	0.54
	1987	7.13	3.92	0.44
	1989	6.34	2.96	0.37

NOTES:
[1] Ratio of interlocking directorates = K/n
  K = Number of directors accepted from other member firms of the same Group.
  n = Total number of directors of the member firms of the same Groups.
[2] The figures for 1977 are based on those of listed companies and life insurance companies, namely exclude unlisted companies and other financial companies.
[3] Averages are simple averages of interlocking directorates ratios of each Group.
SOURCE: Compiled from the 1992 FTC Research Paper on Business Groups.

(iii) Positions within the national economy

The most important aspect of the six major business groups is how these firms stand in the national economy. First, tables 24-9 and 24-10 show group size in terms of total assets, paid-in capital, current profit, etc. Tables 24-11 and 24-12 show how they stand if their subsidiaries are taken into account.

Table 24-9. *Shares of the Six Major Business Groups Over National Economy* (As of FY 1989)*

	Number of Member Firms	Paid-in Capital	Total Assets	Net Worth	Amount of Sales	Current Profits	Profits Before Tax	Number of Workers
		(%)	(%)	(%)	(%)	(%)	(%)	(%)
Mitsui	20	2.51	2.29	3.45	2.81	3.37	3.86	0.62
Mitsubishi	25	2.93	2.37	2.54	2.33	2.32	2.36	0.59
Sumitomo	16	1.95	1.33	1.55	2.23	1.28	1.41	0.33
Total for the Three	61	7.38	5.99	7.54	7.38	6.97	7.63	1.55
Fuyo	25	3.40	2.23	3.45	2.65	2.38	2.52	0.85
Mitsubishi	41	3.82	2.82	3.57	3.13	2.77	2.88	1.03
Sumitomo	41	4.26	3.71	3.52	4.93	2.97	3.03	1.22
Total for the Three	102	9.86	7.55	8.89	8.85	6.67	6.90	2.42
Total for the Six	163	17.24	13.54	16.43	16.23	13.63	14.53	3.97

NOTES:
* The figures are based on those excluding financial companies (163 companies as a whole are analyzed).
  Share over the national economy = K/n
  K = Applicable figures for member firms.
  n = Applicable figures for the total non-financial juridical persons in Japan.
SOURCE: Compiled from the 1992 FTC Research Paper on Business Groups.

Financial institutions are excluded because their asset size is not comparable with those of non-financial companies. The six major business groups occupy a high percentage in terms of net worth, amount of sales and paid-in capital, but do not rank so high in terms of profits (see table 24-9).

To what extent subsidiaries and affiliated companies could be included for this purpose has another difficult aspect for evaluation. Up to 1989, the FTC studies included in their analysis such affiliated companies of which a member firm has more than 10 percent, without making any adjustment (see table 24-12). The 1992 FTC study

Table 24-10. *Shares of the Six Major Business Groups Over National Economy for 1981, 1987, 1989**

	FY	Paid-in Capital	Total Assets	% Amount of Sales
Mitsui	1981	2.17	2.36	2.65
	1987	2.15	2.03	2.51
	1989	2.51	2.29	2.81
Mitsubishi	1981	2.61	2.80	2.86
	1987	2.73	2.22	2.16
	1989	2.93	2.37	2.33
Sumitomo	1981	1.59	1.51	1.87
	1987	1.80	1.38	1.79
	1989	1.95	1.33	2.33
Total for the Three	1981	6.37	6.67	7.38
	1987	6.68	5.63	6.46
	1989	7.38	5.99	7.38
Fuyo	1981	2.90	2.79	2.76
	1987	2.83	2.28	2.40
	1989	3.40	2.23	2.65
Sanwa	1981	3.07	3.02	2.74
	1987	3.21	2.76	2.77
	1989	3.82	2.82	3.13
Daiichi Kangyo	1981	3.90	4.08	4.44
	1987	3.93	3.79	4.65
	1989	4.26	3.71	4.93
Total for the Three	1981	8.20	8.43	8.40
	1987	8.51	7.65	8.22
	1989	9.86	7.55	8.85
Total for the Six	1981	14.57	15.10	15.78
	1987	15.19	13.28	14.68
	1989	17.24	13.54	16.23

NOTES:
* The figures above are based on those excluding financial companies.
  Share over the national economy = K/n
  K = Applicable figures for member firms.
  n = Applicable figures for the total non-financial juridical persons in Japan.
SOURCE: Compiled from the 1992 FTC Research Paper on Business Groups.

Table 24-11. *Shares of the Six Major Business Groups Over National Economy[1] (Including Subsidiaries[2])*

	FY	Number of Companies Subsidiaries	Total	Paid-in Capital Subsidiaries	(%) Total	Total Assets Subsid- iaries	(%) Total	Amount of Sales Subsid- iaries	(%) Total
Mitsui	1981	607	627	0.62	2.76	0.30	2.66	0.48	3.13
	1987	670	690	0.66	2.81	0.64	2.67	0.57	3.08
	1989	743	763	0.61	3.00	0.71	3.00	0.60	3.41
Mitsubishi	1981	563	587	0.71	3.32	0.37	3.17	0.63	3.49
	1987	792	817	0.64	3.37	0.52	2.74	0.49	2.65
	1989	979	1,004	0.61	3.53	0.55	2.92	0.53	2.85
Sumitomo	1981	408	425	0.27	1.86	0.19	1.70	0.35	2.22
	1987	441	457	0.44	2.24	0.38	1.76	0.44	2.23
	1989	550	566	0.42	2.37	0.44	1.77	0.51	2.74
Total for the Three	1981	1,578	1,639	1.61	7.98	0.85	7.52	1.45	8.83
	1987	1,903	1,964	1.74	8.42	1.54	7.17	1.50	7.96
	1989	2,272	2,333	1.64	9.02	1.70	7.69	1.63	9.01
Fuyo	1981	726	751	0.79	3.69	0.53	3.32	0.96	3.72
	1987	757	782	0.80	3.63	0.92	3.20	0.94	3.34
	1989	848	873	0.84	4.24	1.02	3.17	1.02	3.67
Sanwa	1981	1,224	1,261	0.72	3.79	0.49	3.51	0.82	3.56
	1987	1,260	1,301	0.80	4.01	1.01	3.77	1.01	3.78
	1989	1,563	1,604	0.81	4.63	1.05	3.88	1.08	4.21
Daiichi Kangyo	1981	1,260	1,299	1.00	4.90	0.69	4.77	1.14	5.58
	1987	1,508	1,550	1.22	5.15	1.27	5.06	1.33	5.98
	1989	1,704	1,745	1.14	5.40	1.27	4.99	1.43	6.36
Total for the Three	1981	2,693	2,789	1.87	10.07	1.19	9.62	2.10	10.50
	1987	3,057	3,159	2.12	10.63	2.67	10.32	2.32	10.54
	1989	3,545	3,647	2.05	11.91	2.05	9.99	2.55	11.40
Total for the Six	1981	4,271	4,428	3.48	18.05	2.05	17.15	3.55	19.33
	1987	4,960	5,123	3.86	19.05	4.21	17.49	3.82	18.50
	1989	5,817	5,980	3.69	20.93	4.14	17.68	4.18	20.41

NOTES:
[1] The figures are based on those excluding financial companies.
Share over the national economy = K/n
K = Applicable figures for member firms (and subsidiaries).
n = Applicable figures for the total non-financial juridical persons in Japan.
[2] Subsidiaries include domestic companies only.
SOURCE: Compiled from the 1992 FTC Research Paper on Business Groups.

Table 24-12. Shares of the Six Major Business Groups Over National Economy*
(Including Subsidiaries)

	FY	Number of Companies Falling in the Category		Paid-in Capital	Total Assets	Amount of Sales
		Number	(%)	(%)	(%)	(%)
Total for the	1981	157	0.009	14.57	15.10	15.78
Six Groups	1987	163	0.008	15.19	13.28	14.68
	1989	163	0.008	17.24	13.54	16.23
More than 50%	1981	4,271	0.249	3.48	2.05	3.55
owned	1987	4,960	0.247	3.86	4.21	3.82
subsidiaries	1989	5,817	0.309	3.69	4.14	4.18
More than 25% &	1981	4,251	0.248	5.75	2.65	4.10
less than 50%	1987	3,615	0.187	5.78	4.89	3.25
owned subsidiaries	1989	N.A.	N.A.	N.A.	N.A.	N.A.
More than 10% &	1981	3,278	0.191	6.95	3.36	4.29
less than 25%	1987	3,260	0.169	7.20	4.57	3.45
owned subsidiaries	1989	N.A.	N.A.	N.A.	N.A.	N.A.
Total	1981	11,957	0.697	30.75	23.16	27.63
	1987	11,998	0.622	32.03	29.95	25.20
	1989	N.A.	N.A.	N.A.	N.A.	N.A.

NOTES:
* The figures above are based on those excluding financial companies.
  Share over the national economy = K/n
  K = Applicable figures for member firms (and subsidiaries).
  n = Applicable figures for the total non-financial juridical persons.
SOURCE: Compiled from the 1989 FTC Research Paper on Business Groups and the 1992 FTC
  Research Paper on Business Groups.

counted only those firms of which a member firm has 50 percent or more.

By taking into account such firms, the six major business groups occupied 21 percent in terms of paid-in capital, 18 percent in terms of total assets, and 20 percent in terms of total sales (see table 24-11). As a whole, it could be said that the six major business groups share in the national economy is roughly one-fifth.

As a whole, the six major business groups, if combined, could exercise significant economic power in Japan. There is no doubt that if member firms of the same business group came under common corporate control, it would raise serious antitrust concerns. However, because at present there is no sufficient link to connect these member firms within the same business group the FTC policy would be not to allow any member firms such as banks or general trading companies to function as the headquarters of any business group (see Chapter 11 Special Regulation on Stockholdings).[9]

(2) FTC STUDIES ON OTHER ASPECTS OF KEIRETSU

In the first half of the 1970s, general trading companies increased their stockholdings at an extraordinary rate. As of March 1973, eight major trading companies had increased their stockholdings by 71 percent as compared with the previous year. At that point, such stockholdings were equal to 1.8 times as much as their net worths on average, 6.26 percent of their total assets are occupied by stocks (see table 24-13).

After the first oil shock, the rate of stockholding expansion decreased, and by the 1977 Amendment, namely by the introduction of section 9-2, for more than 13 years, the expansion rate was below 10 percent per year.

However, because of the easy availability of equity financing in recent years, general trading companies could expand their net worths very rapidly in the past few years, and as a result, their stock acquisitions started to increase again. It should be remembered that a cross-holding relationship among member firms of a business group compelled new acquisition of stock as much as possible in order to maintain the pre-equity financing level of stockholdings in a particular company, thus would bring about an increase in the value of their stockholdings.

Equity financing would enhance the dispersion of stocks among shareholders, and the stockholding ratio by member firms would decline as a result. Therefore, these member firms were expected to purchase stocks from the stock market at the market price, which necessarily increased the total value of stocks held by these companies. It should also be noted that their net worth expanded more rapidly than the speed of stock acquisitions. Anyway, due to section 9-2 of the Act, it seems impossible to repeat the situation of the first half of 1970s (see chapter 11 (D) Evaluation).

Table 24-13. *Stockholdings of the Eight Major General Trading Companies*[1]

					(100 million yen)
	Total Amount of Stockholdings[2]	Increasing Ratio	Net Worth Ratio[3]	Total Assets Ratio[4]	Equity Ratio[5]
March 1966	1,203	—	86.4	4.30	4.98
March 1967	1,327	10.29	91.1	4.35	4.78
March 1968	1,572	18.38	100.4	4.12	4.10
March 1969	1,949	24.03	114.5	4.26	3.72
March 1970	2,332	19.67	116.6	3.83	3.29
March 1971	2,950	26.48	126.2	3.92	3.11
March 1972	4.012	36.00	152.9	4.54	2.97
March 1973	6.859	70.97	185.2	6.26	3.38
March 1974	7,925	15.54	175.9	5.29	3.01
March 1975	8,064	1.75	158.7	5.32	3.35
March 1976	8,636	7.10	156.2	5.38	3.45
March 1977	9.207	6.61	149.5	5.33	3.57
March 1978	9,210	0.03	143.3	5.61	3.92
March 1979	9,234	0.26	135.4	5.52	4.08
March 1980	9,284	0.54	121.5	4.82	3.97
March 1981	9,836	5.95	112.3	5.06	4.51
March 1982	10,467	6.42	113.5	5.12	4.52
March 1983	10,407	0.57	104.1	4.99	4.79
March 1984	10,532	1.20	101.4	4.78	4.71
March 1985	10,844	2.96	98.0	4.44	4.54
March 1986	11,692	6.99	95.4	5.12	5.37
March 1987	12,590	8.52	86.5	5.67	6.55
March 1988	14,142	12.33	88.2	5.96	6.45
March 1989	15,918	12.56	70.7	5.35	7.56
March 1990	19,305	21.28	67.6	5.08	7.51

NOTES:

[1] The eight major trading companies are Mitsubishi Corp., Mitsui & Co., C. Itoh & Co., Marubeni Corp., Sumitomo Corp., Nissho Iwai Co., Tomen Co., Nichimen Co.

[2] "Total Amount of Stockholdings" is based on those of domestic companies only, and those reported on the balance sheet at the end of each business year of these companies.

[3] "Net Worth Ratio" means the total amount of stockholdings divided by the accumulated total net worths of the eight major trading companies.

[4] "Total Assets Ratio" means the total amount of stockholdings divided by the accumulated total assets of the eight major trading companies.

[5] "Equity Ratio" means the accumulated total net worth divided by the accumulated total assets of the eight major trading companies.

SOURCE: Compiled from the Study Group Report on Distribution and Business Practices etc. and Competition Policy published on June 22, 1990.

(3) STOCKHOLDINGS BY BIG FIRMS IN JAPAN

Companies may have many subsidiaries and affiliated companies around them, and there is nothing wrong with this. But by examining the trends of stockholding by big firms, we can see general trends of concentration. The FTC regularly examined stockholding by big firms using stockholding reports filed under section 10(2) of the Act.

Table 24-14. Top Ten Shareholders of the Top 100 Non-Financial Companies in Japan

	Financial Institutions	Non-Financial Legal Entity	Foreign Firms	Indivi- viduals	Govern- ment	Others	Total
Ratio[1]	55.1	23.4	1.3	2.0	15.5	2.7	100.0
	(61.0)[2]	(27.5)	(5.8)	(2.2)	(0.5)	(3.0)	(100.0)
Per	3.3	9.0	9.3	4.4	62.7	5.9	4.8
Share-	(3.3)	(9.0)	(22.3)	(3.7)	(5.4)	(5.7)	(4.3)
holders							

NOTES:

1 "Ratio" means accumulated percentage of shareholdings by each category of institutions.
2 The figures in parentheses are calculated by excluding NTT and four JR companies which are among the top 100 companies in Japan. These privatized former public corporations are still owned wholly or mostly by the government. Therefore, for objective analysis, these companies are excluded (see chapter 25 Deregulation and Antimonopoly Exemption Laws).
SOURCE: Compiled from the the 1989 FTC Report on Stockholdings by Major Big Companies.

Table 24-15 reveals the interesting trends of Japanese big firms. The table shows that, as of FY 1986, if those firms with more than 10 percent stockholding relationships were counted, the number of affiliated companies of the top 100 non-financial companies was 9,519. Among them, over the past 5-year period, subsidiaries with more than a 50 percent stockholding relationship were increasing, and those with less than a 50 percent stockholding relationship were decreasing.

Probably this meant that Japanese big firms were disposing of their operating divisions more and more as separate companies or establishing new companies in order to enter into new business fields (so-called restructuring).

Table 24-15. Number of Related Companies of Top 100 Non-Financial Companies

Year (FY)	More Than 50%	50% or Less & 25% or More	Less Than 25% & 10% or More	Total
1970[1]	2,808 (36.8%)	3,063 (40.2%)	1,731 (22.7%)	7,602 (100.0%)
1976[2]	3,212 (34.7%)	2,925 (31.6%)	3,119 (33.7%)	9,256 (100.0%)
1981[3]	3,154 (35.5%)	3,053 (34.3%)	2,684 (30.1%)	8,891 (100.0%)
1986[3]	3,899 (40.1%)	2,928 (30.8%)	2,692 (28.3%)	9,519 (100.0%)

NOTES:

[1] As for FY 1970, the figures do not include related companies of 10% exact stockholding ratios.

[2] As for FY 1976, less than 30% & more than 10% figures are used instead of 25% or less & 10% or more figures. 50% or less & more than 30% figures are used instead of 50% or less & 25% or more figures.

[3] As for FY 1981 and 1986, those companies with total assets of less than 100 million yen are excluded. Therefore, only figures for FY 1981 and 1986 are comparable.

SOURCE: Compiled from the 1989 FTC Report on Stockholdings by Major Big Companies.

(C) *KEIRETSU* AND THE STRUCTURAL IMPEDIMENTS INITIATIVE

Keiretsu relationships became one of the targeted areas in SII. The main concerns of the United States are twofold. The first concern is the impact of *keiretsu* relationships on intragroup transactions, and the second concern is *keiretsu* firms' negative impact on mergers and acquisitions, which would effectively prevent the new entry of foreign firms into the Japanese market by eliminating the chance to take over established Japanese firms.

The final report of SII says that

> there is a view that certain aspects of Keiretsu relationships also promote preferential group trade, negatively affect foreign direct investment in Japan, and may give rise to anti-competitive business practices. In order to address this concern, the Government of Japan intends to make Keiretsu more open and transparent and to take necessary steps toward that end. The Government of Japan will take measures in its competition policy and enforce the Antimonopoly Act

strictly, so that business transactions among companies with the background of Keiretsu relationship would not hinder fair competition and thereby have an exclusionary effect on foreign firms attempting to export, market or invest in Japan. (See appendix I.)

More concretely, the FTC will take the following measures. First, the FTC will strengthen its monitoring of transactions among *keiretsu* firms to determine whether these transactions are being conducted in a way that impedes fair competition.

Second, the FTC will set up and publish guidelines that will clarify the criteria regarding the continuity and the exclusiveness of business practices among companies in the same *keiretsu* group. This is spelled out as the part I of the DSBP Guidelines.

Third, the FTC will conduct, regularly, roughly every 2 years, a close analysis of various aspects of *keiretsu* groups, including supplier-customer transactions; financing arrangements among group firms; personal ties, with special emphasis on the role of general trading companies in *keiretsu* groups. Further, the FTC will survey the transactions among companies in specific industries regarding such issues as the effect of cross-shareholding among companies that have transaction relationships (see appendix I).

On *keiretsu* issues, it is to be expected that the FTC's fact-finding role will be great.

(D) *KEIRETSU* AND INTRAGROUP TRANSACTIONS

(1) PROBLEMS OF INTRAGROUP TRANSACTIONS

One of the criticisms against the Japanese *keiretsu* system is its exclusionary effects on outsiders, foreign or domestic.

There are two separate questions to examine from the antimonopoly point of view. One is whether *keiretsu* relationships have any exclusionary effects, and if any, whether they are caused by the existence of *keiretsu* or by some conduct by or with the background of *keiretsu* relationships. Second is whether *keiretsu* relationships have offered unfair advantage to Japanese firms, or more specifically whether Japanese firms have gained any advantage in achieving their international competitiveness due to *keiretsu* relationships.

The first question shall be evaluated from the viewpoint of how corporate structure is organized. It is up to management to organize its corporate structure. Some prefer to have many internal divisions and/or subsidiary companies so that most transactions are done by single and unified corporate decision making. Some prefer to have most transactions with other companies that do not necessarily come within their control, that is, using market mechanisms to set transaction terms.

In Japan, vertical *keiretsu* relationships did develop through various efforts to pursue stable and reliable relationships by the initiative of manufacturers. Stockholding relationships may be a result not a cause of close customer-supplier relationships, or more generally of continuous transactions. It is very common in Japan to ask reliable partners to become stable shareholders.

In particular, stockholding relationships make it easier to have closer technological cooperation, or to share some crucial business information so that joint R & D can be engaged in without much fear of unauthorized disclosure, or a sudden break in ties between partners.

This is an important factor in Japan because, it is said, the court system does not offer an effective and quick remedy to these business disputes, and as a result, Japanese firms tended to become selective in their trading partners in order to avoid future business disputes. Avoidance of business disputes surely reduces business cost, more than the cost needed to select reliable business partners.[10]

The meaning of preferential treatment also needs to be clarified. If trade terms are equal, it is natural to assume that intragroup transactions would be preferred. This is why keiretsu relationships are established. The question is how to define whether trade terms are equal.

The DSBP Guidelines explain that

> there may be a case where a firm, in selecting its trading partners, takes account of such overall business capability of suppliers as steady supply, technical resources, and flexibility in response to the firm's requests, in addition to price, quality, service, and other transaction terms in individual transactions. If total evaluation by the firm from the viewpoint mentioned above, of transaction terms of goods or services to be purchased from the suppliers, results in continuous trans-

action relationships, there would be no problem under the Anti-monopoly Act. (DSBP Guidelines part I-1.)

The other aspect is the fact that maintenance of *keiretsu* relationships requires certain cost sacrificing as well as cost saving aspects. The cost saving aspect is commonly referred to as an insurance effect because member firms can expect financial and other kind of assistance, for example, hiring excess personnel temporarily from other member firms that have undergone serious business difficulty. Of course, member firms will assume implicit responsibility to assist when other member firms are in economic trouble. Sometimes this is very costly.

One such example is a case where five Mitsui Group companies incurred an estimated 166.2 billion yen loss due to the failure of Iran-Japan Petrochemical projects.[11] Or sometimes a main bank will assume a bigger share of the burdens of the economic troubles of its financial *keiretsu* firms. For example, rescheduling of loans, accepting bigger shares for capital increase of the troubled company is expected for member firms. Main banks would normally function to coordinate relief programs for the company.

Frequently indicated merits or demerits, depending upon the viewer's standpoint of this insurance effect, is its tendency toward aggressive investment. In other words, with this insurance effect as well as with the help of the protective stance of the industrial policy authority, it is possible for Japanese big firms to make overly aggressive investment decisions at the time of economic expansion. By their aggressive investment in equipment many Japanese firms could build plants of first-class efficiency, which surely helped them to achieve international competitiveness. Therefore, it is not clear at all whether *keiretsu* relationships did offer significant advantages to Japanese firms. It simply means that its advantages did outweigh its disadvantages due to Japan's state of rapid economic expansion. There is no guarantee that its advantages always outweigh its disadvantages, in particular when the economy is not expanding as rapidly as it used to be.

If *keiretsu* relationships are neutral in their cost saving aspect, the remaining question is whether *keiretsu* would have exclusionary effects on outsiders, in particular foreign firms. As stated above, the FTC takes the view that taking account of overall business capability other than price, quality and services does not pose any problem to the Antimonopoly Act. It means that the exclusionary effects of *keiretsu*, if any, would arise from the conduct of member firms of *keiretsu*, not from the existence of *keiretsu* relationships themselves in Japan.

It was from this point of view that the FTC promulgated the Guidelines Concerning the Continuity and Exclusiveness of Business Transactions Among Firms as part I of the DSBP Guidelines.

(2) FTC STUDIES OF INTRAGROUP TRANSACTIONS

The FTC did a survey on the intragroup transaction ratio in FY 1981 and 1989. Summary figures are shown in tables 24-16 to 24-20. On average, the intragroup sales ratio as well as the intragroup purchase ratio are shown to be declining. There are also big differences among the six major business groups. The Mitsubishi and the Sumitomo Groups showed high percentages on both figures, and the Sanwa and the Daiichi Kangyo Groups showed lower percentages.

Table 24-16. Ratio of Intragroup Transactions[1]

	Intragroup Sales Ratio		Intragroup Purchase Ratio	
	1981	*1989*	*1981*	*1989*
Mitsui	10.4	6.54	11.5	7.65
Mitsubishi	16.6	14.34	18.3	16.07
Sumitomo	12.1	12.23	13.2	12.84
Average[2] for the Three	13.4	11.11	14.8	12.23
Fuyo	9.8	6.37	11.2	7.07
Sanwa	5.5	3.62	5.6	4.15
Daiichi Kangyo	6.7	4.84	6.8	5.29
Average[2] for the Three	8.6	4.86	9.8	5.43
Average[2] for the Six	10.8	7.28	11.7	8.10

NOTES:

[1] *Intragroup sales ratio = K/n*

K = Member firm's sales amount to other member firms of the same Group.

n = Total sales amount of member firms of the same Group.

Intragroup purchase ratio = K/n

K = Member firm's purchase amount from other member firms of the same Group.

n = Total purchase amount from member firms of the same Group.

[2] The figures are based on those excluding financial companies. Averages are simple averages of applicable ratios of each Group.

SOURCE: Compiled from the 1992 FTC Research Paper on Business Groups.

Table 24-17. *Ratio of Intragroup Transactions[1]*
(Manufacturing Companies)

	Intragroup Sales Ratio		Intragroup Purchase Ratio	
	1981	*1989*	*1981*	*1989*
Mitsui	25.4	18.84	16.2	11.95
Mitsubishi	29.6	25.56	21.9	14.97
Sumitomo	31.0	38.11	14.0	16.44
Average[2] for the Three	29.0	27.36	18.6	14.78
Fuyo	16.5	12.65	5.1	3.96
Sanwa	7.3	6.29	6.2	5.24
Daiichi Kangyo	13.3	11.86	9.5	8.17
Average[2] for the Three	14.9	10.38	8.2	5.84
Average[2] for the Six	20.4	16.37	12.4	9.01

NOTES:

[1] *Intragroup sales ratio = K/n*

K = A member manufacturing firm's sales amount to other member firms of the same Group.

n = Total sales amount of member manufacturing firms of the same Group.

Intragroup purchase ratio = K/n

K = A member manufacturing firm's purchase amount from other member firms of the same Group.

n = Total purchase amount from member firms of the same Group.

[2] The figures are based on those excluding financial companies. Averages are simple averages of applicable ratios of each Group.

The above-mentioned is macroeconomic analysis, and cannot claim to be the most authoritative analysis. Because this is a unique aspect of industrial organization, a reliable analytic method is not yet developed. However, by examining the FTC survey on intragroup transactions, one could look at the trend of such transactions in Japan.

Table 24-18 examines the top 30 trading partners of member firms, and shows that unaffiliated domestic companies occupy, on average, 31 percent, in contrast with 20 percent for domestic affiliated companies, and 20 percent for foreign affiliated companies in terms of amount of sales.

Unaffiliated foreign firms are fairly big buying partners, as shown by the figure of 8 percent, on average. In the case of the Fuyo Group, unaffiliated foreign firms seem very important buying partners, as shown by the 20 percent figure.

Table 24-18. Top 30 Trading Partners
(In Terms of Sales Amount)

	Member Firms of the Same Group	Affiliated Companies[1] (Domestic)	(Foreign)	Member Firms of Other Groups	Other Firms (Domestic)	(Foreign)	Others
Mitsui	8.03	19.01	27.00	5.28	36.47	2.67	1.54
Mitsubishi	19.37	13.64	18.06	6.94	28.57	7.85	5.56
Sumitomo	14.89	13.09	24.29	4.55	35.95	4.99	2.25
Average[2] for the Three	13.64	15.48	23.45	5.54	33.94	4.98	2.97
Fuyo	5.37	21.12	16.72	6.85	28.27	19.92	1.74
Sanwa	6.73	27.38	16.61	10.43	27.72	7.62	3.51
Daiichi Kangyo	10.49	23.38	18.82	8.34	27.46	7.67	3.51
Average[2] for the Three	7.95	24.11	17.58	8.56	27.76	11.00	3.03
Average[2] for the Six	10.50	20.26	20.20	7.21	30.52	8.31	3.00

NOTES:
[1] Affiliated companies include every such company of which a member firm has not less than 10% of the stocks.
[2] Averages are weighted averages of applicable ratios of each Group.
SOURCE: Compiled from the 1992 FTC Research Paper on Business Groups.

In terms of purchase, domestic affiliated firms occupy 25 percent, and foreign affiliated firms occupy 28 percent (see table 24-19). On the other hand, unaffiliated domestic firms occupy 21 percent. These figures show that affiliated firms are important sources of purchase. Therefore, it can be said that in terms of purchase, higher intragroup transactions can be seen. This figure seems to show the existence of some difficulty for foreign firms to become among the top 30 trading partners of big corporations in Japan. An increase in this percentage is expected as the fair chance of competition to foreign firms increases.

Besides such macroeconomic analysis on intragroup transactions, the FTC surveyed intragroup transactions with respect to individual items such as mainframe computers. Table 24-20 shows an interesting trend of intragroup transactions on mainframe computers. These numbers seem to show the simple fact that influential manufacturers

Table 24-19. Top 30 Trading Partners
(In Terms of Purchase Amount)

	Member Firms of the Same Group	Affiliated Companies[1] (Domestic)	(Foreign)	Member Firms of Other Groups	Other Firms (Domestic)	(Foreign)	Others
Mitsui	9.31	34.25	27.69	4.75	21.45	0.25	2.30
Mitsubishi	34.95	12.96	18.64	9.50	18.38	5.53	0.05
Sumitomo	22.78	18.02	25.23	3.67	24.83	5.43	0.04
Average[2] for the Three	20.23	23.57	24.58	5.63	21.74	3.27	0.99
Fuyo	13.57	35.53	24.61	3.39	13.46	8.60	0.85
Sanwa	6.88	19.31	33.78	7.65	21.95	9.96	0.37
Daiichi Kangyo	11.59	22.61	33.90	6.23	23.01	2.54	0.12
Average[2] for the Three	10.84	25.46	31.15	5.80	19.93	6.41	0.40
Average[2] for the Six	15.22	24.58	28.08	5.72	20.77	4.94	0.68

NOTES:

[1] Averages are weighted averages of applicable ratios of each Group.

[2] Affiliated companies include every such company of which a member firm has not less than 10% of the stocks.

SOURCE: Compiled from the 1992 FTC Research Paper on Business Groups.

such as NEC, Fujitsu and Hitachi are used widely among big business in Japan. An FTC survey on some more product items was promised at SII.[12]

(E) *KEIRETSU* AND THE DISTRIBUTION SYSTEM AND BUSINESS PRACTICES GUIDELINES

The DSBP Guidelines had clarified illegal practices that are undertaken to establish or maintain continuous transaction relationships, or undertaken to strengthen such relationships, which may result in hinderance of new entries into a market or exclusion of existing ones from the market (see DSBP Guidelines part I).

*Table 24-20. Mainframe Computers Used by Member Firms of the Groups**

| | Member Manufacturers | | Domestic Manufacturers | |
FY	1981	1989	1981	1989
Mitsui	5.30	0.00	43.05	41.34
Mitsubishi	17.73	7.45	44.64	38.51
Sumitomo	67.07	45.57	67.07	46.84
Average^2 for the Three	27.60	16.86	50.08	42.17
Fuyo	30.83	37.71	51.50	53.81
Sanwa	28.15	31.21	57.56	62.08
Daiichi Kangyo	59.59	57.48	70.89	67.74
Average^2 for the Three	42.39	43.20	60.37	62.06
Average^2 for the Six	35.61	33.64	55.65	54.84

NOTES:

* Member computer manufacturers are as follows:
Mitsui—Toshiba
Mitsubishi—Mitsubishi Electric
Sumitomo—NEC
Fuyo—Hitachi
Sanwa—Hitachi
Daiichi Kangyo—Hitachi, Fujitsu
Mainframe computers owned or leased as of December 1990 are analysed. The number of computers amounted to 1,373 as a whole. The data for FY 1981 are as of September 1982. Those computers used by the computer manufacturers themselves are excluded in this analysis.

The Guidelines list the following categories of conducts or practices:

(A) Customer allocation,
(B) Boycotts,
(C) Primary refusals to deal by a single firm,
(D) Restrictions on trading partners of dealing with competitors,
(E) Unjust reciprocal dealings,
(F) Other anticompetitive practices to strengthen continuous transaction relationships,
(G) Acquisition or possession of stocks of trading partners.

Customer allocation, boycotts, primary refusals to deal by a single firm, and restrictions on trading partners of dealing with competitors are nothing new from the *keiretsu* point of view, although it is evident that these conducts could be done with the background of *keiretsu*.

Unjust reciprocal dealings would be regulated as a conduct making use of buying power, and if a firm compels suppliers to deal with it reciprocally, it may create the effect of reducing business opportunities of the firm's competitors or of firms that are unable to accept reciprocal dealings.

In particular, when foreign firms have a code of conduct that prohibits reciprocal dealings to employees, they might have greater difficulty in establishing business relationships with Japanese firms who expect reciprocal dealings.

If directed only at foreign firms, selective price cutting might cause difficulty in getting new customers in Japan. The DSBP Guidelines said that in cases where a firm does business with its customers on condition that the firm reduces its price in response to lower prices offered by its competitors, such selective price cutting arrangements may be illegal if such conduct may reduce the business opportunities of its competitors (see DSBP Guidelines chapter 6, part I)

As to the acquisition of stock, there could be two problems. One concerns the acquisition of stock of its trading partners by way of unfair trade practices. The other concerns exclusionary conduct by means of or by reason of holding stock of trading partners (see DSBP Guidelines chapter 7, part I). The latter is not in itself a type of unfair trade practice, but could function as a means to effect unfair trade practices, as a rebate system can function as a means to secure the effectiveness of unfair trade practices.

In essence, this guideline made clear that the FTC would take into account the continuous relationships among firms when it evaluates the effects on competition of certain conduct with the background of *keiretsu* relationships.[13]

NOTES

[1] These are the products of postwar economic reform programs and the high growth of the Japanese economy. Under prewar *zaibatsu* structure, various *keiretsu* relationships were unnecessary because zaibatsu structure contained everything within its structure and placed them under the control of top holding companies. However, *zaibatsu* dissolution eliminated these unified structures and produced many independent firms, as examined in chapter 1 (B)(2) *Zaibatsu* Dissolution.

When they faced rapidly expanding markets, they did not have the internal structure to cope with such rapidly expanding demand. Therefore, it was inevitable to coordinate transactions among independent firms, thus a network of subcontractors around major industrial firms was rapidly developed. Business groups were revived along the lines of former *zaibatsu* members. Consumer product manufacturers had invested aggressively to enhance access to consumers in domestic markets, thus distribution channelling had resulted.

[2] High growth and changing market conditions necessitated long-term and continuous transaction relationships among these firms. K. Imai, *Japanese Business Groups and the Structural Impediments Initiative,* in K. Yamamura ed., JAPAN'S ECONOMIC STRUCTURE: SHOULD IT CHANGE? (1990), where he argues, "The essence of Japanese industrial evolution has been a sequential learning process associated with sequential, continuous innovation, and Japanese networks of institutions have continuously adapted to promote such learning processes. . . .This pattern of continuous innovation required and created a variety of continuous contracts between users and suppliers. at 177-178.

[3] The Subcontract Act (Act No. 120 of 1956) was one of the political reactions of this phenomenon.

[4] For example, Toyo Keizai (Oriental Economist) has been producing research papers titled *Kigyo Keiretsu Soran* (Complete Data on Business Keiretsu) annually, and documents vast information on major business group firms.

[5] FTC, KIGYO SYUDAN NO JITTAI NI TSUITE (On current situation of Business Groups) (1992), at 9.

[6] For example, Mitsui Toatsu Chemicals and Mitsui Petrochemical Industries are competitors in many fields. The Daiichi Kangin Group, the Fuyo Group and the Sanwa Group contain many competing firms as their members, which suggests a relatively loose interconnection of member firms within these groups.

[7] BUSINESS WEEK, Sept. 24, 1990, at 42, 43, 45. The following comments give insights on *keiretsu* issues, namely, "It did not have to disclose its relations with huge chemical-related companies in the group because they did not financially control each other as defined by U.S. law." at 44. Voluntary disclosure of intragroup transactions is one of the urgently needed tasks for them.

[8] See note 6 of the Distribution System and Business Practices Guidelines, in appendix H.

[9] Secs. 9-2 and 11(1) seem to have very important functions from this aspect.

[10] In the short run, an open procurement policy for parts and raw materials by manufacturers would reduce short-term business costs. On the other hand, selecting stable partners requires additional short-term costs. However, as long as the firm continues a selective procurement policy, switching stable partners from one to the other requires additional cost for the purchaser, and thus discourages them from switching partners frequently.

In addition, speedy coordination among firms in order to cope with changing market conditions and customer needs requires them to be selective about their business partners. For further arguments, see K. Imai, *supra* note 2, at 177-179, 181-183.

[11] After spending billions of dollars for the completion of the project, this huge project was interrupted first by the overthrow of the King of Iran and then by the outbreak of the Iran-Iraq War.

[12] See appendix I. These studies on four items (household electric appliances, shipbuilding, synthetic fibers, city gas) were promised in the FIRST ANNUAL REPORT ON FOLLOW-UP ON SII TALKS (May 22, 1991). In addition, a survey of four other items was promised, namely, paper, sheet glass, automobiles, and automobile parts by the SECOND ANNUAL REPORT (June 30, 1992).

[13] As argued elsewhere, we believe this is the most feasible approach to the *keiretsu* issue.

25

DEREGULATION AND ANTIMONOPOLY EXEMPTION LAWS

(A) IN GENERAL

As is analyzed in part I, one of characteristics of Japanese antimonopoly legislation is the abundance of laws exempting acts from the application of the Antimonopoly Act. In particular, the idea of using cartels as a tool of adjustment is by far the most extensive among all the developed countries.

Based on the theory that, from a positive adjustment point of view, cartels are much more problematic than dominant firms and mergers, an OECD report said "indeed, if government tolerates cartels, they are frequently induced to protect these national producers from international competition."[1]

(1) RATIONALIZATION CARTELS

Many laws were enacted with the specific purpose of rationalizing specific industries to enhance their international competitiveness. These laws authorized MITI to establish a basic promotion plan with yearly enforcement details to achieve the targeted level of efficiency. Compliance with this plan was voluntary; however, if considered necessary, the formation of rationalization cartels could be advised by MITI.

These cartels were meant to promote standardization of products, to specialize in the production of certain kinds of products to achieve scale economies of production, or to conclude sharing agreements of production or processing facilities to reduce production costs, among others.

These special rationalization cartel laws covered the machinery industry, the electronics industry, and the software industry. These laws were enforced from 1956 to 1985. In the early period, there were directed rationalization measures to improve competitiveness, then policy emphasis was gradually shifted to R & D related measures.

The existence of these rationalization laws had great impact because they provided a legal basis for administrative guidance by MITI. Although the actual number of rationalization cartels is not so large, these laws were sufficient to make sure that MITI could get the necessary cooperation from related industries. Formal cartels were used when some kind of compulsion was necessary to effect rationalization measures so that exemption status from the Antimonopoly Act was necessary.

(2) DEPRESSION CARTELS AND EXCESS CAPACITY ELIMINATION CARTELS

In Japan, up to the 1960s, cartels were viewed as a useful tool to eliminate excessive competition (see chapter 3 (B) Change of Industrial Policy). Excessive competition was thought to be the cause of depression, and only by reducing production quantities could depression be reversible. This is why depression cartel provisions were enacted in many exemption laws.

In the late 1970s, reliance on depression cartels declined, and no more strong demand was voiced to relax requirements for depression cartels. However, even in the 1980s it was still the dominant view in Japan that excess capacity was the source of excessive competition and should be eliminated by way of cartels. Proponents argued, that because of excessive competition, entrepreneurs could not eliminate unnecessary capacity on their own initiative.

This view gained momentum because the series of oil shocks had created a so-called structurally depressed industry. It was argued that the need for adjustment was so great and fundamental that private incentive to eliminate excess capacity was insufficient, therefore, cartels to eliminate excessive capacity should be permitted in certain structurally depressed industries. Cartels were viewed as a fair method of sharing the burdens of adjustment equally among troubled companies.[2]

Based on this idea, the Designated Depressed Industries Temporary Measures Act (Act No. 44 of 1978) and its succeeding law, the Designated Industries Structural Improvement Temporary Measures Act (Act No. 53 of 1983) were enacted.

With hindsight, it is dubious whether there existed structurally depressed industries in the true sense. Many of those industrial sectors that were designated under the law had recovered and were successfully operating under the changed circumstances.

As long as the effect of these adjustment mechanisms was limited to within the country, not many problems would be raised. However, when one country takes measures to promote cartels or tolerate cartels to increase the international competitiveness of domestic firms, the negative impact on international trade is unavoidable. Even cartels not officially directed toward increasing international competitiveness might have an indirect negative impact, because it is equal to providing a special subsidy to cartel participants, which could be used as an export subsidy. At least, when export industries are included in such cartelization, the deteriorating effects on international trade might be undeniable.[3]

There were other types of exemption cartel laws directed toward the small business sector to promote rationalization of less competitive industrial sectors or to aid in recovery from a depression. Excessive competition is regarded as a disturbing factor against rationalization of industry or to counter any efforts for recovery from a depression, particularly in the small business sector.

There is still strong policy support for the necessity of small business cartels. However, many small businesses are flourishing as successful exporters, therefore, the fact that only the small business sector is permitted the benefits of the cartel exemption laws cannot provide full justification for such exempted status in the current situation.

(3) CHANGE OF POLICY STANCE

Japan seemed to change its policy stance in the 1980s, and this was evidenced by the repeal of the above-mentioned special laws, such as the Designated Industries Structural Improvement Temporary Measures Act and the Specific Machinery and Information Industry Promotion Temporary Measures Act.

However, these "temporary measures" had lasted nearly 30 years, and the accumulated international trade deteriorating effects caused by such measures are still debated. In the U.S., so-called targeting was specifically questioned in the Trade Act of 1984.[4]

It is difficult to quantify these deterioration effects, but by any means, they could only cause relatively small or almost negligible effects on international trade. However, in view of the unfair nature of the practices, even marginal effects might have a huge negative impact on the international trading system. The international trading system is based on mutual confidence in the fairness of trading partners, and for this reason, cartel policy for the purpose of adjustment would not be tolerated by other trading partners.

(4) REVIEW OF EXEMPTION LAWS

As a matter of domestic policy, toleration of cartels would be inseparable from protection of an industry. When the competent ministry takes a favorable attitude toward cartels, it also takes a favorable attitude toward some kind of protection of the industry. The policy against protectionism goes along with anti- cartel policy as well.

In the early period, the cartel exemption laws did function to limit the territory of the FTC's activities to as narrow a one as possible. Regulated industrial sectors including loosely regulated ones, had been comparatively large in Japan and these cartel exemption laws and other regulatory laws had effectively confined the FTC enforcement activities to non-regulated industries.

In order to overcome this situation and broaden the area where the Antimonopoly Act would be applicable, the FTC had to overcome three kinds of problems.

(1) The first and the most important exception was to abolish the so-called administrative guidance cartels that were used to bypass the Antimonopoly Act without enacting any specific exemption laws. During the mid-1960s, this objective was achieved and, thereafter, no such outright attempt was observed. However, so long as the industrial policy authority took a favorable attitude toward car-

tels, exemption laws were liberally used. Besides, heavy government intervention into business affairs by the industrial policy authority added much difficulty to the FTC's enforcing the Antimonopoly Act as it should be.

(2) The FTC had tried to influence competent ministries in case it had the chance to eliminate unnecessary exempted cartels using its consultation power. (Many exemption laws had a provision to obligate competent ministries to consult with the FTC before approving cartels.)

The FTC also could take a tougher stance toward approving new exempted cartels, and tried to examine various legal requirements more rigidly so that no additional exempted cartels could be formed without convincing specific and urgent necessity. When exempted cartels were going to be extended by competent ministries, the same policy stance was applied by the FTC.

(3) The last problem concerns reexamination of the cartel exemption laws. Even if these laws cannot be utilized easily at present, due to objections from the FTC, the existence of such exemption laws still could have a negative impact on business behavior.

A business might expect that once it fell into serious economic trouble, the law would be employed to offer assistance by way of approving depression cartels. Such attitudes would lessen private incentives to engage in serious business efforts to recover from a depression or economic troubles. This is a fundamental element of a free economy system.

(B) CARTEL EXEMPTION LAWS

(1) CARTEL EXEMPTION LAWS

As of June 1991, there were 56 cartel exemption systems based on 37 laws. The Antimonopoly Act itself provided for two cartel exemptions (depression cartels and rationalization cartels). Exemption systems under the Act Concerning Exemption, etc. from the Antimonopoly Act (Act No. 138 of 1947), which covers various regulated areas, does not provide for major exceptions to antimonopoly policy.

Forty-three cartel exemption systems provided by 26 individual laws more or less constitute true exceptions to the cartel prohibition principles.[5]

The objectives of these cartel exemption systems can be classified as follows:

(A) Recovery from depression,
(B) Facilitating rationalization measures,
(C) Prevention of excessive competition,
(D) Acts of cooperatives,
(E) Export and import cartels,
(F) Government regulated industry cartels,
(G) Others.

Two cartel exemption systems are to be administered by the FTC itself (an FTC authorization case), and 28 cartel exemption systems are administered by the competent minister under 14 laws after having obtained the consent of (an FTC consent case) or having consulted (an FTC consultation case) with or notified to the FTC (an FTC notification case). Concerning these cartels, the FTC can keep records of their current status, and could exercise some influence over permitting or not permitting such cartels.

Most exemption laws were enacted during the 1951-1960 period, and many of them were modeled after the prewar regulatory laws or compulsory cartel laws. In the 1950s, there was no difficulty in including exemption provisions from the application of the Antimonopoly Act when regulatory laws were enacted in spite of the FTC's opposition. What is worse, most of these laws did not contain any provisions with respect to consultation with or notification to the FTC about the formation of cartels. No particular requirements for obtaining approval of cartels were specified in the law.

After 1965, enactment of new exemption laws became few, but by this time the exemption laws had covered so many regulated industrial sectors that no additional need for regulatory laws seemed to exist.

Another serious aspect of cartel exemption laws is the so- called outsider regulation order contained in some of them. When the competent minister thinks it appropriate, he can issue an order to restrict the business activities of non-members of the cartel, thus, in effect, could compel non-members to observe the cartel agreements. This system was modeled after the compulsory cartel laws of prewar days, and based on the spirit of harmony among businessmen that was a matter of business ethics (see chapter 1 (A)(2) After World War I).

As of March 1992, the total number of exempted cartels was 219. At its peak, at the end of FY 1965, this number was 1,079 (see table 25-1). The most drastic decrease occurred in the foreign trade (222 to 29) and small and medium enterprise association cartels (781 to 147). Cartels under the Act Concerning Improvements of Business Connected with Environmental Sanitation dropped from 123 to 37. Table 25-2 shows the breakdown of these cartels.

The number of exempted cartels should be evaluated by the number of product items covered by cartels so that prefecture level cartels can be counted as a single cartel. In this sense, the number of exempted cartels in Japan shall be said to number 45 instead of 219. Table 25-2 shows how these cartels are counted.

Table 25-1. Number of Exempted Cartels*

FY	Number of Cartels	Number of Items	FY	Number of Cartels	Number of Items
1952	53	10	1973	908	233
1953	79	23	1974	788	190
1954	162	31	1975	654	167
1955	248	75	1976	528	150
1956	312	124	1977	535	150
1957	401	170	1978	506	130
1958	509	249	1979	491	121
1959	595	306	1980	489	120
1960	714	349	1981	503	114
1961	868	365	1982	471	105
1962	951	384	1983	436	102
1963	970	397	1984	440	103
1964	999	399	1985	426	102
1965	1079	415	1986	382	99
1966	1040	381	1987	310	87
1967	1003	380	1988	276	73
1968	954	378	1989	261	61
1969	886	347	1990	248	51
1970	845	318	1991	219	45
1971	976	281	1992	161	41
1972	979	285			

NOTE:
*Number of exempted cartels outstanding at the end of each fiscal year (March).

Table 25-2. Objectives of Existing Cartels Exempted from the Antimonopoly Act as of March 1992

Objectives	No. of Items	No. of Cartels	Relevant Acts	Items	Note
1. Protection of small and medium-sized firms	10	147	– Small and Medium-sized Enterprises Organization Act	Mainly fabrics	Cartels mainly formed regionally, prefecture by prefecture. (There are 47 prefectures in Japan.)
	1	37	– Act Concerning Improvements of Business Connected with Sanitation	Barber shops	
	1	2	– Domestic Shipping Association Act		
	3	3	– Acts concerning Fisheries Production Adjustment Association		
2. Export restriction to avert trade frictions	28	28	– Export and Import Trading Act		
	1	1	– Promotion of Marine Products Export Industry Act	Canned mackerel & sardines	
3. To counteract depression	0	0	– Antimonopoly Act	(Shipbuilding, turbine engines for ships)*	
4. Rationalization	0	0	– Antimonopoly Act		
5. To counterbalance monopoly in exporting country	1	1	– Export and Import Trading Act	Silk fabrics from China; (onions from Taiwan)*	
6. Others	0	0	– Fisheries Industry Restructuring Special Measures Act		
Total	45	219			

NOTE:
* ( ) Shows items where exemption cartels were formed within the past 5 years

Currently, no depression cartel is formed under the Antimonopoly Act.

(2) *TRADE IMPLICATIONS OF THE CARTEL EXEMPTION SYSTEM*

It is now widely accepted that the adoption of an adjustment policy in one country may result in the export of the burdens of adjustment to other trading partners. National policy should be clearly prescribed so that other nations can evaluate its impact on international trade. From this perspective, the Japanese cartel exemption system needs a wide range of reevaluation. For most of the current cartel exemption system, use of cartels as a policy tool is not well balanced with their policy objectives. Measures other than cartels could serve for these policy objectives, and some exemption laws could not have any justification under current economic conditions.

In the final report of the Structural Impediments Initiatives the government of Japan had promised that

> the exemptions from the application of the Antimonopoly Act should be at a minimum, and the necessity of existing exemptions will be reconsidered with a view to promoting competition policy. The scope of exemptions will also be reviewed, even in cases where they will be maintained, beginning with the exemptions, if any, which impede import trade or investment. (See appendix I.)

(3) *REVIEW OF THE CARTEL EXEMPTION SYSTEM*

On July 29, 1991, a Study Group on Government Regulations and Competition Policy submitted a report to the FTC on exemption systems of the Antimonopoly Act. This is one of the various study groups organized by the FTC for the purpose of examining issues presented at the SII talks.

The major proposals of this Study Group were as follows. (It should be noted that because drafting works of law is exclusively in the hands of the competent minister, the FTC cannot take any direct action on these laws.[6])

(i) The laws proposed to be abolished

Because the cartel exemption system was never utilized or not utilized in the past 15 years, or the exempted conducts are not considered anticompetitive anymore, the relevant provisions in the laws proposed to be abolished, in principle, are as follows:

(A) The Harbor Transportation Business Act (Act No. 161 of 1951)
(B) The Wholesale Market Act (Act No. 35 of 1971)
(C) The Temporary Measures Act for the Rationalization of the Coal Mining Industry (Act No. 156 of 1955)
(D) The Temporary Measures Act for Adjustment of Pearl Culture, etc.
(E) The Road Transportation Act (Act No. 183 of 1951)
(F) The Car Terminal Act (Act No. 136 of 1959)

(ii) The laws with exemption provisions in government regulated industries

These cartels are used as supplementary means to achieve the regulatory purpose. However, the necessity of regulation itself should be reviewed along with the cartel exemption system in such areas as the insurance industry and the aviation industry.

(iii) Improvement of enforcement

More restrictive administration of the cartel exemption system is proposed in the following areas:
(A) The cartels concerning the restriction of equipment utilization in textile industries (Textile Industry Facilities Temporary Measures Act, Act No. 103 of 1964).
(B) The cartels concerning the restriction of tonnage engaged in coastwise shipping (Coastal Shipping Association Act, Act No. 16 of 1957).
(C) The cartels concerning the restriction of barber shops' fees and methods of business activities (Act Concerning Improvements of Business Connected with Environmental Sanitation, Act No. 164 of 1957).

(D) The cartels concerning the restriction of sales volume and prices of processed fishery products for export (Export Marine Products Industry Promotion Act, Act No. 154 of 1954).
(E) The cartels concerning the restriction of the quality and designs of pearls and smokers' goods (Export and Import Trading Act, Act No. 299 of 1952).

As to these cartels, more limited enforcement or discontinuance of existing cartels is proposed.

(iv) Proposed improvements in administration

The following measures are proposed to improve enforcement procedures of the exemption cartel system:

(A) To prescribe more strict requirements for permitting cartels, such as mandating time limits when cartels are approved, and specifying the kinds of concerted action to be permitted.
(B) Disclosing more detailed data on enforcement on these cartels to insure transparency of enforcement.
(C) Limiting existing outsider control orders, and in the future, considering abolishing such an outsider control order system.

As to proposal (i), the Temporary Measures Act for the Rationalization of the Coal Mining Industry (Act No. 156 of 1955) was abolished.

(C) DEREGULATION AND PRIVATIZATION

(1) PRIVATIZATION

Japanese capitalism's development is owed to some extent to the privatization program effected in the Meiji period. The Meiji government had established many factories such as textile and iron and steel, then sold them to big business concerns (see chapter 1 (A)(1) The Situation Before World War I). Nationalized business was very rare in Japan. The few exceptions were such public entities as the Japan National Railways, the Japan Tobacco and Salt, and the

Nippon Telephone & Telegraphic. The nationwide railway system was established and operated as one branch of the government, then after the war, a public corporation was established by law. The same method was applied to the telephone network and the Nippon Telephone & Telegraphic was established. Besides the above, the government had significant stock in the Japan Airlines Co. as a national flag policy.

In view of the successful program of deregulation in the U.S. and the United Kingdom the Japanese government, in 1981, set up a series of advisory bodies aimed at getting a policy recommendation for reforming government administration systems started.[7] From these studies, a privatization program of publicly held enterprises was begun. Under this program, among others, three giant public corporations, namely the Japan National Railways, the Nippon Telephone & Telegraphic, the Japan Tobacco and Salt were reformed into private companies organized under the Commercial Code (Act No. 48 of 1899).

The Nippon Telephone & Telegraphic became the Nippon Telegraph & Telephone Co. (NTT), and the Japan Tobacco and Salt became the Japan Tobacco Co. (JT). In the case of the Japan National Railways (JR), it was reorganized as five regional operating companies and one freight company. All the stock of these six companies was held by a special public entity called the Japan Railways Liquidation Association.

(2) SALES OF THEIR STOCK

After the privatization program was completed, the stock of NTT, JT or JR related companies was scheduled to be listed at the stock exchange market, so that the government could start to dispose of the stock it held. Because the Japan Railways Liquidation Association must finance the deficits inherited from the Japan National Railways (26.5 trillion yen all told) by selling unnecessary lands and stock of these six companies, there was no legal requirement of government ownership.

In the case of NTT and JT, the government, by law, must hold two-thirds and one-third, respectively, of these companies. As to NTT, no foreign person is allowed to hold NTT stock. The government sold all of the previously held stock of the Japan Air Lines in the early 1980s.

Due to the depressed stock market, sales of these stocks are behind schedule.

(3) DEREGULATION MEASURES

(i) The Privatized area

Monopoly status given by the law as to publicly held enterprises was abolished by the above-mentioned reform, and new entry became possible in such areas as telecommunications and the tobacco sales industry (manufacturing of tobacco has remained a JT monopoly). Salt for household use was under price regulation (the monopoly status of sales of salt is under review at this writing and may be eliminated by 1997).

New entry became possible into telecommunications and tobacco sales. The new common carriers (NCC) entered into the telecommunication field. Long distance telephone service was started by three new comers, the Daini Denden Co., the Nippon Telecom Co. and the Nihon High Speed Telecommunication Co. The Nippon Telecom Co. is a JR-related company and is using a fiber optics network along the Shinkansen railway. The Nihon High Speed Telecommunication Co. is a new entrant using a fiber optics network established along the highway network between Tokyo and other big cities. The Daini Denden is a new entrant using microwave networks established through its own investment.[8]

The international telephone service was also started by two companies, one is owned by the C. Itoh & Co., the Mitsui & Co., and the Hughes Communications Co. The other is owned by the Mitsubishi Corp. and the Mitsubishi Electric Co.

Many car telephone services were started by newcomers. Value Added Network (VAN) service companies had entered into the market since liberalization measures were adopted. Whether market forces are working sufficiently to restore competition in the telecommunications industry is difficult to evaluate as yet. There are arguments in favor of the dissolution of NTT. From the viewpoint of competition, whether NTT's dominant position would not effectively kill new entrants needs close watching.[9]

Some Japanese companies started to sell foreign tobacco in Japan, or joint ventures were formed to sell foreign tobacco.

In the case of JR, each company is in a monopoly position by the nature of its activities, and room for competition was limited. However, rivalries among the five JR companies seem working well in the direction of improving their efficiency.

Privatization and deregulation of these three publicly held enterprises was evaluated in general as a success story. Although they remained as companies whose stock was held directly or indirectly by the government, the impact on their business behavior is obvious. As a company, they started to be profitoriented, and naturally they became cost conscious. Inefficiency cannot be tolerated any more, and cost cutting measures were adopted on their own initiatives.

Best of all, their accounting status was disclosed to the public and they could be evaluated by investors aware of their stock prices once sales of stock schedules were completed. Also, new investment was intensified and diversification into related fields of business was encouraged, thus more efficient use of their resources was made possible. These public entities had huge research capabilities and these capabilities could be utilized for commercial purposes more efficiently than before.

(ii) Financial area

Another area where deregulation had a great impact on the public is the financial sector. Through gradual liberalization measures on interest rates, fixed-term deposits exceeding 500 thousand yen could be set freely by banks as of March 1992. However, the longstanding regulation of interest rates by MOF seems to cause parallel interest rate setting behavior by banks so far. By any means, the public has benefitted by higher interest rates for fixed-term deposits.[10]

The financial market was divided into various markets and submarkets by regulation and intrafinancial sector competition was carefully restricted by licensing requirements. Trust banks and ordinary banks are separated, and within banks, city banks and local banks are distinguished. Before 1989, mutual banks were different from ordinary banks, but as one of the liberalization measures, those mutual banks were transformed into ordinary banks, and the distinction was eliminated.

Like the U.S., banks and security companies are separated by law. After long debates on financial reform and the desirability of a universal banking system, the Financial Reform Act that allowed entry into each financial field through subsidiaries, passed the Diet. Under this Act, banks and security companies are allowed to set up new companies to engage in the securities business or banking business, respectively. The trust bank business would be open for any bank and security company. These reforms will take effect in April 1993.

(iii) Transportation area

In the area of aviation, a so-called double truck or triple truck policy was adopted by the Ministry of Transportation in the 1980s so that two to three airline companies started to compete on the same domestic freight route. Before 1980, the Ministry of Transportation permitted only one airline company to operate on a single domestic route, and only on a heavy traffic route, were two airlines permitted to operate. The Japan Airline Co. (JAL) specialized in international routes, and the All-Nippon Airways Co. (ANA) and the Japan Air System Co. (JAS) specialized in domestic routes, and entry into each other's fields was restricted.

Although price is regulated, increased competition had benefitted the general public in terms of increased service and convenience.

In the area of trucking, the new entry requirement was liberalized and new services such as door-to-door package services by trucking companies were started. Truck fees which must get government authorization to be effective were changed into a notification system, and allowed more flexibility.[11]

(4) ROLE OF COMPETITION POLICY

Privatization and deregulation means more applicability of the Antimonopoly Act. Not only that, deregulation policy can never be complete without enhancement of competition in these industrial sectors. Along with the efforts to eliminate unnecessary exemption cartels, intensified law enforcement activities by the FTC is an important policy mix for deregulation.

Deregulation has important side effects on market access issues. Regulation very particular to Japan would simply mean trade barriers for foreign firms. Such regulation has also problems of nontransparent enforcement by regulatory agencies, and thus would increase the difficulty for foreign firms to engage in business activities in Japan. Therefore, constant evaluation of regulatory laws and policies would be necessary to improve access into the Japanese market.

In this sense, the FTC's contribution is highly anticipated.

NOTES

[1] OECD, POSITIVE ADJUSTMENT POLICIES: SUMMARY AND CONCLUSIONS, CPE/PAP (82) 2 (1st Revision), at para. 24. For further analysis, see A. Uesugi, *Japan's Cartel System and Its Impact on International Trade,* HARVARD INTERNATIONAL LAW JOURNAL (Special Issue), Vol. 27 (1986), at 389-392.

[2] For more detail, see A. Uesugi, *supra* note 1, at 391-392.

[3] *Id.* at 396-397.

[4] Sec. 301(d)(3)(B) of the Trade Act of 1974 as amended by the Trade Act of 1984. This Provision was further tightened by the Omnibus Trade and Competitiveness Act of 1988 (102 Stat. 1107).

As to the criticism on targeting, see FOREIGN INDUSTRIAL TARGETING AND ITS EFFECTS ON U.S. INDUSTRY, PHASE I: JAPAN, U.S. INTERNATIONAL TRADE COMMISSION REPORT TO THE SUBCOMMITTEE ON TRADE OF THE COMMITTEE ON WAYS AND MEANS, U.S. HOUSE OF REPRESENTATIVES (Washington: USITC Oct. 1983).

[5] For more detailed analysis, see A. Uesugi, *supra* note 1, at 401- 408; H. IYORI & A. UESUGI, ANTIMONOPOLY LAWS OF JAPAN (1983), at 137- 160.

[6] See *Report of the Study Group on the Review of the Exemption Systems from the Antimonopoly Act, July 29, 1991,* FTC/JAPAN VIEWS, No. 12 (Sept. 1991), at 40-73.

The FTC does not have law drafting power. Even the Act to amend the Antimonopoly Act needs to be submitted by the Prime Minister's Office to the Cabinet.

[7] M. Uekusa, *Government Regulations in Japan: Toward Their International Harmonization and Integration,* in K. Yamamura ed., JAPAN'S ECONOMIC STRUCTURE: SHOULD IT CHANGE? (1990), at 252-258.

[8] Well before the privatization of NTT was effected, the FTC had been closely examining competitive conditions in the telecommunication services market. See *Study Group Report on Competition Policy in Telecommunication Services,*

FTC/JAPAN VIEWS, No. 2 (April 1988), at 25-32; *Issues Relating to Current Competition Policy in Telecommunication Services, Sept. 14, 1989,* FTC/JAPAN VIEWS, No. 8 (March 1990), at 66-80.

[9] The Study Group was negative on the immediate break-up of NTT, and concerned with abuse of market power by using special status in the industry, such as refusal to connect to its network, predatory pricing by cross subsidization or utilization of intellectual property to eliminate other carriers. See *Issues Relating to Current Competition Policy in Telecommunication Services, supra* note 8, at 69-76.

[10] For a further description of deregulation in the banking sector, see M. Uehusa, *supra* note, 7 at 256-257. He argues, "every bank offers the same rate of interest and shows no apparent inclination to compete. This reflects regulation based on the Temporary Money Rates Adjustment Law, which has in effect blocked any attempt by a bank to assert an independent rate." at 259.

[11] For more information, see *Review of Government Regulations from the Viewpoint of Competition Policy, Oct. 31, 1989,* FTC/JAPAN VIEWS, No. 8 (March 1990), at 5-65.

VOLUNTARY EXPORT RESTRAINTS AND THE ANTIMONOPOLY ACT

(A) VOLUNTARY EXPORT RESTRAINTS

(1) TYPES OF VOLUNTARY EXPORT RESTRAINTS

Voluntary export restraint (VER) is the term used to refer to private or governmental voluntary acts to restrain exports to a particular region or a country in order to avoid trade friction. A mandatory import quota (IQ) is the strictest form of export restraint. In this chapter, we give broad meaning to VER, and examine the legal method used to limit exports on the part of the exporting country. Even under IQs, there could be a voluntary export restraint when there is a need to allocate a fixed export quantity among exporters. In this sense, VERs are not always voluntary acts by exporters, sometimes they are compelled by either the exporting country or the importing country.

VERs are distinguished from international cartels where exporters agree with competitors of the importing country not to export more than the agreed-upon quantity or at no less than the agreed-upon prices. The difference between VERs and international cartels can be seen more or less in the involvement of the government.

There are various terms to describe VERs. One is called a voluntary restraint agreement (VRA) or voluntary restraint undertaking.

This concept normally describes a negotiated agreement between relevant exporters and the government of an importing country whereby the former voluntarily agree to limit their exports to the importing country. The other is called an orderly marketing agreement (OMA). An OMA refers to a bilateral agreement between two related governments to restrain export. OMAs became a formal concept under section 203(a)(4) of the Trade Act of 1974. Under the Act, OMAs can be negotiated as import relief measures in cases where all the requirements under section 201 of the Trade Act of 1974 have been met.[1]

VRAs and OMAs are both government negotiated agreements. However, there are other types of VER in which the exporting country side unilaterally restrains exports in order to avoid trade friction. Sometimes, before VERs were effected only an informal sign of pleasure or displeasure on the current export levels were exchanged at both ends. This is also one type of VER.

Whatever term is used, VERs consist of export restricting cartel activities on the part of the exporting country. On the importing side, there may be a sanction ready to be imposed if the VER has been violated. Or sometimes, disregard of VERs by exporters may trigger protectionist measures and this could be a sufficient sanction to make VERs effective.

Therefore, there is some understanding on the part of the importing country that the restrained level of exports is satisfactory so that no further restrictive action would be taken on the importing country side. It is not important for our analysis whether there are official sanctions ready to be imposed or not in cases of non-observance of VERs, or which of the governments had negotiated the VER.

VERs have several problems. One is the fact that VERs sometimes are indistinguishable from international cartels. When competitors petition the government, and the government negotiates VERs to restrain exports on their behalf, in essence, it is equivalent to an international cartel.

Sometimes VERs were used in response to antidumping charges. For example, VERs were used to set minimum export prices to clear antidumping charges, and thus could go beyond the minimum necessary extent for clearing such charges. In this sense, antidumping duties on individual exporters are preferable and have fewer protectionistic effects than VERs. Sometimes VERs were used to restrain the quantity of exports in order to avoid import relief such as legislated import quotas. These measures taken preventively have more serious restrictive problems than antidumping duties or import relief themselves.[2]

(2) ANTIMONOPOLY PROBLEMS

There are antimonopoly problems on the exporting country side as well as on the importing country side. First, we will examine exporting country side problems. To effect export restraint, there must be exemptions for such concerted action on the exporting side. In Japan this could be done in the following manner.

(A) By using administrative guidance by MITI to restrict export price or quantity.
(B) By forming export cartels under the Export-Import Trading Act.
(C) By using an export licensing system under the Export Control Ordinance, and the Foreign Exchange Trade Control Act (Act No. 228 of 1949).

(B) and (C) give complete exemption status to export cartels. Although (A) is insufficient to provide antimonopoly exemption, when antitrust philosophy was weak it could provide sufficient exemption status, so far as the Japanese side was concerned.

The Export-Import Trading Act (Act No. 229 of 1952) provides for five kinds of export cartels.

(A) Export cartels by exporters (sec. 5),
(B) Cartels on domestic transactions by exporters (sec. 5-2),
(C) Cartels among producers and/or distributors on domestic transactions of commodities for export (sec. 5-3),
(D) Export cartels by exporters' associations (sec 11(2)),
(E) Cartels on export transactions and domestic transactions by exporters' associations (sec. 11(4)).

Export cartels by exporters and export cartels by exporters' associations can be formed by simply notifying to MITI 10 days in advance of their formation (secs. 5(1) and 11(2)). This simplified procedure is based on the idea that when only exporters restrict their export trade, and no domestic transaction is involved, no spill-over effect on domestic markets exists.

The other export cartels involving domestic transactions or producers and distributors of the same products (namely (B), (C), and (E)) require authorization by MITI, although MITI must decide within 20 days after their application (secs. 5-2(3), 5-3(2), 11(5)). Section 33 of the Export-Import Trading Act exempts these export cartels from application of the Antimonopoly Act.

An outsider control order can be issued by MITI under certain circumstances (sec. 28(1)).

(3) NATURE OF EXPORT CARTELS

Export cartels are voluntary in nature. Essentially, it is an act to authorize a private act of cartelization so far as exporting activities are concerned. Besides, free entry and free exist from the cartels are conditional (sec. 5(2)(v), etc.).

However, when outsider control orders are issued by MITI on the products concerned, then MITI is empowered to suspend the exportation of the same products for a period not exceeding 1 year by issuing orders to such violating persons (sec. 28(4)). Under such circumstances, the export cartels may assume a compulsory nature.

(B) POLICY CONFLICTS

As seen above, when VRAs or OMAs are effected, the involvement of either government is clear. There is large concern about the appropriateness of such government involvement in view of free trade or GATT principles. This is why VERs are called a grey area.[3]

On the Japanese side, exporting cartels were used to effect VRAs or OMAs in most cases. This is because when government involvement of the importing country is clear, there is no special and additional need to compel export restraints on the part of the exporting country. This means that when seen from the side of the importing country, they are mere export cartel activities and could be susceptible to attack under the U.S. antitrust laws.

Two related questions are raised. One is whether the negotiating agency, namely the State Department, has such power of negotiation with respect to VRAs, namely, *ultra vires* problems. The other is whether such export cartels are immune from the application of the

U.S. antitrust laws. These questions were raised in the steel case mentioned below.

(1) ADMINISTRATIVE GUIDANCE AND GOVERNMENT COMPULSION

Under the U.S. antitrust laws, when the export restraint was the result of an act of a foreign sovereign, the act of state doctrine precludes inquiry into the legality of such conducts. Besides, a foreign government compulsion defense is available for such exporters when the export restraint is mandatory or compulsory in nature. For example,

> Where collusive private conduct abroad is neither compelled by the foreign government nor capable of being viewed as an act of the sovereign, but merely taken pursuant to a governmental recommendation or request, the risk of antitrust liability is substantial.[4]

As seen above, the nature of export cartels is voluntary in itself, and cannot give rise to a foreign government compulsion defense. In *U.S. v. Watchmakers of Switzerland Information Center, Inc.*, the district court said that

> the defendants' activities were not required by the laws of Switzerland. . . . In the absence of direct foreign governmental action compelling the defendants' activities, a United States court may exercise its jurisdiction as to acts and contracts abroad, if as in the case at bar, such acts and contracts have a substantial and material effect upon our foreign and domestic commerce.[5]

When outsider control orders are issued by MITI, it means all relevant exporters must observe the same restrictions on quantity or price, but still it does not change the nature of the conduct, namely, that those restrictions were agreed to by exporters on their own initiative. Suppose the price or quantity is set by administrative guidance by MITI, are there any differences? The ruling of the U.S. court seems to raise serious doubt as to such a possibility, because administrative guidance, by its nature, does not have direct compelling power.

For this reason, depending on the case, more and more government involvement on the Japanese side could be seen. Let's examine concrete cases.

(C) CASES

VERs have been used continuously as a partial solution to trade friction between Japan and the U.S. The methods used to effect VERs have some connection with the status of the antitrust laws in both countries. In other words, the status of the antitrust policy in both countries was not constant, and VERs affected the way to solve trade frictions on each occasion. This contrasts with how VERs were effected in European countries where export cartels are mostly accepted as sufficient measures from the antitrust viewpoint.[6]

(1) TV CASES

Beginning in June 1968, TV exports to the U.S. have been investigated as to dumping charges, and in December 1970, the Treasury Department had found antidumping law violations as to TV exports from Japan. Japanese exporters had formed export cartels since 1963 under section 5-3 of the Export-Import Trading Act, and under these export cartels, the necessary restriction to avoid dumping charges was effected.

Although this dumping finding became final in March 1971, there remained disputes on the duty amounts, and in April 1980, a settlement agreement on this matter was reached whereby Japanese manufacturers agreed to pay $76 million as antidumping duties and other expenses.

As to color TVs, a section 201 investigation was started in 1976, and after an injury finding was given by the United States International Trade Commission (ITC), the President chose an OMA as an import relief measure, and an OMA was concluded to limit exports from Japan to no more than 1,750 thousand units. The OMA was effective from July 1, 1977 to June 30, 1980.

Export cartels were used to effect the OMA on the Japanese side. These problems were eliminated by Japanese manufacturers' direct investment in color TV factories in the U.S.

(2) STEEL CASES

In response to the rapid increase of steel imports from Japan and EC countries, bills for mandatory import quotas on steel were introduced in the U.S. Congress. The U.S. government favored VRAs and started negotiations with the Japanese and European producers of steel from June to December 1968. As a result, on December 23, 1968, the Japanese and European producers of steel wrote letters to the Secretary of State stating their intentions to limit steel exports to the U.S. to specified maximum tonnages for 1969, 1970 and 1971.

Upon request from domestic producers, extension of the export restraint was negotiated, and in May 1972 a second letter was sent covering the years 1972 to 1974.

In October 1972, the Consumers Union of U.S., Inc. filed an antitrust suit. The district court took the view that "the Executive . . . may enter into agreements or diplomatic arrangements with private foreign steel concerns so long as these undertakings do not violate legislation regulating foreign commerce, such as the Sherman Act" "Executive has no authority under the Constitution or acts of Congress to exempt the Voluntary Restraint Arrangements on Steel from the antitrust laws."[7]

The court of appeals vacated all portions of the district court decision relating to antitrust exemptions, so the issue remained undecided.

Thereafter, the U.S. Congress authorized an OMA as a method of import relief by section 203(a)(4) of the Trade Act of 1974, and *ultra vires* problem was mostly removed. Under this provision of the law, the EC had concluded VRAs starting in November 1982.[8]

As to specialty steel products, upon petition in July 1975, a section 201 investigation was started, and after an ITC finding of injury, an OMA was negotiated by both governments. As a result, exports from Japan were restricted from June 14, 1976 to February 13, 1980 under an OMA.

In January 1984, a section 201 investigation on ordinary steel products was started, and in July 11, 1984, ITC found injury as to five items of steel products. The two governments had negotiated VRAs and in March 14, 1985, a 5-year VRA was concluded whereby a 5.8 percent limit was agreed on for exports from Japan. Carry-over or advance use of these limits was permitted to some extent.

On the Japanese side, export cartels were used to effect these export restraints.

(3) AUTOMOBILE CASE

The automobile case was started in June 1980, when the United Autoworkers of America filed a petition under section 201 of the Trade Act of 1974 for import relief against increased imports of automobiles from Japan. ITC, after investigation, decided that requirements of the Act had not been fulfilled.

Thereafter, many bills in favor of import quotas were submitted in the U.S. Congress, and it looked as if "the only alternative was for the Japanese Government to act on its own accord."[9] However, the steel case has shown that even a VRA in which government involvement was clear was still vulnerable to antitrust suits in the U.S., and the law did not authorize the use of an OMA because of the unfavorable ITC findings.

There was greater antitrust risk for other types of VERs. This is why the method to avoid antitrust risk as much as feasible became the most debated aspect of the automobile case.

> During the month of April 1981, Japanese Government officials consulted regularly with representatives of the Antitrust Division, . . . and the Office of the General Counsel, United States Trade Representatives. These meetings could best be characterized as technical consultations concerning the subtleties of antitrust law, and the vagaries of Japanese commercial statutes.[10]

The method finally adopted was the most complicated one in the history of trade friction between two countries.

MITI issued a directive to each manufacturer of automobiles in Japan indicating the number of passenger cars to be exported to the U.S. during a specified period. The number of passenger cars exported monthly was to be reported to MITI under the Foreign Exchange and Foreign Trade Control Act (Act No. 228 of 1949).

In the directive, MITI makes it clear that the government of Japan will promptly make the export of passenger cars to the U.S. subject to export licensing requirements in accordance with section 48 of the Foreign Exchange and Foreign Trade Control Act, and also

MITI will not issue any licenses for exports in excess of the number of passenger cars specified in the directive.

The directive itself is an administrative guidance, and does not have the force of law. However, once this directive is broken or about to be broken, MITI will utilize its legal power of export control authorized under the Foreign Exchange and Foreign Trade Control Act. It required the government of Japan to amend the current Export Trade Control Order, but it was thought that such action was possible under the law.

The question was whether such a situation was intended to be covered by the export licensing system under section 48 of the Foreign Exchange and Foreign Trade Control Act. Even though there were no precedents in this regard, it was also clear that no one would raise serious objection to such action in Japan.

Therefore, the remaining question was whether this could be evaluated as a foreign government compulsion in the U.S. so that the Japanese automobile manufacturers could use a foreign compulsion defense. It was the government of Japan that decided the number of exportable passenger cars for each manufacturer, and there was no room for automobile manufacturers to discuss or allocate export quantities among themselves.

The Attorney General, by his letter dated May 7, 1981, said that

> in these circumstances, we believe that the Japanese automobile companies' compliance with export limitations directed by MITI would properly be viewed as having been compelled by the Japanese government, acting within its sovereign powers. The Department of Justice is of the view that implementation of such an export restraint by the Government of Japan, including the division among the companies by MITI of the maximum exportable number of units, and compliance with the program by Japanese automobile companies, would not give rise to violations of United States antitrust laws. We believe that American courts interpreting the antitrust laws in such situation would likely so hold.[11]

From 1981 to 1983, the limit was set at 1,680,000 units, and for 1984 it was raised to 1,850,000 units. After 1985, the limit was set at 2,300,000 units. However, because Japanese manufacturers had established factories in the U.S., exports from Japan gradually declined. Since 1987, actual exports have been less than the limit set by the Japanese government.

In March 1992, the government of Japan announced that the limit would be reduced to 1,650,000 units, whereas the actual export level for 1991 was estimated at 1,730,000 units. Therefore, the limit again started to assume a restrictive meaning.

(4) SEMICONDUCTOR CASE

In 1985, the U.S. government started an antidumping investigation on DRAM (dynamic random access memory) and EPROM (erasable programmable read only memory). The U.S. government was also asked to investigate, under section 301 of the Trade Act of 1974. As to the dumping charges, the matter was settled by a "Suspension Agreement" where Japanese manufacturers agreed not to sell those products at less than the fair value in the U.S.

At the same time, both governments had discussed section 301 issues and an international undertaking was agreed to in which DRAM semiconductors of 256 kilobits and above, as well as EPROM dumping charges would be dropped due to the above-mentioned suspension agreement, and the government of Japan promised to monitor the exports of these semiconductors in order to prevent dumping in the U.S. More specifically, MITI will obtain cost and export price data on each item of semiconductors exported to the U.S., and MITI will take measures to stop dumping exports once such facts are revealed by these data.

This agreement also provided that MITI will watch exports to the third market by the same measures. As to market access to Japan, the government of Japan promised to encourage the use of foreign made semiconductors by Japanese users, etc.

The semiconductor case had several characteristics not seen in the previous cases. One is the fact that a bilateral agreement was concluded to make sure no repetition of antidumping would occur in addition to a suspension agreement that should be sufficient to settle antidumping cases. The other is the fact that monitoring of cost and price to the third market were included.

(D) VOLUNTARY EXPORT RESTRAINTS AND INTERNATIONAL TRADE

(1) FREE TRADE PRINCIPLES

Why did VERs take so many forms? The reason may depend on the following two factors at the time they were undertaken.

(A) Whether trade friction had started with the antidumping case or import relief case, or whether there were findings of competent agencies to fulfill legal requirements to take measures under the law.

(B) Whether antitrust law enforcement in the United States and Japan was active enough so that the risk of antitrust suits was high.

Although the authority to negotiate VRAs was supported in court and thereafter authorized by law, it is clear that VRAs or OMAs do not exempt relevant persons from the application of the Sherman Act. There remains serious questions as to the legality of the arrangement under the Sherman Act, and only the theory of implied immunity, the foreign government compulsion defense if accepted by the court, can save them.

First, it is necessary to evaluate VERs in view of the commitment shown or given in the General Agreement on Tariffs and Trade (GATT)

(2) GATT

Article XI of GATT generally prescribes "prohibition or restriction other than duties, taxes or other charges whether made effective through quotas, import or export licenses or other measures . . . on the importation of any product."

Article XIII further says

> No prohibition or restriction shall be applied by the contracting party on the importation of any product. . . or on the exportation of any product. . . . unless the importation of the like product of all third countries or the exportation of the like product of all third countries is similarly prohibited or restricted.[12]

Under GATT, dumping is condemned under article VI, and a countervailing duty to offset any bounty or subsidy bestowed upon the manufacture, production or export of any merchandise is authorized.

Therefore, it seems more justifiable to take measures that are clearly recognized under GATT to counter unfair trading practices by the trading partners. This is because dumping and export subsidies are unfair trading practices and regulation of these unfair trading practices would enhance fairness in the export-import trade, and thus may contribute to maintaining a free trade regime.

However, a so-called escape clause or import relief under section 201 of the Trade Act of 1974 does not have this justification, although such a measure is recognized under GATT. Its motivation is simply to protect domestic industry from a sudden increase in imports.

Among those cases reviewed above, the automobile case had started from import relief, and necessary requirements for section 201 were not satisfied. The rest of the cases started more or less from antidumping charges. Therefore, there existed no compelling reason for the Japanese manufacturers of automobiles to restrict exports to the United States. This could be one of the reasons why a very strong degree of compulsion was used to effect VERs in the case of automobiles.

There is a very clear policy conflict here. Under GATT, no import restrictive measures shall be directed to a particular trading partner, therefore, only unilateral and voluntary conduct on the part of the exporting country can be acceptable from this aspect. However, so long as it is a voluntary and unilateral action, such action has serious risk under the American antitrust laws. It is also dubious because voluntary action tends to exceed the limit provided in the law.

Because an exporting country never contests the validity of such import restrictive measures, when their interest is injured only the third country may contest their validity under GATT. The more markets are internationalized, the more the impact of VERs spreads over the third country. In view of GATT principles, such VERs shall be permissible only when government involvement is very clear.

(3) TREND OF ANTITRUST SENTIMENT

Under the Reagan administration, it seemed that antitrust philosophy was less emphasized compared with the previous administrations, and international considerations were outweighed in these years. This had resulted in the Attorney General's favorable letter in the automobile case. As a whole, the antitrust risk in the 1980s was not high on the U.S. side.[13]

On the Japanese side, in the past there has been no great concern to effect export cartels or export restrictions from the antimonopoly viewpoint. However, the wisdom of the export cartel system and the assumption that pure export cartels may cause no anticompetitive impact on domestic markets is dubious.

Related business attitudes are also relevant to the consideration of what kinds of measures are to be taken. The steel industry has a long tradition of cooperation with the government, and did not have much of a problem to effect the necessary cooperation in enforcing export restraints. In the case of automobiles, related manufacturers tended to be more independent of the government.[14]

(4) POLICY IMPLICATIONS

As seen above, the room for VERs is narrowed by the principles of GATT and the antitrust philosophy of both sides. IQs against a particular trading partner (except as a penalty for unfair trading practices) may raise serious questions under GATT. Therefore, compulsory measures on both ends or on the importing country side, i.e., IQs, government negotiated VRAs, and OMAs have serious problems under the GATT regime.

On the other hand, voluntary measures of export restriction on both ends are indistinguishable from international cartels and may not be acceptable from an antitrust viewpoint. The only remaining choice is a compulsory one on the exporting side (as in the automobile case). A strong antitrust philosophy may also make it difficult to rely on VERs as much as an injured industry may like to.

This difficulty is highly desirable for the maintenance of a free trade regime. In this sense, a strong antitrust philosophy is also desirable as a countermeasure against protectionism. We believe the antimonopoly authority on both sides should have a greater function in finding the way to solve trade frictions.

NOTES

[1] Trade Act of 1974, Pub. L. No. 93-618, 88 Stat. 1978 (1974), 19 U.S.C. §§ 2101-2253 (1976); Sec. 201, 19 U.S.C. § 2251 (1976).

[2] In general, a formal solution has less spill-over effects due to the availability of transparent procedural protection. Informal solutions are preferred to avoid substantive or procedural rigidity to cope with changing circumstances. There are clear trade-offs between lack of procedural protection and flexible adaptation to changing circumstances.

[3] This is called grey because it is not authorized in GATT. Grey areas are one of the multiple subjects of the Uruguay Round.

[4] J. Shenefield, Assistant Attorney General, Antitrust Division, in *Auto Situation, Autumn 1980: Hearing Before the Subcommittee on Trade of the House Committee on Ways and Means, 96th Cong., 2d Sess.* (1980), at 115.

[5] U.S. v. Watchmakers of Switzerland Information Center, Inc., 1963 Trade Cas. 70,600 (S.D.N.Y. 1962), at 77,456-57.

[6] This does not mean that these export cartels are immune from EC competition law. EC competition law could be applied if the EC looks at these export cartels as problematic to their interests.

[7] Consumers Union of U.S., Inc. v. Rogers, 352 F. Supp. 1319 (D.D.C. 1973). The case was appealed by both parties under the name of Consumers Union of U.S., Inc. v. Kissinger, 506 F.2d 136 (D.C.Cir. 1974).

[8] Sec. 805(b)(1) of the Trade and Tariff Act of 1984 (98 Stat. 2948 (1984) was specifically enacted to enforce this agreement. The Agreement on European Communities' Export of Pipes and Tubes to the United States of America, exchange of letters dated Oct. 21, 1982 between representatives of the United States and the Commission of the European Communities.

[9] D. deKieffer, *Antitrust and the Japanese Auto Quotas*, BROOKLYN JOURNAL OF INTERNATIONAL LAW, Vol. 8 (1982), at 62-63. In this article, the author, the General Counsel of USTR, said, "The Reagan Administration did not specify how the Japanese Government would impose these restrictions or what would be an acceptable level of imports." note 20 at 62. However, if this can be characterized as an unilateral action, we could not imagine how any agreement can be found among cartel participants.

[10] *Id.* at 67. In this article, we can find a further interesting characterization, namely, "Ambassador Brock made it clear. . . that this was not a negotiation, and that the Reagan Administration was prepared to accept any decision reached by the Japanese authorities." at 67.

[11] *Id.* at 73.

[12] This universality rule is the key to GATT rules. However, as described in this chapter, it had also prompted nations to move toward informal solutions to trade disputes. Sometimes too rigid a rule would produce undesirable results. The Uruguay Round is expected to formalize the informal aspects in line with the formal mechanism of GATT.

[13] The evaluation of antitrust enforcement during the Reagan administration was mixed. Generally speaking, enforcement shifted toward criminal enforcement of cartel activities and departed greatly from the previous administration in terms of merger regulation, monopoly regulation and regulation of vertical restraints. However, cartel regulation only resulted in many criminal cases against small-scale businessmen, and as a result, big business was relatively relieved from the impact of antitrust regulation. Antitrust laws are evaluated by their impact on the behavior of big business, and if the American antitrust laws had been exerting the same level of impact on big business the negative appearance depicted in the actual enforcement records would not exist. We are doubtful on this aspect, but because our evaluation is based on secondary information, we may be wrong. The point is that the same analysis is necessary as to Japanese antimonopoly policy. Unless the Japanese antimonopoly laws can exert an impact on the business behavior of Japanese big business, it cannot be said that the antimonopoly laws are performing well in Japan.

[14] The difference can be exemplified by the following incidents. As to the automobile industry, C. Johnson wrote that in the late 1960s, following the first round of capital liberalization, "MITI was doing its best to merge the smaller auto firms into keiretsu built around either Nissan or Toyota." See C. JOHNSON, MITI AND THE JAPANESE MIRACLE (1982), at 286. There were 10 automobile manufacturers in Japan (Daihatsu, Fuji, Honda, Hino, Isuzu, Mitsubishi, Nissan, Suzuki, Toyo Kogyo, and Toyota) and MITI succeeded in merging Nissan and the Prince Motor Co., but no other mergers were achieved. MITI could not stop attempts by Honda or Suzuki to move in the auto industry. In addition, contrary to MITI expectations, Mitsubishi had taken steps to form a 65-35 joint venture with the Chrysler Corporation and Isuzu chose to affiliate with General Motors.

In contrast, in keeping with the direction of MITI policy, the top two companies among the six iron and steel companies, Fuji and Yawata, had merged in 1969. The Sumitomo Metal incident in 1965 was the only exception to the generally cooperative relations between the steel industry and MITI. For the Sumitomo Metal incident, see C. JOHNSON, *id.* at 268-271; F. UPHAM, LAW AND SOCIAL CHANGE IN POSTWAR JAPAN (1987), at 176-184.

APPENDICES

Antimonopoly Laws, Regulations and Various FTC Guidelines

ANTIMONOPOLY ACT CONCERNING PROHIBITION OF PRIVATE MONOPOLY AND MAINTENANCE OF FAIR TRADE
(Act No. 54 of April 14, 1947)

CHAPTER 1   GENERAL PROVISIONS

Sec. 1 [Purpose]

This Act, by prohibiting private monopolization, unreasonable restraint of trade and unfair trade practices, by preventing excessive concentration of economic power and by eliminating unreasonable restraint of production, sale, price, technology and the like, and all other unjust restriction of business activities through combinations, agreements and otherwise, aims to promote free and fair competition, to stimulate the creative initiative of entrepreneurs, to encourage business activities of enterprises, to heighten the level of employment and people's real income, and thereby to promote the democratic and wholesome development of the national economy as well as to assure the interests of consumers in general.

Sec. 2 [Definitions]

(1) The term "entrepreneur" as used in this Act shall mean a person, who carries on a commercial, industrial, financial or any other business. Any officer, employee, agent or any other person who acts for the benefit of any entrepreneur shall be deemed to be an entrepreneur in regard to the application of the provisions of the following subsection and of Chapter III [trade associations] of this Act.

(2) The term "trade association" as used in this Act shall mean any combination or federation of combinations of two or more entrepreneurs having

as its principal purpose the furtherance of their common business interest as entrepreneurs and includes one taking either of the following forms: Provided, That a combination or federation of combinations of two or more entrepreneurs, whose stock or other paid-up capital is owned by the constituent entrepreneurs, and whose principal purpose is to operate and which is actually operating a commercial, industrial, financial or any other business for profit shall not be included:

    (i)   Any association incorporated or not incorporated of which two or more entrepreneurs are members (including any position similar thereto);

    (ii)   Any foundation with or without juridical personality of which two or more entrepreneurs control the appointment or dismissal of directors or managers, the execution or continuation of business activities;

    (iii)   Any partnership of which two or more entrepreneurs are members, or any contractual combination of two or more entrepreneurs.

(3) The term "officer" as used in this Act shall mean a director, a partner with unlimited liabilities and executive power, an auditor, or any person with a similar position, a manager, or other employee in charge of business of the main or branch office.

(4) The term "competition" as used in this Act shall mean a situation in which two or more entrepreneurs do or may, within the normal scope of their business activities and without undertaking any significant change in their business facilities or kinds of business activities, engage in any act prescribed in any one of the following paragraphs: Provided, That paragraph (ii) below shall not apply to such competition as provided for in Chapter IV [Stockholding, interlocking directorates, mergers and acquisitions of business]:

    (i)   Supplying the same or similar goods or services to the same consumers or users;

    (ii)   Getting supplies of the same or similar goods or services from the same supplier.

(5) The term "private monopolization" as used in this Act shall mean such business activities, by which any entrepreneur, individually or by combination or conspiracy with other entrepreneurs, or by in any other manner, excludes or controls the business activities of other entrepreneurs, thereby causing, contrary to the public interest, a substantial restraint of competition in any particular field of trade.

(6) The term "unreasonable restraint of trade" as used in this Act shall mean such business activities, by which any entrepreneur, by contract, agreement or any other concerted actions, irrespective of its names, with

other entrepreneurs, mutually restrict or conduct their business activities in such a manner as to fix, maintain, or increase prices, or to limit production, technology, products, facilities, or customers or suppliers, thereby causing, contrary to the public interest, a substantial restraint of competition in any particular field of trade.

(7) The term "monopolistic situation" as used in this Act shall mean circumstances in which each of the following market structures and undesirable market performances exist in any particular field of business where the aggregate total amount of prices (this term refers to the prices of the goods concerned less a sum equivalent to the amount of taxes levied directly on such goods) of goods of the same description (including goods capable of being supplied without making any significant change to their business facilities or kinds of business activities; hereinafter in this subsection referred to as "particular goods") and those of any other goods having a strikingly similar function and utility thereto, which are supplied in Japan (excluding those exported) or the total amount of prices (this term refers to the prices of the services concerned less a sum equivalent to the amount of taxes levied on the recipient of such services with respect thereto) of services of the same description which are supplied in Japan, during the latest one-year period designated by a Cabinet Ordinance, is in excess of fifty billion yen:

(i)   Where the market share (this refers to the ratio accounted for by the aggregate volume (in case it is not appropriate to be calculated by the quantity, the quantity shall be represented in terms of the amount of their prices; the same shall apply hereinafter in this paragraph) of the particular goods and any other goods having a strikingly similar function and utility thereto or by the volume of the services, which are supplied by the entrepreneur or entrepreneurs concerned, to total volume of those supplied in Japan (excluding those exported) of an entrepreneur exceeds one-half or where the combined market share of two entrepreneurs exceeds three-fourths during a given one-year period;

(ii)   Where there exists conditions which make it extremely difficult for any other entrepreneur to be newly engaged in the said particular field of business;

(iii) Where the increase in the price of the particular goods or services supplied by the entrepreneur concerned has been remarkable or the decrease therein has been slight for a considerable period of time in the light of changes occurred in the supply and demand, or in the cost of supplying for such goods or services during such period, and where, in addition thereto, the said entrepreneur has fallen under any one of the following requirements during the said period:

(a) That the entrepreneur has earned profit rate far exceeding that which is established by a Cabinet Ordinance as the norm for the class of business designated by such Cabinet Ordinance to which the said entrepreneur belongs; or

(b) That the entrepreneur has expended a level of selling costs and general and administrative expenses far exceeding one which is considered as the norm for the field of business to which the entrepreneur belongs.

(8) In the event any change has occurred in the economic conditions resulting in a drastic change in domestic industrial shipments and wholesale prices, the amount of prices as prescribed in the preceding subsection may be revised by virtue of a Cabinet Ordinance to reflect such change.

(9) The term "unfair trade practices" as used in this Act shall mean any act coming under any one of following paragraphs, which tends to impede fair competition and which is designated by the Fair Trade Commission as such:

(i) Unjustly discriminating against other entrepreneurs;

(ii) Dealing at unjust prices;

(iii) Unjustly inducing or coercing customers of a competitor to deal with oneself;

(iv) Dealing with another party on such terms as will restrict unjustly the business activities of the said party;

(v) Dealing with another party by unjust use of one's bargaining position;

(vi) Unjustly interfering with a transaction between an entrepreneur who competes in Japan with oneself or the company of which oneself is a stockholder or an officer and his another transacting party; or, in case such entrepreneur is a company, unjustly inducing, instigating, or coercing a stockholder or an officer of such company to act against the interest of such company.

CHAPTER II   PRIVATE MONOPOLIZATION AND UNREASONABLE RESTRAINT OF TRADE

Sec. 3   [Prohibition of private monopolization or unreasonable restraint of trade]

No entrepreneur shall effect private monopolization or unreasonable restraint of trade.

Sec. 4   [Prohibition of particular concerted practices]

Deleted. (Act No. 259 of 1953)

Sec. 5 [Prohibition of private control organization]

Deleted. (Act No. 259 of 1953)

Sec. 6 [Prohibition of particular international agreements or contracts, filing requirement]

(1) No entrepreneur shall enter into an international agreement or an international contract which contains such matters as constitute unreasonable restraint of trade or unfair trade practices.

(2) An entrepreneur who has entered into an international agreement or an international contract (limited to only such an agreement or a contract that belongs to the types which are prescribed by the Rules of the Fair Trade Commission as tending to contain such matters as constitute unreasonable restraint of trade or unfair trade practices) shall, in accordance with the Rules of the Fair Trade Commission, file a report thereof with the Commission, accompanied by a copy of the said agreement or contract (in the case of an oral agreement or contract, a document describing the contents thereof), within thirty days from the conclusion of such agreement or contract.

Sec. 7 [Elimination measures]

(1) In case there exists any act in violation of the provisions of Section 3 [prohibition of private monopolization or unreasonable restraint of trade], or subsection (1) or (2) of the preceding section, the Fair Trade Commission may, in accordance with the procedures as provided for in Division II [procedures], Chapter VIII, order the entrepreneur concerned to file reports, or to cease and desist from such acts, to transfer a part of his business, or to take any other measures necessary to eliminate such acts in violation of the said provisions.

(2) The Fair Trade Commission may, when it finds it particularly necessary, even when an act in violation of the provisions of Section 3 [prohibition of private monopolization or unreasonable restraint of trade] has already ceased to exist, order the entrepreneurs concerned, in accordance with the procedures as provided for in Division II [procedures], Chapter VIII, to take measures to publicize that the said act has been discontinued and order any other measures necessary to ensure elimination of the said act: Provided, That the foregoing shall not apply to cases where one year has elapsed since the date of discontinuation of the said act without recommendation being given to the entrepreneur concerned or without the hearing procedures being initiated with respect to the said act.

Sec. 7-2 [Surcharges]

(1) In case any entrepreneur effects an unreasonable restraint of trade or enters into an international agreement or an international contract containing such matters as constitute an unreasonable restraint of trade, which pertains to the price of goods or services or results in affecting in effect the price of such goods or services by curtailing the volume of supply thereof, the Fair Trade Commission shall order the entrepreneur concerned, in accordance with the procedures as provided for in Division II [procedures], Chapter VIII, to pay to the Treasury a surcharge of an amount equivalent to an amount arrived at by multiplying the sales amount of such goods or services, computed in accordance with the method prescribed by a Cabinet Ordinance, for the period from the date on which the entrepreneur was engaged in the business activities as implementation of such conduct to the date on which the entrepreneur ceased to engage in the business activities as implementation of such conduct (in case such period exceeds three years, the period shall be for three years retroactively from the date on which the entrepreneur ceased to engage in the business activities as implementation of such conduct; hereinafter referred to as "period of such implementation") by six percent (or by two percent for retail business or by one percent for wholesale business): Provided, That in case the amount thus computed falls below five hundred thousand yen, the Commission shall not order the payment of such a surcharge.

(2) In the case of the preceding subsection, the term "six percent" appearing in the preceding subsection shall be "three percent" and the term "two percent" shall be "one percent," if the entrepreneur falls under any one of the following paragraphs:

(i) Any company whose capital or subscription is not more than 100 million yen and any company or individual whose pay-roll employees are not more than 300 persons, whose main activity is to carry on business in the fields of manufacturing, mining, transportation and other kinds of business (excluding the kinds of business stipulated in paragraph (ii) of this subsection and the kinds of business stipulated by the Cabinet Ordinance pursuant to paragraph (iii) of this subsection);

(ii) Any company whose capital or subscription is not more than 10 million yen and any company or individual whose pay-roll employees are no more than 50 persons, whose main activity is to carry on business in the fields of retail trade or services (excluding the kinds of business stipulated in the Cabinet Ordinance pursuant to paragraph (iii) of this subsection); and any company whose capital or subscription is not more than 30 million yen and any company or individual whose pay-roll employees are not more than 100 persons, whose main activity is to carry on business in the wholesale trade (excluding the kinds of business stipulated in the Cabinet Ordinance pursuant to paragraph (iii) of this subsection; or

(iii)   Any company whose capital or subscription is not more than that specified by the Cabinet Ordinance for each kind of business and any company or individual whose pay-roll employees are not more than that specified by the Cabinet Ordinance for each kind of business, whose main activity is to carry on business in fields specified by such Cabinet Ordinance.

(3) Any person who has received an order under the provisions of subsection (1) shall pay the surcharges as provided for in subsection (1) and (2) of this section.

(4) In case the amount of surcharge calculated in accordance with the provisions of subsection (1) or (2) of this section contains a fraction less than ten thousand yen, such fraction shall be disregarded.

(5) In the case the entrepreneur who has committed an act in violation of the provision of subsection (1) above is a company and if such company has ceased to exist through a merger with another company, the violation of such company shall be considered as a violation of the merging company or consolidated company as a result of the merger, and the provisions of the preceding subsections shall apply thereto.

(6) When a period of three years has elapsed from the date of expiration of the period of such implementation (or when a period of one year has elapsed from the date on which the hearing procedures ended in case such hearing procedures had been initiated with respect to such a violation (in case the expiration of the three-year period following the expiration of the period of such implementation, then the date on which the three-year period expired), the Fair Trade Commission shall not order such entrepreneur to pay a surcharge for such violation: Provided, That the foregoing shall not apply to cases where the Fair Trade Commission has ordered to pay the surcharge for the said violation to the Treasury under the provisions of Section 48-2 (1) [surcharge payment order] and thereafter.

CHAPTER III   TRADE ASSOCIATIONS

Sec. 8   [Prohibited acts of a trade association, filing requirement]

(1) No trade association shall engage in any acts which comes under any one of the following paragraphs:

(i)   Substantially restraining competition in any particular field of trade;

(ii)   Entering into an international agreement or an international contract as provided for in Section 6(1);

(iii)   Limiting the present or future number of entrepreneurs in any particular field of business;

(iv)   Unjustly restricting the functions or activities of the constituent entrepreneurs (meaning an entrepreneur who is a member of the trade association; hereinafter the same);

(v)   Causing entrepreneurs to employ such acts as constitute unfair trade practices.

(2) Every trade association shall, when formed, in accordance with the rules of the Fair Trade Commission, file a report thereof with the Commission within thirty days as from the date of its formation.

(3) When any change has occurred to the matters reported under the preceding subsection, the trade association concerned shall, in accordance with the Rules of the Fair Trade Commission, file a report thereof with the Commission, within two months after the end of the business year during which such change occurred.

(4) Every trade association shall, when dissolved, in accordance with the Rules of the Fair Trade Commission, file a report thereof with the Commission, within thirty days as from the date of its dissolution.

Sec. 8-2   [Elimination measures against prohibited acts of trade associations]

(1) When there exists any act in violation of the provisions of the preceding section, the Fair Trade Commission may, in accordance with the procedures as provided for in Division II [procedures], Chapter VIII, order the trade association concerned to file a report, or to cease and desist from such act, to dissolve the said association, or to take any other measures necessary to eliminate the said act.

(2) The provisions of Section 7(2) [measures against already ceased violation] shall apply mutatis mutandis to any act in violation of provisions of subsection (1)(i), (iv) or (v) of the preceding section.

(3) The Fair Trade Commission may, in accordance with the procedures as provided for in Division II (procedures), Chapter VIII, in ordering a trade association to take any of the measures set forth in subsection (1) above or Section 7(2) applicable mutatis mutandis under the provisions of the preceding subsection, when it finds it particularly necessary, at the same time order an officer, manager or constituent entrepreneur (including other entrepreneur when a constituent entrepreneur is acting for the benefit of the entrepreneur; the same shall apply in Section 48 [recommendation to the violator to take elimination measures] (1) and (2)) of the said association to

take measures necessary to ensure the measures provided for in subsection (1) above or Section 7(2) applicable mutatis mutandis under the provisions of the preceding subsection.

Sec. 8-3 [Surcharges against constituent entrepreneurs]

The provisions of Section 7-2 [Surcharge] shall apply mutatis mutandis to cases where an act is committed in violation of the provisions of Section 8(1) [prohibited acts of a trade association] (i) or (ii) (applying only to such an entrepreneur who is a party to an international agreement or an international contract which contains such matters as constitute an unreasonable restraint of trade). In this case, the term "any entrepreneur" appearing in subsection (1) of Section 7-2 shall read "any trade association", the term "entrepreneur concerned" appearing therein shall read "the constituent entrepreneur" (other entrepreneur when a constituent entrepreneur is acting for the benefit of the entrepreneur; the same shall apply hereinafter in this section) of the trade association concerned and the term "such entrepreneur" appearing in subsection (2) of the said section shall read "the constituent entrepreneur of such trade association concerned."

CHAPTER III-II MONOPOLISTIC SITUATIONS

Sec. 8-4 [Measures against a monopolistic situation]

(1) When there exists a monopolistic situation, the Fair Trade Commission may order the entrepreneur concerned, in accordance with the procedures as provided for in Division II [procedures], Chapter VIII, to transfer a part of his business or to take any other measures necessary to restore competition with respect to such goods or services: Provided, That the foregoing shall not apply to cases where the Commission finds that such measures may reduce the scale of business of the said entrepreneur to such an extent that the costs required for the supply of goods or services which such entrepreneur supplies will rise sharply, undermine its financial position and make it difficult for the entrepreneur to maintain its international competitiveness, or where other alternative measures may be taken which the Commission finds sufficient to restore competition with respect to such goods or services.

(2) In issuing an order prescribed in the preceding subsection, the Fair Trade Commission shall give consideration, based on the items prescribed in each of the following paragraphs, to the smooth conduct of business activities by the entrepreneurs concerned, and those associated with them and the stabilization of livelihood for those employed by such entrepreneurs:

(i)   Assets, income and expenditures and other aspects of accounting;

(ii)   Officers and employees;

(iii) Location of factories, workyards and offices and other locational conditions;

(iv) Aspects of business facilities and equipments;

(v)   The substance of patent rights, trademark rights and other intellectual property rights and other technological features;

(vi) Capacity for and situations of production and sales, etc;

(vii) Capacity for and situations of obtaining funds and materials, etc;

(viii) Situations of supply and distribution of goods or services.

CHAPTER IV   STOCKHOLDINGS, INTERLOCKING DIRECTORATES, MERGERS AND ACQUISITIONS OF BUSINESS

Sec. 9   [Prohibition of holding company]

(1) No holding company shall be established.

(2) Any company (including a foreign company; hereinafter the same) shall not operate as a holding company in Japan.

(3) The term "holding company" as used in the preceding two subsections shall mean a company whose principal business is to control the business activities of a company or companies in Japan by means of holding of stock (including shares of partnership; hereinafter the same).

Sec. 9-2 [Restriction on total amount of stockholding by a giant non-financial company]

(1) Any stock company whose business is other than financial (this term refers to those engaged in banking, trust banking, insurance, mutual financing and securities businesses; the same meaning shall apply hereafter) and whose capital is larger than ten billion yen or whose net assets (this term refers to the sum of an amount arrived at by deducting the total liabilities from the total assets listed in the latest balance sheet and the amount by which the net assets have increased as a result of an issuance of new stock in accordance with the provisions of Section 280-2 of the Commercial Code (Act No. 48 of 1899) or as a result of an issuance of new stock by the exercise of pre-emptive right endowed by cum right corporate bonds, or as a result of a merger or the conversion of corporate bonds, if any; hereinafter the same meaning shall apply in this section) are larger than thirty billion yen shall not acquire or hold stock of companies in Japan in excess of its capital or its net assets, whichever is larger (hereinafter referred to as "the

base amount"), if by so doing total amount of acquiring price of such stocks (another price if it is listed so in the latest balance sheet; the same meaning shall apply hereinafter) which it has acquired or holds exceeds the base amount: Provided, That the foregoing shall not apply to the acquisition or holding of such stock in the cases provided for in any one of the following paragraphs;

(i) The acquisition or holding of stock of a company in Japan which has been prescribed by a Cabinet Ordinance and which has been invested in by a juridical person established by the government, or a local public authority, or a juridical person established under a special law whose total amount of capital is owned by the government or whose liabilities may be contractually guaranteed by the government;

(ii) The acquisition or holding of stock of a company in Japan, as prescribed by a Cabinet Ordinance, engaged in a business contributive to the development of industries and the progress of economy and societies, which requires large sum of funds of such a magnitude as to make it difficult to procure by ordinary means;

(iii) The acquisition or holding of stock of a company in Japan whose purpose is to engage in any one or two or more of the following businesses, and which performs business activities pursuant to the objective thereof;

(a) Business undertaken outside Japan (including the business undertaken in Japan which is closely connected with, and incidental to, such business);

(b) Business of investment or long-term loans to foreign governments or foreign juridical persons (including those businesses which are closely connected with, and incidental to, such businesses, hereinafter referred to as "investment and financing business");

(c) Investment and financing business to the companies provided for in the preceding paragraph; or

(d) Investment and financing business to the companies which fall under the purview of this paragraph;

(iv) The acquisition or holding of stock of a company in Japan, as prescribed by a Cabinet Ordinance, engaged in the business provided for in paragraph (ii) above, and in the investment and financing business as provided for in the preceding paragraph;

(v) The acquisition or holding of stock of a company in Japan, established by partially separating the business actually performed by itself, whose issued stock is wholly acquired or owned immediately after the establishment by itself: Provided, That this shall apply only to cases where such stock is held for two years or less from the said company's establishment;

(vi) The acquisition or holding of stock of a company in Japan, established by joint investment with a foreign government, foreign juridical person or foreign national (referred to as "co-investment company" in subsection (5) below) when it is particularly necessary for the operation of its business to take the form of such a co-investment company therein; Provided, That this shall apply only to such cases where authorization of the Fair Trade Commission is obtained in advance in accordance with the provisions of the Rules of the Commission;

(vii) The acquisition or holding of new stock acquired or held due to a stock-holder allocation on currently held stock (excluding the stock held under the provisions of the paragraphs (i) to (iv) inclusive, of the preceding paragraph); Provided, That this shall apply only to cases where such stock is held for two years or less from the date of its acquisition;

(viii) The acquisition or holding of stock as a result of the enforcement of a lien, pledge, mortgage, or as a result of payment in kind; Provided, That this shall apply only to cases where such stock is held for one year or less from the date of its acquisition (or for one year or less from the date on which it is decided to conclude rehabilitation procedures, in case the stock is deemed to have been acquired through payment in kind under the provision of Section 265 [special provisions to Section 9-2 or Section 11 of the Act] of the Company Rehabilitation Act (Act No. 172 of 1952)] ; or

(ix) The acquisition or holding of stock of a company in Japan for an impera-tive reason; Provided, That this shall apply only to cases where approval of the Fair Trade Commission is obtained in advance (or without delay after the acquisition of such stock, in case it is acquired under urgent and imperative circumstances) in accordance with provisions of the Rules of the Fair Trade Commission, and where such stock is held for the period or less stipulated by such approval.

(2) If, as a result of a decrease in the base amount of the stock company as provided for in the preceding subsection, the total amount of the acquisi-tion price of stock held in companies in Japan (excluding the holdings which fall under any one of the paragraphs of the said subsection; the same shall apply in the following subsection) turns out to be in excess of the base amount, the total amount of such acquisition price shall be deemed as the base amount for the purpose of applying the provisions of the preceding subsection during the five years beginning from the date on which the acquisition price exceeded the base amount.

(3) In case the base amount decreases still more during the five-year period under the preceding subsection, the base amount determined prior to such decrease or the total amount of the acquisition price of stock held in companies in Japan as of the date on which the period as provided for in the preceding subsection expired, whichever is the smaller, shall be deemed as the base amount for the purpose of applying the provisions of subsection (1) above during the five-year period. The same shall apply to cases where the base amount decreased still more during the five-year period immediately following such decrease.

(4) The provisions of the preceding two subsections shall not apply to cases where the base amount has increased beyond the amount which is deemed as the base amount then effective under these provisions.

(5) When the Fair Trade Commission grants authorization under subsection (1) (vi), it shall, in advance, consult with the Minister of Finance and the competent minister having jurisdiction over the business in which the co-investment company is engaged.

(6) When the Fair Trade Commission grants authorization under subsection (1) (vi) or approval under paragraph (ix) of the said subsection, the Commission shall, in advance, consult with the minister or ministers who are empowered by virtue of a special law to make recommendations or give instructions with respect to the financial management of the companies which seek to acquire stock and are subject to such authorization or approval.

(7) In case a company which falls under subsection (1) (iii) above ceases to become subject thereto, the provision of the said subsection shall not apply to the holding of stock of such company for one year immediately following the date on which such company ceased to fall thereunder.

(8) In case any company acquires stock of another company in Japan under urgent and imperative circumstances that are subject to an ex post facto approval under subsection (1) (ix) above but fails to obtain such approval, the provision of the said subsection shall not apply to the holding of such stock for one month immediately following the date on which such company failed to obtain such approval.

(9) In the event, as a result of a change in economic conditions, any drastic increase or decrease occurs in the amounts of capital and net assets of the stock companies which rank among the largest two hundred in terms of the size of their capital and net assets (excluding those engaged in financial business; the same shall apply in this subsection), the amount stipulated in subsection (1) may be revised by virtue of a Cabinet Ordinance to reflect such change.

Sec. 10   [Prohibition of particular stockholding by a company, filling requirement]

(1) No company shall acquire or hold stock of a company or companies in Japan where the effect of such acquisition or holding of stock may be substantially to restrain competition in any particular field of trade, or shall acquire or hold stock of a company or companies in Japan through unfair trade practices.

(2) Every company in Japan whose business is other than financial and whose total assets (meaning total amount of the assets according to the latest balance sheet; hereinafter the same) exceed two billion yen or every foreign company whose business is other than financial, shall, in case it holds stock of another company or companies in Japan (including the stock held in the form of trust property of pecuniary or security trust of which it is a trustor or beneficiary and can exercise its voting rights or where such trustor or beneficiary can issue instructions regarding the exercise of such voting rights), submit, in accordance with the Rules of the Fair Trade Commission, a report on such stock held in its name or in the name of trustee as of the end of every business year to the Commission within three months therefrom.

Sec. 11 [Restriction on stockholding rate by a financial company]

(1) No company engaged in financial business shall acquire or hold stock of another company in Japan if by doing so it holds in excess of five percent (ten percent in the case of an insurance company) of the total outstanding stock: Provided, That the foregoing shall not apply to such cases where authorization of the Fair Trade Commission is obtained in advance in accordance with the Rules of the Fair Trade Commission, or to such cases falling under any one of the following paragraphs:

(i)   Acquisition or holding of stock as a result of the enforcement of lien, pledge, mortgage, or of payment in kind;

(ii)   Acquisition or holding of stock by a company engaging in securities in the course of its business;

(iii) Acquisition or holding of stock in the form of trust property of pecuniary or security trust; Provided, That this shall apply only to cases where the trustor or the beneficiary of such trust property can exercise his voting rights or where such trustor or beneficiary can issue instructions regarding the exercise of such voting rights.

(2) Any company whose business is financial, being desirous, in the case of paragraphs (i) and (ii) of the preceding subsection, of holding stock of another company or companies in Japan over the period of one year from the date of such acquisition in excess of five percent of the total outstanding stock, shall, in accordance with the Rules of the Fair Trade Commission, obtain authorization in advance from the Commission. The authorization of the Fair Trade Commission in such case shall be granted with a condition that the company engaged in financial business should promptly dispose of the said stock.

(3) When the Fair Trade Commission grants authorization under the provisions of the two preceding subsections, it shall, in advance, consult with the Minister of Finance.

Sec. 12   [Restriction on acquisition of corporate bonds]

Deleted. (Act No. 214 of 1949)

Sec. 13   [Prohibition of particular interlocking directorates, filing requirement]

(1) Neither an officer nor an employee (meaning in this section a person other than officers in the regular employment of a company) of a company shall hold at the same time a position as an officer in another company or companies in Japan wherever the effect of such an interlocking directorate may be substantially to restrain competition in any particular field of trade.

(2) No company shall coerce another company or companies in Japan in competition with it in Japan, through unfair trade practices, to admit one of its officers concurrently to the position of an officer or an employee of the latter company or companies, or to admit its employee, concurrently to the position of an officer of such company or companies.

(3) Every officer or employee of a company who holds concurrently the position of an officer in another company or companies in Japan in competition with it in Japan, shall, in case the total assets of either one company exceed two billion yen, file, in accordance with the Rules of the Fair Trade Commission, a report thereof with the Commission within thirty days as from the date of assuming the position of such an officer.

Sec. 14   [Prohibition of particular stockholding by a person other than a company, filing requirement]

(1) No person other than a company shall acquire or hold stock of another company or companies in Japan whenever the effect of such acquisition or holding of stock may be substantially to restrain competition in any particular field of trade, or shall acquire or hold stock of another company or companies in Japan through unfair trade practices.

(2) Every person other than a company shall, in case he has come to hold stock of two or more companies mutually competing in Japan in excess of ten per cent of the total outstanding stock of the respective company, file, in accordance with the Rules of the Fair Trade Commission, a report on such stock with the Commission within thirty days as from the date of such holding.

Sec. 15   [Prohibition of particular mergers, filing requirement]

(1) No company in Japan shall effect a merger coming under any one of the following paragraphs:

(i)   Where the effect of a merger may be substantially to restrain competition in any particular field of trade;
(ii)   Where unfair trade practices have been employed in the course of the merger.

(2) Every company in Japan, which is desirous of becoming a party to a merger shall, in accordance with the provisions of the Rules of the Fair Trade Commission, file a report with the Commission.

(3) No company in Japan shall, in the cases coming under the preceding subsection, effect a merger until the expiration of a thirty-day waiting period from the date of the issuance of the receipt of the said report: Provided, That the Fair Trade Commission may, when it finds it necessary, shorten the said period, or extend it by an additional period of time not exceeding sixty days with the consent of the companies concerned.

(4) The Fair Trade Commission shall, where it determines to initiate hearing proceedings or makes a recommendation with a view to ordering the necessary measures relating to the merger in question pursuant to the provisions of Section 17-2 [elimination measures against unlawful acts relating to a company, etc.], do so before the expiration of a thirty-day waiting period as provided for in the preceding subsection, or of any shortened or extended period under the proviso thereof: Provided, That the foregoing provisions shall not apply in cases where there has been a false statement with respect to important matters in the report specified in subsection (2) above.

Sec. 16   [Prohibition of particular acquisitions of business, etc., filing requirement]

The provisions of the preceding section shall apply mutatis mutandis to an act of a company coming under any one of the following paragraphs:

(i)   Acquiring the whole or a substantial part of the business in Japan of another company;
(ii)   Acquiring the whole or a substantial part of the fixed assets used for the business in Japan of another company;
(iii)   Taking on lease of the whole or a substantial part of the business in Japan of another company;
(iv)   Undertaking the management of the whole or a substantial part of the business in Japan of another company;
(v)   Entering into a contract which provides for a joint profit and loss account for business in Japan with another company.

Sect. 17   [Prohibition of evasion]

No acts in whatever form or manner shall be committed to evade such prohibitions or restrictions as provided for by Section 9 to the preceding section inclusive [prohibition of holding company, restriction on total amount of stockholding by a giant non-financial company, prohibition of particular stockholding by a company, restriction on stockholding rate by a financial company, prohibition of particular interlocking directorates, prohibition of particular stockholding by a person other than a company, prohibition of particular mergers, prohibition of particular acquisition of business, etc.].

Sec. 17-2 [Elimination measures against unlawful acts relating to a company, etc.]

(1) Where there exists any act in violation of the provisions of Section 9-2(1) [restriction on total amount of stockholding by a giant non-financial company], Section 10 [prohibition of particular stockholding by a company], Section 11(1) [restriction on stockholding rate by a financial company], Section 15(1) [prohibition of particular mergers] (including such cases where the said provisions are applied mutatis mutandis by Section 16 [prohibition of particular acquisition of business, etc.]) or the preceding section, the Fair Trade Commission may, in accordance with the procedures as provided for in Division II (procedures), Chapter VIII, order the entrepreneur concerned to submit a report, or to dispose of the whole or a part of his stocks to transfer a part of his business, or to take any other measures necessary to eliminate such acts in violation of the said provisions.

(2) Where there exists any establishment of a act in violation of the provisions of Section 9(1) [prohibition of establishment of a holding company] or (2) [prohibition of operation as a holding company), Section 13 (prohibition of particular interlocking directorates], Section 14 [prohibition of particular stockholding by a person other than a company] or the preceding section, the Fair Trade Commission may, in accordance with the procedures as provided for in Division II [procedures], Chapter VIII, order the person violating such provisions to submit a report or to dispose of the whole or a part of his stocks, to resign from his position as an officer in a company, or to take any other measures necessary to eliminate such acts in violation of the said provisions.

Sec. 18 [Measures against the establishment of a holding company or an illegal merger]

The Fair Trade Commission may, in case where any company has been established in violation of the provisions of Section 9(1) [prohibition of establishment of a holding company] or companies that have merged in violation of the provisions of Section 15(2) [filing of merger] and (3) [waiting period of merger], bring a suit to have the said establishment or merger declared null and void.

CHAPTER IV-II   PARALLEL PRICE INCREASES

Sec. 18-2   [Reporting requirement on parallel price increases]

(1) If, in any particular field of business where the total price of goods (this term refers to the price of the goods concerned less an amount equivalent to the amount of taxes levied directly on such goods) of the same description supplied in Japan (excluding those exported; hereinafter the same in this section) or the total prices of services [this refers to the price of the services concerned less an amount equivalent to the amount of taxes levied on the recipients of such services with respect thereto) of the same description supplied in Japan during a one-year period designated by a Cabinet Ordinance, is in excess of thirty billion yen, the ratio of the total amount of such goods or services supplied by the three entrepreneurs, which rank among the three largest entrepreneurs in Japan in terms of volume of supply (this refers to the quantity of goods or services of the same description which one entrepreneur supplied during a given one-year period, and in case it is not appropriate to be calculated by the quantity, the quantity shall be represented in terms of the amount of their prices; hereinafter the same meaning in this section) to the aggregate volume of such goods or services of the same description supplied in Japan during such one-year period (hereinafter referred to as "the aggregate volume") exceeds seven tenths, and if two or more major entrepreneurs (including the largest one) (this term means the five entrepreneurs each of which account for one twentieth or more of the aggregate volume and rank among the five largest entrepreneurs in Japan; hereinafter the same meaning in this section) raise the price they use as the basis of their transactions in such goods or services of the same description by an identical or similar amount or percentage within a period of three months, the Fair Trade Commission may ask such major entrepreneurs for a report, furnishing a statement of reasons for such a raise in the price of such goods or services: Provided, That this shall not apply to price increases effected by entrepreneurs whose price of such goods or services is authorized or approved by, or filed with the competent minister in charge of the business in which the said entrepreneurs are engaged (in case such price shall be filed with the competent minister, this shall apply only to such cases where the competent minister has the authority to order a change in such price).

(2) In the event any change has occurred in the economic conditions resulting in a drastic change in domestic industrial shipments and wholesale prices, the amount of prices as prescribed in the preceding subsection may be revised by virtue of a Cabinet Ordinance to reflect such change.

CHAPTER V   UNFAIR TRADE PRACTICES

Sec. 19   [Prohibition of unfair trade practices]

No entrepreneur shall employ unfair trade practices.

Sec. 20   [Measures against unfair trade practices]

(1) When there exists any act in violation of the preceding section, the Fair Trade Commission may, in accordance with the procedures as provided for in Division II [procedures], Chapter VIII, order the entrepreneur concerned to cease and desist from the said act, to delete the clauses concerned from the contract and to take any other measures necessary to eliminate the said act.

(2) The provisions of Section 7(2) [measures against already ceased violations] shall apply mutatis mutandis to an act in violation of the preceding section.

CHAPTER VI   EXEMPTIONS

Sec. 21   [Natural monopoly]

The provisions of this Act shall not apply to such acts relating to the production, sale, or supply as are done in the proper course of business by a person engaging in railway, electricity, gas, or any other business constituting a monopoly by the inherent nature of the said business.

Sec. 22   [Legitimate acts under special laws and orders]

(1) The provisions of this Act, where there exists a special law concerning a specific industry, shall not apply to legitimate acts of an entrepreneur or a trade association conducted in accordance with such a special law or an order based upon such law.

(2) Such special laws as provided for in the preceding subsection shall be specified by a separate law.

Sec. 23   [Acts under intellectual property rights]

The provisions of this Act shall not apply to such acts recognizable as the exercise of rights under the Copyright Act, the Patent Act, the Utility Model Act, the Design Act or the Trademark Act.

Sec. 24 [Acts of cooperatives]

The provisions of this Act shall not apply to such acts of a cooperative (including a federation of cooperatives) which conforms to the requirements stipulated in each of the following paragraphs and which has been formed in accordance with the provisions of a separate law: Provided, That the foregoing shall not apply to such cases where unfair trade practices are employed, or where competition in any particular field of trade is substantially restrained, resulting in unjust rise of prices:

(i)   Its purpose shall be mutual aid among small scale entrepreneurs or consumers;

(ii)   It shall be voluntarily formed; and the participation in and withdrawal from the cooperative shall be voluntary;

(iii)   Each member shall possess equal voting rights; and

(iv)   If distribution of profits among members is contemplated, the limits shall be stipulated in a law or a Cabinet Ordinance, or in the articles of an association.

Sec. 24-2 [Resale price maintenance contracts]

(1) The provision of this Act shall not apply to legitimate acts performed by an entrepreneur who produces or sells a commodity, the uniform quality of which is easily identifiable and which is designated by the Fair Trade Commission, with another entrepreneur who buys such commodity, in order to fix and maintain the resale price thereof (this term means hereinafter the price at which the latter entrepreneur or a third entrepreneur who purchases from him sells such commodity): Provided, That the foregoing shall not apply if the said act tends to be grossly injurious to the interest of consumers in general, or if it is done against the will of the entrepreneur who produces the said commodity by an entrepreneur whose business is to sell the said commodity.

(2) The Fair Trade Commission shall not designate a commodity under the provisions of the preceding subsection unless it comes under each of the following paragraphs:

(i)   The commodity shall be for the daily use by the consumers in general; and

(ii)   Free competition shall exist with respect to the commodity.

(3) The designation of a commodity under the provisions of subsection (1) above shall be made by a notification.

(4) Legitimate acts performed by an entrepreneur whose business is to publish copyrighted works or by an entrepreneur whose business is to sell

such published works, in order to fix and maintain with another entrepreneur who buys such works the resale price thereof, shall be exempted from the application of the provisions of this Act.

(5) The organization formed in accordance with the provisions of any one of the following Acts shall not be included in the term of "another entrepreneur" who buys commodities or copyrighted works as provided for in subsection (1) or the preceding subsection: Provided, That the foregoing provisions shall, in the case of the organizations formed under the provisions of any one of the Acts mentioned in paragraphs (viii) and (viii-ii) hereunder, only apply to cases where a business cooperative, a minor business cooperative, a federation of cooperatives, a commercial and industrial association or a federation of commercial and industrial associations purchases such commodity as provided for in subsection (2) above or copyrighted works as provided for in subsection (4) above, for the consumption of persons directly or indirectly constituting the said business cooperative, a federation of cooperatives, commercial and industrial associations or a federation of commercial and industrial associations:

(i)   National Public Service Act;
(ii)   Agricultural Cooperatives Act;
(iii)   National Public Service, etc., Mutual Aid Association Act;
(iii-ii) Local Public Service, etc., Mutual Aid Association Act;
(iv)   Consumer Cooperatives Act;
(v)   Fisheries Cooperatives Act;
(vi)   Public Corporation, etc. Labor Relations Act;
(vii)   Labor Unions Act;
(viii)   Small and Medium Sized Enterprise, etc., Cooperatives Act;
(viii-ii) Small and Medium Sized Enterprises Organization Act;
(ix)   Local Public Service Act;
(x)   Forestry Cooperatives Act;
(xi)   Local Public Enterprise Labor Relations Act.

(6) When an entrepreneur as stipulated in subsection (1) above has fixed the resale price under the said subsection and has entered into a contract for the purpose of maintaining it, he shall, in accordance with provisions of the Rules of the Fair Trade Commission, file a report thereon with the Commission within thirty days from the date of the conclusion of the said contract: Provided, That the foregoing shall not apply if the Fair Trade Commission stipulates otherwise in its Rules.

Set. 24-3   [Depression cartels]

(1) Where there exists an extreme disequilibrium of supply and demand for a particular commodity, resulting in circumstances falling under each of

the following paragraphs, the provisions of this Act shall not apply to concerted activities of entrepreneurs (including an act of a trade association which causes its constituent entrepreneurs to undertake concerted activities; hereinafter the same) who produce the said commodity or a trade association consisting of such entrepreneurs (hereinafter referred to as "producers, etc."), which have been obtained authorization under either of the following two subsections: Provided, That the foregoing shall not apply when they employ unfair trade practices or cause any entrepreneur to employ such acts as constitute unfair trade practices:

(i)   The price of the said commodity is below the average cost of production, and a considerable part of the entrepreneurs in the trade concerned may eventually be forced to discontinue production;

(ii) It is difficult to overcome such circumstances as stipulated in the proceeding paragraph by the rationalization of individual enterprises.

(2) When circumstances provided for in the preceding subsection exist, those producers, etc. who desire to effect concerted activities relating to restrictions on output or sales, or on facilities or equipments (excluding such as will impede the renovation or improvement of facilities) may, in order to overcome such circumstances, obtain from the Fair Trade Commission authorization of the said activities in advance.

(3) When circumstances provided for in subsection (1) above exist and if restriction on output of the commodity in a particular trade is found extremely difficult for technical reasons, those producers, etc. who desire to effect concerted activities involving price-fixing may, in accordance with the Rules of the Fair Trade Commission, obtain from the Fair Trade Commission authorization of the said activities in advance. The same shall apply to a price-fixing agreement entered into concurrently with an agreement provided for in the preceding subsection, when the concerted activities have been effected upon authorization under the preceding subsection, and when such concerted activities alone proved to be entirely inadequate to overcome the circumstances stipulated in subsection (1) above.

(4) The Fair Trade Commission shall not grant authorization as provided for in the preceding two subsections unless the concerted activities applied fall under the conditions provided for in the preceding two subsections and conform with each of the following paragraphs:

(i)   That they do not exceed the necessary extent to overcome the circumstances provided for in subsection (1) above;

(ii)   that there is no likelihood of unjustly injuring the interests of the consumers in general, and of related entrepreneurs;

(iii) That they are not unjustly discriminatory;

(iv)   That they do not restrict unjustly participation in or withdrawal from such activities.

(5) When the Fair Trade Commission has authorized or dismissed an application for authorization under subsection (2) or (3) above, or has taken action pursuant to the provisions of Section 66(1) [cancellation or modification of authorization] with regard to authorization under subsection (2) or (3) above, it shall, without delay, make public the fact showing the reason for said action.

(6) The producers, etc. engaged in concerted activities after obtaining authorization under subsection (2) or (3) above shall, without delay, file a notification thereof with the Fair Trade Commission, when they have discontinued the said activities.

(7) The Fair Trade Commission shall, where an objection to authorization under subsection (2) or (3) above has been filed, conduct an open hearing in accordance with the Rules of the Fair Trade Commission.

(8) The Fair Trade Commission shall, prior to granting such authorization under subsection (2) or (3) above, or to dismissing an application thereof, consult with the competent minister in charge of the business concerned. The same shall apply when the Fair Trade Commission intends to take action provided for in Section 66(1) [revocation or modification of authorization, approval or decision] with respect to such authorization under subsection (2) or (3) above.

Sec. 24-4   [Rationalization cartels]

(1) The provisions of this Act shall not apply to concerted activities of producers, etc. who have obtained authorization under the following subsection, where they are found particularly necessary for effecting an advancement of technology, an improvement in the quality of goods, a reduction in costs, an increase in efficiency or any other rationalization of enterprises.

(2) Producers, etc. desirous of undertaking concerted activities regarding restrictions on technology or kinds of product, utilization of facilities for storage of raw materials or products or for transportation thereof, or utilization or purchase of by-products, waste, or scrap in the case provided for by the preceding subsection may, in accordance with the provisions of the Rules of the Fair Trade Commission, obtain authorization from the Fair Trade Commission in advance.

(3) The Fair Trade Commission shall not grant authorization under the preceding subsection unless concerted activities applied for fall under

the conditions provided for in the preceding subsection, and conform with each of the following paragraphs:

(i)   That there is no likelihood of unjustly injuring the interests of users;

(ii)   That there is no likelihood of unjustly injuring the interests of the consumers in general and of related entrepreneurs (excluding customers);

(iii)   That they are not unjustly discriminatory;

(iv)   That they do not restrict unjustly the participation in or withdrawal from such activities;

(v)   That where restrictions on a line of products are imposed differently on participants in the concerted activities, such differentiation is not designed unjustly to concentrate production of a particular product in the hands of any specific entrepreneurs.

(4) The provisions of the proviso to subsection (1) and of subsections (5) to (8) inclusive of the preceding section shall apply mutatis mutandis to the concerted activities as provided for in subsection (2).

CHAPTER VII DAMAGES

Sec. 25   [Absolute liability]

(1) Any entrepreneur who has effected private monopolization or unreasonable restraint of trade or who has employed unfair trade practices shall be liable to indemnify the person injured.

(2) No entrepreneur may be exempted from the liability as prescribed in the preceding subsection by proving non-existence of wilfulness or negligence on his part.

Sec. 26   [Restriction on exercise of the right to claim for damages in court, prescription]

(1) The right to claim for damages in the preceding subsection may not be exercised in court until the decision pursuant to the provisions of Section 48(4) [recommendation decision], Section 53-3 [consent decision], or Section 54 [formal decision] has become final and conclusive in case no decision has been made pursuant to the provisions above.

(2) The right under the preceding subsection shall, upon expiration of three years from the date on which the decision in the said subsection became final and conclusive, be extinct by prescription.

CHAPTER VIII   FAIR TRADE COMMISSION

Division I   Organization and Power

Sec. 27   [Duty and position]

(1) The Fair Trade Commission shall be established in order to attain the purpose of this Act.

(2) The Fair Trade Commission shall be administratively attached to the Prime Minister.

Sec. 27-2   [Affairs under the jurisdiction of the Fair Trade Commission]

The affairs under the jurisdiction of the Fair Trade Commission shall be as follows:

(i)   Matters relating to regulation on private monopolization;
(ii)   Matters relating to regulation on unreasonable restraint of trade;
(iii)   Matters relating to regulation on unfair trade practices;
(iv)   Matters relating to regulation on monopolistic situations;
(v)   Doing surveys and research on business activities or actual economic conditions or making coordination of economic laws or orders, relating to regulation on activities which substantially restrain competition in any particular field of trade, regulation on activities which tend to impede fair competition, regulation in order to prevent excessive concentration of economic power or other regulation on unjust restriction of business activities;
(vi)   Business which is assigned to the Fair Trade Commission based on a law (including an order based on a law), in addition to those stipulated in any one of the preceding paragraphs.

Sec. 28   [Independence]

The chairman and the commissioners of the Fair trade Commission perform their duties independently.

Sec. 29   [Organization, appointment of chairman and commissioners and their status]

(1) The Fair Trade Commission shall be composed of a chairman and four commissioners.

(2) The chairman and the commissioners shall be appointed by the Prime Minister with the consent of both Houses of the Diet from among persons whose age is thirty five or more and who are experts in law or economics.

(3) The appointment or dismissal of the chairman shall be attested to by the Emperor.

(4) The chairman and the commissioners shall be public service officials.

Sec. 30   [Term of office for chairman and commissioners]

(1) The term of office for the chairman and the commissioners shall be five years: Provided, That the term of office for the chairman and the commissioners appointed to fill a vacancy shall be the remainder of the term of office of his predecessor.

(2) The chairman and the commissioners may be reappointed.

(3) The chairman and the commissioners shall retire from the office upon reaching the age of sixty five.

(4) If the term of office for the chairman or the commissioners expires, or a vacancy occurs at the time when the consent of both Houses of the Diet is unobtainable because the Diet is not in session or the House of Representatives is dissolved, the Prime Minister may appoint the chairman or a commissioner from among such persons having qualifications as provided for in the subsection (2) of the preceding section. In this case the subsequent approval of both Houses shall be obtained at the earliest session of the Diet after the appointment.

Sec. 31   [Guarantee of status of chairman and commissioners]

The chairman or a commissioner may not, against his will, be removed from office during his term of office, except in the cases falling under any one of the following paragraphs:

(i)   When he has been adjudicated as incompetent, quasi-incompetent, or in bankruptcy;
(ii)   When he has been dismissed by way of disciplinary punishment;
(iii) When he has been punished for the violation of this Act;
(iv)   When he has been sentenced to imprisonment or heavier penalty;
(v)   When the Fair Trade Commission has decided that he is incapable of executing his duty on account of his physical or mental breakdown;
(vi)   When the subsequent approval of both Houses of the Diet could not be obtained in the case of subsection (4) of the preceding section.

Sec. 32   [Dismissal of chairman or commissioners]

In the case of paragraphs (i) or (iii) to (vi) inclusive of the preceding section, the Prime Minister shall dismiss the chairman or the commissioner concerned from his office.

Sec. 33 [Chairman]

(1) The chairman shall preside over the affairs of the Fair Trade Commission and shall represent it.

(2) The Fair Trade Commission shall choose in advance a commissioner from among the commissioners who acts on behalf of the chairman in case he cannot execute his duty.

Sec. 34 [Quorum and voting]

(1) Meetings of the Fair Trade Commission shall not be declared open and a decision shall not be made without the attendance of the chairman and two or more commissioners.

(2) All decisions of the Fair Trade Commission shall be made by majority votes of the attending commissioners. In case the votes are evenly divided, the chairman shall have the power to decide.

(3) The decision of the Fair Trade Commission under the provisions of Section 31(v) shall, irrespective of the provisions of the preceding subsection, be made with the unanimous concurrence of all commissioners or the chairman except for the commissioner or chairman concerned.

(4) For the purpose of applying the provisions of subsection (1) above, in case the chairman cannot execute his duty, the commissioner chosen to act on behalf of the chairman pursuant to subsection (2) of the preceding section shall be deemed to be the chairman.

Sec. 35 [Staff office personnel]

(1) The staff office shall be attached to the Fair Trade Commission for the discharge of its affairs.

(2) Hearing examiners, not exceeding five in number shall be maintained in the staff office, whose duty shall be to conduct a part of the hearing procedures (excluding the rendering of a decision).

(3) Hearing examiners shall be selected by the Fair Trade Commission from among the personnel of the staff office who have been found to have the necessary knowledge and experience in law and economics to conduct the hearing procedures and to be capable of making a fair judgment.

(4) A public prosecutor, private attorney actually practicing at the time of the appointment, or a person qualified to be an attorney at law shall be among the personnel of the staff office.

(5) Duties to be placed upon the personnel who is a public prosecutor under the preceding subsection shall be limited to matters relating to cases in violation of the provisions of this Act.

Sec. 35-2 [Local offices]

(1) Local offices shall be maintained at necessary places as local organizations of the staff office of the Fair Trade Commission.

(2) The name, location and territorial jurisdiction of each local office under the preceding subsection shall be provided for by a Cabinet Ordinance.

Sec. 35-3 [Administration of personnel]

With regard to the appointment, dismissal, disciplinary measures, and other matters relating to the administration of personnel of the staff office, the provisions of the National Public Service Personnel Act (Act No. 120 of 1947) shall apply.

Sec. 36 [Salaries of chairman and commissioners]

(1) The salaries of the chairman and the commissioner shall be provided for separately.

(2) The salaries of the chairman and the commissioner shall not be reduced in amount against their will while they are in office.

Sec. 37 [Prohibition of certain activities of chairman, commissioners and personnel]

The chairman, each commissioner and such personnel of the Fair Trade Commission as may be stipulated by a Cabinet Ordinance shall not engage in any one of the following activities while he is in office:

(i) Becoming a member of the Diet or of the legislative assembly of a local public authority, or actively engage in political activities;

(ii) Holding any other remunerative position except as permitted by the Prime Minister; or

(iii) Engaging in commerce or any other business for pecuniary gain.

Sec. 38 [Prohibition of expression of opinion]

The chairman, each commissioner and other personnel of the Fair Trade Commission shall not express their views outside the Fair Trade Commission on the existence or non-existence of facts or application of law with regard to a case of violation: Provided, That the foregoing shall not apply to cases provided for in this Act or where the presentation of the results of his study concerning this Act is made.

Sec. 39 [Duty to preserve trade secrets]

The chairman, each commissioner and other personnel of the Fair Trade Commission, or any person who once held such position, shall not divulge or make surreptitious use of trade secrets of entrepreneurs which came to their knowledge in the course of their duties.

Sec. 40 [Compulsory powers of inquiry]

The Fair Trade Commission may, if necessary for the performance of its functions, order government agencies, legal entities established by a special law or an order, entrepreneurs, or organizations of entrepreneurs, or their personnel to appear before the Commission, or may require them to submit necessary reports, information or data.

Sec. 41 [Entrustment of research and surveys]

The Fair Trade Commission may, if necessary for the performance of its functions, entrust government agencies, legal entities established by a special law or an order, schools, entrepreneurs, organizations of entrepreneurs, or persons of learning and experience to carry out necessary research and surveys.

Sec. 42 [Public hearings]

The Fair Trade Commission may, if necessary for the performance of its duties, hold public hearings to obtain views of the public.

Sec. 43 [Publication of appropriate matters]

The Fair Trade Commission may, in order to ensure proper enforcement of this Act, make public any appropriate matters with the exception of trade secrets of entrepreneurs.

Sec. 44 [Reports to the Diet, submission of opinions]

(1) The Fair Trade Commission shall submit to the Diet, through the Prime Minister, an annual report on the enforcement of this Act. In this case, the report shall contain an outline of the report ordered to be submitted under the provisions of Section 18-2(1) [reporting requirement on parallel price increases].

(2) The Fair Trade Commission may submit to the Diet, through the Prime Minister, its views on matters necessary to attain the purpose of this Act.

Division II Procedures

Sec. 45 [Report and detection of violation]

(1) Any person may, when he considers that a fact in violation of this Act exists, report the said fact to the Fair Trade Commission and ask for the appropriate measures to be taken.

(2) The Fair Trade Commission, upon receipt of such report as provided for in the preceding subsection, shall make necessary investigation with respect to the case.

(3) Where any report submitted under the provisions of subsection (1) above specifies in writing any fact or facts in accordance with the Rules of the Fair Trade Commission, and when the Commission decides to take, or not to take, appropriate measures with respect to the case referred to in the report, the Fair Trade Commission shall promptly notify that effect to the person who made such report.

(4) The Fair Trade Commission may, when it considers that a violation of this Act or a monopolistic situation exists, take appropriate measures on its own authority.

Sec. 45-2 [Procedures for measures against a monopolistic situation]

(1) The Fair Trade Commission shall, if it considers that there exists a fact which falls under the purview of a monopolistic situation, and if it decides to take a measure set forth in subsection (3) of the preceding section, make a notice of such action to the competent minister having jurisdiction over business in which the entrepreneur concerned is engaged.

(2) In case a notice under the provision of the preceding subsection has been made, the minister may present to the Commission his view regarding the existence or the absence of such a monopolistic situation and his view regarding other alternative measures which he feels would be sufficient to restore competition as provided for in the proviso to Section 8-4(1) [measures against a monopolistic situation].

Sec. 46 [Compulsory measures for investigation]

(1) The Fair Trade Commission may, in order to conduct the necessary investigation with regard to a case of violation, take any one of the following measures:

(i) Ordering persons concerned with a case, or witnesses to appear for interrogating, hearing their views or collecting reports from them;
(ii) Ordering experts to appear to have them give expert testimony;
(iii) Ordering persons holding accounting books, documents and other matters to submit the same, or to retain such submitted matters; or
(iv) Entering any place of business of the persons concerned with a case, or other necessary places and inspecting conditions of business operation and property, accounting books, documents and other matters.

(2) The Fair Trade Commission may, when it finds it proper, designate, in accordance with the provisions of a Cabinet Ordinance, investigators from among the personnel of the Fair Trade Commission and cause them to take the measures as provided for in the preceding subsection.

(3) Where an inspection is to be conducted by the personnel in accordance with the provisions of the preceding subsection, they shall be required to carry their identification cards and to show it to the persons concerned.

(4) The authority to take action pursuant to the provision of subsection (1) above shall not be construed as one granted for criminal investigation.

Sec. 47 [Investigation record]

The Fair Trade Commission shall, when it has conducted the necessary investigation of a case of violation, keep an investigation record of the main points thereof, and when it has taken any measures as provided for in the preceding section, it shall set out the result thereof.

Sec. 48 [Recommendation to the violator to take elimination measures, Recommendation decision]

(1) The Fair Trade Commission may, when it finds that there exists any act in violation of the provisions of Section 3 [prohibition of private monopolization or unreasonable restraint of trade], Section 6(1) [prohibition of particular international agreements or contracts], or (2) [filing requirement of the same], Section 8 [prohibited acts of a trade association], Section 9(1) or (2) [prohibition of a holding company], Section 9-2(1) [restriction on total amount of stockholding by a giant non-financial company], Section 10 [prohibition of particular stockholding by a company], Section 11 [restriction on stockholding rate by a financial company],

Section 13 [prohibition of particular interlocking directorates], Section 14 [prohibition of particular stockholding by a person other than a company], Section 15(1) [prohibition of particular mergers] (including such cases where the said provisions are applied mutatis mutandis by Section 16 [prohibition of particular acquisitions of business, etc.]), Section 17 [prohibition of evasion] or Section 19 [prohibition of unfair trade practices], recommend the persons who have committed such violation (including the officers and managers of a trade association and its constituent entrepreneurs when the violating act relates to the provisions of Section 8) to take appropriate measures.

(2) The Fair Trade Commission may, if it finds that any act in violation of the provisions of Section 3 [prohibition of private monopolization or unreasonable restraint of trade], Section 8(1) [prohibited acts of a trade association] (i), (iv) or (v) or Section 19 [prohibition of unfair trade practices], has already ceased to exist, and if it finds it particularly necessary, recommend to the person who committed such violation (including the officers and managers of such trade association and its constituent entrepreneurs when the violating act relates to the provisions of Section 8(1)(i), (iv) or (v)) to take appropriate measures.

(3) Any person who has received a recommendation under the provisions of the preceding subsection shall notify without delay to the Fair Trade Commission whether or not he accepts the said recommendation.

(4) The Fair Trade Commission may, when the person receiving the recommendation under the provisions of the preceding two subsections has accepted it, render a decision on the line of the said recommendation without resorting to the hearing procedures.

Sec. 48-2   [Procedures for surcharges]

(1) The Fair Trade Commission shall, when it finds there exists a fact as provided for in subsection (1) [surcharges] of Section 7-2 (including cases where this provision is applicable mutatis mutandis under Section 8-3 [surcharges against constituent entrepreneurs]; hereinafter the same in this section), order the entrepreneur or the constituent entrepreneurs of the trade association (or other entrepreneur in case a constituent entrepreneur is acting for the benefit of the other entrepreneur; hereinafter the same in this section) to pay to the Treasury a surcharge as prescribed in Section 7-2 (1) or (2): Provided, That in case hearing procedures have been initiated with respect to such violating act, such order shall not be issued by such time as such procedures have been completed.

(2) An order prescribed in the preceding subsection (hereinafter referred to as "payment order") shall be made by serving to such entrepreneur a certified copy of such payment order which states the amount of the surcharge

to be paid, the basis of calculation of such amount, the violating act responsible for such surcharge and the deadline for payment.

(3) The deadline for payment of such surcharge as prescribed in the preceding subsection shall fall on a date two months after the date on which such payment order is forwarded.

(4) The Fair Trade Commission shall, when it contemplates issuing a payment order, give in advance, the entrepreneur or the constituent entrepreneur of the trade association concerned, an opportunity to present his views and to submit evidence in support thereof.

(5) If any person is dissatisfied with a payment order, he may, in accordance with the Rules of the Fair Trade Commission and within thirty days from the date on which the certified copy of such order was forwarded, request the Commission to initiate hearing procedures on the said case.

(6) Except in cases where such a decision was rendered pursuant to the provisions of subsection (4) of the preceding section, Section 53-3 [consent decision] or Section 54 [formal decision] with respect to the said violating act, a payment order shall be deemed final and conclusive for the purpose of applying the provisions of Section 26 [restriction on exercise of the right to claim for damages in court, prescription], after the lapse of the period prescribed in the preceding subsection.

Sec. 49   [Initiation of hearing procedures]

(1) The Fair Trade Commission may, in the case of Section 48(1) or (2) [recommendation to the violator to take elimination measures] or in the case where there exists a monopolistic situation (excluding the case provided for in the proviso to Section 8-4(1) [measures against a monopolistic situation]. The same shall apply in Section 54(1) [formal decision], and if it finds that it would be in the public interest to initiate hearing procedures on the case, initiate hearing procedures on the said case.

(2) When a request as prescribed in subsection (5) of the preceding section is filed, the Fair Trade Commission shall, except in cases where it rejects the said request as unlawful by a decision, without delay initiate the hearing procedures on the case which is the subject of such request.

(3) In case hearing procedures have been initiated pursuant to the provisions of the preceding subsection, the payment order issued relating to such case shall lose effect.

(4) The Fair Trade Commission shall, when it contemplates initiating hearing procedures on a case relating to Section 8-4(1) [measures against a

monopolistic situation], consult with the competent minister having jurisdiction over the business in which such entrepreneur is engaged.

Sec. 50 [Complaints, initiation of hearing procedures]

(1) The complaint shall be made in writing, in which the outline of the case shall be stated, and the chairman and the commissioners participating in the voting of the decision to issue the complaint shall sign it and affix their seal thereto.

(2) The hearing procedures shall be initiated by serving a certified copy of the complaint upon a person to be ordered to take such measures (referred to as "elimination, etc. measures" in Section 52(1) [respondent's defense] as provided for in Section 7(1) [elimination measures] or (2) [elimination measures against already ceased violations] (including the cases applicable mutatis mutandis under the Section 8-2(2) and Section 20(2)), Section 8-2(1) or (3) [elimination measures], Section 8-4(1) [measures against a monopolistic situation], Section 17-2 [elimination measures] or Section 20(1) [elimination measures] or such person requesting the initiation of the hearing procedures in accordance with the provisions of Section 48-2(5) [request for initiation of hearing procedures on surcharges] (hereinafter referred to as "respondent").

(3) The respondent shall be ordered to appear on the date of the hearing proceedings.

(4) The date of the hearing proceeding shall be fixed on a day later than thirty days from the date of serving the certified copy of the complaint: Provided, That the foregoing shall not apply when the consent of the respondent is obtained.

Sec. 51 [Answers]

A respondent shall, upon receipt of the certified copy of the complaint, submit an answer without delay to the Fair Trade Commission.

Sec. 51-2 [Entrusted proceedings by hearing examiners]

The Fair Trade Commission may, after issuing a complaint, entrust hearing examiners to conduct a part of the hearing procedures (excluding the decision) in addition to taking the measures under each paragraph of Section 46(1) [compulsory measures for investigation], in accordance with the Rules of the Fair Trade Commission: Provided, That this shall not apply to such person or persons who have performed the duty as the investigator of the said case or those who have intervened in the investigation of the said case.

Sec. 51-3   [Powers of investigators at hearing proceedings]

An investigator designated in accordance with the provisions of Section 46(2) [designation of investigators], may attend hearing proceedings, request evidence to be adopted, and perform other necessary acts.

Sec. 52   [Respondent's defense]

(1) A respondent or his representative may, at hearing proceedings, state the reason why an order of the Fair Trade Commission to take elimination, etc. measures or to pay a surcharge under the provisions of Section 7-2(1) [surcharges] (including such case when the said provisions are applied mutatis mutandis by Section 8-3 [surcharges against constituent entrepreneurs]) in regard to the said case should not be made, submit supporting evidence therefor, request the Fair Trade Commission to interrogate necessary witnesses, to order expert witnesses to testify, to order holders of accounting books, documents and other matters to submit them, or to enter the necessary places and inspect the conditions of business and property, accounting books and other matters, or may interrogate witnesses or expert witnesses who are required to attend the hearing proceedings by order of the Fair Trade Commission.

(2) A respondent may be represented by an attorney at law or any other appropriate persons approved by the Fair Trade Commission.

Sec. 52-2   [Disclosure of reasons for non-adoption of evidence]

In case the Fair Trade Commission has not adopted any evidence introduced by the investigator, the respondent or his representative, the Commission shall state the reason for not having adopted such evidence.

Sec. 52-3   [Non-appearance of respondents]

The Fair Trade Commission may conduct the hearing proceedings even if the respondent or his representative fails to appear on the date of the said hearing proceedings without a justifiable cause.

Sec. 53   [Hearing proceedings, stenographic record]

(1) All hearing proceedings shall be made public: Provided, That when it is found necessary to protect the trade secrets of an entrepreneur, or necessary to the public interest, a hearing proceeding shall not be made public.

(2) A stenographer shall attend all hearing proceedings to record statements made therein.

Sec. 53-2 [Qualification for witness, right to refuse testimony, oath, etc.]

(1) The provisions of Sections 143 to 147 inclusive [principles on quali-fication for witness, relationship between public service secret and witness qualification, responsibility of oneself or close relatives and the right to refuse testimony], Section 149 [qualification for witness, the right to refuse testimony], Sections 154 to 156 inclusive [oath of witness, testimony of estimated matters], Section 165 [expert witnesses], and Section 166 [oath of expert witnesses] of the Code of Criminal Procedures shall apply mutatis mutandis to the procedures by which the Fair Trade Commission or hearing examiners, in the course of hearing proceedings, interrogate a witness, or order an expert to give his testimony.

(2) In such cases as provided for in the preceding subsection, the terms "court," "question", and "defendant" shall read as "the Fair Trade Commission or hearing examiners", "interrogate" and "respondent" respec-tively.

Sec. 53-2-2 [Opportunity to state the case directly to the Commission]

In case the Fair Trade Commission has entrusted hearing examiners to conduct a part of the hearing procedures in accordance with the provisions of Section 51-2 [entrusted proceedings by hearing examiners], if the respon-dent or his representative so requests, the Commission shall give the respon-dent or his representative an opportunity to state their views directly to the Commission: Provided, That this shall not apply to a case in which the hear-ing procedures have been initiated pursuant to the provision of Section 49(2) [initiation of hearing procedures on surcharges] and a decision has been rendered with respect to the violating act of such case pursuant to the provision of Section 48(4) [recommendation decision], the following section [consent decision] or Section 54 [formal decision].

Sec. 53-3 [Consent decision]

The Fair Trade Commission may, after determined to initiate the hearing procedures, when the respondent, admitting the findings of fact and the application of law stated in the complaint, submits to the Fair Trade Com-mission a written statement setting forth that he will accept the decision without resorting to subsequent hearing proceedings, and files a plan setting forth concrete measures which he proposes voluntarily to take in order to eliminate such violation, or to ensure the elimination of such violation, or to restore competition with respect to the goods or services involved in the monopolistic situation, if the Commission finds it appropriate, render a decision on the line of the concrete measures as stated in such plan without subsequent hearing proceedings.

Sec. 54   [Formal decision]

(1) The Fair Trade Commission shall, when it finds after hearing proceedings that violation of the provisions of Section 3 [prohibition of private monopolization or unreasonable restraint of trade], Section 6(1) [prohibition of particular international agreements or contracts] or (2) [filing requirement of the same], Section 8 [prohibited acts of a trade association], Section 9(1) or (2) [prohibition of holding company], Section 9-2(1) [restriction on total amount of stockholding by a non-financial giant company], Section 10 [prohibition of particular stockholding by a company], Section 11(1) [restriction on stockholding rate by a financial company], Section 13 [prohibition of particular interlocking directorates], Section 14 [prohibition of particular stockholding by a person other than a company], Section 15(1) [prohibition of particular mergers] (including such cases where the said provisions are applied mutatis mutandis by Section 16 [prohibition of particular acquisition of business, etc.]), Section 17 [prohibition of evasion] or Section 19 [prohibition of unfair trade practices] exists or that a monopolistic situation exists, order the respondent by a decision to take such measures as provided for in Section 7(1) [elimination measures], Section 8-2(1) or (3) [elimination measures] or Section 8-4(1) [measures against a monopolistic situation].

(2) The Fair Trade Commission shall, when it finds after hearing proceedings that such act in violation of the provisions of Section 3 [prohibition of private monopolization or unreasonable restraint of trade], Section 8(1) [prohibited acts of a trade association] (i), (iv) or (v) or Section 19 [prohibition of unfair trade practices] no longer exists and if it finds it particularly necessary, order, by a decision, the respondent to take the measures provided for in Section 7(2) [measures against already ceased violations] (including cases to which the said subsection is applicable mutatis mutandis in Section 8-2(2) and Section 20(2)).

(3) The Fair Trade Commission shall, when it finds after hearing proceedings that such acts or a monopolistic situation as provided for in subsection (1) did not exist at the time when it issued the complaint, that such acts as provided for in the said subsection or a monopolistic situation existed by the time of the issuance of the complaint, but the said acts or a monopolistic situation have already ceased to exist (excluding the decision under the preceding subsection), or that a monopolistic situation exists and falls under the proviso to Section 8-4(1), make clear the said fact by a decision.

Sec. 54-2 [Surcharge payment order]

(1) The Fair Trade Commission shall, when it finds after hearing proceedings a fact as provided for in Section 7-2(1) [surcharges] (including cases where this provision is applicable mutatis mutandis by Section 8-3 [surcharges against constituent entrepreneurs]), order, by a decision, the respondent to pay to the Treasury a surcharge levied on such violation.

(2) The provisions of Section 48-2(3) [deadline for payment of surcharges] shall apply mutatis mutandis to a decision provided for in the preceding subsection.

Sec. 54-3 [Findings based on evidence]

In rendering a decision as provided for in the preceding two sections, the Fair Trade Commission shall, except in the case of facts not challenged by the respondent or known publicly, find the facts in question based on the evidences examined at the hearing procedures.

Sec. 55 [Meetings for decision]

(1) Decisions shall be made by meeting of the chairman and the commissioners.

(2) The provisions of Section 34(1), (2) and (4) [quorum and voting] shall apply mutatis mutandis to such meetings as provided for in the preceding subsection.

(3) For a decision ordering the respondent or respondents to take the measures provided for in Section 8-4(1) [measures against a monopolistic situation], the decision shall be supported by three or more commissioners or chairman, notwithstanding the provisions of Section 34(2) which are applied mutatis mutandis by the preceding subsection.

Sec. 56 [Closed meetings]

Meetings of the Fair Trade Commission shall not be made public.

Sec. 57 [Form of decision]

(1) Decisions shall be rendered in writing; and the written decisions shall show the fact found by and the application of law thereto made by the Fair Trade Commission and in the case of the decision under Section 54-2(1) [surcharge payment order], the basis of calculating the surcharge; and the chairman and the commissioners participating in the voting shall sign it and affix their seal thereto.

(2) A dissenting opinion may be stated in a written decision.

Sec. 58   [Effective date of decision]

(1) A decision shall take effect from the time when the certified copy of the written decision has been served to the respondent.

(2) Any decision ordering the respondent or respondents to take the measures provided for in Section 8-4(2) [measures against a monopolistic situation] shall not be enforced unless and until such decision becomes final and conclusive.

Sec. 59   [Interventions of the third parties interested]

The Fair Trade Commission may, if it finds it necessary, cause, on its own authority, a third person interested in the result of the decision, to be a party to the hearing procedures: Provided, That it shall in advance interrogate the respondent and the said third party.

Sec. 60   [Interventions of a government agency or public organization]

Any government agency or public organization interested in a case may, if it finds it necessary in the public interest, intervene in the hearing procedures as a party with the approval of the Fair Trade Commission.

Sec. 61   [Opinions of a government agency or public organization]

Any government agency or public organization interested in a case may, in order to protect the public interest, express its views to the Fair Trade Commission.

Sec. 62   [Stay of execution of FTC's order by deposit]

(1) When the Fair Trade Commission has ordered by a decision to cease and desist from acts constituting violations or any other measures in accordance with the provisions of Section 54(1) or (2) [formal decision], the respondent may stay the execution of the said order by depositing such bond or securities as may be fixed by the court until the said decision becomes final and conclusive.

(2) The court ruling under the provisions of the preceding subsection shall be made in accordance with the Act of Procedures in Non-Contentious Matters.

Sec. 63 [Forfeitures of deposit]

(1) In a case where a respondent has made the deposit in accordance with the provisions of subsection (1) of the preceding section and the decision in question has become final and conclusive, the court may, upon application of the Fair Trade Commission, forfeit the whole or a part of such bond or securities deposited.

(2) The provisions of subsection (2) of the preceding section shall apply mutatis mutandis to the court ruling under the provisions of the preceding subsection.

Sec. 64 [Compulsory measures for investigation after decision]

The Fair Trade Commission may, if it considers particularly necessary after a decision rendered in accordance with the provisions of Section 54(1) or (2) [formal decision], take measures or may cause its personnel to take measures in accordance with the provisions of Section 46 [compulsory measures for investigation].

Sec. 64-2 [A reminder for payment of surcharge and measures against delinquency]

(1) If any person fails to pay a surcharge by the designated deadline, the Fair Trade Commission shall press such person to pay the surcharge by serving a written reminder specifying a deadline therefor.

(2) In case a reminder is served pursuant to the provisions of the preceding subsection, the Fair Trade Commission may collect an arrearage charge computed at a rate of 14.5 percent per annum of the amount of such surcharge as prescribed in the said subsection for the number of days intervening between the date immediately following the deadline and the date of payment: Provided, That this shall not apply to cases where the arrearage charge involved is less than one thousand yen.

(3) In case the amount of an arrearage charge, computed in accordance with the provisions of the preceding subsection, contains a fraction of less than one hundred yen, such fraction shall be disregarded.

(4) In case any person on whom a reminder has been served under the provisions of subsection (1) fails to pay a surcharge overdue, the Fair Trade Commission may collect such surcharge based on the example of the national tax delinquency procedures.

(5) The claim on a defaulted surcharge as prescribed in the preceding subsection shall have a lien next to those of the national and local taxes, and the prescription on such claim shall be the same as that of the national tax.

Sec. 65   [Dismissal of application for authorization, etc.]

(1) The Fair Trade Commission shall, when an application for authorization under the provisions of Section 9-2(1)(vi) [application for authorization of holding of stock of joint ventures with a foreign person, etc. by a giant non-financial company], Section 11(1) or (2) [application for authorization of stockholding by a financial company], Section 24-3(2) or (3) [application for authorization of depression cartels], or 24-4(2) [application for authorization of rationalization cartels] or an application for approval under the provision of Section 9-2(1)(ix) [application for approval of stockholding by imperative reasons by a giant non-financial company] has been filed and if it finds the said application to be groundless, dismiss it by a decision.

(2) The provisions of Section 45(2) [investigation in case of report of a violation] shall apply mutatis mutandis to the application for authorization or approval in the preceding subsection.

Sec. 66   [Revocation or modification of authorization, approval or decision]

(1) The Fair Trade Commission may, when it finds, with respect to the authorization or approval as prescribed in subsection (1) of the preceding section, that the facts required for the said authorization or approval have ceased to exist or have changed, revoke or modify such authorization or approval after hearing procedures.

(2) The Fair Trade Commission may, when it finds that further maintenance of a decision is unreasonable and contrary to the public interest due to the changes in economic conditions and to other reasons, revoke or modify it by a decision: Provided, That the foregoing shall not apply if the interest of the respondent may be injured thereby.

Sec. 67 [Urgent injunction]

(1) The court may, upon application of the Fair Trade Commission, when it finds the matter to be one of urgent necessity, order the person doing an act suspected of violation of the provisions of Section 3 [prohibition of private monopolization or unreasonable restraint of trade], Section 6(1) [prohibition of particular international agreements or contracts], Section 8(1) [prohibited acts of a trade association], Section 9(1) or (2) [prohibition of holding company], Section 9-2(1) [restriction on total amount of stockholding by a non-financial giant company], Section 10(1) [prohibition of particular stockholding by a company], Section 11(1) [restriction on stockholding rate by a financial company], Section 13(1) or (2) [prohibition of particular interlocking directorates], Section 14(1) [prohibition of particular stockholding by a person other than a company],

Section 15(1) [prohibition of particular mergers] (including such cases where the said provisions are applied mutatis mutandis by Section 16 [prohibition of particular acquisitions of business, etc.]), Section 17 [prohibition of evasion] or Section 19 [prohibition of unfair trade practices], temporarily to cease and desist from the said act, the exercise of voting rights or the execution of duties as an officer in a company, or may rescind or modify such order.

(2) The court may, upon application of the Fair Trade Commission, when it finds the matter to be one of urgent necessity, order the person who has obtained authorization under the provisions of Section 24-3(2) or (3) [authorization of depression cartels] or 24-4(2) [authorization of rationalization cartels], when there is a reason to suspect, in view of the provisions of Section 66(1) [revocation or modification of authorization], that conditions necessitating revocation or modification of such authorization under Section 24-3(2) or (3), or 24-4(2) have arisen, temporarily to suspend the said authorized activity, or may revoke or modify such order.

(3) The provisions of Section 62(2) [mutatis mutandis application of the Act of Procedures on Non-contentious Matters] shall apply mutatis mutandis to the court ruling under the provisions of the preceding two subsections.

Sec. 68   [Stay of urgent injunction]

(1) The execution of an urgent injunction under the provisions of the preceding subsection (1) or (2), may be stayed by depositing such bond or securities as the court may fix.

(2) The provisions of Section 63 [forfeitures of deposit] shall apply mutatis mutandis to forfeiture of deposit under the provisions of the preceding subsection.

Sec. 69   [Access to records]

Any interested person may request to the Fair Trade Commission, after the issuance of a complaint, to peruse or copy the record of a case, or may ask the Fair Trade Commission for a certified copy of a surcharge payment order or a decision or an abridged copy thereof.

Sec. 69-2   [Service]

With regard to the service of documents, the provisions of Section 162 [service agent], Section 169 [place of service, service by meeting], Section 171 [supplementary service, service by leaving] and Section 177 [certificate for service] of the Code of Civil Procedures shall apply mutatis mutandis. In this case, the terms "marshal" and "court clerk" shall read as "personnel of the Fair Trade Commission" and the term "court" shall read as "the Fair Trade Commission".

Sec. 70 [Matters to be provided for by a Cabinet Ordinance]

Necessary matters with respect to procedures for investigation and hearing proceedings of the Fair Trade Commission, any other matters relating to the disposal of cases as well as those with respect to deposit under Section 62(1) [stay of execution of FTC's order by deposit] and Section 68(1) [stay of urgent injunction] shall be provided for by a Cabinet Ordinance except for such matters as are provided for in this Act.

Sec. 70-2 [Special provisions for appeals]

The decision or any other measures (including the measures effected by an investigator under the provisions of Section 46(2) [designation of and measures by investigators] or by hearing examiners under Section 51-2 [entrusted proceedings by hearing examiners]) that has been rendered by the Fair Trade Commission under the provisions of this Division shall not be appealed under the Administrative Complaint Review Act (Act No. 160 of 1962).

Division III   Miscellaneous Provisions

Sec. 71 [Procedures for designation of unfair trade practices in a specific field of business]

The Fair Trade Commission shall, when it designates specific trade practices in a specific field of business in accordance with the provisions of Section 2(9) [designation of unfair trade practices], first hear the views of entrepreneurs operating in the same line of business as that of the entrepreneurs who employ the said specific trade practices, and hold a public hearing to obtain the views of the public and thereupon shall make the designation after due consideration of the views presented.

Sec. 72 [Designation of unfair trade practices by means of a notification]

Designation under the provisions of Section 2(9) [designation of unfair trade practices] shall be made by a notification.

Sec. 72-2 [Public hearing on a monopolistic situation]

In case the Fair Trade Commission tries to initiate the hearing procedures on a case as prescribed in Section 8-4(1) [measures against a monopolistic situation], the Commission shall hold a public hearing to obtain views of the public.

Sec. 73   [Accusation, report on non-prosecution]

(1) The Fair Trade Commission shall, when it considers that a crime violating the provisions of this Act exists, file an accusation with the Public Prosecutor General.

(2) The Public Prosecutor General shall, when he has taken measures not to prosecute in a case which is the subject of an accusation under the provisions of the preceding subsection, without delay, submit to the Prime Minister through the Minister of Justice a written report stating the said fact and reasons therefor.

Sec. 74   [Public Prosecutor General's request for FTC's investigation, etc.]

The Public Prosecutor General may, when he considers that a crime violating the provisions of this Act exists, notify the Fair Trade Commission of the fact, and request it to investigate and report thereon.

Sec. 75   [Compensation for witnesses or expert witness]

Witnesses or expert witness who have been ordered to appear or to give expert testimony in a hearing proceeding in accordance with the provisions of Section 46(1)(i) [FTC's order to witnesses to appear, etc.] or (ii) [FTC's order to expert witness to appear, etc.], or (2) [investigator's order to the same effect] or Section 51-2 [hearing examiners' order to the same effect], may claim a traveling allowance and fees as provided for by a Cabinet Ordinance.

Sec. 76   [Rule-making powers of FTC]

The Fair Trade Commission may establish rules with respect to its internal disciplines, procedures for disposing cases and any necessary procedures relating to filing a report, applications for authorization or approval and other matters.

CHAPTER IX   SUITS

Sec. 77   [Filing of a suit to quash a decision]

(1) A suit to quash a decision of the Fair Trade Commission shall be filed within thirty days (three months in case of the decision under the provisions of Section 8-4(1) [measures against a monopolistic situation]) from the date on which the decision became effective.

(2) The time period stated in the preceding subsection shall be peremptory.

Sec. 78 [Transmission of records]

The court shall, upon receipt of a suit, request the Fair Trade Commission without delay, to transmit the records of the case concerned (including interrogation records of persons concerned in the case, witnesses or expert witness, stenographic records, and any other matters that may be used as evidences in court).

Sec. 79

Deleted. (Act No. 140 of 1962)

Sec. 80 [Binding authority of FTC's findings]

(1) Findings of fact made by the Fair Trade Commission shall, if established by substantial evidence, be binding upon the court in regard to the suit provided for in Section 77(1) [filing of a suit to quash a decision].

(2) Whether such substantial evidence as provided for in the preceding subsection exists or not shall be determined by the court.

Sec. 81 [Offering of new evidence, reference back of the case to FTC]

(1) A party may plead to the court for offer to introduce new evidence relevant to the case: Provided, That any such offer to introduce new evidence relating to the facts found by the Fair Trade Commission shall have the reason which come under any one of the following paragraphs:

(i) Where the Fair Trade Commission failed to adopt the evidence without good cause; or

(ii) Where it was impossible to adduce evidence at hearing proceedings of the Fair Trade Commission, and there was no gross negligence on the part of the party in failing to adduce such evidence.

(2) In the cases prescribed in proviso to the preceding subsection, the onus shall be on the party concerned to show either of the reasons provided for in the preceding subsection.

(3) When the court finds there is a reason for offer to introduce new evidence under proviso to subsection (1) and it is necessary to examine such evidence, it shall refer the case back to the Fair Trade Commission and order it to take appropriate measures after examining such evidence.

Sec. 82 [Quashing decisions]

The court may quash a decision of the Fair Trade Commission if the decision falls under any one of the following paragraphs:

(i)   If the facts on which the decision is based are not established by substantial evidence, or

(ii)   If the decision is violating the Constitution, or other laws or orders.

Sec. 83   [Reference back of a decision]

The court may, when it finds it necessary that further hearing proceedings shall be conducted in a case where it shall quash a decision of the Fair Trade Commission, refer the case back to the Fair Trade Commission giving the reasons therefor.

Sec. 84   [Request for FTC's opinion on amount of damages]

(1) When a suit for indemnification of damages under the provisions of Section 25 [absolute liability] has been filed, the court shall, without delay, request the opinion of the Fair Trade Commission with respect to the amount of damages caused by such violations as provided for in the said section.

(2) If a counter claim for indemnification of damages under the provisions of Section 25 is made in court proceedings for the purpose of offsetting the other claim, the provisions of the preceding subsection shall apply mutatis mutandis.

Sec. 85   [Original jurisdiction]

Original jurisdiction over any suit coming under any one of the following paragraphs shall lie in the Tokyo High Court:

(i)   A suit concerning a decision of the Fair Trade Commission;

(ii)   A suit concerning indemnification of damages under the provisions of Section 25 (absolute liability); or

(iii)   A suit concerning offenses as provided for in Sections 89 to 91 inclusive.

Sec. 86   [Exclusive jurisdiction of the Tokyo High Court]

Any case stipulated in Section 62(1) [stay of execution of FTC's decision by deposit], Section 63(1) [forfeitures of deposit] (including cases where the said provisions are applied mutatis mutandis by Section 68(2) [stay of urgent injunction]), Section 67(1) and (2) [urgent injunction], Section 97 [administrative fines for contraventions of decisions] and Section 98 [administrative fines for disobeying urgent injunction] shall be under the exclusive jurisdiction of the Tokyo High Court.

Sec. 87   [Special panel in the Tokyo High Court]

(1) A panel of judges invested with the jurisdiction to hear exclusively the suit provided for in Section 85 [original jurisdiction] and such cases as stipulated in the preceding section shall be established within the Tokyo High Court.

(2) The number of judges in the panel under the preceding subsection shall be five.

Sec. 88   [Suit for the cancellation of authorization of depression cartel or rationalization cartel]

A suit for the cancellation of authorization under the provisions of Section 24-3(2) or (3) [authorization of depression cartels], or Section 24-4(2) [authorization of rationalization cartels] may not be filed unless and until a ruling on the objection to the authorization has been rendered.

Sec. 88-2   [Special provisions for suits relating to FTC decisions]

With respect to a suit relating to a decision of the Fair Trade Commission, the provisions of Section 6 [Minister of Justice's guidance, etc. to administrative agencies on suits] of the Act concerning the Authority of the Minister of Justice over the Suits in which Interests of State Are Involved (Act No. 194 of 1947) shall not apply.

CHAPTER IX-II   MISCELLANEOUS PROVISIONS

Sec. 88-3   [Interim measures]

In case any Cabinet Ordinance or Rules of the Fair Trade Commission is instituted, amended or repealed in accordance with the provisions of this Act, necessary interim measures (including those relating to penal provisions) may be provided for by virtue of such Cabinet Ordinance or Rules of the Fair Trade Commission to the extent deemed reasonably necessary as a consequence of such institution, amendment or repeal.

CHAPTER X   PENAL PROVISIONS

Sec. 89   [Penalties against private monopolization or unreasonable restraint of trade, or substantial restraint of competition by a trade association]

(1) Any person committing one of the following offenses shall be punished by penal servitude for not more than three years or by a fine of not more than five million yen:

 (i) Any person who, in violation of the provisions of Section 3 [prohibition of private monopolization or unreasonable restraint of trade], effected private monopolization or unreasonable restraint of trade; or

 (ii) Any person a who, in violation of the provisions of Section 8(1) [prohibited acts of a trade association] (i), effected substantial restraint of competition in any particular field of trade.

(2) An attempt to commit an offense falling under the preceding subsection shall be punished.

Sec. 90   [Penalties against prohibited international agreements or contracts, prohibited acts of trade association, or non-observance of final and conclusive decision]

(1) Any person committing one of the following offenses shall be punished by penal servitude for not more than two years or by a fine of not more than three million yen:

 (i) Any person who, in violation of the provisions of Section 6(1) [prohibition of particular international agreements or contracts) or Section 8(1)(ii) [prohibition of particular international agreements or contracts by a trade association] entered into an international agreement or an international contract which contains such matters as constitute unreasonable restraint of trade;

 (ii) Any person who violated the provisions of Section 8(1) (iii) [limiting the number of entrepreneurs by a trade association] or (iv) [restriction on function or activity of the constituent entrepreneur by a trade association]; or

 (iii) Any person who failed to comply with the decision as provided for in Section 48(4) [recommendation decision], Section 53-3 [consent decision] or Section 54(1) or (2) [formal decision], after it has become final and conclusive.

Sec. 91   [Penalties against holding company, prohibited stockholding or interlocking directorates, etc.]

Any person committing one of the following offenses shall be punished by penal servitude for not more than one year or by a fine of not more than two million yen:

(i)   Any person who, in violation of the provisions of Section 9(1) [prohibition of establishment of a holding company], established a holding company, or violated the provisions of subsection (2) [prohibition of operation as a holding company] of the said section;

(ii)   Any person who, in violation of the provisions of Section 9-2(1) [restriction on total amount of stockholding by a giant non-financial company], acquired or held stock;

(iii)   Any person who, in violation of the provisions of the first part of Section 10(1) [prohibition of particular stockholding by a company], acquired or held stock;

(iv)   Any person who, in violation of the provisions of Section 11(1) [restriction on stockholding rate by a financial company], acquired or held stock; or who, in violation of the provisions of subsection (2) of the said section, held stock;

(v)   Any person who, in violation of the provisions of Section 13(1) [prohibition of particular interlocking directorates], held concurrently positions as an officer of a company;

(vi)   Any person who, in violation of the provisions of the first part of Section 14(1) [prohibition of particular stockholding by a person other than a company], acquired or held stock; or

(vii)   Any person who, in violation of the provisions of Section 17 [prohibition of evasion], committed such prohibitions or restrictions prescribed in the paragraphs above.

Sec. 91-2 [Penalties against failure to file reports, etc.]

Any person committing one of the following offenses shall be punished by a fine of not more than two million yen:

(i)   Any person who, in violation of the provisions of Section 6(2) [filing requirement of specific international agreements or contracts], failed to file a report, or filed a false report;

(ii)   Any person who, in violation of the provisions of Section 8(2) to (4) inclusive [filing requirement of a trade association], failed to file a report, or filed a false report;

(iii)   Any person who, in violation of the provisions of Section 10(2) [filing requirement of stockholding by a company], failed to submit a report, or submitted a false report;

(iv)   Any person who, in violation of the provisions of Section 13(3) [filing requirement of interlocking directorates], failed to file a report, or filed a false report;

(v)   Any person who, in violation of the provisions of Section 14(2) [filing requirement of stockholding by a person other than a company], failed to submit a report, or submitted a false report;

(vi)   Any person who, in violation of the provisions of Section 15(2) [filing requirement of mergers] (including cases where the said provisions are applied mutatis mutandis by Section 16 [filing requirement of acquisitions of business, etc.]), failed to file a report, or filed a false report;

(vii) Any person who, in violation of the provisions of Section 15(3) [waiting period of mergers], effected registration of the establishment of a company by merger or the registration of change in the previously registered entry;

(viii) Any person who, in violation of the provisions of Section 15(3) [waiting period of mergers] which are applied mutatis mutandis by Section 16 [prohibition of particular acquisitions of business, etc.], carried out an act coming under any one of the paragraphs of Section 16;

(ix) Any person who, in violation of the provisions of Section 18-2(1) [filing requirement of a report on parallel price increases], failed to file a report, or filed a false report; or

(x) Any person who, in violation of the provisions of Section 24-2(6) [filing requirement of resale price contracts], failed to file a report or filed a false report.

Sec. 92 [Concurrent punishment]

Any person committing any one of the offenses stipulated in Sections 89 to 91 inclusive [penalties against private monopolization, unreasonable restraint of trade, prohibited acts of a trade association, prohibited international agreements or contracts, non-observance of final and conclusive decision, prohibited stockholding, etc.] may, according to the circumstances, be punished by both penal servitude and a fine.

Sec. 92-2 [Penalties against perjury]

(1) Where any witness or expert witness, who testified in accordance with the provisions of Section 53-2 [qualification for witness, right to refuse testimony, oath, etc.], made a false statement or expert testimony, he shall be punished by penal servitude from not less than three months to not more than ten years.

(2) Where a person committing an offense under the preceding subsection confesses his crime prior to the termination of the hearing proceedings and before the discovery of such offense, the penalty for such offense may be commuted or remitted.

Sec. 93 [Penalties against divulging secrets]

Any person who violated the provisions of Section 39 [duty to preserve trade secrets] shall be punished by penal servitude for not more than one year or by a fine of not more than one hundred thousand yen.

Sec. 94   [Penalties against interference with inspection, etc.]

Any person who refused, obstructed or evaded the inspection as provided for in Section 46(1)(iv) [inspection] or (2) [measures by investigator],
or Section 51-2 [entrusted proceedings by hearing examiners], shall be punished by penal servitude for not more than six months or by a fine of not
more than two hundred thousand yen.

Sec. 94-2   [Penalties against non-compliance with compulsory measures]

Any person coming under any one of the following paragraphs shall be
punished by a fine of not more than two hundred thousand yen:

(i)   Any person who, in violation of such orders as provided for in Section
       40 [compulsory powers for inquiry], failed to appear or to submit a
       report, information or data, or submitted a false report, information or
       data;

(ii)   Any person concerned with a case or any witness who, in violation of the
       order issued to him under the provisions of Section 46(1)(i) [interroga-
       tion of persons concerned with a case or witnesses by the Commission]
       or (2) [measures by investigators], or Section 51-2 [entrusted proceed-
       ings by hearing examiners], failed to appear or to give testimony, or
       gave a false testimony, or failed to submit a report, or submitted a false
       report;

(iii) Any person who, in violation of the order issued to an expert witness
       under the provisions of Section 46(1)(ii) [FTC's order to make expert
       testimony, etc.] or (2), or Section 51-2, failed to appear or to give expert
       testimony, or gave a false expert testimony;

(iv)   Any person who, in violation of the order issued to the holder of the
       matters under the provisions of Section 46(1)(iii) [FTC's order to submit
       documents, etc.] or (2), or Section 51-2, failed to submit the same; or

(v)   Any person who, in violation of the order issued to a witness or an
       expert witness under the provisions of Section 154 (oath of witnesses) or
       Section 166 (oath of expert witnesses) of the Code of Criminal
       Procedures which are applied mutatis mutandis in Section 53-2 [qualifi-
       cation for witness, right to refuse testimony, oath, etc.], refused to take
       the oath.

Sec. 95   [Double punishment]

(1)   When a representative of a juridical person, or an agent, an employee
or any other person in the service of a juridical person or of an individual
has, with regard to the business or property of the said juridical person or
individual, committed a violation as provided for in each of the following
paragraphs, the said juridical person or the said individual shall be punished
by such fine as provided for in the said paragraphs in addition to the punishment of the offender.

(i)   Section 89 [penalties against private monopolization or unreasonable restraint of trade, or substantial restraint of competition by a trade association] Fine of not more than 100 million yen.

(ii)   Section 90 [penalties against prohibited international agreements or contracts, prohibted acts by a trade association, or non-observance of final and conclusive decision], Section 91 (excluding (v)) [penalties against holding company, prohibited stockholding, etc.]. Section 91-2 [penalties against failure to file reports, etc.], Section 94 [penalties against interference with inspection, etc.] Fine as provided for in each of the above sections.

(2) Where a representative, a manager, an agent, an employee or any other person in the service of a non-juridical organization has, with regard to the business or property of the said organization, committed a violation as provided for in each of the following paragraphs, the said non-juridical organization shall be punished by such fine as provided for in the said paragraphs in addition to the punishment of the offender.

(i)   Section 89 [penalties against private monopolization or unreasonable restraint of trade, or substantial restraint of competition by a trade association] Fine of not more than 100 million yen.

(ii)   Section 90 [penalties against prohibited international agreements or contracts, prohibited acts by a trade association, or non-observance of final and conclusive decision], Section 91 (i), (vi) or (vii) (limited to only those relating to (i) or (vi)), or Section 91-2 (i), (ii), (v) or (ix). Fine as provided for in each of the above sections.

Sec. 95-2   [Punishment of representatives of juridical persons who failed to prevent violation]

In case of a violation of Section 89(1)(i) [penalties against private monopolization or unreasonable restraint of trade], Section 90(i) [penalties against prohibited international agreements or contracts relating to unreasonable restraint of trade] or (iii) [non-observance of final and conclusive decision] or Section 91 [penalties against holding company, prohibited stockholding, etc.] (excluding (v)), the representative of a juridical person (excluding those who come under a trade association in case of violation of section 90(i) or (iii)) who failed to take necessary measures to prevent such violation knowingly of the existence of such a plan or who failed to take necessary measures to rectify such violation knowingly of the existence of such violation, shall also be punished by such a fine as provided for in the relevant sections.

Sec. 95-3 [Punishment of directors, etc. of trade associations who failed to prevent violation]

(1) Where a violation of Section 89(1)(ii) [penalties against substantial restraint of competition by a trade association], or Section 90 was committed, a director or any other officer or a manager of a trade association or its constituent entrepreneurs (including another entrepreneur who was acted for by a constituent entrepreneur) who failed to take necessary measures to prevent such violation knowingly of the existence of such a plan or who failed to take necessary measures to rectify such violation knowingly of the existence of such violation, shall also be punished by such a fine as provided for in the relevant sections.

(2) Where a director or any other officer or a manager of a trade association or its constituent entrepreneurs as prescribed in the preceding subsection, is a juridical person or any other organization, the provision of the said subsection shall apply to such director or any other officer or a manager of the said organization.

Sec. 95-4 [Dissolution of trade associations]

(1) The court may, when it considers that the sufficient grounds exist, declare a trade association to be dissolved simultaneously with the imposition of a penalty as provided for in Section 89(1)(ii) [penalties against substantial restraint of competition by a trade association], or Section 90 [penalties against prohibited international agreement or contracts, prohibited acts by a trade association, non-observance of final and conclusive decision, etc.].

(2) When the dissolution has been declared in accordance with the provisions of the preceding subsection, the trade association shall be dissolved by such declaration, notwithstanding the provisions of any other law or order, or articles of association, or any other stipulations.

Sec. 96 [Exclusive accusation by the Fair Trade Commission]

(1) Any offense under Sections 89 to 91 inclusive [penalties against private monopolization or unreasonable restraint of trade, prohibited acts of a trade association, prohibited international agreements or contracts, non-observance of final and conclusive decision and prohibited stockholdings, etc.] shall be considered only after an accusation of the Fair Trade Commission has been filed.

(2) The accusation under the preceding subsection shall be made in writing.

(3) The Fair Trade Commission, in filing the accusation under subsection (1) may, when it considers it appropriate that the declaration under subsection (1) of the preceding section or Section 100(1)(i) [revocation of patent rights or patent licenses] should be made with respect to an offense under the accusation, state the said effect in the said accusation.

(4) The accusation under subsection (1) shall not be withdrawn after public prosecution has been instituted.

Sec. 97 [Administrative fines for contraventions of decisions]

Any person who contravened a decision under Section 48(4) [recommendation decision], Section 53-3 [consent decision] or Section 54(1) or (2) [formal decision] shall be liable to an administrative fine of not more than five hundred thousand yen: Provided, That the foregoing shall not apply when the said act shall be punished under the penal provisions.

Sec. 98 [Administrative fines for disobeying urgent injunction]

Any person who disobeyed a ruling of the court under the provisions of Section 67(1) or (2) [urgent injunction], shall be liable to an administrative fine of not more than three hundred thousand yen.

Sec. 99 Deleted. (Act No. 214 of 1949)

Sec. 100 [Revocation of patent rights or patent licenses and exclusion from government contracts]

(1) The court may, in a case coming under Section 89 [penalties against private monopolization or unreasonable restraint of trade, or substantial restraint of competition by a trade association] or Section 90 [penalties against prohibited international agreements or contracts, prohibited acts by a trade association, and non-observance of final and conclusive decision, etc.] according to circumstances, make the following declaration simultaneously with the sentence of penalties: Provided, That the declaration under paragraph (i) hereunder shall be made only when the said patent right, or exclusive or non-exclusive license for a patented invention belongs to the offender:

(i)   That the patent under patent right, or the exclusive or non-exclusive license for the patented invention to which the offense relates shall be revoked; or
(ii) That the offender shall be barred from becoming a party to a contract with the government for a period of not less than six months and not

more than three years after the date when the judgment became final and conclusive.

(2) When a judgment with the declaration as provided for in paragraph (i) of the preceding subsection becomes final and conclusive, the court shall transmit the certified copy thereof to the Director-General of the Patent Office.

(3) The Director-General of the Patent Office shall upon receipt of the certified copy of the judgment under the provisions of the preceding subsection, revoke the patent right, or the exclusive or non-exclusive license for the patented invention.

UNFAIR TRADE PRACTICES

UNFAIR TRADE PRACTICES
(Fair Trade Commission Notification No. 15, June 18, 1982)

In accordance with the provisions of Section 2(9) of Act Concerning Prohibition of Private Monopoly and Maintenance of Fair Trade (Act No. 54 of 1947), Unfair Trade Practices (the Fair Trade Commission Notification No. 11 of 1953) shall be totally amended as follows and put into force on September 1, 1982.

Unfair Trade Practices

(Concerted Refusal to Deal)

1. Without proper justification, taking an act specified in one of the following paragraphs concertedly with another entrepreneur who are in a competitive relationship with oneself (hereinafter referred to as a "competitor"):

(i)   Refusing to deal with a certain entrepreneur or restricting the quantity or substance of a commodity or service involved in the transaction with a certain entrepreneur; or

(ii)   Causing another entrepreneur to take an act which comes under the preceding paragraph.

(Other Refusal to Deal)

2. Unjustly refusing to deal, or restricting the quantity or substance of a commodity or service involved in the transaction with a certain entrepreneur, or causing another entrepreneur to take any act which comes under one of these categories.

(Discriminatory Pricing)

3. Unjustly supplying or accepting a commodity or service at prices which discriminate between regions or between the other parties.

(Discriminatory Treatment on Transaction Terms, etc.)

4. Unjustly affording favorable or unfavorable treatment to a certain entrepreneur in regard to the terms or execution of a transaction.

(Discriminatory Treatment in a Trade Association, etc.)

5. Unjustly excluding a specific entrepreneur from a trade association or from a concerted activity, or unjustly discriminating against a specific entrepreneur in a trade association or a concerted activity, thereby causing difficulties in the business activities of the said entrepreneur.

(Unjust Low Price Sales)

6. Without proper justification, supplying a commodity or service continuously at a price which is excessively below cost incurred in the said supply, or otherwise unjustly supplying a commodity or service at a low price, thereby tending to cause difficulties to the business activities of other entrepreneurs.

(Unjust High Price Purchasing)

7. Unjustly purchasing a commodity or service at a high price, thereby tending to cause difficulties to the business activities of other entrepreneurs.

(Deceptive Customer Inducement)

8. Unjustly inducing customers of a competitor to deal with oneself by causing them to misunderstand that the substance of a commodity or service supplied by oneself, or terms of the transaction, or other matters relating to such transaction are much better or much more favorable than the actual one or than those relating to the competitor.

(Customer Inducement by Unjust Benefits)

9. Inducing customers of a competitor to deal with oneself by offering unjust benefits in the light of normal business practices.

(Tie-in Sales, etc.)

10. Unjustly causing the other party to purchase a commodity or service from oneself or from an entrepreneur designated by oneself by tying it to the supply of another commodity or service, or otherwise coercing the said party to deal with oneself or with an entrepreneur designated by oneself.

(Dealing on Exclusive Terms)

11. Unjustly dealing with the other party on condition that the said party shall not deal with a competitor, thereby tending to reduce transaction opportunities for the said competitor.

(Resale Price Restriction)

12. Supplying a commodity to the other party who purchases the said commodity from oneself while imposing, without proper justification, one of the restrictive terms specified below:

(i)   Causing the said party to maintain the sales price of the commodity that one has determined, or otherwise restricting the said party's free decision on sales prices of the commodity; or

(ii)   Having the said party cause an entrepreneur who purchases the commodity from the said party to maintain the sales price of the commodity that one has determined, or otherwise causing the said party to restrict the said entrepreneur's free decision on sales price of the commodity.

(Dealing on Restrictive Terms)

13. Other than any act coming under the preceding two paragraphs, dealing with the other party on conditions which unjustly restrict any transaction between the said party and his other transacting party or other business activities of the said party.

(Abuse of Dominant Bargaining Position)

14. Taking any act specified in one of the following paragraphs, unjustly in the light of the normal business practices, by making use of one's dominant bargaining position over the other party:

(i)   Causing the said party in continuous transaction to purchase a commodity or service other than the one involved in the said transaction;

(ii)   Causing the said party in continuous transaction to provide for oneself money, service or other economic benefits;

(iii)   Setting or changing transaction terms in a way disadvantageous to the said party;

(iv)   In addition to any act coming under the preceding three paragraphs, imposing a disadvantage on the said party regarding terms or execution of transaction; or

(v)   Causing a company which is one's other transacting party to follow one's direction in advance, or to get one's approval, regarding the appointment of officers of the said company (meaning those as defined by Subsection 3 of Section 2 of the Act Concerning Prohibition of Private Monopoly and Maintenance of Fair Trade).

(Interference with a Competitor's Transaction)

15. Unjustly interfering with a transaction between another entrepreneur who is in a competitive relationship in Japan with oneself or with the company of which one is a stockholder or an officer and its other party to such transaction, by preventing the formation of a contract, or by inducing the breach of a contract, or by any other means whatsoever.

(Interference with Internal Operation of a Competing Company)

16. Unjustly inducing, abetting, or coercing a stockholder or an officer of a company which is in a competitive relationship in Japan with oneself or with a company of which one is a stockholder or an officer, to take an act disadvantageous to such company by the exercise of voting rights, transfer of stock, divulgence of secrets, or any other means whatsoever.

C

MERGER GUIDELINE

MERGER GUIDELINE: ADMINISTRATIVE PROCEDURE
STANDARDS FOR EXAMINING MERGERS
AND TRANSFERS OF BUSINESS
(Staff Office, Fair Trade Commission, July 5, 1980)

1. Mergers to be notified in a simplified form

(a) The Fair Trade Commission will receive a report of a merger in a simplified form when the merger falls under any one of the following paragraphs:

(1) A merger between companies each of whose total assets are less than 5 billion yen;

(2) A merger that is performed solely for the purpose of carrying out one of the following objectives,

(A) To change the legal status from an unlimited partnership (*gomei kaisha*), limited partnership (*gosi kaisha*) or unlimited liability company (*yugen kaisha*) to a stock company (*kabusiki kaisha*), or from a stock company to an unlimited liability company;

(B) To change the nominal value of a unit of shares issued by a stock company.

(b) As for mergers falling under (a) above, the Fair Trade Commission will, in principle, examine the filed report only. However, this does not apply to mergers that the Fair Trade Commission finds to be exceptionally important cases, for example, where the market share of any of the parties, or the combined market share of the parties concerned is the largest and 25 percent or more in any relevant market where any of the parties operate, and in addition new entry into the market is considered difficult.

(Note: In this case, the total assets of any of the parties shall be calculated by adding those of the companies that are in substance controlled by the parties and those of the companies that in substance control the parties.)

2. Standards to select mergers for closer examination among those mergers notified in a regular form

Among those mergers that do not fall under any one of the paragraphs mentioned in 1 above, the cases that fall under any one of the following paragraphs will be examined closely.

(a) In any relevant market where any of the parties operates, the market share of any of the parties to the merger or the combined market share of the parties concerned:

(1) is 25 percent or more,

(2) is the largest and 15 percent or more, or

(3) is the largest and the difference between the market share and that of the second or the third largest company is substantial;

(b) In any relevant market where any of the parties operates, the market share of any of the parties to the merger or the combined market share of the parties concerned is ranked among the top three companies and the combined market share of the top three companies is 50 percent or more;

(c) In any relevant market where any of the parties operates, the number of competitors is considerably small;

(d) The total assets of any of the parties to the merger are 100 billion yen or more, and those for the other parties are 10 billion or more.

(Note: In determining whether the merger falls under any one of the above paragraphs, the FTC will take into account those companies that are in substance controlled by the parties and those companies that in substance control the parties.)

3. Matters to be considered in the course of examination of the mergers

In conducting an examination of mergers that fall into any one of the above-mentioned paragraphs to see whether the mergers may substantially restrain competition in any particular field of trade, the Fair Trade Commission will distinguish the mergers, in principle, according to their types, namely, horizontal mergers, vertical mergers and conglomerate mergers. For each type of merger, the Fair Trade Commission will take into account the following matters.

In cases where the merger has more than two aspects, the merger will be examined as to each aspect.

(Note: 1 A horizontal merger is one between companies in direct competition.

2 A vertical merger is one between companies that are in a transaction relationship with each other, such as a merger between a manufacturer and its distributors.

3 A conglomerate merger is one that is not classified as either horizontal or vertical, such as a merger between companies that operate in different lines of business or between companies that operate in different geographical markets.)

(a) Horizontal mergers

Recognizing that horizontal mergers bring about a reduction in the number of competitors and directly affect competition, the Fair Trade Commission will examine the merger by taking into account the matters described in (1) mainly, along with the matters described in (2).

(1) Market share after the merger

Market share of the parties after the merger; the parties' rank in terms of market share; the difference between the market share of the parties and those of competitors and the extent of change in these matters caused by the merger.

(2) Situation of competition in each of the relevant markets where the parties concerned operate;

(A) Situation of competition in the markets where any of the parties operates

The number of competitors; the change in the market share; and the difficulty of entering into the market, etc.

(B) Situation of the markets that are interrelated with the market in question

Existence of substitutable goods; the degree of the substitutability; conditions in the neighboring markets and any other related matters that may affect competition in the market in question.

(C) Overall business capability of the parties after the merger

Overall business capability of the parties after the merger such as their capability for acquiring raw materials, technological capability, marketing capability, credit accessibility, conditions of business (including the degree of financial difficulty), and any other matters that may affect competition in the market in question.

(D) Character and environment of the market

Character and environment of the market such as growth possibilities of the market, and environment of the market such as current business conditions in the domestic market and situations in overseas markets for the same kinds of goods.

(b) Vertical mergers

As to vertical mergers, the Fair Trade Commission will examine them by considering the following matters, in addition to the matters described in (a) above.

(1) Degree of foreclosure

The degree of influence the merger exerts on the business activities of competitors of each of the parties concerned, such as whether the merger will deprive the competitors of their important customers or suppliers, or diminish competitors' accessibility to them.

(2) Degree of the increase of entry barriers

Such matters as whether the merger or increase of vertical integration stimulated by the merger will considerably increase the minimum necessary amount of capital required to enter into the market.

(c) Conglomerate mergers

As to conglomerate mergers, the Fair Trade Commission will, in principle, examine them by considering the following matters, in addition to the matters described in (a) above.

(1) Degree of potential competition between the parties concerned;

(A) As for product extension conglomerate mergers, the degree of substitutability or interrelationship between the goods or services supplied by the parties. As for geographical extension conglomerate mergers, the geographical closeness of the market where each of the parties operates.

(B) Positions of the parties in their respective markets.

(C) Degree of influence that one party to the merger exerts on the other parties.

(D) Degree of potentiality for one party to the merger to enter into the market where the other parties operate.

(Note: A product extension conglomerate merger is one between companies whose goods or services are not in direct competition with each other but are interrelated with each other (including the interrelationship regarding production or distribution methods). A geographical extension conglomerate merger is one between companies that are engaged in the same line of business but whose markets are geographically different from each other.)

(2) Degree of competitive advantage of the parties after the merger

The effect of the merger on the business activities of the parties' competitions, for instance, through the increase in the competitive advantage of the company after the merger caused by the increase in overall business capability such as the parties' capability to acquire raw materials, technological capability, marketing capability and credit accessibility.

(3) Degree of the increase in entry barriers

Whether the minimum necessary amount of capital required to enter into the market will remarkably increase after the merger.

4. Application mutatis mutandis to transfers of business

1 to 3 above are applicable mutatis mutandis to transfers of business. In this case, the following paragraph shall be added as 1 (a)(3)

"(3) Transfers of business by a newly established company in case the company was established by a company to separate some units of its business from itself."

D

STOCKHOLDING GUIDELINE

STOCKHOLDING GUIDELINE: ADMINISTRATIVE PROCEDURE STANDARDS FOR EXAMINING STOCKHOLDING BY COMPANIES

(Staff Office, Fair Trade Commission, September 11, 1981)

The Fair Trade Commission will examine stockholdings by companies in the following way:

(1) The Fair Trade Commission will examine whether there exists a joint relationship between companies due to stockholding based on the standards listed in 1 below.

(2) Then, among the cases where a joint relationship between companies due to stockholding can be found, the Fair Trade Commission will select cases that fall under the standards listed in 2 below; and

(3) Finally, the Fair Trade Commission will examine those selected cases to determine whether the effect of the stockholding may substantially restrain competition taking into account the matters listed in 3 below.

1. Standards for the examination of joint relationships between companies due to stockholding

In these standards, a joint relationship between companies due to stockholding includes not only a case where a company that holds the stock of domestic companies (hereinafter called "stockholding company") is able to control, through the stockholding, the business activities of a company whose stocks are held by the stockholding company (hereinafter called "stock issuing company"), but also a case where the stockholding company is able to exert a considerable influence on the business activities of the stock issuing company.

(a) Stockholding cases that fall under any one of the following paragraphs shall be deemed to involve a joint relationship between companies due to stockholding.

(1)   Where the stockholding ratio (percentage of stocks held by stockholding company to the total outstanding stocks of stock issuing company) is 50 percent or more;

(2)   Where a stock issuing company satisfies the requirements for an "affiliated company" provided by Section 8(4) of the "Rules concerning the Term, Forms and Methods for Completion of Financial Reports, etc." (Ministry of Finance Ordinance No. 59 of 1963).

(Note:

1.   The stockholding ratio may be calculated by adding those stocks held by the subsidiary (a company more than half of whose total outstanding stocks are held by a stockholding company), the affiliated company and the like to those stocks held by the stockholding company, when necessary.

2.   Section 8(4) of the Rules;
"In this rule, an affiliated company means a company that satisfies the following requirements;

"(1)   Between 20 percent and 50 percent of its voting stock is substantially controlled by the other company (including a subsidiary in the event the other company has such a company);

"(2)   Its financial and operational policies are importantly influenced by the other company through relations in such fields as personnel, financial, technology and transactions.")

(b) Stockholding cases that do not fall under (a) above shall, in principle, be examined to see whether joint relationships between companies due to stockholding is involved, by selecting cases coming under any one of the paragraphs listed in (1) below and then by taking into account the matters listed in (2) below.

(1)   Standards for selecting cases for which joint relationships between companies due to stockholding is involved

(i)   Where the stockholding ratio is 25 percent or more,

(ii) Where the stockholding ratio is 10 percent or more and less than 25 percent, and at the same time any one of the following conditions can be found.

(A) Where the stockholding company is the largest shareholder.

(B) Where the stockholding company is among the top three shareholders and the stockholding company and the stock issuing company (hereinafter each will be referred to as "party") compete with each other.

(C) Where the stockholding is related to the formation of a joint venture company (a company jointly established or acquired based on contracts, etc. by two or more companies to perform business operations necessary for the pursuits of joint interests), and the stockholding company competes with other companies investing in such a joint venture company.

(2) Matters to be considered in examining whether joint relationships between parties due to stockholding are involved.
Matters listed in (i) shall be primary considerations and matters listed in (ii) shall be considered supplementarily.

(i) Stockholding ratio, etc.

(A) Stockholding ratio,

(B) The stockholding company's rank among shareholders, degree of difference among their stockholding ratio and degree of dispersion of stockholding ratio, and other relations among shareholders,

(C) Relations between the parties such as whether the parties compete with each other and whether they hold each other's stocks.

(ii) Other matters to be considered in examining whether joint relationships between parties are involved due to stockholding.

      (A)   Whether a person who is or was an officer or an employee of one party has become an officer of the other party,

      (B)   Transactional relations between the parties,

      (C)   Cooperative business relations, technological assistance and other contractual relations between the parties,

      (D)   Financial assistance relations etc. between the parties.

2. Standards for selecting cases for closer examination

In examining whether the effect of stockholding may substantially restrain competition, the Fair Trade Commission will select among those cases that are found to involve joint relationships between parties according to the standards described in 1, and will examine closely those cases that come under any one of the following paragraphs.

However, the above will not apply to cases where the stock issuing company is established by a stockholding company and all of whose stocks are acquired by the stockholding company.

(a) In any relevant market where any of the parties operates, the market share of any of the parties or the combined market share of the parties concerned;

    (1)   is 25 percent or more,

    (2)   is the largest and 15 percent or more, or

    (3)   is the largest and the difference between the market share and that of the second or the third largest company is a quarter of the largest company's market share or more;

(b) In any relevant market where any of the parties operates, the market share of any of the parties or the combined market share of the parties concerned is ranked among the top three companies and the combined market share of the top three companies is 50 percent or more;

(c) In any relevant market where any of the parties operates, the number of competitors is less than 7;

(d) The total assets of any of the parties are 100 billion yen or more, and those for the other parties are 10 billion or more;

Standards for selecting cases for closer examination where the parties concerned engage in a retailing business shall be governed by the Retail Merger Guideline (see Appendix E).

(Note: In determining whether the stockholding falls under any of the above paragraphs (a) to (d), the Fair Trade Commission will take into account those companies 25 percent or more of whose total outstanding stocks are held by the parties, and those companies that hold 25 percent or more of the total outstanding stocks of the parties.)

3. Matters to be considered in examining restraint of competition caused by stockholding

As to cases selected according to the standards described in 2 above, examination of stockholding to see whether their effect may substantially restrain competition in any particular field of trade will be conducted by classifying the stockholdings, in principle, into three types, namely, horizontal, vertical and conglomerate. For each type of stockholding, the Fair Trade Commission will take into account the following matters.

In cases where "a particular field of trade" is examined as to stockholding cases involving retailing businesses, 2. "Particular Field of Trade" of Retail Merger Guideline shall be applied.

In cases where the stockholding has more than two aspects, the stockholding will be examined as to each aspect.

(Note:
1. A horizontal stockholding is one between companies in direct competition.
2. A vertical stockholding is one between companies that are in transaction relationships with each other, such as stockholding between a manufacturer and its distributors.
3. A conglomerate stockholding is one that is not classified as either horizontal or vertical, such as a stockholding between companies that operate in different lines of business or between companies that operate in different geographical markets.)

(a) Horizontal stockholding

Recognizing that horizontal stockholding brings about reduction in the number of competitors and directly affects competition, the Fair Trade Commission will examine the stockholding by taking into account the matters described in (1) mainly, along with the matters described in (2).

(1) Market shares of the parties where a joint relationship between the parties is found due to stockholding

  (A) Market share of the parties after a joint relationship is found between the parties due to stockholding, the parties' rank in terms of market share; the difference between the market share of the parties and those of competitors and the extent of change in these matters caused by the stockholding.

    (B)   Extent of the closeness of the joint relationship between the parties due to stockholding;

(2)   Situation of competition in each of the relevant markets where the parties concerned operate;

    (A)   Situation of competition in the markets where any of the parties operates
The number of competitors; the change in the market share; and the difficulty in entering into the market, etc.

    (B)   Situation of the markets that are interrelated with the market in question
Existence of substitutable goods; the degree of the substitutability; conditions in the neighboring markets and any other related matters that may affect competition in the market in question.

    (C)   Overall business capability of the parties
Overall business capability of the parties such as their capability for acquiring raw materials, technological capability, marketing capability, credit accessibility, conditions of business (including the degree of financial difficulty), and any other matters that may affect competition in the market in question.

    (D)   Character and environment of the market
Character and environment of the market such as growth possibility of the market, and environment of the market such as current business conditions in the domestic market and situations in overseas markets for the same kinds of goods.

(b) Vertical stockholding

As to vertical stockholding, the Fair Trade Commission will examine it by considering the following matters, in addition to the matters described in (a) above.

(1)   Degree of foreclosure
The degree of influence the stockholding exerts over the business activities of competitors of each of the parties concerned, such as

whether the stockholding will deprive the competitors of their important customers or suppliers, or diminish competitors' accessibility to them.

(2)   Degree of the increase of entry barriers
Such matters as whether the stockholding or increase in vertical integration stimulated by the stockholding will considerably increase the minimum necessary amount of capital required to enter into the market.

(c) Conglomerate stockholding

As to conglomerate stockholding, the Fair Trade Commission will, in principle, examine it by considering the following matters, in addition to the matters described in (a) above.

(1)   Degree of potential competition between the parties concerned;

(A)   As for product extension conglomerate stockholding, the degree of substitutability or interrelationship between the goods or services supplied by the parties. As for geographical extension conglomerate stockholding, the geographical closeness of the market where each of the parties operates.

(B)   Positions of the parties in their respective markets,

(C)   Degree of influence that one party exerts on the other parties.

(D)   Degree of potentiality for one party to enter into the market where the other parties operate.

(Note: A product extension conglomerate stockholding is one between companies whose goods or services are not in direct competition with each other but are interrelated with each other (including interrelationship regarding production or distribution methods);

A geographical extension conglomerate stockholding is one between companies that are engaged in the same line of business but whose markets are geographically different from each other.)

(2) Degree of competitive advantage of the parties where a joint relationship is found due to stockholding

The effect of the stockholding on the business activities of the parties' competitions, for instance, through the increase in the competitive advantage of the parties after a joint relationship is found due to stockholding caused by the increase in the overall business capability such as the parties' capability to acquire raw materials, technological capability, marketing capability and credit accessibility.

(3) Degree of the increase in entry barriers

Whether the minimum necessary amount of capital required to enter into the market will remarkably increase after the stockholding.

[4 and 5 are not translated]

E

RETAIL MERGER GUIDELINE
(Extract)

ADMINISTRATIVE PROCEDURE STANDARDS FOR EXAMINING MERGERS OR TRANSFERS OF BUSINESS IN THE RETAILING SECTOR

(Staff Office, Fair Trade Commission, July 24, 1981)

1. Standards in Selecting Mergers which are to be Closely Examined

Regardless of part 2 of the Administrative Procedure Standards for Examining Mergers or Transfer of Business ("Standards to select for closer examination among those mergers notified in a regular form"), for mergers in the retailing sector, those mergers which fall into any one of the following categories shall be closely examined:

(a) In each of more than three administrative districts (the district is principally considered as that of a city) where the merging parties are competing, the combined market share of the merging parties calculated in annual retail sales is 25 percent or more in proportion to the total annual retail sales of retailers belonging to the same type of retailing ("types of retailing" pertain to different kinds of retail stores, namely, department stores, mass-merchandising stores and general retail stores) and at the same time the combined market share becomes the largest in any field of any particular type of retailing;

(b) Combined annual sales of the merging parties amounts to 500 billion yen or more (except the cases where the increased amount of sales resulting from a merger is less than 30 billion yen);

(c) Merger involves more than 2 companies each of whose annual sales is 150 billion yen or more.

Note 1. Following are definitions for department-stores, mass merchandising stores and general retail stores;

(1) Department Stores: Those whose sales floors cover 1,500 m² or more (3,000 m² or more in the case of department-stores located in the 23 special wards of Tokyo and the cities designated by a Cabinet Ordinance), and which deal with a wide variety of commodities daily consumed by general consumers, excepting those which fall into the category of mass-merchandising stores.

(2) Mass-Merchandising Stores: Those whose sales floors cover 500 m² or more and which aim at obtaining mass sales by attracting customers through the adoption of low prices sales combined with self-service methods.

(3) General Retail Stores: Retail stores which do not fall into the categories of department-stores and mass-merchandising stores.

Note 2. In judging the type of retail stores among those described above from (a) to (c), which category a certain retail store falls into, the FTC shall include in its analysis not only the merging parties themselves, but also companies that own 25 percent or more of the total outstanding stock of any of merging parties, and the companies 25 percent or more of whose total outstanding stocks are owned by any of merging parties.

2. "Particular Field of Trade"

In carrying out examinations under the Antimonopoly Act of the mergers selected for closer examination according to the standards described in 1, "particular field of trade" is determined after looking into the individual nature of each case. However, the types of retailing, geographical areas of the markets and the kinds of goods handled which form the elements in such determination are generally taken into account in the following ways.

(a) Distinction according to the types of retailing

(1) Types of retailing are typically classified into department-stores, mass-merchandising stores and general retail stores according to the

differences in facilities of the stores, the variety of commodities handled, marketing policies, shopping attitudes of general consumers and other factors.

Among these types of retail stores, general retail stores are mostly small in their scale of operations, and usually carry only a limited variety of commodities. On the other hand, so-called large-scale retail stores composed of department stores and mass-merchandising stores generally solicit customers from larger areas due to the wider variety of commodities in the larger-scale stores, and they provide services characteristically distinct from general retail stores, for instance, fulfilling most customers' shopping needs within one store. Moreover, among large-scale stores, department stores and mass-merchandising stores each have different individual characteristics to a considerable degree, and consumers have different shopping motivations in selecting between the various types of stores. The difference between the stores is caused by the following factors: department stores solicit customers by extending the scope of the consumers' selection of goods, through the adoption of a person to person sales method and through the carrying of a wide variety of branded goods, many of which are top quality; mass-merchandising stores on the other hand solicit customers through the appeal of low prices without a wide variety of branded goods; through the adoption of self-service methods and by carrying principally convenience goods.

Due to the nature of their operations, especially with respect to department stores and mass-merchandising stores, marked competition generally exists among retailers belonging to the same type of retailing, although retailers belonging to all three different types of retailing compete with one another.

However, the degree of competition among retailers belonging to different types of retailing varies depending on the scale and features of the retailers' shops, their variety of goods sold, their shops' locations, and the shopping attitudes of general consumers. Therefore, in the examination of a "particular field of trade," those aspects should be taken into account. The following conclusions may be drawn:

(A) In big cities such as Tokyo, Osaka and Nagoya, each of the different types of retailing, namely, department stores, mass-merchandising stores and general retail stores in many cases form a "particular field of trade." This is because each type of retailing has considerable individuality, and competition between retailers belonging to different types of retailing is relatively weak;

(B) In local cities, the degree of competition between department stores and mass-merchandising stores is greater than in the case of big cities, and therefore a "particular field of trade" may in many cases contain both types of stores;

(C) When relatively small to medium sized mass-merchandising stores are involved in mergers, the judgment of a "particular field of trade" may in many cases require consideration of among other things, the degree of their competition with general retail stores.

(2) As for department stores and mass-merchandising stores, country-wide department stores[1] and large-scale comprehensive country-wide mass-merchandising stores[2] may sometimes be judged to form distinct "particular fields of trade" among stores belonging to the same type of retailing. The factors that could lead to such a finding include: an advantage over other retailers who belong to the same type of retailing in terms of sales ability, planning ability, ability to develop new products, purchasing power, ability to create new branches and the ability to obtain credit.

(b) Geographical Market Areas

(1) Geographical market areas in the retail business are generally considered to be regionally restricted (the so-called "regional markets") as competition generally involves sales of goods to consumers near the locations of the stores.

The geographical area of the regional markets is determined by the proximity of the consumers who shop in the stores. Usually this is determined by considering the location of one store, but if several stores are located so close together that they form one combined business district, the district which includes the locations of these stores composes the relevant local market.

Note   "Country-wide department stores" and "large-scale comprehensive country-wide mass-merchandising stores" respectively mean the following kinds of stores:

(1) Department stores whose headquarters are located at Tokyo, Osaka or Nagoya and at the same time have 5 or more stores which are located in 3 or more prefectures;

(2) Mass-merchandising stores which carry a wide variety of goods including foodstuff, garments and household items, and which at the same time have 50 or more stores located in 5 or more prefectures including 2 or more of the following: Tokyo, Osaka and Nagoya.

(2) Areas of regional markets vary depending on the retailers' business operations, type of goods sold, location of the stores and amount of shopping space, facilities such as parking lots and public transportation, the density of retail stores in the area, the degree of advertising activity, and shopping activity by consumers around the location of the store. Accordingly, a case-by-case analysis of these aspects is necessary.

As a general approximation (and depending on the specific nature of the local markets), the areas of regional markets are considered to correspond to the areas of cities designated as administrative districts, except in instances of big cities.

(3) The areas of markets for the kinds of retail stores listed above in (a) (2) may sometimes be considered as country-wide as well as regional markets. In order to be classified as country-wide market such factors as sales and planning ability, product development, purchasing power, credit standing, location and the existence of potential competition would be considered.

(c) Determination according to the range of goods sold

(1) "Particular field of trade" for department stores and aggregate mass-merchandising stores (mass-merchandising stores which cover a wide range of goods such as foodstuff, garments and household items) is principally determined by the entire range of goods sold in stores of a similar kind. However, depending upon the nature of the relevant market, competition may sometimes be analyzed by dividing the market into several submarkets, for example into food-stuff, garments and household items. Alternatively, it may be divided into approximately 10 relying on the classification of commodities for department stores established under the classification of retail businesses in the Statistical Survey of Commerce.

(2) Mass-merchandising stores which are not classified as aggregate mass-merchandising stores, "particular field of trade" may sometimes be composed not only of the whole range of goods sold, but also as to each of the major kinds of goods sold (relying on the classification of commodities sold by various kinds of retail stores in the Statistical Survey of Commerce).

F

PATENT AND KNOW-HOW LICENSING GUIDELINES

GUIDELINES FOR THE REGULATION
OF UNFAIR TRADE PRACTICES WITH
RESPECT TO PATENT
AND KNOW-HOW
LICENSING AGREEMENTS

(Staff Office, Fair Trade Commission,
February 15, 1989)

Introduction

1. The Fair Trade Commission, on May 24, 1968, had announced Guidelines for International Technology Introduction Agreements and had specified outstanding restrictions among those which are liable to come under unfair trade practices in international technology licensing agreements on patent or know-how.

   The FTC relied on this Guidelines when it reviewed international contracts or agreements filed under Section 6(2) of the Antimonopoly Act.

2. In view of recent trends of increasing significance of importance as well as the number of international technology licensing agreements (those agreements between Japanese entrepreneur and foreign entrepreneur) and of technology licensing agreements among Japanese

entrepreneurs, the FTC had formulated the Guidelines for the Regulation of Unfair Trade Practices with respect to Patent and Know-How Licensing Agreements.

3.   The legal framework to protect intellectual property rights such as patent has a procompetitive effect by giving stimulation to research and development for entrepreneurs, and could work as a promoter to introduce a new market or new technology.

Also, technology transactions could have a procompetitive effect when, as a result of technology transactions, new business entities can enter a market, when the number of competing entities increases, or when the technology will be utilized more efficiently.

Therefore, transfer of technology should be promoted, and it is expected that transfer of technology could be promoted through clarification of examining standards by way of guidelines.

On the other hand, if certain types of restrictive conditions are imposed in technology licensing agreements, they might cause an anti-competitive effect.

In view of such nature of restrictions, it is as a matter of course that impacts on competition should be evaluated individually as to each case when it is examined whether restrictions contained in technology licensing agreements constitute unfair trade practices.

However, impacts on competition may vary depending on types of restrictive conditions.

Therefore, after taking our enforcement experience into consideration as well, the following three types of outstanding restrictions contained in patent and know-how licensing agreements which occupy a large part of technology licensing agreements are identified as much as possible in this guidelines.

(a) Such restrictions which are considered, in principle, not to fall under unfair trade practices.

(b) Such restrictions which may fall under unfair trade practices.

(c) Such restrictions which are highly likely to fall under unfair trade practices.

As to restrictions which are described as "may fall under unfair trade practices", such determination will be made, in addition to the requirements stipulated in each paragraphs, after the position of licensor and licensee in a relevant market, the conditions of a relevant market, the duration of restrictions imposed, etc. are examined as a whole.

On the other hands, as to restrictions which are described as "highly likely to fall under unfair trade practices", such restrictions are considered to constitute unfair trade practices unless specific justifiable reasons could be presented.

4.   Examining standards stipulated in this guidelines are applicable without any discrimination to those patent and know-how licensing agreements among Japanese entrepreneurs as well as those between Japanese entrepreneur and foreign entrepreneur.

However, so far as restrictive conditions contained in patent and know-how licensing agreements between Japanese entrepreneur and foreign entrepreneur are concerned, examining standards in this guidelines are applicable insofar as restrictive conditions can influence competition within a Japanese market.

5.   As stated above, impacts on competition within a Japanese market should be evaluated individually as to each case when it is examined whether restrictions contained in technology licensing agreements constitute unfair trade practices.

Thus, clearance request from contracting parties is expected to increase. Therefore, at the same time with announcement of this guidelines, a clearance system on patent and know-how licensing agreements is established, and any clearance request filed by foreign entrepreneurs as well as by Japanese entrepreneurs will be responded in a proper way.

6.   Examining standards in this guidelines could be applicable to reciprocal licensing agreements or licensing agreements among more than three parties such as cross-licensing agreement, patent pool, multiple licensing agreement, etc.

Because this guidelines are to clarify examining standards for unfair trade practices as to patent and know-how licensing agreement, it is a matter of course that Section 3 of the Antimonopoly Act (Prohibition of Private Monopolization or Unreasonable Restraints of Trade) and other Sections could also be applicable to such cases where technology licensing agreements are used as a means to effect unreasonable restraint of trade.

Thus, as to reciprocal licensing agreements or licensing agreements among more than three parties, other aspect than unfair trade practices need to be examined.

7.   A licensing agreement which licenses both patent and know-how could be regarded as a patent licensing agreements and a know-how licensing agreements, therefore, as to restrictive conditions contained in such hybrid licensing agreement, examining standards in each Part will be applied depending on which technology restrictive conditions are related to.

Part 1   Patent Licensing Agreements

1. Restrictions which are considered, in principle, not to fall under unfair trade practices

> Among restrictions contained in licensing agreements on patent or utility model rights (hereinafter referred to as "patent licensing agreements"), which are considered, in principle, not to fall under unfair trade practices (This is defined as those practices designated as unfair trade practices in the FTC Notification No. 15 of 1982. This Notification is referred to as "General Designation" hereinafter.) since they are thought to be within a proper exercise of patent rights or utility model rights, or to have only a negligible effect on competition, the following are outstanding.
>
> Hereinafter, when referred to as "patent", "patent rights", "patented goods (Goods covered by patent rights are referred to as "patented goods". Goods produced by employing patented process are also included. hereinafter the same)", they also include "utility model", "utility model rights", "goods covered by the utility model rights" respectively.

(1) Separately granting a license to manufacture, use, sell, etc.

(2) Granting a license for a limited period within the life of patent rights.

(3) Granting a license for a limited area within the whole area covered by patent rights.

(4) Restricting exploitation of patent rights to a specified field of technology.

(5) Requiring minimum production or minimum sales volume of patented goods, or minimum use of patented process.

(6) Making it obligatory for the licensee to inform the licensor of knowledge or experience newly obtained by the licensee regarding licensed patent, or to grant the licensor non-exclusive license with respect to an improved or applied invention, etc. by the licensee, insofar as the licensor bears similar obligations and obligations of both parties with respect to informing the other party or granting non-exclusive license are roughly balanced in substance.

(7) Making it obligatory for the licensee to maintain certain standards of quality for patented goods, raw materials, components, etc., insofar as such obligation is confined to an extent necessary for guaranteeing the effectiveness of licensed patent (This condition applies when the licensor guarantees the licensee specifically the effectiveness of licensed patent. hereinafter the same), or for

maintaining the goodwill of trademark, etc. (This condition applies only when the licensor grants a license on trademark, etc. to the licensee. hereinafter the same)

(8) Making it obligatory for the licensee to procure raw materials, components, etc. from the licensor or a person designated by the licensor, insofar as restrictions on quality of raw materials, components, etc. or any other restriction is insufficient to guarantee the effectiveness of licensed patent, or to maintain the goodwill of trademark, etc; Provided, That such obligation is confined to an extent necessary for guaranteeing the effectiveness of licensed patent, or for maintaining the goodwill of trademark, etc.

(9) Restricting ability of the licensee's to export patented goods into an are falling within one of the following paragraphs.

 a) The licensor has registered his patent rights on patented goods in the area.
 b) The licensor has been conducting a continuous marketing activity on patented goods in the area.
 c) The licensor assigns the area as an exclusive sales territory to a third party.

(10) Restricting the licensee's export price or export volume of patented goods, or making it obligatory for the licensee to export through the licensor or a person designated by the licensor, insofar as the licensor allows the licensee to export to the area falling within one of the paragraphs a), b) or c) mentioned in (9) above; Provided, That such restriction or obligation is confined to a necessary extent.

(11) Making it obligatory for the licensee to use production or sales volume or price of finished product as a basis for royalty in order to facilitate its calculation, or making it obligatory for the licensee to use consumption of raw materials or components, etc., which are necessary for producing patented goods, as a basis for royalty in order to facilitate its calculation.

(12) Making it obligatory for the licensee to accept licensing of more than two patents as a package, insofar as such restriction is necessary for guaranteeing the effectiveness of licensed patent.

(13) Providing that royalty continues to be charged after the expiration of patent rights, insofar as it constitutes installment payment or extended payment of royalty.

(14) Providing that licensor can terminate licensing agreements if the licensee challenges the validity of licensed patent.

(15) Making it obligatory for the licensee to use his best efforts to exploit licensed patent.

2. Restrictions which may fall under unfair trade practices

Among restrictions which may fall under unfair trade practices in patent licensing agreements, the following are outstanding.

The determination whether restrictions fall under unfair trade practices will be made, in addition to the requirements stipulated in each paragraphs, after the positions of licensor and licensee in a relevant market, the conditions of a relevant market, the duration of restrictions imposed, etc. are examined as a whole.

(1) Making it obligatory for the licensee not to handle substitutable goods or similar goods which are in competition with patented goods (hereinafter referred to as "competing goods"), or not to employ substitutable technology or similar technology which is in competition with licensed patent (hereinafter referred to as "competing technology") during the term of licensing agreements.

- This restriction could fall under unfair trade practices in such cases where competing companies are deprived of important customers or the chance of business with them, or the licensee is deprived of freedom to select his goods or technologies, thus it could result in the reduction of competition in a relevant market (possibly falling under Articles 11 or 13 of the General Designation).

(2) Making it obligatory for the licensee to sell patented goods through the licensor or a person designated by the licensor, or not to sell to a person designated by the licensor.

- This restriction could fall under unfair trade practices in such cases where the licensee is deprived of an important means of competition, namely freedom to select sales outlet, and thus it could result in the reduction of competition in a patented goods market (possibly falling under Article 13 of the General Designation).

(3) Making it obligatory for the licensee to inform the licensor of knowledge or experience newly obtained by the licensee regarding licensed patent, or to grant the licensor non-exclusive license with respect to an improved or applied intervention, etc. by the licensee.

However, such cases are excluded where the licensor bears similar obligations and obligations of both parties with respect to informing the other party or granting non-exclusive license are roughly balanced in substance.

- This restriction could fall under unfair trade practices in such cases where it could result in setting transaction terms in a way unduly disadvantageous to the licensee, by such reasons as the licensor does not bear similar obligations, or obligations of both parties are not well balanced in substance (possibly falling under Clause 3 of Article 14 of the General Designation).

(4) Making it obligatory for the licensee to use trademark, etc. designated by the licensor for patented goods.

- This restriction could fall under unfair trade practices in such cases where business activities of the licensee is unjustly restricted by the licensor by depriving of the licensee's freedom to select trademark, etc., which is one means of competition, thus it could result in the reduction of competition in a relevant market (possibly falling Article 13 of the General Designation).

    This restriction could also fall under unfair trade practices in such cases where the licensee is forced to continue the use of trademark, etc. after expiration of patent rights because of his continued use of the trademark, etc. during the term of licensing agreements, thus it could result in setting transaction terms in a way unduly disadvantageous to the licensee. (possibly falling under Clause 3 of Article 14 of the General Designation).

(5) Restricting quality of patented goods, raw materials, components, etc.
    However, obligation for the licensee to maintain certain standards of quality for patented goods, raw materials, components, etc. are excluded where such obligation is confined to an extent necessary for guaranteeing the effectiveness of licensed patent, or for maintaining the goodwill of trademark, etc.

- This restriction could fall under unfair trade practices in such cases where it could result in the reduction of competition in a market of raw materials, components, etc. or in a market of patented goods, because quality of patented goods or quality of raw materials, components, etc., which should be freely decided by the licensee, is unduly restricted (possibly falling under Article 13 of the General Designation).

(6) Making it obligatory for the licensee to procure raw materials, components, etc. from the licensor or a person designated by the licensor.

However, such cases are excluded where restrictions on quality of raw materials, components, etc. or any other restriction is insufficient to guarantee the effectiveness of licensed patent, or to maintain the goodwill of trademark, etc. and such obligation is confined to an extent necessary for guaranteeing the effectiveness of licensed patent, or for maintaining the goodwill of trademark, etc.

- This restriction could fall under unfair trade practices in such cases where the licensee is deprived of freedom to select his sources of raw materials, components, etc., and thus it is deemed as an unfair means from the viewpoint of efficient competition, or where it could result in the reduction of competition in a market of raw materials, components, etc. (possibly falling under Article 10 of the General Designation).

(7) Restricting ability of the licensee to export patented goods.

However, such cases are excluded where restricted area falls into within one of the following paragraphs.

a) The licensor has registered his patent rights on patented goods in the area.

b) The licensor has been conducting a continuous marketing activity on patented goods in the area.

c) The licensor assigns the area as an exclusive sales territory to a third party.

- This restriction could fall under unfair trade practices in such cases where freedom of the licensee to export patented goods to the area not covered by patent rights is restricted, and thus it could result in the reduction of competition in an export market (possibly falling under Article 13 of the General Designation).

(8) Restricting the licensee's export price or export volume of patented goods, or making it obligatory for the licensee to export through the licensor or a person designated by the licensor.

However, such cases are excluded where the licensor allows the licensee to export to the areas falling within one of the paragraphs a), b) or c) mentioned in (7) above, and such restriction or obligation is confined to a necessary extent.

- This restriction could fall under unfair trade practices in such cases where freedom of the licensee to export patented goods to the area not covered by patent rights is restricted, and thus it could result in the reduction of competition in an export market (possibly falling under Article 13 of the General Designation).

(9) Making it obligatory for the licensee to pay royalty based on products or service other than patented goods.

However, such cases are excluded where the licensor makes it obligatory for the licensee to use production or sales volume or price of finished product as a basis for royalty in order to facilitate its calculation, or the licensor makes it obligatory for the licensee to use consumption of raw materials or components, etc., which are necessary for producing patented goods, as a basis for royalty in order to facilitate its calculation.

- This restriction could fall under unfair trade practices in such cases where it could result in setting transaction terms in a way unduly disadvantageous to the licensee (possibly falling under Clause 3 of Article 14 of the General Designation).

(10) Making it obligatory for the licensee to accept licensing of more than two patents as a package.

However, such cases are excluded where such restriction is confined to an extent necessary for guaranteeing the effectiveness of licensed patent.

- This restriction could fall under unfair trade practices in such cases where the licensee is deprived of freedom to select his technology, and thus it is deemed as an unfair means from the viewpoint of efficient competition, or it could result in the reduction of competition in a technology market (possibly falling under Article 10 of the General Designation).

  This restriction could also fall under unfair trade practices in such cases where the licensee is forced to pay extra royalty or the duration of royalty payment is extended, thus it could result in setting transaction terms in a way unduly disadvantageous to the licensee (possibly falling under Clause 3 of Article 14 of the General Designation).

(11) Imposing unilaterally disadvantageous condition to the licensee for the termination of licensing agreements, such as terminating licensing agreements unilaterally or terminating them immediately without affording an appropriate notice by reasons other than unenforceability of licensing agreements due to insolvency, etc.

- This restriction could fall under unfair trade practices in such cases where it could result in setting transaction terms in a way unduly disadvantageous to the licensee (possibly falling under Clause 3 of Article 14 of the General Designation).

(12) Making it obligatory for the licensee not to challenge the validity of licensed patent.

- This restriction could fall under unfair trade practices in such cases where patent rights continue to exist for technology which otherwise could not obtain any patent rights, and use of technology by other business is eliminated, thus it could result in the reduction of competition in a relevant market (possibly falling under Article 13 of the General Designation).

   This restriction could also fall under unfair trade practices in such cases where the licensee may have to continue to pay royalty for technology which otherwise could be used without any royalty, thus it could result in setting transaction terms in a way unduly disadvantageous to the licensee (possibly falling under Clause 3 of Article 14 of the General Designation).

3. Restrictions which are highly likely to fall under unfair trade practices

   Among restrictions in patent licensing agreements which are considered to constitute unfair trade practices unless specific justifiable reasons can be presented, the following are outstanding.

(1) Restricting resale prices of patented goods in Japan.

- The licensor, under this restriction, restricts freedom of pricing which forms a basis of competition for wholesalers and retailers, therefore it is highly likely to impede fair competition (possibly falling under Article 13 of the General Designation).

(2) Restricting sales price of patented goods by the licensee in Japan.

- This restriction, by restricting freedom of pricing of the licensee, will lead to a significant limitation of competitive ability of the licensee, and could result in the reduction of price competition in a patented goods market.

   Further, this restriction cannot be justifiable by such reason as securing royalty. Therefore, it is highly likely to impede fair competition (possibly falling under Article 13 of the General Designation).

(3) Making it obligatory for the licensee not to handle competing goods, or not to employ competing technology after the expiration or termination of licensing agreements.

- After the expiration or termination of licensing agreements, this restriction could have no such justification as securing royalty for the licensor based on sales by the licensee. Therefore, it is highly likely to impede fair competition (possibly falling under Articles 11 or 13 of the General Designation).

(4) Restricting use of licensed technology in spite of the expiration of patent rights, or making it obligatory for the licensee to pay royalty for use after the expiration of patent rights.

- Anyone should be able to use licensed technology freely after the expiration of patent rights, and the licensor has no authority to limit the use of technology concerned, or to compel payment of royalty for use after the expiration of patent rights. Therefore, it is highly likely to impede fair competition (possibly falling under Article 13 or Clause 3 of Article 14 of the General Designation).

(5) Restricting research and development activities by the licensee himself or joint research and development with a third party regarding to licensed patent or its competing technology.

- Under this restriction, the licensor restricts freedom of research and development activities of the licensee which are an important means of competition, and also limits business activities of the licensee in a product or technology market in the future, thus it could have an important and long term impact on these markets. Therefore, it is highly likely to impede fair competition (possibly falling under Article 13 of the General Designation).

(6) Making it obligatory for the licensee to assign the licensor the right on an improved or applied invention, etc. by the licensee or to grant the licensor exclusive license (such case where licensee grants a license exclusively for the licensor by agreeing not to exploit the invention by himself in the licensed territory is included.) with respect to an improved or applied invention, etc. by the licensee.

- This restriction could result in undue enhancement or maintenance of the dominant position of the licensor in a relevant market. This restriction could further impede incentive for research and development of the licensee, and thus it could impede development of new technology by restricting freedom of the licensee to use knowledge, experience and modification or to grant a license to a third party. Thus it could result in the reduction of competition in a product or technology market (possibly falling under Article 13 of the General Designation).

When the licensor does not bear similar obligations, or obligations of both parties are not well balanced in substance, this restriction could result in setting transaction terms in a way unduly disadvantageous to the licensee (possibly falling under Clause 3 of Article 14 of the General Designation).

Part 2   Know-How Licensing Agreements

1. Restrictions which are considered, in principle, not to fall under unfair trade practices

Among restrictions contained in licensing agreements on know-how (only those technological know-how related to industrial use are covered. Non-secret know-how is excluded hereinafter the same. Hereinafter those licensing agreement are referred to as "know-how licensing agreements".) which are considered, in principle, not to fall under unfair trade practices, since they are thought to have only a negligible effect on competition, the following are outstanding.

(1) Granting a license for a limited period insofar as licensed know-how remains secret.

(2) Restricting exploitation of licensed know-how to a specified field of technology.

(3) Requiring minimum production or minimum sales volume of goods manufactured exploiting licensed know-how (Hereinafter referred to as "licensed goods".), or minimum use of licensed know-how.

(4) Making it obligatory for the licensee not to handle substitutable goods or similar goods which are in competition with licensed goods (Hereinafter referred to as "competing goods".), or not to employ substitutable technology or similar technology (Hereinafter referred to as "competing technology".) for a short period after the expiration or termination of licensing agreements, insofar as it is difficult to prevent unauthorized exploitation of licensed know-how by such restrictions as use ban after the expiration or termination of licensing agreements; Provided, That such obligation is confined to an extent necessary for preventing unauthorized exploitation of licensed know-how.

(5) Making it obligatory for the licensee to inform the licensor of knowledge or experience newly obtained by the licensee regarding licensed know-how, or to grant the licensor non-exclusive license with respect to an improved or applied invention, etc. by the licensee, insofar as the

licensor bears similar obligations and obligations of both parties with respect to informing the other party or granting non-exclusive license are roughly balanced in substance.

(6) Making it obligatory for the licensee to maintain certain standards of quality for licensed goods, raw materials, components, etc., insofar as such obligation is confined to an extent necessary for guaranteeing the effectiveness of licensed know-how (This condition applies when the licensor guarantees the licensee specifically the effectiveness of licensed know-how. hereinafter the same), or for maintaining the goodwill of trademark, etc.

(7) Making it obligatory for the licensee to procure raw materials, components, etc. from the licensor or a person designated by the licensor, insofar as restrictions on quality of raw materials, components, etc. or any other restriction is insufficient to guarantee the effectiveness of licensed know-how, or to maintain the goodwill of trademark, etc., or such obligation is vital for protection of the secrecy of licensed know-how; Provided, That such obligation is confined to an extent necessary for guaranteeing the effectiveness of licensed know-how, or for maintaining the goodwill of trademark, etc., or for protecting the secrecy of licensed know-how.

(8) Restricting ability of the licensee to export licensed goods into an area falling within one of the following paragraphs.

  a) The licensor has registered his patent rights on licensed goods in the area.
  b) The licensor has been conducting a continuous marketing activity on licensed goods in the area.
  c) The licensor assigns the area as an exclusive sales territory to a third party.

(9) Restricting the licensee's export price or export volume of licensed goods, or making it obligatory for the licensee to export through the licensor or a person designated by the licensor, insofar as the licensor allows the licensee to export to the areas falling within one of the paragraphs a), b) or c) mentioned in (8) above; Provided, That such restriction or obligation is confined to a necessary extent.

(10) Making it obligatory for the licensee to use production or sales volume or price of finished product as a basis for royalty in order to facilitate its calculation, or making it obligatory for the licensee to use consumption of raw materials or components, etc., which are necessary for producing licensed goods, as a basis for royalty in order to facilitate its calculation.

(11) Making it obligatory for the licensee to accept licensing of more than two know-how as a package, insofar such restriction is necessary for guaranteeing the effectiveness of licensed know-how.

(12) Providing that royalty continues to be charged after licensed know-how has become publicly known due to reasons for which the licensee it not responsible, insofar as it constitutes installment payment or extended payment of royalty, or insofar as a royalty is charged for use after licensed know-how has become publicly known for a short period thereafter during the term of licensing agreements.

(13) Providing that the licensor can terminate licensing agreements if the licensee challenges whether licensed know-how has become publicly known.

(14) Making it obligatory for the licensee not to disclose licensed know-how to a third party insofar as licensed know-how remains secret.

(15) Making it obligatory for the licensee to use his best efforts to exploit licensed know-how.

2. Restrictions which may fall under unfair trade practices

> Among restrictions which may fall under unfair trade practices in know-how licensing agreements, the following are outstanding.
>
> The determination whether restrictions fall under unfair trade practices will be made, in addition to the requirements stipulated in each paragraphs, after the positions of licensor and licensee in a relevant market, the conditions of a relevant market, the duration of restrictions imposed, etc. are examined as a whole.

(1) Making it obligatory for the licensee not to handle competing goods, or not to employ competing technology during the term of licensing agreements.

- This restriction could fall under unfair trade practices in such cases where competing companies are deprived of important customers or the chance of business with them, or the licensee is deprived of freedom to select his goods or technologies, thus it could result in the reduction of competition in a relevant market (possibly falling under Articles 11 or 13 of the General Designation).

(2) Making it obligatory for the licensee to sell licensed goods through the licensor or a person designated by the licensor, or not to sell to a person designated by the licensor.

- This restriction could fall under unfair trade practices in such cases where the licensee is deprived of an important means of competition, namely freedom to select sales outlet, and thus it could result in the reduction of competition in a licensed goods market (possibly falling under Article 13 of the General Designation).

(3) Making it obligatory for the licensee to inform the licensor of knowledge or experience newly obtained by the licensee regarding licensed know-how, or to grant the licensor non-exclusive license with respect to an improved or applied invention, etc. by the licensee.

However, such cases are excluded where the licensor bears similar obligations and obligations of both parties with respect to informing the other party or granting non-exclusive license are roughly balanced in substance.

- This restriction could fall under unfair trade practices in such cases where it could result in setting transaction terms in a way unduly disadvantageous to the licensee, by such reasons as the licensor does not bear similar obligations, or obligations of both parties are not well balanced in substance (possibly falling under Clause 3 of Article 14 of the General Designation).

(4) Making it obligatory for the licensee to use trademark, etc. designated by the licensor for licensed goods.

- This restriction could fall under unfair trade practices in such cases where business activities of the licensee is unjustly restricted by the licensor by depriving of the licensee's freedom to select trademark, etc., which is one means of competition, thus it could result in the reduction of competition in a relevant market (possibly falling under Article 13 of the General Designation).

    This restriction could also fall under unfair trade practices in such cases when the licensee is forced to continue the use of trademark, etc. after licensed know-how has become publicly known because of his continued use of the trademark, etc. during the term of licensing agreements, thus it could result in setting transaction terms in a way unduly disadvantageous to the licensee (possibly falling under Clause 3 of 14 of the General Designation).

(5) Restricting quality of licensed goods, raw materials, components, etc.

However, obligations for the licensee to maintain certain standards of quality for licensed goods, raw materials, components, etc. are excluded where such obligation is confined to an extent necessary for guaranteeing the effectiveness of licensed know-how, or for maintaining the goodwill of trademark, etc.

- This restriction could fall under unfair trade practices in such cases where it could result in the reduction of competition in a market of raw materials, components, etc. or in a market of licensed goods, because quality of licensed goods or quality of raw materials, components, etc., which should be freely decided by the licensee, is unduly restricted (possibly falling under Article 13 of the General Designation).

(6) Making it obligatory for the licensee to procure raw materials, components, etc. from the licensor or a person designated by the licensor.

However, such cases are excluded where restrictions on quality of raw materials, components, etc. or any other restriction is insufficient to guarantee the effectiveness of licensed know-how, or to maintain the goodwill of trademark, etc., or where such obligation is vital for protection of the secrecy of licensed know-how, and such obligation is confined to an extent necessary for guaranteeing the effectiveness of licensed know-how, or for maintaining the goodwill of trademark, etc., or for protecting the secrecy of licensed know-how.

- This restriction could fall under unfair trade practices in such cases where the licensee is deprived of freedom to select his sources of raw materials, components, etc., and thus it is deemed as an unfair means from the viewpoint of efficient competition, or where it could result in the reduction of competition in a market of raw materials, components, etc. (possibly falling under Article 10 of the General Designation).

(7) Restricting ability of the licensee to export licensed goods.

However, such cases are excluded where restricted area falls into within one of the following paragraphs.

a) The licensor has registered his patent rights on licensed goods in the area.

b) The licensor has conducting a continuous marketing activity on licensed goods in the area.

c) The licensor assigns the area as an exclusive sales territory to a third party.

- This restriction could fall under unfair trade practices in such cases where freedom of the licensee to export licensed goods is restricted, and thus it could result in the reduction of competition in an export market (possibly falling under Article 13 of the General Designation).

(8) Restricting the licensee's export price or export volume of licensed goods, or making it obligatory for the licensee to export through the licensor or a person designated by the licensor.

However, such cases are excluded where the licensor allows the licensee to export to the areas falling within one of the paragraphs a), b), or c) mentioned in (7) above, and such restriction or obligation is confined to a necessary extent.

- This restriction could fall under unfair trade practices in such cases where freedom of the licensee to export licensed goods is restricted, and thus it could result in the reduction of competition in an export market (possibly falling under Article 13 of the General Designation).

(9) Making it obligatory for the licensee to pay royalty based on products or service other than licensed goods.

However, such cases are excluded where the licensor makes it obligatory for the licensee to use production or sales volume or price of finished product as a basis for royalty in order to facilitate its calculation, or the licensor makes it obligatory for the licensee to use consumption of raw materials or component, etc., which are necessary for producing licensed goods, as a basis for royalty in order to facilitate its calculation.

- This restriction could fall under unfair trade practices in such cases where it could result in setting transaction terms in a way unduly disadvantageous to the licensee (possibly falling under Clause 3 of Article 14 of the General Designation).

(10) Making it obligatory for the licensee to accept licensing of more than two know-how as a package.

However, such cases are excluded where such restriction is confined to an extent necessary for guaranteeing the effectiveness of licensed know-how.

- This restriction could fall under unfair trade practices in such cases where the licensee is deprived of freedom to select his technology, and thus it is deemed as an unfair means from the viewpoint of efficient competition, or it could result in the reduction of competition in a technology market (possibly falling under Article 10 of the General Designation).

This restriction could also fall under unfair trade practices in such cases where the licensee is forced to pay extra royalty or the duration of royalty payment is extended, thus it could result in setting transaction terms in a way unduly disadvantageous to the licensee (possibly falling under Clause 3 of Article 14 of the General Designation).

(11) Imposing unilaterally disadvantageous condition to the licensee for the termination of licensing agreements, such as terminating licensing agreements unilaterally or terminating them immediately without affording an appropriate notice by reasons other than unenforceability of licensing agreements due to insolvency, etc.

- This restriction could fall under unfair trade practices in such cases where it could result in setting transaction terms in a way unduly disadvantageous to the licensee (possibly falling under Clause 3 of Article 14 of the General Designation).

(12) Making it obligatory for the licensee not to challenge whether licensed know-how has become publicly known.

- This restriction could fall under unfair trade practices in such cases where the licensee may have to continue to pay royalty for technology which otherwise could be used without any royalty, thus it could result in setting transaction terms in a way unduly disadvantageous to the licensee (possibly falling under Clause 3 of Article 14 of the General Designation).

3. Restrictions which are highly likely to fall under unfair trade practices

Among restrictions in know-how licensing agreements which are considered to constitute unfair trade practices unless specific justifiable reasons can be presented, the following are outstanding.

(1) Restricting resale prices of licensed goods in Japan.

- The licensor, under this restriction, restricts freedom of pricing which forms basis of competition for wholesalers and retailers, therefore it is highly likely to impede fair competition (possibly falling under Article 13 of the General Designation).

(2)   Restricting sales price of licensed goods by the licensee in Japan.

- This restriction, by restricting freedom of pricing of the licensee, will lead to a significant limitation of competitive ability of the licensee, and could result in the reduction of price competition in a licensed goods market.

    Further, this restriction cannot be justifiable by such reason as securing royalty. Therefore, it is highly likely to impede fair competition (possibly falling under Article 13 of the General Designation).

(3)   Making it obligatory for the licensee not to handle competing goods, or not to employ competing technology after the expiration or termination of licensing agreements.

   However, such cases are excluded where such obligation covers for a short period after the expiration or termination of licensing agreements, and it is difficult to prevent unauthorized exploitation of licensed know-how by such restrictions as use ban after the expiration or termination of licensing agreements.

- After the expiration or termination of licensing agreements, this restriction could have no such justification as securing royalty for the licensor based on sales by the licensee. Therefore, it is highly likely to impede fair competition (possibly falling under Articles 11 or 13 of the General Designation).

(4)   Restricting use of licensed technology even though licensed know-how has become publicly known due to reasons for which the licensee is not responsible, or making it obligatory for the licensee to pay royalty for use after licensed know-how has become publicly known.

   However, such cases are excluded where royalty is charged for use after licensed know-how has become publicly known for a short period thereafter during the term of licensing agreements.

- Anyone should be able to use licensed technology freely after licensed know-how has become publicly known due to reasons for which the licensee is not responsible, and the licensor has no authority to limit the use of technology concerned, or to compel payment of royalty for use after licensed know-how become publicly known. Therefore, it is highly likely to impede fair competition (possibly falling under Article 13 of Clause 13 of Article 14 of the General Designation).

(5) Restricting research and development activities by the licensee himself or joint research and development with a third party regarding to licensed know-how or its competing technology.

- Under this restriction, the licensor restricts freedom of research and development activities of the licensee which are an important means of competition, and also limits business activities of the licensee in a product or technology market in the future, thus it could have an important and long term impact on these markets. Therefore, it is highly likely to impede fair competition (possibly falling under Article 13 of the General Designation).

(6) Making it obligatory for the licensee to assign the licensor the right on an improved or applied invention, etc. by the licensee or to grant the licensor exclusive license (such case where licensee grants a license exclusively for the licensor by agreeing not to exploit the invention by himself in the licensed territory is included) with respect to an improved or applied invention, etc. by the licensee.

- This restriction could result in undue enhancement or maintenance of the dominant position of the licensor in a relevant market. This restriction could further impede incentive for research and development of the licensee, and thus it could impede development of new technology by restricting freedom of the licensee to use knowledge, experience and modification or to grant a license to a third party. Thus it could result in the reduction of competition in a product or technology market (possibly falling under Article 13 of General Designation).

  When the licensor does not bear similar obligations, or obligations of both parties are not well balanced in substance, this restriction could result in setting transaction terms in a way unduly disadvantageous to the licensee (possibly falling under Clause 3 of Article 14 of the General Designation).

G

UNJUST RETURN OF UNSOLD GOODS GUIDELINE

GUIDELINES CONCERNING THE UNJUST RETURN OF UNSOLD GOODS UNDER THE ANTIMONOPOLY ACT

(Staff Office, Fair Trade Commission,
April 21, 1987)

Introduction

In Japan's distribution system, it is common practice for consumer products purchased for sale by retailers or wholesalers to be returned to the seller if unsold, though the specific customs vary substantially depending on the product and the distribution stage. Groups representing merchants that supply goods to large retailers have for some time been making presentations to the Commission calling for the prohibition of this practice in those cases where it seems unfair under the provisions of the Antimonopoly Act. There has also been foreign criticism that the practice of returning unsold goods constitutes a barrier to market participation by those wishing to sell foreign goods in the Japanese market.

In Japan new consumer goods are developed in rapid succession, and many are manufactured in anticipation of market trends. The distribution sector is fiercely competitive. In this environment, the Japanese practice of returning unsold goods is an integral part of transaction conditions among partners dealing with each other on a continuing, long-term basis. From the economic viewpoint, the custom of returning goods facilitates the introduction of new products and offers a number of other advantages, including better ability to respond quickly to regional shifts in supply and demand. There are also problems, however. The practice increases distribution costs, leads to easygoing management habits in businesses who are able to return unsold goods, and can impose an unfair burden on businesses accepting returned goods.

These and other circumstances must be taken into account when studying the application of competition policies to the practice of returning goods. Efforts must be made to discover ways of retaining the advantages of the practice while eliminating its disadvantages.

This document presents the Commission's thinking on the application of the Antimonopoly Act to regulate the unjust return of unsold goods. It is hoped that this document will help to ensure fair trade by preventing unjust returns from occurring.

1. Legal Restraints on Unjust Returns

In general the practice of returning unsold goods is not covered by the regulations provided under the Antimonopoly Act. However, when there are differences in the status of the parties to a transaction and the party with an advantageous status employs that status to force the other party to accept unwarranted returns of unsold goods, thereby damaging that party, the returns can be regarded as an abuse of dominant bargaining position and subjected to regulation under the Antimonopoly Act.

The unjust return of unsold goods can be regulated under the provisions of Article 14, paragraphs 3 and 4, of *Unfair Trade Practices* (FTC Notification No. 15 of 1982; hereinafter referred to as "General Designations"). In addition, when the unsold goods are returned by large retailers to their suppliers, regulations can be applied under the provisions of Article 1 of *Specific Unfair Trade Practices in the Department Store Industry* (FTC Notification No. 7 of 1954; hereinafter referred to as "Specific Designations for the Department Store Industry").

2. Interpretation of General Designations

The following stipulations are provided in Article 14, paragraphs 3 and 4, of the General Designations:

> (Abuse of dominant bargaining position)
> Article 14. Taking any act specified in one of the following paragraphs, unjustly in the light of the normal business practices, by making use of one's dominant bargaining position over the other party:

3. Setting or changing transaction terms in a way disadvantageous to the said party;

4. In addition to any act coming under the preceding three paragraphs, imposing a disadvantage on the said party regarding terms or execution of transaction.

The viewpoint of the Commission with regard to the application of these stipulations to returns of goods is as follows.

(1) Dominant bargaining position

The phrase "dominant bargaining position over the other party" is understood as a situation in which the party purchasing goods enjoys a relatively superior bargaining position over the supplier, irrespective of whether the purchaser has a monopolistic or an oligopolistic position in the market, and is therefore capable of unfairly causing losses to the other party. The existence of such an advantage must be determined individually and specifically, taking into account such factors as overall differences in business capabilities (according to a comparison of capital, numbers of employees, gross sales, etc.), the trading relationship (including the degree of dependence on the transaction and the need to trade on a continuing basis), and the supply-and-demand situation for the goods being traded.

(2) Unjust return of unsold goods

a. Two conditions must be taken into account before the return of unsold goods by a party that enjoys a dominant bargaining position is judged to be an act that is taken unjustly in the light of normal business practices and that imposes a disadvantage on the other party. Here, "normal business practices" are defined as practices that are acceptable from the viewpoint of maintaining and promoting fair competition. In this sense, a practice cannot automatically be justified simply because it conforms to existing business customs.

Condition 1: A clear prior understanding was reached between both parties at the time of purchase to the effect that the return of goods is permitted under the terms of the transaction.

Condition 2: The risk burden from the return of unsold goods under the terms of the transaction is not disadvantageous to the other party when seen in relation to the other transaction conditions.

The need to return unsold goods and the circumstances under which the goods are returned must also be taken into account in deciding on specific cases.

b. In general, businesses engage in transactions on the basis of mutual understanding, after taking into account all the conditions relating to the transaction and calculating the advantages and disadvantages. The same is true of transactions between unequal parties that provide for the return of unsold goods.

If it is not clearly understood by both parties prior to the transaction that the terms of the transaction provide for the return of unsold goods, the party whose trading position is weaker may incur losses that could not be taken into account beforehand when goods are returned. Such a case may be deemed an unjust return of goods.

When one party to a transaction is superior in status to the other party and the burden of risk to suffer a disadvantage associated with the return of unsold goods is only on the party whose status is inferior, in view of the terms of transactions such as margins this may also be deemed an unjust return of goods.

c. Regardless of the preceding two conditions, the return of unsold goods shall not be deemed unjust under the following circumstances: First, returns due to reasons attributable to the supplier, such as where the goods supplied were defective or differed from those ordered; second, returns due to the specific circumstances of a party to the transaction where the party accepting the returns will clearly not incur any loss and where the request by one party for the returns is accepted by the other party.

3. Interpretation of Specific Designations for the Department Store Industry

The following stipulations are provided in Article 1 of the Specific Designations for the Department Store Industry:

Article 1: The return to a supplier of all or part of goods purchased from the said supplier by a department store (including, here and hereinafter, actions that amount in essence to the return of goods, such as the conversion of the purchase agreement into a consignment sales agreement or the replacement of the goods), except under one of the circumstances defined in the following paragraphs.

1. If the goods delivered are soiled, damaged, incomplete, or in any other way imperfect due to reasons attributable to the supplier, and the

said goods are returned to the supplier within a reasonable period of time from the date of delivery.

2. If the goods delivered are different from those ordered, and the said goods are returned to the supplier within a reasonable period of time from the date of delivery.

3. If it is the normal trade practice in general wholesale transactions other than those between the department store and the supplier to return goods within a certain period of time from the date of delivery or up to a certain amount of the total supplied, and the goods are returned to the supplier within the period of time or up to the amounts that constitute the said normal practice.

4. If the goods are returned to the supplier subject to the payment by the department store of any costs that would normally be incurred in the return of goods and subject to the agreement of the supplier.

5. If the goods are returned in response to a request from the supplier in a case where the supplier will profit directly from the disposal of the said goods after they are returned.

When a large retailer that can be characterized as a department store, as defined in the Specific Designations for the Department Store Industry, has purchased goods from a supplier whose trading status is inferior to that of the large retailer, the retailer is prohibited from returning the goods to the supplier except under the circumstances defined in each paragraph of Article 1, such as where the goods are imperfect due to reasons attributable to the supplier. In applying the provisions of Article 1, paragraph 3, the Commission will determine whether the return of goods constitutes a normal trade practice according to whether or not the following conditions are fulfilled.

Condition 1: A clear prior understanding exists between both parties at the time of purchase to the effect that the return of goods is permitted.

Condition 2: The risk burden from the return of unsold goods under the terms of the transaction is not disadvantageous to the other party when seen in relation to the other conditions of transaction.

Condition 3: The period during which unsold goods may be returned is, in principle, understood beforehand by both parties.

The need to return unsold goods and the circumstances under which the goods are returned must also be taken into account in deciding on specific cases.

DISTRIBUTION SYSTEM
AND BUSINESS PRACTICES
GUIDELINES

THE ANTIMONOPOLY ACT GUIDELINES
CONCERNING DISTRIBUTION SYSTEM
AND BUSINESS PRACTICES

(Staff Office, Fair Trade Commission, July 11, 1991)

Introduction

1. Practices regarding distribution system and business transactions have been formed with various historical and social backgrounds, and they differ from one country to another. And there is the need to review them from time to time in order to change them for the better. In accordance with the increasing globalization of economic activity and the enhancement of Japan's international status, and under increased need to enrich national life, Japanese distribution system and business practices, too, are called on to change in the direction of further protecting consumers' interests and making the Japanese market more open internationally. For this purpose, it is essential to promote free and fair competition and enable the market mechanism to fully perform its functions: more specifically, to make sure that [1] firms be not prevented from freely entering a market, [2] each firm can freely and independently select its customers or suppliers, [3] price and other transaction terms can be set via each firm's free and independent business judgement, and [4] competition be engaged in by fair means on the basis of price, quality and service.

This set of the Guidelines is intended to contribute to preventing firms and trade associations from violating the Antimonopoly Act and helping in the pursuit of their appropriate activities, by specifically describing, with respect to Japanese distribution system and business practices, the types of conduct which may impede free and fair competition and violate the Antimonopoly Act.

2. Part I of these Guidelines sets forth guidance under the Antimonopoly Act concerning the continuity and exclusiveness of transactions among firms, mainly keeping in mind transactions of producer goods and capital goods between producers and users, and Part II states guidance under the said Act concerning transactions in distribution, mainly keeping in mind transactions in the distribution process in which consumer goods reach their consumers.

However, there is no difference in guidance under the Antimonopoly Act between transactions of producer goods and capital goods and those of consumer goods. That is, if there are business practices regarding transactions of consumer goods which are not described in Part II but in Part I, the guidance provided in Part I shall apply to them. And if there are business practices regarding transactions of producer goods and capital goods which are not described in Part I but in Part II, the guidance provided in Part II shall apply to them.

Furthermore, Part III provides guidance under the Antimonopoly Act concerning sole distributorship for the entire domestic market, regardless of the nature of goods. If there are business practices which are not described in Part III but in Part I or II, the guidance provided in Part I or II shall apply to them.

In addition, although these Guidelines provide guidance mainly with respect to goods, the same guidance shall fundamentally apply to service trade.

3. Among the types of conduct described in these Guidelines, "Customer Allocation" and "Boycotts" in Part I, and "Resale Price Maintenance" and so forth in Part II, in principle constitute violations of the Antimonopoly Act. On the other hand, regarding other types of conduct, whether or not each conduct constitutes a violation of the Antimonopoly Act is to be judged on a case-by-case basis, analyzing its effect on competition in a market.

These Guidelines provide guidance on major types of business practices which may present a problem under the Antimonopoly Act, with respect to distribution system and business practices. The Guidelines, however, do not cover all types of practices which may present a problem. For example, price fixing cartels, supply restriction cartels, purchase volume cartels, and bid riggings, which are not covered in the Guidelines, in principle constitute violations of the Antimonopoly Act. Accordingly, it is to be judged on a case-by-case basis whether other types of business practices not provided in these Guidelines may present a problem under the Antimonopoly Act.

There may be cases where it is difficult for firms and others to know whether or not particular practices may present a problem under the Antimonopoly Act in the light of these Guidelines. Accordingly, at the publication of the Guidelines, a prior consultation system concerning distribution system and business practices shall be established in order to respond to specific consultations (see Appendix II).

PART I THE ANTIMONOPOLY ACT GUIDELINES CONCERNING THE CONTINUITY AND EXCLUSIVENESS OF BUSINESS PRACTICES AMONG FIRMS

1. There sometimes could be seen continuous transaction relationships with specific customers or suppliers, mainly in transactions between firms of producer goods and capital goods.

However, if business relationships between firms continue over a long period of time due to each firm's choice of trading partners on its own independent judgement based on price, quality, service, and other transaction terms, there would be no problem from the viewpoint of the Antimonopoly Act.

Furthermore, there may be a case where a firm, in selecting its trading partners, takes account of such overall business capability of suppliers as steady supply, technological capabilities, and flexibility in response to the firm's requests, in addition to price, quality, service, and other transaction terms in individual transactions. If total evaluation by the firm from the viewpoint mentioned above, of transaction terms of goods or services to be purchased from the suppliers, results in continuous transaction relationships, there would be no problem under the Antimonopoly Act.

If, however, any firm consults with another firm to mutually respect of or to place priority to the existing business relations to ensure the continuation of such relations, or engages in such conduct as concertedly with another firm excluding competitors, competition to win customers in a market is to be restrained and entries of new competitors hindered, which result in restraining competition in the market. Moreover, if any firm does business with its trading partners on condition that the latter shall not deal with the former's competitors, or the former applies pressure on the latter to prevent it from doing business with the former's competitors, adverse effects on competition in a market is to be produced, including prevention of new entrants from entering the market.

2. There sometimes could be seen cases where firms mutually hold each other's stocks to have stable stockholders, or hold stocks of their trading partners to facilitate their transactions.

Since acquisition or possession by a company of another company's stocks may affect competitive order, such acquisition or possession is regulated in various ways under the Antimonopoly Act. Any company may acquire or possess stocks of another company freely in principle, so long as it does not contravene these regulations.

However, even if acquisition or possession of stocks of another company in itself is not subject to the regulations of the Antimonopoly Act, should a firm, in carrying on transactions with its trading partners whose stocks are owned by it, prevent them from doing business with its competitors, by making use of the stockholding relationships, or for the same reason, give priority to transactions with them, it would have adverse effects on competition in a market, including prevention of newcomers and others with no stockholding relationship, from entering the market.

Furthermore, so-called business groups have been formed by means of holding stocks by a specific firm of many of its trading partners, or mutually holding stocks and dispatching executives among firms belonging to different industries. Transactions between firms belonging to the same business group can be considered in the same light as described above.

3. What follows in Part I, keeping in mind transactions of producer goods and capital goods between producers and users, describes guidance under the Antimonopoly Act primarily on business practices undertaken to establish or maintain continuous transaction relationships, or undertaken on the strength of such relationships, which may result in hindrance of new entries of firms into a market or exclusion of existing ones from the market, chiefly from the viewpoint of regulation of unreasonable restraint of trade and unfair trade practices.

CHAPTER I CUSTOMER ALLOCATION

1. Viewpoint

Such conduct of a firm in concert with any other firm or firms, or of a trade association as mutually respecting existing business relations without contending for customers or agreeing not to enter a market where another firm has already engaged in business activities, is sometimes employed for the purpose of securing the continuation of existing business relations in a situation where many firms are engaged in continuous transactions. Such conduct is most likely to lead to an attempt to exclude new entrants from the market for the purpose of ensuring the effectiveness of that conduct.

Such conduct, which restricts competition for customers, is in principle illegal.

2. Concerted Restrictions by Firms on Competition for Customers

In cases where a firm, concertedly with any other firm or firms, engages in the following types of conduct, for instance, and if competition for customers is thereby restricted and competition in a market becomes substantially restrained, such conduct constitutes unreasonable restraint of trade and violates Section 3 of the Antimonopoly Act (Note 1):

(1) Customer Allocation

  [1] Manufacturers concertedly arrange mutually not to deal with customers of other firms;
  [2] Distributors concertedly restrain each other from winning over customers from other firms by offering lower prices;
  [3] Distributors concertedly arrange to require payment of a rectification charge when one of the distributors deals with any customer of other firms;
  [4] Manufacturers concertedly arrange to require each other to register customers, and refrain from dealing with any customer other than those registered; or
  [5] Distributors concertedly restrict customers which each of the distributors deals with.

(2) Market Allocation

  [1] Manufacturers concertedly restrict each other's sales territory;
  [2] Distributors concertedly arrange not to start sales activities in any area where other firm or firms have already engaged in sales activities;
  [3] Manufacturers concertedly restrict standards and kinds of products to be manufactured by each firm; or
  [4] Manufacturers concertedly arrange not to start manufacturing any kind of products already being manufactured by other firm or firms.

(Note 1) Even in the absence of an explicit agreement, if a tacit understanding or a common intent is formed among firms regarding customer allocation or market allocation, thereby substantially restraining competition in a market, this in itself constitutes a violation of the Antimonopoly Act. The same shall apply in Part 1.

3. Restrictions by Trade Associations on Competition for Customers

In cases where a trade association, in connection with its member firms' activities, undertakes any of such conduct as described in the foregoing Section 2(1)[1] through [5] or (2)[1] through [4], and if competition for customers among member firms is thereby restricted and competition in a market becomes substantially restrained, such conduct constitutes a violation of Section 8(1)(i) of the Antimonopoly Act. Even if the conduct does not cause substantial restraint of competition in the market, it in principle constitutes a violation of Section 8(1)(iv) of the Antimonopoly Act, because it unjustly restricts the functions or activities of member firms.

CHAPTER 2 BOYCOTTS

1. Viewpoint

Even if free and fair competition results in compelling a firm to exit from a market or to fail to enter the market, it would present no problem under the Antimonopoly Act.

It is, however, in principle illegal for a firm, in concert with its competitors, customers or suppliers, etc., or for a trade association to prevent new entrants from entering a market or exclude existing firms from the market, because such conduct impairs the freedom of firms to enter a market, which is a prerequisite for effective competition.

There are a variety of types in which concerted refusals to deal (boycotts) may take place, and their extent of effect on competition may vary with, among other things, the market structure as well as the degree of probability that such conduct would prevent a firm from entering a market or exclude a firm from the market. A concerted refusal to deal, if it makes it very difficult for a firm to enter a market, or its effect is to exclude a firm from the market, judging from, among other things, the number and position in the market of the firms concerned as well as characteristics of the products or services concerned, thereby resulting in substantial restraint of competition in the market, is illegal as unreasonable restraint of trade. A concerted refusal to deal, even if it does not cause substantial restraint of competition in a market, is, in principle, illegal as unfair trade practices, because it generally tends to impede fair competition. In the case of a trade association arranging for a concerted refusal to deal, such conduct is illegal as substantial restraint of competition by trade associations, or obstruction of competition by them (conduct to limit the number of firms in any particular field of business; to unjustly restrict the functions or activities of member firms; or to induce any firm to engage in such acts as constitute unfair trade practices).

2. Refusals to Deal in Concert with Competitors

(1) In cases where competitors concertedly engage in, for instance, the following types of conduct, and, if the conduct makes it very difficult for any firm refused to deal with to enter a market, or its effect is to exclude the refused firm from the market, thereby resulting in substantial restraint of competition in the market (Note 2), such conduct constitutes unreasonable restraint of trade and violates Section 3 of the Antimonopoly Act.

[1] Manufacturers concertedly, in an attempt to exclude price-cutting distributors, refuse or restrict the supply of products to such distributors;

[2] Distributors concertedly, in an attempt to prevent new entries by competitors, refuse to supply products to new entrants as well as cause their suppliers (manufacturers) to refuse to supply products to new entrants;

[3] Manufacturers concertedly, in an attempt to exclude imported products, inform distributors of their intention to refuse to supply products if the distributors deal in the imported products, and thereby causing the said distributors to refuse to deal in the imported products; or

[4] Finished product manufacturers concertedly, in an attempt to prevent competitors from entering a market, inform material suppliers of their intention to refuse to deal if the suppliers provide the materials to new entrants, and thereby causing the material suppliers to refuse to supply to the new entrants.

(Note 2) In cases where a concerted refusal to deal brings about such situations as follows, competition in a market shall be found to be substantially restrained:

[1] In case where it is made very difficult for any firm manufacturing or selling products superior in price and quality to enter a market, or in case where such a firm is to be excluded from the market;

[2] In case where it is made very difficult for any firm adopting innovative selling methods to enter a market, or in case where such firm is to be excluded from the market;

[3] In case where it is made very difficult for any firm having superior overall business capabilities to enter a market, or in case where such firm is to be excluded from the market;

[4] In case where it is made very difficult for any firm having superior overall business capabilities to enter a market where no active competition is taking place; or

[5] In case where a concerted refusal to deal is conducted toward any potential entrant, and if it makes it very difficult for the potential entrant to enter a market.

(2) Any type of conduct described in (1)[1] through [4] above, undertaken in concert by competitors, even if the conduct does not cause substantial restraint of competition in a market, is in principle illegal as unfair trade practices (Violations of Section 19 of the Antimonopoly Act, Article I (Concerted Refusal to Deal) of the General Designation).

3. *Refusals to Deal in Concert with Customers, Suppliers, etc.*

(1) In cases where a firm or firms concertedly with their customers, suppliers, etc., engage in, for instance, the following types of conduct, and if the conduct makes it very difficult for any firm refused to deal with to enter a market, or its effect is to exclude the refused firm from the market, thereby resulting in substantial restraint of competition in the market, such conduct constitutes unreasonable restraint of trade (Note 3) and violates Section 3 of the Antimonopoly Act.

[1] Distributors and manufacturers concertedly, in an attempt to exclude price-cutting distributors, undertake such conduct that the latter refuses or restricts the supply of products to such distributors and that the former refuses to deal in the products of those manufacturers which have supplied their products to such distributors;

[2] A manufacturer and its distributors concertedly, in an attempt to exclude imported products, undertake such conduct that the latter does not deal in the imported products and that the former refuses to supply products to those distributors selling the imported products;

[3] Distributors and a manufacturer concertedly, in an attempt to prevent other distributors from entering a market, undertake such conduct that the latter refuses to supply products to new entrants and that the former refuses to deal in the products of those manufacturers which have supplied their products to such new entrants; or

[4] Material manufacturers and a finished product manufacturer concertedly, in an attempt to exclude imported materials, undertake such conduct that the latter does not purchase the imported materials, and that the former refuses to supply materials to those finished product manufacturers which have purchased the imported materials.

(Note 3) For any conduct to constitute unreasonable restraint of trade, it is required that any firm in concert with other firms, "mutually restrict their business activities" (Section 2(6) of the Antimonopoly Act). The content of restrictions of business activities in this context does not need to be identical in all firms (for example, distributors and manufacturers), but is sufficient if the conduct restricts the business activities of each firm and is for the purpose of achieving a common purpose, such as the exclusion of any specific firm.

As for examples of cases where competition in a market shall be found to be substantially restrained through refusals to deal in concert with customers, suppliers, etc., see Note 2 above.

(2) Any type of conduct described in (1)[1] through [4] above, undertaken by any firm concertedly with its customers, suppliers, etc., even if the conduct does not cause substantial restraint of competition in a market, is in principle illegal as unfair trade practices (Article 1 (Concerted Refusal to Deal) or 2 (Other Refusal to Deal) of the General Designation).

4. Refusals to Deal Arranged by Trade Associations

In cases where a trade association engages in, for instance, the following types of conduct, and if the conduct makes it very difficult for any firm refused to deal with to enter a market, or its effect is to exclude the refused firm from the market, thereby resulting in substantial restraint of competition in the market (Note 4), such conduct violates Section 8(1)(i) of the Antimonopoly Act. Furthermore, in any case where a trade association engages in the following types of conduct, even if such conduct does not cause substantial restraint of competition in a market, such conduct, in principle, violates Section 8(1)(iii), 8(1)(iv), or 8(1)(v) (Article 1 (Concerted Refusal to Deal) or 2 (Other Refusal to Deal) of the General Designation) of the Antimonopoly Act.

[1] A trade association composed of distributors, in an attempt to exclude imported products, prohibits member firms from dealing in the imported products (Section 8(1)(i) or 8(1)(iv) of the Antimonopoly Act);

[2] A trade association composed of distributors and manufacturers induces member manufacturers to supply products only to member distributors and not to outsiders (Section 8(1)(i) or 8(1)(iv) of the Antimonopoly Act);

[3] A trade association composed of distributors, in an attempt to exclude outsiders, applies pressure on manufacturers dealing with member distributors, by requesting the manufacturers not to supply products to outsiders or through other means (Section 8(1)(i) or 8(1)(v) of the Antimonopoly Act);

[4] A trade association composed of distributors, in an attempt to prevent competitors of member firms from entering a market, applies pressure on manufacturers dealing with member distributors, by requesting the manufacturers not to supply products to those new entrants or through other means (Section 8(1)(i) or 8(1)(v) of the Antimonopoly Act);

[5] A trade association composed of distributors restricts new membership in the association and causes manufacturers dealing with member distributors to refuse to supply products to outsiders (Section 8(1)(i), 8(1)(iii), or 8(1)(v) of the Antimonopoly Act); or

[6] A trade association composed of service providers restricts new membership in the association under the circumstances where it is difficult for the service providers to carry on business without membership (Section 8(1)(iii) of the Antimonopoly Act).

(Note 4) As for examples of cases where competition in a market shall be found to be substantially restrained through concerted refusals to deal arranged by trade associations, see Note 2 above.

CHAPTER 3 PRIMARY REFUSALS TO DEAL BY A SINGLE FIRM

1. Viewpoint

Basically speaking, it is a matter of freedom of choice of trading partners for a firm to decide which firm it does business with. Even if a firm, considering such factors as price, quality and service, decides not to deal with a certain firm at its own judgement, there would be fundamentally no problem under the Antimonopoly Act.

However, exceptionally, even a refusal to deal by a single firm is illegal in cases where the firm refuses to deal as a means to secure the effectiveness of its illegal conduct under the Antimonopoly Act. A refusal to deal by a single firm may also present a problem in cases where the firm refuses to deal as a means to achieve such unjust purposes under the Antimonopoly Act as excluding its competitors from a market.

2. Primary Refusals to Deal by a Single Firm

In cases where a firm engages in such conduct as [1] below as a means to secure the effectiveness of its illegal practice under the Antimonopoly Act, such conduct is illegal as unfair trade practices (Article 2 (Other refusal to deal) of the General Designation).

Moreover, in cases where an influential firm in a market engages in such conduct as [2] or [3] below as a means to achieve such unjust purposes under the Antimonopoly Act as excluding its competitors from a market, and if such conduct may make it difficult for the refused firm to carry on normal business activities, such conduct is illegal as unfair trade practices (Article 2 (Other Refusal to Deal) of the General Designation):

[1] An influential manufacturer in a market (Note 5), by causing its distributors not to deal with its competitors, reduces business opportunities of the competitors, and prevents them from easily finding alternative trading partners, and, with a view to ensuring the effectiveness of such conduct, refuses to deal with distributors not yielding to this request (Article 11 (Dealing on Exclusive Terms) of the General Designation shall also apply to such conduct);

[2] A material manufacturer influential in a market, in an attempt to prevent its customers (finished product manufacturers) from manufacturing for themselves some of the materials supplied by the material manufacturer, stops the supply of main materials which have been supplied to the finished product manufacturers; or

[3] A material manufacturer influential in a market, in an attempt to exclude competitors of its customers (finished product manufacturers) which have close relations with it (Note 6) from the said finished product market, stops the supply of the materials which have been supplied to these competitors.

(Note 5) As to the definition of "an influential firm in a market," see Note 7 below.

(Note 6) A firm "which has close relations" with another firm means one having common interests with the other. Whether or not a firm has close relations with another firm is to be judged on a case-by-case basis, taking comprehensively into consideration such factors as stockholding relationship, interlocking or dispatching of directorates, trading and financing relationship, and common membership of so-called business groups. The same shall apply in Part I.

CHAPTER 4 RESTRICTIONS ON TRADING PARTNERS OF DEALING WITH COMPETITORS

1. Viewpoint

If a firm deals with its customers or suppliers on condition that the latter does not deal with the former's competitors, the latter is to be unable to deal with other firms, and this may also reduce the business opportunities of the competitors. Moreover, there is the concern that, where firms are doing business with one another on a continuous basis, it may become easier for them, for the purpose of maintaining the existing business relations, to put pressure on their customers or suppliers not to deal with their competitors.

Such conduct infringes on the freedom of choice of trading partners, and at the same time tends to reduce business opportunities of competitors, and, therefore, may pose a problem under the Antimonopoly Act.

2. Restrictions on Trading Partners of Dealing with Competitors

In cases where an influential firm in a market (Note 7), by means of the following manners, engages in transactions with its trading partners on condition that the trading partners shall not deal with competitors of the firm or another firm having close relations with the firm (Note 8), or causes the trading partners to refuse to deal with those above-mentioned competitors, and if such conduct may result in reducing business opportunities of the competitors and making it difficult for them to easily find alternative trading partners (Note 9), such conduct is illegal as unfair trade practices (Articles 2 (Other Refusal to Deal), 11 (Dealing on Exclusive Terms), or 13 (Dealing on Restrictive Terms) of the General Designation) (Note 10).

[1] An influential material supplier in a market, by notifying or suggesting to its customers (manufacturers) that it intends to discontinue the supply of materials to the customers if they carry on business with other material suppliers, requests the customers not to carry on business with other material suppliers (Article 11 of the General Designation);

[2] A finished product manufacturer influential in a market requests an influential parts manufacturer not to sell parts or to restrict the sales of parts to competing finished product manufacturers, and obtains consent from such parts manufacturer to that effect (Articles 11 or 13 of the General Designation);

[3] An influential financial firm in a market provides finance for an influential distributor on condition that the distributor exclusively deals with a manufacturer having close relations with the financial firm; or

[4] An influential manufacturer in a market causes its customers (distributors) not to accept an offer of transactions by a specific manufacturer attempting to enter the market (Article 2 of the General Designation).

(Note 7) Whether a firm is "influential in a market" is in the first instance judged by a market share of the firm, that is, whether it has no less than 10% or its position is within the top three in the market (meaning a product market which consists of a group of products with the same or similar function and utility as the product covered by the conduct, and competing with each other judging from geographical conditions, transactional relations and other factors.)

Nonetheless, even if a firm falls under this criterion, the firm's conduct is not always illegal. In cases where the conduct may result in reducing business opportunities of the competitors and making it difficult for them to easily find alternative trading partners, such conduct is illegal.

In case of a low-ranked or newly-entered firm which has a market share of less than 10% and whose position is the fourth or later, the conduct usually would not result in reducing business opportunities of the competitors and making it difficult for them to easily find alternative trading partners, and such conduct is not illegal.

The same shall apply in Chapters 5 through 7 of Part I with regard to whether a firm is "influential in a market."

(Note 8) In addition to cases where a contract or an agreement between a firm and its trading partners stipulates that the trading partners shall not deal with the firm's competitors, if any artificial means is taken by the firm to secure the effectiveness of such restriction, the firm shall be found as dealing with the trading partners on a condition that restricts transactions with the competitors.

(Note 9) Whether or not "such conduct may result in reducing business opportunities of competitors and making it difficult for them to easily find alternative trading partners" is to be determined on a case-by-case basis, taking comprehensively into account the following factors:

[1] Structure of the market (market concentration, characteristics of the product, degree of product differentiation, distribution channels, difficulty in new market entry, etc.);

[2] Position of the firm in the market (in terms of market share, rank, brand name, etc.);

[3] Number of parties affected by the conduct at issue and their positions in the market; and

[4] Impact of the conduct on business activities of the affected parties (extent, manner, etc. of the conduct).

As an element of market structure listed in [1] above, other firms' behaviors are also to be considered. For example, in cases where two or more firms respectively and parallelly restrict transactions with their competitors, it is more likely to result in reducing business opportunities of the competitors and making it difficult for them to easily find alternative trading partners, compared to cases where only one firm does.

The same shall apply in Chapters 5 through 7 of Part I with regard to whether such conduct "may result in reducing business opportunities of competitors and making it difficult for them to easily find alternative trading partners."

(Note 10) In cases where there is such proper justification under the Antimonopoly Act, in restricting transactions with competitors as follows, such restriction is not illegal:

[1] In case where a finished product manufacturer which commissions
parts manufacturers to make parts, supplying materials to them,
requires them to sell the parts made with the materials exclusively
to itself; or

[2] In case where a finished product manufacturer which commissions
parts manufacturer to make parts, supplying materials and providing
know-how (meaning those technologies related to industrial use and
excluding those that are not secret in nature), requires them to sell
parts exclusively to itself, and if such restriction is deemed necessary for keeping the know-how confidential, or preventing unauthorized exploitation of it.

CHAPTER 5   UNJUST RECIPROCAL DEALINGS

1. Viewpoint

(1) In cases where transactions are continuously taking place between
firms, the parties to the transactions, mutually selling products required by
each other, may engage in reciprocal dealings (meaning transactions in
which the purchases by one party of the other party's products are linked
with the sales of the one party's products to the other party) in order to keep
the existing business relationship as long as possible, and maintain mutual
trust between the transacting parties. Such dealings may take place not only
between directly transacting parties, but also between one party and another
firm having close relations with the other party.

(2) If each firm reciprocally deals with another as a result of its free choice
of suppliers of products with better price, quality, service, and so forth, it
does not present any problem under the Antimonopoly Act.
    However, if one firm, by making use of its buying power, makes condi-
tions on or compels the other to deal reciprocally, the conduct may infringe
the latter's free choice of trading partners, or create the effect of reducing
business opportunities of the former's competitors or of firms that are
unable to accept reciprocal dealings, and may present a problem as unjust
reciprocal dealing.

(3) In cases where a firm establishes a department or appoints personnel to
supervise both purchases and sales, and has the department or personnel
compare and check data on such purchases and sales, and systematically
maintain lists of the volumes of purchases from and sales to each specific

firm, or exchanges lists of customers and suppliers between the purchases and sales departments, and if such conduct is carried out in order not to ensure recovery of credits but to have its purchase records from specific firms reflect on the sales of its products to those firms, such conduct is most likely to invite unjust reciprocal dealings.

2 Reciprocal Dealings by Making Use of Buying Power

(1) In cases where an influential firm in a purchase market deals with the other party (supplier) on a continuous basis by means of the following manners on condition that the other party purchases the firm's products, and if such conduct may result in reducing business opportunities of firms not buying or unable to buy products from the influential firm, or of competitors of the influential firm and making it difficult for those firms to easily find alternative trading partners, such conduct is illegal as unfair trade practices (Article 13 (Dealing on Restrictive Terms) of the General Designation) (Note 11):

[1] The influential firm, indicating that it would terminate or reduce purchases from the other party unless the other party purchases the firm's products, requests the other party to purchase the firm's products;

[2] The procurement personnel in the influential firm, suggesting that the influential firm's purchases would be affected, requests the other party to purchase the firm's products;

[3] The influential firm, setting a sales target of its products for each transacting party on the basis of the amount of purchases from the latter, and indicating that the latter's failure to attain this target would result in a reduction in the volume of purchases by the firm from the latter, requests the latter to purchase a large enough amount to meet the sales target;

[4] The influential firm, revealing the comparative list of each transacting party's purchases from and sales to the firm and suggesting that it would otherwise purchase only a corresponding volume, requests additional purchases by each party; or

[5] In response to the other party's offer to sell, the influential firm, indicating that it would purchase the other party's products if the other party purchases services supplied by the firm or its designated firm, requests the other party to purchase the services.

(Note 11) If there is such proper justification under the Antimonopoly Act, that for one party to a transaction to ensure the quality of the products to be supplied by the other party, the former's supply of materials for the particular products to the latter is considered necessary, such conduct is not illegal (the same shall apply in 3 below).

(2) Furthermore, in cases where a firm, by making use of its buying power (Note 12), engages in any type of the conduct described in (1)[1] through [5] above, or any of the following types of conduct to the other party, and if the other party, under the circumstances in which the conduct takes place (including the firm's position in a market, relationship between the firm and the other party, market structure, and the extent and manner of the request or proposal), is to be compelled to purchase products from the firm, such conduct is illegal as unfair trade practices (Article 10 (Tie-in Sales, etc.) of the General Designation):

[1] Though the other party has expressed its intention not to purchase, the firm, saying that it has purchased services from that party, makes a request to the party and induces it to purchase the firm's products; or

[2] In spite of the absence of proposal by the other party to purchase, the firm unilaterally sends its products to that party, and offsets the products' total value against the unpaid balance due the latter.

(Note 12) In cases where a firm makes use of buying power of another firm having close relations with it, as well as buying power of its own, consideration is to be given to such use of buying power (the same shall apply in (3) below).

(3) In cases where, between firms having continuous business relations, the one party which is relatively in a dominant bargaining position over the other party (Note 13), by making use of that position, unjustly in the light of normal business practices, induces the latter which sells its products to the former, to buy products sold by the former or its designated firm, such conduct impairs transactions based on free and independent judgement by firms. Therefore, in cases where a firm in a dominant bargaining position induces the other party which sells its products to the firm, to buy products sold by the firm or its designated firm, by resorting to such conduct as described in (1)[1] through [5], or (2)[1] or [2] above, the conduct is illegal as unfair trade practices (Article 14 (Abuse of Dominant Bargaining Position) of General Designation).

(Note 13) One party in transaction shall be found to be "in a dominant bargaining position over the other party" in such cases where the latter is obliged to accept the former's requests even if they are excessively disadvantageous to the latter, since discontinuance of transaction with the former would significantly damage the latter's business. In making this finding, consideration is to be given to such factors as degree of dependence on the former, position of the former in a market, changeability of customers, and supply and demand situations of the product.

3. Reciprocal Dealings Based on Voluntary Consent Between Firms

In cases where firms having continuous business relations engage in reciprocal dealings based on voluntary mutual arrangements such that each party should purchase products from the other on condition of reciprocity, such reciprocal dealings are different from the cases in 2 above, in which one party unilaterally induces the other party to buy its products, and they present no problem except where a market is significantly to be foreclosed. One party to such dealings may give priority to transactions with the other party purchasing the one party's products, and the one party would respond only reluctantly to offers from competitors of the other party. As a result, these competitors would lose business opportunities to deal with the one party. Therefore, reciprocal dealings, even if based on voluntary consent, are illegal in the following cases:

(1) In case where an influential firm in a market, based on voluntary consent with the other party to a continuous transaction, engages in reciprocal dealings, in which both parties purchase products on condition that each party mutually purchase the other's products, and if such conduct may result in reducing business opportunities of other firms selling the products which are the object of said reciprocal dealings and making it difficult for such other firms to easily find alternative trading partners, such conduct is illegal as unfair trade practices (Article 13 (Dealing on Restrictive Terms) of the General Designation); or

(2) In case where a firm, based on voluntary consent, purchases products from the other party on condition that the latter buy products from another firm having close relations with the former, such conduct is to be assessed in accordance with the thinking described in (1) above. The same shall apply to reciprocal dealings, based on voluntary consent, among firms belonging to the same so-called business group.

CHAPTER 6   OTHER ANTICOMPETITIVE PRACTICES ON THE
            STRENGTH OF CONTINUOUS TRANSACTION
            RELATIONSHIPS

In addition to the conduct described above up to Chapter 5, the following types of conduct, for instance, on the strength of continuous transaction relationships, may present a problem under the Antimonopoly Act.

510 / *Appendix H*

1. Restriction on Dealings with Competitors by Price Meeting

(1) Reducing prices by a firm of its products in accordance with market conditions is indeed a manifestation of competition, and can be positively evaluated from the viewpoint of competition policy. However, in cases where the firm does business with its customers on condition that the customers continue business with the firm if the firm reduces its price in response to lower prices offered by its competitors, such conduct may reduce business opportunities of its competitors, and may present a problem under the Antimonopoly Act if a market is significantly to be foreclosed.

(2) In cases where an influential firm in a market, as a means to maintain continuous transaction relationships with its customers, continues business with such customers on conditions that the terms of any proposal made by the former's competitors be made known to the former, and that if the former reduces its sales price to the same level as or to a more attractive level than the price quoted by the competitors, the latter will not deal with the competitors or will maintain the volume of transaction with the former at the same level as before, and if such conduct may result in reducing the competitors' business opportunities and making it difficult for the competitors to easily find alternative trading partners, such conduct is illegal as unfair trade practices (Articles 11 (Dealing on Exclusive Terms) or 13 (Dealing on Restrictive Terms) of the General Designation).

2. Abuse of Dominant Bargaining Position on the Strength of Continuous Transaction Relationships

In cases where a firm in a dominant bargaining position on the strength of continuous transaction relationships, engages in such conduct that render unjust disadvantage in the light of normal business practices to its customers regarding terms or implementation of transactions, such conduct may impede the customers' transactions based on their free and independent judgement, or place other firms intending to deal on reasonable terms and the firm's competitors at a competitively disadvantageous position. Such conduct is illegal as unfair trade practices (Article 14 (Abuse of Dominant Bargaining Position) of the General Designation).

Whereas abuse of dominant bargaining position on the strength of continuous transaction relationships is apt to occur in transactions between a parental firm and its subcontractors (subcontract transactions), such conduct in subcontract transactions violates Section 4 of the Act Against Delay in Payment of Subcontract Proceeds, etc. to Subcontractors.

(For supplementary reference)

Act Against Delay in Payment of Subcontract Proceeds, etc. to Subcontractors (Act No. 120 of 1956) (excerpt)

Section 4 (Prohibited Conduct of Parental Firms)

(1) No parental firm shall, in case it gives a manufacturing commission or repairing commission to a subcontractor, effect any one of the following types of conduct:

i. Refusing to receive the work from a subcontractor without reason for which a subcontractor is responsible;

ii. Failing to make payment of subcontract proceeds after the lapse of the date of payment;

iii. Reducing the amount of subcontract proceeds without reason for which a subcontractor is responsible;

iv. Causing a subcontractor to take back the things relating to its work after receiving the work from the said subcontractor without reason for which the subcontractor is responsible;

v. Unjustly fixing a conspicuously lower amount of subcontract proceeds than the price ordinarily paid for the same or similar contents of work.

(The rest is omitted.)

CHAPTER 7 ACQUISITION OR POSSESSION OF STOCKS OF TRADING PARTNERS AND ANTICOMPETITIVE EFFECT

1. Viewpoint

(1) Since the acquisition by a company of stocks of another company may have effect on competitive order, the Antimonopoly Act prohibits the acquisition or possession of such stocks where its effect may be substantially to restrain competition in any particular field of trade. In addition, from the viewpoint of preventing excessive concentration of economic power, there also are provisions which prohibit establishing holding companies and restrict stockholdings by giant non-financial companies or financial companies (Note 14). However, a company may acquire or possess stocks of another company freely so long as it does not contravene these regulations.

(2) Even where the acquisition or possession of stocks by a company is not in itself subject to regulation, if a firm uses its holding of stocks of its trading partners as a means to restrict transactions by the said partners with the firm's competitors or unreasonably refuses to deal with any other firm of which it holds no stocks, such conduct may reduce business opportunities of new entrants and other firms with no stockholding relationship, and accordingly may present a problem under the Antimonopoly Act.

Whereas a firm may enter into a stockholding relationship with its trading partners with a view to facilitating transactions between them, if the former, by making use of its dominant bargaining position, acquires stocks of the latter, such conduct may present a problem under the Antimonopoly Act.

(3) When such conduct as constituting unfair trade practices has been committed, the Fair Trade Commission may order, besides a cease and desist order, any necessary measure to eliminate the conduct (Section 20 of the Antimonopoly Act). Therefore, in cases where such conduct as constituting unfair trade practices has been committed by a firm by means or by reason of the holding of stocks of its trading partners, the Commission will order the firm to cease and desist the conduct, and furthermore, if it is considered necessary, in order to eliminate the violation, to have the firm dispose of the stocks, because the violation is repeated or highly likely to be repeated, despite the cease and desist order, so long as the stockholding relationship continues to exist, the Commission will order the firm to dispose of the stocks in question.

If the acquisition or possession of stocks of the other party is achieved by means of unfair trade practices, the Fair Trade Commission may order any necessary measure, including the disposal of the stocks in question, to eliminate the violation (Section 17-2 of the Antimonopoly Act).

(Note 14) Regulations of acquisition or possession of stocks by a company under the Antimonopoly Act

[1] Prohibition of stockholding, etc. which would result in substantial restraint of competition (Section 10 of the Antimonopoly Act):
In cases where the effect of acquisition or possession of a domestic company's stocks may be substantially to restrain competition in any particular field of trade, such acquisition or possession is prohibited.

[2] Prohibition of holding companies (Section 9 of the Antimonopoly Act):
The formation of a company whose principal business is to control the business activities of domestic companies by means of stockholding and the transformation of a company to become such a holding company in Japan are prohibited.

[3] Restriction on total amount of stockholding by giant non-financial companies (Section 9-2 of the Antimonopoly Act):
A company having no less than 10 billion yen in capital or 30 billion yen in net assets (excluding financial companies described in [4] below) is prohibited from acquiring or holding stocks of domestic companies in excess of its capital or its net assets, whichever is larger.

[4] Restriction on stockholding by financial companies (Section 11 of the Antimonopoly Act):
Financial companies (meaning banks, trust banks, insurance companies, mutual financing associations and securities companies) are prohibited from acquiring or holding more than 5% (10% in the case of insurance companies) of the stocks of any domestic company.

2. Formation of Stockholding Relationship by Unfair Trade Practices

Whereas a firm, with a view to facilitating transactions or for some other purpose, sometimes acquires or holds stocks of any of its trading partners, or has any of them acquire or hold its own stocks, the following types of conduct undertaken as a means to do so, is illegal.

(1) Acquisition of stocks of trading partners by unfair trade practices

A company is prohibited from acquiring or holding stocks of any domestic company by means of unfair trade practices (Section 10 of the Antimonopoly Act). Acquisition of stocks of trading partners is illegal when it is achieved by a method which in itself constitutes unfair trade practices as well as by making the normal business activities of the trading partners difficult by means of unfair trade practices.

Acquisition of stocks by a firm of its trading partners by any of the following means, for instance, constitutes unfair trade practices and violates Section 10 of the Antimonopoly Act:

[1] A finished product manufacturer in a dominant bargaining position, by requesting its parts supplier to let it acquire stocks of the latter, or suggesting that the latter's failure to comply with the request would invite the former's refusal to deal with the latter, or imposition of unjustly disadvantageous terms on the latter, forces the latter to issue new stocks for allocation to third parties or take some other step which enables the former to acquire stocks of the latter (Article 14 (Abuse of Dominant Bargaining Position) of the General Designation); or

[2] An influential finished product manufacturer in a market, by inducing a material producer which supplies materials to a parts manufacturer, with whom the finished product manufacturer has no stockholding relationship, to refuse further supply of the materials to the parts manufacturer, makes the normal business activities of the parts manufacturer difficult and as a result the finished product manufacturer acquires stocks from stockholders of the parts manufacturer (Article 2 (Other refusal to deal) of the General Designation).

(2) Causing Trading Partners to Hold Stocks by Using Dominant Bargaining Position

In cases where a firm in a dominant bargaining position, by making use of that position, undertakes the following types of conduct, for instance, and thereby unjustly in the light of normal business practices, induces its trading partners to offer economic benefits or renders a disadvantage to them regarding transaction terms, such conduct is illegal as unfair trade practices (Article 14 (Abuse of Dominant Bargaining Position) of the General Designation):

> [1] A finished product manufacturer in a dominant bargaining position, by making use of that position, suggests to its parts supplier that the latter's failure to subscribe to stocks to be issued by the former would result in the former's suspension of dealings with the latter, and thereby obliges the parts supplier to subscribe to the stocks to be issued; or
>
> [2] A manufacturer in a dominant bargaining position, by making use of that position, supplies its products to its distributor which owns stocks of the manufacturer on condition that the distributor does not dispose of the stocks.

3. Exclusionary Conduct by Means or by Reason of Holding of Stocks of Trading Partners

In cases where a firm holds stocks of or is in a cross stockholding relationship with any of its trading partners, even if the proportion of stockholding is not particularly high, the former can use its position as a stockholder to influence decision-making processes by the latter, and may thereby engage in such conduct as impairing the latter's independent judgement in selecting trading partners, etc. Furthermore, in cases where a firm has a relationship of either unilateral or cross stockholdings with its trading partners, the firm may refuse to deal with other firms having no stockholding relationship with it, with the intent of excluding them from a market. Such conduct may impair the choice of trading partners through their own independent judgement based on price, quality, service, and other transaction terms. It may also reduce business opportunities of new entrants or other firms having no stockholding relationship, and may present a problem under the Antimonopoly Act.

(For cases where a firm and its trading partners are in a parent–subsidiary relationship, see Appendix I "Transactions between Parent and Subsidiary Companies.")

(1) Restrictions on trading partners' dealings with competitors by means of stockholding

In cases where an influential firm in a market, holding stocks of any of its trading partners, engages in the following types of conduct, for instance, and if such conduct may result in reducing business opportunities of competitors and making it difficult for them to easily find alternative trading partners, such conduct is illegal as unfair trade practices:

[1] An influential finished product manufacturer in a market notifies its parts supplier, whose stocks it holds, of its intention to dispose of the stocks and suspend business with the said supplier if the latter sells parts to the former's competitors who are attempting to enter the market, or makes suggestions to that effect, and thereby discourages the latter from dealing with the said competitors (Article 2 (Other Refusal to deal) of the General Designation); or

[2] An influential manufacturer in a market, by making use of its position as a stockholder, induces its distributor, whose stocks it holds, to give consent to the effect that the latter will deal only in the former's products (Article 11 (Dealing on Exclusive Terms) of the General Designation).

(2) Refusals to deal by reason of presence or absence of stockholding relationship

It is basically a matter of freedom of choice of trading partners for a firm to decide which firm it does business with.

However, in cases where an influential firm in a market, in any of the following manners, for instance, refuses to deal with other firms having no stockholding relationship with it, with a view to excluding them from the market, and if such conduct may make it difficult for the refused firm to engage in normal business activities, such conduct is illegal as unfair trade practices (Article 2 (Other Refusal to Deal) of the General Designation):

[1] An influential finished product manufacturer in a market stops purchasing from a parts manufacturer which has no stockholding relationship with it, with a view to excluding the competitors of a parts manufacturer which does have a stockholding relationship with it; or

[2] An influential parts manufacturer having a stockholding relationship with a finished product manufacturer, rejects a proposal for purchases of parts by a firm attempting to enter the finished product market, by reason of the absence of stockholding relationship with the parts manufacturer.

PART II THE ANTIMONOPOLY ACT GUIDELINES CONCERNING TRANSACTIONS IN DISTRIBUTION

1. Scope of the Guidelines

In order to sell its products, a manufacturer tends to conduct a variety of marketing activities, not only in connection with direct transactions with customers but also extending to the level of retailers and consumers. In cases where as a part of those marketing activities, a manufacturer interferes in, or influences, sales prices of distributors, kind of products they sell, their sales territories, their customers, etc., it is most likely to impede competition among distributors and among manufacturers.

On the other hand, it is most likely to have anticompetitive effect if a large-scale retailer seeks to utilize its dominant bargaining positions over its suppliers, on the strength of buying power.

This Part, mainly keeping in mind transactions in the distribution process in which consumer goods reach their consumers, provides guidance under the Antimonopoly Act on the following types of conduct, from the viewpoint of regulation of unfair trade practices: [1] conduct by manufacturers (Note 1) vis-a-vis their distributors regarding restrictions of sales price, products handled, sales territories, customers, etc., provision of rebates and allowances, and interference in management; and [2] transactions between retailers and their suppliers, with regard to coercion to purchase, return of unsold goods, request for dispatch of salespersons to shops, coercive collection of contributions, and request for frequent delivery in small lots.

(Note 1) The term "manufacturer" shall include a sole distributor, wholesaler or the like which conducts marketing activities as a principal.

2. Unjust Low-price Sales and Discriminatory Pricing

As an issue under the Antimonopoly Act in relation to distribution, in addition to these two types of conduct, there is the matter of unjust low-price sales and discriminatory pricing.

Unjust low-price sales and discriminatory pricing as defined below are prohibited under the Antimonopoly Act as unfair trade practices:

[1] Without proper justification, supplying a commodity or service continuously at a price which is excessively below cost incurred in the said supply, or otherwise unjustly supplying a commodity or service at a low price, thereby tending to cause difficulties to the business activities of

other entrepreneurs (Article 6 (Unjust Low-price Sales) of the General Designation).

[2] Unjustly supplying or accepting a commodity or service at prices which discriminate between regions or between the other parties (Article 3 (Discriminatory Pricing) of the General Designation).

As to unjust low-price sales and discriminatory pricing relating to them, the Fair Trade Commission has already provided guidance on them in the Guidelines Concerning Unjust Low-price Sales under the Antimonopoly Act published in 1984, and will address these practices properly in accordance with these Guidelines.

CHAPTER 1   RESALE PRICE MAINTENANCE

1. Viewpoint

(1) It is one of the most basic matters in a firm's business activities that it independently determines its own sales price, in keeping with conditions in a market, and moreover this secures competition among firms and consumer choice.

In cases where, as one aspect of marketing activities, or as requested by distributors, a manufacturer restricts sales price of distributors, it is in principle illegal as unfair trade practices, because it reduces or eliminates price competition among distributors.

(2) In cases where a manufacturer's suggested retail price or quotation is indicated to distributors as a reference price, such conduct itself is not a problem (Note 2). In cases where the price is not merely given as a reference price, however, and the manufacturer seeks to restrict resale price of the distributors by causing them to keep the reference price, such conduct falls under the conduct described (1) above, and is in principle illegal.

(Note 2) In cases where a manufacturer sets a suggested retail price, it is desirable that the manufacturer does not use such representations as "True Price" (seika), "Set Price" (teika), or the figures of the price alone, but non-binding expressions such as "Reference Price" (sanko kakaku) or "manufacturer's suggested retail price", and that in case of announcing the suggested price to distributors and consumers, the manufacturer clearly states that the suggested retail price is given solely for reference and that each distributor should determine its resale price independently.

2. *Restrictions of Resale Price*

(1) Restrictions by a manufacturer of sales price of distributors (resale price) are in principle illegal as unfair trade practices (Article 12 (Resale Price Restriction) of the General Designation).

(2) Whether resale prices have been restricted is to be judged based on the determination of whether any artificial means is taken to secure the effectiveness in attaining sales at the price indicated by the manufacturer.

In the following cases, it shall be judged that the effectiveness in attaining sales at the price indicated by the manufacturer is secured:

[1] In case where a written or oral agreement between a manufacturer and its distributors causes the distributors to sell at the price indicated by the manufacturer. Examples are as follows:

    a. In case where a written or oral contract provides that sales are made at the price indicated by a manufacturer;

    b. In case where distributors are required to pledge in writing to sell at the price indicated by a manufacturer;

    c. In case where a manufacturer only starts dealing with such distributors that accept such condition that they sell at the price indicated by the manufacturer; and

    d. In case where a manufacturer deals with distributors on conditions that the distributors sell at the price indicated by the manufacturer and that unsold goods are not to be discounted but to be repurchased by the manufacturer.

[2] In case where any artificial means, such as imposing or suggesting to impose economic disadvantage if sales are not made at a manufacturer's indicated price, causes distributors to sell at the indicated price. Examples are as follows:

    a. In case where curtailment of shipments or any other economic disadvantage (including reduction of quantities shipped, raising of shipment price, reduction of rebates, refusal to supply other products; hereinafter the same) is imposed in the event that sales are not made at a manufacturer's indicated price or in case where a notification or suggestion to that effect is made to distributors;

    b. In case where rebates or other economic rewards (including lowering of shipment price, supplying of other products; hereinafter the same) are provided in the event that sales are made at a manufacturer's indicated price, or in case where a notification or suggestion to that effect is made to distributors; and

    c. In case where a manufacturer causes distributors to sell at the manufacturer's indicated price by the following means:

(a) Collecting sales price reports, patrolling retail establishments, conducting price supervision by salespersons dispatched to shops, examining ledgers or records of retailers, and so forth in order to ascertain whether sales are being made at the manufacturer's indicated price;

(b) Identifying price-cutting distributors by making use of secret marks and requesting wholesalers who supplied goods to such distributors not to sell to them;

(c) Buying goods from price-cutting distributors and requesting such distributors or wholesalers who supplied them to buy the goods or pay the cost of their purchases; and

(d) Transmitting complaints to price-cutting distributors from nearby distributors with regard to low-price sales, and requesting the price-cutting distributors to end such sales.

(3) In cases where discriminatory treatment in the form of refusals to deal or provision of rebates, and so on, has been used to secure the effectiveness of restrictions on resale price, such conduct itself is illegal as unfair trade practices (Articles 2 (Other Refusal to Deal) or 4 (Discriminatory Treatment on Transaction Terms, etc.) of the General Designation).

(4) In (2) above, the price indicated by a manufacturer to distributors includes both a specific price and any of the following types of price level:

a. Price to be within x% discount from the manufacturer's suggested retail price;

b. Price to be in a specific range (no less than Y yen and no more than Z yen);

c. Price to be approved in advance by the manufacturer;

d. Price to be not less than that charged by nearby stores; or

e. Price to be suggested by the manufacturer to the distributors as the lowest limit by such means as warning the distributors selling below a specific price level.

(5) The guidance regarding restrictions on resale price described in (2), (3) and (4) above shall apply not only to conduct by a manufacturer vis-a-vis direct customers but also to conduct vis-a-vis secondary wholesalers or retailers which are indirect customers, either directly or indirectly via wholesalers (Articles 12, 2, or 4 of the General Designation).

(6) In cases where in the following kinds of transactions, a direct purchaser from a manufacturer only functions as a commission agent, and if it is recognized that in substance the sale is being done between the manufacturer and its ultimate purchasers, even if the manufacturer instructs resale price to the direct purchaser, it is usually not illegal:

[1] In case of consignment sales, and if the transaction is made with a consignor on its own risks and account so that a consignee bears no risk beyond that associated with its obligation to exercise the care of a good manager in storage and handling of goods, collection of payments, and so on, i.e., is not liable for loss of goods, damage to them, or for unsold goods; or

[2] In case of transactions where a supply price is negotiated and decided directly between a manufacturer and a retailer (or user), and the manufacturer instructs a wholesaler to deliver goods to the retailer (or the user), and if the manufacturer is deemed, in substance, to sell the goods to the retailer (or the user), under such circumstances that the wholesaler is charged only with responsibility for physical delivery of the goods and collection of payment, and a fee is paid for such work.

CHAPTER 2 VERTICAL NON-PRICE RESTRAINTS

1. Viewpoint

(1) A manufacturer tends to conduct a variety of marketing activities directed to distributors handling the manufacturer's products, not only at direct customers but extending as far as the retail stage. A number of managerial advantages are identified with such marketing activities to distributors, but in cases where the marketing activities involve restrictions of products handled by distributors, distributors' sales territories or customers, etc. (hereinafter referred to as "vertical non-price restraints"), the following problems may arise (Note 3).

[1] Interference in business activities conducted by distributors through creative efforts;

[2] Maintenance of final sales prices as a result of dependence of distributors on a manufacturer, and cooperative behavior by the manufacturer and the distributors together;

[3] Restriction or elimination of inter-brand competition (competition among manufacturers and competition among distributors carrying different brands of products) and intra-brand competition (competition among distributors carrying the same brand of products);

[4] Higher barriers to entry by other manufacturers and distributors; and

[5] Reduced consumer choice.

(Note 3) Since the above problems are most likely to arise particularly in the case of restrictions on products handled by distributors, it is desirable that distributors be capable of handling those products that match the needs of consumers on their independent judgement.

(2) Generally speaking, the effect of vertical non-price restraints on competition in a market differs according to the types of restrictions and specifics of each case. Vertical non-price restraints include the following two categories:

[1] those which shall not be considered illegal based on types of restraint, but examined on a case-by-case basis, to analyze their effects on competition in a market, from such viewpoints of whether competitors such as new entrants would be excluded and whether price competition of the product covered by the restriction would be impeded, taking account of various factors, including the position of a manufacturer in a market; and
[2] those which usually tend to impede price competition and are considered in principle illegal, regardless of the position of a manufacturer in a market.

(3) As to whether or not vertical non-price restraints have been imposed by a manufacturer, as is the case of restrictions on resale price described in 2 of Chapter 1 above, it shall be found that restrictions have been imposed not only in cases where a contract or other means of arrangement between the manufacturer and distributors can be found, but also in cases where any artificial means, such as imposing economic disadvantage on distributors who do not comply with the request of the manufacturer, is taken to secure the effectiveness of the restrictions.

2. Restrictions on Distributors' Handling of Competing Products

(1) Restrictions on distributors' handling of competing products include the following types of restraint imposed by a manufacturer:

[1] Making it mandatory for distributors to handle only the manufacturer's products;
[2] Restricting distributors from handling competitors' products;
[3] Prohibiting or restricting distributors from handling specific products, such as imported products, that compete with the manufacturer's products, or from handling products from a specific firm; and
[4] Restricting distributors from handling competing products by means of requiring the distributors to sell such a large volume of its products as is close to their capacity.

(2) In cases where a restriction on handling of competing products is imposed by an influential manufacturer in a market (Note 4), and if the restriction may result in making it difficult for new entrants or competitors to easily

secure alternative distribution channels (Note 5), such restriction is illegal as unfair trade practices (Articles 11 (Dealing on Exclusive Terms) or 13 (Dealing on Restrictive Terms) of the General Designation).

(Note 4) Whether "a manufacturer is influential in a market" is in the first instance judged by a market share of the manufacturer, that is, whether it has no less than 10% or its position is within the top three in the market (meaning a product market which consists of a group of products with the same or similar function and utility as the product covered by the restriction, and competing each other judging from geographical conditions, relations to customers, and other factors).

Nevertheless, even if a firm falls under this criterion, the restriction by the manufacturer is not always illegal. In cases where the restriction "may result in making it difficult for new entrants or competitors to easily secure alternative distribution channels," such restriction is illegal.

In cases where a restriction on handling of competing products is imposed by a low-ranked or newly-entered firm which has a market share of less than 10% and whose position is the fourth or later, the restriction usually would not result in making it difficult for new entrants or competitors to easily secure alternative distribution channels, and such restriction is not illegal.

The same shall apply in the remainder of Part 11 with regard to whether a firm is "influential in a market."

(Note 5) Whether or not a restriction "may result in making it difficult for new entrants or competitors to easily secure alternative distribution channels" is to be determined, taking comprehensively into account the following factors:

[1] Structure of the market (market concentration, characteristics of the product, degree of product differentiation, distribution channels, difficulty in new market entry, etc.);

[2] Position in the market of the manufacturer that imposes the restriction (in terms of market share, rank, brand name, etc.);

[3] Number of distributors affected by the restriction, and their positions in the market; and

[4] Impact of the restriction on business activities of the distributors (extent, manner, etc. of the restriction).

As an element of market structure listed in [1] above, other manufacturers' behaviors are also to be considered. For example, in cases where two or more manufacturers respectively and parallelly restrict handling of competing products, it is more likely to result in making it difficult for new entrants or competitors to easily secure alternative distribution channels, compared to cases where only one manufacturer does.

The same shall apply in the remainder of Part 11 with regard to whether a restriction "may result in making it difficult for new entrants or competitors to easily secure alternative distribution channels".

(3) The guidance given in (2) immediately above shall also apply to cases where a manufacturer causes wholesalers to restrict retailers' handling of competing products (Article 13 (Dealing on Restrictive Terms) of the General Designation).

3. Restrictions on Distributors' Sales Territory

(1) Restrictions on distributors' sales territory include the following types of restraint imposed by a manufacturer:

[1] Assigning a specific territory to each distributor as the area of primary responsibility and requiring the distributor to carry out active sales activities within each territory (establishing the area of primary responsibility, without restriction on sales outside the area and not falling under [3] or [4] below; hereinafter referred to as "area of responsibility system");

[2] Restricting the area where a distributor may establish business premises such as stores, or designating the place where such premises are to be established (restricting the location of business premises, and not falling under [3] or [4] below; hereinafter referred to as "location system");

[3] Assigning a specific area to each distributor and restricting the distributor from selling outside each area (hereinafter referred to as "exclusive territory"); and

[4] Assigning a specific area to each distributor and restricting the distributor from selling to customers outside each area upon request (hereinafter referred to as "restriction of sales to outside customers").

(2) Area of responsibility system and location system

It is not illegal for a manufacturer to adopt the area of responsibility system or location system, for the purpose of developing an effective network for sales or securing a better system for after-sales service, except where such restriction falls under exclusive territory or restriction on sales to outside customers.

(3) Exclusive territory

In cases where an influential manufacturer in a market (Note 6) assigns exclusive territory to distributors, and if price level of the product covered by the restriction is likely to be maintained (Note 7), such restriction is illegal (Note 8) as unfair trade practices (Article 13 (Dealing on Restrictive Terms) of the General Designation).

(Note 6) Whether a manufacturer is "influential in a market" is in the first instance judged by a market share of the manufacturer, that is, whether it has no less than 10% or its position is within the top three in the market.

Nevertheless, even if a firm falls under this criterion, the restriction by the firm is not always illegal. In cases where "price level of the product is likely to be maintained" by the restriction, such restriction is illegal.

In case of a low-ranked or newly-entered manufacturer which has a market share of less than 10% and whose position is the fourth or later, price level of the product usually would not be maintained by exclusive territory, and such restriction is not illegal.

(Note 7) Whether or not "price level of the product covered by the restriction is likely to be maintained" is to be determined, taking comprehensively into account the following factors:

[1] Actual conditions of inter-brand competition (market concentration, characteristics of the product, degree of product differentiation, distribution channels, difficulty in new market entry, etc.);

[2] Actual conditions of intra-brand competition for the product (degree of dispersion in price, business types of distributors dealing in the product, etc.);

[3] Number of distributors affected by the restriction, and their positions in the market; and

[4] Impact of the restriction on business activities of the distributors (extent, manner, etc. of the restriction).

For example, in cases where exclusive territory is assigned to distributors by an influential manufacturer in a market under the circumstances where inter-brand competition does not work well due to oligopolistic structure of the market and advanced product differentiation, price competition for the product of the manufacturer's brand may be impeded, and the price level of the product is likely to be maintained.

The same shall apply in the remainder of Part II with regard to whether "price level of the product is likely to be maintained."

(Note 8) In case of test marketing of a new product or sale of local souvenirs, price level of the product usually would not be maintained by territorial restriction, and such restriction is not illegal.

(4) Restriction of sales to outside customers

In cases where a manufacturer imposes restriction of sales to outside customers on distributors, and if price level of the product is likely to be maintained, such restriction is illegal as unfair trade practices (Article 13 of the General Designation).

(5) The guidance given in (2), (3), and (4) immediately above shall also apply to cases where a manufacturer causes wholesalers to restrict retailers' sales territory (Article 13 of the General Designation).

4. Restrictions on Distributors' Customers

(1) Restrictions on distributors' customers include the following types of restraint imposed by a manufacturer:

[1] Requiring each wholesaler to supply only to certain retailers, so that the retailers may buy only from that wholesaler (hereinafter referred to as "requirement of designated accounts");

[2] Preventing distributors from buying and selling products among themselves (hereinafter referred to as "prohibition of sales among distributors"); and

[3] Prohibiting wholesalers to sell to price-cutting retailers.

(2) Requirement of designated accounts

In cases where a manufacturer imposes requirement of designated accounts on wholesalers, and if price level of the product covered by the restriction is likely to be maintained, such restriction is illegal as unfair trade practices (Article 13 (Dealing on Restrictive Terms) of the General Designation).

(3) Prohibition of sales among distributors

In cases where a manufacturer prohibits sales among distributors for the purpose of preventing its products from being sold to price-cutting distributors, and if price level of the product is likely to be maintained, such restriction is illegal as unfair trade practices (Article 13 of the General Designation).

(4) Prohibition of sales to price-cutters

In cases where a manufacturer causes wholesalers not to sell to a retailer on account of the retailer's price-cutting (Note 9), price level of the product is likely to be maintained, and such restriction is in principle illegal as unfair trade practices (Articles 2 (Other Refusal to Deal) or 13 of the General Designation).

Moreover, in cases where a manufacturer stops shipments to a distributor that has been its direct customer, on account of the distributor's price-cutting (Note 9), price level of the product is likely to be maintained, and such conduct is in principle illegal as unfair trade practices (Article 2 of the General Designation).

(Note 9)   Whether or not such restriction is "on account of the retailer's (the distributor's) price-cutting" is to be objectively judged based on actual conditions of the transactions, including the manufacturer's response to other distributors, and related circumstances.

5. Restrictions on Retailers' Sales Methods

(1) Restrictions on retailers' sales methods include the following types of restraint imposed by a manufacturer:

[1]   Calling for demonstration-sales of the product;
[2]   Calling for customer delivery service for the product;
[3]   Instructing conditions for quality control of the product; and
[4]   Calling for shelf space or a display area exclusively for the product.

(2) In cases where restrictions on the retailers' sales methods (excluding those on sales price, sales territory and customers) are recognized to have rational reasons for the purpose of ensuring proper sales of the product, such as related to assuring the safety of the product, preservation of its qualities, maintenance of the goodwill of its trademark, and so on, and if the same restrictions are applied to other retailers-customers on equal terms, such restrictions in themselves do not present a problem under the Antimonopoly Act.

However, in cases where restrictions on retailers' sales methods are used as a means to restrict sales price, handling of competing products, sales territory or customers (Note 10), their illegality is to be judged on the basis of the guidance set forth for each type of conduct described in Chapter 1 and 2 through 4 of Chapter 2 (Articles 11 (Dealing on Exclusive Terms), 12 (Resale Price Restriction), or 13 (Dealing on Restrictive Terms) of the General Designation).

(Note 10)   For example, in cases where a manufacturer stops shipments only to price-cutting retailers among those which do not observe the restrictions on sales methods on account of their non-observance of the restrictions, the manufacturer usually shall be found to restrict sales price by means of the restrictions on sales methods.

(3) Furthermore, in cases where a manufacturer imposes the following types of restriction on advertisements and representations as one kind of sales methods, price level of the product is likely to be maintained, and such restriction is in principle illegal as unfair trade practices (Article 13 of the General Designation):

[1] In case where a manufacturer restricts the price shown at stores or in handbills etc. or prohibits price advertisings; or

[2] In case where a manufacturer causes magazines, newspapers or other advertising media in which the manufacturer put advertisements, to reject such advertisements that give prices or announce price-cutting.

(4) The guidance described in (2) and (3) immediately above shall also apply to cases where a manufacturer causes wholesalers to restrict retailers' sales methods (Article 13 of the General Designation).

CHAPTER 3 PROVISION OF REBATES AND ALLOWANCES

1. Viewpoint

The nature of rebates and allowances provided by a manufacturer to its distributors (in general, meaning money paid on a systematic or case-by-case basis, separately from the billing price for goods; hereinafter referred to as "rebates") is diverse, including those that have the nature of adjusting the billing price, and those that have the purpose of promoting sales. Thus, rebates are paid for a variety of purposes, and rebates as one element of price also have the aspect of promoting price formation in keeping with actual conditions in a market. Accordingly, the provision of rebates in itself does not necessarily present a problem under the Antimonopoly Act.

There are cases, however, where depending on the ways that rebates are provided, they may restrict business activities of distributors and present a problem under the Antimonopoly Act (Note 11).

(Note 11) In cases where a manufacturer discretionally provides rebates without clear basis, and particularly if such opaque rebates account for a large percentage of distributors' margin, they can give rise to the effect of making it easy for the manufacturer to conform the distributors to its sales policy, and are most likely to restrict business activities of the distributors. For this reason, it is desirable for manufacturers to make clear the basis for payment of rebates, and inform their distributors of it.

2. Cases Where There Is a Problem under the Act

(1) Rebates used as a means of restrictions on distributors

In cases where rebates are provided as a means of restricting distributors' sales price, handling of competing products, sales territory, or customers, etc. (for example, in such cases that rebates are reduced if the distributors do not sell products at the price indicated by the manufacturer), their illegality is to be judged in accordance with the guidance described in Chapters 1 and 2 above (Articles 11 (Dealing on Exclusive Terms), 12 (Resale Price Restriction), or 13 (Dealing on Restrictive Terms) of the General Designation).

Furthermore, the conduct of discriminating the provision of rebates depending on the price, handling of competing products, or the like, if it has the same or similar function as the imposition of illegal restrictions on distributors, such conduct itself is illegal as unfair trade practices (Article 4 (Discriminatory Treatment on Transaction Terms, etc.) of the General Designation). The same shall also apply to (2), (3), and (4) below.

Also, the same shall apply to cases where a "repayment system" (under which a manufacturer collects all or a part of the margin from distributors and pays it back after a certain period) is used as a means of or has the same or similar function as the imposition of illegal restrictions on the distributors.

(2) Coverage rebates

A manufacturer sometimes provides rebates to its distributors according to the percentage of sales of the manufacturer's products in the total business of each distributor during a specific period, or according to the share that the manufacturer's products have in the display of all goods at the distributor's store.

In cases where the provision of rebates of these kinds (coverage rebates) has the function of restricting the handling of competing products, its illegality is to be judged in accordance with the guidance described in 2(2) of Chapter 2 (Restrictions on Distributors' Handling of Competing Products) above.

That is, in cases where an influential manufacturer provides coverage rebates, and if the provision has the function of restricting distributors' handling of competing products and may result in making it difficult for new entrants or competitors to easily secure alternative distribution channels, such provision is illegal as unfair trade practices (Articles 4, 11, or 13 of the General Designation).

(3) Remarkably progressive rebate

At times a manufacturer in providing volume rebates, may set a rebate rate progressively, according to a ranking of distributors based on criteria such as quantity of products supplied to each distributor during a certain period. While progressive rebates have the aspect of promoting price formation in keeping with actual conditions in a market, if the rate is remarkably progressive, they have the function of encouraging the preferential handling of that manufacturer's products over those of others.

In cases where the provision of remarkably progressive rebates has the function of restricting the handling of competing products, its illegality is to be judged in accordance with the guidance described in 2(2) of Chapter 2 (Restrictions on Distributors' Handling of Competing Products) above.

That is, in cases where an influential manufacturer provides such rebates, and if the provision has the function of restricting distributors' handling of competing products and may result in making it difficult for new entrants or competitors to easily secure alternative distribution channels, such provision is illegal as unfair trade practices (Articles 4, 11, or 13 of the General Designation).

(4) Rebates that have the function of requiring designated accounts

At times a manufacturer may provide rebates directly or through wholesalers even to retailers who are indirect customers of the manufacturer, in accordance with the purchases by each retailer of the manufacturer's products. In cases where the manufacturer provides such rebates, and if the amount of rebates to each retailer is calculated solely on the purchase amount of the manufacturer's products purchased from a specific wholesaler by each retailer, it is most likely to have the function of requiring designated accounts.

In cases where the provision of such rebates has the function of requiring designated accounts, its illegality is to be judged in accordance with the guidance described in 4(2) of Chapter 2 (Requirement of designated accounts) above.

That is, in cases where price level of the product is likely to be maintained by the provision of rebates that have such function, such provision of the rebates is illegal as unfair trade practices (Articles 4 or 13 of the General Designation).

CHAPTER 4   INTERFERENCE IN DISTRIBUTORS' MANAGEMENT

1. Viewpoint

At times a manufacturer provides in transaction contracts with its distributors, the interference in the management of the distributors as a condition for doing business with it. The concrete obligations in each contract may vary, but there are cases where it is made obligatory for the distributors to obtain advance permission from, or to consult with, the manufacturer before making changes in their articles of incorporation, business lines, amount of capital, officers, major stockholders, products to deal in, and sales methods, or cases where the distributors are required to submit ledgers and other documents for inspection. Such interference in the management of distributors is undertaken in order to diffuse the sales policy of the manufacturer, or for various reasons including provision of managerial guidance, securing recovery of credits, collection of marketing information, and so on, and the interference in itself does not necessarily present a problem under the Antimonopoly Act.

However, depending on the methods and extent of interference in the management of distributors, business activities of the distributors may be restricted, or unjust disadvantages may be imposed on the distributors; in such cases there is a problem under the Antimonopoly Act.

2. *Cases Where There Is a Problem under the Act*

(1) In cases where interference in the management of distributors is used as a means of restricting the distributors' sales price, handling of competing products, sales territory, or customers, its illegality is to be judged in accordance with the guidance described in Chapters 1 and 2 above (Articles 11 (Dealing on Exclusive Terms), 12 (Resale Price Restriction), or 13 (Dealing on Restrictive Terms) of the General Designation).

(2) In cases where a manufacturer's interference in the management of distributors is regarded as, by making use of its dominant bargaining position over the distributors, imposing unjust disadvantage on the distributors in the light of normal business practices, such as onerous restrictions or obligations regarding other lines of business, sales quantities, etc., it is illegal as unfair trade practices (Article 14 (Abuse of Dominant Bargaining Position) of the General Designation).

(3) In franchise system, regarding interference of a franchisor (franchise headquarters) in the management of its franchisees, reference should be made to the Guidelines Concerning Franchise System under the Antimonopoly Act (published on September 20, 1983).

CHAPTER 5 ABUSE OF DOMINANT BARGAINING POSITION BY RETAILERS

1. Viewpoint

(1) While transaction terms or conditions are basically to be negotiated and determined between the parties to transactions based on their independent business judgement, in cases where a retailer in a dominant bargaining position over its suppliers, by making use of that position, engages in coercion to purchase, return of unsold goods, request for dispatch of salespersons to shops, coercive collection of contributions, or request for frequent delivery in small lots, such conduct is most likely to present a problem under the Antimonopoly Act as abuse of dominant bargaining position.

The regulation of abuse of dominant bargaining position under the Antimonopoly Act aims at eliminating these types of conduct if they are likely to impede fair competition among retailers or among suppliers.

(2) A retailer shall be found to be "in a dominant bargaining position over its suppliers" in such cases where the suppliers are obliged to accept the retailer's requests even if they are excessively disadvantageous to the suppliers, since discontinuance of transaction with the retailer would significantly damage the suppliers' business. In making this finding, comprehensive consideration is to be given to such factors as degree of dependence on the retailer, position of the retailer in a market, changeability of customers, and supply and demand situations of the product.

(3) The remainder of this Chapter provides cases where specific types of conduct by a retailer vis-a-vis suppliers are illegal under the Antimonopoly Act. The same fundamentally shall apply to cases where the same or similar conduct is engaged by a wholesaler or user by making use of its position as a purchaser.

(4) Abuse of dominant bargaining position is regulated, in general, as unfair trade practices, under Article 14 (Abuse of Dominant Bargaining Position) of the General Designation, and regarding the conduct of large-scale retailers such as department stores and supermarkets vis-a-vis their suppliers, in addition to Article 14 of the General Designation, "Specific Unfair Trade Practices in the Department Store Industry" (Fair Trade Commission Notification No. 7 of 1954), which regulates retailers having no less than a certain number of square meters of sales area and selling a large variety of goods for ordinary use to general consumers, shall apply to it.

In cases where a business relation between a retailer and its supplier falls under parental firm-subcontractor transaction under the Act Against

Delay in Payment of Subcontract Proceeds, etc. to Subcontractors, and if it also comes under manufacturing commission of products, such as manufacturing and supplying of goods bearing the brand of the retailer (so-called "private brand" goods), this Act shall apply to it.

2. Coercion to Purchase

(1) Viewpoint

A retailer, at times, by making use of its relations with suppliers, requests the suppliers to purchase goods or services from itself. In cases where a retailer in a dominant bargaining position requests suppliers to purchase its goods or services, the suppliers, even if not wishing to purchase them, are forced to do so out of concern about adverse effect on future transactions with the retailer, and it may present a problem as abuse of dominant bargaining position.

(2) Cases Where There Is a Problem under the Act

In cases where a retailer in a dominant bargaining position, causes suppliers to purchase its goods or services, or those of the firm designated by the retailer, by the following ways, it causes unjust disadvantage in the light of normal business practices to the suppliers and is illegal as unfair trade practices (Article 14 (Abuse of Dominant Bargaining Position) of the General Designation):

[1] Requesting to purchase by employees of the retailer who can influence purchasing from the suppliers, such as buyers;
[2] Requesting to purchase systematically or deliberately;
[3] Requesting to purchase repeatedly or shipping products unilaterally, when a supplier has expressed no intention to purchase, or when even in the absence of such an expression it is clearly recognized that the supplier has no intention to purchase; or
[4] Requesting to purchase in such ways as to indicate that failure to do so would influence future transactions, or using such selling methods as to indicate that effect.

3. *Return of Unsold Goods*

(1) *Viewpoint*

Although return of unsold goods has advantages such as facilitating the introduction of new products, or providing better ability to respond quickly to regional shifts in supply and demand, in cases where a retailer in a dominant bargaining position returns unsold goods to its suppliers only at its convenience, such conduct is most likely to render unjust disadvantage on the suppliers and to present a problem as abuse of dominant bargaining position (Note 12).

(Note 12) In cases where the conditions under which goods may be returned have not been clearly set forth between the parties to the transaction, such a problem is most likely to arise, and it is desirable that retailers set forth clearly those conditions with their suppliers in advance.

(2) *Cases Where There Is a Problem under the Act*

In cases where a retailer in a dominant bargaining position returns unsold goods to its suppliers (meaning to return the purchased goods from the suppliers, and including such conduct deemed in substance as return of goods, such as replacement of a purchase contract by a consignment sales contract, or exchange of goods), and if it falls under one of the following cases, it is to cause unjust disadvantage in the light of normal business practices to the suppliers, and is illegal as unfair trade practices (Article 14 (Abuse of Dominant Bargaining Position) of the General Designation):

[1] In case where the circumstances and conditions to return goods have not been clearly determined between the parties, and thereby causing the suppliers to suffer unforeseeable disadvantage (Note 13); or

[2] In case where goods are returned in the following manners, and thereby causing the suppliers to suffer disadvantage (Note 13) (Note 14);

    a. Return of goods soiled or damaged through no fault of the suppliers. Examples are as follows:

        (a) Return of display goods that have become soiled;

        (b) Return of goods bearing the retailer's price labels difficult to take off with no damage;

        (c) Return of goods on account of their having aged beyond a period set by the retailer that is shorter than the manufacturer's "best-tasting" period (Note 15);

    b. Return of a retailer's private brand goods;

    c. Return of goods for inventory clearance at the end of a month or accounting terms; and

d. Return of goods because of remodelling of the shop or changes of its display based on the retailer's own decision (Note 16).

Regarding return of unsold goods, reference should also be made to the Guidelines Concerning Unjust Return of Unsold Goods under the Antimonopoly Act (published on April 21, 1987).

(Note 13) Return of unsold goods in the following cases would cause no disadvantage to the suppliers, and is not illegal: (a) In case where the retailer account for the loss to be usually incurred by return of goods with the consent of the suppliers; (b) In case where the goods supplied are soiled, damaged, or defective due to any reason attributable to the suppliers; or (c) In case where the goods supplied are different from those ordered.

(Note 14) Such return as described in [2] is illegal, even if the circumstances and conditions to return goods have been clearly set forth between the parties.

(Note 15) This shall not apply to such cases where goods are returned at a short time before the expiration of best-tasting period, taking account of the period for consumers to spend from their purchase to consumption, and if specific conditions of such return have been clearly determined in advance between the parties.

(Note 16) This shall not apply to such cases where seasonal goods are returned because of changes of display at the end of sales term, and if specific conditions of such return have been clearly determined in advance between the parties.

4. Request for Dispatch of Salespersons to Shops

(1) Viewpoint

A manufacturer or wholesaler dispatches its employees or others (hereinafter referred to as "salespersons") to retailers such as department stores or supermarkets to sell their products or products they have supplied. These salespersons are dispatched based on two reasons. On the one hand, a manufacturer or wholesaler dispatches salespersons for the purpose of publicizing and promoting the sale of the products manufactured or supplied by it, directly to consumers at retail shops. On the other hand, the salespersons are dispatched at the request of retailers to supplement the latter's knowledge of the products and salesmanship, or shortage of labor.

While dispatch of salespersons has the aspect of enabling the manufacturer and wholesaler to directly grasp the trend of consumer needs, and of supplementing a shortage in the retailers' specialized knowledge of the products, if salespersons are dispatched only at the convenience of retailers in a dominant bargaining position, such conduct is most likely to render unjust disadvantage on the dispatching manufacturer or wholesaler, and to present a problem as abuse of dominant bargaining position (Note 17).

(Note 17) In particular, in cases where the conditions for dispatch of salespersons have not been made clear between the parties, such a problem is most likely to arise, and it is desirable that retailers set forth clearly such conditions as job specifications, working hours, and term of dispatch, with their suppliers in advance.

(2) Cases Where There Is a Problem under the Act

In cases where a retailer in a dominant bargaining position, by making use of that position, has its suppliers dispatch their salespersons for sales or other activities, and if it falls under one of the following cases, it is to cause unjust disadvantage in the light of normal business practices to the suppliers, and is illegal as unfair trade practices (Article 14 (Abuse of Dominant Bargaining Position) of the General Designation).

The same shall apply to cases where a retailer, in place of the dispatch of salespersons, causes the suppliers to bear the equivalent cost of such personnel:

[1] In case where the circumstances and conditions for dispatch of salespersons have not been clearly determined between the parties, and thereby causing the suppliers to suffer unforeseeable disadvantage (Note 18); or

[2] In case where in comparison to the direct benefits obtained by the suppliers through the dispatch of salespersons, the suppliers are caused to suffer disadvantage (Note 18) (Note 19). Examples are as follows:

(a) In case where the dispatched salespersons are engaged in taking inventory, changing displays, or doing clerical work not directly related to the sales promotion activities of the products from the suppliers, and thereby causing the suppliers to suffer disadvantage; and

(b) In case where the dispatched salespersons are engaged in the sale of products from the suppliers and the cost of dispatching the salespersons is larger than the benefits directly obtained by the suppliers through the increased volume of sales attained by such sales activities.

(Note 18) In cases where the retailer bear the normal cost for dispatch of salespersons with the consent of the suppliers, such request would cause no disadvantage to the suppliers, and is not illegal.

(Note 19)   Such request as described in [2] is illegal, even if the circumstances and conditions for dispatch of salespersons have been clearly set forth between the parties.

5. Coercive Collection of Contributions

(1) Viewpoint

At times a retailer may request suppliers to defray monetary contributions or other financial burdens for the cost of special events, advertising, etc. (hereinafter referred to as "contributions"). There exist cases where suppliers do benefit from the burden of contributions through increased sales of the products supplied by them, if, for example, the contributions are to be spent for special events or advertising for sales campaigns jointly undertaken by the retailer and the suppliers. However, in cases where a retailer in a dominant bargaining position for its own conveniences causes suppliers to make contributions, it is most likely to cause unjust disadvantage to the suppliers, and to present a problem as abuse of dominant bargaining position (Note 20).

(Note 20)   In cases where the conditions for making contributions have not been clearly determined by the parties, such a problem is most likely to arise, and it is desirable that retailers set forth clearly those conditions with their suppliers.

(2) Cases Where There Is a Problem under the Act

In cases where a retailer in a dominant bargaining position causes suppliers to make contributions, and if it falls under one of the following cases, it is to cause unjust disadvantage in the light of normal business practices to the suppliers, and is illegal as unfair trade practices (Article 14 (Abuse of Dominant Bargaining Position) of the General Designation):

[1]   In case where the amount of contributions, the basis for calculation and the purpose for expenditure have not been made clear between the parties, and thereby causing unforeseeable disadvantage to the suppliers; or

[2]   In case where the retailer causes the suppliers to make contributions in the following ways, and thereby causing disadvantage to the suppliers (Note 21):

    a.   Requesting contributions for special events, redecoration of sales premises, advertising, etc. which do not contribute to promotion of sales of the products from the suppliers;

b. Requesting contributions exceeding the range of direct benefits obtained by the suppliers through promotion of sales of the products, reduction of costs, etc.;
c. Requesting contributions for reasons related to the retailer's adjustment in settling account;
d. Under an arrangement that rebates would be provided to the retailer in case of attaining a certain volume of sales by the retailer in a certain period, requesting such rebates despite the failure to attain the volume; or
e. Requesting the reduction of billing price, after the products have been purchased from the suppliers, without liability of the suppliers.

(Note 21) Such request as described in [2] is illegal, even if the conditions of contributions have been clearly set forth between the parties.

6. Request for Frequent Delivery in Small Lots

(1) Viewpoint

While recently large-scale retailers have been developing systematization of purchasing activities, such as on-line ordering system, establishing distribution centers, they, in relation to those activities, sometimes request suppliers to make frequent delivery in small lots (to make a delivery-lot smaller and frequency of deliveries higher) and to bear the expense of such systematization.

The systematization of purchasing activities sometimes encourages rationalization of order and delivery operations and benefits not only consumers but also suppliers. However, in cases where a retailer in a dominant bargaining position for its own conveniences requests suppliers to make frequent delivery in small lots or to bear the cost arising from the systematization, in the name of, for example, charges or fees for using an on-line ordering system, or a distribution center, without concretely indicating the basis or ratio for such burdens, it is most likely to cause unjust disadvantage to the suppliers, and to present a problem as abuse of dominant bargaining position (Note 22).

(Note 22) It is desirable that retailers fully discuss with their suppliers lest the retailers unilaterally causes the suppliers to bear the burden arising from the systematization of purchasing activities or frequent delivery in small lots.

(2) Cases Where There Is a Problem under the Act

In cases where a retailer in a dominant bargaining position causes suppliers to make frequent delivery in small lots or to bear the burden arising from the systematization of purchasing activities, and if it falls under one of the following cases, it is to cause unjust disadvantage in the light of normal business practices to the suppliers, and is illegal as unfair trade practices (Article 14 (Abuse of Dominant Bargaining Position) of the General Designation):

[1] In case where the retailer requests the suppliers to make frequent delivery in small lots and thereby causes them, without full discussion with them, to supply goods at a remarkably lower unit price than that considered to be equivalent to the price ordinarily paid (Note 23), even if the suppliers requested the retailer to raise the unit price by reason of a large increase of delivery cost;

[2] In case where the retailer, without full discussion with the suppliers about the burden of cost arising from the systematization of purchasing activities and the basis for its calculation, requests them to bear the burden, and thereby causes them to suffer disadvantage; or

[3] In case where the retailer unilaterally requests the suppliers to bear the cost arising from the systematization of purchasing activities, beyond the benefits to be gained by them (Note 24).

(Note 23) Whether or not a unit price is "considered to be equivalent to the price ordinarily paid" is to be judged, taking comprehensively into account such factors as the previous unit price and unit prices of other suppliers under the same or similar conditions of frequent delivery in small lots.

(Note 24) Such request as described in [3] is illegal, even if the conditions of the burden have been clearly set forth between the parties.

PART III   THE ANTIMONOPOLY ACT GUIDELINES CONCERNING SOLE DISTRIBUTORSHIP

1. There are cases where a firm, domestic or foreign, supplying the products it handles, grants to another firm an exclusive distributorship covering the entire domestic market. Such firm given an exclusive distributorship is called a sole agent or a sole import distributor (hereinafter referred to as "sole distributor"; and a firm granting an exclusive distributorship is hereinafter referred to as "supplier"; and a contract concluded between them as "sole distributorship contract"). Sole distributorship contracts can reduce the cost and risks of suppliers for new entry into markets and encourage sole

distributors to undertake organized marketing activities, and then there are many cases where foreign firms utilize sole import distributorship contracts in entering domestic markets.

2. As stated above, sole distributorship contracts can generally contribute to promote competition. However, depending on the market position of the product covered by such contracts as well as the contracting parties, or their behaviors in markets, such contracts may function to impede competition in the markets. This Part, focusing on sole distributorship contracts, provides guidance under the Antimonopoly Act from the viewpoint of regulation of unfair trade practices.

With the promulgation of these Guidelines, the Examination Guidelines on Unfair Trade Practices in Sole Import Distributorship Contracts, Etc. (published on November 21, 1972) and the Guidelines Concerning Unreasonable Obstruction of Parallel Imports under the Antimonopoly Act (published on April 17,1987) are repealed.

3. Chapter 2 of Part Ill deals with restrictions imposed by one party to a sole distributorship contract on the other. Part 11 shall be referred to with regard to resale price maintenance, vertical non-price restraints, and other restrictions which a sole distributor in its marketing activities imposes on distributors.

Chapter 3 of Part Ill deals with unreasonable obstruction of parallel imports, regardless of whether they are stipulated in a sole distributorship contract, or carried out by a supplier or a sole distributor. It shall also apply to such obstruction that are carried out toward distributors by a sole distributor at its own discretion.

CHAPTER 1   SOLE DISTRIBUTORSHIP CONTRACTS BETWEEN COMPETITORS

1. Viewpoint

There are cases in which a sole distributorship contract is concluded between competitors. The conclusion of a sole distributorship contract between a supplier and its competitor, while it is expected that entry into a market by the supplier itself or through another firm would enable the supplier to function as an effective competitive entity and help promote competition in the market, could either eliminate competition between the two parties or help reinforce and expand the market position of the firm that serve as a sole distributor. This may result in impeding competition in the market. Whether a sole distributorship contract between competitors would have such effect of impeding competition depends on the market position of a firm that becomes a sole distributor, the overall business capability of a supplier, actual situations in the market concerned, and other factors.

2. Cases Where There Is a Problem under the Act

(1) In cases where a firm to serve as a sole distributor either manufactures or markets the same kind of products as the one covered by the contract (meaning a group of products with the same or similar function and utility as those of the product covered by the contract and in competition with each other; hereinafter the same in Chapter 1), and if the firm has a market share of no less than 10% and is ranked within the top three in the domestic market of the products, the conclusion of a sole distributorship contract with the supplier of the product may have an anticompetitive effect. To determine whether the conclusion of the contract has an anticompetitive effect, how much effect it would have on competition in the market is to be examined on a case-by-case basis, taking comprehensively into account the following factors. If it is recognized that the conclusion of the contract has an anticompetitive effect, it is illegal as unfair trade practices (Article 13 (Dealing on Restrictive Terms) of the General Designation).

[1] The market share and rank of a firm to serve as a sole distributor, the extent of their differentials with the firm's competitors and the extent of their changes caused by the conclusion of the contract;

[2] Overall business capability of a supplier (sales amount, brand value, market position in other markets, etc.);

[3] The market share and rank of the product covered by the contract in the domestic market;

[4] Actual situation of competition in the market (number of competitors, fluctuations in market shares, difficulty in new market entry, etc.);

[5] Characteristics of the product covered by the contract, the degree of competition between products produced or marketed by a sole distributor and the product covered by the contract; the presence or absence of closely comparable substitutes, and the sales price of the product covered by the contract; and

[6] Actual situation of distribution for the product covered by the contract (difficulty in new entry into distribution, etc.).

(2) In cases where a firm to serve as a sole distributor has a market share of no less than 25% and is ranked top, whether or not the conclusion of the contract has an anticompetitive effect is to be judged on a case-by-case basis, as in the case of (1) above. In general, however, conclusion of a sole distributorship contract between a firm in such a strong position and a supplier in competition with the firm is highly likely to have an anticompetitive

effect. Therefore, each contract is to be carefully examined, paying special attention to the following factors:

[1] Whether the overall business capability of the supplier is not large; and
[2] Whether the product covered by the contract has already held a not insubstantial market share in the domestic market.

3. Cases Where There Is No Problem under the Act

(1) In case of either 2(1) or 2(2) above, if a sole distributorship contract is concluded for the purpose of newly selling the product in the domestic market for a short term (while the meaning of "a short term" depends on the types of the product covered by the contract, three (3) to five (5) years is considered as a standard), or if the product covered by the contract is produced in accordance with the technology provided by the firm to serve as a sole distributor or under consignment contract by the firm, the conclusion of the contract presents, in principle, no problem under the Antimonopoly Act.

(2) In cases where a firm to serve as a sole distributor, manufactures or markets the same kind of products as the one covered by the contract, and if the firm has a market share of less than 10% or is ranked the fourth or later in the domestic market, the conclusion of a sole distributorship contract with the supplier of the product presents, in principle, no problem under the Antimonopoly Act.

CHAPTER 2 MAJOR RESTRICTIVE PROVISIONS IN SOLE DISTRIBUTORSHIP CONTRACTS

1. Cases Where There Is a Problem Under the Act

(1) Resale price maintenance

The guidance provided in Chapter 1 of Part 11 (Resale Price Maintenance) shall apply to any conduct by a supplier to restrict its sole distributor's sales price or to cause the sole distributor to restrict sales price of firms which purchase the product covered by the contract from the sole distributor for sales (including other firms that purchase the product from the said firms for sales; hereinafter referred to as "distributors").

(2) Restrictions on handling of competing products

[1] Restrictions on handling of competing products during the term of the contract.

The guidance provided in 2 of Chapter 2, Part II (Restrictions on Distributors' Handling of Competing Products) shall apply to cases where a supplier restricts its sole distributor from handling competing products or causes the sole distributor to restrict its distributors from handling competing products during the term of the contract. Provided, however, that during the term of the contract, if the supplier does not restrict handling of competing products which have already been handled by the sole distributor, it presents, in principle, no problem under the Antimonopoly Act.

[2] Restrictions on handling competing products after the termination of the contract.

In cases where a supplier restricts its sole distributor from handling competing products after the termination of the contract, such conduct would restrict business activities of the sole distributor and obstruct entry into the market, and it presents, in principle, a problem under the Antimonopoly Act. Provided, however, that in cases where such restriction is imposed with such proper justifications as the necessity for preventing confidential information (including marketing know-how) from being diverted and only to an extent necessary for such prevention, it presents, in principle, no problem under the Antimonopoly Act.

(3) Restrictions on sales territory

[1] The guidance provided in 3 of Chapter 2, Part II (Restrictions on Distributors' Sales Territory) shall apply to any conduct by a supplier to cause its sole distributor to restrict distributors' sales territories in the domestic market;

[2] In cases where a supplier requires its sole distributor not to actively market the product covered by the contract in areas outside the territory for which the sole distributor is granted the exclusive distributorship for the product (hereinafter referred to as "approved territory"), or the sole distributor causes the supplier to discourage its direct customers located outside the approved territory from actively marketing the product in the sole distributor's approved territory, it presents, in principle, no problem under the Antimonopoly Act.

(4) Restrictions on customers or suppliers

[1] The guidance provided in 4 of Chapter 2, Part II (Restrictions on Distributors' Customers) shall apply to any conduct by a supplier to restrict its sole distributor's customers or to cause the sole distributor to restrict distributors' customers;

[2] In cases where a supplier requires its sole distributor to buy the product covered by the contract exclusively from the supplier or from the parties it designates, it presents, in principle, no problem under the Antimonopoly Act.

(5) Restrictions on sales methods

The guidance provided in 4 of Chapter 2, Part II (Restrictions on Retailers' Sales Methods) shall apply to any conduct by a supplier to restrict its sole distributor's sales method for the product covered by the contract or to cause the sole distributor to restrict distributors' sales methods.

2. Cases Where There Is No Problem under the Act

While a supplier, in exchange for granting an exclusive distributorship of the product covered by the contract, sometimes imposes on its sole distributor the following restriction or obligation, it presents, in principle, no problem under the Antimonopoly Act.

[1] Setting a minimum volume or value of the product covered by the contract to be purchased or sold; or

[2] To make the best efforts to sell the product covered by the contract.

CHAPTER 3 UNREASONABLE OBSTRUCTION OF PARALLEL IMPORTS

1. Viewpoint

(1) In case of a sole import distributorship contract, a product covered by the contract can be imported by way of channels other than that arranged between the contracting parties (such importation of the product is hereinafter referred to as "parallel import"; it assumes the importation of genuine products, which does not infringe any trademark right).

Parallel imports are considered to promote price competition in a market, and accordingly, obstruction of parallel imports presents a problem under the Antimonopoly Act, if it is conducted to maintain price level of the product covered by the contract.

(2) In cases where products being sold as parallel import goods are not genuine products but counterfeit products, owners of trademarks may request to cease and desist from selling such products, on the ground of trademark infringements. In addition, taking necessary measures to maintain goodwill of trademarks under the following situations present, in principle, no problem under the Antimonopoly Act:

[1] In case where consumers may misunderstand parallel import goods with different specification or quality are identical to the product handled by a sole distributor, because of false representations of origin or other reasons; or

[2] In case of parallel import of trademarked goods which were legitimately sold in foreign markets, if goodwill of the product handled by a sole distributor may be damaged because of such reasons as threats to consumers' health or safety caused by deterioration of the parallel import goods.

(3) In case of domestic products, if the same or similar conduct as in case of parallel import goods is carried out, viewpoint on it is basically the same as stated above, and the guidance described below in this Chapter shall apply.

2. Cases Where There Is a Problem under the Act

(1) Preventing any parallel importer from purchasing genuine products in overseas markets

There are cases where parallel importers are prevented from buying genuine products through overseas distribution channels, in order to maintain price level of the product covered by the contract. Such conduct curtails or eliminate price competition between the product handled by the sole distributor and the parallel import goods and deviates the extent necessary for the sole import distributorship system to function properly.

Accordingly, such conduct is illegal as unfair trade practices, in cases where the following types of conduct are employed by a sole distributor or supplier to maintain price level of the product covered by the contract (Articles 13 (Dealing on Restrictive Terms) or 15 (Interference with A Competitor's Transaction) of the General Designation).

[1] In case where a parallel importer makes an offer of purchase to the supplier's overseas customer, the sole distributor or supplier induces the overseas customer not to sell to the parallel importer; or

[2] The sole distributor or supplier induces the supplier's overseas customer, to stop selling to the parallel importer by such means of tracing the supply channel of parallel import goods by checking their serial numbers or the like, and providing the information to the supplier or its overseas customer.

(2) Restriction on distributors' handling of parallel import goods

Distributors should be free to choose whether or not to handle parallel import goods. In cases where a sole distributor transacts business with its distributors on condition that they shall not handle parallel import goods or in any manner induces the distributors not to handle parallel import goods, and if such conduct is employed to maintain price level of the product covered by the contract, it is illegal as unfair trade practices (Articles 13 or 15 of the General Designation).

(3) Restriction on wholesalers of selling the product covered by the contract to retailers handling parallel import goods

Distributors (wholesalers) should be free to sell the product purchased from a sole distributor, to any retailer of its own choice. In cases where a sole distributor induces its distributors not to sell the product covered by the contract to a retailer that is handling parallel import goods, and if such conduct is employed to maintain price level of the product covered by the contract, it is illegal as unfair trade practices (Articles 13 or 15 of the General Designation).

(4) Interference with marketing of parallel import goods by alleging them as counterfeit

Owners of trademarks may request to cease and desist from marketing any counterfeit of their products on the ground of trademark infringements.

However, in cases where a trademark owner requests a firm handling parallel import goods to cease and desist from selling them, alleging, without adequate reasons, that they are counterfeit and infringes his trademark (Note 1), and if such conduct is employed to maintain price level of the product covered by the contract, it is illegal as unfair trade practices (Article 15 of the General Designation).

(Note 1)   If such conduct is carried out, a retailer may refrain from handling parallel import goods out of fear that such allegation in itself might be detrimental to the retailer's reputation, even if the parallel import goods are genuine and the parallel importer can prove them as such.

(5) Cornering parallel import goods

When a retailer attempts to sell parallel import goods, there may be cases where a sole distributor may come to the store and corner the goods, thereby obstructing transaction of parallel import goods (Note 2). If such conduct is employed to maintain price level of the product covered by the contract, it is illegal as unfair trade practices (Article 15 of the General Designation)

(Note 2) If parallel import goods advertised to consumers are cornered by a sole distributor, consumers who come to buy the goods may allege as "bait and switch advertising" and the retailer's reputation may be injured. Cornering of the parallel import goods may also place psychological pressure on the retailer to stop selling parallel import goods and deter it from handling them.

(6) Refusal to conduct repairs or the like on parallel import goods

It is common for a sole distributor to set up repair service and keep in stock of repair parts, commensurate with its volume of supply of the product. Consequently, there may be cases where it is not available for the sole distributor to comply with requests for repair of parallel import goods or to provide the required repair parts. Accordingly, even if the sole distributor refuses to repair parallel import goods under the objective circumstances which make the sole distributor unable to comply with the requests for repair, or makes differences in terms and conditions of repair or the like between the goods handled by it and the parallel import goods, such conduct in itself presents no problem under the Antimonopoly Act.

However, in cases where it is extremely difficult for any party other than a sole distributor or its distributors to repair parallel import goods or to obtain necessary repair parts, and if the sole distributor refuses repair work or supply of repair parts or induces the distributors to refuse such repair work or supply of repair parts, solely on the ground of being parallel import goods, such conduct is illegal as unfair trade practices, if it is employed to maintain price level of the product covered by the contract (Article 15 of the General Designation).

(7) Obstruction of advertising activities for parallel import goods

Depending on ways and means, advertising activities for parallel import goods might constitute infringement of trademark rights, or cause confusion with the business operations of a sole distributor, due to similarities of advertising and the like, and may constitute violations of the Unfair Competition Prevention Law. In such cases, discontinuation of such advertising activities may be requested.

However, in cases where a sole distributor induces publishers of magazines, newspapers, and other media not to carry advertisements on parallel import goods or in any manner obstructs the advertising activities of parallel import goods without proper justification, and if it is employed to maintain price level of the product covered by the contract, such conduct is illegal as unfair trade practices (Articles 13 or 15 of the General Designation).

APPENDIX I TRANSACTIONS BETWEEN PARENT AND SUBSIDIARY COMPANIES

In cases where a firm (parent company) owns stocks of another (subsidiary company), whether or not transactions between the two companies are subject to the regulation of unfair trade practices depends on the following:

1. In cases where a parent company owns 100% of stocks of a subsidiary, it is usually recognized that transactions between them are in substance equivalent to intra-company transactions, and the transactions in principle are not subject to the regulation of unfair trade practices.

2. Even in cases where a parent company owns less than 100% (in principle, more than 50%) of stocks of a subsidiary, and if it is recognized that transactions between them are in substance equivalent to intra-company transactions, the transactions in principle are not subject to the regulation of unfair trade practices.

3. In cases where transactions between a parent company and a subsidiary company are recognized to be in substance equivalent to intra-company transactions, and if the parent company restricts business activities of a third party that deals with the subsidiary, for example, in such cases where either a contract between the parent and subsidiary or instructions given by the parent causes the subsidiary to restrict sales price of the third party, such conduct of the parent company is subject to the regulation of unfair trade practices.

4. In 2 and 3 above, whether or not transactions between a parent company and a subsidiary company are in substance equivalent to intra-company transactions is to be determined on a case-by-case basis by means of comprehensive examination of various factors, including:

[1] Ratio of stocks of the subsidiary held by the parent;
[2] Situation regarding dispatch of directors from the parent to the subsidiary;
[3] Situation regarding interference of the parent in financial matters and business policy of the subsidiary; and
[4] Business relationship between the parent and the subsidiary (ratio of the subsidiary's transaction with the parent in the total volume of transaction, etc.).

In cases where a parent imposes the same or similar restrictions on other firms as on a subsidiary, it is usually recognized that the restriction is imposed on the subsidiary as one of the other parties to transactions and the transactions between the parent and the subsidiary are in principle subject to the regulation of unfair trade practices.

APPENDIX II PRIOR CONSULTATION SYSTEM REGARDING DISTRIBUTION SYSTEM AND BUSINESS PRACTICES

Although these Guidelines are intended to provide guidance on major types of conduct regarding distribution system and business practices which may pose a problem under the Antimonopoly Act, there may be cases where it is difficult for firms to judge whether a particular practice may present a problem under the Antimonopoly Act in the light of the Guidelines. Accordingly, as described below, a prior consultation system regarding distribution system and business practices shall be established to respond to specific consultations.

Informal consultations including general inquiries on these Guidelines shall continue to be treated as before.

1. Business Practices Which May Be the Object of Prior Consultation

Prior consultation may be requested concerning specific conduct contemplated by a firm or firms, or by a trade association, and which is relevant to the types of conduct described in the Guidelines.

2. Parties Who May Apply for Prior Consultation

A firm or firms, or a trade association, domestic or foreign, contemplating to engage in specific conduct which may be the object of prior consultation may apply for prior consultation. In cases where proposed conduct is to be carried out through a contract, either party as well as both parties of the contract may apply for prior consultation, and in case of an application from the one party of a contract, inquiries from the other party will be conducted with the consent of the applicant, if deemed necessary.

3. How to Apply for Prior Consultation

Any party requesting prior consultation shall submit an application for prior consultation in the attached form with relevant data and materials to the Secretary-General of the Fair Trade Commission. Applications may also be lodged at Local Offices.

In addition, foreign parties may file their applications at the Consultation and Complaint Unit for Foreign Firms established at the External Affairs Office.

For further information on how to apply for prior consultation or how properly to fill out the form, please contact any office in charge of prior consultation listed in the Annex.

4. Reply to Prior Consultation

(1) The Staff Office of the Fair Trade Commission, in response to an application for prior consultation, examines whether the conduct contemplated as described in the application would constitute a violation of the Antimonopoly Act and notify its judgment to the applicant in writing. A time limit or other conditions may, if deemed necessary, be attached to this reply.

(2) If the reply states that the proposed conduct will not violate the Antimonopoly Act, no legal measures will be taken against that conduct. However, this treatment does not apply to cases where false information has been described in the application; where the applicant deviates from the scope of the conduct described in the application; or where conduct contrary to the conditions set forth in the reply is carried out.

5. Withdrawal of Reply to Prior Consultation

Following the reply in accordance with 4(1), to the effect that the proposed conduct would not violate the Antimonopoly Act, the whole or a part of the reply may be withdrawn in writing, in cases where changes of the facts, upon which the judgment was made, take place, such as conspicuous changes in the applicant's position in the market and in the situation of the market, or where it is considered inappropriate to hold on to the reply. In such cases, no legal measure will be taken against the conduct under prior consultation until the withdrawal of the reply.

6. Publication of Prior Consultation

Except for those parts containing trade secrets, the contents of prior consultations and the replies thereto (including withdrawal of such replies) shall be published in summary form, so long as there is no objection to it.

I

THE FINAL REPORT ON JAPAN–U.S. STRUCTURAL IMPEDIMENTS INITIATIVE TALKS (May 22, 1991) (Extract)

EXCLUSIONARY BUSINESS PRACTICES

I. BASIC RECOGNITION

Maintenance and promotion of fair and free competition is an extremely important policy objective, which not only serves the interest of the consumers but also increases new market entry opportunities including those of foreign companies. Based upon such recognition, the Government of Japan will implement wide-ranging measures.

1. Enhancement of the Antimonopoly Act and its enforcement.
2. Greater transparency and fairness in administrative guidance and other government practices.
3. Encouragement of transparent and non-discriminatory procurement procedures by private companies.
4. Facilitation of patent examination disposals including a shorter examination period.

II. MEASURES TO BE TAKEN

1. ENHANCEMENT OF THE ANTIMONOPOLY ACT AND ITS ENFORCEMENT

The Government of Japan or the Fair Trade Commission (FTC) will take the following actions, including legislative action, which are necessary or appropriate in achieving the goals set forth in the Report regarding enhancement of the Antimonopoly Act and its enforcement.

(1) Resorting More to Formal Actions

The Fair Trade Commission (FTC) will strictly exclude, through resorting more to formal actions, activities violating the Antimonopoly Act, by expanding and enhancing the investigatory function of the FTC and increasing its proof-collecting capacity against illegal activities. Especially, the FTC will rigorously deal with such conduct as price cartels, supply restraint cartels, market allocations, bidrigging, and group boycotts, and will take formal actions against them when they are found violating the Antimonopoly Act.

In addition, a system for consultations and complaints from foreign businessmen and foreign firms was established in the FTC on June 8 and a special official (Officer in charge of Consultation from Foreign Firms) was appointed, in order to make it easier for foreign businessmen and foreign firms to have consultations or make complaints concerning the Antimonopoly Act, to report cases of violation of the Act, and in order for the FTC to address such cases as violations of the Antimonopoly Act promptly and adequately.

(2) Ensuring Greater Transparency

In order to ensure transparency, to enhance the deterrent effect and to prevent similar illegal activities from occurring, the contents, including the names of the offenders, the nature of the offense and circumstances surrounding it, of all formal actions such as recommendations and surcharge payment orders will be made public. Warnings will also be made public other than in exceptional cases.

(3) Increase in Budgetary Allocation

In June this year, the Government of Japan increased the number of personnel in the FTC investigation department and created new divisions:

  (a) Allocation of 25 new officials (129 → 154), resulting in a 20% increment in staff,

(b) Establishment of one new office for strengthening violation detection (1 → 2 offices),

(c) Establishment of two new divisions for enhancing investigative functions (6 → 8 offices),

(d) Establishment of one new division in the Osaka Local Office for enhancing investigative functions of local offices (1 → 2 offices).

The Government of Japan will continue with its efforts to steadily improve and strengthen the FTC.

(4) Surcharges

In order to enhance enforcement against violations, the Government of Japan plans to submit a bill to revise the Antimonopoly Act to the Diet during the next regular session, to raise the surcharges against cartels so that they effectively deter violations of the Antimonopoly Act. A consultative group consisting of scholars and other experts has been set up under the auspices of the Chief Cabinet Secretary, to consider the concrete contents regarding the raising of surcharges. Moreover, group boycotts will also be regulated as cartels if they substantially restrain competition, and will be subject to surcharges if they influence prices.

(5) Resorting to Criminal Penalties

More criminal penalties will be utilized in the future, by the FTC's accusation of illegal activities violating the Antimonopoly Act to seek criminal penalties for them.

Relevant governmental agencies (the Ministry of Justice, prosecuting authority and the FTC) have initiated coordination in enhancing systems to cope adequately with any case violating the Antimonopoly Act. As a specific measure, a liaison-coordination was set up in April between the Ministry of Justice and the FTC, to examine matters such as accusation procedures. The group is working with a view to reaching a conclusion by the end of this year. There is also a plan to establish a point of contact between the prosecuting authority and the FTC for exchange of opinions and information on concrete problems of each case being considered to be accused.

The FTC will, from now on, actively accuse to seek criminal penalties on the following cases, and this policy was made public on June 20:

(a) Vicious and serious cases which are considered to have wide spread influence on people's livings, out of those violations which substantially

> restrain competition in certain areas of trade such as price cartels, supply
> restraint cartels, market allocations, bidrigging, group boycotts and other
> violations.
>
> (b) Among violation cases involving those businessmen or industries who are
> repeat offenders or those who do not abide by the elimination measures,
> those cases for which the administrative measures of the FTC are not con-
> sidered to fulfill the purpose of the law.

On June 20, 1990, the Minister of Justice, in a publicly released statement, called on all the chief prosecutors, on the occasion of the Annual
Meeting of Chief Prosecutors, to provide to the FTC any relevant information on Antimonopoly Act violations they have obtained during the course
of investigation or otherwise. In addition, he directed all the chief prosecutors to make special efforts to vigorously pursue cases where the FTC has
accused a criminal violation of the Antimononopoly Act.

(6) *The Damage Remedy System*

A study on the effective use of the current damage remedy system provided in the Section 25 of the Antimonopoly Act is currently undertaken by
a study group set up in the FTC, in order that any individual party suffering
damage from violation of the Antimonopoly Act can resort effectively to
damage remedy suits. The study group has publicized the results of its
deliberations on June 25. The FTC will implement the recommendations of
the study group, effective immediately, and will take necessary measures,
including the following, so that the current damage remedy system will be
able to be effectively utilized:

> (a) In order to deter violations of the Antimonopoly Act through proper and
> swift recovery of damages caused by such violations, the FTC intends to
> play a more active role in damage remedy suits under Section 25 of the
> Antimonopoly Act.
>
> (b) In order to alleviate plaintiffs' (injured parties') burden of proof concern-
> ing violation and damage, the FTC will take the following measures:
>
>> aa. the FTC will describe its findings on the violation as concretely and
>> clearly as possible in its document of decision.
>>
>> bb. when the FTC submits its opinion pursuant to Section 84 of the
>> Antimonopoly Act, it will describe as much as possible its judgment
>> on the relevance or causal relations between violations and damages,
>> the amount of damages, and the measure used for its calculation. The
>> FTC will also append as far as possible, the materials and the data
>> which are the bases of its views.

cc. the FTC will, upon request of the court, submit to the court materials and data necessary to prove the existence of violations, or the amount or causation of damages. Plaintiffs (injured parties) will be permitted, according to the civil procedures, to review such materials and data upon receipt by the court.

dd. the FTC will retain originals or copies of materials and data obtained in the course of investigations resulting in formal decisions of violation of the Antimonopoly Act that might be relevant to proof of violation, or the amount or causation of damages, in a private damage action based on such violation.

(c) The FTC will fully publicize the damage suit system under Section 25 of the Antimonopoly Act.

(d) The FTC will take necessary actions, including measures similar to those listed in paragraph (b) above, to ensure that the private damage remedy can be utilized effectively when the FTC finds that a trade association has violated the Antimonopoly Act.

Moreover, with regard to the question of filing fees of private damage remedy suits based upon the section 25 of the Antimonopoly Act, the Ministry of Justice and the FTC will continue to study the matter as to whether or not there is room for improvement.

(7) Effective Deterrence against Bidrigging

(a) The Government of Japan will continue to make efforts to eliminate bidrigging on government-funded projects. In this regard, procuring agencies will rigorously deal with any bidrigging cases, and will vigorously apply against firms found to have engaged in such bidrigging administrative measures, including suspension from designation, that are effective in deterring bidrigging activities. Moreover, such procuring agencies will increase their vigilance against bidrigging activities on their procurements, and will on their own judgment report relevant information regarding such activities to the FTC.

(b) The FTC will enforce the Antimonopoly Act strictly against bidrigging in all industries.

(c) The National Coordinating Committee for Implementation of Public Works Contract Procedures (NCC) has revised its model guideline on designation suspension, extending the period of suspension and expanding the district of application of suspension in Antimonopoly Act violation cases. Through this revision, in certain cases, the minimum period of designation suspension has been doubled and it is to be applied on a nationwide level.

Upon the above-mentioned revision, governmental agencies and public corporations have been taking steps to revise their guidelines on designation suspension, and most of them have completed the revision of the guidelines in an expeditious manner since June this year.

(d) In reviewing the fines provided in the Criminal Code, the Ministry of Justice is considering an increase in the maximum fine under the Criminal Code 96-3 concerning bidrigging, and will endeavor to amend the Criminal Code to that effect at the earliest time possible.

2. GOVERNMENT PRACTICES

(1) The Government of Japan has been making strenuous efforts to promote deregulation. On the basis of the recommendations of the Provisional Council for the Promotion of Administrative Reform, a Cabinet decision on Deregulation Policy Proposals was adopted. Based upon these Proposals, improvements in the system and its implementation will be made as soon as possible, through such means as expeditious considerations in the relevant Councils.

(2) Administrative Guidance

In order to ensure comprehensive and government wide transparency and fairness of administrative guidance, the Government of Japan will ensure that administrative guidance conforms with its intention that administrative guidance does not restrict market access or undermine fair competition. The Government of Japan will implement its administrative guidance in writing as much as possible. It will make the administrative guidance public when it is implemented, unless there are strong reasons not to do so, for example, when it is related to national security or when a publication of the administrative guidance causes, or may cause, such harm as might result from divulgence of trade secrets.

(4) With regard to the exemptions from the application of the Antimonopoly Act, they are exceptional dispositions exempting certain special cases from the general rules of the Antimonopoly Act. The exceptional treatment has therefore always been kept to a minimum.

The exemptions from the application of the Antimonopoly Act should be at a minimum, and the necessity of existing exemptions will be reconsidered with a view to promoting competition policy. The scope of exemptions will also be reviewed, even in cases where they will be maintained, beginning with the exemptions, if any, which impede import trade or investment.

No recession cartel based upon the Antimonopoly Act is currently in effect. The FTC will not allow recession cartels to be used to impede imports.

DISTRIBUTION SYSTEM

I. BASIC RECOGNITION

Concerning the distribution system in Japan, the Government of Japan attaches great importance to the enrichment of consumer life in Japan through further improving efficiency, ensuring market access, and building physical infrastructure. Based upon such recognition, the Government of Japan will promote the implementation of a broad spectrum of measures:

1. The distribution of import freight will be accelerated and its cost will be reduced by the improvement of airports, harbors, and other import infrastructure.

2. Customs clearance procedures and other import procedures will be further expedited to correspond to the increasing trade volume, while maintaining such functions as realizing a proper and fair sharing of the tax burden, and ensuring the health and safety of the people.

3. Deregulation of the distribution system will be further promoted with regard to a variety of laws and regulations, such as the Large-Scale Retail Store Law, with a view to enriching consumer life in Japan.

4. As to trade practices concerning distribution, an improved environment will be sought from the standpoint of promoting competition and securing market openness.

5. Wide-ranging measures with lasting, structural impact will be implemented in order to expand imports, thereby improving the efficiency of Japan's market structure including the distribution system.

II. MEASURES TO BE TAKEN

3. Deregulation

(2) Regulation concerning premium offers and advertisement

The regulation of premium offers by the Act Against Unjustifiable Premiums and Misleading Representation, including that by Fair Competition Codes, is designed to ensure fair competition in the market place and to protect consumer interests. Obviously, this system is not intended to be an impediment to new entry by foreign or domestic firms, and the Fair Trade Commission (FTC) has enforced and will continue to enforce this system so that it does not impede such new entry.

The FTC, however, is currently reviewing all existing Fair Competition Codes on premium offers so that they will not work as impediments to new entry by foreign or domestic firms, and will give priority to completing this review, and any relaxation as necessary, as early as possible with respect to Codes relevant to foreign trade or investment. As part of such an undertaking, the regulation by the Fair Competition Code on Premium Offers in Chocolate will be relaxed for the second time in July this year. The regulation of eight Codes will also be relaxed as early as possible this year and, among them, newspaper advertisements with coupons are scheduled to be allowed by this summer.

In reviewing the Codes, the FTC will hear the opinions of foreign firms and foreign businessmen.

Guidance on Fair Trade Conferences by the FTC will be tightened lest they take any action beyond their proper objectives.

4. Improvement of trade practices

(1) The FTC received a recommendation on June 21 from the "Advisory Group on Distribution Systems, Business Practices and Competition Policy," consisting of scholars and business experts.

The main contents of the recommendation are as follows.

(1) The FTC should formulate guidelines concerning the Antimonopoly Act enforcement with regard to marketing policy by manufacturers towards distributors and by distributors towards manufacturers in the field of consumer goods' distribution, taking fully into account merits and demerits of concerned business conduct from the viewpoint of competition policy.

In formulating the guidelines, the following points should be taken into consideration.

a. To alleviate excessive interference into business activities of trading partners, and to promote more active and independent business conduct.
b. Especially to promote price competition among companies.
c. To enhance openness of markets in order that new entrants, whether domestic or foreign companies, can more freely enter the market or perform more active business activities,

The guidelines may include the following types of conduct and other issues.

a. Resale price maintenance.
b. Suggested retail or wholesale prices by manufacturers which come under resale price maintenance.
c. Non price vertical restraints (restraints on dealing with competitors' products or imported goods, territorial or customer restriction, and restraints on sales methods), interference into distributors' business, rebates or allowances, return of unsold goods, dispatching salespersons to shops, systematizations regarding purchasing of commodities by large scale retailers, coercion into purchase, and coercive collection of contribution, which fall into unfair trade practices.
d. Group boycott formed among competitors or among trading partners which falls into private monopolization or unreasonable restraints of trade when they substantially restrain competition in certain fields of trade or else which fall into unfair trade practices.
e. Application of the Antimonopoly Act regarding unfair trade practices to dealings between parent and subsidiary companies.

(2) Although sole import agent agreements are an important instrument for new entry of imported goods, it may sometimes cause anti-competitive effects upon domestic distribution. Therefore, the FTC has to review its current guidelines by clarifying its interpretations with regard to manufacturers' import, sales at high price in domestic markets, and undue inhibition of parallel imports, in order to effectively tackle these anti-competitive effects.

Furthermore in case foreign companies or sole import agents are engaged in anti-competitive conduct, the FTC has to apply the Antimonopoly Act strictly.

(3) Individual companies, especially big companies, should desirably enhance their legal affairs division and make compliance programs, etc. in order to prevent violations of the Antimonopoly Act.

The FTC, based on these recommendations, will formulate and publish guidelines by the end of FY 1990 which will clarify, as concretely and clearly as possible, the criteria regarding the enforcement of the Antimonopoly Act so that fair competition with regard to trade practices in the distribution sector will not be hindered. In formulating such guidelines, drafts will be made available in advance to the agencies concerned at home and abroad, so that they may provide comments to the FTC before the guidelines are finalized. The FTC will strictly enforce the Antimonopoly Act according to these guidelines.

The FTC has enhanced its investigation system so that it can intensify information gathering on illegal activities under the Antimonopoly Act and strictly eliminate such activities. The FTC will continue its endeavor to enhance steadily its investigation system.

(2) The Ministry of International Trade and Industry (MITI), after hearing the opinions of foreign business organizations in Japan and having received a recommendation from the Council on June 20, formulated and presented to the industries concerned on June 25, a guideline for improving trade practices aiming at simplification, clarification and increased transparency of trade practices. The MITI is encouraging the industry concerned to take positive steps to improve trade practices. Contact points for processing complaints from foreign businesses will be established in MITI and the industries concerned.

KEIRETSU RELATIONSHIPS

1. BASIC RECOGNITION

Certain aspects of economic rationality of Keiretsu relationships notwithstanding, there is a view that certain aspects of Keiretsu relationships also promote preferential group trade, negatively affect foreign direct investment in Japan, and may give rise to anti-competitive business practices. In order to address this concern, the Government of Japan intends to make Keiretsu more open and transparent and to take necessary steps toward that end. The Government of Japan will take measures in its competition policy and enforce the Antimonopoly Act strictly, so that business transactions among companies with the background of Keiretsu relationship would not hinder fair competition and thereby have an exclusionary effect on foreign firms attempting to export, market or invest in Japan.

The Government of Japan will also implement a wide range of policies to facilitate the entry of foreign enterprises into the Japanese market.

II. MEASURES TO BE TAKEN

1. Strengthening the Function of the Fair Trade Commission

(1) The Fair Trade Commission (FTC) will strengthen its monitoring of transactions among Keiretsu firms, including but not limited to, those which have cross shareholding relationships, to determine whether these transactions are being conducted in a way that impedes fair competition. If such monitoring reveals that the effect of the cross shareholding may be a substantial restraint on competition, the FTC will restrict cross shareholding or order transfers of shares held in the cross shareholding to remedy the illegal situation; if the monitoring reveals that cross shareholding is used as a

means of effecting an unfair trade practice, the FTC will take appropriate measures, including restriction on cross shareholding or transfers of shares held in the cross shareholding, to remedy the illegal situation. Further, if such monitoring reveals that anti-competitive practices are occurring, the FTC will take appropriate measures to prevent and remedy the anti-competitive practices. The FTC will include in its annual report any results and such actions as have been taken.

In this connection, on June 21 this year, the "Advisory Group on Distribution Systems, Business Practices and Competition Policy" established by the FTC, consisting of scholars and business experts, issued recommendations with respect to the continuity and the exclusiveness of the transactions among companies in the same Keiretsu group whether or not cross shareholding is involved. Main contents of the recommendations are as follows:

(1) Although continuous trade relationships may have been formed due to certain reasonable motives, impediments to competition, such as entry barriers, should be removed. For this purpose, regarding the exclusiveness in transactions among companies where a continuous trade relationship or a shareholding relationship exists, the FTC should establish guidelines setting out the conduct which may be illegal under the Antimonopoly Act. The guidelines should include following types of conduct:

a. Cartels regarding customer restrictions, and market allocation cartels, among competitors.
b. Group boycotts formed among competitors or among trading partners which fall into private monopolization or unreasonable restraint of trade when they substantially restrain competition, or else which fall into unfair trade practices.
c. Unilateral refusals to deal, exclusive dealing, coercing to deal or mutually beneficial reciprocal dealing, and other anti-competitive conduct associated with continuous trade relationships, which fall into unfair trade practices.
d. When shareholding is used as a means of insuring the effectiveness of conduct listed in a, b, and c above, or when dealing is refused etc., because of the absence of a shareholding relationship, the FTC should clarify its interpretation that such conduct could be regulated from the viewpoint of unfair trade practices. Furthermore, when it is envisaged that unfair trade practices can not be eliminated effectively without ordering disposition of stocks, the FTC can order such disposition.

(2) Individual companies especially big companies, should desirably enhance their legal affairs division and make compliance programs, etc., to prevent violations of the Antimonopoly Act and other exclusionary practices. It is also desirable to improve transparency of presidents' meetings within corporate

groups through such means as providing the public with information on their activities.

On the basis of the recommendations, the FTC will set up and publish guidelines by the end of FY 1990, which will clarify, as concretely and clearly as possible, the criteria regarding the enforcement of the Antimonopoly Act with respect to the continuity and the exclusiveness of business practices among companies in the same Keiretsu group, with a view to ensuring that business practices among companies in Keiretsu groups will not hinder fair competition, and thereby contributing to the promotion of fair and more open transactions among them without any discrimination against foreign firms. In formulating such guidelines, drafts will be made available in advance to the agencies concerned at home and abroad, so that they may provide comments to the FTC before the guidelines are finalized. The FTC will strictly enforce the Antimonopoly Act in accordance with the guidelines.

(2) The FTC will conduct regularly, roughly every two years, analysis of various aspects of Keiretsu groups, including supplier-customer transactions, financing arrangements among group firms, personal ties, and special emphasis on the role of general trading companies in Keiretsu groups. The results of these analyses will be published. The FTC will take steps, including stricter enforcement of the Antimonopoly Act, to address anti-competitive and exclusionary practices uncovered in the FTC analyses. Furthermore, the FTC will survey the transactions among companies in specific industries regarding such issues as the effect of cross shareholding among companies which have trade relations.

(3) The Chief Cabinet Secretary will issue a statement which affirms that the Government of Japan will implement a wide-range of measures so that Keiretsu relationships will not hinder fair competition and transparent transactions and thereby the entry of foreign firms into the Japanese market will be facilitated as well as calling upon keiretsu firms for their cooperation to that effect.

BIBLIOGRAPHY

SELECTED BIBLIOGRAPHY OF THE JAPANESE ANTITRUST LAW IN ENGLISH AND GERMAN (1970-1991)

Abell, Mark, Japanese Anti-trust Law and Patent and Know-how Licensing. EIPR 11 (1990), 413.

American Bar Association, Joint Comments on the Japan Fair Trade Commission Antimonopoly Act Enforcement Guidelines, Antitrust Law Journal 60 (1991), 291.

Anchordoguy, Marie, "A Challenge to Free Trade? Japanese International Targeting in the Computer and Semiconductor Industries" in: Yamamura (1990), 301.

Antimonopoly Legislation, Antimonopoly Legislation of Japan (Masanao Nakagawa, ed.), 1984, text of various statutes including a brief comment.

Ariga, Michiko, Merger Regulation in Japan. Texal Int'l Law Forum (1969), 112.

_____, Efforts to Revise the Japanese Antimonopoly Law, Antitrust Bulletin 21 (1976), 703.

_____, "Regulation of International Licensing Agreements under the Japanese Antimonopoly Law" in: Doi/Shattuck, Patent and Know-How Licensing in Japan and the United States, 1977.

_____, Chapter "Japan" in: Von Kalinowski (ed.), Competition Laws of the Pacific Rim Countries, vol. 6, chap. 1-20, 1989 et seq.

566 / *Bibliography*

Baum, Harald, Vertrautes und weniger Vertrautes—einige Überlegungen zum japanischen Internationalen Privat und Verfahrensrecht, in: Menkhaus (ed.), Das japanische Recht, revised for 1992.

Brown, Ronald G. & Uesugi, Akinori, Japanese Regulation of Ocean Freight Shipments, Journal of Maritime Law and Commerce 11 (1980), 293.

Coles, Isobel, see: Krauss, Ellis S.

Covey, J. Amanda, Vertical Restraints under Japanese Law: The Antimonopoly Study Group Report, Law in Japan 14 (1981), 49.

Davidow, Joel, The New Japanese Guidelines on Unfair Practices in Patent and Know-How Licenses: An American View. World Competition (Geneva) 12 (1989), 4.

Distribution System, Distribution System and Business Practices in Japan, EPA Paper 1989.

_____, Japan's Distribution System and Options for Improving U.S. Access, USTIC Publications (Washington) 2291 and 2327, 1990.

Dore, Ronald, "An Outsider's View" in: Yamamura (1990), 359.

Eubel, Paul (ed.), Das japanische Rechtssystem, 1979.

The Fair Trade Commission, FTC/Japan Views, Bulletin on Information and Opinion from the Fair Trade Commission of Japan, 1988 et seq.

Futatsugi, Yusaku, Japanese Enterprise Groups, 1986.

Grice, Geoffrey & Oda, Hiroshi, Japanese Banking, Securities & Antimonopoly Law, 1988.

Hadley, Eleanor, Antitrust in Japan, 1970.

Haley, John Owen, Antitrust Policy in Postwar Germany and Japan, speech at the Conference on the political management economic change in postwar Japan and the Federal Republic of Germany, unpublished, 1982.

_____, Antitrust Enforcement: A Comparative Study of German and Japanese Law, 1982.

_____, Japanese Antitrust Law; Commentary and Cases, 1982. Antitrust Sanctions and Remedies: A Comparative Study of German and Japanese Law, Washington Law Review 59 (1984), 471.

_____, "Administrative Guidance versus Formal Regulation: Resolving the Paradox of Industrial Policy" in: Saxonhouse/Yamamura, Law and Trade Issues of the Japanese Economy (1986), 107.

_____, "Weak Law, Strong Competition and Trade Barriers: Competitiveness as a Disincentive to Foreign Entry into Japanese Markets" in: Yamamura (1990), 203.

Hashimoto, Goro, Application of U.S. Antitrust Laws and Japanese Antimonopoly Law to International Trade, 1986.

Henderson, Dan Fenno, Foreign Enterprise in Japan: Laws and Policies (1973).

Herinckx, Yves, Le Droit de la Concurrence au Japon, Rev. Dr. Int. Dr. Comp. (1985), 320.

Hwang, Shen-Chang, Das japanische Antimonopolgesetz im Lichte des deutschen Kartellrechts, 1968.

Imai, Kenichi, "Japanese Business Groups and the Structural Impediments Initiative" in: Yamamura (1990), 167.

Irie, Kazutomo, see: Komiya, Ryutaro.

Ishida, Hideto, Anticompetitive Practices in the Distribution of Goods and Services in Japan: The Problem of Distribution Keiretsu, Journal of Japanese Studies 9 (1983), 319.

Iyori, Hiroshi, "Antitrust and Industrial Policy in Japan: Competition and Cooperation" in: Saxonhouse/Yamamura, Law and Trade Issues of the Japanese Economy (1986), 56.

_____, "A Comparative Analysis on Japanese Competition Law: An Attempt to Identify German and American Influences" in: Die Japanisierung des westlichen Rechts (1990), 227.

Johnson, Chalmers, MITI and the Japanese Miracle, 1982.

Kitagawa, Zentaro (ed.), Doing Business in Japan, 6 vols. plus appendices and statutes. 1980 et seq.; Vol. 5 "Security Transactions, Antimonopoly Regulations, Taxation" (1989), comments on the Antimonopoly Law by Michiko Ariga, Hiroshi Iyori, Mitsuo Matsushita and Akinori Uesugi.

Komiya, Ryutaro & Irie, Kazumoto, "The U.S.–Japan Trade Problem: An Economic Analysis from a Japanese Viewpoint" in: Yamamura (1990), 65.

Krauss, Ellis S. & Coles, Isobel, "Built-in Impediments: The Political Economy of the U.S.–Japan Construction Dispute" in: Yamamura (1990), 323.

Kugai, Takahashi, The Relaxation of Antitrust Policy in the U.S. in Comparison with Antimonopoly Policy in Japan, 1985.

Maruyama, Shuhei, see: Menkhaus, Heinrich.

Matsuo, Marota, Mergers and Acquisitions under Japanese Law, Antitrust Law Journal 52 (Fall 1983), 1011.

Matshushita, Mitsuo, The Antimonopoly Act of Japan and International Transactions, Japanese Annual of International Law 14 (1970), 1.

_____, Export Control and Export Cartels in Japan, 20 Harvard Int'l L. J. (1979), 103.

_____, "Protection of Technology and the Liberal Trade Order: A Japanese View" in: Yamamura (1990), 271.

_____, Introduction to Japanese Antimonopoly Law, 1990.

_____ & Schoenbaum, Thomas, Japanese International Trade and Investment Law, 1989.

Menkhaus, Heinrich & Maruyama, Shuhei, "Vertrieb, Transport und Lager-haltung" in: Drobnig/Baum (ed.) Japanisches Handels- und Wirtschaftsrecht, revised for 1992.

Miyagi, Junichi, Relationship Between Antitrust Laws and Regulations in the U.S. and Japan, 1985.

Miyamoto, Satoshi, Tension Between Antitrust Laws and Patent Laws and its Recent Transition: Comparative Study Betwen the U.S. and Japan, 1990.

Nakagawa, Masanao, see: Antimonopoly Legislation.

Nakazawa, Toshiaki & Weiss, Leonard, The Legal Cartels of Japan, Antitrust Bulletin 34 (1989), 641.

Nanto, Dick, Japan's Industrial Groups, The Keiretsu: Congressional Research Service, The Library of Congress, 1990.

Negishi, Akira, Legislation concerning Security of Some Business Areas for Small and Medium-Sized Enterprise and Antimonopoly Act, Kobe Law Review Int 13 (1979), 25.

_____, The Business Groups and the Distribution System, and the Antimonopoly Law, Kobe Law Review Int 18 (1984), 33 and 19 (1985), 39.

_____, Administrative Guidance and the Japanese Antimonopoly Law, Rabels Z 49 (1985), 277.

_____, "Kartellrecht" in: Drobnig/Baum (ed.), Japanisches Handels-und Wirtschaftsrecht, revised for 1992.

Note, Trustbusting in Japan: Cartels and Government Business Cooperation, Harvard L R 94 (1981), 1064.

Oda, Hiroshi, see: Grice, Geoffrey.

Ohara, Yoshio, International Application of the Japanese Antimonopoly Act, Swiss Review of International Competition Law 28 (1986), 5.

_____, New Japanese Guidelines for the Regulation of Restrictive Clauses in Patent and Know-How Licensing Agreements, IIC (1990), 645.

Okada, Toshihiro, The Large-Scale Retail Stores Law—its Outline and Problems, Japan Business Law Letter 1990/2, 6.

Palenberg, John, see: Toyama, Kozo.

Pape, Wolfgang, "Kartellrecht" in: Eubel (ed.), Das Japanische Rechtssystem, 461.

_____, Gyoseishido und das Antimonopolgesetz in Japan, 1980.

_____, Nichttarifäre Handelshindernisse in Japan, RIW (1990), 726.

_____, "Kartellrecht" in: Menkhaus (ed.), Das Japanische im japanischen Recht, revised for 1992.

Rahn, Guntram, "Gewerblicher Rechtsschutz" and "Urheberrecht" in: Eubel (ed.), Das Japanische Rechtssystem, 417 and 445.

Ramseyer, Mark R., Japanese Antitrust Enforcement After the Oil Embargo, Am J of Comp L 31 (1983), 395.

_____, The Costs of the Consensual Myth: Antitrust Enforcement and Institutional Barriers to Litigation in Japan, The Yale Law Journal 94 (1985), 604.

Rodatz, Peter, Japanisches Kartellrecht in: Frankfurter Kommentar zum GWB, 2nd ed. 1982 et seq., vol. 1, appendix C.

Roehl, Thomas W., An Economic Analysis of Industrial Groupings in Post-War Japan, 1983.

Sanekata, Kenji, Administrative Guidance and the Antimonopoly Law, Law in Japan 10 (1977), 65.

_____, Antitrust in Japan: Recent Trends and Their Socio-Economical Background, Univ. of British Columbia L R 20 (1986), 379.

Saxonhouse, Garry, Industrial Restructuring Japan, Journal of Japanese Studies 5 (1979), 273.

Schoenbaum, Thomas, see: Matsushita, Mitsuo.

Shoda, Akira, Die neue Entwicklung und Problematik des japanischen Antimonopolgesetzes, WuW (1976), 621.

_____, Antimonopoly Law Violations and Compensatory Damages, Law in Japan 16 (1983), 1.

_____, "Kartellrecht" in: Menkhaus (ed.), Das Japanische im japanischen Recht, revised for 1992.

Tateishi, Norifumi, see: Toyama, Kozo.

Toyama, Kozo/Tateishi, Norifumi/Palenberg, John, Trade Friction, Administrative Guidance and Antimonopoly Law in Japan, Case Western Reserve J of Int L 15 (1983), 601.

Tsukamoto, Koichi, Joint Ventures and Antitrust Laws, 1986.

Uekusa, Masu, "Government Regulations in Japan: Toward Their International Harmonization and Integration" in: Yamamura (1990), 237.

Uesugi, Akinori, Japanese Antimonopoly Policy—Its Past and Future, Antitrust L J 50 (Summer 1982), 709.

———, Japan's Cartel System and Its Impact on International Trade, Harvard Int Law Journal 27 (1986), 389.

———, see: Brown, Ronald G.

Wassman, Ulrike & Yamamura, Kozo, "Do Japanese Firms Behave Differently? The Effects of Keiretsu in the United States" in: Yamamura, "Japanese Investment" (1989), 119.

Weiss, Leonard, see: Nakazawa, Toshiaki.

Yamada, Naoyoshi, Vertical Restraints and Antitrust Laws: Comparative Study of U.S. and Japan, 1988.

Yamamura, Kozo, "Success that Soured: Administrative Guidance and Cartels in Japan" in: Yamamura/Vandenberg, Policy and Trade Issues of the Japanese Economy: American and Japanese Perspectives, 1982.

——— (ed.), Japanese Investment in the United States: Should we be concerned?, 1989.

——— (ed.), Japan's Economic Structure: Should it Change?, 1990.

———, The Burden of an Economic Superpower: Transforming Japanese-Efficiency into World Efficiency, unpublished paper of February 1990.

——— see: Wassman, Ulrike.

Yamauchi, Koresuke, Internationales Konzernrecht in Japan, ZGR (1991), 235.

Yazawa, Makoto, International Transactions and the Japanese Antimonopoly Law, Law Asia 4 (1973), 169.

Young, Michael K., Administrative Guidance in the Courts: A Case Study in Doctrinal Application, Law in Japan 17 (1984), 120.

———, Japanese Antitrust Policy and Practice: Competition, Patterns of Governance and Participation, 1986.

Zerdick, Axel, Die präventive Funktionskontrolle in Japan, 1970.

ABOUT THE AUTHORS

Hiroshi Iyori, Commissioner of the Japanese Fair Trade Commission from 1986 to 1991, is currently an advisor to the Mitsubishi Research Institute. He also holds the position of Professor of Law, Chuo University and is the long time Director of the Association of Economic Jurisprudence and of the Association of Japan International Economic Jurisprudence.

Before being appointed as Commissioner of the Fair Trade Commission, Mr. Iyori held many important assignments within the Commission. He has served as Secretary-General and as Director General of the Investigation Bureau and of the Economic Bureau, as well as Deputy Secretary-General for General Affairs. Earlier, he held the Directorships of the General Affairs Division, the Coordination Division, the Trade Practices Division, and the International Transaction Division.

Akinori Uesugi is currently Director, Trade Practice Division, Fair Trade Commission. He has responsibility for rule making on unfair trade practice and enforcement of the resale price maintenance system. Mr. Uesugi also serves as Lecturer of Law, Chuo University, a post he has held since 1991.

Prior to his present assignment he first served as First Secretary, Embassy of Japan, Washington, D.C. (1981 to 1984), and then, in succession, he held various offices for the Japanese Fair Trade Commission: first as Director of the Industrial Research Division, then as the Director for the Corporate Affairs Division, the International Transaction Division, and the Second Investigation Division and, until recently, as Director of the Management and Planning Division.